TO PROTECT
AND
TO SERVE

Also by Joe Domanick

*Faking It in America: Barry Minkow
and the Great ZZZZ Best Scam*

TO PROTECT
AND
TO SERVE

The LAPD's Century of War
in the City of Dreams
·······················
Joe Domanick

POCKET BOOKS

New York   London   Toronto   Sydney   Tokyo   Singapore

POCKET BOOKS, a division of Simon & Schuster Inc.
1230 Avenue of the Americas, New York, NY 10020

Library of Congress Cataloging-in-Publication Data

Domanick, Joe.
    To protect and to serve : the LAPD's century of war in the city of dreams /
Joe Domanick.
        p.   cm.
    Includes index.
    ISBN 0-671-75111-5
    1. Los Angeles (CA).   Police Dept.   2. Police—California—Los
Angeles.   I. Title.
    HV8148.L7D66   1994
    363.2′0974′94—dc20   94-19984
                                                                                CIP

First Pocket Books hardcover printing November 1994

10   9   8   7   6   5   4   3   2   1

POCKET and colophon are registered trademarks of
Simon & Schuster Inc.

Printed in the U.S.A.

For Judy Tanka . . .
and Theresa too . . .

Acknowledgments

I first became interested in the LAPD not as a police groupie or reporter, but as a newly arrived immigrant to Los Angeles in the mid 1970s. I'd come from Queens, New York, where nobody gave the police much thought except to wonder where they were when a local wolf pack started to crowd around in a subway car.

But the LAPD was different, and I soon became intrigued with the department's all-pervasive policing, and with its power, autonomy, and ability to silence its critics dead in their tracks. The LAPD seemed to have carte blanche to do what it wished, and I couldn't understand how such a situation could exist in one of America's leading cities. This book is an attempt to answer that question.

Over the years, many people have taken the time and trouble to encourage and help me in the task. Twelve years ago, when I was a graduate student at USC's School of Journalism, three of my teachers—Joe Saltzman, Sue Horton, and Pat Dunavan—were particularly helpful, not only in assuring me that the LAPD was a great story, but in pumping up my confidence, shaping my ideas, visualizing the work, and asking the right questions.

Leonard Leader, the wonderful historian of Los Angeles in the twenties and thirties, and also a teacher at the journalism school at that time, then shared his insights with me. It was he who suggested that I look at Joseph Gerald Woods's extraordinary UCLA doctoral dissertation, *The Progressives and the Police,* which pointed me in the right direction and provided the building blocks for my analysis of the LAPD in the first half of the twentieth century.

The work of the *Los Angeles Times* media critic David Shaw served the same purpose in my interpreting of the Los Angeles press and its relationship to the LAPD. And David Johnston's investigative reporting for the *Los Angeles Times* and Lennie LaGuire's and Mark S. Warnick's series on police shootings in the Los Angeles *Herald Examiner* were key in helping me understand the nature of shootings by LAPD officers and the problems with their subsequent investigations. Bella Stumbo's 1982 two-part profile of Daryl Gates was equally as invaluable a resource for me. And so were the political reporting and columns of Bill Boyarsky of the *Los Angeles Times* and of Harold Meyerson of the *L.A. Weekly* in helping me fathom the politics of Los Angeles. This was true not only of them, but of the scores of reporters for the *Los Angeles Times, Herald Examiner,* and *Daily News,* who, since 1979, have covered the LAPD under frequently difficult circumstances. After the shooting of Eulia Love in 1979, the *Los Angeles Times,* in particular, was methodical in its detailed coverage of the department, and was an irreplaceable source. Journalist Charles Rappleye was also extremely gracious in helping me understand the influence of organized crime in Los Angeles in the 1920s and 1930s. And David Dotson, Jim Fisk, and Zvonko G. (Bill) Pavelic were extraordinarily patient and candid in helping me understand the inner workings of the LAPD.

Among the scores of other LAPD officers, past and present, with whom I spoke, the following were also generous in sharing their expertise, and deserve special thanks: Steve Fisk, Jack White, Ed Davis, Joe Dircks, Tom Reddin, Stanley Sheldon, John Kinsling, Irvis Lester, George Aliano, Rocky Washington, Janine Bouey, Harold Sullivan, Carl McGill, Ed Williams, Thomas Windham, Mike Rothmiller, William Rathburn, Jack Holstead, Roger Murdock, Paul Harrison, Garland Hardeman, David Klinger, and Jesse Brewer.

Others whose insights and expertise proved useful were: Ethel Narvid, May Churchill, Stephen Reinhardt, William Mason, Maury Weiner, Zev Yaroslavsky, Sam Yorty, Dennis Swanson, Wayne Satz, Jim Bellows,

Acknowledgments

Joel Sappel, Stanley Sheinbaum, Melanie Lomax, Dan Garcia, Reva Tooley, Duane Peterson, Leon Gilbert, Tony Bouza, James Fyfe, Mark Fabiani, R. Samuel Paz, Hugh Manes, Don Jackson, Karol Heppe, Ted Watkins, Raye Cunningham, Dave Lynn, Leo Cortez, Mark Ridley-Thomas, Ramona Ripston, Charles Stewart, Frank Wilkinson, Stephen Yagman, Cynthia Anderson, Rhonda Moore, Johnny May Carter, Charles Davis, and Derrick Mims.

I am also indebted to Michelle Meyers, Hugh Bonar, Anne Bergman, John DiGregorio, Stacie Stukin, and Sally Schultheiss for their spirit and determination in assisting me in fact-checking, researching, and manuscript preparation. And to Dace Taube at the Regional History Center at the University of Southern California; to Carolyn Cole of the Los Angeles Public Library; to Robert Freeman, assistant archivist at the Los Angeles City Clerk's Office; and to the staff at the UCLA Library's Department of Special Collections.

Additionally, I'd like to express my thanks to Kit Rachlis at the *L.A. Weekly,* where the genesis for this book first appeared. To John Blanton, for once again being the right man at the right time. To my agent at ICM, Kris Dahl, who showed me how to transform the abstract into the concrete, and then went out and sold it. To my editor, Jane Rosenman, who cheered me on, edited me down, and never lost faith. To Matthew Futterman, whose insights, patience, and professionalism were always deeply appreciated. To David Deitch, the fabulous doctor. To Eric Boorman for his patience above and beyond the call of duty. To Charlie Lerman, for helping me to get there. To Dan Abatelli, the man who taught me style. To Clancy Sigal, the man who taught me to write, and who took it as his mission never to let me forget Queens. To Frances Ring, who took it as hers to relentlessly cheer me on. To Catherine, Carol, Anthony, and Andrea Domanick, my family, my loves. And most especially to Jack Langguth, without whose guidance, inspiration, and example this book would never have been written.

Contents

·········

PART 3—THE GODFATHER AND THE SUBVERSIVE

PART 4—UNDER SIEGE

Contents

Contents

PART 7—CAN'T WE ALL GET ALONG?

PART 1

PROLOGUE: SILENCE OF THE LAMBS

....

CHAPTER 1

The
Black Prince

·······················

Deep in his bones he must have known it would all come down to this—to a fat woman in a red dress bellowing at him as his city went up in flames.

"Say what you gonna do," the woman had screamed as he was being introduced. "It's your police department. Say what *you* gonna do!"

Sailing up and over the roar of boos, her crackling continued nonstop as Tom Bradley, the mayor of Los Angeles, tried to settle into his speech. In front of him, two thousand black bodies were crushed inside the main chapel of the First AME Church; and hundreds more had overflowed into its lobby, basement, and packed anterooms.

"I was shocked," Bradley tells them, "I was stunned—"

"No," shouts the fat woman, breaking through the ceaseless, low-level din. "Don't tell us that. Tell us what you gonna *do!*" The question, like a demanding echo, ripples through the crowd. "Yes, tell us! What*cha* gonna do? What*cha* gonna do?"

Leaning his long, dark, still-powerful frame into the podium onstage, Tom Bradley—his face a perfect mask except for the slight twitching of his right cheek; his voice as neutral as if he were dedicating a local supermarket—plods on, seemingly oblivious. "I don't know where they were," he says, "they certainly weren't watching that videotape."

The heat inside is oppressive, the tension palpable.

Above the entrance to the church, a banner has been placed. "Brothers," it reads, "Come Help Us Stop The Madness." Below the stage, tiny monitors on the local TV cameras make a joke of both the banner and the evening's purpose: to keep the city calm in the wake of the acquittals in the Rodney King beating trial that had been announced just hours before.

One is tuned to Parker Center—the LAPD's downtown headquarters, which is in imminent danger of being stormed by a venomous, outraged mob. Rocks fly through its plate-glass windows as a wooden guard post on the building's front lawn burns bright orange.

A second is broadcasting every white man's worst nightmare: truck driver Reginald Denny lying like a fallen embryo on his knees and elbows at a busy South Central intersection while five or six homies gleefully smash their boots, their fists, a fire extinguisher, and then a brick into his curly, blond head.

". . . I've received hundreds of calls from across . . . the country," Bradley continues.

But by now it's already too late. The fat lady in the red dress, like most of the rest of the congregation of Los Angeles' preeminent African-American church and the heart of its bourgeoisie, is busy fanning herself, is busy going through her pocketbook, is busy making herself busy. It's as if following the unloading of her contempt, she and the others had telepathically written and signed a message they are now sending up to Bradley, up to the native son who for twenty-one years as an LAPD officer had provided them their one glimmer of hope on a police force they've hated as passionately as any cracker-filled sheriff's department has ever been hated in the deepest heart of Dixie. A message to a man they'd sent to City Hall as one of two of Los Angeles' first elected black city councilmen; who'd spoken for them during the rebellion in Watts; and whom they then worked so hard to send to live in the mayor's fourteen-room, French-colonial mansion among the palatial homes and leafy elegance of Hancock Park. For eighteen years, they—the members of the First AME and the other churches of black South Central—had been Tom Bradley's bedrock of support. Even in the dog days of the late eighties—when the mere mention of his name would bring a derisive snort from the corner men chugging back their eighteen-ounce cans of

Olde English 800, or a cool, mocking smile from the young brothers and sisters trying to avoid the Bloods and Crips and make it at Trade Tech or LACC—he had remained as close to Harlem's Adam Clayton Powell-Black-Prince as L.A. had ever produced.

But the subtext of the message they are beaming up to Tom Bradley on this late April night in 1992—on the eve of the worst American insurrection of the twentieth century—is that all of that has finally, irrevocably changed; while its central thrust is even more emphatic: "Sit down," it reads. "Shut up. Take a look at why it took the Rodney King video for you to finally take a stand, when that kind of shit's been going down every day for years, as you, being *black* and an ex-cop, knew better than anybody. Take a look at how Daryl Gates's been dancing you around. Take a look at what you did when at the height of your power they were gunning down Eulia Love over an unpaid gas bill and were choking every brother that didn't kiss their ass during routine traffic stops. Take a look at how irrelevant you've been during eighteen years in office."

It wasn't fair, of course. None of it. But what did they know? What did any of them know? The public, the press, the ACLU; the political scientists from Claremont and USC and UCLA with their bar graphs and neat yellow maps with the blue flags in them, endlessly pontificating about the "changing demography of Los Angeles," and about what a "liberal city" L.A. was. Why, Los Angeles had elected a black mayor with a black population that had never exceeded 18 percent they'd write in their little Sunday op-ed pieces in the L.A. *Times*. It had voted for Carter, gone for Dukakis. Even *Mondale* had carried the city. The surface sheen of L.A.'s politics, that's all they seemed to understand. Not how weak the position of mayor was in Los Angeles. Not the real interplay of power. At least not where the LAPD was concerned.

Did they really think that because Otis Chandler had gone to Andover and Stanford, hung out with some brothers on the track team and in the Air Force, and brought the L.A. *Times* from its omnipresent right-wing domination of the city into a kind of squishy liberalism that *that* would somehow transform the LAPD? Did they really think the editorial page of the *Los Angeles Times* could change the kind of police force that the homeowners' associations, the real estate barons, and the downtown WASPs, Westside Jews, and Japanese corporate heads wanted? Did they really think that when black South Central hooked up with the city's then liberal Jewish electorate and got Tom Bradley into the mayor's office—

and the crew-cut Republicans from the Valley in their checkered sports coats out—that he would wave a magic wand and reform the department?

This wasn't, after all, the Duluth PD he was dealing with. He was dealing with the Golden Boys. With the department that for the past forty years had been presented on television as the personification of cool professionalism on "Dragnet"; as the cutting edge of tactics and technology on "S.W.A.T."; as the epitome of sheer white-bread wholesomeness on "Adam 12"; and as white-knight urban warriors holding the "Thin Blue Line" as their fleet of helicopters whirled overhead and they proned-out black South Central and Cholo-infested Pico-Union on the nightly news.

Long before Tom Bradley took office, they had written the book on look-sharp, take-charge, big-muscle law enforcement. For decades they had exported new chiefs along with the LAPD philosophy to police agencies all over the South and Southwest; and played guru to visiting law-enforcement dignitaries from such countries as Japan, Taiwan, and Chile who had come to learn at the feet of the masters.

And all along, the department had taken care—no, had taken gleeful *pride*—in pointing to their city-charter mandated independence, and telling politicians and critics to get fucked. Over the years, they became not just a police force, but AMERICA'S COPS.

Which was why it was so unfair to single out Tom Bradley for refusing to pick up the gauntlet when it was thrown first by LAPD chief Ed Davis, and then by his successor Daryl Gates. Why, you barely needed half the fingers of one hand to count the number of politicians willing to stand up and publicly criticize the Los Angeles Police Department before the beating of Rodney King.

The L.A. *Weekly,* for example, had summed up the stance of almost the entire city council with just the title of a lead story about that institution *after* the King beating. "Silence of the Lambs," they'd called it. Now, the city council, *they* had understood about the LAPD's power. They had understood L.A. was not San Francisco or New York. They knew who held the door for whom in Los Angeles. They had always understood— even if it would now take hot coals under their armpits to get them to admit it—what it would cost to take on an LAPD that spied on the state attorney general, that backed down critical California governors, and that caused even police commissioners to nervously check their rearview mirrors following any thought that might have displeased the chief. That's why, almost to a man and woman, the council had done nothing. Had sat out the entire fiasco following the world-famous videotape featuring Rodney King's kidneys, arms, legs, and head and the LAPD's solid-aluminum, two-foot-long, Monadnock PR-24 batons. They knew that to challenge the most powerful, most independent, most arrogant, most feared, and most political big-city police department in the nation meant the real possibility of it all coming down to that late-April night in 1992. To blood on the tracks. And to their political careers on the line.

It all seemed so completely absurd, so askew, so perversely amusing to politically savvy visitors from places like New York, Boston, or Chicago. But this was L.A. And this was the LAPD, as Tom Bradley had always known better than anyone else.

For another ten minutes, in the same flat, neutral southern-California tone that he'd used to conceal so much over so many years, Tom Bradley continued his speech. Then to the faintest ripple of applause given only because of the let's-hear-it-for-the-mayor urging of the evening's emcee, it was over. For perhaps the first time in his seventy-four years, the man who'd come within a hair of being California's first black governor, and whose name just a decade before had been seriously mentioned for the short list for vice president, literally shuffled, as bent-shouldered, he exited the stage.

The Keepers of the Flame

·························

Eighteen months earlier, in the autumn of 1990, Daryl Francis Gates, the chief whose police department had been obsessing the residents of South Central for decades, had also stepped to a podium to make a speech: the commencement address to the seventy-six cadets about to graduate from the Los Angeles Police Academy. He wore a navy blue uniform whose shirt was tailored to perfectly hug his trim, wiry torso. On his chest, multiple rows of brightly colored military ribbons and an over-size, silver-plated LAPD badge contrasted vividly against his police blues—as did the numerous gray longevity stripes on his sleeve that indicated his forty-one years on the force. Tucked low over his blue-gray eyes, the visor of his service cap seemed to have more scrambled eggs than did Douglas MacArthur's on his return to Corregidor. The hat both made him look his self-described five-foot-ten and one-half inch height and hid the thinning hair he artfully combed over the balding areas on his already high forehead. The hair, however, along with the sagging skin between the four silver stars he wore on each collar, and the squint and frown lines in his deeply tanned face, were the only visible signs that he was nearing sixty-five.

Minutes before, as if to prove the point, he had stood utterly—almost imperiously—still and straight in the morning sun, facing the rigid ranks of blue-uniformed cadets for what seemed an eternity. Then unexpectedly a command was bellowed, and the pumped-up recruits had grunted something unintelligible back as they simultaneously dressed it up and snapped to attention. As Gates stepped forward an instant later, the first rank whipped out their sixteen-round, 9mm, double-action semiautomatic Berettas and in one blurred movement propelled their muzzles back, locked their forearms, and presented their weapons for inspection. It was a defining moment—an LAPD moment: Joe Wambaugh's New Centurions ready to hit the streets and eliminate the lice—an assignment the LAPD took very seriously. Far more seriously than most other police agencies.

Afterward, back at the dark wood podium that had been set up on the small dirt and grass area that served as both the academy's drill field and track, Daryl Gates laid out—as he did every chance he got—the myth and the glory of the LAPD.

"Some years ago," he tells his troops, "a young officer came up with a motto for the Los Angeles Police Department that's been patented and used all over the United States. . . . 'Hey,' he said, 'do you know what this job is all about?' " Skipping a beat, Gates then gives the officer's answer: " 'To protect and to serve.' " Reverently, like a wedding vow, Daryl Gates repeats the phrase, "To protect and to serve . . . Think about it," he tells the cadets, who are now sitting in neat rows of folding chairs in front of him, intently listening.

Behind him, framed by the tranquil brown hills and low-slung, weathered buildings of the fifty-five-year-old Academy, are the cadets' families. Most have an Orange County chapter of Mothers Against Drunk Driving look to them. Los Angeles as it used to be. They had mostly disappeared from L.A. in the decades following the Watts insurrection in the sixties—fleeing to the safe far reaches of the San Fernando Valley and Orange County. They were people who, if you'd ever smoked a joint, had radical hair, cruised with a beer, felt an aversion to the fifties, or had a trace of anarchy in your soul, always caused a slight ache in the pit of your stomach. Even the blacks and Latinos present had that *look*. In fact, had it not been for the substantial numbers of black, brown, and female faces among the cadets and in the crowd, 1959 would surely have been the year that crossed your mind.

Of course, many of those black, brown, and female cadets had been forced on Daryl Gates and his department by the courts strong-arming the city into a consent decree that required each recruit class to be composed of at least 25 percent minorities and women. But over the years, Daryl Gates had grudgingly begun to accept the inevitable, and to welcome them into "the LAPD family." "The LAPD isn't white, black, or brown; it comes in only one color: blue," he would say. Which did not mean that any female or so-called minority should expect to be promoted any quicker than anyone else, or should covet his or her share of those disproportionately numerous, much coveted special assignments that got an officer out of uniform and out of a patrol car, home at night and on weekends, and served as essential stepping-stones to promotions. No, they'd wait their turn like everyone else. Besides, as far as the veteran macho-men of the LAPD were concerned, the way the city was going the department would soon all be theirs anyway.

Los Angeles certainly no longer belonged to WASPs with names like Gates, Davis, Parker, and Fisk. Not with all those impoverished, undoubtedly illegal Mexicans, Salvadorans, and Guatemalans in Pico Union and East L.A. And it wasn't as if it were *just* Pico Union and East L.A. They were everywhere now: the eastern reaches of Hollywood, moving in on the blacks in South Central, even crossing the Hollywood Hills and the Santa Monica Mountains to envelop whole areas of the San Fernando Valley, the last affordable white, suburban bastion of the city. No longer could white Angelenos move to the Valley, harmonizing to the happy lyrics of that very special Gordon Jenkins Valley song: "I'll forget my sins, I'll be makin' new friends, Where the West begins and the sunset ends. 'Cause I've decided where yours truly should be ... it's the San Fernando Valley for me."

Now it was the San Fernando Valley for *them*, too. True, they hadn't rolled into the predominantly Jewish Westside yet, but with six-hundred-square-foot bungalows going for half a million dollars, nobody else was rolling in there either. Latinos were 40 percent of the city's population now and growing. Forty percent. And most of them were barely scratching out a living. Was there a maid, a baby-sitter, a busboy, a cook, a gardener, a janitor, or a nonunion construction or factory worker in L.A. who spoke anything but Spanish? Sure, only 11 percent of them voted, but just wait until they were all legal and organized.

And in addition to them was the endless sea of Koreans, Thais, and Vietnamese who had washed over Central City and mid-Wilshire, competing with the Latinos who were there, *too*. Hollywood and Fairfax were busting with Armenians, Arabs, Israelis, Russian Jews, and God knows what else. And the blacks, of course, were still in South Central, even if their percentage of the total population had declined to about fourteen. But then again, with all those Latinos pouring over the border, *everybody's* percentage was declining. Why by the early 1990s the top-rated radio station in the 10-million-listener Los Angeles–Orange County radio market wouldn't be one programming gangster rap, heavy metal, easy-listening, or angry right-wing talk-show hosts, but KLAX-FM, a Spanish-language station playing endless tracks of *ranchera*, that is, *Mexican* country music. That's right. Of *all* the radio stations in the Los Angeles metropolitan area, the number one Arbitron-rated station had Spanish-speaking DJs playing Mexican music. It was amazing what was happening to the city.

The migration of the third world into a city that had once prided itself on being both literally and figuratively the "white spot" of America had swelled Los Angeles' population to 3.5 million people and completely transformed its social fabric. During the sixties, seventies, and eighties the city had gone from the neat WASP community it had once been—Ronald Reagan's 1920s Main Street vision of urban America—into a teeming modern-day version of New York's Lower East Side of ninety years ago. They, and the blacks, had taken over Los Angeles. In the Los Angeles school district—the second largest in the nation after New York City—almost half of the 641,000 kids, for example, didn't even speak English. Which wasn't surprising considering that over 70 percent of the parents in the district were immigrants, and 87 percent of the students were nonwhite.

The department would be next. And right beside them when they took over would be the women. Who would have believed it? Women officers with their braided hair tucked under their caps, working patrol on a police department that for decades had routinely defined policing in operational and tactical Marine Corps elite-unit military terms. How tall could they be? Five foot two? Five three? In the old days when Bill Parker had made the LAPD the self-proclaimed best police department in the world, everyone had known with whom they were dealing when they encountered a Los Angeles police officer. The motorcycle cops all looked like Arnold Schwarzenegger prototypes clad in jackboots and tailored uniforms that seemed as if they'd been copied from models in an SS war museum. The SWAT team resembled a highly secretive, ski-masked, antiterrorist military unit. And the patrol officers really *did* look like Martin Milner and Kent McCord on "Adam 12": five foot ten or more, overwhelmingly white males, high-school educated, probably veterans, with a contact-sports background and clean, traditional, Anglo-Saxon values and beliefs.

Not now. Now, in addition to the women, you had homosexuals de-manding—*demanding*—their place on the department. "Who," as Daryl Gates himself had once asked, "would want to work with one?"

Less than thirty years ago, the city had been white and Protestant, a neat and orderly community where a family could go out for dinner at restaurants with names like Bob's Big Boy and leave their doors un-locked. It was simple life in the big city. Now it was becoming a horror, a West Coast version of New York. Nobody, however, was going to turn the officers of the LAPD into slump-shouldered, big-bellied, long-haired cops dangling cigarettes out of their mouths while they held up lampposts, like in New York City. Not on Daryl Gates's watch. He might be the last of the white big-city chiefs of police, but he was still very much around.

"To protect and to serve . . ."

Continuing with his speech, Daryl Gates lets that sink in for a moment. Then he goes on, "The law, you must have a reverence for the law. A secular reverence for the law."

A secular reverence for the law. He had learned that from Bill Parker, as he had so much else. Bill Parker's stamp, in fact, was not only on him, it was everywhere in L.A.—everywhere in the Southwest—where there was a cop. Forty years earlier, Daryl Gates had been a soft-spoken rookie barely on the street a year when he was yanked out of traffic control and made the chauffeur and bodyguard for Parker, who'd just been appointed the new chief of police.

Bill Parker was an iron-fisted, God fearing alcoholic so stern and icy that "Star Trek" creator Gene Roddenberry—himself a former LAPD officer—was said to have based the character of Spock on him. It was Parker who started the modern-day LAPD breed. Bill Parker who had taught his protégé Daryl Gates the essential philosophy of policing that Gates, Ed Davis, the LAPD hierarchy—the entire department—would follow as if sent down by Moses from the Mount: Give no slack and take no shit from anyone. Confront and command. Control the streets at all times. Always be aggressive. Stop crimes before they happen. Seek them out. Shake them down. Make that arrest. And never, never, admit the department had done anything wrong.

And it was Bill Parker who had grasped the power of the chief of police in Los Angeles and redrawn the hierarchical flow chart in a way that city officials couldn't help but understand: "The police commission doesn't run the police department, *I* run the police department," he would sum up. By the seventies, Chief Ed Davis would contemptuously dismiss rumors that he might run for mayor, a sad, weak position that controlled little and was always at the mercy of the city council. He didn't want to be mayor, he said, because he already *had* more power than the mayor.

Civil rights, Vietnam, the social revolution of the sixties, Watergate, had passed. The city's racial, cultural, and class transformation was complete. But nothing in the code or the philosophy of the department had changed. Most especially nothing in its leadership. The special LAPD pugnaciousness that went beyond cop machismo, that seemed the product of long nights spent tossing and turning—struggling to invent new ways to outrage everyone who did not totally back the department—remained under Daryl Gates. Just weeks before the speech he was now giving, for example, he had told a U.S. Senate committee how he thought the problem of recreational drug use should be dealt with. "Casual drug users," he said, "should be taken out and shot." Now *there* was an outrageous line made even more so by Daryl Gates's straight-faced delivery and the fact that he was commanding thousands of police officers who, in many judgment-call situations, were licensed to kill. Local reporters, however, had examples that stretched for a mile of such taunting, deliberately provocative remarks and insults that Daryl Gates, like Bill Parker and Ed Davis before him, had made over the years—any one of which would have gotten them fired in other cities.

But in L.A., as Daryl Gates knew—as everyone knew—they wouldn't dare *try*. And he was of no mind to resign. Even after twelve years as chief, and forty-one on the force. He had plans for the department. Plans for his 8,400 officers who worked the LAPD's eighteen geographic divisions and patrolled the sprawling 465 square miles of Los Angeles. Plans to expand his department. It was common knowledge that the LAPD had the fewest police per resident of the nation's six largest departments, just 2.5 per thousand. There was hardly a time, after all, that either Gates or his tightly controlled, smoothly oiled public relations division failed to mention it. That the department was policing a horizontal, easy-to-traverse city, however, was rarely if ever brought up. Nor was the fact that the LAPD had more civilians assisting them than did the cops in many other cities; or that the department was top-heavy with officers in special units as opposed to those actually out on patrol. Nevertheless, crime *was* increasing, the department *was* stretched thin, and it was Daryl Gates's *mission* to see that the LAPD was increased to ten thousand officers.

With his large hands slicing through the air for emphasis, Gates continues addressing the cadets:

"You wear on your chest a badge that's unlike any other badge anywhere, the badge of the Los Angeles Police Department."

By now his voice, which is normally soft—and his syntax, which usually resembles the convoluted meanderings of a George Bush—has been transformed. The tremor has deepened a dramatic, rhythmic octave—displaying as much passion as is possible for a man so tightly wound.

"It [the badge] is unique," he tells them, "because it . . . represents a department that has never known a major scandal. . . . No major scandals like you have in New York or Chicago or Philadelphia or the other major cities in the country."

No major, *modern-day* scandals. Daryl Gates had always been proud of that. The department had always been proud of that. No major scandals. *Controversies,* yes. Too many to count. But for forty years, ever since Bill Parker, the department's reputation for honesty had been almost as well deserved as it had been shrewdly publicized. The unspoken credo was simple: If you beat the shit out of someone, we'll back you 100 percent; but if you take even one penny, your ass is ours.

Daryl Gates had continued that tradition over his tenure as chief, even as he looked for new opportunity. For several years, "scared to death," as he frequently said, "because [he] couldn't turn the president down," he had waited for the call from George Bush offering him "the only jobs he would have considered": drug czar or head of the CIA. But the call never came. And the feelers he had put out to the state Republican hierarchy about running for governor of California had been insultingly— condescendingly—dismissed, as if he were a loose cannon, a right-wing kook.

As for running for mayor, that had long ago ceased being an option. The city was too liberal and Democratic to elect him, even though whites, less than 40 percent of the population, still made up 65 percent of the registered voters. He was too much of a lightning rod. And Daryl Gates was the kind of man for whom just the *thought* of retiring to his condo in San Clemente with nothing to do but work on his tan was a constant source of anxiety. Retirement was *old* personified. Retirement was no chauffeur and no bodyguard and no 8,400 awestruck men and women snapping to attention and hanging on your every word. Retirement was obscurity.

So he had now committed himself indefinitely to the LAPD, to his $180,000-a-year salary, and to his plans. He would get Michael Milken paroled to his care and use the fallen financial icon of the eighties to develop a partnership between business, the LAPD, and government. He would oversee the building of a new, expanded LAPD headquarters downtown. He would surpass Bill Parker's record sixteen years as chief and outlast Mayor Tom Bradley, the man he probably detested more than any other in public life. And with the new officers in his expanded department, he would increase the power of the LAPD, putting even more uniformed officers into public school classrooms to teach his antidrug crusade through the department-controlled and -operated DARE program. There would be LAPD cops in the classroom, LAPD officers everywhere, pumping up the department's—and his—power and reach. Why not? He was, after all, unique as a civil servant. Like a federal judge, he could only be fired for cause. There was no mandatory retirement age for the chief of police in Los Angeles. He could serve for life.

Besides, the city was falling apart. The Bloods and Crips and the local *vatos locos* had been going nuts for years, ever since the manufacturing-based economy in South Central and East L.A. had collapsed in the late seventies, and Ronald Reagan had decided at the same time to decimate the nation's CETA programs. By the mideighties, unemployment among black and Latino males in South Central was approaching 45 percent, and the city's annual toll of gang killings was topping three hundred a year. Countrywide, the number was nearing 700. Every day it seemed the Metro section of the *Times* or the local TV stations carried a story about some six-year-old black or Salvadorian kid being gunned down in gang cross fire on his or her way to school.

But when it had really gotten out of hand, when they had stopped killing just each other and the people in their neighborhoods and started spraying bullets around *Westwood*—located as it is just thirty seconds from UCLA, two minutes from Ron and Nancy Reagan's retirement home in Bel Air, and five from Beverly Hills—to whom had the leaders of Los Angeles turned? To Daryl Gates and the LAPD, that's who. And it hadn't been just the mayor and the city council. It was also the VIPs and others who were there today listening to Daryl Gates speaking at the Academy, the people who were among his core constituency—the downtown corporate CEOs, the car dealers, the real-estate agents, and bankers, the aerospace executives, the insurance brokers, the owners of small businesses, the homeowners groups and businessmen associations, the white lower-middle class in the Valley—they had also turned to the department, almost pleading for him to do something.

And he had responded by intensifying what had been the cornerstone of the department's policing in the city's ghettos for decades: drawn guns and orders over loudspeakers, "Out of the car . . . on your knees . . . hands behind your neck," while all the time, the whirl of one of the department's eighteen Bell Jet Ranger or French-made Aerospatiale helicopters armed with state-of-the-art surveillance technology buzzed overhead, serving as ambience, like in *Boyz in the Hood*. Then he had ordered the gang sweeps—flooding the streets with cops, proning out and rounding up almost twenty-five thousand black or brown males—anyone, it seemed, under forty not wearing a suit or tie who happened to be on the street at the wrong time.

Subsequently, Daryl Gates's popularity seemed to grow along with the weekend body count from the killings. One in three black males in California between twenty and twenty-nine was either in jail, in prison, on probation, or on parole, and still the slaughter continued unabated. Despite the soaring number of gang killings, the L.A. *Times* had printed a poll showing that 74 percent of the city approved of the job the LAPD was doing. His tough talk and simple solutions were popular. At least *he* hadn't given up.

Just days after he gave his suggestion that casual drug users should be shot, for example, he had received from the civilian members of the police commission—a commission appointed by his liberal rival Tom Bradley—not a rebuff, but a cake with candles. They had wheeled the cake into the weekly police commission hearing, a token to celebrate the anniversary of his fortieth year on the force. Within days, the LAPD's press relations office announced that Gates had also received a $300,000 book advance for his memoirs. He was becoming both rich and famous: playing himself in an idolatrous episode of the TV cop show "Hunter" and garnering headlines by bringing former first lady Nancy Reagan with him on a drug raid. Outfitted in a navy blue LAPD windbreaker with NANCY inscribed on the front, she had first freshened up her makeup in a special LAPD trailer before going with the chief to a suspected South Central rock house. There she watched as it was smashed into and then gingerly stepped around the handcuffed cokeheads on the floor.

"I have chiefs all over the country who have these badge collections," says Daryl Gates, now nearly shouting as he reaches for the apex of his address. "And they're forever coming up to me and saying, 'Hey! Can I get a badge from the LAPD? It's the only one I don't have.' And I always tell them proudly, 'That's the only one you're *not* going to get. Unless,' " says Daryl Gates, pounding the podium, " 'you wanna go through the Los Angeles Police Academy—If-You-are-Qualified-Chief!' . . . If you are qualified." Softly, he adds, "Three things, folks, three things: reverence for the law . . . to protect and to serve . . . and pride in a badge that shines because of the people who wear it."

Then, spreading his arms, Gates ends his speech: "Welcome to the greatest family of all—the LAPD family!"

Around him, beaming parents, and the brothers, sisters, and friends of the cadets, cameras in tow, happily click away, while off to the west, beyond the parched, eucalyptus-studded hills surrounding the Academy, the endless sprawl of Los Angeles sparkles in the November sun.

In 1949, Daryl Gates had stood on this same dirt and grass field as a graduating cadet. His ascendancy in the following decades had almost exactly coincided with the department's golden age. And on this same field had also marched the fabled chiefs who'd made the LAPD the dynasty it was today: James Edgar Davis, William Parker, Edward M. Davis.

Like him, they had devoted their careers to building the department, and their public lives to exemplifying the traditions of the LAPD. As the CIA had belonged to the boys from Yale, the NYPD to New York's Irish Catholics, so, too, had the LAPD belonged to them. Their ghosts were everywhere at the Academy, and their legacies never seemed more secure. It was perfectly understandable, therefore, that Daryl Gates had not an inkling of the raging inferno that was to come, or that on this day, both he and the LAPD legend he so revered had reached their high-water mark. It was easy, after all, to forget on a day like this that the Los Angeles Police Department was not only theirs.

In the winter of 1940, Tom Bradley, too, had marched onto that Police

Academy field, an outsider who never really became a part of the LAPD tradition, although, undoubtedly, he would have loved to have been included.

But it was a measure of the success of James Edgar Davis, Bill Parker, Ed Davis, and Daryl Gates that so much of Tom Bradley's public life would nevertheless revolve around the LAPD, even though he had quit the force in 1961. It was also a mark of their success that it wouldn't be until the spring of 1991, at least twenty-five years late, that Tom Bradley would find himself locked in mortal, epoch-defining combat with Daryl Gates and the ghosts that stood behind him over a motorist named Rodney King; and that a year later, they would watch with the world as their city went up in flames.

PART 2

PEORIA WITH PALMS

. . . .

CHAPTER 1

The Past Meets the Future

• •

Out of the corner of his eye Tommy Carr could see the chief of police of Los Angeles. But he couldn't *hear* him. And hearing James Edgar Davis—or rather hearing the chief's overdue command for him to raise his Colt .38—was becoming almost an obsession for Carr. An obsession that was now increasing in direct proportion to the rapidly expanding ash that was dangling from the cigarette in the mouth of Lt. Joe Dircks.

Standing laterally and about fifteen or twenty feet from Carr on the dirt and gravel shooting range of the Police Academy, Dircks had lit the cigarette on cue. He'd done his part. It was Chief Davis who was making Tommy Carr more nervous with each passing second by failing to give the command. It was Davis who kept ignoring them in spite of the fact that they were constantly looking over at him, trying to figure out exactly what it was he was waiting for. Davis who should have been more considerate. Carr, after all, was new to the LAPD pistol team. And this day in 1937 was the first time he was really participating in a shooting exhibition. The first time, with the public looking on, that he was going to shoot a lighted cigarette out of the mouth of a tall, thin man standing sideways in a blue uniform five or six yards away from him.

Unlike Tommy Carr, Chief of Police James Davis and Lt. Joe Dircks—

who were gambling and hunting partners as well as close friends—had been putting on shooting demonstrations for over eight years now, ever since 1929. Two or three times a week they'd go to Rotary and Elks clubs, to high schools, and to women's organizations such as the Daughters of the American Revolution. Davis would first give a speech, and then both of them would display their marksmanship.

James Davis was always impressive. At five feet seven inches tall and a weight that ranged from 220 to 250 pounds, he was a broad, massive Texan who was once described by his most fervent critic—the Reverend Robert "Fighting Bob" Shuler—as "a man with a pink complexion who looks like he had a massage every morning and his fingernails manicured."

On the LAPD pistol team that he had founded, Davis was known as a good but not a great shot, as someone never quite able to draw the department's $16 monthly "distinguished expert" bonus pay, or the solid-gold medal with a platinum bar and diamond that went along with it. Certainly, he wasn't good enough, as Joe Dircks was quick to point out, "that you'd feel comfortable holding a cigarette or anything *else* in your mouth when he was shooting."

Dircks, on the other hand, was both the Academy range master as well as one of the two or three best marksmen on the pistol team, and looked the part. The slow-talking son of a Colorado homesteader, he had the lean, hard appearance of a central-casting stand-in for Randolph Scott in a forties B western.

Together over the past year, they'd also been running and participating in additional shooting demonstrations at the newly completed Police Academy. James Davis had used prison labor to get it built: Okie trustees straight out of the *Grapes of Wrath,* homeless Depression vagrants, and drunks doing 180 days for public intoxication. Afterward, determined to show it off and generate good-will for further construction, he'd begun the shooting exhibitions.

Warming up the school and club audiences before the demonstrations, James Davis would tell them how "in the old days, a test of a man's marksmanship was to snuff out the flames in a line of candles." And *that,* he'd add, was exactly what he intended to do.

Meanwhile, Joe Dircks would be busy unloading the huge leather satchel crammed with white chalk, decks of playing cards, clay pigeons, cigarettes and cigars, two or three kinds of ammunition, and a gigantic spotlight. While Davis continued talking, Dircks would carefully light the room, trying always to precisely place the beam so that the light—which affects a shooter's aim—was exactly the same for each demonstration. Next, on a nearby wall, he'd mount a steel-backed two-by-twelve-inch board with ten drilled holes in which birthday candles had been placed.

Ceasing his talk, Davis would then turn and rapidly fire six rounds from his little .22 Whitman—managing always to instantly extinguish the flames. Of course the audience was never made aware that the swift drafts of air from the bullets whizzing anywhere near the candles was in itself enough to blow them out.

Joe Dircks always followed this by the stunt Tommy Carr was getting set to perform: the shooting of a cigarette or a piece of chalk or candles or a card out of Davis's or another officer's mouth, hand, or ear.

By now, the exhibitions at the Academy had also settled into a pattern: to the background sounds of bluebirds chirping, .38s popping, and the Academy's artificial waterfall cascading over a rock garden arduously built by the trustees, James Davis would give a speech to groups of about thirty invited guests. Each week came different faces who were otherwise interchangeable: rich downtown businessmen who ran the city, their power-brokering attorneys, well-connected real-estate speculators, small-time entrepreneurs, film-industry executives, and movie stars as famous as little Shirley Temple and Freddie Bartholomew. Anyone who James Davis thought might be even remotely useful to him or to the department's image was welcome.

Late every Wednesday morning they would ride up to the Academy, driving the twisting roads through the pastel cottages in the tranquil villages of Chavez Ravine and Echo Park. In the lounge above the Academy's white adobe cafeteria, lunch was served and the chief would speak. Usually he talked about one subject: communism. Communism, and the subgroups that, he was certain, revolved around it: unions, union men and union organizers, liberals and subversives (there was no difference) and vagrants, drunks and drug addicts. His Red Squad was considered by the Los Angeles chapter of the ACLU to be "the most lawless and brutal" in the country. And he himself was thought of even by contemporaries such as reporter Harold Story of the then ultra-right-wing *Los Angeles Times* as "a burly, dictatorial, somewhat sadistic, bitterly antilabor man who saw communist influence behind every telephone pole."

Residents of Los Angeles, James Davis believed, were either "citizens of economic value" or they were not. "Known narcotic addicts," as he would tell his luncheon guests, should be arrested *on sight* under the state's vagrancy laws and slammed into jail for six months. There, they would be deprived of coffee, milk, sugar, tobacco, candy, cards, reading material, games, visitors, or the chance for parole. They were entitled, he'd say, to only a Bible and "beans and abuse."

Following his luncheon speech, Davis's guests would line up to be formally presented with LAPD detective-lieutenant badges. Invariably, the day's finale was a short walk to the pistol range to view the shooting exhibition, which usually proceeded as it had so far this day. That is, while Joe Dircks lit a cigarette, James Davis would busy himself giving yet a second, more casual talk. Then, at a moment of his choosing, he'd turn from his audience and bellow the command that Tommy Carr was now anxiously awaiting: *"R-a-i-s-e pistol!"* After the shooter had done so, Davis would then pause and boom what was meant to sound like a spontaneous afterthought: "No! Wait! J-u-s-t a minute here, Lieutenant. W-a-i-t j-u-s-t a minute. *I'll* hold that cigarette. In the Los Angeles Police Department a superior officer never asks a man to do anything he wouldn't do himself."

And with that, he would march dramatically forward in a stiff, shoulders-back gait that reminded his friend and fellow cop Irvis Lester of a pouter pigeon—"the kind that sticks out his breast and struts as he walks."

His intercession was always exciting with its spur-of-the-moment edge, the possibility of real danger, and Davis's own, very real charisma. For in spite of his enormous girth, James Davis did not have the look, at least in his navy blue uniform or tailored three-piece business suit, of a soft, classic, Oliver Hardy fat man. Instead, there was a solidity, an energy, to his bulk—as if the tight fabric of his clothing was being pressed to bursting by flesh that was not exactly muscle, but not quite flab.

And today, striding toward Joe Dircks, everything had been going as planned. Davis had reached out, snatched the cigarette from Dirck's mouth, and carefully wrapped a piece of white paper around its end—a necessary step that was both practical and macho, enabling him to extend the cigarette's length and to avoid the appearance, if only by proxy, of touching Dircks's lips.

He'd taken so long talking, however, that by the time he'd completed wrapping the paper around the cigarette, all that was left for Carr to shoot at was the paper, a tremendous ash, and a tiny white butt. Nevertheless, as he always did during the routine, James Davis placed it in his mouth.

The tension, already high among the audience, was only heightened by Davis's unfailingly stern demeanor. He had lips that moved so rarely when he talked that his words seemed to tumble through the spaces in his teeth. That, along with a strong chin and jaw atop a bull neck, gave his face a cast-in-concrete look. When he smiled, which was seldom, it was quick and short—as if he'd impetuously given something away and wanted immediately to snatch it back.

It was his eyes, however, that revealed the full, intense force of his personality. Blue-gray, they stared out like two piercing bullets. Bending forward to talk, he'd lean his head into your face, his eyes never for a moment leaving yours. The effect caused men to avoid speaking with him unless absolutely necessary, and women to whisper of how they felt undressed by his gaze. Even if he hadn't been a policeman, wrote a reporter for the old *Los Angeles Record*, "you'd wonder if you had forgotten to hide the body."

Standing absolutely still now, Davis waited as Joe Dircks waved his right arm and barked, "Raise pistol!"

Fiercely concentrating, Tommy Carr took aim and, on command, fired. Joe Dircks looked at Davis, then stared back astounded at Tommy Carr. He had missed. He had missed everything. It was amazing, really. The LAPD pistol team was among the very best in the country. Almost everybody on it had won a national or international championship. This was the first time anybody had missed *everything* since the Badge Day luncheons at the Academy had begun. Nevertheless, Carr squared himself and fired again. Usually, the shooter tried for the end of the cigarette, knocking off just the ash. But there had been so little cigarette left, when the second bullet blasted into the burned-down butt located just startling inches from James Davis's lips, the ash, paper, and tobacco splattered all over his face, neck, and chest.

Instantly, reflexively, James Davis's right hand rose to check himself out, to make certain that it was merely ash and tobacco on his face, and not parts of himself. But almost as quickly, he snapped his hand back down to his side. Off to his left, his riveted guests were staring, transfixed. James Davis had always cultivated his image as a fearless top marksman almost as diligently as he had his tough-cop, crime-fighting persona— blending the two as if he were some kind of nineteenth-century frontier lawman instead of the chief of police of one of the nation's fastest-growing cities.

In 1931 at the National Pistol Matches at Camp Perry, Ohio, for example, he had invented and won the right-handed, left-handed pistol championship of the United States. Ever since 1917 when he'd been involved in a Chinatown gun battle and witnessed another officer's shooting arm broken by a suspect's bullet, he'd practiced shooting both right- and left-handed. Practice, of course, is everything in pistol shooting, a physical act that requires time for an arm to develop the strength to hold, sight, and fire a pistol. So shooting both left- and right-handed was an uncommon stunt really, more than a mark of skill, and the winning of the match didn't mean much. Except that James Davis had practiced and that nobody else had. And that he *wanted* it. He had understood the drama, the showmanship, of shooting. It was only the intervention of his wife, in fact, that had prevented James Davis from using his eight-year-old son Charlie for holding a piece of chalk while he blasted it out of the boy's hand. *That* was drama, his son standing there holding that chalk, trusting him to shoot it out. *That* was an image.

An image that was now at work on James Davis. An image that made him now fear checking himself out to ensure that it wasn't part of his nose lying there on his cheek, but merely some shattered pieces of paper and tobacco. He'd survived a scandal, been called a thief and been publicly described as a simple puppet of Harry Chandler and the L.A. *Times*. Those were business. But a coward? Unmanly? No, those were words with which he couldn't live. Not even with the possibility of people *thinking* them. Hadn't the whole point of his intercession been, after all, to show his courage? To display his bravery in the most public of ways? And hadn't he told a reporter that he'd once refused an order to "throw up [his] hands" when "a revolver was thrust into [his] ribs" during a search in a darkened room because it wouldn't have been "dignified" to do so? Yet to the cops standing by who regularly watched the exhibition, it was obvious by the strained look on James Davis's face that he was deeply frightened—and at war with himself about what to do. Officers assigned to the Academy such as rookie patrolman John Kinsling were catching each other's eyes and literally biting their lips to keep from laughing. Knowing Davis as they did, the entire sequence of events was hysterical: his missed cue, the ashes and tobacco smearing him, the stricken look that had crossed his face.

Suddenly, however, James Davis made up his mind and broke the tension. As if charged by a surge of electrical current, his open palm whipped up and wiped his entire face. But no one present, and most particularly not his officers, laughed. An inadvertent laugh could seriously stall a career.

James Davis was a man of enormous power, which on this day in 1937 was perhaps at its apex. The youngest chief in the history of the Los Angeles Police Department, Davis, by now, was also L.A.'s longest-serving chief of police, having already been in office for nine years. In those years, the department had broken all arrest records and initiated both the dragnet and the bum blockade. His Red Squad had become nationally famous, leading the way in breaking strikes and suppressing subversives. And almost single-handedly, he had wrestled from the city the northern hills of Elysian Park and had them placed in the hands of the private association that he headed known as the Los Angeles Police Revolver and Athletic Club. Then he'd overseen the building of the Police Academy. So successful was he that after the Academy's completion, a bronze plaque—still prominently displayed—was hung outside its main building. It read:

In Memorial

James E. Davis

Through Whose Vision, Leadership and Untiring Efforts This Police Training and Recreational Training Center was Established

Vain and formal, James Davis was, moreover, one of those angry short men who always wanted to be tall. Invariably, he gave his height as five ten and bitterly bemoaned the fact that he wasn't taller. "I wish my thighs were in accordance with the rest of my body," he once complained to Irvis Lester. "If they were, I'd be about as tall as anyone in the department. When I sit down at a table, I *look* tall. But not when I'm standing. It's my thighs, they're just not in proportion."

No one on the department ever dared call him Jim. Not even Joe Dircks. Nor did he call his assistant, Lt. William H. Parker, Bill. No. It was always lieutenant. Lieutenant this, lieutenant that. Once on a rainy Badge Day afternoon in the Academy lounge, Parker was talking with

John Kinsling before the luncheon started. A taciturn South Dakotan with ten years on the force, Parker was highly respected, having already managed to put himself through law school, pass the bar, and draw up the bylaws governing the Police Academy for Davis. During Badge Day, he and Kinsling were expected to mingle with Davis's guests, massage their egos, answer questions, and sell the department.

Spotting the two, Davis approached them and, ignoring Kinsling, whose rank made him not important enough to be addressed, said to Parker, "Lieutenant, you're shirking your duties; make yourself available to these people. Now."

For Kinsling, the incident was petty and embarrassing, but inconsequential. It was 1937, the height of the Depression, and as a twenty-four-year-old rookie, he was happy just to have a job. It wasn't until decades later that he realized that he'd been standing with the two men who would come to symbolize the LAPD. In James Davis he was seeing the personification of the department in the first half of the twentieth century. And in Bill Parker, the architect of its future.

Fighting Bob's People

••••••••••••••••••••••

Fourteen years earlier, enormous clouds of smoke had burst from the flashlight cameras of the news photographers who were busily snapping pictures of the Reverend Robert Shuler. At that moment Shuler himself was busy, almost frantically trying to calm an angry crowd packed to suffocation in an ornate anteroom of the office of the mayor of Los Angeles. The role of pacifier did not come easily to a man affectionately known to his followers as Fighting Bob, but that day in June of 1923 he had felt it necessary to act. The situation was clearly getting out of hand. As pastor of the Trinity Methodist Episcopal Church, Shuler, together with the Reverend Gustav Briegleb and other outraged local ministers, had brought the members of their flocks to City Hall to protest the LAPD's lax enforcement of the city's vice laws, and the ineffectiveness of its vice squad. Prominent on the squad, and a man Fighting Bob seemed to particularly detest, was James Davis, who was already a rising star within the department. He just couldn't get it into his head, Shuler would say, how a man as pampered and fastidious looking as Davis could ever be a good policeman.

Despite Shuler's pleas, his followers began standing on chairs, screaming and pushing—surging forward to within just a few feet of Mayor

George Cryer himself. A politician not known for his strength of character, Cryer seemed incapable of response. In fact, as the furious crowd booed and heckled a police spokesman hastily summoned by Cryer to defend his administration, the mayor could be seen behind his desk looking numb and dumbfounded, as inch by inch, moment by moment, he slumped ever deeper into his chair.

Stepping forward and raising his hands, Bob Shuler finally managed to quiet his supporters, who had been lustily cheering his every word even as they booed almost every utterance of the LAPD's spokesman. We're not here, he told them, to accuse the mayor or chief of police of dishonesty, of graft, or payoffs. But God knew, as did they, that something was grievously wrong with the LAPD's vice enforcement. The city was obviously rife with sin and corruption, and something, he told the mayor and the crowd, would have to be done. Immediately.

The very next day, reported the *Los Angeles Record,* "a sweeping investigation of the Police Department," and a simultaneous "search of cheap rooming houses, soft drink parlors and pool halls to round up vags [vagrants] and questionable characters" was ordered. It was an impressive display of Bob Shuler's strength. And over the next years he and his fellow clergymen would demonstrate that strength again and again, much to the consternation of successive police chiefs and vice squad officers like James Davis. In a city whose culture, with the exclusion of Hollywood, had virtually been run by Protestant ministers for the past two decades, Bob Shuler was a man of influence.

He'd been born in a log cabin in Virginia's Blue Ridge Mountains, and for a time before coming to Los Angeles, he was a circuit-riding Methodist minister in Texas. Once he'd established himself in L.A. he publicly attacked the city's Catholics, was jailed for contempt of court, and was sued for libel by the mayor. It was no matter.

Through *Bob Shuler's Magazine,* and his radio station, KGEF, he influenced an enormous population (at one time estimated to be the largest religious radio audience in the world) that went far beyond his substantial bedrock, fundamentalist congregation.

He was far from the only local minister with that kind of influence. Shuler's colleague, the Reverend Dr. Gustav Briegleb of St. Paul's Presbyterian Church, was almost as powerful. It was Briegleb who convinced the police commission to regulate public dancing to ensure that dancers' cheeks or heads not touch, that the hand of a male not be permitted anywhere but on a female's back between her shoulder and waist, and that a female's right hand rested nowhere but in her partner's left palm. Banned as well was "music suggestive of bodily contortions." The regulations were no aberration. Not in the Los Angeles of the 1920s, where Isadora Duncan had been barred from dancing, and the LAPD had shut down Eugene O'Neill's *Desire Under the Elms;* not in the L.A. of the thirties, where the department had thrown the entire seventy-member cast of the play *Lysistrata* into the Lincoln Heights jail. There were, after all, few American cities where the notion of a pure, sinless metropolis had been taken so seriously for so long. And fewer cities still had reacted with such a powerful disgust to their own histories or had a police department with a vice detail known as the Purity Squad.

The sole purpose of the railroad tracks that cut down the middle of Alameda Street in the late 1890s seemed to have been to move customers, as if the railroad itself were part of some adult-fantasy theme park. As the Southern Pacific trains rolled slowly past, women inside the hundreds of narrow, cell-like structures lining the street began to stir—patting their small beds and checking their washstands and chamber pots before they emerged to sit on their windowsills. There, calling out to the passengers, they would expose themselves to their potential clients. The downtown section of Los Angeles they worked was known then as the Tenderloin, and it contained hundreds of gambling dives and dozens of saloons as well as the rooms or "cribs" of the prostitutes. It was the last in a series of flourishing red-light districts that had been a staple of Los Angeles ever since the Gold Rush. By the turn of the century, however, it had all been driven underground, brought down by the forebears of Robert Shuler and Gustav Briegleb, brought down by the people who had come to Los Angeles, made it theirs, and then painted its culture a dull, anemic gray.

They began arriving in earnest in 1883, when the railroad tracks of the Southern Pacific finally entered the city. Enticed by brilliant promotional advertising that saturated the nation, and by ticket prices as low as one dollar, they had poured into Los Angeles from the Midwest and elsewhere. In 1887, the new Santa Fe line alone would bring more than one hundred thousand tourists, settlers, and land speculators, who, in that year, would boost real estate sales to more than $100 million. People would literally get off the train and, on *that day,* buy land and property.

It was no accident. A small group of visionary local businessmen, together with the railroad barons, had made it happen. They owned huge tracts and needed people to purchase them. Comfortable, middle-class people with money to spend and invest. And thanks to their national advertising, they got them. By the 1890s, Los Angeles' population, which had been just under twelve thousand in the 1880s, had reached one hundred thousand. For the next thirty years they kept coming: the native sons and daughters of Illinois, Ohio, Nebraska, Minnesota, Iowa, and Missouri, just a generation or two removed from the bleak states of New England. They were hard working farmers who'd sold their land; ne'er-do-well salesmen looking to score; small-town lawyers, dentists, and schoolteachers; the tubercular; the invalid; the wealthy widow or pensioned spinster; the speculators in stocks and real estate. They were all part of what Charles Fletcher Lummis, the pioneering editor of the *Los Angeles Times,* later called "the least heroic migration in history . . . [undertaken] by and large, by the most comfortable immigrants, financially, in history." Welcomed for their white skin, Protestant heritage, and intrinsic conservatism, it was they who would create an economy so vital, transformative, and expansive that it would seem to exist on its own, like a ravished, self-mutating organism. And it was they who would control the social, political, and cultural life of Los Angeles until the early 1960s. Hollywood glamour and Hollywood's image would become synonymous with the city. But *they,* the sons and daughters of the American heartland, would define the real L.A.

From the start they had been determined to achieve control of their city and then hold it tight. They might have needed blacks, Catholics, Jews, Mexicans, Chinese, Japanese, Filipinos, Italians, and other foreign-born immigrants for their sweat labor, but they would not permit them to mongrelize and corrupt their culture. No, Los Angeles would remain the "white spot" of America. Would remain, as John Porter, the teetotaling, Bible-quoting Iowa transplant who successfully ran for mayor in 1929, put it, "the last stand of native-born Protestant Americans." In this they would be remarkably successful. And instead of Los Angeles growing into a Mediterranean cultural mecca, or into a free-flowing forum of social, political, and artistic ideas like New York or San Francisco, the city and its surrounding communities—Glendale, Inglewood, Pasadena, and Burbank—would develop into a region of stifling homogeneity.

In 1902 they passed laws prohibiting prostitution and gambling. In

1906 they limited the number of saloons to two hundred, part of the national trend toward prohibition that by 1917 would see twenty-seven states outlaw alcohol. In 1919 the entire country would do so with the Volstead Act, paving the way for America's criminal cartels. By 1913, Los Angeles was also forbidding sexual relations between unmarried people, a law that was strictly enforced. Gambling laws, meanwhile, were being so rigidly interpreted that LAPD officers were tracking down candy machines that occasionally returned a nickel instead of a gum ball.

They formed groups and organizations such as the Anti-Saloon League, the Anti-Racetrack Gambling League, and the Sunday Rest League to reflect their passion and to ensure that the people of Los Angeles would live according to their vision of the world. Even by the Victorian standards of the day, the puritanical atmosphere they created in Los Angeles was astoundingly intrusive. There existed in the city, as Willard Huntington Wright wrote in the *Smart Set* in 1913, "a stupid censorship so incredibly puerile that even Boston will have to take second place. . . . Los Angeles is overrun with militant moralists, connoisseurs of sin, experts of biological purity."

Titillating scandals of Hollywood stars like Fatty Arbuckle, multiple marriages and divorces of various movie queens and leading men, eccentric revivalist preachers like Aimee Semple McPherson, and the weird cults and political movements of Southern California would come to be misinterpreted by the rest of the country as signs of a flourishing individuality. But in reality, as the great historian of California, Carey McWilliams, has pointed out, these were all precisely the symptoms of a *lack* of power and diversity; were, in fact, evidence of people's inability to affirm their individuality. Underneath the happy veneer of sunshine and palms, thousands of people—characters straight out of a Nathanael West novel—were sitting in their cottages at night silently screaming. Nightlife, street life, street vendors (Los Angeles was the only major American city that outlawed street vending), and crowds all lead to noise, filth, disorder, diversity, rebellion, anarchy, drinking, gambling, and sex and were therefore to be discouraged.

And the Los Angeles Police Department was expected to do the discouraging. It was then and there that the seeds for the invasive philosophy of policing that would dominate the culture and politics of Los Angeles throughout the twentieth century were planted.

*　　*　　*

In part, the rigid, homogenized culture that the new middle class institutionalized was a reaction to the city's history. Before California entered the Union, Los Angeles had been a minor Mexican pueblo with a population of about fifteen hundred. But the Mexican-American War of 1848, and the violent years of the Gold Rush that followed, had transformed the town into a lethal mix of cowboys, merchants, miners, drifters, hustlers, pimps, hookers, gamblers, drunks, gunmen, thugs, and thieves. Los Angeles' twin claims to fame as the "toughest town" in the West and the murder capital of California soon spawned vigilante groups, who regularly rounded up, tried, and lynched suspected criminals. Heavily armed mobs would snatch prisoners from jail and hang them from trees, corral gateways, the portico of City Hall, and once, even from the mast of a ship. Rarely did the few ineffective sheriffs or marshals do anything but look on.

In 1871 the bloody apocalypse came when a Chinese merchant shot and killed a white man in his store, sparking the Chinatown Massacre. A raging mob shot or hanged more than twenty Chinatown residents, wounded dozens more, and then looted and burned their businesses.

From its inception as a full-fledged police department in 1877, the LAPD had been underpaid and demoralized. Patrolmen, who owed their patronage and jobs to city council members, had been expected to remove weeds from vacant lots, pick up dead animals from the street, and inspect sewers in addition to the traditional tasks of law enforcement. The bobbies in London might have been widely respected. But police in Los Angeles, like those in most big American cities, were regarded as thuggish enforcers of the rich man's laws who'd been selected for their job, as one of Los Angeles' first black policemen later put it, with "the unquestioned presumption [among] those in authority . . . that a burly, two-fisted knuckle-buster who could flatten a violator with one blow made an ideal policeman." Turn-of-the-century America was overflowing with farm boys, immigrants, and working men who perfectly fit *that* description, and the skimpy pay reflected the job's meager qualifications. Predictably, American cops became not just thugs, but *corrupt* thugs, objects of ridicule and scorn, Mack Sennett's Keystone Kops. Throughout the 1890s this impression was only reinforced by widespread corruption scandals within police departments as far-flung as New York, Chicago, Philadelphia, Baltimore, Atlanta, San Francisco, and Kansas City.

In Los Angeles the paltry salaries of many LAPD officers had been supplemented by the money they'd received from local brothel owners and gamblers in the then legal, downtown red-light district—a supplemental income that was eliminated when the district was shut down. But the beat cops still needed the money, and the new reformers were determined to keep funding and salaries for the department as low as possible. It was a situation that made the taking of payoffs almost inevitable. Moreover, the reformers had also eliminated many traditional sources of political funding, while civil service reform had eliminated patronage. Yet as patrolmen needed supplemental income to make a decent living, politicians desperately needed money to wage their campaigns. Inevitably brothel and saloon owners, gamblers, and hustlers once again financed almost every major politician seeking public office, as they had done in the past. It was a symbiosis that enabled both criminals and politicians to survive despite the reformers. But it fatally poisoned the city's politics and all but destroyed the integrity of its police department.

From 1902 to 1909, three mayors elected as reformers failed to get reelected, and five police chiefs were forced to retire. The department's dual allegiance to the reformers and their almost prurient fascination with weakness and lust on one hand, and to the gangsters, businessmen, and politicians either running or acquiescing in the city's prostitution, gambling, liquor, and drug trade on the other, was leading to an institutional schizophrenia. Zealous enforcement had to be repeatedly demonstrated, but nothing truly effective could be done by a chief of police who owed his job to frequently corrupt politicians. The LAPD's dilemma in serving two of its major constituencies, each with conflicting goals, would corrode its soul for decades to come. But it was its third master, the rich, driven businessmen of downtown L.A., who would turn the department into a strong-arm goon squad.

CHAPTER 3

San Francisco Blues

••••••••••••••••••••••

Always on the minds of Harrison Gray Otis, Harry Chandler, and their business allies who ran Los Angeles had been San Francisco. San Francisco, blessed as it was with one of the world's great harbors, with a capital base derived from its forests and gold mines, with its magnificent river system for moving goods, and always, *always* with its forty-year head start on L.A.

While Los Angeles had been engaged first in vigilante excess, and then in the precarious businesses of tourism and land speculation, San Francisco was already the rich, powerful queen of California's cities. By the turn of the century, it had grown into a major industrial center with a work force that was among the most highly unionized in the world. With those advantages, Otis and Chandler—the twin titans of L.A.'s business establishment and the co-owners of the *Los Angeles Times*—reasoned that the only way for Los Angeles to possibly compete with San Francisco was to build a strong industrial base, keep the unions out and wages low. That they were able to succeed in all three was testimony to their fierce resolve.

Born in a log house in Marietta, Ohio, in 1837, Harrison Gray Otis grew up to become a seething, unforgiving man as violently outspoken as he was combative. At fourteen he became a printer's apprentice and, during the Civil War, was twice wounded while serving as a Union Army captain. Thirty years later, during the Spanish-American War, he earned the rank of brigadier general in the Philippines and the right to be referred to for the rest of his life as General Otis. In 1882 at the age of forty-five, he came to Los Angeles. The following month he bought into the *Times,* becoming its publisher. By 1886 he controlled the paper outright.

Harry Chandler, Otis's assistant and future son-in-law, would perfectly complement him, providing the calculating logic, cool stability, and long-term vision that Otis lacked. Together they were an extraordinary team, building their fortune and running Los Angeles for the next seventy years; brilliantly shaping public policy to benefit their empire, enhance their power, and amass their fortunes. They and their business partners owned over a hundred thousand acres of semiarid grazing land in the San Fernando Valley; land whose value would soar if only they had water. To irrigate them, they bought key acreage hundreds of miles north of the city in the lush, verdant Owens Valley. Then they had the city charter changed, cut the city's water commissioners in on the impending deal, and watched as a massive 230-mile aqueduct constructed with taxpayer money brought water from the Owens Valley to their land. When it was over, they had sucked both the water and the life out of a thriving agricultural valley and annihilated its farmers. But *they* had become wildly rich, making over $100 million in profits as they subdivided and sold off land now suitable for orchards, farms, and development. The water they'd bought, when combined with the bright, perennial Southern California sun, would soon make Los Angeles among America's richest farm counties.

And to export both the petroleum from the city's rapidly expanding oil industry and the produce and goods from the lands they owned, they and their allies annexed the sleepy port town of San Pedro and connected it to Los Angeles by mapping out a sixteen-mile, gerrymandered corridor. Then they had the shallow port dredged and deepened with public funds. Like the Owens aqueduct, it would become a cornerstone of both Los Angeles' future and Otis's and Chandler's fortune, connecting Los Angeles to vast new areas of the world's trade.

Using the city's new, abundant water supply as leverage, Los Angeles and its Otis-and-Chandler-led businessmen also devoured the communities surrounding the city, sweeping farther west and south in the San

Fernando Valley, annexing the distant beach town of Venice, and absorbing huge areas of the Santa Monica Mountains and their flatlands that today include Hollywood, Westwood, Bel Air, and Brentwood.

But to truly succeed, to completely impose their will and realize their vision, they had to keep their workers' wages low. Far below that of San Francisco. That meant breaking the unions. A task Harrison Gray Otis took very seriously indeed. In 1890, during one of Los Angeles' periodic recessions, he unilaterally proclaimed a 20 percent reduction in the wages at the L.A. *Times,* and then refused to even negotiate with the unions. In retaliation, they engaged him in a bitter twenty-year strike. Los Angeles suddenly became a focal point in the larger war being played out all over the nation between industry and a labor movement desperate to organize as both sides poured enormous resources into the battle. A battle that would prove as momentous in shaping the character of the Los Angeles Police Department as would the puritanical nature of the city's middle class.

Together, Otis and Chandler founded the Merchants and Manufacturers Association (M&M), an organization that not only spoke and acted for them, but controlled many of the city's politicians as well as its police. In 1909, at the Association's bidding, the City Council passed a law curtailing union organizing and limiting free speech. In the decade that followed, the council also enacted one of the most restrictive antipicketing statutes in the nation and passed the Red Flag Law, which made it a felony to display a red flag in ''opposition to organized government.'' Failure to *salute* the flag would carry a twenty-year maximum sentence. They were just three of many such antiunion and antiradical laws passed in Los Angeles. What General Otis, Harry Chandler, and the M&M wanted, they got.

In 1910, as the *Times'* twenty-year strike and lockout continued, the brewery and the metal workers also went on strike. For at least two of the strikers, it was the last straw. On an October morning, six momentous explosions hit the nerve center of the antiunion movement—the printing plant of the *Los Angeles Times.* Twenty-one *Times* employees died in the blasts, which the *Times* called ''the crime of the century'' and ''one of the worst atrocities in the history of the world.''

It's impossible to exaggerate just how stunning and unmitigated a disaster the dynamiting of the *Times* was for L.A.'s labor movement. Particularly after two structural-iron workers, the brothers J. B. and J. J. McNamara pleaded guilty in a deal engineered by their attorney, Clarence

Darrow. The strikers had been used to hard, lean times, and the McNamara brothers had become a cause célèbre, a rallying point, proof once again of the evil of their big-business enemies—personified by Harrison Gray Otis—who, they felt, had framed and scapegoated the brothers. Their admission of guilt robbed the movement of its martyrs and disillusioned the city's labor movement. In the mayoral election of 1911 the Socialist candidate, who earlier had won the primary overwhelmingly, was routed. Not only the Socialist Party but the city's labor movement was dead. For decades afterward, visitors from London, New York, Chicago, or San Francisco would be struck by the lack of a working-class style, of a certain pride, a joie de vivre, a feeling that the city belonged to the people whose sweat made it go, as well as to those who owned it. Sustaining a style and attitude was difficult when the right to picket, the secondary boycott, free speech, and any effective opposition to the white, Republican power elite and the middle class who ruled the city had been all but crushed. Los Angeles' politics would now mirror its social and cultural homogeneity. Like zealously limiting cultural diversity, declaring a city "the last citadel of the open shop" was to declare it an almost closed society. The noose around the neck of the people of L.A. would be very tightly knotted from then on.

The bombing was also a watershed event for the LAPD. It placed the department unequivocally, passionately, and irrevocably in the business of spying, surveillance, and repression, much as the bombing of Haymarket Square in 1886—in which seven policemen were killed and seventy people were injured—had done for the police department of Chicago.

Following the bombing, the number of men on the department doubled to five hundred; and the LAPD set up a file system that contained records on almost three hundred thousand people. Records, according to the LAPD's Annual Report for 1913, that "were said to be more complete than those of any other city except New York." By 1916, the LAPD also had another unit to rival the Purity Squad. It was known as the Strong-arm Squad.

CHAPTER 4

The Company Man

•••••••••••••••••••••••

He'd arrived in Los Angeles in 1911, wearing the same Army uniform in which he was discharged a week earlier. For seventeen months he'd been an artilleryman in a mule-riding mountain battery in the Philippines, and for six or seven fruitless days following his discharge, he had searched for work in San Francisco. On his first days in Los Angeles he was still searching.

A couple of years on the road picking cotton, mucking out stables, clerking in grocery stores, and three more in the Army had already drummed home the grim choices available to a dirt-poor but ambitious turn-of-the-century Texas farm boy like himself. There were the endless grunts and rivers of sweat shed by the drones in the farms and factories. There was the rage and resistance of the union men, the Reds, and the gangsters who wound up with their spirits crushed or jailed in cages like animals. Or there were the get-by jobs of a chauffeur, clerk, salesman, or petty bureaucrat. At twenty-two James Davis was a man of calculating intellect who'd emerged from the Army with $154 in his uniform pocket, an education that scarcely went beyond grade school, and no family on which to rely. For him, the choice was really no choice at all.

He'd been born into the hard, joyless world of small-town northern

Texas in 1889 among tough, silent, uncompromising people loath to reveal their emotions or display any weakness. His mother was a stern, priggish woman devoted to the Northern Methodist Church who abhorred tobacco, liquor, dancing, cards, and the theater. His nearly as devout stepfather was a deacon in the church, and the superintendent of the Sunday school. Not until he was sixteen did James Davis ever see anyone dance or play cards. And in all of his childhood he saw liquor in his home only once.

His childhood "left [him with] the impression," James Davis's son would later say of his father, "that if he had ever committed one small sin in this world, he was going to fry in hell for eternity." It was a lesson that James Davis would take to heart, both personifying and rebelling against it his entire life.

On his first full day in Los Angeles, he rented a cheap hotel room, bought a suit, shirt, and tie, and began searching for a job. Within a month he found one as a patrolman on the Los Angeles Police Department. His ranking, as he described it to an interviewer nearly two decades later, was impressive: number four out of five hundred applicants. It's uncertain, however, exactly what that meant. Perhaps it was simply a reflection of his military experience, because there was no written entrance exam. Or training. None in the law and none in marksmanship. The newly hired patrolman received only a little lecture, a bit of advice about not getting involved in family quarrels, and the guidance of a street cop who would help break him in during his first three or four days on the job. After that, he was on his own. Any qualifying tests would come later.

Two months after his arrival in Los Angeles, James Davis purchased his gun, handcuffs, billy club, keys, brass buttons, and uniform and along with twenty-five other men was sworn into a Los Angeles police department that was then doubling in size from 250 to 500 as the city's population surged to almost 325,000. His pay was $75 a month, rising to a top of $100.

Immediately upon hitting the street, James Davis ran into trouble. As he was walking his beat, "two rather nice women said hello," he later recounted, "and offered to chat." One was approaching middle age, the other, her daughter, was about nineteen. Visits to the women's home followed. Davis sat on the porch and "once or twice" even accepted their invitation into the house. It was "silly," he knew, to do so, but after all, their friendship was "perfectly ordinary." When the woman's husband—who worked nights—began to overhear gossip, he complained, and the department sent out investigators, who were told that James Davis had become a pest, a man impossible to get rid of. L.A.'s new chief of police, Charles Sebastian—who would himself later be accused of carrying on affairs with several women—called Davis into his office and dismissed him with a single sentence: "You had better look for another job."

Moving to Arizona, he took a job as a street car conductor, then drifted farther east, working as a machinist's helper and a railroad fireman. His new jobs featured sweat, tedium, backbreaking toil, little respect, and no glory. A rookie cop's pay of $75 a month might not have been much, but at least the work was secure and relatively easy. So he wrote a letter to Chief Sebastian asking for a second chance and, when told he could reapply, returned to Los Angeles. There, in early July of 1912, he was reappointed to the LAPD. "I determined at that time," he would later say, "to go as far as I could in the service and wipe out any false opinions that had been built up about me."

Always, thereafter, a certain tension—a tearing at his soul so intense it went far beyond mere hypocrisy—would mark James Davis's career as the fire and brimstone of his upbringing had marked his character. Every subversive Red, union organizer, homeless Okie, hapless drunk, strung-out junkie, or two-bit bookie would become a chance for James Davis to display his vigilance in upholding the strict letter of the law. Every gambling, prostitution, and bootlegging operation organized by his well-connected sponsors, and ignored by him, was, on the other hand, an equally useful opportunity for advancement.

That tension would also play itself out in his private life. For every bottle of beer he'd turn down, there would be a woman, as Joe Dircks would recall, whom James Davis felt compelled to ravish on a marble slab in the steam room of the Police Academy, in a Pullman berth on a moving train, or in a clandestine tryst at the home of his latest conquest. For every cigarette scorned there was a poker game to be played; for every muscle rigidly held in check and every emotion left unexpressed, there was a greasy chicken-fried steak to be wolfed down as his weight ballooned. But it was precisely this inner dichotomy that would become James Davis's survival skill in a Los Angeles where the Lord's avenging angels and the devil's temptations had been forced, almost since the city's inception, to live side by side.

His new assignment was in the heart of the action: the LAPD vice squad. Sprinting over roofs and squeezing through transoms, shinnying up drainpipes and stepping over cornices, James Davis spent the next four months raiding lottery joints, Chinese fan-tan parlors, and Japanese whorehouses; arresting junkies and drug dealers; and busting those selling or giving away liquor without a license. He found it all exhilarating. Outsmarting your prey, the thrill of the chase, the almost sexual surge of power when you made an arrest—*that* was the heady wine of police work, for James Davis as for many young cops. The con, the game, the power, the hazy line between protection and oppression, was what working in vice was all about. And it was to vice that James Davis would come back again and again throughout his career.

One evening a young woman named Edna Kline got off a streetcar on Tenth and Western, and the eager, pink-cheeked James Davis, all buffed nails, intense blue eyes, creased pants, and air of self-confidence, struck up a conversation with her. They quickly began dating, and when Edna Kline began teaching in 1915, they were married. It was a good marriage for James Davis. Not only was Edna Kline a schoolteacher, but a member of the Highland Park Methodist Church and a past president of the Santa Monica Epworth League. For a young officer in a highly Anglo-Saxon, Protestant institution such as the LAPD, a wife like Edna Kline was a distinct asset.

For his first nine years on the force James Davis's salary would never exceed $100 a month. Still they managed to buy a $600 hillside lot in the then semirural working-class district of Silverlake, just northwest of downtown L.A. There they built the tiny, two-bedroom, six-hundred-square-foot bungalow in which they would live for the rest of their lives and raise five children. It was striking how dumpy and boxlike the house looked from the outside, and how gloomy and claustrophobic it felt within. The stiff-backed, right-angled mission furniture that they purchased for $350 felt as uncomfortable as it looked. It, along with a bookcase filled with bound sets of the *National Geographic* magazine, and a stand-up globe by James Davis's straight-backed rocking chair, set the house's severe motif. And although James Davis enjoyed his women and poker, he never brought that side of him into the house, where the ban on smoking, alcohol, and profanity was absolute.

As he rose through the ranks of the LAPD on a vice squad whose lingua franca was graft, the payoff, and the take, he remained in that house, almost it seemed, as a point of pride. Would he be living *here*, the house almost shouted, if he didn't have to?

By the end of 1914, James Davis was receiving tip-offs from bellboys about poker games in hotel rooms; peeking through windows and boring small observation holes in walls; following room-service waiters into suites where card games were taking place; using fire ladders to scale buildings; being lowered on ropes from roofs; and crawling through air shafts and windows with the zeal of a modern-day DEA agent on a drug raid—all the while "observ[ing]," as the *Los Angeles Record* would later put it, "gambling, liquor selling and immorality." The vice squad was small then, three to eight men, but it was supplemented by a Chinatown squad of seven, and by the Purity squad. Warrantless searches and entries were rarely a problem back then. As James Davis would later say of his habit of breaking down doors, "to secure material evidence and exhibits, we had to effect quick entrance, and when that involved breaking a door, we didn't hesitate."

In one month alone he and his partner would randomly stop and search almost twenty-five hundred suspects—finding weapons, he'd later boast, on about eighty. The doors he would kick down over the course of his career would number, by his own estimate, "at least one thousand," and the number of times he drew his gun on someone, "no more than two dozen." And if a guy got lippy, no one hesitated to knock him on his ass. If you wanted to shake him down and search him, you did it. Decades later the LAPD would take that practice of stopping, searching, and arresting citizens on the flimsiest of pretexts and develop it into an entire philosophy of law enforcement, proudly giving it a name. "Proactive policing," they'd call it. In that, as with so much else, James Davis would be a harbinger—a pioneer—of things to come.

Earle Kynette was a smart boy, a comer. Even as a recruit with the LAPD cadet class of 1925, his ambition stood out; it was there in the intensity of his body language, and in the frantic manner he studied for his weekly exams. In fact, Earle Kynette was about as tightly wound and emotional a man as one was likely to encounter in a profession whose primary business is other people's trouble, and where a certain detached, studied cool had evolved by necessity. There was something about him, everybody agreed, that was troubling, something that seemed slightly off. It was apparent in the swift offense he took to the most innocent remark, and in the way he'd let you know that there were lines he'd have no trouble crossing to get what he wanted, a characteristic that caused his few friends to describe him as high-strung, and others as crazy.

Few people doubted, therefore, that when Capt. James Davis, now the acting commander of vice, visited the Police Academy at the Armory on Jefferson Boulevard to select some graduating cadets, Earle Kynette would be chosen. His appearance as much as his intense drive assured it. Earle Kynette was ugly, but not so ugly that he stood out. And at about five feet eight inches, his height, like that of Davis, was ideal for a vice man who wanted to blend in with dirty-necked laborers in a makeshift speakeasy, or to stake out a card game or bootleg joint without being noticed.

As he strode into the Armory, James Davis moved down the ranks and carefully picked eight men, including Earle Kynette. Kynette had reportedly joined the LAPD at the urging of Albert Marco, then the boss of L.A.'s organized prostitution, and later he would be fired and then reinstated for shaking down and extorting money from hookers. But always he would remain James Davis's dirty-job man.

Davis had waited nine long years before making sergeant in 1921, but then his promotions had come with a dizzying rapidity: detective lieutenant in 1922, and in 1924 his current position as acting captain of vice, commanding what had recently been expanded into an entire vice division. The expansion was part of the department's recruitment of over 900 new men, an acknowledgment of L.A.'s emergence as a major metropolis whose population would triple over the course of the 1920s, reaching about 1.5 million by 1930.

Over the years James Davis had been assigned to a fraternity within a fraternity, to the heart of the LAPD's operations: Central Vice. The men working there were a breed apart, able to set their own loose standards, free to roam the entire city often serving as bagmen for City Hall and the department, picking up the payments from brothels, speakeasies, and gambling houses.

Many big-city police departments in the twenties and thirties had such men working in and out of vice. Men impatient with legal niceties, notorious for their brutality, and notable for their willingness to do whatever it took to get the job done and ensure that they more than just survived financially. The LAPD was overflowing with them. In just one fifteen-month period during 1922–23 more than one hundred members of the twelve-hundred-man force had been discharged for brutality or corruption.

The problem flowed from the top. From 1915 to 1923, eight police chiefs had served under four scandal-plagued city administrations. During those years, mayors, DAs, and city councilmen had been taking campaign money and sometimes payoffs from madams, bootleggers, and gamblers, then looking the other way as their contributors continued in business. As a result of that, and of Prohibition, organized crime was flourishing in Los Angeles in the 1920s. Not big-time, high-profile, Al Capone, machine-guns-blasting, Chicago-style crime—although bootleggers like Milton B. "Farmer" Page and the volatile Sicilian-born Jack Dragna, who was trying to muscle in on Page's action, were shooting at each other in what became known as the Bootleg Wars. But the organized prostitution, gambling, and bootlegging in L.A. was significant, and most importantly, so corrupting it was rotting the fabric of both the city government and the LAPD.

At its center was Kent Kane Parrot, a handsome man with sharp, combative eyes, a stubborn jaw, and a boyish grin. The *Los Angeles Times,* which disliked Parrot as it disliked anybody it did not control, once called him "a swaggering, more or less insolent and altogether colorful personality [of] imposing physique and magnetism." And power. He was, said the *Record,* "the de facto mayor," while George Cryer, L.A.'s mayor in *fact,* and nominally Parrot's boss, was really nothing more than "Parrot's Puppet." Indeed, according to the *Times,* if one was looking for "the place to get action," it was unnecessary to search any further than Kent Kane Parrot's anteroom. A graduate of the law school at USC, where he'd been a football star as well, Kent Kane Parrot came to his behind-the-throne power when George Cryer was elected mayor in 1921. Immediately Parrot knew what he had to do to keep himself and his man Cryer in office, and to make them both rich. They'd promise every Protestant minister, every reform-minded voter, every temperance group and anti-sin league in town to absolutely eliminate vice. Then, they'd systematically protect the vice operations that paid them off. Around Parrot was a loose, protected syndicate led by Charlie Crawford, a local saloon owner. It included bootlegger and casino operator "Farmer" Page; Bob Ganz, who controlled the slot machines; Albert Marco, who ran the city's prostitution; and gambler and former LAPD vice detective Guy McAfee, who became known while working vice for whistling "Listen to the Mockingbird" over the phone to tip off his gambling associates of impending raids.

In the midtwenties a rival faction led by Jack Dragna and John Rosselli, men with Eastern Mafia connections, began to challenge Kent Kane Parrot's and Charlie Crawford's organized-crime operations. Parrot and Crawford had organized vice locked up in L.A. But thanks to Prohibition Dragna and Rosselli managed to carve out their own small niche by bootlegging. Then they set up a local outpost for the mob's nationwide horse-racing wire service, a step crucial to the prosperity of the city's bookmakers. The splashy, sometimes bloody rivalry between the two competing organizations would engender embarrassing local headlines that made it necessary for LAPD chief R. Lee Heath, and his captain of vice, James Davis, to take steps to keep the Bob Shulers and Gustav Brieglebs off their backs and out of their faces.

So troops were sent out to knock down doors, sweep the streets clean of vagrants and other undesirables, and fill the foul, airless Central City Jail. Afterward, their vigilance would be spread all over the front pages of the local papers. The vast majority of the vice arrests, of course, would be for petty offenses—hip-flask liquor busts, freelance hooking, small-time gambling, people in Little Italy who were drinking wine with dinner— while the big, connected bootleggers and brothels continued to thrive. But no matter. Heath and Davis had produced *numbers*. By the mid-1920s the need to produce those numbers would all but cast the LAPD's pattern of omnipresent policing in stone. The Shulers and Brieglebs wanted a pure city. Big business wanted a docile workforce. What choice did the department have? In 1927–28, *before* the Depression, over twelve thousand arrests were made for vagrancy. And by the decade's end, fifty thousand people a year were being arrested in Los Angeles.

It's hard to say how much money Parrot's operation was making. Most of the local papers avoided mention of the city's corruption. L.A.'s image as America's "white spot" was at stake, and boosterism had more than ever become the city's ethos as it busily sought to promote itself to Eastern investors. But the Internal Revenue Service claimed that Albert Marco, who ran the city's prostitution, banked $500,000 between 1922 and 1924. A top liquor smuggler, Tony Cornero, complained he paid out

$100,000 for police protection he never received; and his girlfriend told the *Record* that Cornero made $500,000 in two years. Those kinds of revelations and a scandal involving yet another police chief, Louis Oaks, who was discovered in the back seat of a car with a bottle of whiskey and a half-naked woman, had convinced Mayor George Cryer and Kent Kane Parrot that a reformist police chief with impeccable credentials was needed. The heat had to be taken off, if only temporarily.

August Vollmer, the trailblazing criminologist who lectured at Berkeley and served as its village chief of police, was chosen. Vollmer had become renowned for his theories of scientific policing and his advocacy of modern technology, intensive training, and professional police standards. Needing a large city to test his theories, he agreed to run the LAPD for a year.

In just that one year between August of 1923 and August of 1924, Vollmer made extraordinary strides. He added well over eight hundred men to the force and founded the LAPD's police school to train them, commissioned five new police stations, instituted a ninety-day training course for recruits, and started a statistical bureau and a daily crime-summary report. He stressed the importance of courtesy, appearance, and cooperation with community organizations, emphasized respect for the Constitution, and instituted mobile teams or "Crime Crushers," which flooded high-crime areas with police—vastly increasing arrests for hold-ups and burglaries. He convinced the city council to provide money for sixty-three new patrol cars, sixty motorcycles, and seventy police sirens; had the entire department take the U.S. Army's Alpha Intelligence Test; increased its fingerprint experts from two to nineteen; and began an academic association between the department and the University of Southern California.

These reforms moved the LAPD toward "professionalization" earlier than other big-city police departments. The benefits were so immediately obvious that professionalization would be widely and almost uncritically applauded. This was particularly true in the LAPD, where "profession-alization"—despite the department's corruption—would be handed down through James Davis to his successors like the Holy Grail. James Davis, after all, loved efficient traffic control, bull's-eye marksmanship, rigorous training, and defending the city from the forces of destruction. He fed off it. He knew, of course, that doing what he was told was essential in keeping his job. But within these limitations, he wanted an efficient, highly regulated police department that stood for absolute law and order. In this he was truly August Vollmer's disciple, and he would pass on many of Vollmer's lessons to men like his young assistant, Lt. Bill Parker. An emphasis on formal education and training (it was James Davis who would expand Vollmer's school into an academy); modern management techniques, a reliance on technology, a strict adherence to formalized rules and instructions—all of them would surely lead to greater efficiency. And weren't high wages, better pensions and working conditions, and most particularly independence from corrupting outside influence laudatory goals for police officers and departments? Clearly Vollmer and other visionary criminologists' concepts of professionalization *were* an answer to dealing with corruption and lawless police behavior.

But as Joseph Gerald Woods has pointed out, no one questioned what might happen if the ceaseless, ever-accelerating emphasis on training, and faceless paramilitary policing, along with the ever-expanding power and independence of police departments from civilian control, was carried to its ultimate conclusion. No one questioned if one day all this might lead to police departments that were powerful, independent political entities in their own right, and a criminal justice system that would become a criminal justice *industry*. If few people before Eisenhower had thought to warn of the spreading power of the military-industrial complex, fewer still in the twenties and thirties had an inkling that professionalization—along with shrewd political maneuvering by the police protective leagues and unions—might one day lead to precisely the problems the LAPD would face decades later. No one understood the cure might be as bad as the disease. No, at the time, professionalization, like clean government, was basic enlightened stuff. And it was August Vollmer, more than any other chief in the first half of the twentieth century, who was responsible for bringing it to the LAPD. It was impossible, of course, for him to have changed the culture of the department in just one year. But he had planted the seeds for a third major force, which along with strong-arm policing and rigid enforcement of the law, would characterize the LAPD long after the corruption had disappeared.

CHAPTER 5

The Survivor

....

It was all happening so fast that it's difficult to imagine how James Edgar Davis could even taste the ham and eggs and pancakes and bacon placed before him on this bright, extraordinary morning in March of 1926. Nor was the rapid turn of events the only bedazzling aspect of the day's happenings. There were also the men now set to eyeball him. The richest, most powerful, most prestige-laden men in Los Angeles. Men guaranteed to make anyone in James Davis's position more than a little intimidated. It was just fifteen years earlier, after all, that he'd been ignominiously dismissed from the department. And only five since he'd been a lowly sergeant. Now here he was, a cohonoree along with outgoing LAPD chief R. Lee Heath, sitting at a head table at a posh outdoor banquet being thrown by three hundred of the titans of California.

Two years ago, August Vollmer had left office and been succeeded as head of the LAPD by Heath. Today's breakfast was to publicly mark the latest changing of the guard: Heath's retirement and the ascension of James Edgar Davis into the post of chief of police of Los Angeles.

Rising to speak as their hosts sat under huge shade trees sipping morning coffee, R. Lee Heath and James Davis traded careful platitudes, Heath telling the Breakfast Club audience how James Davis had every quality needed to run the LAPD and James Davis praising Heath as "the best chief of police Los Angeles ever had."

The studied blandness of their remarks was understandable. This was certainly not the place to do or say anything controversial. The members of the Breakfast Club, after all, weren't some kind of police groupies, but the very men then presiding over a city awash in deals and action—a city in the thrall of one of the most dynamic decades in its history. From 1920 to 1924 alone, 400,000 new people had settled in Los Angeles on land that was now bringing enormous profits to many of the men of the Breakfast Club. By the end of the boom years of the twenties, Los Angeles would absorb an astounding 600,000 heartland Americans ready to hustle or invest their money as the city's population surged to almost 1.5 million. Within a quarter-century L.A. had grown from a city in a league with Paterson, St. Joseph, and Syracuse into one of America's largest metropolises. Only four cities in the entire country were now larger.

Harry Chandler, the preeminent member of the Breakfast Club as he was of any club he chose to join, was in the forefront of that real estate boom. By the mid-thirties, Chandler, as owner and publisher of the *Los Angeles Times,* would be not only the absolute master of the paper that dominated the region's media and politics, but a land baron who owned 2 million acres of real estate. Real estate that surrounded Los Angeles and stretched north to the Tehachapis, south to Baja, and east into the San Bernardino Mountains. In addition, he would sit on the board of directors of more than fifty corporations; be a pivotal player in tourism, manufacturing, and real estate; serve as a crucial catalyst in luring the rubber and aircraft industries to Southern California; and be an instrumental force in the building of the Coliseum, the Hollywood Bowl, and Cal Tech—all of which enhanced his massive real estate holdings.

His guiding principle had remained the same as in the old days when he'd run the city with the now departed Harrison Gray Otis and the tiny group of bankers, businessmen, and attorneys from the old-line downtown law firms. The same as that of the members of the Breakfast Club, the Jonathan Club, the Los Angeles Athletic Club, the California Club, and of the Merchants and the Manufacturers Association. The same as the residents of Hancock Park, Pasadena, and San Marino, whose wealth and status, they were certain, depended on that principle. The principle of keeping the city ever expanding and the unions out. And in those matters, in matters of organized labor and of strikes, dissidents, and vagrants, they intended that their control of the LAPD remain unquestioned.

Other believers, either in attendance that day to honor Davis and Heath or on the Breakfast Club's advisory committee, were Guy Barham, who represented the interests of William Randolph Hearst; the region-shaping financiers Marco Hellman, William W. Mines, and William May Garland; United States senator Samuel Shortridge and ex-senator Frank Flint; Louis B. Mayer, the autocratic godfather of MGM and a major power in the Republican Party and local politics; Dr. Robert Millikan, the president of Cal Tech; and Dr. Rufus B. Von Kleinsmid, the president of USC.

What they most wanted in a new chief of police, James Edgar Davis had in abundance: an absolute loyalty to their interests, and an unquestioning willingness to do as he was told. He would be officially sworn in as L.A.'s thirty-fourth chief of police on April 1, 1926—April Fools' Day—a portentous, inadvertent reminder of the extraordinary minefield over which he now had to run. But if James Davis got the joke, he wasn't laughing. For it *was* a mine field.

First, he had to continue to protect Kent Kane Parrot's approved vice operations. If you owed the mayor, you owed Kent Kane Parrot. And James Davis owed the mayor. He'd been chosen by the police commission under the new city charter of 1925, which meant that they—all appointees of Mayor George Cryer and Parrot—could also fire him. Never mind the new charter's stipulation about the commission being independent of the mayor. Cryer had already taken care of that by gathering the commissioners' letters of resignation in advance. They'd do what he said.

Second, James Davis had to appease the Shulers and Brieglebs of the city with lots of high-profile tough-on-crime posturing. So he put together a fifty-man "Gun Squad" and said of gangsters, "I want them brought in dead, not alive." And of two rum-running brothers: "If the courts won't eliminate them, I will." To his men he warned that he would "reprimand any officer who shows the least mercy to a criminal." He would back up his law-and-order repertoire with the ceaseless intimidation and arrest of thousands of men working punishing jobs who were guilty of nothing more than looking for a little release: a sweet drink or two or maybe a woman at the end of a hard week. They would provide his numbers.

Keeping Harry Chandler and the men of the Breakfast Club happy was James Davis's third, and easiest, task. They may have been at opposite ends of America's economic and class structure, but they couldn't have been more in tune ideologically, and James Davis understood what was required. Dissent was to be squelched. The Red and Vagrancy squads unleashed.

Fourth, James Davis had to back his troops. Although he issued a bulletin forbidding the beating of prisoners, the *Los Angeles Record* maintained that Davis was constantly sending a different message: "He looks upon the refusal of brother officers to admit beating up a suspect as perfectly natural. . . . Like many other police officials, he is inclined to excuse policemen who beat up citizens when they say they don't like policemen."

And finally—finally—James Davis had to keep it all together. And to do that, he would have to deal with the department's enemies, the really smart critics—the ones who bothered to look hard and carefully and were thoughtful enough to connect all the dots—*they* would have to be watched. And if necessary neutralized.

Nevertheless, James Davis loved being chief. He loved the respect. He loved the authority. He loved playing the role and the women it got him. He loved greeting VIPs. He loved the spit and polish and the way the Mexican *federales* would send their generals up to Los Angeles to observe *his* troops. And he loved running a tight ship, the ship in this case being the city of Los Angeles. As the *Record* put it after a lengthy interview: "Davis quite honestly and sincerely believes that the country would be much better off if the whole question of constitutional rights was forgotten, and everything left to the discretion of the police. . . . It is an axiom with Davis that constitutional rights are of benefit to nobody but crooks and criminals, and that no perfectly law-abiding citizen ever has any cause to insist upon 'constitutional rights.' " Indeed, James Davis wanted every resident of Los Angeles to be fingerprinted, and their record kept on file by the LAPD. It would help the department function more efficiently, he believed, and make the city a better place to live. Barring that, he proposed the fingerprinting of all "domestics."

In his war on crime, criminals—and the general public—always had tactical surprises awaiting them. Among his most innovative was the first—and at the time the only—use of the dragnet. It was a perfect name for a fishing expedition, a perfect precursor to proactive policing.

During the dragnet, officers from a hundred-man "emergency squad" would fan out across ten or twelve major boulevard intersections. Then eight men—two on each corner—would be deployed at each of the intersections, stopping and examining all passing vehicles and searching any "suspicious characters."

While a dragnet may have been a useful tactic for the French during a major insurrection such as the Battle of Algiers, it generated an enormous number of complaints from the citizens of relatively tranquil L.A. It wasn't just the indignity, but the inconvenience. Glendale and Beverly Boulevard, for example, had five traffic-packed roads coming together at one intersection, and it just happened to be a frequent target of the dragnet. But when James Davis heard of the complaints, his reaction was incomprehension: "Today the public has an automobile complex. It resents being stopped and looked over, even though the stopping and examining is for the protection of the honest and law-abiding section of the community. . . . In the old saloon days men didn't think anything of being stopped and searched for concealed weapons." But it wasn't over the dragnet that James Davis first ran into trouble. It was over the issue of the department's enemies.

Clad only in his underwear, Carl Jacobson slid into the bed. Next to him were two glasses, an open whiskey bottle, and the invitingly nude body of Helen Ferguson. Suddenly the lights went out, a flashlight was thrust into his face, and several pairs of powerful hands grabbed him from behind. They belonged to three LAPD officers, who then arrested the stunned city councilman on charges of lewd conduct and vagrancy.

The initial reaction to Carl Jacobson's arrest was what one might expect: the usual mixture of feigned shock and titillation, not much different from what it would be today if the bottle of whiskey by the bedside were an eighth of an ounce of coke. Jacobson, after all, was a popular, respected city councilman who was married with two kids.

The entire focus of the scandal changed, however, when an outraged Jacobson demanded and got a jury trial and was quickly acquitted. A subsequent grand-jury investigation made it apparent why. Carl Jacobson had been set up. As a fierce, righteous critic of the LAPD and its connections to organized vice, it was his misfortune to have been among the first of a long list of critics of the LAPD to be targeted in a new, greatly expanded definition of the enemy. No longer were they just Reds, radicals, and union organizers. Now they'd also become good, mainstream reformers who were critical of the LAPD and City Hall.

The entrapment of Carl Jacobson was clumsy and ill-conceived from the start. It would turn out that Helen Ferguson—whom Jacobson did admit to having had an "immoral interest" in—wasn't Helen Ferguson at all, but Mrs. Callie Grimes, the sister-in-law of vice detective Frank Cox. Through him, she had been promised a down payment of $2,500 and $100 a month thereafter to get Jacobson to disrobe in her bedroom. Her payments were to be provided by Albert Marco, who headed the city's prostitution during the twenties, and who had been, along with the LAPD, the object of Jacobson's scathing attacks.

Testifying before the grand jury, Helen Ferguson/Callie Grimes swore she was told that if she did what was asked, she would have the full support of at least one police commissioner, the DA, and James Davis.

After several hung juries the case was finally dropped. But it demonstrated the extraordinarily incestuous relationship between the city's prosperous, connected gangsters and the cops working at the heart of the LAPD's most powerful and most autonomous units. It also displayed the department's willingness to use the Intelligence Squad to defend the political interests of the mayor as well as its own. There would be more such missions, and the officer James Davis selected to head the squad, and to carry them out, had to be equal to the task. The man he finally chose was the one he'd plucked out of the Police Academy to serve in his vice division: Earle Kynette.

By the winter of 1929, it was clear that James Davis was not holding it together. Old cases were lingering in the public's mind and coming back to haunt him. The trial of the officers who'd set up city councilman Carl Jacobson had concluded just that summer, and Albert Marco had recently been indicted and convicted in a highly publicized trial. There was also the particularly embarrassing case of a young kidnapped boy named Walter Collins. The LAPD had outraged the public by returning a similar-looking boy to Collins's mother, vehemently insisting he was her son. When she and everyone who knew her boy protested that the child was *definitely not* hers, the LAPD first threatened to throw her in jail, and then placed her in a psychiatric ward.

That case was followed by the one that would not go away. Harry "Bathhouse" McDonald, who had been paying vice squad commander Max Berenzweig and his men $100,000 a year to be permitted to run his large bootlegging operation, was arrested and, once in custody, started to talk. As a result, both Berenzweig and one of his detectives, James Howry, were indicted and skipped town to avoid prosecution.

McDonald's arrest, however, had been prompted not by the LAPD, but by information developed by a grand jury. And people began asking, not unreasonably, how it was that he and other gangsters like Albert Marco could have flourished for so long with a big-talking law-and-order chief like James Davis in charge. And why it was that Berenzweig—a personal friend of Davis's who'd been fired from the department and then reinstated when Davis became chief—was commanding a vice squad without a regular appointment as a police officer. He was, after all, a man with one of the most notorious records in the department, a man considered so "incompetent and unqualified" that he'd been unable to pass the civil service exam.

Sixty-two officers, according to federal authorities, were involved in the McDonald case and others related to it. McDonald himself named thirty officers—many of them high ranking—as being on the take, fifteen of whom were eventually indicted by the grand jury. Concurrently, ten separate police-misconduct cases were being tried all over the city. As 1929 neared its end, James Davis's situation had moved from grim to pathetic, and in late October the police commission charged him with incompetence and neglect of duty.

Two months later on December 30, 1929, with the newly elected mayor John Porter giving him just a few hours to make up his mind, James Davis agreed to a demotion to deputy chief. He would now be in charge of the turgid Traffic Bureau and have his salary reduced from $500 to $400 a month.

He was replaced by Roy "Strongarm Dick" Steckel, a rough-hewed version of James Davis whose chief claim to fame had been his arrest of Albert Marco after a Venice Beach shooting. Steckel's refusal of Marco's bribe offer as he made the arrest had been well publicized during Marco's trial, and as a result, Steckel had become something of a folk hero.

The jury foreman at that trial was John Porter, who then rode the glory of the Marco case to victory during his ardent antivice campaign for mayor in 1929. As mayor, Porter, an avowed prohibitionist, went to Europe to secure the 1932 Olympic Games for Los Angeles. While in France at a ceremonial banquet, he caused a minor sensation by indignantly refusing to toast the president of France *and* the president of the United States because the glasses on the table were filled with wine. At home in Los Angeles, he brought new meaning to sentimental evangelism when he ordered the LAPD to stop all traffic at precisely three o'clock in the afternoon of Good Friday to allow the magnificence of Christ's crucifixion, redemption, and resurrection to seep into the city's consciousness.

But despite his promises to purify Los Angeles, Porter's use of the department for political intrigue and spying only further tarnished the department's reputation. By 1933 and the next election, both he and Steckel were out, and James Davis was back in.

The rumors of James Davis's impending return had begun flying even before Frank Shaw, the newly elected mayor, took office. Shaw, a former wholesale grocery salesman from Joplin, Missouri, had been both a Los Angeles city councilman and a county supervisor. He was known, according to a member of a committee that had investigated his actions as a supervisor, as a man who always took "good care of his friends in the industry in return for political support." In 1934, that committee, which was investigating the food service at Los Angeles County's General Hospital, issued a report excoriating the hospital's waste, low quality, sometimes spoiled food, overstaffing, and the handing out of sweetheart contracts to local food suppliers. Responsible for much of the problem, wrote the committee, was Frank Shaw.

When "Strongarm Dick" Steckel heard the rumors that Shaw was thinking of replacing him, he cut short a visit to his boyhood home in Indiana, hopped on a plane, and hurriedly returned to Los Angeles. There, while James Davis coolly took target practice at the LAPD pistol range, Steckel met for two hours behind closed doors with the police commission. Three days later he was clearing his personal belongings out of the chief's office. Now Steckel would head Traffic.

He had never had a chance. It had all been preordained. "Local political figures, none of whom are police commissioners," as the *Daily News* put it, had secretly met at a downtown hotel and reached the decision to appoint James Davis the new chief of police. "All of the interests," said the *News,* were there: the *Times;* the "badge, gun and uniform" interests; the "meat to the city jail" interests; the "furniture for rooming houses and massage parlors" interests; and the representatives of organized vice.

The way Davis's friend—former LAPD deputy chief Irvis Lester—saw it, there were really only two ways to go: "You could either have a dummy in there [as chief] who didn't know what was happening and work around him, which was never very successful because those guys just came and went. Or you could have a smart guy who was your man and work through him or his subordinates. [With Davis] . . . they decided to put their own guy back in there.''

Frank Shaw, the new mayor, had known what he wanted, which was peace. He did not want the *Times*—which during his mayoral campaign had been one of his bitterest opponents due to his mildly prolabor stances —to continue as his enemy. He did not want the *Times* to continue asking if Frank Shaw had claimed Canadian citizenship during World War I to avoid the draft, or to run additional stories charging ''that jobs paid for with public money have been traded for votes and support for Shaw.'' Nor did he wish to deal with the *Times* circulating photos of checks made out to him and signed by local gangsters while he was sitting on the Los Angeles County Board of Supervisors, copies of which the *Times* allegedly had lying within a thick file the paper had compiled on him. James Davis's return to chief had been the price of that peace. After that, serious money could be made with the men who controlled L.A.'s bootlegging, speakeasies, gambling, and whorehouses.

Harry Chandler and the L.A. *Times,* for their part, also knew exactly what they wanted: their lapdog back. Chandler had always maintained an undisguised proprietary interest in the LAPD—closely monitoring the actions of its chiefs and their subordinates, judging them by how well they directly served the interests of the *Times,* and adjusting the paper's reporting and evaluation of crime accordingly. Throughout the tenure of Frank Shaw, the *Times* would keep its part of the deal, studiously ignoring the administration's corruption even as it took place right under the noses of the paper's most astute reporters.

And Frank Shaw, too, kept his word, rendering unto Harry Chandler what was Harry Chandler's: the total subservience of the police department to his wishes in those matters, such as labor organizing and left-wing political activism, that he found threatening.

Organized vice's slice of the deal would be the same as the new mayor's administration, that is, they would be let alone to deal with city officials and rational cops who wanted to do business and make money just as they did.

And James Davis, James Davis got to be chief again.

CHAPTER 6

Bum Blockades

••••••••••••••••••••••••

They came to California a half century after the first wave of heartland Americans had arrived. And although possessing similar names, their circumstances could not have been more different. They were, as Steinbeck wrote in the *Grapes of Wrath*, from "Kansas, Oklahoma, Texas, New Mexico; from Nevada and Arkansas families, tribes, dusted out, tractored out. Carloads, caravans, homeless and hungry; twenty thousand . . . a hundred thousand . . . two hundred thousand . . . seven generations back Americans . . . Oakies . . ."

It was the drought, and the Dust Bowl winds, coupled with a Depression America without unemployment insurance, social security, or federal welfare benefits, that, by 1932, had caused the transformation of 2 million Americans into homeless, jobless, wandering vagabonds routinely and often violently routed from town to town. That, and a jobless rate of 25 percent. In one year alone, Southern Pacific Railroad guards threw almost seven hundred thousand of them off its trains. Thirty-nine states then had residency requirements for welfare benefits, and early on, many communities had developed a policy to confront and deal with these people whom the *Los Angeles Times* referred to as "invading hordes": arrest them for being incompetent, dim-witted, poor, unemployed, young, unlucky, unconnected, broken down, and tapped out; arrest them, in short, for having the audacity to be in the condition they were in. And then give them a cheap breakfast and ship them across the next county line.

Their relentless wandering was as pointless as it was pathetic. As an aide wrote to Secretary of the Interior Harry Hopkins: "This transient thing is funny, men unable to get work in California and en route to the Kansas wheatfields, actually meet up in Denver with men unable to get work in the Kansas wheatfields and on their way to California."

Earlier, enormous efforts had been made to lure people to L.A. by civic boosters such as the *Los Angeles Times* and the All-Year Club. Those efforts had been astonishingly successful, and that success had continued into the Depression. Only now it was viewed as a decidedly mixed blessing. Fortified by a million-dollar budget during the boom years of the twenties the All-Year Club had aggressively—almost stridently—promoted southern California as a virtual paradise, a place where you could "sleep under a blanket every night all summer."

About one hundred thousand of the homeless, destitute, and unemployed had already migrated to California by late 1931, with about seventy thousand of them alone going to Los Angeles. The "indigents," the *Los Angeles Times* warned, were "pouring into the state at the rate of 2,000 a week . . . [a] situation . . . which threatens to break the financial back of California."

Something, James Davis felt, had to be done. And if no one else in California had the guts, had the backbone to act, then he would. Even if what he finally decided on, was, in the words of former LAPD deputy chief Bernard Caldwell, "as illegal as hell."

In February of 1936, James Davis came up with his plan. He would repel "the refuse of other states" by building on his dragnet of a decade earlier, expanding its logistical possibilities from that of a pathetic, small-scale occupation of an L.A. street corner to nothing less than the embargo of an entire state. In a move startling in its extraterritorial assumptions, he would dispatch his officers—that is, the police of the city of Los Angeles—to the major points of entry along *California's* borders with Oregon, Nevada, and Arizona, where he'd once and for all put a stop to these people who, in the words of the *Times*, had "no definite purpose in coming into the state." He would send the LAPD north to the counties of Siskiyou, Modic, and Del Norte; south to San Bernardino, Riverside, and

Imperial; east to Nevada, Mono, and Inyo. Then he would see to it that his officers blocked access from sixteen of the most critical highways and rail crossings straddling the state line.

One million five hundred thousand dollars, James Davis promised the Breakfast Club, would be saved from "thieves and thugs" and another $3 million in welfare payments. "We will concentrate," Davis said when making his announcement, "on vagrants who come into the state by stealing rides on trains or hitchhiking. Those vagrants do not come here to seek work but to go on relief, to beg or to enter [into] crime." Davis's plans also envisioned erecting "concentration camps" (a term not as loaded in 1936 as it is now) in which to imprison those waiting deportation. "We hope," he concluded, "that this . . . assignment will become advertised throughout the country and discourage such persons from heading for California." Thus, among the many events of the 1930s for which the LAPD would become notorious, began one of the most extraordinary: the bum blockade.

On February 6, on the Arizona border, LAPD officers stopped and asked 227 men the terse, unsmiling questions being asked at entry points throughout the state: "Any money? Any work?" When the answer was no, the travelers were given a blunt choice: thirty to eighty days at hard labor for vagrancy and nonpayment of train fare, or turning around and going back from where they came.

The sheriff of Modoc County, however, refused to deputize the fourteen LAPD officers assigned to his county's border with Nevada and Oregon. "I've stood for a lot and tried to be fair," he told them, "but you have violated all the rules of decency." The blockade was clearly wildly unconstitutional. But California's Republican governor, the ex-Iowan Frank Merriam, was remarkably circumspect. Commenting later on L.A.'s decision to send officers to the border, Merriam said that it was "up to them, if they can get away with it."

Meanwhile, just east of the California state line in Reno, Nevada, a large white billboard with a drawing of a baton-wielding, blue-uniformed cop with his palm thrust out had been erected. Above his hand was the word "Stop!" and a painted stop sign. And next to it, in larger, black, officious block letters, was the phrase "Los Angeles City Limits."

At the very same time in Los Angeles, James Davis, who had himself once been as close to broke as you could get without actually *being* broke, was unleashing a specially augmented "flying squadron" of thirty detectives and forty-five patrolmen on the city's "loafers . . . panhandlers, dissolute persons, suspicious characters, and others with no visible means of support," and appealing to housewives on radio broadcasts "to call the police department if beggars appear at [your] doors." Empathy, identity, or outrage was for priests, communists, social workers, anthropologists, and union organizers, not cops like James Davis. Sweeps and roundups of destitute and marginal men had, in any case, been a regular, unquestioned feature of the LAPD's policing operations for decades. But these, the latest roundups he had ordered, were different from those of the past. Now, the special "flying squads" of LAPD officers weren't only "sweeping through," in the words of the *Times,* "the tangled other-world habitat . . . combing hobo jungles, beer halls, poolrooms and public parks . . . the habitual hangouts of Los Angeles' ne'er-do-wells." No. On these raids his officers were also rounding up "indigent families, single women, juveniles and men unable to work because of illness or infirmities," and then providing them with special funds from the Los Angeles County Relief Administration for railroad tickets back to their "legal homes."

No institution supported James Davis more than Harry Chandler's *Times,* whose view of the blockade could not have been clearer. If it was an outrage, as some critics were charging, well, said the *Times,* "let's have more outrages." For, as the paper explained, "it is the kind of outrage that ought to have been perpetrated in California several years ago. If it had, we would have been saved . . . many millions [in] . . . tax money that has since gone to the support of the indigent from other states. . . . If it had, our citizens would have been spared many of the depredations of our present army of imported criminals. . . ."

Ironically, however, in 1936, James Davis had asked Capt. Bernard Caldwell to write "a report on the effects of the invasion by the Dust Bowl refugees" on Los Angeles. Caldwell did so and, using data from the Chamber of Commerce, the tax rolls, and anecdotal information from LAPD detectives, was amazed by what he found. Not only were many of the transients not the parasites they were being made out to be, but were often hardworking assets. Davis seemed surprised, Caldwell later recalled, when he told him.

For two months the blockade proceeded, petering out as negative publicity sparked court injunctions. The Fourteenth Amendment, federal judge Leon Yankwich pointed out, "provides that we are citizens of the

United States and not citizens of the several states, and that as such a man shall be free from interference in moving himself or his goods from one state to another. Evidently Jim Davis hasn't heard about that one yet."

The local raids were a different story. They continued for the next several years, becoming an exalted crusade for James Davis, who cited a 25 percent drop in purse snatchings, burglaries, and robberies, and a new low in vagrancy and panhandling arrests, as proof of their validity.

Predictably, James Davis's actions earned him the praise of the *Times,* which favorably compared him to England's sixteenth-century Queen Elizabeth, who, it was to be remembered, had "launched the first war on bums."

William F. "Red" Hynes's nickname came not from the color of his hair, which was brown, but from the zeal that was key to his rapid rise to notoriety. A St. Louis native, he'd spent seven years in the Army before joining the LAPD in 1921. Two years later, he received his career-defining assignment: the infiltration of the International Workers of the World, or IWW. He'd already joined the Communist Party as part of his cover, so when the maritime strikes of 1923 threatened to shut down the port of San Pedro, he was prepared to serve as both a spy and agent provocateur. It took a singular man to infiltrate the IWW, then the elite corps of the labor movement, but Red Hynes managed not only to do so, but to become the secretary of its strike committee and the editor of its strike bulletin. Afterward, Hynes took the witness stand, faced the men whom he had betrayed, and provided the key testimony against them. A Justice Department official would later give him credit for doing "more than any other person to help the government in their operation against the IWW throughout the nation during [their] general strike," and for "breaking up the IWW in Southern California."

Following the loss of his cover, Red Hynes was permanently assigned to the Red Squad, and in 1927, with the rank of temporary captain, he was made its commanding officer by James Davis. His devotion to the Merchants and Manufacturers Association and the Better America Federation would subsequently become legendary. And reciprocal. They would provide him with strikebreakers, economic analysis, the constant cheerleading and backup manpower of the American Legion, and their political savvy. More significantly, Red Hynes, a patrolman raised to the rank of temporary captain, would have their enormous power conferred upon *him.* He was their surrogate. He had their proxy. In Los Angeles in matters of public meetings in auditoriums, rented halls, parks, vacant lots, and streets; in the enforcement of local, state, and federal laws; in matters concerning the distribution of pamphlets, leaflets, and political literature and "all forms," as Hynes himself described it, "of sedition and treasonable activities," Red Hynes would reign supreme, his word was law, he was the final arbiter.

Always he would be in *their* service, outside the LAPD hierarchy. They spoke, Red Hynes acted, and James Davis and the politicians of Los Angeles acquiesced. They, the captains of industry in L.A., assisted Hynes by setting the political climate within the press, within the police commission, within the city council and the state legislature. Through them, Red Hynes would shine as his targets were publicly exposed and discredited.

In 1930, he brought so many documents, dossiers, photos, and exhibits before the House Special Committee to Investigate Communist Activities in the United States that he became an overnight superstar in law enforcement circles and quickly found a niche as a consultant to fledgling Red squads throughout the country.

Locally, he'd make joint public appearances with prominent members of the Better America Federation or accompany James Davis and Joe Dircks when they held their shooting exhibitions before the Elks, Rotarians, or Daughters of the American Revolution. Pointing to a chart, he'd sound the alarm, explaining how the communists had formed octopuslike organizations whose tentacles were reaching down into virtually every street in Los Angeles.

Red Hynes was also permitted to make money on the side. In fact it was often his big business sponsors who employed him. According to Joe Dircks, he had a private eye business that sold embarrassing information from the vast store of department and private files that he had amassed. But he made his real money from part-time strike-breaking consultations. Occasionally, the business became full-time. In 1934, Hynes took a leave of absence and worked for the Fruit and Vegetable Growers of the Imperial Valley, whose striking employees, according to the National Labor Board, were living in conditions that were "primitive or even savage." During the strike, the union's headquarters was bombed, and strikers— and sometimes their families—were gassed, beaten, jailed, and held incommunicado, often for weeks. When, for example, A. L. Wirin, an attorney for the ACLU, traveled to the Imperial Valley to address striking lettuce workers, he was kidnapped, beaten, "threatened with burning, and left barefoot in the desert, eleven miles from the nearest town." Afterward, he sued a variety of officials, including Red Hynes.

That same year Hynes was also paid more than $7,000 to help break the Los Angeles Railway strike. Generally, he received about $50 a day for his expertise, a gold mine for Red Hynes considering that his rank of captain was a temporary rating and he was earning only a patrolman's salary of $170 a month. Yet he frequently played open, no-limit stud poker with James Davis, Joe Dircks, and others, and he regularly attended the horse races out at Santa Anita, where he'd sometimes bet and lose the equivalent of his patrolman's monthly salary on a single race.

But the city received more than its money's worth from the man whom James Davis had ordered to "redouble his efforts against labor." Under Hynes the Red Squad was relentless in looking for what L.A.'s Left in the twenties and thirties would come to describe with grim humor as "the 'mysterious' documents." A phrase that covered any paper, placard, or book whose mere existence provided the justification for shutting down a meeting or confiscating an organization's records. For a concert sponsored by the John Reed Club of Hollywood, for example, a program schedule announcing "mass chants, a play and the singing of 'The Internationale' " was enough to do the trick and cause the concert's cancellation. During one eight-month period from January to September of 1932, the police, led by the Red Squad, would raid thirty-six meeting halls, and beat seventeen people during the raids and another twenty-seven while in jail.

As much as a quarter of the department—five hundred men—were put on alert when the Reds and radicals scheduled demonstrations. Red Hynes referred to those times as shove days. If the communists demonstrate, said Hynes, "the policemen will shove and keep on shoving until the parade is disrupted." Shoving was not all they did. During the San Pedro maritime strike of 1934, they'd hold a prisoner's arm or leg rigid over a chair and then snap it; on other occasions they used brass knuckles and slingshots on unarmed people. "Side by side with modern bureaus . . . the Los Angeles police . . . express a theory of law enforcement more openly opposed to the Constitution than any I have yet encountered," wrote Jerome Hopkins, one of Herbert Hoover's appointees to the National Commission on Law Observance and Enforcement in the early 1930s.

Red Hynes also launched his squad south into Long Beach and east to Pasadena to break up meetings. Which was amazing really, given that both were cities with police departments and governmental structures as separate and distinct from Los Angeles'—except for their proximity—as say, San Diego's or Bakersfield's.

And he successfully demanded that the Depression-strapped owners of town halls in Los Angeles such as the Shrine, the Olympic, the Philharmonic, and the Trinity Auditorium refuse to allow the Reds and others he deemed subversive to use their facilities.

Red Hynes also pioneered the tactic of equating criticism of the department with subversion, a technique that the LAPD would later develop into an art form. He publicly cursed "the damnable vilification and vicious attacks by [the] metropolitan dailies." He explained how their attacks were "based on propaganda from Moscow." He pointed out how the *Los Angeles Record*'s criticism of his squad was based on a policy of "glorification of avowed Communists, anarchists, criminals, and malcontents." And he urged citizens to "force the cessation of articles criticizing the police department." Despite his complaints, he and his men had no fear of the press. As one of his squad members told some reporters who began citing a Supreme Court decision when they were arrested: "You'll learn pretty soon that the Supreme Court isn't running Los Angeles."

And he believed in object lessons. Once during a city council session, the Red Squad dragged the prominent ACLU attorney Leo Gallagher into a small anteroom off the council chambers, smashed his glasses, ripped his clothes, blackened both his eyes, and left him with numerous contusions and abrasions, thereby sending a message to all those interfering in the political process. As Hynes explained to the council the following day, he didn't believe in the use of force unless resisted, but if his men were resisted, he didn't want to see them on the floor, he "wanted to see the Communists on the floor." It was his heyday, but Red Hynes's heyday was also the beginning of his demise.

By the mid-1930s, with a quarter of America's workforce unemployed, those who wanted to transform a frigid, failing economic system, be on the right side of history, change the world, and save humanity were precisely those most attracted to communism in America. They were no sixties Marxist weekend warriors. No Ivy League college kids waving around Mao's little red book or picture postcards of Che as they phoned home to Mom and Dad in Scarsdale or Marin for an advance on their allowance to buy some reefer. They were serious people, hardened by strikes and beatings, people willing to take on cops as well as capitalists. The abomination of the Hitler-Stalin pact of 1939 was still several years away. FDR and the economic buildup of World War II had not yet saved the system for capitalism. The danger of the Reds for men like Harry Chandler, James Davis, and Red Hynes was so real they could taste it. They were organizing hunger strikes and marches, organizing people— who, as one city councilman described them, were nothing more than "a bunch of bums in ragged clothes"—three hundred thousand of whom were unemployed in Los Angeles County alone in 1933. They were subverting law and order with publications like *The Hunger Fighter,* which ran headlines like: "Bread: Not Police Clubs!" They were cutting too close to the bone, referring to the Red Squad with insulting accuracy as "the pampered pet of the Merchants and Manufacturers Association, the Chamber of Commerce . . . the city council and . . . the county politicians." The organizing battles in New York, Detroit, and Chicago might have been better publicized, but in Los Angeles they were just as bitterly fought. And nowhere was the alarm greater than in Los Angeles. The threat was all too clear.

Vicious strikes that were as much about the political soul of a nation as they were about money were spreading all over the city, feeding off Franklin Roosevelt's election and the newly acquired legal right to organize that had been granted by the National Labor Relations or Wagner Act. By the end of the decade, the CIO was organizing the local oil and rubber workers, and strikes were breaking out all over the Los Angeles region. There were strikes in the film, trucking, garment, millinery, furniture, and meatpacking industries—a particularly violent, ugly railroad strike—and two epoch-defining struggles by the tough, militant West Coast maritime workers led by the indomitable communist Harry Bridges of the International Longshoreman's Association. Twice, once in 1934 and then again in '35, the longshoremen struck—37,000 of them crippling every port along the West Coast from Seattle to San Diego—5,000 strikers in Los Angeles alone. During 1936, over 10,000 workers in Los Angeles took part in fifty strikes. That same year, a scene occurred that would have been unthinkable just five or six years earlier. Thirty-six thousand people representing 142 Los Angeles unions mocked all those decades of Harry Chandler's shrewd calculations and all of those years of

Red Hynes's hard work by marching uncontested down the middle of Broadway. By the year's end, membership in the city's unions had risen to 65,000.

Two years earlier, in 1934, the muckraking journalist, novelist, and utopian political activist Upton Sinclair had run for governor of California on the then radical platform of free speech, free mass transportation, a progressive state income tax, the repeal of the regressive sales tax, the public ownership of vital utilities, and a humane social welfare system. Despite the fact that the *Times* and its allies spent massively to deliberately distort his record, Sinclair and his movement to End Poverty In California through "revolution by the orderly processes of majority rule" had garnered almost nine hundred thousand votes.

At the same time, a Democratic president offering a New Deal to America's workers was beginning to fundamentally alter the relationship of business and labor. And Los Angeles' leaders were discovering that they had no choice but to loosen their grip if they wanted Southern California to be a part of a national market in an America undergoing fundamental transformation. The emergence of Southern California as a pivotal hub in America's transcontinental industrial base was already taking place, and by the end of the decade it would be all but secured. National, unionized industries or those that would soon be, such as General Motors, Chrysler, Studebaker, Willys, Firestone, Dow Chemical, General Foods, and General Cable were all opening plants in or near Los Angeles. Democrats were now registered in greater numbers than Republicans in both the city and county of Los Angeles. By the end of the decade the LAPD would become far less a policy arm of the city's business establishment and the mayor than it had been before. But the tradition within the department of intolerance of political dissent, and of spying and keeping dossiers on anyone who criticized the status quo, would remain an integral part of the department's culture, one that would rise up again and again.

Meanwhile, other events were at work. Local events that would, with lightning swiftness, compel far more dramatic change within Los Angeles, and most particularly the LAPD, than anybody could have imagined.

CHAPTER 7

Clark Kent

••••••••••••••••••••••••

Within minutes of the call, James Davis had issued orders for a ticket on the first flight back to L.A. Slowing him down, stopping his rush home, proved impossible, even though it made little sense. By the time he got back, the damage would be done, the news already spread all over the papers. But before many in his party had even heard the sketchy details of the bomb blast, James Davis had left Mexico and was flying to Los Angeles.

He'd been in Mexico City for several days participating in the 1938 International Pistol Matches along with the rest of the crack LAPD pistol team he'd done so much to organize. Conveniently, the mayor's brother and alter ego, Joe Shaw, had been with him on the trip, while the mayor himself was away in Washington, D.C.

So they were all out of town when it happened. All out of town when, on the morning of January 14, 1938, Harry Raymond strolled out of his Boyle Heights home and into his garage, unlocked his car, stepped on the starter, and as he started the engine, simultaneously ignited a massive bomb that shattered windows of houses for blocks around, tore the engine from his car, blew his garage into a heap of splintered wood, glass, and roofing, and drove about 150 pieces of that wood and glass and metal into his body while breaking his arm and leg.

Raymond, the former chief of police of San Diego and of Venice before it had become part of Los Angeles, was a shrewd, cynical, amoral, hot-tempered ex-LAPD detective, your basic hard-eyed, bullheaded, dirty-work cop; Chandler's Bogart character, but without the flickering spark of decency. On the LAPD, Harry Raymond had been the icy ideal against which all others of his breed were measured. As a detective he worked on celebrated cases like the Mary Pickford–Douglas Fairbanks kidnapping; but he'd also twice been forced to resign during embarrassing scandals like the attempted framing of city councilman Carl Jacobson. Earlier, he'd been fired by the Venice PD after being sued for making repeated false arrests, knocking out a fellow policeman during a fight, and being indicted by a grand jury for extortion. That case had only been dismissed when his accuser, in mortal fear of Harry Raymond, fled the state.

Now, in late 1937, Harry Raymond, a hired gun, was working as a private eye for a local watchdog group known as CIVIC: Citizens Independent Vice Investigating Committee. Its name spoke for itself, and it would probably have remained just another antivice organization attempting to gather evidence and make connections between the cops, politicians, and organized vice had it not been for Harry Raymond's investigative skills. Raymond had gotten evidence that a key campaign aide to Mayor Frank Shaw had promised an appointed job to one of the city's top gamblers, and received money from another; and that that money had then been used to help finance Frank Shaw's 1933 campaign for mayor. (Earlier, the grand jury had found evidence linking James "Sunny Jim" Bolger, Frank Shaw's campaign manager—who was now working out of James Davis's office—to those very same gamblers. When the funds later turned up in the bank account of his mother, Bolger refused to answer any questions about it before the grand jury.) Not only had Harry Raymond gathered the evidence, but he'd been preparing to go into court and present it when his car was blown up, and the government and police department of Los Angeles were thrown into crisis.

It quickly became apparent to James Davis that the bombing was not going to go away. The blast had destroyed too much property, shattered too many windows, riddled Harry Raymond with too much shrapnel, garnered too many headlines, and seemed too obviously connected to the LAPD and City Hall.

Already CIVIC had banded together with the Federation for Civic Betterment—and a broad umbrella coalition of church groups, social and fraternal organizations, business associations, and labor unions disgusted with the city's corruption—to mount a recall effort. They meant to do nothing less than oust Mayor Frank Shaw from office and rid the city of the regime that James Davis served, and to which he owed his job and was irrevocably tied. And the impetus was the bombing. And Clifford Clinton, of course.

He was out to get James Davis, out to get them all. And it was difficult to imagine him failing. Difficult to imagine even a publicity-mad U.S. attorney with the full weight of the federal government behind him having the tenacity and indomitable will of Clifford Clinton, the man who had founded CIVIC, now the source of James Davis's woes.

Clinton was the son of Salvation Army captains devout and theatrical enough in their own right to have been married in a public ceremony during a Salvation Army meeting by none other than the daughter of the organization's founder, Evangeline Booth. When he was four, his parents took him on a two-year missionary tour of China. When they returned in 1906, Clifford Clinton's father then opened a soup kitchen. Clifford Clinton worked in the back cooking and cleaning, and he would never forget it, or where he came from. He grew up to be an energetic, square-jawed, serious man whose thick glasses and slicked-back hair gave him the determined look of Clark Kent about to transform himself into Superman, an image that would not prove inappropriate. In 1931 he moved to Los Angeles and opened the first of his "restaurants of the Golden Rule." There, patrons—as his cafeteria pamphlet entitled "Food for Thought" spelled out—could "dine for free if not pleased." For five cents he offered a "five-course dinner" of soup, bread, salad, Jell-O, and coffee, and during the height of the Depression he served meals that either cost a penny or were free. Nevertheless, he was a registered Republican, and an astute enough businessman that he eventually parlayed Clifton's Cafeteria into a second restaurant, two hotels, and a fifteen-room Hollywood mansion complete with tiled swimming pool.

In 1934, he'd been appointed to the committee that had investigated the negligence and corruption of the food service at the county hospital and pointed the finger at Frank Shaw. It was the first time that Clifford Clinton crossed swords with Frank Shaw. It would not, by far, be the last.

After leaving the County Board of Supervisors and becoming mayor in 1933, Frank Shaw had instituted what the socialist journalist and political activist Reuben Borough called the "Shaw spoils system." City contracts were awarded without competitive bidding, and people in city government were paid to use designated contractors. Early in his tenure, for example, members of Shaw's administration met with the head of the Los Angeles Poultry Council and offered to sponsor legislation that would eliminate "80 percent of the small operators." In return for the "organizing" of the local poultry industry, they asked for a $5,000 payment up front, and $500 a month thereafter. The man who was to receive the money, according to the head of the Poultry Council, was Mayor Frank Shaw's brother, Joe Shaw.

From his corner-pocket office in City Hall, Lt. Joseph E. Shaw, United States Navy (Ret.), would put the steel in his brother Frank's backbone and organize the administration's graft. The old guys, the men who under Charlie Crawford had dealt with Kent Kane Parrot, were out. Instead, Joe Shaw chose to align himself with the Italians: with Jack Dragna, who was operating his own local branch of the Costa Nostra family; and with John Roselli, the man who would often personally pay him off. Joe Shaw also placed the right people in the right slots.

His chief bagman was Pete Del Gado, one of those charming, happy-go-lucky men who was always in financial trouble, loved living beyond his means, and perpetually had his hand either out or in your pocket. He couldn't have been better suited for the job. He was a big, handsome, well-built Mexican American who loved women and a good time and always needed money. It seemed almost preordained, therefore, that he would eventually hook up with Frank and Joe Shaw. As their contact, Pete Del Gado got his cut and a promotion to the temporary rank of captain.

The Shaws' man in police headquarters was James Davis's personal secretary, James "Sunny Jim" Bolger—Frank Shaw's former campaign manager; the same James Bolger who had taken the Fifth Amendment in 1934 when questioned by the grand jury about his ties to organized gambling.

Joe Shaw also sold LAPD jobs, the answer keys for exams governing the choice assignments such as the motorcycle squad, and promotions. Sergeants' exams, with a guarantee of promotion, for example, went for $500. Whatever any of it cost, it was worth it. Becoming a motorcycle officer meant $25 extra a month, a lot of money when a policeman's monthly salary was just $200.

Inevitably, questions were raised. Once Joe Dircks went to see civil service commissioner Bill Cormack to complain. He was always number eleven on the list for promotion to permanent lieutenant, he said. Cormack replied that Dircks had nothing to complain about. The ranking on the list, based on honest competition, after all, *started* at number eleven. The first ten positions, Dircks was given to understand, had gone to those who bought them.

As for the vice squad, all the Shaws had to do was build on what was already there. Many of the older lieutenants and captains who'd worked vice back in the twenties were either still doing the same or were easily reassigned. How much money was being made is difficult to say. According to the police commission, one LAPD robbery detective of no particular distinction made over $200,000 in vice-connected income over four years during the Shaw administration.

The local vice squad in areas like Venice or the Valley got their cut. Central Vice, free to roam the entire city serving as the ultimate enforcer of the organized operations, got theirs. And the rest of the take went all the way up the line to the central organizer, Joe Shaw. If an ordinary patrolman came upon a brothel or gambling house, he'd report it to the vice squad. If nothing happened, he'd assume it was protected. But he knew better than to make the arrest. At the same time, James Davis could boast of the arrests of those *not* part of the organized operation, without mentioning they were often using information garnered from the underworld people they were working with. And with a straight face he could declare, as he did in 1934, that "organized racketeering had been reduced to an irreducible minimum." He had the numbers. People were being hauled in by the thousands, and so successfully that a Frank Shaw re-election campaign brochure in 1937 could cite a 9 percent increase in gambling and lottery arrests compared to the previous administration and point out how prostitution arrests were also up. But on LAPD vice it was now understood: the old syndicate guys were out and Dragna and Rosselli and a new boy named Bugsy Siegel were in.

*   *   *

Nineteen thirty-five and thirty-six were years to give Clifford Clinton serious pause. Professional "floppers" began inexplicably sliding and falling in his cafeteria, causing a string of lawsuits. Customers began suing for food poisoning. Stink bombs were set off. His local taxes were suddenly raised. The city health department inspected his two restaurants and forced him to make $10,000 in improvements. In 1937, he'd even had a bomb explode in the basement of his home, buckling part of the floor and destroying some of the house's rafters.

It was in January of that year that Superior Court Judge Fletcher Bowron nominated Clinton to serve on the Los Angeles grand jury. Bowron was a conservative man, a former private secretary to the reactionary Republican governor F. W. Richardson, and an ex-beat reporter working the county courthouse. In the pressroom a perpetual poker game had been played. Most of the reporters would sit in, a one-man press pool would cover whatever was breaking, and the information would be bought back to the game's participants. Then they would all rewrite and file the same story. Fletcher Bowron was never part of the game. Instead, he would be bent over a law book, studying for the bar examination. In his years as an attorney and then a judge, Fletcher Bowron had watched the city's rich, powerful, and politically well-connected come to court and, through manipulation and bribery, walk away free. Many of his fellow judges had quite knowingly taken campaign funds from local gambling interests. And as a result, he had come to this conclusion: "There [was] only one way to stop corruption," and that was "by the forthright action of an honest grand jury."

Bowron, like so much of L.A.'s Protestant middle class, was not seeking to right vast injustices or engage in great social causes. His Christianity was not that of redemption through utopian transformation. He was a decent, prodding, honest man who seemed to take visceral offense at vice, corruption, and the weaknesses of human nature. In this he was like so many of his fellow Republican reformers who'd made the fight against vice the central political issue in Los Angeles for over half a century.

Traditionally, a majority of the nineteen-member grand jury had consisted of safe, pliant members whose loyalties lay with the reigning political powers. But with his appointment of Clifford Clinton to the 1937 grand jury, Fletcher Bowron would change the rules of the game. On that grand jury, Clinton began a deeply embarrassing exposé of the Shaw administration and James Davis's LAPD. He conducted highly publicized tours of red-light areas. He photographed prostitutes soliciting, pinball machines clanking, and police officers conducting friendly, unofficial visits to gambling halls. He would tell the police about a brothel or gambling house, inform the newspapers of its location, and monitor the arresting officers as they made their raid. He compiled lengthy lists of gambling houses and brothels and then had names and photos printed on the front page of the *Citizen News*. He issued subpoenas to witnesses of the attempted murder of gambler Les Bruneman, a leader of the old, established syndicate. That attempted killing had taken place after Jack Dragna and John Rosselli (who by 1937 was controlling the movie industry's International Alliance of Theatrical and Stage Employees) had joined with Bugsy Siegel and announced that henceforth they were to receive a cut of all the city's gambling proceeds. When Bruneman rebelled, he was shot. And when he recovered he was shot again—sixteen times, after which there was no recovery. Bruneman's killing would contribute to the atmosphere of corruption enveloping the city; an atmosphere so pervasive that it led John Bogue, one of Clifford Clinton's renegade allies on the grand jury, to claim that six hundred brothels, two hundred gambling houses, and eighteen hundred bookie joints were doing business in the Los Angeles area.

Clinton and his allies also laid out the philosophical underpinnings of their charges in the grand jury's minority report: "A portion of the underworld profits have been used in financing campaigns . . . of . . . city and county officials in vital positions. . . . The district attorney's office, Sheriff's office, and the Los Angeles Police Department work in complete harmony and never interfere with . . . important figures in the underworld. The police investigation squad is spending its . . . budget . . . not on the investigation of crime, but to build up a file of dossiers designed to intimidate respectable citizens whose only crime consists of their unswerving opposition to the present city administration." But Clifford Clinton had done more than garner headlines on the grand jury. He had hired Harry Raymond.

The bombing had done more than just riddle Harry Raymond's body with scores of hideous wounds. In the simple-minded stupidity of its conception and the clumsiness of its execution, it had also inadvertently managed to outrage public opinion and unite the city's most disparate forces. A not so simple task.

The mood of the local papers, most of which had been skeptical of Clinton's accusations, now changed. Even the *Times,* which gave James Davis and Frank Shaw plenty of space to defend themselves, was now offering no more than lukewarm support.

It was all turning into a nightmare for James Davis. All of it. Talk of a recall was no longer talk. Petitions were being circulated and a professional agency had been hired to oversee the operation. The success of such an effort, as James Davis knew, would be the end of his career. The Intelligence Squad, the Red Squad, the Vice Squad, the links between the Shaws, the illegal gambling joints and whorehouses, the payoffs, the graft—none of it would bear the kind of scrutiny the bombing was already stirring up. And there he was, smack in the middle, with all signs pointing to Earle Kynette and the Intelligence Squad.

Earle Kynette. Fired and rehired for shaking down hookers, Earle Kynette had originally worked vice. James Davis had promoted him to sergeant, then assigned him to the Intelligence Squad. A creature separate and apart from Hynes's Red Squad—which focused on "enemies" of the government and big business—the Intelligence Squad's raison d'être was to spy on, compromise, and intimidate critics and foes of the department and the mayor. By the late thirties, Kynette was heading the squad as an acting captain and working out of the mayor's office.

For months Kynette and his Intelligence unit had been spying on Harry Raymond. They climbed telephone poles to tap and monitor his calls. They sat in stakeout cars for numbing hours on Harry Raymond's street. They established a surveillance post in a house across the street from his and bored holes in it to spy on Harry Raymond. They snuck around the premises of Harry Raymond's house, where one night, George Sakalis, a Greek vegetable-wagon driver who lived next door, spotted them and told them to leave. Less than a week later they returned, beat and robbed him, and told him, "Keep your mouth shut." Harry Raymond wasn't the only one the Intelligence Squad had been spying on. They surveilled over fifty prominent people, including the district attorney, Byron Fitts, two of the five members of the County Board of Supervisors, the publisher of the *Citizen News,* and, of course, former grand juror Clifford Clinton. It was the Intelligence Squad's job, as James Davis later pointed out, "to check on the activities of . . . criminal political elements . . . attempting to destroy confidence in the police department."

After a hurried seven-day investigation, James Davis declared Earle

Kynette and the members of his Intelligence Squad completely innocent of the bombing. For a short time he even placed Kynette in charge of the bombing investigation, whereupon Earle Kynette, with his and Davis's usual lack of imagination and disrespect for people's intelligence, suggested that Harry Raymond might have set off the explosion himself, accidentally using an excessive amount of dynamite.

But there was little else James Davis could do. It was too big to cover up. Calling the bombing an "unspeakable outrage," District Attorney Byron Fitts had started presenting evidence to the new grand jury on February 5, and by the eighteenth they'd handed down indictments against Earle Kynette and two members of his Intelligence Squad.

Earle Kynette went on trial in April of 1938, three months after the bombing. During the proceedings the judge would characterize James Davis's testimony as "a debris of words." "My memory is not sufficiently clear to state that I directly ordered Captain Kynette to keep Raymond under surveillance but . . . I did not order Kynette not to do so," testified James Davis. Most of the nineteen-man Intelligence Squad would decline to testify, including seven who refused to account for their whereabouts on the day before the bombing took place. George Sakalis, the Greek vegetable dealer who lived next door to Raymond, would identify Kynette and one of his fellow defendants as the two men in Raymond's garage the night before the bombing, and as the same men who subsequently beat, robbed, and ordered him to keep quiet.

The mind-set that had propelled the LAPD and the Intelligence Squad for decades was at last publicly crystallized by the revelation that scores of files had been kept on anyone even remotely critical of the department. They ran from the crusading liberal journalist and editor Carey McWilliams, through the dour, conservative judge Fletcher Bowron. The general public had never known about that before, and now here was irrefutable proof. It was devastating. All of it. Devastating for the Shaws. For James Davis and the LAPD. And most especially for Earle Kynette. When the jury came back they returned a guilty verdict on three of the four counts, and the judge, equally impressed by the evidence, gave Earle Kynette two years to life in San Quentin Prison. Kynette's lieutenant was convicted of the explosives charge, and a sergeant was acquitted. Kynette and the lieutenant were also fired. But in a reflection of recent civil-service job-security reforms, seven of the Intelligence Squad officers who'd refused to testify and been placed on suspension were immediately returned to duty by a Board of Rights made up of their fellow officers. James Davis, however, was forced to dissolve the Intelligence Squad. It was a victory that would prove Pyrrhic as the squad came back under a different guise a decade later. But the trial of Earle Kynette had laid bare the soul of the LAPD, and Clifford Clinton and the hundreds of church, business, labor, and community leaders who had been fighting Frank Shaw could not have wished for more.

On September 16, 1938, Frank Shaw was ousted as mayor and Fletcher Bowron elected as his successor. It wasn't even close. Bowron received about 233,000 votes, Shaw less than 122,000 as he became one of the first big-city mayors in American history to be recalled. All of the major newspapers, with the exception of the *Times,* had opposed him. And the support of the *Times* had been tepid at best. Why not? What would be the point of Harry Chandler going all out to save damaged goods like Frank Shaw? Fletcher Bowron, after all, was a good conservative, and Harry Chandler felt confident that Bowron would not do the unthinkable, that is, would not fire James Davis or abolish the Red Squad.

But Harry Chandler was wrong. James Davis would go. How, after all, could a reform mayor like Fletcher Bowron allow him to stay? There was no way reform could go forward with James Davis as chief. Within a month after the election, and despite a last-minute plea on his behalf by his admirer J. Edgar Hoover, James Davis was forced into retirement by the Bowron administration. In April 1939, twenty-three other high-ranking LAPD officers submitted forced resignations. Over the following six months forty-five more ranking officers would resign.

Pete Del Gado fled to Mexico and married well.

Joe Shaw eloped to Reno with his secretary, acquiring a wife and silencing a potential troublesome witness against him. Nevertheless, he was found guilty of sixty-six counts of corruption. Later, however, his conviction was reversed on appeal.

As Harry Chandler had been wrong about Fletcher Bowron retaining James Davis as chief, so, too, was he wrong about the Red Squad, which Bowron abolished in 1938. Red Hynes's honorary captaincy was taken away from him, and he was reassigned to a far Westside beat eighteen miles from the heart of downtown, where he worked until his retirement in 1943.

* * *

A few months after his resignation in 1938, James Davis became the chief of security for Douglas Aircraft. Through the midforties, when there was a lot of cash around, James Davis and Joe Dircks made money playing cards at Douglas and downtown in the Biltmore. It was a good time until Davis had a heart attack and had to quit Douglas. He was 250 pounds. "Mama," he would say afterward when Joe Dircks would stop by his house, "I'm going down to the store with Joe and get him some chocolates." And Edna Davis would tell him that he wasn't fooling anybody, that it was for himself that he wanted that candy. Undeterred, James Davis would walk into the kitchen, get out a box of chocolates and a bottle of milk, and sit there and eat as he chatted with Dircks. Physically weakened, James Davis was now in a household, as his son Charlie later put it, "dominated by women, forced to do 'unmanly' chores like washing the dishes, reduced to having to shave under his armpits to cut down on his body odor." It was a terrible thing for Charlie Davis to witness. But that was now his father's life, until June 29, 1949, when, while visiting a friend who had a ranch near Helena, Montana, he suffered a stroke and died at the age of sixty. His legacy, along with that of Harry Chandler and Robert Shuler, would run deep in the LAPD for the next half century, despite reforms. But in his obituary in the *Los Angeles Times,* which ran eleven paragraphs, no mention—not one—was made of the increasingly grotesque controversies that had plagued his years in office, the scandal that had brought him down, or his role in one of the most tumultuous eras in Los Angeles history.

PART 3

THE GODFATHER AND THE SUBVERSIVE

·························

CHAPTER 1

The Godfather and the Subversive

••••••••••••••••••••••••••

They would jog in formation past the tiny cottages of the Mexican village of Chavez Ravine, then turn and head up to the surrounding hills. There were seventy-eight of them—seventy-eight men who constituted the LAPD's first cadet class in three years, the first class since the great scandal, the first class since the recall of Mayor Frank Shaw and the forced resignation of James Davis. They were the class of 1940.

They had gone through a decade of cataclysmic poverty and were now standing on the brink of a war from which America would emerge supreme over half the world. The Battle of Britain was already being fought. The war was coming for America, too. It was there in the headlines and in the factories of the growing war industry.

The unflagging joblessness of the Depression had been their defining experience, as it had been for their entire generation; and they were forever mindful of the advice of their parents, of their neighbors, of every practical person caught up in the debacle of the thirties: "Go work for the city, it's steady" . . . "Mr. Schwartz at Goodyear's on layoff now" . . . "I'm in construction and I haven't worked for a year and a half . . . get a job with the city."

For the most part they were the sons of small-town, Midwestern, Anglo-

Saxon America: the children of small-business people, of salesmen, grocers, small-time realtors, shopkeepers and farmers from east of the Rockies who'd come to Los Angeles looking for that new start in the promised land, each of them, in his or her way, trying to disprove F. Scott Fitzgerald's famous line that there were no second acts in American lives.

They were delivery men, gas station attendants, college dropouts; men of modest circumstances and unformulated long-term aspirations. Their culture was middlebrow, and their politics—following their flirtations with FDR—would be uncomplicated and reflexively right-wing. They were genial, friendly, well-mannered, and most had at least a high school education at a time when a high school diploma still had some meaning attached to it. Better educated than their predecessors, they had a different look to them—that of a certain kind of administrator or businessman. The cops before them—the James Davises and the Joe Dirckses—were really the last gasp of Los Angeles as a John Ford western. Raw, tough men were now increasingly out of place in a big, complex city. And the Harry Raymonds and Earle Kynettes—the hard-eyed, low-rent thugs who looked the part in those photos and newsreels of the time; the detectives who'd casually induce screams from suspects during interrogations; the muscle-headed Ward Bond detective to Bogart's private eye; they, too, were a dying breed.

But the men of the class of 1940 lacked qualities that the old-time cops had in abundance: color, passion, style. They were not, in short, characters, but men in many ways produced on the same one-mold cookie-factory assembly line. In the movies, Ronald Reagan would play them, as later he would represent them in politics. In World War II, they were "our boys." In Los Angeles, they would epitomize the homogeneity of the masculine world of the 1950s and form the leadership core of the new LAPD.

They called themselves the Shields. The name was a way of emphasizing that they were the first class to have the LAPD's newly numbered copyrighted badges; a way to distinguish themselves and their shields from the old detective-lieutenant badges that citizen friends of the department would flash to get out of a speeding ticket or drunk-driving bust; badges that James Davis had distributed as freely as a hired clown gives out hard candy at a rich kid's birthday party. It was a new era in L.A. There was a new chief of police not indebted to the old leadership. And most importantly there was a new mayor—the staid, austere, honest

Fletcher Bowron. And there were the Shields. Seventy-eight men culled from five thousand applicants.

The first time they encountered Lt. Bill Parker, they were sitting in a Police Academy law class. Parker the lawyer, Parker the Police Protective League activist, Parker the former assistant to James Davis and already a minor legend within the department, was there to teach them about the law, and about honesty in enforcing it.

Bill Parker revered the law as he hated imprecision and disorder, finding even a hint of anarchy intolerable. He therefore gave no slack to thieves or to the kind of cops who'd bust in a head if they got a look they didn't like. That kind of behavior was not permissible. Not in his presence. Once in the late twenties, when he was an acting sergeant working the desk at Central Booking, a prisoner began giving the arresting officers some lip and they replied by starting to beat him senseless. Which was common practice in those days. If a guy got lippy, you'd knock him on his ass. Nobody made a big issue out of it. But Bill Parker spoke up and told them to knock it off: "You don't hit him in here. Take him someplace else and book him if you want to start that stuff, you're not going to hit him here."

It wasn't that Bill Parker was any bleeding heart; he believed in the strongest enforcement of every law, and in the fullest atonement and maximum punishment. His bleak view of human nature, in fact, permitted nothing less. In his mind, America was "the most lawless nation on earth" and "man the most predatory of all [in] the animal kingdom." An omnipresent police force—a "thin blue line"—was, he felt, society's only salvation. It was unlikely, therefore, that compassion was what had motivated Bill Parker. It was more that he hated seeing human fallibility among police officers, particularly when it was they—and only they— who stood between civilization and moral anarchy. It was a belief that would become first his mandate, and then his all-consuming passion. Order. Order was everything.

In this, and so much else, he was the future of the LAPD, as he would be its architect. And within the class of 1940 were the men who'd help him build it. Of those sitting in the law class that day, one, Edward M. Davis ("Crazy Ed," as the hippies and radicals called him three decades later) would write the rules, the regulations, the manual—the bible that cops live by—for Bill Parker's LAPD, and then go on to become one of his successors as chief. A second, Jim Fisk, a proud, God-fearing Christian known to the troops as "the nigger inspector," would become Bill Parker's liaison and flack catcher to L.A.'s Negroes when Chief William H. Parker finally decided to throw them a bone. Fisk would never become chief as a result, although he'd twice score highest on the civil service exams for the job. (A third cadet, Tom Reddin—who would also go on to be chief—would enter the Academy just three months later.) So with Parker at the Academy as he taught his law class, it was a virtual summit conference attended by a group of men who would become the LAPD's key leadership in the fifties, sixties, and seventies. Except for another cadet in the room with them that day. *His* path, Tom Bradley's path, and Tom Bradley's future, would be very different.

Often in the lead on their runs through the hills of the Academy, loping up a slope, skin glistening in the sun, would be Tom Bradley, his towering black figure dressed in regulation white ducks and T-shirt. His stride displayed the smooth, effortless motion of the star UCLA quarter miler he had been; his carriage so erect and graceful that people would use the word *statuesque* to describe him. As he entered the Academy with the class of 1940, Tom Bradley, at 22, already possessed all the gifts and insights he needed to maneuver in the overwhelmingly WASP world of prewar Los Angeles.

His daunting six-foot-four-inch height was complemented by a preternatural alertness, a keen intellect, an astonishing physical magnetism, a fine integrated public-school education, and three years as a student at UCLA. Coffee-colored and handsome, he was so physically imposing that all eyes would turn his way when he entered a room. Yet there was something absolutely unintimidating about him as well. Something that enabled Bradley to disarm white people—even those whose fear or hatred of blacks was intense and visceral—and place them at ease without him in any way having to shuffle. He had a soft smile that he'd use right away, a willingness to really listen without interrupting, and a warmth that made his whole face beam—a laugh that made you laugh at his laugh. His quick intelligence and winsome capacity for getting to the core of what people were talking about, moreover, allowed him to give back to the speaker the essence of what he or she had just said, an attribute that both complimented those speaking and highlighted the intense attention he was paying them.

He'd grown up on the streets of East Los Angeles, one of four children of a mother two generations removed from slavery who worked as a maid and seamstress, and of a former sharecropping cotton-picking father, who, before deserting the family, worked as a cook, waiter, railroad porter, and odd-job man. Early on, Tom Bradley had gotten a taste—just a taste—of the brutal, oppressive life his parents had left behind in a small log cabin in Calvert, Texas. At the age of six, as they were working their way to Los Angeles, he went out to pick cotton in a field just outside of Yuma, Arizona. Hunched over, working the rows, he watched his cousin pick up a ball of hard, still-green cotton, hurl it violently, and kill a coiled rattlesnake set to strike. As Bradley left the field at the end of the day with his hands virtually encrusted in cuts, holes, and bruises, and his left shoulder throbbing from the weight of the cotton sack, he knew—even at that young an age—that he never wanted to go back.

On that trip from Texas to Los Angeles in 1924, Tom Bradley's entire family had slept in their old jalopy because they couldn't find a boardinghouse that admitted blacks. He was only six, but decades later he could still recall the mashed-potato and baloney sandwiches his mother would prepare in the morning to eat that day because no diners would serve them; and he would find himself unable to shake that poor-boy feeling that came over him in odd ways. Like socks. He had never had enough as a boy, and once he'd reached adulthood, he'd buy drawers and drawers of them, more than he could ever possibly wear, brand-new socks that would remain unused for years.

Lee Bradley, his father, deserted his family within a few years of their arrival in Los Angeles, leaving his mother, Crenner Hawkins, to raise their four children alone. She was a tiny woman who remained resolutely upbeat despite a lifetime of drudgery picking cotton and cleaning, cooking, and sewing in white people's homes. It was a struggle only intensified by the Depression, her lack of education, the loss of five children in infancy, and her husband's desertion. Cleaning and washing for various families throughout Los Angeles, she traveled to South Grand Avenue one day, across town to Hollywood on another day, and worked the rest of the week in different houses throughout the city. Money was tight and Hawkins moved her family often, rarely to a better place.

Sundays they took a streetcar to the distant but properly middle-class New Hope Baptist Church and spent the day and evening there. She believed in the power of the Lord and sought to instill His righteousness in her children. Once, when Tom Bradley was ten or eleven, after being told by friends at school how ridiculously easy it was to steal a candy bar from a local grocery store, he took one. When his mother asked how he'd gotten it without any money, he told her the truth, received a beating, and was hauled back to the store and made to confess to the grocery man. She did not intend to lose her son to the street. Perhaps as a result, he grew up a young man with the small-town, middle-class values of hard work, self-discipline, and doing for yourself, values that, had he been white and more prosperously born, might well have led him into business and the Republican Party. "In my neighborhood," he would later say about his boyhood, "there were many who would prefer to get out and steal and vandalize rather than . . . get a job, rather than make some contribution to life. I refused to go along with that crowd."

For the most part, his growing up in Los Angeles was an experience that a self-satisfied, prewar, white America living outside of the Deep South could point to with pride, as if to say, "See that, look at him, a credit to his race, living proof that the Negro's lot is not so bad, if only they would work hard and apply themselves." He had lived in integrated neighborhoods and gone to integrated public schools, among them one of the city's best, Polytechnic High, where out of thirteen hundred students he'd be one of just over one hundred African-Americans. There, he starred as a high-school quarter miler, setting the then record for Los Angeles in the 440 dash, and making All City tackle on the 1936 football team. In 1937, he was also named All Southern Californian Track Champion as well as All City in the quarter mile.

Like Malcolm X, another poor black boy who'd gone to integrated schools, Tom Bradley was aware early on that he had great potential and stood out among the whites around him because of it. Malcolm would later bitterly complain about the distinction. About, for example, being voted class president by his white classmates, an experience, he said, that made him feel "like a pink poodle." Tom Bradley, by contrast, used it to his advantage. When the administration at Polytechnic suggested he serve as a mediator when racial tensions ran high, Tom Bradley obligingly interceded.

Doggedly, he ran for election for president of the school's Boys League. When his white opponent saw he'd be campaigning against a no-suit-owning black boy so poor that his kindly elementary-school teacher had felt compelled to bring in old clothes for him to wear, he quickly proclaimed "image" as the theme of his campaign. Image. It was an un-subtle message to the student electorate. A constant reminder that Tom Bradley could not possibly represent *them* to the downtown businessmen he'd have to meet. Appropriating the family's only suit—which belonged to his brother and which on Tom Bradley appeared almost foolishly oversize—he determined that what he "didn't have in suits, [he'd] try to make up for in cleanliness." Each day, he got up early, scrubbed one of his two dress shirts, and brought one of the pairs of pants from his brother's two-pants suit to the cleaners. When the election came, he won. He had beaten the white man at his own game.

Even then, as a student leader, he was tightly wound, self-contained, and supremely controlled. Those who knew Bradley then described him exactly as others would decades later: "You could know Tom Bradley for a hundred years and you still wouldn't know him." "Even in high school and college Tom kept his mouth shut," said James O'Neil, an old friend, years afterward. "He figured it out better than I did that if you're going to get by, you don't volunteer a thing." The only indications he'd ever give of being upset were a narrowing of his eyes, a twitch of his right cheek, and a tightening of his lips.

Like Malcolm X—who was told by a teacher that he had to be "realistic about being a nigger"—Tom Bradley was less harshly advised to forget about taking academic courses and preparing for college. Making those kinds of plans will "just break your heart," a teacher told him. "Take some studies that are going to lead you to manual labor because that's about as much as you're going to be able to hope for." Already an expert at stoically ignoring inadvertent insults, Tom Bradley ignored the advice.

As his reward, he received the blessings, recommendations, and support of his track and football coaches at Polytechnic and was awarded a full scholarship to UCLA. There he'd preceded Jackie Robinson by a year.

In his junior year, he decided to take the patrolman's exam for the LAPD, later describing his decision as something of a lark, done on the spur of the moment and urged on him by some friends who were on their way to take the test. But once having passed the exam, he quit UCLA in order to take the appointment. It was the Depression. This was a *job*. Money in the hand and a chance for some respect in a jim crow America where respect was as hard to come by for a black man as a decent paycheck.

On the eve of his entering the department, after already having passed the written, oral, and physical examinations, he arrived at the Police Academy for his medical. The name of the doctor working for the department was Vance. Every black American back then knew a Dr. Vance. Knew a gatekeeper. Vance was one of the LAPD's primary gatekeepers. Others were on the oral board. They gave the oral examination and served the same function as Vance: to make sure that the smallest possible number of blacks, Mexicans, and other undesirable outsiders were admitted into the LAPD family. Nothing was ever really said, but then no real effort was made to conceal what was going on either. Examining Bradley, it was obvious that Vance could barely contain his distaste. There were scores of reasons he could have chosen to fail Tom Bradley on his medical—a slight hearing impairment, less than perfect eyesight. The one he picked, however, happened to be exactly the wrong choice. "We can't take you," he told Bradley. "You've got a heart murmur." A heart murmur? Was he insane? Tom Bradley hadn't only been running track, he'd been running the *quarter mile*. And almost every day for years— pushing his body to its maximum. Bradley immediately appealed, passed another examination given by a city doctor not on the LAPD payroll, and in September 1940 entered the Los Angeles Police Academy.

As Tom Bradley was preparing to enter the LAPD, Bill Parker, who'd lectured him and Ed Davis and Jim Fisk at the Academy that day in 1940, was fighting to move up the departmental ladder. He was only a lieutenant, but even then, he was intimidating. Razor-sharp smart, self-assured to the point of arrogance, he never asked what you thought. He told you how it was. Brash, defensive, and determined, he would rarely admit to a mistake. And he would not back down.

He was born in 1902, and the place names of his youth seemed to foreshadow his mind-set and worldview: Lead, where he spent his early childhood; Deadwood, where he went to high school; the Black Hills and Badlands of South Dakota.

Much of those years are so steeped in the myth ground out by the LAPD's relentless public relations machine that it's difficult now to divorce fact from the PR fantasy that would make Bill Parker a legend.

His father, William Parker II, a superintendent in a gold mine, was rarely mentioned in approved bios and press releases except to point out that he "was buried in the same cemetery as Wild Bill Hickok—the man who brought law enforcement to Deadwood."

His uncle had been a prosecutor, and his grandfather—William Henry Parker—was, as Jack Webb tells it in his pungently idolatrous biography of Parker, *The Badge,* "one of the great frontier peace officers when there was no middle ground between right and wrong. After the gunslingers had been quieted, he had gone on to Washington as a congressman; so the boy [Bill Parker] knew that, though the fight may be dangerous, courage and honesty win out in the end."

Despite Webb's florid prose, there is no doubt that Bill Parker was a man of that hard, barren place, of that simpler, agrarian time, and of the end of that Victorian era.

In high school he played football, was on the debating team, and worked part-time either as a hotel detective or in a Deadwood "ladies' ready-to-wear store," where—as he himself later put it, perhaps tongue-in-cheek—he would "display lingerie in the town's [seven] brothels."

He was a serious drinker, but never a philanderer. Bill Parker was too much the Catholic for that, too much the altar boy at St. Ambrose's charged with lighting the furnace on bleak, bitterly cold Midwestern Sunday mornings before mass.

He believed in the Church, in its training, in its inherent moral superiority, and in the responsibility that went with it. "There was," therefore, "less excuse for a Catholic failing as a citizen," as he would later point out to Catholic Youth groups, "than for one who had not had the benefit of Catholic training."

With his family he moved to Los Angeles in 1923, getting a job first as an usher at the California Theater, and then as a cab driver. But what he needed—what all his life he would seem to need—was to answer the Call, to respond to that which had an even greater pull on him than did the Church. So in 1926, he entered the local night school for poor working boys anxious to join the bar: the Los Angeles College of Law. For the next year he'd sit and study his books at a cabstand outside the Biltmore Hotel while awaiting fares. The following year he joined the LAPD, walked a beat on the graveyard shift, and then switched to day classes. In 1930 he graduated and was admitted to the California bar.

It was a terrible time for young lawyers from no-name schools to open a practice or get a job. But a sergeant's pay was $225 a month. He took the test and placed third out of sixteen hundred applicants. There may have been an arrogance about Bill Parker, but he was no fool. The LAPD offered not only security in the Depression, but a chance to shine. There were, at the time, no more than a handful of men on the LAPD with college or law degrees. So he stayed. As a sergeant he became known for being obstinate, ornery, demanding, a stickler for the rules, a bookman who believed in giving the department its money's worth, and for expecting the troops to do the same.

It was the same reputation he'd later have with his peers. In command classes for the department's captains at the Police Academy in the early forties, if anybody had an idea that wasn't Bill Parker's, he'd attack it aggressively, outspokenly. Never mind their feelings, he said what he thought, and nobody could lay a glove on him.

Later he would simultaneously take both the deputy chief's and inspector's exams and miss about fifteen questions out of perhaps four hundred. When he got his results, he lodged a formal protest over every question he missed and refused to deal with the civil service staff who normally heard such disputes, insisting instead on being heard by the Civil Service Commission. On the day of the hearing, he got up and argued every single question he'd missed. And by the time he was through, the commission had conceded more mistaken answers than had William H. Parker.

He was neither too thin nor too fat and looked sharp in his LAPD blues. And he had that quality that in a quasi-military organization is far more significant than most lay people understand. He had presence, command presence. His bearing exuded authority, and his style was so deliberately reserved and no-nonsense that it bordered on the antithesis of style. In its way it said as much about him as tailored uniforms and pearl-handled revolvers said about George Patton. Nor was he a personality boy. Never would Bill Parker try to overwhelm you with a smile, joke, pat on the back, or arm around the shoulder. The mere posing of a question about whether he would have placed an arm around a colleague or subordinate would, in fact, evoke a look of utter incredulity from those who knew him.

By the midthirties he had risen to lieutenant and was working as an administrative assistant to James Davis. Although normally outspoken, Bill Parker never went out of his way to criticize or challenge the corruption daily staring him in the face as he served James Davis and shared the same suite of offices with "Sunny Jim" Bolger—Shaw's personal emissary to the LAPD and James Davis's personal secretary. In those days you either got on the take or closed your eyes and worked around it.

Even then, even alongside the stiff pomposity of James Edgar Davis, Bill Parker's inability to be comfortable within himself stood out. On fishing trips in the high Sierras with James Davis and his sons—when even the fastidious Davis would wear old clothes—Bill Parker would appear neat and well dressed, looking exactly as he should. His manner, as always, would remain precise; there was no buddy-buddy bantering or camaraderie between him and James Davis, whom he always called "Chief." Rather he related to Davis—who was not to be jollied in any case—as an adjutant would to an imposing general, as a man determined to show himself as even more responsible and serious than the ponderous, unsmiling James Davis.

But Bill Parker's tenure as an administrative officer to James Davis would prove invaluable. He was able to observe the lines of power; learn the details of running the department; absorb the politics inherent in the chief's job; and plug into the intrigue, gossip, sins, peculiarities, transgressions, and problems of future rivals and private citizens whose names came across the chief's desk. L.A. was a small town then, at least in terms of serious players.

It was in the Fire and Police Protective League, however, that Bill Parker first teethed on political tactics and learned about political power. The League, a cops and firemen's union by another name, had developed in the early thirties, a time when pay raises were nonexistent and arbitrary dismissals frequent. Officers with twelve, fourteen, even nineteen years of service were being dismissed and left with no—with zero—pension benefits. Other than getting shot or doing time in an Alcatraz cellblock with some lowlife you'd once locked up, the thought of finishing a career with zero pension benefits was a police officer's worst nightmare. Ostensibly, they were protected from arbitrary dismissal under Section 202 of the city charter, which had passed in 1925. It provided for a trial board of three captains to judge an officer. But the civilian police commission could—and did—dissolve the board whenever it rendered a verdict the commission didn't like.

So in 1931, the city charter was amended and sworn officers were given a substantial "right" to their positions. But the chief still did not have to accept the trial board's verdict. If a chief fired an officer and the board found him innocent, he could—and did—ignore their finding. The board could not force him to reverse the firing.

In 1934 and 1937 Bill Parker joined with Earl Cooke, another League official and LAPD officer-attorney, and rewrote Section 202 of the city charter, which the League then had placed on the ballot. Spread over eight pages of the charter, it was an astounding piece of work. The rights of all LAPD officers were vested and codified, the internal discipline system cast in stone. Henceforth, there would be a one-year statute of limitations on bringing charges, and a guaranteed right to counsel and a public hearing. Plus—and this was key—only a cop could now judge another cop. Only a Board of Rights, designated as a legal entity—and composed solely of other cops—could judge and fire an LAPD officer. No longer could they be overruled. Not by the police commission. Not by the chief of police. Only three ranking LAPD officers, whom the *accused* could choose from six names drawn from a box—thus maximizing the chance for a sympathetic jury—would have that power and right. Only men who were part of the code, men inherently sympathetic to certain kinds of police misconduct, such as beating someone who tried your patience or clearly deserved it, or shooting some guy in the line of duty who shouldn't have been shot, had that power. Now, only brother officers would gather the facts of your case. Now, the chief of police could decrease but not increase penalties. Now, the rank and file, from the beat cop up through the deputy chiefs, were free from a chief's discipline if the penalty was more than a thirty-day suspension. Nor was that all.

Parker, Cooke, and the other moving forces in the League—who wrote, strategized, financed, and campaigned for the amendment's passage—took their autonomy one crucial step further and gave the *chief* the same rights they had. He, too, would be protected by 202. He, too, needed that protection. Hadn't Joe Shaw, after all, been practically running the vice squad? So the chief's job was also made a "substantial property right," not to be taken away from him by suspension or firing except for "good and sufficient cause shown upon a finding of 'guilty' of the specific charge or charges . . . after a full, fair and impartial hearing before the [Board of Civil Service Commissioners]."

If zero for a pension was a cop's worst nightmare, the procedures laid out by Parker and Cooke in order to find a chief guilty and remove him were a politician's. First would come a headline-making public confrontation between the chief and a part-time police commission whose police staff was beholden to the chief and not to them, a commission appointed by a weak mayor, a commission that would have to draw up a sworn complaint delineating the facts and charges.

Next, the chief would be entitled to a full hearing before the civil service board in which he had the right to cross-examine witnesses. He could cross-examine the mayor, the commissioners, *anybody,* with the press, like a pack of hungry wolves, braying hard outside the hearing room. What a circus it would be. Then, a chief could halt or drag out the proceedings at any time by claiming the charter had been violated and taking the case into Superior Court.

Third, if a chief were fired, he could then sue in state and federal court over alleged violations of his constitutional or procedural rights. And finally, he could again go back into Superior Court to challenge any verdict.

It was a potential quagmire that could drag on for years, one that any politician would be insane to get involved in. And the League, and Bill Parker and Earl Cooke, got it passed. If Bill Parker had done nothing else, that alone would have merited him a place in LAPD history. He and Earl Cooke and the rest of the League activists had given the chief of the Los Angeles Police Department the lifetime tenure, free of accountability, of a Supreme Court justice and laid the cornerstone on which the department's future autonomy and power would rest. The League had seen its opportunity, struck, and won with a timing that couldn't have been more perfect. The midthirties had been years of tremendous tumult and dissatisfaction with the LAPD. The grand jury was finding corruption under every overturned stone, Clifford Clinton was leading a citizens' crusade against Frank Shaw, and James Davis and the department were becoming an increasingly intolerable joke. It was their moment.

The vote on the 1937 charter amendment protecting the chief passed by more than ten thousand votes, 79,336 to 69,380, dramatically altering the history of Los Angeles. With the approval of the electorate, a weird balkanization had taken place. A quasi-military organization had declared itself independent of the rest of city government and placed itself outside the control of the police commission, City Hall, or any other elected public officials, outside of the democratic system of checks and balances. Bill Parker, the man who helped to write the statute, would be the first to realize it.

By the early 1940s Bill Parker had risen to the rank of captain and was heading the Accident Investigation Bureau. Then he went into the Army and came back a minor hero. During the Second World War, he served as a lieutenant and then a captain in the occupation forces in Europe. In his twenty-six months there, he helped draft the plans for establishing police departments and prisons in occupied Germany; and during the Normandy invasion, he'd been awarded a Purple Heart for a minor shrapnel wound. Later, he would also receive the French Croix de Guerre with Silver Star.

In 1947, back on the department for two years, he made inspector. By the end of the year he'd become the odds-on favorite to place first on the list for chief of police, should there be an opening. His chance would come when Brenda Allen's name hit the headlines in 1949.

Allen was the queen of Hollywood madams, hers among L.A.'s most lucrative, upscale call-girl services, with a daily take in 1949 dollars that was said to be $1,200. She lived in West Hollywood, off the Sunset Strip, in the same area out of which most of L.A.'s bookmakers operated.

During an FBI search of her home, Elmer Jackson, an LAPD vice detective (and 1940 classmate of Bradley, Davis, and Fisk), was told to stay and watch Brenda Allen while the search was being conducted. Jackson was young, handsome, and ambitious. He and Allen quickly became lovers. One night when they were parked together, a holdup man stuck a gun through Elmer Jackson's open window. Jackson pulled out his hide-away pistol and shot the stickup man dead. About a year later, a reporter from the *Daily News* discovered that the woman who had been with Elmer Jackson that night was Brenda Allen.

The subsequent headlines lead to a grand jury investigation. Brenda Allen testified before that grand jury that she had paid Jackson $50 a week for each woman she employed, and other sums to other vice squad members. Hollywood Vice was also reported to have been shaking down prostitutes, homosexuals, and drug addicts, and padding expense accounts.

Following the damaging grand jury testimony, C. B. "Jack" Horrall was forced to retire after eight years as chief. A native of small-town Indiana, Horrall was a heavyset, bald-headed man who was not very articulate and certainly not sophisticated. He loved his friends and having them around and left much of the running of the department to his friend Assistant Chief Joe Reed, which led to his downfall. Horrall and Reed were later indicted for perjury, but their cases were thrown out. Elmer Jackson and a lieutenant were also indicted for extortion. Just ten years after the Shaws, and here it was, a similar scandal, on a much smaller scale, happening again.

Simultaneously, the LAPD was being embarrassed by one of the most sensational crime stories ever to hit Los Angeles: the murder of Elizabeth Short, the sad, famous Black Dahlia. Her death was the kind of case Americans love, crossing as it did the nexus where puritanical outrage meets sexual titillation. A seventeen-year-old runaway from Massachusetts, Short was slim, statuesque, black-haired, and porcelain-skinned, with a rose tattoo on her upper thigh. By twenty-two she was posing for porno pictures in Los Angeles. In early 1947 she ended up in a vacant L.A. lot with her mouth slashed from ear to ear, her body spread-eagle, punctured, bruised, mutilated, burned, and ever-so-slowly tortured before it was cut cleanly in half at the waist. Despite the LAPD's putting over fifty detectives on the case, her killer was never found.

There was no place in the white spot for that sort of thing, or for Brenda Allen and Elmer Jackson. What was needed was a high-profile campaign of police reform. A campaign that would reassure the citizens that the LAPD wasn't going back to its bad old ways, but was instead developing into a new force with a new chief who would keep the lid on the town. A chief with vastly increased powers, a strong chief, would be good for business and good for civic order. He could create a new police department, but stand for the old-time religion of big business, social conformity, rigid morality, and strict law and order. Cowtown L.A. Hicksville, the rube's paradise, was gone. Brenda Allen and the Black Dahlia was the first drama of the new Los Angeles that had, more than ever, to be kept on a short leash and contained. What was needed was an enemy and a war. And the enemy that was chosen—the mob—was no pipe-dream bogeyman.

Jack Dragna and Johnny Rosselli had been operating with Joe Shaw in the thirties, and Rosselli had also been busy shaking down the International Alliance of Theatrical Stage Employees (IATSE). Bugsy Siegel, Meyer Lansky and the mobs' man on the West Coast, had had a piece of the gambling ships operating in the Long Beach and Santa Monica harbors—beyond the three-mile limit—before then California attorney general Earl Warren had closed them down in 1939. But in 1947, after his vision of the great casino in the dunes of Las Vegas had cost Meyer Lansky, Frank Costello, and the mob $6 million, Siegel had his face splattered all over his wife's Beverly Hills living room by carbine bullets. Jack Dragna had probably facilitated Siegel's killing for the mob, just as he had also tried to kill Mickey Cohen, who was then collecting $250 a week gambling juice from almost every one of L.A.'s bookmakers. Moreover, Dragna was known to have ties to the L.A. county sheriff's department. There were other reasons as well to be concerned about organized crime. Ex-members of the LAPD, working in the office of California attorney general Fred Howser, had set up offices in the Biltmore Hotel in an unsuccessful attempt to organize a statewide protected gambling ring. And, at about the same time, Jim Fisk, now a vice-squad lieutenant with a tough reputation among bookmakers, had raided the office of the Guarantee Finance Corporation and found "thousands of betting markers" and a file showing that 160 agents had been taking bets totaling $7 million annually. Perhaps $450,000 of that was being paid for protection to the sheriff's department. The thread was there. It was undeniable.

But by the end of the 1940s Jack Dragna was over sixty and over the hill. In 1953, he would be ordered deported to Italy and hounded by the INS until he died in 1956. Johnny Rosselli, Dragna's longtime running partner—who'd been released from prison in 1947 after being jailed for his IATSE shakedowns—was past his prime and marginalized. And Siegel was dead.

In the dozen years Fletcher Bowron had been mayor, most of the old-time vice cops and corrupt bureaucrats and politicians had been flushed out of the system, the gambling ships had been closed, and the state of California had tightened controls on both the racetrack gambling wires used by bookies and the manufacturing of gambling equipment. Legalized prostitution in parts of Nevada, and especially the glitzy legal gambling in Las Vegas, would siphon off the most ardent players and revelers from Southern California. When his time came to deal with the mobsters he so hated, Bill Parker would thus be extremely lucky, and extremely skillful in using the threat of the mob for his own ends. But before he got the chance, he'd first have to deal with a retired Marine Corps general named William Arthur Worton.

After Mayor Fletcher Bowron's police commission had forced the resignation of Chief Jack Horrall, he named William Worton to temporarily lead the department until a permanent successor could be chosen. Worton, a retired marine corps general, wanted to put his personal stamp on the LAPD, and he went at it with vengeance. He revered training and reinstated the old ninety-day training program at the Police Academy. Then he ordered large-scale and continuous transfers—reshuffling secretaries along with police officers, breaking up cliques, cutting off ties that had endured years, letting in a huge gust of fresh air, and taking the heat from a lot of outraged, calcified people. At the same time he met with rank-and-file officers and invited their observations and recommendations. And he brought back Earle Kynette's old Intelligence Squad. It was only a decade since it had been abolished, but now, justified by the specter of Eastern gangsters trying to infiltrate and organize Los Angeles, it was back.

One of Worton's first acts was to select Bill Parker to head a sensitive new unit known as Internal Affairs that would investigate corruption and misconduct by police officers. Parker's service as an administrative officer, his cowriting of the department's internal discipline system while on the League, and his work as a department prosecutor on trial boards, all made him the ideal candidate. When it was combined with his frosty, not-one-of-the-boys persona, his knowledge of where the bodies were buried, his reputation for honesty, and his willingness to go after other cops, Bill Parker was a powerful message just waiting to be sent.

Like civil service safeguards and a re-activated Intelligence Squad, a strong Internal Affairs division riding herd over a department with a notorious history of corruption made perfect sense. And in cases of graft and payoffs, or infractions such as sleeping on duty or misconduct off duty, the system would work. Investigations would be vigorous, the punishment harsh. But in police shootings and brutality, discipline would depend on how strongly the chief wanted to pursue such cases, and in the decades to come pursuit would be tepid at best, setting up additional problems. Theoretically, the district attorney could always indict a police officer for a *criminal* act. But with Internal Affairs—that is, the police themselves—handling most investigations, and the DA beholden to the LAPD to investigate almost all of his other cases within the city, rarely, if ever, did that happen, unless Internal Affairs referred cases to him. In time, any complaint of misconduct by an LAPD officer, whether it originated with the DA, the city attorney, the city council, the mayor, or the police commissioner, would be investigated by Internal Affairs, further strengthening the LAPD's autonomy. Thus, the department would have it all covered. The entire process of police misconduct— from complaints lodged against individual officers through investigation and then judgment—would now be handled internally by LAPD officers.

And there was more, an extra worker, a side benefit for the department.

Each time an LAPD killing or other outrage led to cries for a civilian review board, the department would discount it by simply pointing to the Internal Affairs division. There was no need for a civilian review board, no need for any kind of civilian oversight, they would say. We already have a vigorous mechanism of investigation and punishment in place. Undoubtedly all this was not the intent of William Worton, but that would be the way it played out.

For the first nine months things went smoothly between William Worton and Bill Parker. Until Worton began to forget his place, to forget he was an outsider, to forget there were civil service rules and regulations— powerfully written, tamperproof, and unequivocal—governing just exactly who got to be chief of the Los Angeles Police Department. And those rules didn't include former generals with no police experience who'd probably never *seen* a city civil service exam. Three months, six months, even nine months to brace things up, let in a little fresh air, and serve as a figurehead was one thing; but Worton was talking about staying an additional year to make certain his programs were properly implemented. A suggestion that was unacceptable to Bill Parker, who was waiting in the wings. Further, in a dramatic departure from the independence that Parker and the others in the Protective League had worked so hard to achieve, Worton was also advocating the appointment of a civilian manager named by the mayor and approved by the city council to serve a single three-year term. The manager would oversee virtually everything but day-to-day police work, which the chief would handle. William Worton not only liked the idea, but wanted to be the first to hold the post. Civilian control. He was talking about civilian control. It was not just unacceptable, it was outrageous, and the League and Bill Parker began applying pressure. "The League very much opposed [the idea] of an interim chief like Worton coming from the outside," says former LAPD deputy chief Harold Sullivan, who served on the League with Parker in 1946 and 1947. "Historically, that had been our position. There was a question of his legality as soon as a chief's list was created. And when they tried to extend—[Worton's tenure], *that* was clearly illegal."

And in fact, the selection of a new chief was spelled out in civil service law: the police commission was required to choose the new chief from the three top-scoring applicants on the civil service list. Worton was delusional if he thought he could get around it, or that there was any stomach for yet another charter amendment, and one fiercely opposed by the League. It was a joke. He'd have to go. Asking around about the three top contenders, Fletcher Bowron questioned Irvis Lester about the type of chief Bill Parker might make, and Lester told him, "A piss-poor one . . . He's right at the top [of the list], but he's too bossy to just let people do their job. He'd always be second-guessing them. He thinks that he, and only he, knows it all." But in the end it would all come down to William H. Parker and to a man who was his polar opposite, Thaddeus Brown.

In the eyes of Thad Brown, his detectives could do no wrong. If they were drunks, he'd carry them. If the boys decided to get a little piece of a suspect, well, he probably deserved it. That was the attitude of Thaddeus Brown, the LAPD's chief of detectives. He loved to drink, loved his men, and they loved him. He had little formal education, but by the early thirties Thad Brown had become a legendary LAPD detective. His specialty—and he developed it into an art—was getting people to tell him all their sins. He knew how to put them at ease, how to be the gentle father or helpful brother. He was a likable native of Missouri, a stocky man of about five feet eleven inches who dressed neatly in conservative cop suit and hat and always played the good cop. His nonthreatening attitude and body language, and the decent, kindly way he'd talk to everyone were like a gift from God, wonderfully offset by his hard-nosed investigative instincts. His stable of informants was among the very best: an LAPD officer who'd gone underground and become a high-ranking official in the local Communist Party; bartenders and bar patrons all over the city; a barber in Watts; the heads of tongs in Chinatown. Thad Brown, like a smart reporter, cultivated them all. He had multiple sources and the wisdom not to bust them for petty shit. "You don't get any information in church" was his motto, and as a result, far better than most, he knew what was really going on in the city. He was a practitioner of old-school nuts-and-bolts police work. Never mind this going to school and getting degrees, this scientific policing, this "professionalization." Every good cop knew that 90—no, 95—percent of the cases they solved were solved because somebody had snitched out somebody else. And Thad Brown was a cop, not a man with a message. His core value was loyalty. He was of the boys and one of the boys.

Bill Parker, on the other hand, *had* to overwhelm you with his intellect and fervently believed police officers had to be vigorously trained and highly moral. They were, after all, literally the saviors of civilization as we know it.

When the time came to choose between them, the police commission was divided, but leaning three to two for Brown. Then right before the vote, one of Brown's key supporters unexpectedly died. Thad Brown told his backers to go ahead and vote for Bill Parker. He did not, he'd later explain, want to serve as chief "with Bill Parker behind me with his knife out." The commission then voted unanimously for Parker.

Although William Worton initiated a number of reforms for which Bill Parker would receive credit, Worton had in mind one reform that Parker, once in office, refused to institute: the integration of the department's black officers.

For a man of his age and background, Worton's attitude on race had been relatively enlightened. When he took over the department, he met with local black leaders and promised that both the LAPD's racism and its brutality would end, and that the LAPD would be integrated.

One day in 1949 he called Lt. Rocky Washington, a black, twenty-year LAPD veteran and one of the department's two black lieutenants, into his office. "Where are you working?" he asked. "Special [plainclothes] detail . . . gangster squad," Washington told him, adding that he'd made lieutenant in 1940 and during the war had been in the LAPD War Activities Office, working with the air-raid wardens. The latter was an assignment that fifty years later still rankled Rocky Washington, filling him with rage and shame. He'd been in his prime then, and what had they given him but "a piece of crap, a *nothing* assignment." Worton listened and then told Washington he'd decided to utilize him as he would any other lieutenant, which meant in charge of a watch in a regular LAPD division. He was going back East, he said, and he'd find out how integration had been handled in other departments. "When I come back," Worton added, "I'll put you where you belong." And he did, assigning Washington to the night watch in the Central Division after he returned. The white officers in Central immediately threatened a revolt. "They didn't figure," says Washington, "that a white officer should be subordinate to a black man." Word went around, in fact, that all of the officers in Central—every one of them—was going to ask for a transfer out of the division. But it never materialized. Neither, however, did Worton's promised integration plans. His time was too short and he left too soon. And when Bill Parker took over, he put integration on hold for a *very* long time.

*   *   *

In August 1950, Bill Parker became the chief of police of the City of Los Angeles. The LAPD would never be the same. In the days following his appointment, he promised "with all the fiber of [his being to] see to it that crooked rats who would change the City of Angels to the city of *diablos* will not do so"; and that the LAPD would "work for the community, not rule it."

Bill Parker knew his constituency, knew those whose support he needed, and he wasted no time in courting them. From his work with the League in the thirties and forties he was familiar with the veterans on the city council, knew how to talk to politicians, and how to sell them. Reporters, too. The Protective League had always courted the press when legislation concerning them came up, and Bill Parker had learned the importance of taking reporters out for dinner and drinks, of making sure they got a bottle of liquor at Christmas, and that good relations were maintained with their editors. That was how the department got bigger budgets and cops got raises.

During his first few years in office, by former LAPD deputy chief Harold Sullivan's account, Bill Parker would make over a thousand speeches. He'd go to breakfasts, lunches, and dinners and speak before crucial groups such as the Chamber of Commerce, the Downtown Business Men's Association, and the Merchants and Manufacturers Association. He'd even travel out to the city's distant reaches in the Valley and South Bay, leaving no stone unturned in his efforts to promote the LAPD, expand its power, and transform its image.

Almost immediately it began to work. You saw it on the street in the way Parker's men carried themselves, in their starched, creased appearance, in the way they eyed you, and in the way they spoke. Bill Parker was something more than just a police chief. He was the force around which it would all gravitate. He had the ego, he had the will, he had the vision, and he had the need. The words, the analogy, he would have found an abomination, but there could be no question about it. Bill Parker was nothing less than the godfather—*il capo di tutti capi*—of the New Centurions.

CHAPTER 2

The Grip

••••••••••••••••••••

Summoning him into his office in late 1950, Bill Parker didn't offer Ed Davis the job, he told him that he would take it. A new department manual—a procedural talmud—had to be written as part of the massive, top-to-bottom overhaul of the department that Parker was undertaking. And Ed Davis was clearly the best-qualified person for the task. Throughout much of the forties, Davis had led a small team that had redesigned and rewritten the department's "Daily Training Bulletin" into a series of roll-call minilessons that spelled out how to deal with street-level situations such as making vagrancy arrests or handling landlord-tenant disputes. The bulletins had become immensely popular with the troops both for their imaginative, easy-to-understand content and slightly salacious cartoons.

What Parker now wanted from Lt. Ed Davis was for him to oversee a comprehensive revamping of the department's manual, which was dense, stilted, and in some areas twenty, thirty, even forty years out-of-date. It was a massive undertaking that would eventually grow to five thick, loose-leaf books covering field regulations, departmental organization, and clerical procedures. But Ed Davis was more than up to it.

He was a man who believed in self-discipline. Rigid self-discipline and rigorous hard work, that was the thing. All that was its antithesis appalled him. Like desks. Desks had drawers to put away unfinished business. He worked on a table, where you could see what had not been completed, and if you were a serious person, you would not leave until that work had been attended to. His was the nineteenth-century mind-set of Henry Ford, with his emphasis on industriousness as salvation, and the best advertisement for that philosophy was himself. He would attend USC (where he'd graduate with honors), rise to the presidency of the Protective League, have a family, and do volunteer work at his church all the while he was climbing the ladder of the LAPD.

He was a big man, standing six feet tall and weighing about 190 pounds, with a determined, theatrical presence about him. "Even in those days," former LAPD chief Tom Reddin would later recall, Ed Davis was "a great one for posturing. He smoked a pipe and would hold on to the lapel of his coat while smoking, [and he made] a big production of tapping that pipe and lighting it." In the years since he'd graduated from the Academy, Davis had grown a mane of hair that he wore long and wavy, and a mustache, which was also unusual for a cop of the time. When he walked, it was with a bearlike, tough-guy shuffle.

He was born in 1916, the son of a dyer of materials for women's clothing and a housewife, and raised in South Central L.A. when South Central was not synonymous with Watts and Bloods and Crips. When it was a tranquil area of stable neighborhoods; when it was still white, largely Protestant, and filled with working people and the lower-middle class. Ed Davis loved that small-town Los Angeles, loved that L.A. of what he would call the "average man." He was tuned into those people—his people—and as he rose through the ranks, he would unfailingly reflect their passions and perceptions. In the midthirties, while still attending Fremont High, his father had a serious heart attack, and he'd been forced to go to work. Finishing school at night at twenty-four, he had entered the Police Academy class of 1940.

Ed Davis did an outstanding job on the manuals. And when they were finally published, they almost immediately became the much-copied prototype and standard by which others throughout the nation were judged. They were useful tools, but their real significance lay in what they represented: Bill Parker's determination to apply the principles and techniques of modern business management to the creaky, cumbersome, bureaucratic behemoth that the LAPD, like most big-city police departments, had become. Bill Parker believed in technology and in the precepts of twentieth-century scientific management and research as fervently as he believed in nineteenth-century morality. Believed in it so passionately that he'd built an entire LAPD division, Planning and Research, around it. It was a sharp, insightful innovation, soundly conceived and led by Parker and precisely executed by the rest of the LAPD hierarchy. He streamlined the command structure, combining divisions and reducing the number of people reporting directly to him from fourteen to eight. He had officers sick days systematically tracked. That assignment, too, was given to Ed Davis, because it was *he,* as Davis himself later pointed out, who ''had imagination.'' Davis proceeded to put together a calendar on which he plotted the sick days of a group of officers suspected of constantly taking time off for reasons other than their health. He charted their conduct over a ten-year period, finding patterns of abuse: officers with drinking problems calling in sick after payday as they went on benders, and others who had seasonal jobs, such as selling Christmas trees, who were out sick for the same periods year after year. Planning and Research also developed methods for streamlining booking procedures, tracking stolen cars, analyzing crime patterns, and deploying officers far more efficiently.

Parker would also strengthen and institutionalize the department's passion for strict traffic and pedestrian control, a mania that left visitors from all over the country, from all over the world, stunned, incredulous, and outraged over a jaywalking ticket they'd just received for failing to walk seventy-five yards to the closest intersection to cross the street. Parker had studied at the traffic school the insurance industry was funding at Northwestern University and had absorbed its message—a message that could cut the industry's costs and liability: reduce accidents by stringently enforcing the law. The upside was that it worked. By the end of 1953, Los Angeles's traffic deaths were the lowest in the nation for cities with a population of over one million. Achieving those figures while both the number of registered vehicles and the population were growing by hundreds of thousands made the accomplishment even more impressive. The downside was that it would produce a system that made you feel like your city belonged to someone else, some faceless, omnipotent being. You could never relax, you had to follow every rule—whether walking or driving—all the time, ever fearful that some stiff, gigantic motorcycle cop with an attitude would swoop down on you. As many as fifteen thousand jaywalking tickets a year would be written. (''They write tickets or they don't ride bikes," Harold Sullivan, who headed Traffic Division under Bill Parker, used to say of his motorcycle officers.) In the years to come, Mexican day laborers would be written up for drinking a beer in front of their overpriced, rented bungalows after a hard day's work. Bingo games would be busted; dart throwers arrested for making dollar-a-game bets in a local bar, and junkies would be booked after parking in front of a methadone clinic as they arrived to receive treatment. It was like basic training. Like the Army. Like being a guest in someone's house whom you didn't know very well. You were always aware that this was their house, not yours. So it was with the streets of Los Angeles.

And so it was with the department. For Bill Parker, a police force that wasn't "professional" wasn't a department. He was a professional and his men would be professionals. That was both his ideal and the image he was determined to display. He would start with the best new meat. All recruits would undergo a stringent background investigation, pass highly competitive exams, and meet rigid height, weight, education, intelligence, and psychiatric standards. And once they were accepted in the department, they would be trained as professionals.

Professionals. It was an idea whose time had come, a concept that criminologists such as August Vollmer and Orlando W. Wilson had advocated for years but that had remained largely unrealized due to the Depression and then to the war. Training. Education. The scientific method. Technology. Standards. Peer review. Self-regulation. Independence from politics. Square-jawed police officers, not flaccid, potbellied cops. That was professionalism. And now was the time—it was the postwar era. There was money to spend and hundreds of thousands of exservicemen were going to school on the G.I. Bill. There were programs like the Traffic Education School at Northwestern, a Community Relations Program at Michigan State University, the FBI's school for fast-track local police officers in Quantico, Virginia, and the California Council on Criminal Justice. Locally there were the courses offered by the community and state colleges, and especially the program in public administration at USC being taught by Jim Fulton, a ranking LAPD officer. All would leave their mark, all would contribute to the professionalization that Bill Parker would make a sacred, central tenet of his administration. His men, the men of the LAPD, would behave in his image. No longer would they be underpaid and have their integrity, their professionalism, bought for a ten-dollar bill.

Between 1950 and 1966 the LAPD's budget would quadruple, and by 1956 the LAPD had become the best-paid police department in the nation, attracting a higher caliber of men than ever before.

But Bill Parker's vision extended beyond professionalization. Society was running amok. The Victorian values of his youth had been abandoned. America was in the last rancid stages of decay. For L.A. to remain the "white spot," and not become, God forbid, Rio, the people needed to be policed by officers superior to their own venal selves. His officers had to be stronger, smarter, and cleaner living. Their jawlines would be straighter, and their hearts far purer than the general public's. They would know, when they hit the street, that they were superior to the people they were encountering. They would stand at least five feet nine inches and be white and male high school athletes with military experience (you automatically received a ten-point bonus on your civil service ranking for military experience). They would be Andy Hardy as war hero.

The standards for his new officers would be grounded in the research and statistical analysis of police science and his own Planning and Research Division. The height requirement was just one example. The minimum was set at five feet nine inches, a measurement not arrived at casually. Five feet nine was then the average height of the American male. Bill Parker's officers had to be at least that tall. They would look down, the general public up.

That feeling of uniqueness, superiority, and esprit de corps would be summed up by the concept of the twenty-fifth man. Just the fact that you were in the Academy at all, they'd inform new recruits, proved you were some kind of superman. Twenty-four others had applied along with you, been found wanting, and had washed out. You made it. You were the twenty-fifth man. Of course, your being the twenty-fifth man was contingent on your actually making it through the Academy, and then through the probationary period that followed, which in those days, like standards, actually meant something.

And who better to make Bill Parker's dream a reality than the drill instructors who personified the traditions of America's elite military units—the Corps, the Airborne. They were born for the task. So they were sought out. It all made perfect sense. America had just won a righteous war in which millions of men and women had served in the armed forces. Well, policemen, as Bill Parker was unflaggingly pointing out, were fighting in a continuous war, too, weren't they? Wasn't that what the concept of the "thin blue line" was all about? So shouldn't some of the men who'd been DIs or combat veterans be used as DIs at the Academy? Why shouldn't men like Frank Walton, who'd served as a major under Pappy Boyington in the Corps, have some input into devising the training? And shouldn't someone like Merrill Duncan, who'd been a captain in the Marines, be in charge of the physical training, be in charge of the drill, of the stress? Hell, who knew better how to take the Corps' state-of-the-art stress training, tear down boys, and then build them back into the proud fighting machines that had enabled America to rule over half the earth? And as they were the experts, shouldn't they be permitted to function in an atmosphere that enabled them to get the job done? In an atmosphere that Tom Reddin—who was superintendent of training in the early 1950s—would later characterize as "permissive"? In an atmosphere that allowed them to flourish? They did not immediately turn the Academy into the epitome of the Jones-you-are-one-sorry-motherfucker school of stress training that it was to become. They started out by doing, says Reddin, just "enough to test the guy's control, to put him under pressure, not to break him."

Back then, a cadet was still permitted to walk on the sidewalks as if he were a human being. He didn't then have to flatten up against the wall whenever an Academy staff member passed in the hallways or bang on the training-board door so hard that it rattled the door hinges. Nor was he required to stand braced at rigid attention behind the black line in the gym with the rest of his class on the first day of training as the instructors set the tone by literally screaming in his face as if he were some dumb-ass, eighteen-year-old Iowa hayseed going through Marine Corps drill camp down in Camp Pendleton. None of that. The only formation then was in the morning when you showed up for inspection and they looked you over to ensure your appearance was up to standard. And, of course, on graduation day. It was different then, at the beginning. They hadn't taken the concept of fear and humiliation as a teaching tool and expanded it to its logical conclusion. They hadn't perfected high-stress training into an art form. All of that didn't really lock in until sometime in the 1960s. In the early and midfifties, you were an LAPD cadet, a gentleman, and were to be treated as one. You were always addressed by your title—which was Cadet—and not, as was later the case, as "scumbag" or "worm" or whatever was the latest derogatory term out on the street.

But the nucleus of the rigid, military training that would follow was there, even then. And after a while, the influence of DIs and other like-minded instructors began having a powerful impact on Academy training. Eventually, says Tom Reddin, it went from a case of "whatever you want to do we like it, to the inmates running the institution."

The military model would become the standard for police departments throughout southern California. Few if any of the surrounding police agencies had any real standards of training. And it was the Los Angeles Police Academy to which they'd turn, and that would set those standards and show the way. In time, members of the LAPD hierarchy would become the chiefs of police of the communities surrounding Los Angeles such as Beverly Hills and Pasadena, head departments in Southwestern cities such as Dallas and Ft. Worth, and go on to lead organizations like the California Highway Patrol. Through them and the Academy, Parker's training and philosophy would spread.

Not only was it perfect for the type of officer Bill Parker wanted, it was also ideal for Bill Parker's philosophy of policing. If you had fewer than five thousand men to police over 450 square miles of a city with a rapidly expanding population as was the case with the LAPD in the early fifties, you needed to develop a strategy and tactics to deal with it. Which Bill Parker did. He took James Davis's stop-and-search and dragnet techniques, and Bob Shuler's and Harry Chandler's conception of a culturally limp, politically obedient city, put it all together, and gave it a name: "proactive policing."

L.A. was sprawling and horizontal, not vertical. Its citizens' beliefs had already begun to mirror the city fathers' aversion to the crowd. They'd been made part of the game by the successful lobbying of the auto, oil, and rubber industries to have the region's mass-transit system dismantled, and by the concurrent growth of L.A.'s suburbs following World War II. The city's skinny sidewalks—designed to speed traffic; and its houses without front porches whose architectural design directed the dwelling's gravity and action toward the backyard illuminated that aversion. Los Angeles was a place that seemed to loathe street life and the teeming masses mingling together.

For decades the LAPD had reflected the loathing with its raids on "undesirables," with dragnets, with its mindless vice enforcement, with its rage at union demonstrators and marches and its annoyance at crowds in open spaces. That was the LAPD Bill Parker had come of age in. And that was the LAPD he would continue. Not because of any pressure from a Robert Shuler or orders from the *Los Angeles Times*. But because he wished it. *Il capo di tutti capi.*

It was a philosophy for its time: the pre–Earl Warren Supreme Court, for James Davis's L.A., for the early fifties. But it would be obsolete almost as soon as it was instituted. Its underpinning was dominion, control, The Grip. Walking a beat, knowing the residences of a neighborhood, using discretion in making arrests, serving as a safety valve, as a mediator, as a social-agency facilitator or problem solver was out. Patrol cars with faceless occupants detached from the community; enforcing all laws and keeping an intense twenty-four-hour surveillance over an equally faceless population—The Grip was in. Authority would be centralized, tasks defined, discretion limited, arrests—the numbers—emphasized. Never should an officer be out there waiting for a crime—victim or victimless, petty or serious—to happen. Instead he should be seeking one out or—and here was the key—stopping it before it happened. To do that, you had to know a criminal by his appearance and demeanor. You had to check him out. You had to hit the street hard and be aggressive. If people were on the streets, they were suspect. Grab everybody and sort them out until you find someone who fits whatever it is you're looking for. After that, come up with a reason for having stopped him. There was always probable cause. The suspect was weaving over the centerline, he failed to come to a complete stop at a stop sign—whatever. As Daryl Gates would later put it, "If someone looked out of place in a neighborhood, we had a little chat with him. If a description of a thief could be obtained, we stopped everyone fitting that description, even if it meant angering dozens of innocent citizens. . . . Using these proactive tactics [the] LAPD would become the most aggressive police department in the country." For blacks and Latinos in white neighborhoods this meant being spotted, circled, checked out, and "moved" every few blocks, moved back to where they belonged. Meanwhile, in South Central and East L.A., where they did belong—and where all many young men had was the corner, and where street life was the pillar of their social life—Parker's proactive policing had another meaning. What it meant was constant mind games, hassles, intimidation, and shakedowns by the cops, as well as the acquisition of arrest records for minor offenses such as loitering or suspicion of truancy. In 1956 alone, when crime was low and had yet to become the issue it is now in America, the LAPD would arrest 220,000 people, about 10 percent of the population of Los Angeles, and, as Bill Parker would point out, "over twice the number it would take to fill the Memorial Coliseum."

Over the years, the message was drummed into your head at the Academy and on the street: you are a cop, you are in charge, you have to show everyone you are in charge. Be decisive. Have command presence. Seek out the crime. That was the emphasis. That, and this admonishment: you never, never backed off. You never loosened The Grip. When the cadets graduated, the message was reaffirmed on the street.

Once, for example, a couple of drunks were fighting in a house out in the Valley. One of the drunks waved a gun at the other, who then left and called the police. The immediate reaction was to surround the house, call for the drunk to surrender, and if he didn't, to teargas him. A lieutenant drove over to the scene and said, "Wait a minute, let's think this out. The guy's in his own house, it's legal for him to have a gun there, and both he and his friend were both drunk out of their minds. So why don't we just pack it up and go back to the station house, take a crime report, see if we can get a filing, and we'll come back when he's sober and book him on a warrant."

The suggestion was unheard of and the lieutenant severely criticized. Everyone thought him afraid, unmanly, a sissy boy. And even though the lieutenant had done what was required and analyzed the situation correctly, his suggestion was not okay. We'll get him tomorrow, we don't quite have it, so let's back off, was never okay for the LAPD that Bill Parker built.

With a faith in their philosophy that was almost mystical, Bill Parker and his successors would send the troops out across the city like an elite, mobile army of occupation. That faith would lead to a seventeen-helicopter, one-fixed-wing, seventy-five-officer LAPD Air Support Division—"the largest airborne municipal law enforcement system in the world." It would fly eighteen hours a day, seven days a week. And when those Bell Jet Ranger 206-Bs flew over L.A. with additional choppers "borrowed" from the Army in the LAPD's "anti–urban guerrilla" exercises, the sound rivaled Robert Duvall and the First Cav approaching that doomed Vietnamese hamlet in *Apocalypse Now*.

But more typically the helicopters would be used in the department's all-pervasive quest to control the streets. "We watch for people running, that is, people who aren't dressed as joggers," one LAPD pilot would say, describing his mission. "We try to figure out what they're running from, while keeping track of them. . . . A suspect running away from something may change clothes, but he'll never change his shoes. So we check the shoes. . . . We watch for, maybe, a guy standing by the curb, with a lot of people driving up to talk to him. That could be drugs.'' As for the implications of a fleet of helicopters shining 33-million candle-powered, "night sun" spotlights on people during routine patrol, well, that was the price of safe streets. Besides, if you weren't doing anything wrong, what was the problem?

When the bedrock for all of it had been laid in the fifties, J. Edgar Hoover was at the height of his power; a drunken Joe McCarthy had become an amazingly powerful force in American life by using tactics so crude and transparent they were comical; and the Hollywood Ten were being hauled before the House Un-American Activities Committee. It was witch-hunt time, a good time for Bill Parker to launch his version of law and order. But while Parker's timing was perfect, it was also fleeting. Within five years of his ascendancy to chief, the civil rights movement would emerge and begin to transform the way a new generation of Americans thought about blacks and other minorities, while the legal authority to stop people on suspicion would begin to be undermined by the courts. No longer would it be legal—in theory if not in practice—to stop a kid just because he looked too young to be driving a car, or to shake down some coon in a white neighborhood because he looked out of place there. Stopping a car or a pedestrian and checking him out to see if he had an outstanding warrant or criminal intent or had violated the law in *any* way, and then popping him one as a way of putting the fear of God into his ass, was running contrary to both Earl Warren's Supreme Court and the new spirit of the times. Soon both state and federal courts would begin ruling that the results, "the fruits," as they say, of those kinds of stops were inadmissible in court. In the early 1950s, when Bill Parker had instituted proactive policing, you didn't need a hell of a lot of cause to stop anybody for anything in the state of California.

Then came 1955. LAPD vice detectives planted secret microphones in the homes of a number of local gamblers including Charles Cahan, the "boy bookie," and used the wiretap information to arrest him. Afterward, the California Supreme Court ruled that the department had gotten the evidence through illegal trespass and had violated the Fourth Amendment guarantee against unreasonable searches and seizures. For the first time the Fourth Amendment exclusionary rule of the U.S. Constitution was applied to California police. For Bill Parker and the LAPD, *that* was the start of it, the start of the courts—both state and federal—handing down decisions restricting the rights of cops to go on fishing expeditions or to use thin, imaginative, or nonexistent reasons for stopping, searching, questioning, intimidating, and bugging people. And it was an outrage.

Bill Parker railed against the Cahan decision, calling it and similar rulings "a death warrant for law enforcement" and the prelude to "a policeless state." "The positive implication drawn from the Cahan case," he declared, "is that activities of the police are a greater social menace than are the activities of the criminal. This, even as a suggestion, is terrifying." And with that, Bill Parker allowed the Cahan ruling to go unenforced in Los Angeles. "Chief Parker could not believe that decision," says Jack White, a former LAPD commander and chief investigator for the district attorney, "and no matter how many cases of illegal search and seizure there were, there was never an officer disciplined for a search-and-seizure violation. Officers were just not disciplined for violating somebody's rights in that fashion. So I guess as a young policeman I knew that I could do what I had to, to get the job done."

Each time a state or federal court expanded citizens' rights and restricted unconstitutional police practices, the attitude and focus of the LAPD under Bill Parker and his successors would be not to find the best way to comply with the law, but the best way to work around it. The assumption, the philosophy, the fuel, and the dynamic of The Grip all demanded a righteous fight. The law was one thing. The job, and The Grip, quite another. So each time a new restrictive ruling came down, quality thought was given and ways were found and adjustments made to circumvent the intent of the decision. If the courts ruled, for example, that you may not search the interior of a vehicle without probable cause, that is, without seeing drugs or other contraband—well, rather than understanding this is a protection that must be afforded people if their rights to privacy and their expectations of privacy are not to be abused, the letter of the law would be examined and a way would be found so you could. Did he make a sudden movement? Well, he was probably concealing something under his seat; therefore, in order to protect yourself, you can look under the seat. Officers' stories would be gotten straight. One officer's account would always confirm the other's. There would be no deviation from what was decided. It would be the suspect's word against that of two or more sworn police officers.

Another way was to learn that art of carefully—very carefully—writing reports so that most of the cases they filed wouldn't be thrown out for lack of probable cause. Officers wouldn't necessarily lie—although outright lying certainly took place—they'd just leave things out, like the names and versions of events of unfriendly witnesses; or would make a situation seem much worse than it actually was in order to justify their stop. Creative report writing, too, would become an ingrained part of the LAPD's policing.

Criticism would be answered by counterattack. In 1960, Ed Davis, then a captain and a former vice president of the Fire and Police Protective League, gave a typical response, telling the Chamber of Commerce in a speech that campaigns for police review boards, both locally and throughout America, were part of a "national conspiracy" to "emasculate law enforcement." As such, he added, they "did not displease the Communist Party."

All of this blurred the difference between a police force and an occupying army, the difference between making arrests and reducing crime. To be truly effective, a police force has to work together with the populace, have the vast majority on its side. Thad Brown had had it right. Solutions to serious crimes—murder, rape, robbery—almost always come because somebody tells a cop this is who did it, this is how they did it, and this is where they threw the gun.

Bill Parker's new LAPD would first downplay and then forget that the job of a police officer only assumes a military mode when there's an insurrection, riot, or major disaster; and that the rest of the time it's one or two cops together, dealing with someone face-to-face, following laws, procedures, and departmental policies, while trying to do some high-level, serious problem solving. But analytical skills, the ability to arrive at appropriate solutions to problems, would be deemphasized at the Academy, while the philosophy of Bill Parker's new LAPD would be to cause problems by stopping people for no really good reason.

That training, that philosophy, would, over the years, produce the LAPD's signature patrol image: the flint-eyed or mirrored-sunglasses-wearing robocop. "The entire essence of an L.A. officer's training and development at the Academy," says Jack White, who went through the Academy in 1957, "was that we were the people who had the responsibility for eliminating the lice from the community. It was a responsibility that was taken very seriously."

"If you'd gone to an [LAPD] roll call, what you would have seen was

how much the LAPD defined policing in military terms," says criminology professor and former New York City police lieutenant James Fyfe.
"Everything was discussed as military operations and tactics, as opposed
to human relations."

Over the years, the trend would deepen. A training program that emphasized physical stress and prided itself on being the "West Point of
police training" would change into a program so cooled out by macho
overkill that ex-LAPD officer Joe Wambaugh would start a novel about
the LAPD with a scene at the Academy of one cadet applying a choke
hold to another during a training exercise and almost killing him. The
personas, experiences, and attitudes of Wambaugh's characters would
prompt his editor to suggest what would seem an astounding title for a
book about a police force from laid-back southern California. Why don't
we call it, he suggested, *The New Centurions.*

CHAPTER 3

The Mythmakers

·····················

Nancy Davis, future wife of a governor of California and a president of the United States, had just finished *The Next Voice You Hear,* a B-picture thriller for MGM about the atomic bomb, when Sgt. Stanley Sheldon spotted her at the Police Academy. Sheldon, who headed Bill Parker's public-relations unit, had noticed that she was marching with the color guard on the drill field as they rehearsed for the following day's graduation ceremonies. When he asked just exactly who this woman was, and why she was parading around with the color guard, he found out that Nancy Davis, MGM starlet, had been selected sweetheart of the graduating cadet class, just like at West Point. Not only was she scheduled to march and pass in review, Sheldon found out, but also to accompany Bill Parker when he inspected the troops.

Sheldon immediately became concerned. It was 1951, and although Bill Parker had been in office for only one year, Sheldon knew Bill Parker. He knew that the graduation was Bill Parker's spotlight and Bill Parker's stage, and that there could only be one star. And his instincts proved exactly right. Bill Parker was furious when informed. He didn't want any precedent started, he said, and he didn't want to be involved in any embarrassing publicity stunt involving some fledgling actress hoping to garner publicity for herself and her new movie. Moreover—and this was left unsaid but understood by Sheldon—the local television stations, in some of the first coverage of its kind the LAPD was to receive, were going to be there, cameras running, and God damn, this was *his* moment. See to it, Parker instructed Sheldon, that this doesn't happen.

The next morning Sheldon arrived early at the Academy as the cadets went through their final rehearsal. Off to the side was Nancy Davis posing for some cameramen from MGM. Sheldon called her over and explained the situation and the bottom line: no marching and no inspecting. Well, recalls Stanley Sheldon, Nancy Davis got huffy; she was strong-willed even then. But mindful of the excellent relations the department had with MGM, Stanley Sheldon came up with a solution that he laid out to Nancy Davis: she could sit in the front row of the reviewing stand with the dignitaries, and the MGM crew could get pictures of that. Then, when the ceremony was over, Sheldon would reassemble the color guard, and with the eucalyptus- and pine-studded hills of Elysian Park in the background, she could march with them toward the camera. Well, what could she say? The MGM publicity people were already there. She was going to be in the front row. She would get to march. It was half a loaf.

Then Sheldon went and talked to Bill Parker and convinced him that the compromise was sensible. After giving it some thought, Bill Parker agreed. After all, Nancy Davis marching with the color guard might make a newsreel, but it wasn't the thing that was going to play on TV that night. And that night, sure enough, on television sets throughout Los Angeles there was Bill Parker reviewing the graduating LAPD cadets alone.

Bill Parker may have been blunt and abrasive, but he prized good publicity and knew its value, and as a result his reign as chief would become as much a triumph of style as substance.

During the midthirties Parker had handled publicity for James Davis, and among his duties was preparing Davis's speeches. To assist him in the writing of one of them, he turned to Stanley Sheldon, an LAPD officer who'd graduated from Hollywood High, spent a couple of years at UCLA and USC, and then knocked around in radio selling ads, making commercials, and doing occasional stints as an announcer.

Stanley Sheldon would turn out to be a perfect PR man. He wasn't slick, he wasn't brash, he wasn't oozing charm. Rather he was just the opposite. He had weight, he spoke slowly, earnestly, as if finding just the right word was the most important thing in the world, and he radiated seriousness of purpose. Tall, broad-shouldered and handsome, he was like a kindly uncle who'd taken a crash course on the full curriculum of Madison Avenue tricks and techniques and turned out to be an honor student. He had a taste for it, believed in it. Decades later, he would pinpoint the source of the serious criticism the LAPD was then undergoing: why, it was because "they haven't been out there singing their own song and telling their own story." He was enamored with Hollywood and knew his way around, having grown up in and around it. By the midthirties, he had joined the LAPD and was producing star-studded stage shows to raise money for the L.A. Police Relief Association, for the LAPD's American Legion Post, and for James Davis's Police Revolver and Athletic Club. The shows usually ran about two weeks, and every other night or so there would be a different guest host—stars like Jack Benny, Gene Autry, Donald O'Connor, Red Skelton, Edward Arnold, Bing Crosby and, of course, Bob Hope. Hope would take at least two nights of the show's run, and accompanied by Jane Russell or some other curvaceous female, do a little skit. Autry and his horse Champion would do a Saturday matinee for the kids.

Once established, the shows—which were held at the Coliseum and Shrine Auditorium—came under the imprimatur and sponsorship of four of the city's most influential and powerful organizations: the Merchants and Manufacturers Association, the Los Angeles Chamber of Commerce, the Junior Chamber of Commerce, and the Downtown Business Association. It was they who would spread the word to their membership, who would in turn purchase and distribute blocks of tickets.

But they were not the only ones working for the success of the shows, which ran until the midfifties. The Los Angeles Newspaper Publishers Association, the Motion Picture Industry Association, the Theatre Authority, Inc., the radio industry, the Hollywood Coordinating Committee, the American Guild of Variety Artists, and the fledgling television industry, all donated to the cause.

Sheldon got permission for the stars to waive their usual fee. Once he got Edward Arnold to chair the guest committee, the shows started to take off. The Earl Carroll Girls agreed to perform, and one year, because they were engaged in a run at another theater, the department sent a bus to pick them up between shows and rush them—with red lights glaring, sirens blaring, and a motorcycle escort clearing the way—to the benefit. Chief Many Treaties, who headed an association of Indian motion-picture actors, agreed to do a performance featuring a powwow and dancing. Clarence Muse signed on to sing "Old Man River," and Bo Jangles and the high steppin' Nicholas Brothers did their acts.

The shows also usually contained "stirring patriotic prologues" like the one that featured the Los Angeles Police Post American Legion band and motorcycle drill team opening the 1952 show. Called "The Free Way" and "specially written" for the police show production, the lyrics tied together the highway system then being built throughout Los Angeles with "human ideals"—both of which were "truly symbolic of the American Way of Life." With a stage setting featuring a "faithful reproduction of the intersection of the world-famous Hollywood Santa Ana and Arroyo-Harbor freeways . . . [and] Civic Center skyline" as background, they sang:

> We're on the Freeway, upon the Highway, that's the
> place to be.
> We're on the Right Way, there is no Left Way,
> Let's go, the road is straight and clear.
> There are no bars ahead, there are no signs of red
> All the land is free for you and me.
> We're on the Freeway, upon the Highway
> The American Way of Life.

In the early 1940s, newly appointed sergeant Stanley Sheldon and Capt. Bill Parker had worked together developing a ten-officer Traffic Education Section, which functioned as a public-relations unit for the entire department. Compared to the FBI's well-oiled, groundbreaking propaganda machine, the unit was laughably naive. But it did have one innovative feature: it made its own movies. Sheldon had become intrigued with the use of educational films by business and understood, as did Hoover, their powerful potential. His goal was to reshape the department's image and to hammer home the need for strict adherence to traffic laws in a city becoming increasingly dependent on the automobile. The insurance industry was already becoming a powerful lobby within the LAPD, so Parker was receptive.

Using a 16mm camera, Sheldon and his police officers made three-reel movies like *Motors on Parade,* which promoted the motorcycle squad. One key scene shows a buxom Southern California sweater girl cheerfully accepting a jaywalking ticket. It was crude, but like the police shows, it was a start. And the leap from using movie, show-business, and advertising techniques to raise funds to expand the tiny unit in the traffic division into a PR machine mythologizing Bill Parker and the department would not prove great. Not with Stanley Sheldon. With him Parker had found his P. T. Barnum, his spin doctor, his link between the cop's world of cynical reality and the fantasy world of show business. He was the man who would whisper in his ear the primacy of image and media manipulation. The techniques were there, in the air of Hollywood, of course, permeating the entire city. It was only a matter of time before someone on the LAPD realized their value.

By the 1940s, the film industry had become a key business second only to agriculture in Los Angeles. Thirty to forty thousand workers were turning out 90 percent of the films then produced in the United States, while twenty-five national radio shows, using Hollywood actors and technicians, were being broadcast out of a handful of Los Angeles radio stations.

The studios depended on the police for cordoning off streets during shoots, for issuing permits, and for allowing uniformed off-duty and retired officers to provide security during these shoots. Mayors and city councilmen, moreover, received substantial financial support from movie-industry people like Louis B. Mayer and organizations such as the Motion Picture Industry Association. During the 1934 gubernatorial election, in fact, Mayer had joined with the L.A. *Times* to produce a series of phony newsreels that deliberately and successfully distorted the record of the populist Socialist-Democratic candidate Upton Sinclair and helped defeat him. They showed scenes like an old lady frightened that a Sinclair victory would take away her tiny home, and bums gleefully awaiting Sinclair's election so they could swarm into California. That campaign against Sinclair was also the first in American history to use a public relations firm.

The industry also needed to protect its stars and other key players from career-destroying scandals in an era dominated by Calvinistic morality. Carousing wild men like Errol Flynn and homosexual stars were constantly being picked up by the LAPD, but never booked. Howard Hughes and Busby Berkeley were rumored to have been involved in auto accidents that resulted in deaths, but managed never to go to jail. Looking the other way when Hollywood stars were involved went back to the days of the murder of William Desmond and through the mysterious circumstances under which women in their prime such as Jean Harlow and Lupe Velez died. Calls would be made, and charges either not filed by the police or dropped by the DA. In turn, Warner Brothers, 20th Century-Fox, Columbia, MGM—all the major studios—drew their security chiefs from local law enforcement. It helped keep things smooth. It bought them access. It kept everybody happy.

But the image of cops that Hollywood had been turning out left people like Bill Parker and J. Edgar Hoover enraged. In the teens and 1920s that image was of Keystone Kops, buffoons. By the thirties they were worse than buffoons. In many of the fifty or so B gangster movies Hollywood was churning out every year, they were corrupt, brutal oafs. In the early years of the decade, many of those films had mirrored a disgust with the Depression that had made romantic, underground Robin Hoods out of Bonnie Parker and Clyde Barrow, Machine Gun Kelly, Pretty Boy Floyd, Ma Barker and her boys, Baby Face Nelson, and John Dillinger. Edward G. Robinson in *Little Caesar,* Paul Muni in *Scarface,* and James Cagney in *Public Enemy,* played the gangster as flawed hero.

Recognizing the awesome power of the movies and radio, J. Edgar Hoover set up a public-relations section that saw to it that *all* criticism of the FBI was responded to, and that movie and radio scripts dealing with the Bureau were approved by the Bureau.

But what Hoover (and later Parker) wanted was to place their imprimatur on the movies, to have cops portrayed as sanitized, uncomplicated heroes and those they were pursuing as the personification of evil. In 1934, Hoover got much of what he wanted when the film industry instituted a production code of censorship. "Correct standards of life shall be presented," the Code would read, "and the sympathy of the audience shall never be thrown to the side of crime, wrong-doing, evil or sin." Cops would still occasionally be portrayed as venal and stupid as private eyes like Raymond Chandler's Philip Marlowe constantly outsmarted them. But the gangster as a complicated cultural character—that imbecilic sociology, that communistic shit—was out.

None of this had been lost on Bill Parker and Stanley Sheldon. And when their opportunity came in the person of Jack Webb, they were ready. Webb was a volatile, intensely ambitious journeyman actor with an overly developed sense of the dramatic, who had gotten a part in a police movie called *He Walked by Night.* Dark and wiry, with a nervous energy then popular among young actors in the late forties, he had a few small parts like the one he scored in *Sunset Boulevard,* but never anything close to matching his ambitions.

On the set of *He Walked by Night,* Webb became friendly with one of Thad Brown's detectives, a veteran LAPD officer named Marty Wynn. Wynn also had ambitions, having listed himself and his partner with various casting agencies as a technical director—the position in which he was working when he met Webb. One day Webb told him about a short-lived radio program he'd done in San Francisco, a private-eye show called "Novak for Hire." He wanted to do a similar radio show, but about police detectives, and he needed the expertise and story ideas of Wynn and other LAPD detectives. With Wynn's help, Webb got the department's cooperation, and in June of 1949, "Dragnet" debuted on NBC radio as a summer replacement.

But from his first days in office, Bill Parker had been wary of the show. Which was not unusual. Parker saw the potential for impropriety and embarrassment to himself and the department in virtually every situation. One thing that bothered him in particular about "Dragnet" was the casual, almost nonexistent ground rules under which his officers were assisting the show. Wynn and his partner, who were working for Webb as technical advisers, weren't doing any police work—not a dime's worth. Instead, they were spending all their time down at the studio advising Webb or consulting with his writers. Thad Brown, in his easygoing way, had given them carte blanche to do what they wanted. The show had barely been on the air a year and already they were each receiving $125 a week from Webb—about half their LAPD salary. An LAPD salary they weren't earning. It wasn't that there was any big-time money or big-time abuse of the public trust going on; it was the appearance of the thing. These men were giving nothing to the department. It may not have been corrupt, but it had the stench of corruption about it.

But there was something more: control. Control, absolute control of the product. The lesson of the thirties, the lesson of the Hollywood code and J. Edgar Hoover and the FBI, that would be the price of his cooperation. His opportunity would come in 1952, when Webb, whose radio show had been a big success, wanted to take it to television. To TV, the box that was in less than 4 million homes in 1950. To TV, whose numbers in American households would increase to 10 million in the following year. To TV, where even more than on radio, Webb would need the LAPD's cooperation. On television you could see things, see if the police work, the station house, the squad car, seemed right, seemed authentic. And authenticity was a major component of what Webb, as a producer and in his persona as detective Joe Friday, was trying to sell. To do so, he was going to need a lot more technical advice than he had on radio. And he was going to need double the story ideas, which the show had been getting for free from LAPD detectives who'd been happily telling their war stories to Webb's writers.

Parker and Sheldon told Webb they'd continue and expand the association, but only if he agreed to some new ground rules. First, if LAPD officers wanted to work as technical advisers, they'd have to take vacation time or compensatory overtime; no more spending city time on the set. Next, the advisers would have to come from the office portrayed in the story. If it was a homicide story, the technical adviser would have to be from the homicide squad—someone really qualified to give the advice.

This last was fine with Jack Webb. Perfect, in fact. Within the framework of total unbelievability—within the notion of police officers who never lied, stole, cheated, had sex, slugged a lowlife, tricked a witness, or acted in any way other than as neutered Eagle Scouts—everything on "Dragnet" had to be completely authentic. Technical authenticity, Webb had realized early on, was a key element of his success, and he became a fanatic about it. "He duplicated everything," former LAPD chief Tom Reddin would later recall. "When you walked on a 'Dragnet' set that was supposed to be a replica of the police business office, you could bet it was an exact replica." He made a plaster cast of a rock used as a paperweight in an LAPD office and then used it in the duplicated office on the set. He re-created a door to precisely resemble one at City Hall, going to great lengths to copy both its heavy brass hinges and the exact thump of that particular door. And, of course, there was always a technical adviser right there on the set showing them the correct procedures, and how things were done. Minus, to be sure, the ugly grit. But it was *technically* authentic, that was the thing. "The Streets of San Francisco," "Hawaii Five-O," "Highway Patrol"—why, the police work in those shows was atrocious. There was Broderick Crawford, as the *chief* on "Highway Patrol," running around taking calls as if he were a young, green rookie, and solving crimes as if he were a detective sergeant. It was ridiculous. A joke.

But control, control would be Parker's most crucial stipulation. Without it, there could be no deal. Each script would have to be submitted to Sheldon and the Public Information Division well in advance of shooting. Webb would have to agree to the stipulation in a signed, binding, lawyer-approved exchange of letters. Complete script control. They had it certified. And it would be tightly, very tightly, enforced. People were watching all over America.

There was, for example, the case of the script submitted about a woman in a bedroom dying from an illegal abortion. On the dresser was a used scalpel and other implements. It was too bloody. There was a sexual connotation. It wouldn't do. It was not approved. Then when Webb wanted to make his first "Dragnet" movie and call it *711*—after Joe Friday's badge number—the department also had to cut him down to size and let him know that the imprimatur of the LAPD would not be on any film with the title *711*. As Webb undoubtedly knew, "711" had gambling connotations. If he wanted a badge number for the title, he could use something like 714. And when the movie was made, *Badge 714* it was.

When Stanley Sheldon saw the item in *Daily Variety,* he immediately grabbed the telephone, dialed Jack Webb's number, and left a message with an assistant. "You tell Webb to call me right back," he said. Sheldon was uncharacteristically enraged by the story he'd just read, and not only because of its description of what Webb intended to do. That had been bad enough. But it was also a glaring violation of their understanding—of their deal—that he, Stanley Sheldon, now a captain in charge of the LAPD's Public Information Division, had to read about it in one of the trades. This was already the summer of 1953. By now Webb *knew* he was to clear anything to do with "Dragnet" through him.

Christ, how could he have made such a blunder? Didn't he read the newspapers? Wasn't he aware that J. Edgar Hoover had just launched a major, highly publicized campaign against the use of that highly derogatory word that Sheldon had just spotted in *Variety;* that outrageous word that the International Association of Chiefs of Police had decried as insulting to the entire profession of policing? And if he was, why then was he using that very word as the title for the syndicated episodes of "Dragnet" that he was now selling? Why then, as the item in *Variety* had pointed out, had he decided to call those shows "The Cop"? It was an outrage. They were police officers. Professionals. And here was Webb, who was supposed to be on their side, using *cop* in a title associated with the LAPD. Using the word that every two-bit hood was placing after the adjectives *dirty* or *damn* or *crooked,* and just as they were dying to stamp it out.

Sheldon and Parker had already stopped Webb from using that same offending word after the first twenty or so television episodes of "Dragnet." But by then the damage had been done and the line Webb had uttered at the top of every show had become one of the most quoted in television history: "My name's Friday, I work here, I'm a cop." After that, the "cop" part had been changed to "I carry a badge." It was none too soon. The show had been wildly, extraordinarily popular almost from the moment it had aired—one of those network-making television programs back in the fifties, like Uncle Miltie's or "I Love Lucy." One of those shows which, as you walked your dog on a balmy evening, you could hear from every house the blaring of its theme music. A theme that in the case of "Dragnet" would become as famous as any six or seven bars of music in television history: "Bom-ba-bom, bom-ba-ba-bom-baaah." That theme, along with Webb's clean, neat, polite, humorless, and militaristically efficient persona; along with the lack of sex and the lack of violence; along with the righteous, professional police protecting society against truly evil criminals—all of it had been an astounding coup for Bill Parker and the LAPD. Joe Friday and his partners may have been bloodless automatons who spoke in clipped, emotionless sentences, but then it was a cool, stoic, sexless time. It was a good image, a "white spot" image, a safe American image at a time when "Americanism" was viewed as the Holy Grail, nonconformity a communist plot, and the lines between right and wrong were crystal clear. "Dragnet" showed L.A. as it should be shown: sunny, white, clean, and orderly; the LAPD as pressed and efficient.

When the N.Y.P.D. was portrayed on TV, its officers would be shown as mentally and physically disheveled, cynical and weary men and women burned out from dealing with all that New York dirt and grit. Parker and Sheldon had been smarter with "Dragnet." Within a few years it had gained enormous fame for Bill Parker and the kind of favorable, almost gushing publicity for his department that money couldn't buy. In addition to the sanctified image of Friday and his colleagues, there was the show's conclusion, which consisted of a solemn rendering of the tough sentences each of the criminals on that week's show invariably received. And then there was a voice-over announcing how "you have just seen 'Dragnet,' a series of authentic cases from official files.... Technical advice for 'Dragnet' comes from the offices of Chief of Police W. H. Parker, Los Angeles Police Department.'' Even on the extremely rare occasions when Webb tackled a potentially controversial subject like a police officer on the take, as he had in the early fifties, it was done with the searing sanctimony that was a hallmark of "Dragnet." On one of the earliest shows—aired before the word *cop* had been declared unusable—Webb had done an episode about a dishonest officer, climaxing it with an angry Joe Friday lecture: "You get this through your head, mister. You're a bad cop . . . a bad cop. [The public's] not gonna read about . . . the rookies pounding their feet flat out in the streets . . . the guy in robbery who stopped two slugs last night. They're gonna read about you. One crooked, thieving cop. . . . Every kid in school with a cop for a father will have to fight his way out today because of you. . . . The people who read it in the papers, they're gonna overlook the fact . . . that we washed our own laundry and we cleaned this thing. . . . They're gonna . . . overlook every last good cop in the country."

It was more than just good publicity. With "Dragnet," Webb and Parker had found that point where propaganda meets entertainment and serves both. By the 1953–54 season, "Dragnet" had become the second-highest-rated show on network television, behind only "I Love Lucy."

You would have thought, therefore, that Stanley Sheldon and Bill Parker would have been appreciative of "Dragnet," grateful to Webb, and understanding of any problems he might be having. But that was not the case. When Webb returned Stanley Sheldon's call, Sheldon was not in the least sympathetic. He started with, "What's this I see in *Daily Variety?*" and ran through all the problems this was going to cause with Hoover and the Chiefs Association and ended by warning that he was going to tell Parker about it. "See if he'll come down to NBC and talk to some of the executives," Webb almost pleaded. Sheldon promised he'd try. "But Jack," he warned as he signed off, "this is *bad.*"

And it was. Bill Parker, who was rarely approachable even with good news, was incensed. You tell them, Bill Parker all but shouted, that if they don't immediately change "The Cops" to something that we approve, we'll completely sever all connections. Everything. The department's name, the use of our badge and advisers—everything. As for going to their office? If they want to talk to me, he told Sheldon, they can come down to *my* office.

As Bill Parker had commanded, Stanley Sheldon then met with Webb and NBC vice president John West. West was a tall, handsome, imposing-looking man who greeted Webb and Sheldon in his office with the easy assurance of one used to giving orders and making decisions.

He listened courteously as Sheldon laid out why he and Bill Parker so loathed that word *cop* and couldn't possibly approve its use. He even showed him Hoover's and the Chiefs Association's objections to it. When Sheldon finished, West spun around, picked up the phone, and dialed New York. Sheldon listened intently as the conversation went back and forth: "How many contracts do we have for the syndicated release of 'The Cop,' " West asked. Then, a pause. "I see. Well, put me through to . . ." Sheldon didn't catch the name. A moment later West was explaining the situation to someone on the other end of the line. After a minute or two of silence on his end, John West hung up the phone, turned to Sheldon and Webb, and unapologetically pronounced the mighty National Broadcasting Company's decision: "They absolutely refuse. They've already got all these contracts drawn up and they're not going to rewrite them."

Desperate now, Webb got in touch with Gen. David Sarnoff, the founder and chairman of the board of NBC, and a titan of the industry. Sheldon agreed to give Webb one day. One day! This to the man who had made Parker and the police department of what was still—literally—not a major-league city, famous throughout America. One day. And Webb was grateful. The very next day he called. He'd spoken directly to Sarnoff, he said, and NBC had agreed to all of the department's demands. Shortly thereafter, Bill Parker received a letter from Jack Webb. He realized, wrote Webb, that the title "The Cop" was "detrimental to the entire police profession," and that the character of Sgt. Joe Friday was "identified by millions of viewers with the Los Angeles Police Department." And he wanted Parker to know that he was "so appreciative of the assistance granted by your Department, without which the making of 'Dragnet,' would have been *impossible*" (a word that Webb felt compelled to underline). Among the steps the network was taking, wrote Webb, again underlining his words, was the *"exercise of extreme care in the distribution of the films so that commercial sponsors will in no way be embarrassing to the law enforcement profession."* "Due credit," Webb assured Bill Parker, would be given "to your office for the idealistic and professional reasons behind [the title] change." "I am sorry," Webb wrote in closing, "that this had to occur, but trust that it has been adjudicated to your complete satisfaction."

John West must have thought he was in New York, dealing with some functionary, some city worker, some garbage commissioner. John West must not have realized that Bill Parker's name was the *only* one ever mentioned on "Dragnet" out of all the members of the LAPD; must not have been reading the enormous piles of paper that Stanley Sheldon's Public Information offices were churning out about Bill Parker, the lawmen's lawman. Jack Webb would never make the same mistake again.

During the midseventies, Webb began developing a new series about an LAPD canine unit. When he sent over some scripts to the LAPD's Public Information Division, a memo on the scripts appeared in the division's biweekly report: "Except for some deviations in the concept from true life situations," read the memo, "the scripts are technically correct and, more important, do not portray the department in any way except favorably." Then, referring to the two LAPD sergeants who were hired by Webb as technical consultants, the memo went on: "They understand that their role is to protect the department's interests and to oversee the production to the extent that police officers are portrayed properly and consistently with department policy." Nothing had changed.

Back in the fifties, of course, network censorship of any show was clumsy and heavy-handed. The armed forces would routinely check out scripts before agreeing to cooperate with a studio. The Hayes office was still busy censoring, and the Legion of Decency was on the march. As was the LAPD. In 1956, for example, an official from the International Associations of Chiefs of Police contacted Stanley Sheldon and asked if he could do something about what they viewed as the proliferation of anti-police movies then being released. Movies like *Bad Cop* and *Shield for Murder*. Sheldon sent a letter of complaint to Geoffrey M. Shurlock, the vice president and director of the Motion Picture Association of America's Production Code. Shurlock made no promises to Sheldon in his return letter. But his tone and a few strategically placed sentences said a great deal. "I trust," he wrote, "we will not have too many scripts dealing with policemen as heavies. *So far, you are acquainted with all that have been submitted to this office* [italics added]. . . ."

"In the last few months [I've made] three public addresses on the work

of the Production Code. In all of them I took time out to compliment the
Los Angeles Police Department on the assistance they are giving the
Hollywood motion picture industry in avoiding offense in this respect.''
It *was* the censorious fifties, but still the letter's unwritten assumption was
surprising. Here was the LAPD—a local, unelected arm of government—
assuming that it had the right to pressure the film industry not to make
films it deemed offensive. J. Edgar Hoover, with decades in office, tens of
thousands of dossiers, and the power of the federal government behind
him, had that kind of pull. But the fact that the chief of police of Los
Angeles and his functionaries felt they also had it said a lot about how far
Parker and the LAPD had come.

The department always seemed especially imaginative in finding ways
to squeeze Webb. The LAPD badge used on the show was kept in a
felt-lined box in Stanley Sheldon's desk, to be brought back and forth by
the technical adviser on that particular day's shoot. The plastic decals
with the LAPD insignia that could be put on and taken off the show's
black-and-white Fords (which were identical to those used by the department) were also in the possession of the technical advisers. But Webb
never minded, never minded any of it, according to Stanley Sheldon. And
having little choice, Webb eventually became a thorough and complete
true believer. In 1970, just prior to the publication of ex-LAPD sergeant
Joseph Wambaugh's *The New Centurions,* Webb asked to read it. Even
before its publication, the book was considered highly controversial
within the LAPD, depicting the department as it did, warts and all. Wambaugh gladly sent it to Webb, hoping to both catch his interest and win his
support. But when Webb returned the manuscript, ''it weighed,'' said
Wambaugh, ''three pounds more than when I dropped it off. Every place
there was an objectionable word or line [was] marked with a paper clip,
and the damn thing had about a thousand paper clips.''

From the first, Parker had permitted himself to be used in the department's mythmaking efforts, holding more press interviews than any local
chief in history, and allowing stories to be planted in the press that he,
who so prided himself on his honesty, should have found shameful. A
Reader's Digest article entitled ''Why Hoodlums Hate Bill Parker'' was
typical. In the story, which ran six pages, Bill Parker heroically battled his
way through a series of frightening encounters. First, he took a ''long-
bladed knife'' of a ''badly wanted maniac called Jack the Ripper'' who

"stood over six feet tall, weighed at least two hundred pounds, [and] had long arms and small, close-set eyes . . ." "Then," the article continues, Bill Parker, who was "quick on the draw even by TV standards," got "into a face-off with another cop who was beating a bail bondsman, and stood him down." Still further on in the story, Parker, then a sergeant, is sent on a suicide mission by a lieutenant who "believed that . . . Bill Parker had been getting too many good breaks." Parker's mission was to disarm a "berserk shopkeeper" armed with a repeating shotgun who was holding two employees hostage. "Calmly, persuasively, [Parker] walked up to the man holding the shotgun and snatched it out of his hands." "He never asks one of us," the writer quoted an "old timer" as saying, "to take on a job he wouldn't be willing to do himself, and alone." Then, using the department's favorite phrase, the article described how Bill Parker had built "the best big city police force in America."

By 1955 Stanley Sheldon had made captain and was heading the Public Information division. Every third-rate police force had a press officer, of course, but the LAPD now had an entire *division.* Twenty employees staying busy banging out a barrage of favorable stories, images, and pictures heralding the department's every achievement and innovation, grinding out the legend of the Golden Boys. They fed their stories not only to the local newspapers, but throughout Southern California. Not just big ones like the *Times* and the *Examiner,* but black and Hispanic newspapers and radio stations, and 150 throwaway weekly newspapers. They clipped stories both for the Intelligence Division and for their own use from magazines all over the country. They had a motion picture unit. They scheduled the full-time police band, which made promotional appearances all over the region. They read the scripts for "Dragnet" and other shows, such as "Adam 12." They had a speakers bureau, which matched requests for speakers from the department to just the right people. They wrote most of Bill Parker's speeches. They had promotional programs in the schools and with organizations like the American Legion. They published their own magazine, *The Beat,* which Sgt. Gene Roddenberry did a lot of work for. They put out glossy, colored annual reports that replaced the drab, lifeless ones that had preceded them. And they put Parker himself on television with a show called "The Thin Blue Line," where he'd directly answer any stupid, unfounded criticism of himself or the department.

When the new LAPD building was completed, they made a film about its construction, and then, once it opened, another about the wonderful work being done within. In the department's new auditorium, they would show the film, narrated by Bill Parker, to groups of schoolchildren and VIPs. A tour of the building, conducted by an attractive in-uniform policewoman, would follow.

Within the headquarters they designed a set—an actual set—that was a precise replica of Bill Parker's office. They took pictures of the venetian blinds behind his chair, pictures of the hall of justice, which framed the view from his office window, pictures of everything, and got it so right you couldn't tell it from Parker's real office. Then they put in trolleys and other equipment for the television crews. When Parker wanted to make a speech or hold a press conference, they'd wait until the press corps was all set up, then phone down to his office, and Parker would then come over to the room, sit down, and proceed. Even then, with television still in its infancy, they knew its power—"Dragnet" had taught them—and they knew how to use it.

And Stanley Sheldon's division made sure when you turned on your set, you'd see something to do with the LAPD. They did small local spots, three or five minutes, such as "Wanted Persons," which featured blown-up mug shots and an in-studio officer who'd tell the viewer all about the suspect. There was a show hosted by the actress Betty White, on which an LAPD officer showed photos of missing juveniles. They were local, they were short, but White's show was on five days a week, and the "Missing Persons" segment was broadcast on Channel 5 throughout the broadcast day.

The department's control of the local media had its roots both in the culture of the police press and in local events. The police in big-city America had often been covered by beat reporters who shared the same limited educations and backgrounds as most police officers. "Consequently," as L.A. *Times* media critic David Shaw would later point out, "the public came to look on the reporters who regularly covered them— and on the press in general . . . as part of the police department . . . as 'cops without guns. . . .' The police and reporters grew to like each other, and when necessary to cover up for each other."

But in L.A. it went further. The city's oligarchy, led by the *Los Angeles Times,* had always wanted to perpetuate the city's ethos—growth and land speculation. And they demanded of the press total support of the myth of L.A. as a white spot, and a deliberate closed-eyes distortion of reality.

Thus crime news and police news was either studiously ignored or sanitized and written about in such an oblique style that it took a great deal of knowledge along with a decoder key to decipher a story's meaning. Of the five or six Los Angeles dailies, only one, the *Record,* did any real muckraking, investigative journalism. But even in its heyday the *Record,* a workingman's paper that shut down in 1935, had limited influence. Still, without the *Record,* as police scholar Joseph Gerald Woods pointed out in his 1973 doctoral dissertation on the LAPD, it would have been impossible for him to have written his thesis.

In 1956, the men of Stanley Sheldon's Public Information Division were joined by a media-massaging press relations officer. His job was to manage the news, leak to the department's friends, and punish its enemies. (The LAPD issued the area's all important press cards.) The Public Information Division, the press relations officer, they were the mythmakers and early spin doctors; they were the men who, in collaboration with the soft, receptive press corps and product-hungry Hollywood producers, would create the legend of the Golden Boys.

From "Dragnet" there would flow more than twenty-five LAPD police shows on network television. They'd range from the lethally dull, white-bread goodness of "Adam 12" through the glitzy "21 Jump Street" and "The New Breed"—spreading the word and carrying the LAPD's water throughout America. "Mod Squad." "Felony Squad." "Blue Thunder." "The Blue Knight." "S.W.A.T." "Hunter." "Strike Force." "Chopper One." "The Rookies." "Jigsaw John." "Renegades." "T.J. Hooker." For twenty-five consecutive seasons at least one LAPD police show was being aired on network television.

Young men—and increasingly young women—from all over the country, awestruck by the almost mythic image of the LAPD portrayed on the television screen, would come to L.A. to join the department. They did not come specifically—at least as far as one knows—to join the Los Angeles County Sheriff's Department, an organization of comparable size, offering roughly equivalent pay and benefits—a police force no better or worse than the LAPD. But the Sheriff's Department had not been a hit on TV.

In the summer of 1970, after Parker was gone, the legacy lived on. Sgt. Dan Cooke of the LAPD press relations office gave a reporter a guided tour of Parker Center. Pointing to a room, Cooke, a white-haired man who favored the tweedy, pipe-smoking, lanky look of a precounterculture Oxford don, explained its purpose. It was used, he said, to disseminate news to the press corps during emergencies. Reflecting back on 1968 and the assassination of Bobby Kennedy at the local Ambassador Hotel, Cooke told the reporter of the clamorous situation back then as newsmen from all over the world had converged on the room. There had been a feeding frenzy, said Cooke, and in the tradition of desperate journalists covering a monumental story, they had become pushy, rude, and demanding. It had been tawdry, unseemly, *disorderly,* and Cooke could hardly contain his disdain as he recalled the scene: "It was our local press people who told them to 'cool it.' The local reporters let them know that whatever approach they may use with the police where they come from, that isn't the way things are done here. When we have news that we're able to release, we release it, and release it to all the press at the same time." Dan Cooke later added, "We have an amazing corps of newsmen." And it was understandable that he thought so. For in 1970, he and his colleagues still had most of the Los Angeles press corps right where Stanley Sheldon had them in the fifties: under their thumbs.

CHAPTER 4

Whiter Than White

••••••••••••••••••••••

When Tom Bradley was growing up in Los Angeles in the twenties and thirties, race had not yet become the city's central obsession. L.A. had been far too white and Anglo-Saxon, far too dominated by its rich businessmen and churchgoing middle class for the small, powerless enclaves of Mexicans, Asians, and African-Americans scattered throughout Los Angeles to be anything more than a minor curiosity. Fan-tan games in Chinatown would be raided, pachucos' heads knocked in, and racially mixed couples coming out of the Apex Club, the Club Alabam, and other legendary jazz nightclubs on South Central's Central Avenue in the thirties and forties might get harassed or beaten. But it was no different in L.A. than in other cities.

In 1940, good jobs for blacks were almost nonexistent in corporate America, in the professions, academia, or in the construction or craft unions. Racial prejudice was insidious, widespread, and unapologetic. In Los Angeles, blacks were not permitted to teach in the city's high schools or junior highs, and only one of the city's twenty-two hospitals would admit them. Total segregation in national institutions like the armed forces was the norm. Exclusion from organizations like professional baseball went virtually unquestioned. Joe Louis's being permitted to fight and defeat a white man for the heavyweight championship of the world created a sensation on Central Avenue, in Harlem, and throughout black America. Sure it was a crumb, but at least it was something. That's how bad it was. Working as a policeman offered Tom Bradley—offered any black man—not only the security of a good-paying civil service job, but a chance for a little respect, for a hard-to-find touch of dignity. That Bradley's opportunity would come from a Los Angeles Police Department composed of men—as Bill Parker would later point out—who were either "conservative, ultraconservative, or very right-wing" was the ultimate irony.

It was always strange, therefore, for the African-Americans living in the tiny wood-framed cottages or two-story apartment boxes of East and South Central L.A. to see a cop so tall, so handsome, so formidable, so *black,* as was Tom Bradley, residing in their neighborhood. Strange for a young black kid in the 1940s to have this LAPD officer who looked like a movie-star-fantasy version of what he hoped *he* would look like when he grew up stare at him as he was getting out of his car and acknowledge his presence, his *humanity,* with a dazzling smile. And to do so at a time when most black males in the movies or on radio were head-scratchin' Stepin Fetchit Negroes.

Often in those years, a black cop or a black boss would be tougher for many blacks to deal with than whites in a similar position. They had things to prove and to deny. Not Tom Bradley. His street reputation was all that any good, effective cop—black or white—could have hoped for: tough, fair, human. Human. Sure he was out to prove something. Was there any middle-class African-American in those years who could escape it? But it wasn't at *your* expense. If the style of the time was for cops to either bark or condescend when talking to black people, it was not Tom Bradley's style. And consciously or unconsciously, Bradley's refusal to fall into the traditional black cop's role as bad nigger would have long-term payoffs for him. In the years to follow he would find himself cut off by his color from the kind of advancement that Ed Davis, Jim Fisk, Tom Reddin, and Daryl Gates would enjoy. But the goodwill he'd engendered on the street, his keen ability to spot and grasp opportunities, and sheer good fortune would all combine to enable Tom Bradley to find a way to use the LAPD for his own devices.

*   *   *

His first three days out of the Police Academy had been spent directing traffic and sucking in exhaust fumes in downtown Los Angeles, an assignment he'd later describe as the worst of his entire LAPD career. After several months working patrol in South Central, however, he received an astounding gift, an almost unheard of opportunity to work in plainclothes in the Juvenile Division. Usually, a cop had to work five or six years in uniform before getting that kind of assignment. But Bradley had the city's rapidly expanding black population and his UCLA college background working for him. The opportunity was golden and he would not waste it. To the juvenile officer's traditional parameters of investigations and informal probation and counseling, he developed a year-round football and track program—soliciting equipment and assistance from the coaches and athletes of USC and UCLA. Then he began setting up youth programs at local churches, community centers, playgrounds, and YMCAs. "Wherever my natural work would take me," he'd later say in that dull, vague, gray idiom he grew to use in public, "I became associated with those groups and with their activities."

The exuberance Tom Bradley felt about the progress he was making in juvenile was tempered in 1943 by the Zoot Suit Riots. There they were, a precursor of the searing racial turbulence that would mark America's cities in the decades to follow. It was the start of the war, and thousands of servicemen were packed into induction centers and points of debarkation all over Los Angeles, brimming with the volatile energy of cooped-up young men. The electric red cars that then traversed the region were ushering the sailors and GIs from the Chavez Ravine Naval Base and other military installations quickly and smoothly into the heart of L.A. There, they'd mingle with young Mexican American and black men, some of whom Tom Bradley was then supervising. Many wore zoot suits—the long-jacketed, big-shouldered, big-kneed, and narrow-cuffed outfits that were then the rage. Like rock and roll a decade later, and the Panthers and hippies a decade after that, the zoot suiters seemed a direct assault on Anglo-Saxon America, on all that was straight and white and therefore good. It was a textbook case of race and loathing rubbing up against each other, of youthful ebullience turned to rage. Here they were getting set to go over and fight for their country, and here were these cartoon greaseballs and jungle bunnies running around slick and free. So they beat their ass without interference by the LAPD. Afterward, hundreds of Chicanos and African-Americans in and out of zoot suits were arrested. Among those beaten were some of Tom Bradley's off-duty Negro colleagues.

Negroes. It was clear even then that the Negroes—previously cooped up in sharecropping Dixie—were coming to *your* neighborhood. In 1920 there had been only about fifteen thousand of them in L.A. By 1930 it was thirty-five thousand. But it wasn't until the early forties that the extraordinary internal migration of African-Americans from the fields of the South to jobs in the big cities of the North and West had begun to obsess white Los Angeles as it would the rest of white urban America. Once they started coming, their influx was astounding. Between 1942 and 1945, two hundred thousand African-Americans, drawn by the demand for the half million workers needed in the aviation, steel, rubber, and shipbuilding industries, would arrive in a city whose black population had barely topped sixty-two thousand in 1940. By 1950, more than 170,000 had settled permanently in Los Angeles, cramped into the narrow confines of South Central L.A. and its surrounding communities—almost 9 percent of the city's population, and growing. They were here, but they were not real Americans.

So the zoot suiters were beaten; twenty-three innocent Chicanos were jailed in 1942 for a murder at Sleepy Lagoon that they did not commit; and 110,000 Japanese Americans, many of them native Angelenos, were imprisoned en masse in 1942.

They never wrote down the rules, although the LAPD had had black officers since before the turn of the century. But everybody in the department knew them. First, the maintenance of segregation always took precedence over efficient law enforcement. Second, black and white officers were forbidden to work together, and if a black officer called in sick, his partner was told to either just stay home or was given a make-work task, like guarding the station house—whatever it took to avoid having him work with a uniformed white cop. Third, blacks promoted above the basic rank of police officer almost always worked plainclothes. To have African-American officers with stripes on their shoulders would have put them in a position of supervising white officers. When blacks first started working in patrol cars in the twenties and thirties, for example, they would be segregated and restricted to the midnight shift. The department didn't want white people to see a black officer in a patrol car.

They were assigned primarily to the Newton Station in black L.A., or to directing traffic downtown. Working Hollywood or in the Valley? The mere thought of that was a joke. Not until the early fifties were blacks permitted to work in elite units like motorcycles or accident investigation.

It was the same for Mexican Americans. Take detectives. There were more Latino than black detectives, of course, because the Latinos were bilingual. But still, they worked *Mexican* homicides, Mexican robberies. White detectives would have to be overwhelmed with cases before a Mexican or black detective worked a white homicide. The juvenile units in Watts and Newton Street were all black; the units in Seventy-seventh Street and the University division, all white.

When the LAPD found itself with two black uniformed lieutenants in the forties, they were assigned to a new, all-black midnight shift especially created for them. "A whole new standard," Tom Bradley would later recall, "was put into operation. Ordinarily one lieutenant and three sergeants would be on a particular watch [but] here they had two black lieutenants assigned . . . and no sergeants. . . . They were not even permitted to command a watch involving blacks and whites." It was also common knowledge that they, or any other African-American, had about as much chance of making captain as they did of making chief.

Negroes, even the best of them, it was felt among many in the LAPD, simply did not make really good officers. They were sloppy in their work, had a different set of morals from whites, and were natural hobnobbers with pimps and pushers. It was sort of their way of life, the order of things. Even their own people didn't respect them. The white officers, in fact, told a story, complete with high-pitched Butterfly McQueen Southern drawl, about a black woman calling the police for assistance and screaming when an African-American officer showed up: "The white law! I want the *white* law! Don't come in *my* house. I don't want no colored police. Send me the white law!" No black officer had ever spoken to another who had experienced such a situation, but the story made the rounds for decades nevertheless.

It wasn't that blacks couldn't be promoted or get into a good unit. Tom Bradley went to plainclothes faster than most whites because he *was* black, and bright, and well qualified. The unit to which he was sent was considered a good assignment. The department needed black officers in detective or plainclothes units where they'd blend into the black community. It was the easy thing, the efficient thing, to do. "You could send

Negro officers to do tough jobs in the Negro belt," as Thad Brown once said, "and there would be no beef."

For a black officer to have challenged any of this would have raised the ugly specter of disloyalty. And there was no worse notation for an African-American cop to have in his jacket than that charge. Betrayal is always in who is defining it, and loyalty to each other is everything for cops, always. No nuances, no exceptions. But never, in the case of black cops, was loyalty assumed. It was up to them to prove it. To prove they were whiter than white, and that their fellow cops and the department came first. None of this Negro-dignity, black-pride shit, you're a cop. Caught in the middle of conflicting loyalties. That was the bind, the strain, black cops would always be in.

There were other reasons, too, for the impotence of the LAPD's black officers. Their small number, usually 2 to 4 percent of the force, and local politics. In a city like Chicago, African-American politicians had some clout, even in the forties. Oscar DePriest and William L. Dawson, for example, who were two of the first black Northern, big-city congressmen, had come out of Chicago. If a black cop there had a problem with discrimination, he had an appeal—his political connection. In Los Angeles, black officers like Tom Bradley had nobody to whom they could turn. There were a few judges, but until the early sixties, no city councilmen. Nobody. For years Rocky Washington, who'd come on the force in the twenties, had just one source of influence—a white guy who knew a couple of people at City Hall. But he couldn't do much. The guy, after all, was just a driver in public works. The city's politicians were all lily-white and local black organizations ineffective. Nor was there a black officers association or even an informal network of black cops.

So secure was the department about its racial segregation that only halfhearted excuses to justify it were offered. They amounted to little more than outright assaults on your intellect. Decades later, Stanley Sheldon would give the department's segregation cover stories: "Blacks couldn't work together with whites for several reasons. The first is that when it comes to eating, the white man wants to eat in one place, say Clifton's Cafeteria, and the other guy wants soul food at Joe's Ribs. It would have just caused problems. Another was that blacks preferred to work with each other. They could jive-talk together."

But Tom Bradley had been lucky, and less of this had touched him than other black officers. By the late 1940s, he had already made sergeant and was working as a detective when he received a call from Jim Fisk, who wanted him in administrative vice—the unit that worked directly out of the chief's office investigating other cops. A black gang-squad had just been caught on the take, and Fisk, who remembered Bradley from the Academy, asked him to head a new one. Bradley took the job. As with his organizing of sports events while working in juvenile, Bradley would use his time in vice to his benefit. Many of the people whom he arrested for gambling and other minor crimes would become some of his strongest supporters when he left the department.

Then, in 1955, he was given an even sweeter plum, an assignment in Stanley Sheldon's Public Information Division, working in a new program called community relations. Its function was to ease police-community tensions in minority neighborhoods, and to provide favorable stories about the department to weekly community newspapers—the first such police program of its kind in the nation. Bradley was free to roam the entire city promoting the LAPD, and because he worked out of the chief's office, no one in the field interfered with him. Much of his time was spent massaging the black media, particularly the city's major black weeklies, the *Sentinel*, the *Sun*, the California *Eagle*. He'd drive around Los Angeles trying to smooth things over and deal with both the real complaints and the rampant rumors about the LAPD's brutality and discourtesy, while at the same time attempting to place positive stories about the department in the papers. When the department's first black motorcycle officer was assigned in 1955, for example, Bradley arranged for both his picture and an accompanying article to appear on the front pages of the *Sentinel* and the *Sun*, both of which played the story big.

He also traveled the city holding meetings with about one hundred community organizations concerned with race and intergroup relations. Through them, he began to develop a base of political support throughout Los Angeles. The city was changing, growing more black, more Mexican, more Jewish, and more liberal. Tom Bradley was astute enough to recognize what was taking place and ambitious enough to move on what lay before him: a growing citywide network of progressive political activists responding to the city's changing character. He would plug into it and use it to his maximum advantage. Why not? He'd gone to a good white high school and been among its best students. He'd gone to UCLA, the future white-boy frat school of Republicans like Bob Haldeman and John Ehrlichman. And he was working in public information with cops like Gene

Roddenberry, who were far more cosmopolitan and tolerant than the average LAPD officer. Once, Roddenberry rented a summer house down in Newport Beach and had the public information officers down for a barbecue. Although Bradley and his wife, Ethel, were the only blacks present, they "fit in," recalls Stan Sheldon, "beautifully." Bradley, in fact, even led the group sing. For a black LAPD officer in a segregated department, for a black man in a city that in the forties and fifties had virtually no ranking black elected or appointed officials, Tom Bradley's career in the LAPD had been astoundingly smooth. Almost blessed.

CHAPTER 5

The Seven Dwarfs

....

That entire day in August of 1957, radio station KMPC interspersed its regular programming with tributes especially recorded to air on "Chief Bill Parker Day" in Los Angeles. And in they came: from Vice President Richard M. Nixon in Washington D.C.; from Chicago and its police chief, George Ottewis, who, more importantly, was also the president of the International Association of Chiefs of Police; from Sacramento and California's Republican governor, Goodwin J. Knight; and from the State's Democratic attorney general, Edmund G. (Pat) Brown. Tributes from the commissioner of the California Highway Patrol, from the mayor of Los Angeles, from the district attorney, from the president of the police commission, and from the sheriff and fire chief of Los Angeles County were all broadcast that day. Bill Parker Day.

The celebration was to mark the seven years since the appointment of Parker as chief of police of Los Angeles, and the almost three decades to the day since he'd joined the LAPD. It was thus a double-pronged cause for celebration, and both the department's adroit public relations apparatus and the downtown business community that constituted his major constituency were clearly going all out for Bill Parker. That morning, the *Los Angeles Times* ran a story on the testimonial luncheon that was to be held for him at the sumptuous Biltmore Hotel in the afternoon. Below it was an illustration drawn by Chester Gould, the cartoonist and creator of America's then most famous cop, Dick Tracy. It pictured the literally square-jawed Tracy shaking hands with a beaming Bill Parker as he said, "Congratulations, Chief William H. Parker!"

It was a wonderful touch, another image added to the growing mythology surrounding the chief, and one that would surely have made America's second most famous cop—and ardent Parker nemesis—J. Edgar Hoover, seethe with jealous rage. Hoover didn't like Bill Parker, in fact detested him, both because in just seven years as chief of police, Parker had already started to rival Hoover as Wise Man of Law Enforcement, and because Parker was constantly challenging Hoover's oft-stated position that the Mafia didn't exist. Parker, in turn, despised Hoover. In addition to Hoover's attitude about the Mafia, there was the FBI's propensity to publish ever-soaring crime statistics for Los Angeles that invariably made Bill Parker livid. Particularly when the *Los Angeles Times* would run headlines, as it did in 1958, proclaiming that the "F.B.I. Says L.A. [Is] Crime Center of Nation." In turn, Parker labeled Hoover a "compiler of statistics over which he does not take the responsibility for accuracy" and sarcastically pointed out how "the FBI shows great interest when stolen property moves across a state line, but little interest when some criminals or criminal mobs move from state to state."

The mere fact J. Edgar Hoover felt crowded by Bill Parker said a lot about the enormous power Parker had accrued, a power that in just seven years had made him easily the most powerful public official in Los Angeles, and after Tracy and Hoover, the most influential lawman in America. When Nikita Khrushchev came to America in 1959 and asked to visit Disneyland, it was cleared by the FBI but vetoed by Bill Parker for "security reasons." Bill Parker did not wish it, and it did not happen. *Il capo di tutti capi.* That power, along with its twin dividends, fear and worship, were much in evidence on this afternoon at the Biltmore.

Led by the Los Angeles Chamber of Commerce, Bill Parker's testimonial luncheon had *thirteen* cosponsors, including the holiest institutions of the old guard: the Merchants and Manufacturers Association, the Better Business Bureau, and the Downtown Business Men's Association. There was also the Los Angeles Newspaper Publishers Association, the Greater Los Angeles Press Club, the Motion Picture Producers Association, the Southern California Broadcasters Association, the American

Legion, and even the local chapters of AFL and CIO—even the labor unions. By the end of seven years, Bill Parker had them all—an entire city of admirers, more than eight hundred of whom were now overflowing a Biltmore ballroom and spilling into the corridors.

Inside, the master of ceremonies, ex-Hollywood hoofer and future Republican United States Senator George Murphy—front man for Southern California's hard-right millionaires just as Ronald Reagan would later be—worked the crowd: "Bill held the record for having the world's largest law library ever carried in a taxicab," Murphy told them, alluding to both Parker's studying for the bar while driving a cab, and to the fact that Parker had just been admitted to practice before the U.S. Supreme Court—an honor of which he was inordinately proud. This was followed by the presentation of an endless stream of commendations, such as the one from the L.A. city council pointing out how Parker had made the LAPD "a model for police and administrators throughout the world." Then came a lionizing speech—also with a global reference—from the president of the Chamber of Commerce, who called Parker "one of the top police administrators in the world." After which, the man himself strode to the podium.

It was a time to bask in the limelight, to take it all in, to allow the warm glow of satisfaction to wash all over him. It was an opportunity—a perfect opportunity—for one of his patented, increasingly shrill attacks on godless communism, creeping socialism, misguided liberals, do-good judges, and America's moral decay. But instead, with the well-calibrated instinct of a rock or film star who knows that giving less is sometimes giving more, he thanked his wife, thanked those assembled, and sat down. Ninety seconds. He gave them just ninety seconds. And why not? He'd already said all he needed to in his speeches over the years. Proved what he had to by his performance in office. Wasn't that, after all, why they were all there?

That same year, on an escalator in Sun Valley, Idaho, after a hotel banquet that had been held to mark the end of Mobil Oil's 1957 economy run, Bill Parker danced. Snaking behind him, up and down the escalators, was a conga line of police executives, journalists, and Mobil Oil officials. Conga dancing! Frolicking. Bill Parker, dour, autocratic, abrasive; Bill Parker, an obnoxious, sloppy, sarcastic drunk, was frolicking. And it wasn't the first time on the trip, one of Mobil's annual long-distance races from Los Angeles. On the way to Sun Valley, they had stopped in Albuquerque, New Mexico. After a long bout in the club car drinking the double shots of bourbon deluxe he called Parker Specials, Bill Parker had then joined with Slim Barnard, the automobile editor of the *Los Angeles Examiner,* and one or two others, and gotten off the train. Every year Barnard would plan the kind of shit-faced-drunk-throwing-restraint-to-the-winds escapade that frat-house boys a decade later would refer to as a "zoo" and gleefully recount the next day. This year Barnard had brought some old high-school band uniforms that resembled those of the Salvation Army. At the Albuquerque stop, he briefly exited the train along with Bill Parker and one or two others, who were now wearing those uniforms and carrying a drum and some cymbals. They proceeded to play at the station, pretending to be Salvation Army workers and actually receiving some donations for their efforts. It was a sociable thing on a sociable trip among men who understood each other.

But Bill Parker, who had been known as a good-time drunk as a younger man, had grown increasingly alcoholic, and increasingly nasty and buffoonish when he drank. He slurred his words, stumbled in and out of cars, and sometimes had to be literally carried home. Awkwardly prancing about shaking his arms doing a Sioux Indian dance he'd learned in his youth in South Dakota, or regularly throwing up after downing his predinner bourbons in his house, among friends, was one thing. Showing up late, hungover, and still drunk to review the Rose Parade with the mayor, and then giggling uncontrollably, quite another. "Whiskey Bill," they were calling him behind his back. He knew he had to stop. But it was not an easy addiction to break. He cared nothing for sports, women, or travel, and little for films or books that weren't police manuals or police related. He had no children and no sense of humor when sober. His life was the LAPD—twelve to fourteen hours a day, seven days a week. The department was him, he was the department. Now in his fifties, a heavy drinker and two-pack-a-day smoker at a time when exercise beyond high school or college was for fitness freaks, Bill Parker's health was failing. His heart was giving out.

And not only that. He had made a fool of himself on that Sun Valley run. Beyond just the dancing and the Salvation Army tomfoolery, Bill Parker had shot off his mouth about a major murder case then under investigation, and the news that he had done so, along with word of his drunken public behavior, had gotten back to Norris Poulson, the *Times*-sponsored mayor, who had called him on it. Called *him,* Bill Parker, on it. It was intolerable. Some *Los Angeles Times* lacky chiding *him.* Him in the wrong. Him vulnerable. He would drink no more. And when he stopped drinking, he stopped smoking. Cold. Bill Parker, a man of fragile ego wound astoundingly tight, would now have *no* way to unwind.

The seven deputy chiefs who served under Bill Parker were called the seven dwarfs because they were both dwarfed and marginalized by him. He deliberately kept them in a constant state of turmoil and promoted their differences so astutely that no three could ever agree on anything. "His attitude," recalls Tom Reddin, the man who succeeded him as chief, "was, 'If they're fighting with each other, they're going to leave me alone.' " Each would have his separate little fiefdom—patrol, traffic, detectives, and each would function separately. Public Information, although now a division, was headed by Stanley Sheldon, a captain, and not a deputy chief as it had traditionally been. Sheldon was good, Sheldon was loyal, and most importantly, Sheldon reported directly to him. Bill Parker had no wish for a big office —for a rival power center—to be built up under some deputy chief who coveted his job.

And they were all, as far as Bill Parker was concerned, coveting his job. Out of that certain knowledge, and Bill Parker's volcanic style, domineering nature, and profound conviction of his infallibility, flowed staff meetings—on those rare occasions when he held staff meetings—that were almost always a nightmare. He was, after all, a visionary. The man who'd taken that corrupt piece of shit that was the LAPD and made it his own As he would not be replaced, so he would not be told. The best you could do to avoid being "put on the pan [and] needled," as Deputy Chief Harold Sullivan put it, was to find a time when Parker was approachable, go into his office, and "throw out your idea. And then leave him, and let him mull over it." And you had better be right. "I heard him criticize Ed Davis once in the fifties at a seminar up in Fresno," says Irvis Lester, "and I just cringed for Davis. He'd just presented something, and Bill got up and made it seem as if that was the most childish, stupid, silly thing anybody had ever said. And it was right in front of all these officers from all over the country. It was embarrassing."

Bill Parker had seen what had happened to C. B. "Jack" Horrall when he had trusted his deputy chief—his *only* deputy chief—and wound up with Brenda Allen in his lap. But healthy suspicion had long since given way to both obsession and paranoia with Bill Parker. Shut down to the fresh and innovative, he delegated little and gave his proxy to no one. It was the way he had built the department. *Il capo di tutti capi.*

CHAPTER **6**

The Victorian
••••••••••••••••••••••

Bill Parker's triumphs brought him no joy. They were mere background static on a radio unceasingly blaring forth the real news, news that Bill Parker could feel like an ache in his bones: America was in deep, epoch-defining, turning-point trouble. And it was too soft, self-absorbed, undisciplined, and hedonistic to realize it. For over a decade, in thousands of speeches he had warned of the imminent threat posed by the communists, criminals, and society's growing permissiveness, and of the inherent dangers of criticizing the police. His speeches were fierce, blunt tirades filled with historical allusions supplied by speechwriters such as Gene Roddenberry; filled with the gut instincts of the Southern California, right-wing warrior disgusted with the excess of the New Deal and alarmed by the soft pink trust the liberals had placed in the Soviet Union—a trust that had produced nothing but the Iron Curtain, the Korean War, and the threat of nuclear annihilation. It was hard for him, *very* hard, he would say in speech after speech, "to believe that society could continue to violate all the rules of human conduct and expect to survive." He was a titan in a city of political pygmies, so what was he to do but mount his bully pulpit and strike out at all those causing the crisis engulfing America—a crisis so profound, as Parker noted in 1956, that it was causing "the crime-increase rate'' in America to ''more than double the rate of increase in church membership.''

He was sure of the people to blame for this ruinous situation, and he would lay it out over his sixteen-year tenure as chief. The liberals. Those linking crime to poverty and social conditions. The press, which was constantly ''feeding upon . . . an inherent rebellion against authority,'' ''molding distrust of police,'' and deeming police failures ''worthy of far more space than police successes.'' The criminal justice system, which by its leniency, by its parole policies, bore ''the major responsibility for crime in Los Angeles.'' The state legislature, which wanted to give over California to a ''hedonistic philosophy'' by passing laws legalizing sex between adult homosexuals. And the courts, which were busily throwing out perfectly good laws, such as the Los Angeles ordinance making it a crime for a known prostitute to be in a room with a man ''identified'' as a customer. That was all the proof that had been needed for an arrest in Los Angeles. Unlike state law, no evidence of solicitation or money changing hands was required. When the California Supreme Court overturned that law, Bill Parker called the decision what it was: ''a Bill of Rights for prostitutes.'' The courts were creating a ''policeless state,'' at a time when America was already the ''most lawless nation in the world.'' At a time when the ''criminal army in our midst'' already numbered ''6 million.'' At a time when organized crime was out of control. At a time when only one Mafia murder, as Bill Parker told it, had ever been solved in the entire history of the United States. It was only the vigilance of his Intelligence Division that was keeping the mob out of L.A. They had compiled dossiers on ten thousand members of the American underworld. He never wavered, never ceased his steady staccato warnings: the mob and communists, the mob and the Reds.

It was the communists who were furthering the trade in heroin and marijuana, watching approvingly as those drugs were used like trench tools to dig the hole into which America was sinking ever deeper into moral degeneracy. And those women in the Women's Strike for Peace, their demonstrations, as Bill Parker pointed out, had ''been well noted in the Kremlin and they are happy about the whole movement.'' He saw it, saw it all, and did his best to spread the word. That was what distinguished him from the crass opportunism of Richard Nixon, the drunken buffoonery of Joe McCarthy, and the insatiable lust for power of J. Edgar Hoover. Bill Parker *believed.*

*   *   *

There was no one to oppose him in Los Angeles. No one to slap Bill Parker down to size. No one to challenge either his politically charged speeches or how he ran the department. No one, in any case, who cared to. He had the support of the new mayor—the right-wing congressman and creature of the *Times*—Norris Paulson, who'd defeated Fletcher Bowron in a bitter 1953 campaign. And more importantly he had behind him the money people who had created Richard Nixon and still ran Los Angeles: Norman Chandler, son and heir of Harry; Asa Call; the secretive group of businessmen known as the Committee of Twenty-five, who pulled the strings, passed on all important decisions, and served as the city's shadow government; the large old-line law firms; the major corporations; and the city's big developers. Not all were overt supporters of Bill Parker, but in the main they were well satisfied with his leadership. He was giving them a police department that was no longer an embarrassing, corrupt joke as they sought to become a major world metropolis. Through "Dragnet" and other police shows, in fact, Parker's LAPD was actually helping to promote the city. Equally good for business was the department's relentless patrolling of the city, which kept things safe and orderly. The perception of the LAPD, of Parker's LAPD, was fresh, new, different. And wasn't that, after all, the image of Los Angeles they all wanted to portray? It was very simple. They'd run the city, and he'd run not only the police department but everything even remotely connected to it.

He knew he was impenetrable, knew that all he had to do was keep his legs closed. Having cowritten the charter reforms that gave him his power, Bill Parker had taken them and systematically reduced the police commission to what one commissioner would describe with disgust "as an impotent rubber stamp." The commission was supposed to set policy and oversee the department, but that was a joke. The idea that five businessmen or lawyers meeting one afternoon a week could stand up to a fierce, shrewd, contentious chief of police who controlled the flow of information to the commission, who held the careers of the officers on the commission staff in the palm of his hand, who had a rigid agenda, a popular mandate, and ironclad civil service protection, was exactly that: a joke. The commissioners were chosen by the mayor for geographic diversity as political paybacks, or to watch out for the mayor's interests. To the extent that they had constituent agendas, they often clashed. They were citizen volunteers, pillars or would-be pillars of the establishment, who had businesses to run or bosses to whom they were accountable forty or fifty hours a week. It was a wonder, in fact, that they had a spare moment to do anything meaningful, what with the commission's meetings being consumed with the endless task of granting or rescinding commercial permits and licenses for various businesses all over the city. That was really the only power the commission had under Bill Parker. By law, they had no power over the budget, and none over discipline short of drawing up charges to fire the chief—a situation that was impossible to imagine. Five faceless, pressed-for-time, politically constrained amateurs versus a consummate professional was a contest that was really no contest at all. The easiest thing, the prudent thing, was to acquiesce, to go along. "We relied on Parker an awful lot," John Ferraro, a city councilman who had served on the police commission for thirteen years, would later say, "and maybe that's why we got the rubber-stamp image. But you know, Parker was usually right—he wasn't wrong very often." Relying on Parker. It was smart, it was easy. Just as it was easy for the commissioners to feel honored to be serving on *the* prestigious plum of all city commissions. As it was easy to enjoy the privilege of carrying a commissioner's five-starred badge, and of being picked up in a limo to lunch with the celebrity chief whose name appeared in big bold letters every week on a network television show that had become a national institution. Under Bill Parker, says Jack White, who as an LAPD captain headed the commission's investigations division, the police commission "really didn't have any-thing to do other than just sit back and kind of watch the fire burn."

If any commissioner chose not to, there was always an option: he could resign in protest. That is, he could make a small noise, cause a stir for a day or two, and be gone, changing nothing. In 1959, that was driven home to Herbert A. Greenwood, an African-American attorney then serving on the commission. Greenwood had been deluged by questions about the number of blacks on the department and in the middle and higher ranks, and the types of assignments they were receiving. When he asked for the information, Bill Parker refused to give it to him. Instead, he flew into a rage, accusing Greenwood of wanting the information so that he could attack him. Nor would Parker give Greenwood access to the department's gambling arrests (Greenwood rightly suspected that blacks were being arrested at a far higher rate than whites) or allow him or the other com-missioners to question officers who'd been involved in serious brutality complaints.

So Herbert Greenwood held a press conference to explain why he had resigned in what the *Los Angeles Times* described as "a huff." He told the reporters about a motion he'd made for the commission to investigate a recent controversial killing of a black man by a police officer. The man, an uninvolved witness to a street fight, had been grabbed by an officer who'd arrived on the scene and judo-flipped, breaking his neck and killing him. Bill Parker, as Herbert Greenwood recounted it, was enraged at even the suggestion of an outside—that is, of a police-commission investigation—of what he considered to be his police department. "We know all about that [incident]," Parker told him. "The man died of a broken neck. There's no need for more investigation." Then he looked at Herbert Greenwood and added that he was fed up—fed up—with Greenwood "yelling brutality every time anything happened." That was Bill Parker's attitude toward troublemakers on the Los Angeles Police Commission. "He rules the force with an iron hand," Hugh Irely, another commissioner who resigned in frustration, would say. Herbert Greenwood put it another way: "We don't tell him, he tells us."

It was a bad thing, among the worst possible legacies Bill Parker could have passed on to his successors, this business of "attacks" on the police being attacks on America. Implicitly, it challenged democratic civilian rule, in the same way that MacArthur had explicitly challenged Harry Truman. But there was no Harry Truman in L.A. to teach Bill Parker the chain of command.

Criticism—fair or petty, tough-minded analysis or sloppy thought, personal or directed at the department—it was all the same to Bill Parker. It all had to be fought. A generation of LAPD officers would watch him, and they, too, would find themselves unable to tolerate the normal give-and-take of public discourse. They, too, would act as if they were operating out of the brain of Richard Nixon. It was strange, its own thing, as unrepresentative as Southern-plantation-town politics or a one-party, on-the-take Tammany Hall machine. A powerful governmental agency was operating unchecked, and almost nobody was noticing. When Herbert Greenwood resigned from the police commission, he talked about discrimination within the LAPD, and the "unhealthy attitudes" that condoned it. But the unchallenged power of the Los Angeles chief of police, combined with an institutional ego so frail it could hardly stand the slightest criticism, *that* was the really unhealthy attitude.

CHAPTER 7

The Property of the Chief

••••••••••••••••••••••

Bill Parker loved intelligence, loved it as a young beautiful woman with ambition loves a rich old man, loved it because he knew what it could do for him. Like J. Edgar Hoover, he dealt in information, and with it he could intimidate, discredit, or destroy his enemies, dry up dissent, and render impotent all those alien to his values and critical of the LAPD. Understanding the value of information, he held it dear. Once in office, he issued a directive that the files of the Intelligence Division were his files, "the property of the Chief of Police," "official police records not subject to subpoena" or to perusal by others. Most importantly he understood how the mere threat of files, tapped phones, undercover cops, agent provocateurs, and spies looking through your garbage could stifle dissent and bring protest to a screeching halt. Everybody, after all, had a skeleton in the closet and something to hide.

The intelligence-gathering model adopted by Bill Parker was the same as that followed by the KGB, by Hoover's FBI, and by the International Association of Chiefs of Police: get it raw, get it all, and keep everything on everybody. You'll never know, went the theory, when it might come in handy. As the Chief's Association's own history put it: "Intelligence was seen as the gathering of as much information as possible in order to fit seemingly irrelevant facts into an overall pattern. Because it was often impossible during the initial gathering stages to be certain how the information would eventually be used, intelligence officials felt it was unwise to exclude any data.'' Intelligence-gathering ''Soviet-style,'' it was called, so named, went the story, because the Russians had subscribed to every U.S. journal in existence and, by clipping, sorting, and analyzing, had been able to acquire an enormous amount of classified material. Bill Parker's LAPD would do the same. ''Every time somebody went to a meeting,'' says former LAPD assistant chief David Dotson, ''we wrote down everybody who was there because this guy might go to another meeting [and talk to] another pinko, and eventually we'd get a big enough file so we would say *he's* a pinko. That's an exaggeration, but that was the mind-set.''

Parker had created the Intelligence *Division* from the small unit of about four detectives and a lieutenant that had been authorized by William Worton. Then he brought in a captain and assigned twenty officers to it. Within Stanley Sheldon's Public Information Division a civilian employee did nothing but read, underline, cut, and paste clippings from newspapers from all over the county, matching them up with names on a list he'd been given. A list, that Sheldon, spreading his arms wide, would recall as being ''this long.'' Added Sheldon, ''That stuff went [directly] to Intelligence. I never saw it.''

Operating without any publicly stated rules or guidelines, the number of people assigned to the division grew to eighty-four by 1969. Little more than a year later, after Intelligence was split in half to form the Organized Crime Intelligence Division and the Public Disorder Intelligence Division, the number rose to 188, a figure that excluded the intelligence units working within vice and narcotics. But they were needed. As ''a football coach who has the other teams thoroughly scouted can exploit their weaknesses and overcome the strengths of the other team,'' so, too, would the LAPD, Ed Davis would explain.

As the LAPD's files began to bulge, they bulged like the FBI's, with half-truths and outright lies, with total distortions, unsubstantiated rumors, and misinformation. After he became chief of the LAPD in 1967, Tom Reddin sat at his desk and called for what he knew would be there, his intelligence file. And it was. ''The notions'' in it, he would later recall, ''were almost laughable, and most of them were wrong.''

They indicated an indifference to the truth, and a lack of discrimination, analytical competence, and political sagacity that, thought Reddin, was embarrassing. And he was of them. Bill Parker's paranoia, Bill Parker's fears, were seeping into the department's file cabinets.

The rationale for the Intelligence Division in the early fifties was the mob. The mob was coming to town, and it had to be thwarted. Worldwide criminal cartels were planning to take over Los Angeles; Frank Costello was just drooling to make L.A. another Chicago. The alarm was nothing new. Italian and Jewish gangsters from the East had been used as a support-your-local-police rallying cry in Los Angeles since the 1920s. And the potential *was* present for their infiltration. And Bill Parker's Airport Squad, which met incoming planes and intimidated mobsters before they could settle into L.A., was extremely effective in keeping them out of the city. This too was nothing new. Meeting out-of-town gangsters as they arrived in town was an LAPD tradition that went back to James Davis in the thirties. They'd wait at the train station, meet the guy, pound his head into the men's-room sink, and send him back out of town. Under Parker, the focus switched to the Airport Squad, which existed into the sixties. "Before they could claim their luggage," as Daryl Gates would later say, "we had officers out there to greet them . . . [and] literally put them on the next plane home." But an intelligence unit of the size and scope that William Worton had envisioned—perhaps a dozen well-trained, highly knowledgeable men with expertise in organized crime—should have been enough to deal with any mob problems.

But the opportunity for Bill Parker's Intelligence Division to go *beyond* organized crime was so golden, and the time so ripe, however, that he could not possibly have passed it up. The Korean War, Stalin's megalomania, and the horrors of his regime had opened the door to massive political surveillance by the federal government. In the sixties, the Panthers, the Weathermen, and the anti-war movement would open it even further. It would have been unimaginable for Bill Parker's LAPD not to have been a part of it. In the early fifties, as Parker told a meeting of local police officials who had gathered together to better pool their resources to fight organized crime: "This plan goes deeper than a means of saving Los Angeles from the stigma of vice. We are protecting the American philosophy of life. It is known that Russia is hoping we will destroy ourselves as a nation through our own avarice, greed, and corruption in government. Hence, this program has a wider application than in the Los Angeles area alone."

Once Bill Parker's LAPD was walking down that road, it was only to be expected that it would strive in the spirit of the new LAPD to be the biggest, the best, and most efficient at the job. It was like a circle had been closed, and a missing piece put back into the institutional heart of the department. James Davis, Red Hynes, and Earle Kynette, like Freddie Krueger in those *Nightmare on Elm Street* movies, were back.

Bill Parker was tapped into the files; they were, after all, by his own declaration, *his* files, and he would personally use them on stupid things that posed no threat, things he should have been too busy to deal with. In 1957, Ethel Narvid was working as a volunteer in the campaign of a young, liberal Los Angeles Democrat named Jim Corman, who was running for the city council. Corman had all the right credentials for an era marked by a rampant anticommunism and glorification of "Americanism": he was a Methodist from Kansas, a veteran of the Marines, and a district leader in the local Lions Club. Ethel Narvid did not. She was a Jew from Brooklyn. Her parents hadn't been communists but they had been liberals, and probably socialists. She herself was a liberal New Dealer. Corman's campaign had been a loosely organized grassroots affair, and Narvid had gravitated to the unofficial position of campaign manager. After he had won, Corman asked Narvid to become his deputy on the city council. Almost immediately, it became clear that her nomination was in trouble. She was a Jew and a woman, two groups still not particularly welcome around City Hall. But more important, Bill Parker had a file claiming she was a communist. And Bill Parker had personally called the president of the city council to tell him. No matter that immediately after the war she had gone with her husband—an Army major in the Judge Advocate's Office—to occupied Europe, found a job with the U.S. government, been checked out and given a top-secret security clearance. Her family background was enough. After a bruising process, Narvid's appointment was finally approved, but only because Jim Corman was unassailable and therefore not open to intimidation, and because Bill Parker had nothing even remotely of substance on Narvid. But it was a sign of how closely Bill Parker was monitoring and influencing local political affairs that he would invest himself trying to defeat a staff member of a freshman on a fifteen-member city council.

Bill Parker's attention, however, would focus beyond the trivial. In 1963, he intervened in the Democratic nomination for the U.S. Senate, torpedoing the candidacy of California's attorney general Stanley Mosk by leaking embarrassing information of Mosk's marital infidelities with a former prostitute.

And he would ensure that another liberal who was formerly the attorney general of California, Edmund G. (Pat) Brown, the two-term governor of California, would cause him no trouble by bugging and spying on Brown while he was governor, and compiling a massive file of him.

Frank Wilkinson had within him a righteous call equal to that of Bill Parker's. He'd grown up in upper-middle-class comfort in Beverly Hills, the son of Dr. A. M. Wilkinson, respected elder in the Hollywood Methodist Church, head of the Protestant Men's Movement of Southern California, friend to Robert Shuler, and guide and mentor to Clifford Clinton in forming CIVIC and in taking on the Shaws in 1938.

At Beverly Hills High School he'd headed Youth for Herbert Hoover and fought hard against the election of Franklin Roosevelt. His activism wasn't just political, it was a question of morality. The very existence of Prohibition was at stake. Roosevelt was wet. Hoover dry. Frank Wilkinson had been the first president of the Hollywood Young People's Chapter of the Women's Christian Temperance Union. While his brother and sister decided they would follow in their father's footsteps and become medical doctors, Frank Wilkinson wanted passionately to serve the Lord and enter the Methodist ministry. At UCLA he was chair of the student board of the religious conference and pledged Sigma Alpha Epsilon, running for student body president as the candidate of the fraternities and sororities.

In 1936 his family sent him to the Middle East to experience Christmas Eve in the Holy Land. It would be beautiful. A cleansing, star-filled, Christ-laden, silent-holy-night. But at the Church of Nativity, where Christ was said to have been born, he saw literally hundreds of starving beggars. One, a woman, a child really, approached him barefoot and raggedy, nursing two babies. Her eyes caught his. They were filled with red, running sores oozing a horrific liquid that was dripping into the faces of her babies. And she was blindly reaching for him, for his coat, his arm, his hand. Asking for money. Begging for what was the equivalent of one-tenth of a penny. That night, Frank Wilkinson had his epiphany. He tried to help the beggars, he lived with them, and in the process decided preaching was a fraud.

* * *

By 1951, Frank Wilkinson had become a committed social activist who was working for the Los Angeles Housing Authority as its public relations officer. Slum clearance and low-income public housing had become popular, and in 1949 when Congress passed a federal housing act, Los Angeles was one of the first cities to qualify for funds. Previously, Fletcher Bowron, now in this thirteenth year as mayor, had gained the support of the city council for a massive slum-clearance project to be followed by the building of ten thousand units of low-income, integrated public housing in areas like Chavez Ravine and Bunker Hill—areas much coveted by large, powerful real estate interests including the Chandlers. Integrated, low-cost, *public* housing was a volatile combination in the America and the Los Angeles of the 1950s. "Creeping socialism," it was called. And Bill Parker, like the monied interests he viewed as his core constituency, did not like it. He ordered a study showing that juvenile delinquency rates were higher in a local housing project than in adjacent slum areas, and then was embarrassed when the political activists working with the Housing Authority were able to show that the "adjacent areas" had been cleared of housing six months before they had reportedly been studied.

One day during a court proceeding in which Frank Wilkinson was serving as an expert witness, he was suddenly asked by an attorney for a landlord what organizations, political or otherwise, he had belonged to since 1929. In the attorney's hand was a dossier filled with information passed on to him by Bill Parker. When Wilkinson replied that that was irrelevant, the judge ordered Wilkinson to answer. Wilkinson, who to this day denies ever having been a communist, refused, and the real estate lobby demanded that the House Un-American Activities Committee come to town to investigate. The stage was set. Bill Parker, meanwhile, visited Fletcher Bowron and handed him a file filled with the "subversive associations" of Frank Wilkinson and nine other employees of the Housing Authority. Bowron told him he had known Frank Wilkinson since he was a boy, had worked with his father, and that Frank Wilkinson was no subversive and he wouldn't fire him.

There it stood until 1953, when the housing projects had become the central issue in an ugly Red-baiting mayoral campaign that pitted Bowron, Wilkinson, and the Christian thing to do against the right-wing congressman Norris Poulson, who'd been handpicked by the *Times* and a powerful coterie of downtown real estate interests.

Three days before the election—*three days*—Bill Parker acted. Appearing as a star witness at a televised state legislative hearing, Parker testified about Frank Wilkinson and the other subversives in the Housing Authority, then dramatically recounted how Fletcher Bowron had taken the dossiers that he had been vigilant enough to bring to Bowron's attention and tore them up right before his eyes. On election day, Fletcher Bowron, who along with Clifford Clinton, had done more than any other man alive to clean up the city and the LAPD, was overwhelmingly defeated with the well-timed assistance of LAPD reform chief William H. Parker. With Bowron went the plans to clear out L.A.'s slums. Left holding the land, the city turned it over for a song to Walter O'Malley— who'd just broken the hearts of millions of people in Brooklyn to line his already fat pockets—for his now *Los Angeles* Dodgers.

By 1975, the LAPD Intelligence Division that Bill Parker had set in motion had amassed almost 2 million dossiers on fifty-five thousand individuals and at least two hundred lawful groups, including the PTA, the National Organization for Women, the World Council of Churches, Operation Breadbasket, and the Beverly Hills Democratic Club. It had undercover agents who were having affairs with a major Hollywood star and with an official of the ACLU. It had a spy in the mayor's office in the person of his driver; an officer so deeply infiltrated in the Communist Party that he'd gone to the Soviet Union. It had secret caches of files hidden in public storage areas. The head of the Organized Crime Intelligence Division (OCID) was reporting directly to the chief of police about the personal lives of politicians, entertainers, and critics as well as legitimate targets. Police commissioners were paranoid that their homes and offices were being bugged and their phones tapped. Men, usually with little more than a high school education working in a profession not known for its cosmopolitan nature or cultural or political sophistication, were gathering information and rendering judgments on the lives of thousands of law-abiding citizens of Los Angeles. A system designed for espionage was being abused domestically not just by J. Edgar Hoover's FBI, but by police departments in cities like Los Angeles, where a local police chief was gathering material of a private nature that should not have been of interest to a policeman. The only thing his Intelligence Division would miss, it seemed, was the insurrection in Watts, for which he and his department would prove to be totally unprepared.

CHAPTER 8

The Betrayer
·····················

Sitting in his office that day in 1959, Bill Parker saw a highly critical story about the LAPD in the *Los Angeles Sentinel*. Another critical story. Why was all this criticism coming from these black weeklies? For much of the 1950s negative stories in the *Sentinel* and the city's other black weekly, the *Sun*, had been the only really negative stories in the local press, as well as one of the few ways the local black community had of getting its grievances publicized. The department's relations with L.A.'s black community had never been good, as they had never been good in most of America's big cities. But the huge influx of blacks into the city in the forties and fifties was already making Los Angeles a whole new world for white cops. Their traditional alienation and racism, the department's segregation, and the department's aggressive proactive policing of a population it clearly despised were all having their effect. Even the mild-mannered *Sentinel*—a paper that never passed up an opportunity to lecture its readers on the virtues of law and order—felt compelled to reflect their readers' outrage. The situation in Los Angeles had moved from not good to appallingly bad.

In South Central, the man was *always* breathing down your neck. The city's population by 1960 was about 2.5 million. In the two and half years from 1960 through mid-1962, the LAPD would have "contacts" with over 2 million citizens, arrest nearly 500,000, and issue over 1.5 million citations. By then almost 14 percent of the population, and with a large amount of crime being committed by and against blacks, the city's African-Americans were finding themselves—as they had throughout the fifties—on the receiving end of a large share of all that proactive law enforcement. And feeling forever hassled, disproportionately hassled, by a police department whose philosophy it *was* to hassle people. In areas like South Central, in fact, it was what they did—their raison d'être. Just hanging in the street, just jiving with the fellas on the corner, got you checked out. Driving in a car with one or two other black males got you stopped, *anything* could get you stopped and get you a ticket. A ticket that for a variety of reasons you could not or did not pay. Then it would go to warrant and the next time you were stopped, you'd be arrested and hauled to the Seventy-seventh Street Station. There, you'd be reminded of who *they* were, and who you were. The booking officers were the Centurions. You, you were the occupied people to be kept in line. There to be shoved, insulted, punched, and prodded, toyed with and fucked over while you kept your mouth shut or got your ass really kicked. That was the Seventy-seventh Street Station in South Central in the fifties and sixties. What went on was no secret. Certainly not in South Central, although the white cops, to this day, deny it. But it was bad. In 1960 alone $1 million in brutality and misconduct claims were filed against the LAPD.

Yet Bill Parker, who'd once threatened to throw an officer out of *his* booking station for hitting a prisoner, was permitting it to go on at the Seventy-seventh—or at least doing nothing to stop it. Instead, he would issue dismissive, contempt-filled statements or reply caustically whenever the subject of police brutality was raised. So black weeklies like the *Sentinel* would editorialize: "Hardly a day passes without someone showing up at [our] offices with physical evidence of beatings and accusations [against local policemen]." Or, as it pointed out on another occasion: The LAPD is led by a chief who, "by his public statements and acts, has shown either an abysmal ignorance or an unbelievable contempt for the Negro and Mexican American communities."

It was those kinds of comments, and the kinds of stories he was seeing almost weekly in the black press, that were driving Bill Parker crazy. It was embarrassing the department—*his* department—the greatest sin that Bill Parker could imagine. And it was happening under Tom Bradley's watch. Bradley was supposed to be on duty twenty-four hours a day in his role as community relations officer, ready to, as Stanley Sheldon put it, "research a complaint" and "give them the *true* facts." Yet, either through his incompetence—and nobody thought Tom Bradley incompetent—or through his active collusion, these stories were appearing. Just where were they getting this stuff? Daryl Gates would later allege that Bill Parker received an intelligence report stating that "instead of talking the department up," Bradley was "providing negative information to dissident groups, saying unfavorable things about Parker and the LAPD."

True or not, Tom Bradley was sending Bill Parker memos warning of all the problems and the mounting, searing rage within the black community. Memos that seemed to understand the complaints of the agitators and so-called leaders of the black community better than the department's difficulties. Memos that seemed to indicate that it was the *department* that was at fault.

Bradley didn't seem to realize that it wasn't Bill Parker or the department that had the problem. It was *they,* these minority groups, who were out of step with the real people of L.A.—with the vast majority of white Angelenos who adored the department and were close to deifying Parker. Hadn't Immaculate Heart College, after all, given him their Bill of Rights Freedom Award?

Not that he, Bill Parker, hadn't made a few ill-advised statements, to be sure. Before the U.S. Civil Rights Commission in 1959, he expressed his feelings about the city's Mexican Americans: "Some of these people have been here since before we were, but some of them aren't far removed from the wild tribes of Mexico." It was a sentiment then widely shared. In some parts of Mexican-American East L.A., the streets and sidewalks were still unpaved and door-to-door mail service was just beginning. As with the zoot suit riots and mass indictments of those "Sleepy Lagoon" greaseballs—it was all part of an L.A. attitude toward Mexican Americans as old as Sonoratown. Bill Parker had matured as a man in that tradition. What did they expect from him?

On Christmas Eve of 1951, after seven young Mexican Americans had gotten into a fight with two police officers in a bar and had been hauled to the Central Station and systematically and horribly beaten, hadn't he acted? He'd been in office barely more than a year and "Bloody Christmas," as it came to be known, was his first test of how minorities would be treated. When it was all over, two officers were forced off the depart-

ment, eight others were indicted, and thirty-six received official reprimands.

He'd taken action back then. But over the years, he and the city had
changed. Those Negroes kept pouring in. *Pouring* in. And as he would
point out in 1962, almost one-half of all the murders and "vicious physical assaults" committed in Los Angeles were committed against blacks,
mainly by other African-Americans. That had to be contained. People all
over the city were becoming fearful.

So he told the truth when he spoke before the National Conference of
Christians and Jews and said that "certain racial groups" committed "a
disproportionate share of the crime." And he told the truth when he said
that the LAPD wasn't interested in *why* that was so. What the department
was "interested in [was] maintaining order. The fact that the group would
not be a crime problem under different socioeconomic conditions and
might not be a crime problem tomorrow," he said, did not "alter today's
tactical necessities." Tactical necessities, that was it. He would respond
by doing what was tactically necessary. And by telling his truth. And if
people got angry at him for saying those things, then so be it. This whole
concept of community relations was a two-edged sword to begin with. It
was good—excellent—spin control, but there was something about it that
went against Bill Parker's disdain for social-work policing, against his
belief that people didn't like cops and never would; something about
encouraging people to become involved with the department. Long term,
where could it lead? To civilians interfering with the professionals and
thinking they had a right to have input into the department and how it was
run, that was where. But he'd agreed to it, and now all it was getting him
was a never-ending stream of so-called police brutality stories, like the
ones the *Sentinel* was now running.

So enraged did Bill Parker become at the story that he strode into his
outer office, looked at his aide John Kinsling, and said four words: "Get
rid of Bradley." Then, red-faced, he whirled around and added, "I want
him out of there. Now!" Kinsling immediately told Stanley Sheldon, who
said he understood and would put Bradley on the next transfer list, which
came out twice a month. No, no, Kinsling told him, Parker said *now*. And
immediately Bradley was transferred to the Wilshire Division. Bill Parker
decided Tom Bradley had committed the cop's cardinal sin, that his
loyalty lay more with the black community than with the LAPD. That
Tom Bradley was not a good soldier, was too involved with politics, was

too involved with his law studies at Southwestern School of Law, was too involved with his career outside the department, and was pushing him. Pushing him with his reports of complaints from the black community, and pushing him with these requests to integrate the patrol cars.

So Bill Parker ordered Tom Bradley out of community relations, out of his special assignment, forbade him, in fact, all special assignments, and sent him into isolation. Henceforth Tom Bradley would work in uniform, out in the Wilshire Division. There, decreed Bill Parker, he would stay.

Tom Reddin, meanwhile, was working in the detective bureau and wanted to bring in some more black detectives. Bradley's name came up and he looked perfect for the job. He was a sergeant. He already had experience as a detective. He had an excellent educational background, and now that he was working in uniform he was available.

So Reddin went to Thad Brown, the chief of detectives, and said, "We oughta bring Bradley in here." "I don't think Parker will ever hold still for it," Brown told him. Reddin suggested they try anyway and put Bradley's name on the transfer sheet.

Shortly thereafter both Reddin and Brown were summoned into Parker's office. He was furious, literally livid. "Who's responsible for this?" he asked, pointing at the transfer list. When Reddin said he was, Parker picked up the transfer sheet, threw it across the room, and screamed, "That man will never work any special assignment as long as I'm chief. Now get out of here!"

Bill Parker was true to his word. Tom Bradley made lieutenant—with his background and record it was hard under civil service to deny him— but he remained in Wilshire, on the graveyard shift.

There he was, one of the very few black lieutenants in the department's history; about to finish law school, with three years as an undergraduate at UCLA; experienced throughout the department; big, sharp, smart, good-looking and still relatively young. The civil rights movement was in full flower, the city was really starting to change. The department could have had this impressive, innately conservative black officer out there once again buying some goodwill, generating some favorable PR, keeping the department just ahead of the curve so that real trouble could be avoided. But Bill Parker wouldn't hear of it. In spite of increasing pressure on the department from L.A.'s growing black, Chicano, and Jewish communities, Bill Parker wouldn't budge. He had banished Tom Bradley. Tom Bradley had betrayed the department. He'd stay banished.

Tom Bradley's feelings for Parker, on the other hand, were more complex and ambivalent. Both the cop in him and his ordered, middle-class nature seemed to admire Parker, whom he described in 1978 as "a man of brilliant intellect, an eloquent spokesman, a tough disciplinarian, a man who, perhaps more than any . . . helped to set a pattern of professional standards for the police department in this city as well as across the nation . . ." It was the carefully measured, finely calibrated assessment of a black politician then leading a multiethnic city, not that of a black man who had repeatedly clashed with Parker and was well aware of his virulent racism. But by then Parker was long gone. Why should Bradley have bothered to stir up that old, in-the-past shit? Why stir all *them* up, when in just two years he would run for governor of California and be required to be whiter than white?

In any case, after he had made lieutenant in 1960, Bradley notified Parker that some of his men had volunteered to work together in an integrated patrol car. It wasn't the first time Bradley had asked Parker to integrate patrols, he'd broached the subject at a staff meeting while he was in community relations, but Parker had sent back word for Bradley to forget it. This time, however, he agreed to let Bradley do a limited experiment.

On the very first day, the patrol car involved began to get "calls" and, according to Bradley, a "very sick kind of treatment and abuse from fellow officers, not only from our division but all over the city. It became such a nasty situation that the white officer involved . . . came to me and asked if he could be relieved from the assignment."

Parker could have stopped it, stopped all of it with just a word. He could have ordered the integration of the entire department right then and there had he chosen to. He'd been chief for a decade, and it was *his* department in a way it never has been anyone else's before or since. He was the man. *Il capo di tutti capi.* But he chose not to.

And without Parker's support, Bradley's integration experiment turned into a predictable fiasco. It wasn't as if Bradley had been trying to wildly accelerate a process that was already moving. By the late fifties the department's segregation had scarcely changed from what it was when Tom Bradley had joined the force almost twenty years earlier. Blacks could still not work with whites on patrol, were still relegated to South Central, still could not work the San Fernando Valley, and were still not admitted into many of the department's elite units. There were still only two black lieutenants and none above the rank of captain. Rocky Washington had tried to make captain. Four times he took and passed the exam, and four times he failed to get promoted.

One night he left an LAPD banquet at the Biltmore Hotel at the same time as Bill and Helen Parker were leaving. They were parked on one side of the street, and Washington, who had just gotten into his car, was on the other. Unexpectedly, Helen Parker shouted over to him, "Lieutenant, have you made captain yet?" And Washington yelled back, "No, uh, uh." "Why not?" she demanded. Washington shrugged and said, "I don't know, ask the chief," and Parker, as his car pulled out, called back, "You mean ask *Civil Service!*"

Only when Sam Yorty successfully campaigned for mayor in 1961 and pledged to integrate the LAPD did the department's segregation end. It was then that Bill Parker decided to integrate the LAPD himself. Bill Parker never liked to be upstaged. "Quietly he sent out the word," recalls Jim Fisk. "There was no written order. I was an area commander, and I drove around giving the order, word of mouth, to all my captains, telling them they had to integrate." Eight years after the Supreme Court had proclaimed school segregation dead in the South, thirteen years after William Worton had pledged to integrate the LAPD, and fourteen years after Harry Truman had ordered the integration of the American armed forces, Bill Parker had finally, grudgingly integrated the LAPD. During the forties and fifties the department had been a closely knit, Anglo-Saxon, Protestant organization (Bill Parker was the first Catholic chief), small enough so that almost everybody knew, or knew of, everybody else. It was a family as well as a fraternity. At best, black officers were stepbrothers, relegated to certain assignments, precluded from working with the real family members. At worst, they were unwanted poor relations forced on people who wanted nothing to do with them. For a long time Bill Parker, Big Daddy, had seen no reason to let the bastard children into the big house.

Tom Bradley's reputation as arrogant and disloyal only increased after his failed attempt to integrate the patrol cars. It was unfathomable, a real head-shaker to people in the department who liked Tom Bradley, how he'd gone bad, crossed over.

As a watch commander in Wilshire, Tom Bradley only compounded his problems. He insisted on seeing every report, on inspecting arrestees to make sure they didn't have any marks on them, on checking on the bookings to ensure they were justified. And if they brought someone in on a bullshit charge, say, drunk in public, and he lived in the neighborhood, Bradley would tell him to just take the guy home. And they'd leave and take the guy to the Hollywood station instead and book him there. And laugh about it, and about Tom Bradley. Bradley's actions, as Daryl Gates later wrote, were "viewed as taking care of his friends rather than supporting his men." It was ironic—but part of the schizophrenic nature of being a black cop—that what should have been Tom Bradley's greatest asset, his integrity, turned out in the eyes of many in the department to be his greatest liability.

Internal Affairs, the unit that oversees and investigates the conduct of police officers, hauled him in for questioning because he was publicly supporting a candidate for the city council who had been critical of the LAPD.

The handwriting was on the wall. He saw what he'd been too blind to see as a younger man: that there was really no place for uppity, self-respecting Negroes like himself in a police department that was constantly reminding him of his blackness even as it simultaneously demanded that he forget it. So Tom Bradley decided to zero in on his law studies and prepare for the bar and his retirement.

But he never forgot the insults. He would mask his rage behind a flat stoicism, cataloging the stupid slights, and then transcending them. But that didn't mean they were forgotten. Not the trip he took as a grown man from Michigan to Los Angeles where he was forced to sleep in his car on the side of the road because no motel would take him in. Not the vacation trip he took with his wife and two daughters to Vancouver, B.C., when he encountered the same problem. With his children watching, he would tell the L.A. *Times,* brightly lit vacancy signs would suddenly shut off as he was told there were no vacancies, and half-empty restaurants would insist they were booked up. It was the only time, he would later say improbably, that he ever recalled getting really angry.

In his head, he kept "a long, long list" of the local stores and restaurants that refused to serve or do business with him, even when he was wearing his LAPD uniform. Among them was a downtown store that featured large-size clothing for men and that had refused him credit. "If a Los Angeles police officer can't qualify for credit, who can?" he asked, "his usual pleasant, measured voice," according to the *Times*, "edged with steel." He never "stepped a foot into that store again."

In 1950 he'd called his former Academy classmate Jim Fisk and asked for a favor. Fisk was active in his church and lived about four blocks west of Crenshaw in a white neighborhood. He seemed the ideal person to help Tom Bradley move to a better area. *His* area. So Bradley asked Fisk if he could help him find a house on the west side. "I'll see what I can do," Fisk told him. But he never got back to Bradley. "I didn't have the guts," Fisk later said. "Those were the days of breaking down barriers, and I just didn't have the guts to go against custom."

The young Malcolm X or Richard Wright's Bigger Thomas reacted to that kind of draining, almost unconscious insult by exploding. Tom Bradley settled on another solution: be four times better than any white man. Be whiter than white.

At Polytechnic he'd set the record for Los Angeles in the 440 dash, made All City tackle in 1936 and in 1937 was All Southern Californian Track Champion as well as All City in the quarter mile. Rage had at least partly fueled his determination. The rage that was later exacerbated by unanswered letters written to corporations like Gillette asking why they never showed Jackie Robinson or any other black athletes in their ads. The rage at the insults he faced at work. During his twenty-one years on the LAPD, Tom Bradley had completed law school, passed the bar, and become an attorney, accomplishments much heralded when attached to the name of Bill Parker, but only grudgingly acknowledged when it came to Tom Bradley. In those twenty-one years he'd worked on a police department filled with many men less than him in every sense. Some accepted and even helped him in what for a black cop was a storybook early career. But many treated him with the condescension or contempt that was the fashion of the time, and some filled his personnel file with racist evaluations. Those kinds of indignities had killed a lot of black men. But Tom Bradley's pride was a tempered one, tempered with a politician's sense of reality, and of the possible. Tom Bradley was a survivor; his forte was dealing around the edges, working for that gradual change. "It never occurred to me to become an activist," his daughter Lorraine would later say. "Like Daddy, I always thought I could do more good by setting a positive example."

CHAPTER 9

Integrating the Garbage

••••••••••••••••••••••

Sam Yorty, the new mayor of Los Angeles, was a small man with wavy hair and a nice smile who had the look and feel of someone who, had he not gone into politics, would have been selling refrigerators in a suburban Sears: Ronald Reagan with a quicker mind and a cheaper suit.

He'd grown up in Nebraska, the son of an Irish housewife and a German-Irish contractor who early on injured his back in a fall from which the family's fortunes never quite recovered. Young Sam grew up poor, and at seventeen he headed to Los Angeles. A little man from a humble background, he always had big ambitions. In 1961 he had squeaked into the mayor's office with a margin of victory delivered by the most diverse groups in Los Angeles: white suburban housewives and the city's rapidly expanding black and Latino communities. The themes he used to get their votes were equally as disparate. To the housewives he promised to do away with the trash-collection system, which required them to sort their tin cans from the rest of the garbage, a small inconvenience but enough of an annoyance to win him some votes. And to L.A.'s blacks and Mexican Americans, he promised to integrate the Los Angeles Police Department. And in a sense Yorty had done so. For it was that campaign promise that had pressured Bill Parker into moving on the issue. Sam Yorty also promised to name a new police commission that would no longer be a Bill Parker rubber stamp. "I wouldn't have faith in this commission," he declared at a press conference during the home stretch of his campaign. "I would want my own people, who will back the police department and also be fair to all the people of the city." Once in office, said Sam Yorty, he would give Bill Parker some serious schooling in public relations.

Then, shortly after his election, Yorty held a press conference and charged that Bill Parker had used his Intelligence Division to spy on him, his aides, and contributors—on "hundreds of people." It was, said Yorty, "perfectly obvious that the department was used to check the history from childhood to the current date of everybody even remotely connected with my campaign." Perfectly obvious that the LAPD had conducted a "gestapo operation." Next month, vowed Sam Yorty, when he was sworn in as mayor, he would use his power of "subpoena" to get to the bottom of the episode.

When Bill Parker learned of all this, he reacted as if a slightly annoying fly were buzzing 'round his head. "I've survived changes in other administrations and I'm still here," he said. "I have no intention of retiring." Then he added, "I read in the papers that he [Yorty] wants to talk to me; I assume he'll get in touch."

They met in Yorty's home high atop a hill in the San Fernando Valley, and afterward went to a restaurant on Ventura Boulevard. There, all "conflicts" were "clarified to their mutual satisfaction," as they later declared in a joint statement. Together, they also asked the DA to halt the investigation of Yorty's spying charges against Parker. Later in the day, when Yorty accidentally ran into the district attorney at the Biltmore Hotel, he seemed a bit frantic, "bracing up" the DA as he urged him to drop the inquiry.

Afterward, a rumor made the rounds that Bill Parker had shown up at their meeting with an attaché case bulging with Sam Yorty's intelligence files, and that when he returned, the briefcase was empty. It was a story filled with cop and reporter overkill. Bill Parker, overall, didn't need any bulging briefcase. A mere whisper in Yorty's ear would have sufficed. With the kind of background Sam Yorty had, it would have been a miracle if Bill Parker had not had a bulging file on him going back to the days of Red Hynes. He'd been elected to the state assembly at just twenty-seven as a fiery New Deal progressive and was rumored in those early years to have been the lover of the equally fiery communist activist Dorothy Healy. He'd gone on to become a perennial candidate for mayor and for the city council. In 1949 he was reelected to the state assembly and the following year won a congressional seat. During the fifties he lost two runs for the United States Senate and in 1960 supported Richard Nixon over John F. Kennedy for the presidency. "I can not take Kennedy" was his theme that year, as with the merest nod to subtlety, he accused the man soon to be the nation's first Catholic president of taking "advantage of his religious affiliations." The following year he was elected L.A.'s mayor, at last winning the post that had eluded him ever since the days back in 1938 when his radical allies had deserted him and supported the more electable Fletcher Bowron as their mayoral candidate against Frank Shaw. "From that day on," said the socialist journalist Reuben Borough, "[Sam Yorty] was a Red-baiter, [without] a shred of those old progressive principles left in him."

It would have been impossible, in any case, for Sam Yorty as mayor to have indulged in the trappings of power or the lifestyle he so relished without a rapprochement with Bill Parker. For his schedule in office was less than taxing. "I'd be in the police building, and at ten o'clock in the morning a helicopter would [fly over]," says Tom Reddin. "That was the mayor going to work . . . he'd come to work by police helicopter almost every day . . . and he'd be there from about ten to twelve. . . . [Then] his driver would meet him and take him wherever he wanted at noon, and nobody would ever see him again." "Wherever he wanted," according to Reddin, usually had to do with an "assignation apartment" on the Sunset Strip. Yorty would be chauffeured to the apartment, pull into a convenient back-lot parking space, get out, step into an elevator, go up three floors, and enter a huge apartment with gold mirrors and bathrobes in the closet. There, he would enjoy the afternoon.

Over the years Yorty had gone from ardent New Dealer to right-wing Democrat. By the midsixties he would become the outspoken defender of the frightened white middle class, hoping to ride the same wave of fear, discontent, and indignation that would propel his fellow ex–New Dealer Ronald Reagan into the governor's mansion in Sacramento in 1966. In any case following his initial meeting with Bill Parker there would never again be any question that Bill Parker ran the LAPD and got what he wanted.

But Yorty got something in return. That same year Tom Reddin, the newly appointed chief of the LAPD, received a call from one of Mayor Sam Yorty's assistants. He wanted him, recalls Reddin, to put a tail on Otis Chandler, the young and mildly liberal new publisher of the *Los Angeles Times*, to "get something on Otis that we could use to get him off the back of both the department and Yorty." When Reddin refused, Quinn seemed surprised. "Parker would have done it," he said. Then Yorty's office sent over another mayoral aide who also brought up the fact that Parker would have cooperated and was also surprised that Reddin wouldn't. Reddin was surprised, too. Not just that they'd asked, but that as a result of dealing with Parker they'd so matter-of-factly assume that Reddin would spy on a *Chandler*, on the publisher of the *Los Angeles Times*. On the scion of the most powerful family in Southern California, not some starlet sleeping with the leader-of-the-month of the local chapter of the Black Panthers. But they kept on telling Reddin, over and over, that Parker would have done it, Parker would have done it. And undoubtedly he would have. For a political price.

CHAPTER 10

The Black Nirvana

·······················

Walking the streets of the black neighborhoods of Los Angeles in the spring of 1965, Tom Bradley had felt it building. In offices, stores, parks, churches, and meeting halls, the pent-up rage and hatred of the LAPD was pouring out, so strong people seemed unable to contain it any longer, so powerful you could almost taste it. So omnipresent that Tom Bradley had actually "predicted," as he later put it, "that this growing hostility and friction between the police department and a large segment of the black community could result in a major confrontation." But nobody was listening. Nobody who mattered. The *Los Angeles Times,* which didn't have a black reporter on staff, and the rest of the white media certainly weren't headlining the story. That wasn't their job. Their job was what it had always been: to boost and shape the image of Los Angeles as pure and untouchable, not to cover the complaints of some marginal, newly elected Negro councilman who seemed bent on tarnishing that image.

Tom Bradley had been out of the department practicing law for less than four years, and it was just two years earlier that he'd run for a seat on the city council. That had been his first campaign. Together with Speedy Curtis—a dynamic, black ex-cop who was serving as his advance man—he would circulate flyers and dance in and out of traffic, thrusting campaign material into the open windows of cars, trying to whip up people's interest and to build up the voter recognition he needed to complement the political connections he'd been nurturing ever since his days in vice and public affairs.

In the fifties and early sixties, he'd strengthened those ties as a volunteer in local Democratic clubs, and most especially in the liberal, biracial clubs of the California Democratic Council (CDC). Always immaculately, precisely turned out, tie never, ever loosened or undone, he canvassed the tenth councilmanic district with Curtis, working from early morning to late into the night. His hard work and those connections had paid off. In a highly diverse district where blacks comprised only one-third of the population and just 15 percent of the voters, he had won.

Nineteen sixty-three had been a breakthrough year in Los Angeles politics. Two other African-Americans, Billy Mills and Gilbert Lindsay, were also elected to the city council, albeit from heavily black districts. Before them no African-American had ever been elected to anything in Los Angeles. In fact, they hadn't even had started voting as a block until John F. Kennedy's campaign in 1960. Whatever political power did exist had been restricted to the local black churches and weekly newspapers, neither of which had much influence. But Sam Yorty had shown in his successful 1961 run for mayor that the black vote could be courted as a block, and that it had significance.

What was most extraordinary about Tom Bradley's victory, however, had little to do with the black vote. What was extraordinary was that in a time of increasing fear and racial polarization and in a district where neighborhoods were changing almost overnight, Tom Bradley had garnered enough white votes to win.

The hordes, those invading, alien black hordes were coming to Los Angeles as they were coming to big cities throughout America, instilling fear and loathing in their wake. In the span of less than twenty-five years, the number of African-Americans in Los Angeles County had increased almost ninefold, with the biggest increase by far coming within the confines of the city where, by 1965, blacks comprised 16 percent of the population. Oh, there was some goodwill among white people to be sure. There were those who sympathized with the astounding injustice that had been visited on black Americans. There were the Jews, for whom repression and segregation cut all too close to the bone, and there were those caught up by the righteous passion of Martin Luther King and the civil rights movement. It was that—all of that—that Tom Bradley had tapped into.

But already the Pharaohs, the Bartenders, and other black gangs were springing up in South Central L.A., and the area's low-income housing projects like Jordan Downs, Nickerson Gardens, and Aliso Village were becoming to Los Angeles what Cabrini Green was to Chicago: horror shows featuring desperation and depravity, mini-bantustans in what was once the heart of L.A. At the same time the local high schools—Jefferson, Washington, Fremont, Jordan—were already deteriorating, as the center of South Central expanded ever outward into surrounding areas like Inglewood and West L.A., and white Los Angeles raced to Orange County and the Valley.

South Central and the surrounding neighborhoods of Willowbrook, Avalon, Florence, Exposition, and particularly an area known as Watts were experiencing a jobless rate two to three times that of the rest of L.A. County. It was all there, the entire litany: crime rates were astronomical and upward of 60 percent of the people were on welfare. The schools were overcrowded, understaffed, and underfunded. The high school drop-out rates were soaring. The dismantling of the mass-transit system had made Los Angeles's public transportation the worst of any big city in America. It would frequently take hours riding on a bus to get to work. And South Central's aging housing stock, two-thirds of which was owned by absentee landlords, was rapidly deteriorating to the point of dilapidation. In 1964 white Californians reacted to that deterioration by voting two to one to overturn the state's fair-housing law. All of it, all of the problems of black urban America. There in abundance in the sprawling neighborhoods of South Central in 1965. There, despite the calm-looking, tree-lined side streets and neat, sun-baked swatches of green lawns that disguised it. There, within the heart of a city the rest of America still imagined was peopled by nothing but beach boys, movie stars, and perennially smiling suburban families living in five-thousand-square-foot ranch-style homes.

But South Central and the surrounding black neighborhoods were places with wounds rubbed raw by rage, poverty, envy and insanity. And by Bill Parker's police department. In the two-year period from 1963 to 1965, sixty black Angelenos would be killed by the police, twenty-seven of whom were shot in the back. Thousands of other young black men were simultaneously harassed in the street or beaten at the police station houses on Seventy-seventh Street, Georgia Street, or Juvenile Hall. "Many times," the veteran South Central community activist Ted Watkins would later recount, "I'd see a white policeman drop-kick a guy and laugh and say, 'Well, this is the first nigger I've kicked today.' I've seen that with my own eyes." Middle-class, suit-wearing blacks like the publisher of the *Sentinel* were being shaken down and harassed as well. Middle-aged and wearing a suit? So what? They could be making book, pushing numbers, pimping, dealing drugs. Brutal policing in black ghettos certainly wasn't unique to Los Angeles, but the LAPD's probing, invasive style was making the situation in L.A. even more combustible than elsewhere. That and its quickness to resort to violence at the slightest provocation. That and Bill Parker's unwillingness to concede there was anything at all that he or his department might be doing wrong.

When Tom Bradley tried to tell the white people downtown that the black people of South Central, the good Negroes—not just the wild-talking, dashiki-wearing brothers with mile-wide 'fros, not just the gang-hangers, but good, solid, churchgoing people—were deeply unhappy with the LAPD, he'd be met by The Wall. By this lead and steel wall of resistance from the mayor and city council, from the media, and from most white Angelenos. None of them seemed open to even considering the possibility that the complaints had any validity. And most of all not Bill Parker.

They were after his job. CORE, the NAACP, the ACLU, they were all trying to snatch it away. Roy Wilkins, the national president of the NAACP, had specifically criticized Bill Parker's LAPD in 1962. Officers had stopped two Muslims who were working for a dry cleaner and who thus had a suspicious amount of clothing in their car. Shots were fired, by whom was unclear, but seventy-five LAPD officers quickly massed at the local Muslim temple and sprayed the building with bullets as they entered. When they left, one Muslim was dead, four seriously wounded, and one permanently disabled. Three LAPD officers were also injured. Malcolm X, then a spokesman for the Nation of Islam, had also attacked Bill Parker over the same incident, accusing him of "filling his men with hatred of the black community" and of being "intoxicated with power." Wilkins from the NAACP, Malcolm X from the Muslims, James Farmer from the Congress of Racial Equality, all of them, Bill Parker believed, were after his job. Something was happening as America approached the midsixties, and nobody, least of all Bill Parker, knew what it was. What he did know was that the line, the line had to hold.

So when a group of local black ministers predicted, like Tom Bradley, that Los Angeles was on the verge of a racial confrontation that would "tear the city apart," Bill Parker responded. He declared that there was danger of "manufactured incidents" taking place if officers worked alone. From then on, he ordered, there would be two-man patrol cars in South Central and other black areas.

Mounting racial tensions in America had caused Harlem, Chicago, Philadelphia, and Jersey City to flare up in flames in the summer of '64. "Antipolice" violence was increasing in Los Angeles and was a constant threat, Parker pointed out. Still, a Harlem or Chicago was unlikely in L.A. Hadn't the conservative, business-oriented, Negro Urban League just ranked Los Angeles among the very best cities in the nation for African-Americans to live? Wasn't it true as Bill Parker himself had said in 1964 that "Los Angeles has never had segregation problems or problems of frustration similar to those elsewhere in the country"? Wasn't it all just a "highly organized minority" that was trying to undermine law enforcement in the name of some "new order of theoretical human rights"?

That was it. Two World Wars, a Great Depression, the massive migration from the farms of the South to the cities of the North and West, and a civil rights revolution had all taken place in Bill Parker's lifetime. And he was talking about the problems of America's cities as a struggle between "socialistic" and "capitalistic" values. It was as if it were still the nineteenth century and not the twentieth. "There was no realization," Tom Reddin would later say, "that a riot could happen here. There was no thinking about how you could cope with it . . . no sincere attempt to work with the community. . . . It was the product of calcification of the chief executive." Bill Parker had brilliantly transformed his department into a smooth, efficient machine. But efficient at what?

CHAPTER 11

Caught Flat-footed

·····················

From a pickup truck that had pulled up alongside of Lee Minikus came a voice. "See that man," said the pickup's driver as he pointed at a 1955 Buick Special, "I think he's drunk." Minikus, a veteran California Highway Patrol motorcycle officer, hadn't noticed the Buick, but when he looked over, the car did appear to be speeding, so he followed it as the driver, a young black man, made his way up El Segundo Boulevard into the small black community of Watts, which abutted South Central. Minikus, a lone white face in a sea of African-Americans, ordered the driver of the car to stop, walked over, and looked directly at a twenty-one-year-old neighborhood resident named Marquette Frye. One look was enough. This guy, thought Minikus, was clearly drunk. But he put him through the drill anyway—through the usual field sobriety tests that look like playground hopscotch but determine whether you're about to spend the night in jail. Frye was drunk, but he was happy drunk, and he joked as he went through the routine, putting on a show for the crowd that had been outside trying to cool off and was now gathering around to watch on this sweltering, insufferably hot evening of August 11, 1965. So good-natured was Frye, in fact, that he was even making Minikus laugh. When the tests confirmed that Frye was drunk, and Minikus informed him he was under arrest, Frye, as Minikus later told it, couldn't have been more cooperative; was, in fact, "real nice about it." The entire incident was on its way to being about as pleasant an arrest as a cop could make. Until Marquette Frye's mother, Rena, who lived only two blocks away, arrived on the scene along with his brother Ronald and began haranguing Marquette for being drunk. Now Marquette Frye was beginning to look like a kid, a fool, a chump. That was bad. When Lee Minikus reached over to actually take Marquette Frye into custody, he found out how bad. Marquette Frye jumped back, went into a rage, and began telling Lee Minikus just exactly what he thought about him and his bullshit arrest. Meanwhile, the crowd was really beginning to grow, "idle hands," as Bill Parker later put it, being "the devil's workshop." So Minikus's partner, who'd arrived on the scene earlier, radioed for some backup.

The best thing, the most prudent thing given the tensions of the times, would have been to back off, tell him to lock up his car, and let the guy go. This wasn't murder, armed robbery, or hit and run. Nobody'd been hurt. And drunk driving was viewed far less seriously in 1965 than today. But Minikus had already made the arrest. If he let Marquette Frye go now, he wouldn't have been backing off, he'd have been backing down. He couldn't do it. As the crowd continued growing to perhaps four hundred, and the backup officers arrived, Marquette Frye tried to slip away—to disappear and become invisible in the milling, increasingly menacing throng. And as he did so, one of the officers smashed his baton into Marquette Frye's forehead. Minikus then grabbed Frye and tried forcing him into a nearby patrol car. It was then that Frye's brother punched Minikus in the kidney, while his mother leapt on the CHP officer's back and tore at his shirt. Meanwhile, the crowd, which would reach about one thousand people, was growing ever bolder and increasingly turbulent. Minikus and the other officers finally wrestled the three Frye family members into a patrol car and sped off with them. Then an officer turned to a woman whom, he said, spit on him and grabbed her. As she struggled, he shoved her into a patrol car, which was quickly surrounded by the crowd. More reinforcements arrived, and finally—through a shower of rocks and bottles—the police retreated with their prisoner. The mob then began belting innocent, oblivious white motorists driving through the intersection with rocks and bottles. The Watts insurrection had begun.

* * *

The days that followed were a disaster for the entire city of Los Angeles, but most especially for Bill Parker and his police department. Part of the reason was Parker's health. He was ill, mortally ill with a ballooning aorta—a heart aneurysm in the principal artery carrying blood from his heart that had rendered him, at sixty-three, a man of greatly diminished vigor. The drive, the energy, that had enabled him to make thousands of speeches and to transform the LAPD during the 1950s was no longer there. He tried to play it down. He was not interested in the anonymity of retirement, of endless days spent sitting in the living room of his home in the hills of Silver Lake with his wife, Helen, and their pet Weimaraner, Lex, while somebody else ran his police department. But when the insurrection and rioting in Watts erupted, he simply was not physically able to take personal charge of its suppression. Nor was he—or anybody else in the department—prepared to take charge and to deal with the chaos and rage, with the widespread looting and mindless violence, with the *revolt* that was taking place. It was still a new thing in American law enforcement, this kind of massive racial insurrection. There had been violent protests and riots in Chicago in 1919, in Harlem in 1935 and '43, and in the summer of '64 in four different Eastern cities. But not on this scale. And the closest thing the LAPD had to a plan was the old, outmoded antipicket, antilabor techniques for demonstrations from the 1930s. Riot control back then had been union control: wedge formations, flailing batons, small contingents of cops barreling through the demonstrators, splitting the protesters in half, dispersing them in two different directions and then surrounding the leaders and hustling them away from the site. The remaining strikers or demonstrators would then, like a chicken with its head cut off, run around aimlessly until the protest petered out. If there was something bigger, you formed a perimeter and let it play itself out.

But this thing in Watts had no leader. It was no demonstration, no strike. Nor was it confined to a couple of blocks outside a factory. And it wasn't dying down. No. It was taking place in an area encompassing over forty-six square miles, over an area roughly the size of San Francisco. And in those forty-six square miles people were shooting at police officers, hurling Molotov cocktails and sniping at firemen, burning buildings, setting whole blocks on both sides of the street ablaze, breaking windows, looting stores, overturning cars, beating innocent people. It was something new. A large-scale uprising. Somewhere between ten and seventy-five thousand of the area's five hundred thousand residents were actively involved. Bill Parker's oft-predicted anarchy had come to pass. "One person," as he later put it, "had thrown a rock, and then like monkeys in a zoo, others had started throwing rocks."

That Bill Parker had some inkling of what should have been done to try to stop what was now happening may have been reflected about three weeks earlier when he called Jim Fisk into his office. Fisk, who by then had risen to the rank of inspector, was the only one on his staff—the only one he knew in the department—said Bill Parker, who had "any interest in blacks." And right then and there he told Jim Fisk he was appointing him director of community relations. Fisk didn't know whether to be flattered or appalled. "At the time," as Fisk later recalled, to be thought of as "having good relations with the black community was to be considered a traitor."

The uprising had started on Wednesday evening and by Friday had turned into a full-scale riot so completely—so horribly—out of control that it reached the point where Bill Parker had to do what he was loath to: ask the assistance of the National Guard. At the same time, while designating Tom Reddin as the man now in overall charge of combating the violence, Bill Parker made what was for him a startling admission: "Don't ask me how to fight the riot," he said to Reddin, "I never fought one. Nobody's ever fought a riot like this. How should we know?"

Nobody knew who was in charge. Parker, who had created the Seven Dwarfs so that he could never be upstaged, circumvented, or replaced, for whom the word *control* was a mantra, had told Tom Reddin that he— Reddin—was in charge, while at the same time neglecting to inform Roger Murdock, the chief of patrol, who'd been running the department's operations since the outbreak of the rebellion. As a result, the command structure was thrown into even more confusion, and Reddin and Murdock wound up giving conflicting orders, which Bill Parker did nothing to rectify. "Just call me every morning at eight o'clock and tell me what happened the night before so I can be well informed with the press," he told Reddin.

Among those on the other end of those orders was Daryl Gates, a young inspector, serving during the rebellion as a field commander. Roger Murdock would give him one set of directions during the day, and Tom

Reddin, different instructions at night. Finally, Gates approached Reddin and said, "I wish you guys would make up your mind who's in charge here."

In spite of the vast investment in time and money the LAPD had poured into its Intelligence Division—the department had been caught flat-footed when Watts exploded. Bill Parker had created this highly mobile, technologically up-to-the-minute paramilitary organization whose efficiency was its pride and discipline its obsession, and it had virtually collapsed in the face of the unrest. Communications broke down. The department's various geographic divisions were sectioned off on different radio frequencies as opposed to one system throughout the city, and it became impossible for patrol cars brought in from areas like San Pedro or the San Fernando Valley even to talk to the cars from Central L.A. Downtown, it was mass confusion. Scores of LAPD officers were sitting in an auditorium at the department's headquarters waiting to be deployed, while 150 sheriff's deputies were standing by at the 190th Street Station. But nobody knew where to deploy them. The information flow had so broken down that the Command Center under Reddin and Murdock had to use motorcycle cops to shuttle messages back and forth from headquarters to the field because they couldn't talk on the radio. Officers could be sent down to Watts, could be a visible presence, but they couldn't be effectively directed into any kind of a coordinated strategy. There were other, equipment-related problems like an insufficient supply of tear gas and shotguns. But the real problem lay with a stunning tactical miscalculation: to pull back and avoid inflaming the situation, to retreat, form a perimeter, and let whatever was taking place within calm down, and then take it back. But fires, looting, and violence were breaking out all over Watts— all over this massive area known as South Central. They weren't taking back streets, they were giving up the streets. "We got there . . . formed squads, and handcuffed some people," Harvie Eubank, an LAPD officer at the time, would later say, referring to the initial disturbance after the arrest of Marquette Frye. "We went down both sides of the street, we had everybody contained and back in their houses." Then at about three in the morning, an LAPD inspector came up and told us to clear out. "We don't want to start a riot," he said. "I want you people to pull back." "We did start pulling back," continued Eubank, and "that's when they started breaking into the liquor store, looting it . . . started coming out of the houses . . . started firebombing. . . . When people started to see we were pulling back, they were setting fires block by block. We were several blocks from the location when we saw the smoke, and the first thing you know flames were going everywhere.''

The inspector on the scene that evening conveying the orders to pull back was Daryl Gates. Decades later, although acknowledging it was "obvious we were not equipped to deal with the situation at all," he would still express his disgust at the decision, and of how Deputy Chief Roger Murdock had "ordered us to retreat. . . . It turned out to be faulty wisdom, but, ordered to withdraw, we did. I felt pretty shitty about this, thinking it an unwise decision.'' But in an internal police report he wrote shortly after the tumultuous events of the evening of August 11, 1965, Gates seemed to have concurred: "A sweep of the area on foot was thought to be inadvisable at the time, primarily because of a lack of sufficient personnel and the belief that the disorder would subside by itself.'' Rocks were being thrown at his men from everywhere, Gates wrote in a follow-up report, and it "would take a large number of personnel to establish complete control.'' The LAPD had either allowed itself to be run out of Watts or decided it was not worth defending. Then it stood by and watched as it—along with vast sections of black L.A.— were consumed in flames. A little over a quarter of a century later that decision would come back as an eerie, powerfully haunting echo.

A massive show of force was what was needed. And on the third night the National Guard, which had been requested earlier in the day, arrived. It would take almost fourteen thousand Guardsmen, sheriff's deputies, and highway patrolmen along with the entire LAPD to finally bring the insurrection and riot, block by block, to a halt. Watts and vast areas of South Central were charred, wasted shells. The signature jive of a local black DJ, KGFJ's Magnificent Montague's "Burn, baby, burn!'' became the anthem of a rebellion that may have been cathartic and self-affirming but in the end would also prove mindlessly self-destructive; the first in a series of blows that would devastate South Central. Thirty-four people, the vast majority of them African-Americans, died. Over one thousand were wounded, and almost four thousand arrested. More than six hundred buildings were burned, destroyed, or damaged, at a cost of $40 million. Every one of the 103 LAPD patrol cars that entered the riot area was damaged. It was, at the time, the worst American insurrection and riot of the century.

Bill Parker's reaction made it clear that he had learned nothing from Watts. About two weeks afterward, he appeared on "Meet the Press" and blamed it on the Highway Patrol. If his officers had made the arrest, he assured the nation, "this riot would not have occurred." It was "the lack of training and experience on the part of the officers who made the arrest" that was at fault. Nor, he would add on another occasion, did he consider Watts to be "a race riot, since the rioters were all Negroes." What it was, said Bill Parker, was "people [giving] vent to their emotions on a hot night when the temperature didn't get below seventy-two degrees." With that dismissal Bill Parker also had a warning. "It is estimated that by 1970, forty-five percent of the metropolitan area of Los Angeles will be Negro," he told a local television audience. "If you want any protection for your home . . . you're going to have to get in and support a strong police department. If you don't, come 1970, God help you."

CHAPTER 12

Insulting Reactions

··

Sitting in the ornate chambers of the Los Angeles City Council, Bill Parker was unable to contain himself any longer. Turning to the council president, he asked if he might make a statement and then, not waiting for a reply, shot to his feet and shouted out his indignation: "It has not yet been established," he told the dozen or more astounded council members, "that the Watts riots were caused by the Los Angeles Police Department—regardless of the assertion of one of our former members." One of our former members? Well, there could be no question about whom he was referring to, and as if on cue, Tom Bradley, joined by three or four other council members, also jumped up, clamoring to be heard. But Bill Parker, although already weakened by his heart condition, would not yield. Over the din he continued, "A recent public opinion survey of the Watts riot made by the California Highway Patrol relegated the police faction [of the causes of the insurrection] to fifth position." Then he added, "I deeply resent statements in a public body that the police department was responsible."

With that, Tom Bradley, normally the model of decorum, told Parker that he ought to go into the room where the council proceedings were taped and listen to see if he could hear such a statement—which, Bradley asserted, "was never made."

The question over which Parker and Bradley were clashing had powerful implications: the establishment of an inspector general independent of the chief of police who would investigate citizen complaints against police officers. It was a key recommendation of the McCone Commission, which had been appointed by California governor Pat Brown to investigate the causes of the insurrection. But when Bradley unsuccessfully proposed it to the city council, Bill Parker was incensed. "Independent" meant he and his successors could not control it. And Bill Parker, like Tom Bradley, knew that he who controls the investigative process determines the outcome and ultimately controls discipline. Bill Parker was unwilling to give away anything. But *that* would surely have been the last thing he'd have given up.

So it went with Bill Parker and Tom Bradley over the fall of '65 and winter of '66. Every inquiry by Bradley or his fellow black councilman Billy Mills, every statement that had about it the merest whiff of criticism or suggestion of reform of his LAPD was met by Bill Parker with the fierce, indignant, unyielding outrage of a parent defending his errant, spoiled child against the world.

Not to have embraced some of the McCone Commission's recommendations, not to have bought some time with moderate blacks like Bradley until the heat was off, not to have come up with his own recommendations—which both he and the department could live with—showed just how out of touch Bill Parker had become. He'd been fighting the city's Tom Bradleys every step of the way. Their clashes on the council floor and in the press would be played out over innocuous matters like bullhorns and substantive ones like inspector generals. But for Bill Parker, the ailing commanding general of the old WASP order, and for Tom Bradley, the vigorous, ascendant young prince of the new L.A., they all went to the heart of the matter.

Take the bullhorn controversy. Testifying before the council about the causes of the insurrection in September of '65, Bill Parker stated that there was mounting evidence of an organized effort to escalate the violence and keep it going. An unarmed youth toting a bullhorn had been spotted directing both the traffic and the riots, said Parker. The department, he said, had identified both the youth and his organization but was not at liberty to reveal any until it obtained "legal evidence."

Tom Bradley seemed to understand there was more at stake in Parker's accusations than just some bullshit about a bullhorn. That what Parker was really talking about was how Watts would be defined. Had it been a riot in which black radicals schooled in Marx and Che and Trotsky fired up the city's punks and criminals? Had it been fueled by those radicals and by the prodigious amounts of T-bird and malt liquor and reefer that those punks and criminals were consuming while the rest of L.A.'s good, decent, *content* Negroes watched in horror? Or was it a combination of that, and of deep, ingrained factors from poverty to rage, not the least of which was a thuggish, uncomprehending police department?

In any case, Tom Bradley wouldn't leave the bullhorn question alone. He had backed Bill Parker into a corner, then left him no way out, pressing Parker to name the organization, to name the "youth." Frustrated, flustered, Bill Parker finally snapped at Bradley, "Why don't you [just] disregard this? You know the question was answered, yet you persist." Bradley must have sensed that he had Bill Parker, that Parker had taken a description by a local television reporter of a man with a bullhorn directing traffic (a man, as Bradley had already discovered, who was an antipoverty worker who'd gotten the instrument from none other than the LAPD's Watts substation) and was trying to float it as some proof of a revolutionary conspiracy. So Bradley had a reply. "It's a question of judgment," he told Bill Parker.

The tarnish was spreading on his Golden Boys, and later that afternoon Bill Parker exploded. "I think you are trying to pin this [uprising] on the police," he told Bradley. "[And] I'll go to my grave thinking this was your intention." He announced, "This is not an inquiry, it's an inquisition!"

But while Tom Bradley may have scored an occasional point, he never won big with the LAPD. City council members remained "so reticent to get into a situation of fighting the police department" that, as Tom Bradley later put it, "you couldn't get two or three votes on any issue of that kind." And indeed, seven months after Watts, Bradley joined by the other two African-Americans on the city council, voted against a resolution "commending Police Chief William H. Parker for his conduct in the field of human relations." It passed, eleven to three.

In 1968, after a series of police shootings had once again outraged

South Central, Tom Bradley, still maintaining delusions of change, again called for an investigation. And once again he was met by The Wall.

Then, like a good fiscal conservative he'd turned around and opposed a costly change in the pensions of police officers and firemen that would allow their retirement pay and benefits to float ever upward with the cost of living. Although as a retired cop he would personally have benefited, he saw within the proposal, as he later put it in untypically dramatic fashion, the "seeds of disaster for the taxpayers." So he worked against the plan, only to see it pass as a ballot initiative. His opposition would never be forgiven or forgotten by the Protective League and its rank and file. Who the hell did the guy think he was?

Such was the power of the LAPD and such were the racial and ideological divisions within the city, that Tom Bradley's measured, ever-so-reasonable criticisms and calls for reform made him both a hero in South Central and among liberals, and a despised object of scorn among many cops. It wasn't much, what he was saying, in fact, it was mild, eminently reasonable. But unlike almost any other public official, at least he was speaking out, showing some balls, some sense of proportion. As a result, Tom Bradley would be thrust into the leadership of a new emerging liberal coalition in Los Angeles, while at the same time having laid upon him the accusation that has come to be among the most dreaded of all by politicians—particularly those who happen to be black and mildly liberal in a city with an overwhelmingly white electorate. Henceforth, Tom Bradley would be known as antipolice.

Like the city council sessions following Watts, Bill Parker found the McCone Commission hearings an insult. "The thing that irritates me," he told the commission, which had been appointed by California governor Pat Brown to investigate the causes of the insurrection, "is that you have all laid back there with bits of information . . . and asked questions on them as if you were cross-examining a defendant in a criminal action. . . . I resent having to deal this way." Bill Parker had had things his way for so long that he failed to realize the gift that Pat Brown had given him. Brown, a consummate politician, was facing a bruising reelection campaign the following year. The student protests at Berkeley in 1964 had made many voters angry, and Pat Brown had been harshly criticized for not having cracked down a lot harder on those frizzy-haired, dope-smoking, free-love freaks. He had also strongly supported the state's fair-housing law, a loser if there ever was one, that two-thirds of the electorate had voted to overturn. So much for principle. Pat Brown now had his own troubles. The vast majority of people in California were appalled by Watts. It was prudent to name a conservative man of stature to head the commission—more prudent still to name an entire commission that was decidedly conservative and let them take the heat. It was a wise strategy, and when the right chairman is selected, as was later the case in New York when Mayor John Lindsay chose Whitman Knapp to look into the police-corruption allegations stirred up by Frank Serpico, it can work brilliantly. You get credit for the appointment and the reform that's necessary without political fallout because someone to your right with impeccable establishment credentials has made the critical findings and recommendations. You were just passing them along. The man Pat Brown chose to head the investigative commission, John A. McCone, however, was no Whitman Knapp. True, he had the right pedigree: San Marino millionaire industrialist, Republican member of the boards of some of America's wealthiest corporations, recently retired director of the Central Intelligence Agency—he had it all. Except the detachment needed to leave his staff alone to develop a rounded picture of the events that transpired and the grace to let the chips fall where they may. Screw that. "Mr. McCone was the kind of guy who knew what caused it all before he started," Samuel L. Williams, a black attorney who served on the commission's staff, later told the *Los Angeles Times*. The messenger would be the message. McCone set the tone: meetings would be closed to the public; civil rights leaders and social scientists disregarded; an independent, impartial expert on police practices would *not* be hired to serve on the commission's staff.

Serving on the commission in addition to McCone was the vice chairman, a downtown corporate lawyer, a Democrat, and the future U.S. Secretary of State, Warren Christopher; a conservative black judge and ex-LAPD officer, Earl C. Broady; and the ultimate behind-the-scenes L.A. man of power and puller of strings, the downtown Republican businessman Asa V. Call, who, as the *Times* pointed out, "showed up at one of the [commission's] few public neighborhood gatherings . . . in a chauffeur-driven limousine." The panel's eight members weren't all conservative, but they were all stalwart establishment figures, most without links to the black community or experience in race relations.

The commission's final report, "Violence in the City—An End or a Beginning?" was received with outrage by blacks, liberals, and journalists familiar with the story. The California State Advisory Committee to the U.S. Commission on Civil Rights called it "elementary, superficial, unorganized and unimaginative . . . [displaying] a marked and surprising lack of understanding of the civil rights movement . . . [that] failed totally to make any findings concerning the existence or nonexistence of police malpractice."

But the commission's findings weren't quite a whitewash. The myth of Los Angeles as the African-American nirvana was dispelled. Housing, said the report, was bad, transportation terrible, unemployment very high, and the schools in great need of improvement. "The existing breach between rich and poor, black and white, in Los Angeles," concluded the commission prophetically, "could blow up one day in the future."

Moreover, the commission pointed out the police commission wasn't leading the department, and people were rightly dissatisfied with the LAPD's complaint procedure. It even suggested an entirely new internal disciplinary system—the outside inspector general that Tom Bradley had advocated. But when it came to assessing responsibility, it lapsed into the language of caricature. What had caused Watts to explode? "The economic and sociological conditions in our city that underlay the gathering anger which impelled the rioters to escalate the routine arrest of a drunken driver into six days of violence." That was that. The commission would acknowledge the "bitter criticism" and "recurring charges" of "police brutality," but go no further. In fact, as the city council had done, they praised Bill Parker and the LAPD, although it wasn't quite the council's glowing affirmation: "Despite the depth of feeling against Chief Parker expressed to us by so many witnesses," the commission wrote, "he is recognized, even by many of his vocal critics, as a capable chief who directs an efficient police force that serves well this entire community." But it didn't matter. None of it mattered. White people were scared. They didn't want change. Even without Bill Parker's bombast and the department's constant harassment and casual brutality, by 1967 riots and insurrections had broken out in 150 American cities, and there would be more—many more—to come. That year, President Johnson convened another panel called the Kerner Commission after its chairman, Gov. Otto Kerner of Illinois. In its report on those 150 riots and rebellions, it wrote, in a line that would become famous before its truth came to pass with such terrible swiftness it became a cliché, that the United States was in danger of becoming "two societies, one black, one white—separate but unequal." In the decades to come, lip service would be paid to reforming the LAPD, and to community relations. But it was all nonsense, window dressing. The political will wasn't there, in or out of the department. The Kerner Commission had found the truth and had spoken it. Bill Parker, too, knew the truth.

Sam Yorty, now in his second term, reacted to the insurrection in Watts by playing the outraged defender of the frightened white middle class. Yorty, Tom Bradley would later tell the *New York Times,* "used to be known as a man who would not tolerate any kind of racial slur. He'd walk out of a party if they started telling anti-Negro jokes. But then came the Watts riot. [And] when the mayor came down hard on the side of Chief Parker and the police, he got a lot of mail supporting his position." A lot of mail. Seventy-five thousand people wrote or telegraphed Sam Yorty at City Hall supporting his tough stance on Watts, while only 337 had been opposed. After that, Yorty, who had helped integrate the notoriously racist fire department, spurred Bill Parker into integrating the LAPD, and who had appointed blacks to many of the city's important commissions, seemed a different man. In 1966, he went with Bill Parker to Sacramento and warned the Criminal Procedure Committee of the California State Assembly that unless an antiriot bill was passed, Los Angeles would face "urban guerrilla warfare." The bill was vaguely worded, and when members of the committee began questioning its constitutionality, Sam Yorty could barely stop himself from throwing up his hands in disgust. Look, he said, "I can tell when a committee is going to flyspeck a piece of legislation. Let's leave that to the courts. We are constantly subjected to psychological warfare and threats, we face urban guerrilla warfare—an absolute plan to burn and sack a city! We are dealing with facts." Sam Yorty's facts, however, were meager: stacks of handbills and placards from the perennially marginal Progressive Labor Party, which, he pointed out, was a "Peking-dominated communist organization."

Then, dramatically pointing to a huge map delineating "South Los Angeles' ghetto boundaries," and noting the high concentration of factories there, he proclaimed, "This highly inflammatory literature and the map of the industrial heartland of Los Angeles goes to the point of saying it should be burned out!"

With both white and black college students carrying around Mao's little red book, revolutionary literature with headlines like "The Revolt in Watts and the Coming Battle" and "Reactionary Violence Must Be Met by Revolutionary Violence" did have a certain ring of authenticity. And Sam Yorty and Bill Parker were playing it for all it was worth. "We are sitting on a powder keg," Parker, who had earlier asked the L.A. city council to double the size of his police department, told the committee. Relations between the black community and the LAPD were so tense, he said, that "we're talking about putting moats around all our new buildings. . . . The seeds of another major riot have been sown. Legally the police are unable to neutralize the agitators." Then, emotionally, he told the committee, "I'm recuperating from a cardiac condition and I can't take this sort of thing much longer."

His testimony was passionate, but Sam Yorty's was so compelling that a sympathetic Republican committee member asked the mayor if he would mind if the proposed bill was called the Yorty Antiriot Act. And when Sam Yorty replied that he didn't care what it was called, as long as it was passed, the bill was so named.

If any further proof was needed that Sam Yorty had become the sixties equivalent of a cheerleading Laker Girl for the LAPD, it came about a year later when ten thousand antiwar marchers massed at Century City, a huge complex of offices and hotels adjacent to Beverly Hills, to protest a speech that was to be given by President Lyndon Johnson. As they peacefully marched down the Avenue of the Stars toward Johnson's hotel, they were met by thirteen hundred LAPD officers wearing helmets, carrying guns, and holding batons, which they started swinging as they turned on the overwhelmingly white, middle-class men and women with a frightening, never-to-be-forgotten ferocity. In the days that followed, "Mayor Sam," as he had come to be known, was ready with an explanation. "The hard core of the demonstrators," he told the New York Times, had "pushed the dupes forward," and "of course, some of those people smeared themselves with red paint to make it look like blood."

CHAPTER 13

The Legacy
•••••••••••••••••••••••

They still loved him. Loved him more than ever. Not in spite of Watts, but because of Watts. He was there for them like some mythic father figure speaking out and protecting them against forces they could not comprehend: civil rights marchers, antiwar demonstrators, student protesters, long-haired hippies, free love, drugs, and now riots. What was happening to their America? Bill Parker knew. He'd been talking about it now for his entire sixteen years as chief—the moral rot, the anarchy, the communists, the decay, the blacks and their social "revolution." Earlier in 1966, after an LAPD officer had shot and killed a black man, Leonard Deadwyler, as he was rushing his pregnant wife to the hospital, Bill Parker was asked what he intended to do about the killing. "I am going to do nothing," he replied. "Bova [the officer who had killed Deadwyler] is not suspended. . . . Police are not supposed to stand by and watch a car speeding down the street at eighty miles per hour. This twenty-three-year-old officer did something he thought would successfully conclude a police action. All he is guilty of is trying to do his job. . . . More people defended Oswald [President Kennedy's assassin] than defended Bova." That was it. No apology. Only a counterattack. And he'd been right, and people, his people, loved him for it. That was evident by the almost deafening standing ovation that more than one thousand Marine Corps veterans had given to Bill Parker as he made his way back to his seat at the head table at the banquet at which he was being honored. In his hand was the specially inscribed plaque he'd just received from the men of the Second Marine Division Association at their seventeenth annual reunion. Only a month before, in June of 1966, he'd returned to work looking pale and gaunt, still a shadow of his former self after his major heart surgery the previous October. But he now was back. And here on a Saturday night, on July 16, in the Pacific Ballroom of the Statler Hilton Hotel, he was being feted and presented an award, along with the actress Betty Hutton and the comedian Joe E. Lewis. It wasn't the first such dinner Bill Parker had attended since his operation. In March, at the Biltmore, over twelve hundred people had gathered at a banquet hosted by the Greater Los Angeles Press Club, which had named Bill Parker its Headliner of the Year. Jack Webb, who was the affair's master of ceremonies, had joked then that Bill Parker "made more news in the past year than Batman, Sandy Koufax, and Don Drysdale." Later, the Press Club, still almost lily-white and overwhelmingly male, presented him with a gold-plated lifetime membership.

The award presented to him that evening from the Second Marines was special, as the Press Club card had been special. Everything after his operation was special now to Bill Parker, who felt lucky to be alive and, at sixty-four, had been given a new lease on life. It was a gift he intended to take advantage of. There was work to be done, a lot of work. He had received more than a thousand letters and telegrams during his recuperation at the Mayo Clinic's St. Mary's Hospital in Minnesota and had been encouraged and energized by them. They, too, were proof, if any were needed, of his popularity. "L.A. needs you!" That was their tone, their sentiment, Bill Parker had proudly recalled. The same sentiment that was now filling his ears with the applause of a thousand Marine veterans as he sat down at his table, leaned back in his chair, gasped for air, and died.

His death was played by the *Los Angeles Times* as if he'd been a sitting head of state. For four consecutive days it ran the story on its front page. Thirty-six hours after his fatal Saturday-night heart attack—thirty-six hours after the news had gone out on TV and radio airwaves across Los Angeles—the *Times* gave the event breaking-story status, running a front-page Monday-morning headline and a mammoth lead story, replete with glowing tributes from Sam Yorty, former mayor Fletcher Bowron, Governor Pat Brown, the California attorney general, L.A. city councilmen, county supervisors, police commissioners, officers on the beat, and the head of the Fire and Police Protective League. One picture in particular dominated the coverage. It showed Bill Parker in smiling conversation with the martyred John F. Kennedy, a powerful image in those years when JFK, then dead less than three years, was a national icon.

They laid his flag-draped casket in state, in the rotunda of City Hall. Then they buried him. Three thousand five hundred mourners, including sixty visiting police chiefs, overflowed the downtown cathedral of St. Vibiana and spilled out onto Main Street. There, they listened to the service—presided over by James Francis Cardinal McIntyre—over loud-speakers, while Monsignor Patrick Roche eulogized "the luminous qual-ity" of Bill Parker's life, and the "holy impatience [with which he] surged to meet the horse charging toward the apocalypse of our times."

Thomas Kilgore, the Western representative of the Southern Christian Leadership Conference, sounded the single sour note. "His death," said Kilgore, was "a loss in the sense [that] he put together a strong, disci-plined police force. But I think [it] will be a relief to the minority com-munity, who believes he woefully misunderstood the social revolution taking place." It was true.

Bill Parker was a white man's white man, a creature of the nineteenth century, born at a time when millions of Americans still regarded black people as cotton-pickin' darkies, a subservient race apart. How could he understand Black Panthers? How could he understand young men smok-ing reefer and refusing to fight for their country as he'd done? What did the Kilgores of the world expect? In other cities like New York where a mayor chose his own chief and he served at the mayor's pleasure, an anachronism like Bill Parker would have been eased out, despite his popularity. The Kilgores could have made themselves felt politically. But not in L.A. Power was still too tightly held. Parker was too shielded by fear and the city charter. So the *Times* and the *Herald* in their eulogizing editorials spoke the dominant view. Bill Parker, wrote the *Times,* was "the man who devoted his life to making this the best-policed city in the nation." "He had been the recipient of scores of honors and awards," said the *Herald,* a record that "even brought him world renown."

The legend of the Golden Boys would have Bill Parker as an almost mythic figure—the white knight who fought his way to the top and single-handedly cleaned up the department's historic corruption. But that struggle was fought and won by Clifford Clinton, Fletcher Bowron, and the hundreds of churchgoing reformers and Depression-radicalized men and women who successfully brought down the Shaws and James Davis. And when Brenda Allen's prostitution operation threatened their reforms, it was Fletcher Bowron who acted with power and swiftness and forced the resignation of Chief Jack Horrall and his top assistant.

But there were areas where the department wasn't merely selling the lie of the legend. Bill Parker did make a certain kind of honesty—that of refusing to take payoffs and bribes (as opposed to doing what was necessary to get the job done)—the ethos of the department. And through tough investigation and harsh punishment he cemented that ethos and sent a message: that kind of misconduct would not be tolerated. It was a natural extension of who he was: he refused to use a city car except for city business, paid careful attention to who paid for a meal, and lived much of his life in an exceedingly modest home. When he died, his estate consisted of that home and about $13,500 in personal property. After him there would be LAPD officers who formed a burglary ring in Hollywood, and LAPD officers who hired themselves out as contract killers. But they were renegades, anomalies, not what Bill Parker's LAPD stood for.

The political support he engendered for the department wasn't any PR delusion either. It enabled the LAPD to offer salary and fringe benefits that—when combined with the "Dragnet" public-relations hype—began to attract recruits from all over the country.

His absolute gut-level hatred of East Coast gangsters did make Los Angeles inhospitable for them. But the legal action in nearby Las Vegas, Earl Warren's crusade against gambling, and the fact that Jack Dragna and Johnny Rosselli were over the hill by the early fifties were equally important. But he knew his constituency as he knew his gut. And he used the fear of organized crime to rebuild the intelligence squad into a division and turn it from gangsters to other predators L.A. had no place for: Reds, alleged Reds, liberals, civil rights activists, and critics of the department. This time, however, Bill Parker, not some hack politician, controlled it.

Troop deployment, investigative techniques, and police procedures grounded in scientific theory, he instilled them all in the LAPD, having learned well the lessons of August Vollmer. And when he did, they were fresh, overdue, and innovative. But when the fires came to Watts, Bill Parker had not a clue why they were burning. He understood in theory for he was well versed in sociology and even social psychology; but he had no visceral understanding about exactly what was happening or why. He was too much the white man, too much the old man, too much the closed-down cop. "We're on the top, and they're on the bottom," he would say after the Watts rebellion. It was the remark of a gloating seventeen-year-old, not of a mature public official.

The reforms he'd worked for all his life—the necessary reforms that protected the department from being used as a political tool—would become distorted under him, and in time, deeply self-serving, bureaucratic impediments to reform. Bill Parker created an unaccountable bureaucratic power. Then he showed the entire city, the entire nation, that the chief of police of Los Angeles was not just some goddamn civil-service department head running the harbor in San Pedro or picking up garbage or putting out fires, but instead was one of the most important players in the political life of the city. His message was clear: independence from "political interference" meant nobody fucked with his department, but he could pop anybody he wished. Politicians would come and go, but Bill Parker and his descendants would impose their values, say what they pleased, ignore the political winds, and with no mandatory retirement age, stay as long as they wished. Over the next quarter century, they and the LAPD would be at the center of the city's public life.

And he took the police culture, as inbred and insular a beast as exists in America, and made it more so, isolating LAPD officers even further from the community than they were in other big cities, deliberately setting his cold, Joe Friday, New Centurion professionals apart from the rest of the city. The arrogance of power began filtering down the ranks. They were superior to civilians. They were the lice exterminators. And blacks, Latinos, gays, freaks, punks, hippies, artists, street people, students, protesters, political dissidents, and all questioners of authority knew it. "The L.A. cops are idealists, almost fanatical in believing the righteousness of their case," said rock star Jim Morrison in 1969. "They have a whole philosophy behind their tyranny." That philosophy—proactive policing— would also become the department's pride. The department would go after them all and insist on enforcing every law with a weird Germanic zeal. Bill Parker passed that on, too. Not only to the LAPD, but to police departments throughout Southern California.

Finally, Bill Parker produced a system where the stairway to success was education, "professionalism" was the byword, and civil service was

God. But that system would perpetuate discrimination against the department's blacks and Latinos, discouraging their promotions and entry into specialized units. This, too, he passed on to his successors as if from the Mount.

And because Parker always knew he was right, it was only natural that the hierarchy that developed under him would know they were always right, too. Their world would stop with his death in 1966. The opening shots in the torrent of change that white, Anglo-Saxon America would undergo had been fired in Watts. The two incandescent decades after World War II when America had stood alone and reigned supreme over half the earth were already dying. Vietnam, and then the economic re-emergence of Japan and Germany, would modify that reign internationally; while at home, the mass migration of millions of impoverished blacks from the South, and of Hispanics and Asians, would continue to transform the face of America's cities. And nowhere, save perhaps New York, Detroit, or Miami, was all this more apparent than in Los Angeles. And no leaders would prove less suited by background and inclination to deal with these cataclysmic changes than the men formed and led by William H. Parker. Like Ronald Reagan, they were all about the past. But Los Angeles, of course, has always been about the future.

PART 4

UNDER SIEGE

....

CHAPTER 1

False Breezes

·····················

In January 1967, six months after Bill Parker's death, Sam Yorty urged his police commissioners to choose Tom Reddin as the LAPD's new chief. Yorty liked Reddin, who was a deputy chief. They were both gregarious, ruddy-faced, glad-handing Irishmen who loved a good story and a funny joke, would talk to anyone, and shared an ambition born out of the grinding poverty of their childhoods. Unlike Ed Davis and Jim Fisk, his two competitors for the job, Reddin had attended college only sporadically and never graduated. Instead, he joined every professional organization he could, and relied heavily on his big man (6'4", 215 pounds), twinkle-eyed charm. He seemed to know everybody on the force and to have a moment to share with them before he'd walk away with their names mentally filed for future reference. He was a good listener and at least gave the appearance of understanding other people's point of view, a rare gift in Bill Parker's LAPD.

Under Parker, he'd been given the delicate, thankless task of cleaning out the drunks, slackers, has-beens, incompetents, and cronies from Thad Brown's Detective Bureau—all the deadwood that Brown couldn't bear to deal with himself. It was a measure of his diplomatic skills that he'd emerged without being labeled a hatchet man, his popularity still intact.

Later, as Watts was turning into a debacle, Bill Parker had placed Reddin in cocharge of the department's response. And while no one on the LAPD could take pride in his performance, Reddin's reputation was undamaged. As he worked the troops and the professional organizations, Reddin also worked the community, attending meetings, laying on the charm, making vital grassroots contacts. Ed Davis, by contrast, had spent his off-duty time in the Protective League, much the route Parker had taken. Jim Fisk, a "bookish man," a "PR man," as Sam Yorty would later describe him, was never really in the running in Sam Yorty's eyes even though he'd placed number one on the chief's list before Yorty chose Reddin in January of '67. Sam Yorty had made his disdain for Fisk, the department's community-relations specialist and "nigger inspector," very clear to his police commissioners.

Despite his popularity on the force, Tom Reddin soon ran into trouble with the department's hard-core, hard-line macho men. The very qualities that had brought him to the top—his willingness to meet and listen to anyone, to be cool and radiate quiet authority, to not make enemies or pick fights unnecessarily, the fact that he was not, by nature, bellicose or combative—all now began to work against him. It all went against the culture of the department. The military vets, the guys who were smart but not real smart, the white men with attitudes, were dominant. Their credo was simple: if you were at war, compromise with the enemy was appeasement; if you were a soldier, it was weakness. And the enemy was very broadly defined. So Reddin's attending virtually the entire calendar of events at the new, glamorous Los Angeles Music Center with his socially conscious wife, Betty, and being seen and photographed with the rich and famous of Los Angeles's cultural elite, just didn't sit well with the macho men. Nor did his going to UCLA—into Kosher Canyon, the despised home of all those wire-haired Jewish radicals and militant black and brown Panthers—to take evening classes with his wife. To take classes in subjects like drama, modern art, archaeology, and "Man in Contemporary Society." His wife, he would later say admiringly, hadn't let him "become a one hundred percent law enforcement officer" consistently acting as if "there was nothing else" in the world. Instead she had kept him "a whole person," not a "police beast."

But Reddin's social life was nothing compared to the changes he started making within the department. They were marginal really, a difference in tone and attitude more than in substance. The LAPD under Tom Reddin would continue to represent the people American big-city police departments always had: the monied and middle classes, the property owners and business interests. That wasn't going to change under Tom Reddin, who was no social theorist. Still, it was an extraordinarily difficult time to be a big-city chief of police. One segment of society was in rebellion, the other in reactive fear. The Black Panthers, the counterculture, the antiwar demonstrations—so much shit was happening that any savvy police executive after Watts would have recognized what needed to be done: meet with some of their leaders, meet with the Panthers, with H. Rap Brown, with anybody who wanted to meet and complain about the police. And let them posture, talk their talk, and vent their anger. Then give them a few things that really cost you nothing, that even help you. Expand community relations from about 4 to 120 officers, put Jim Fisk in charge, and let them catch some flack. And if Fisk was able to get a grant that employed some ex-cons as liaisons between the department and the community, why not try it out? And if petty-ass traffic tickets in South Central and in Watts were particularly galling to the impoverished people who lived there, well, give them warnings instead. And if black leaders are asking people to turn on the headlights during the day of his funeral as a way of honoring Dr. Martin Luther King after he'd been assassinated, well, then ask your patrolmen to turn on the goddamn headlights. All of these things, Tom Reddin did. And he set up community councils where officers met with local residents around the city, and he created an inspector general to monitor complaints and report directly to him.

And he might as well have gone ahead and kissed their asses, too. Working with ex-cons. Turning on your headlights to honor one of the biggest troublemaking flouters of the law in the history of the United States. Having a Community Relations Program and letting punks and Black Panthers spray their spittle in your face as they talked about your mother. People in the department not only despised it, they wouldn't comply. Maybe one-quarter turned on their headlights to honor King, but mostly it was a joke, and Tom Reddin and Community Relations head Jim Fisk were the punch lines.

It was a bum rap, of course; on things that really mattered, Tom Reddin had proven where he stood. He stoutly defended the bloody police riot that had occurred during the 1967 antiwar demonstrations in Century City and came down hard on the Watts community-alert patrol when its more militant, sometimes armed members began trailing around LAPD patrol cars, monitoring their arrests and threatening to make citizens' arrests of the officers if they witnessed any police brutality. Nor did he modify the provocative surveillance of almost every move made by almost every Black Panther in the city. He permitted the heir to Red Hynes's Red Squad, the fearsome 55-member Metropolitan Division, to grow to 220 members. And under the command of Deputy Chief Daryl Gates, these officers would go out and, as Gates put it, "roust anything strange that moved on the streets." The "shake, rattle, and roll boys" they were called within the department; their very presence on a scene designed to immediately convince people of the wisdom of driving quickly but carefully home and going to bed.

And under Reddin the use of helicopters had also been vastly expanded. They were valuable tools for policing in specific situations, but as an omnipotent part of the department's routine patrol, they became an oppressive feature of the city's culture.

In a volatile time, Tom Reddin's police department had become Bill Parker's with a ready ear, occasional smile, and a hint of a promise of better times in the future. It was a start toward something better, a tentative attempt to go beyond incessant prowling and attempts to set arrest records, and to move to something that in the long run might have produced a less hostile standoff between the LAPD, the city's liberals, and the young black men of South Central.

But the LAPD was this huge, bloated vessel that would take years to turn around, and a powerfully willed, highly motivated chief to steer it. Before anything could really settle in, Tom Reddin, at the age of just fifty-two, announced his resignation in April of 1969. He was quitting to become a television commentator on local station KTLA. They'd offered him $500,000 for three years with a two-year option, a salary almost six times the approximately $32,000 a year he'd been making as chief. He was tired, he would later point out, of putting in a seventy to eighty-hour workweek. He'd just had a physical exam in which he'd failed the treadmill test. He had things to say "to broaden the base of public understanding." Perhaps, he also no longer had the stomach for the conflict between his instincts and the loyalties that the job required. It had been a tumultuous two and a half years in Los Angeles: another near-riot in Watts; a shoot-out with the Panthers; a police riot in Century City; and Sirhan Sirhan blowing Bobby Kennedy's brains out in a pantry in the once-Hollywood-glamorous Ambassador Hotel. In any case, his decision turned out to be a disaster. His voice didn't broadcast well. He couldn't time his commentaries to end at the allotted time. He hated reading off a teleprompter, hated having to smile and sparkle while he made ridiculous happy talk with the anchor. He looked stiff. He felt wooden. Eventually KTLA took Tom Reddin off the air. He would then make an abortive run for mayor and lose badly before starting his own private-security firm. There he would sit in his office on Sixth Street, watching—as Ed Davis and then Daryl Gates fought with the world—thinking about what might have been.

One of the proudest symbols of LAPD law and order had also developed on Tom Reddin's watch: the Special Weapons and Tactics teams or SWAT. It was all so new, so cutting-edge back in 1969: sixty men in five-man squadrons trained and dressed like assault commandos, armed with AR-180 semiautomatic weapons, AR-15 semiautomatic rifles, twelve-gauge shotguns, tear-gas guns, a .243-caliber long rifle, and .45-caliber pistols, policing an American city. Then deputy chief Daryl Gates would claim credit for the name, although he had originally wanted to call the unit the Special Weapons Attack Teams. But Ed Davis, then also a deputy chief, was appalled by the notion of the word *attack* being in its title and insisted on the change. But its new name and image was perfect in the eyes of Bill Parker's protégé, associating the LAPD and its copycat departments in the South and West even more strongly with the world of the paratrooper and the Marine commando as opposed to a civil police negotiating and emergency unit. The teams would train in secret "deep in the San Fernando Valley" and meet regularly to train and "trade expertise" with the Marines at Camp Pendleton, according to Gates.

The need for some unit to deal with crisis situations was undeniable. Skyjackings, shoot-outs and hostage-taking were becoming a very real threat. And police departments were reacting accordingly. In Detroit in 1967, the police gunned down three men outside of the Algiers Motel, and the Chicago PD would brutally riot during the '68 Democratic Convention and literally assassinate Black Panther leader Fred Hampton and Mark Clark in 1969. But no one ever dreamed (at least not until David Koresh and more than eighty of his followers were incinerated in Waco almost twenty years later) that SWAT's meeting with the Symbionese Liberation Army (SLA) would end in the hellish nightmare that it did. The SLA was everybody's worst nightmare, but particularly anybody white and over forty. Led by a black revolutionary named Cinque, they had kidnapped Patricia Hearst—the twenty-year-old granddaughter of Californian newspaper titan William Randolph Hearst—from her apartment in Berkeley in February of 1974. Several months earlier the ragtag, multiracial group of young revolutionaries, caught up in the fervor of the time, had ruthlessly shot and killed the totally blameless superintendent of schools in nearby Oakland, leaving most Americans appalled.

After imprisoning Patty Hearst in a closet and brainwashing her, Cinque and the others then turned her out, in much the same way a pimp would turn out a young prostitute, transforming her into a revolutionary who was now called Tanya. Beyond the horror of it all, beyond the obvious insult to law and order, beyond the violation of the very heart of one of the California establishment's most prominent families, was the racial trauma the kidnapping involved. Patricia Hearst, previously an ordinary upper-class California debutante, was now robbing banks and serving the revolution, brainwashed and conquered by a wild black revolutionary. It confirmed every sexual fear that the white man had about every young black stud, every fear that millions of Americans had about all these revolutionary movements.

In May of 1974 the SLA arrived in Los Angeles. During the shoplifting of a pair of socks from a sporting goods store, Patty Hearst fired off about fifty rounds as cover while two SLA members—William and Emily Harris—fled. Most of the handful of people who constituted the SLA—including the Harrises—wound up in a small yellow bungalow in South Central L.A. When the LAPD received a tip, they surrounded the house with 225 officers. Despite the fact that nobody knew if Patty Hearst—at best an innocent kidnap victim, and at worst a brainwashed kidnap victim—was inside, a firefight quickly ensued. And with America looking on in gape-mouthed fascination, network television broadcast it all live. Over nine thousand rounds of ammunition were fired as police tear-gas canisters touched off a fire that quickly consumed the small wood-frame house. Patty Hearst, it turned out, hadn't been in the house, but six others were. Daryl Gates, who was among those in charge that night, said he was sickened by the sight and that "the memory of the fire devouring six people will always haunt me." But he also said this about the SWAT team: "They were intrepid; they were brilliant in their deployment; their execution was flawless. Soon, other law enforcement agencies began mounting their own SWAT teams. The whole nation had watched the shoot-out—live, on TV. Clearly SWAT had arrived."

*   *   *

Like those who worked on Eugene McCarthy's 1968 antiwar candidacy and Bobby Kennedy's star-crossed run for the presidency, the people who worked on Tom Bradley's mayoral campaign a year later would always remember it. By then, Bradley was not only the most prominent black politician in Los Angeles, but among the city's most prominent politicians, period. His decision to try becoming L.A.'s first black mayor would inspire over five thousand volunteers. History, they believed, was about to be made, and they were about to help make it.

Watts had been a booster rocket, accelerating the suburban migration and white flight that had characterized Los Angeles and the rest of the nation since the end of World War II. But L.A. still had the film industry and was fast becoming the center of the recording and television business as well. An economic boom was on the horizon. By the midsixties, tens of thousands of artists, designers, writers, critics, musicians, and architects from all over America, Europe and Asia were migrating into Los Angeles as they had to New York in the forties and fifties. Along with them, in first a trickle and then a tidal wave, came Mexicans, Salvadorans, Guatemalans, Armenians, Chinese, Koreans, Vietnamese, Filipinos, Iranians, Samoans, and Soviet Jews. Within a decade, they would transform the face of Los Angeles.

But 1969 belonged to earlier, more established immigrants: to the affluent liberals of L.A.'s largely Jewish Westside and to its African-Americans from South Central's black wards and churches; to them and to the women's organizations and labor unions and liberal clergy; to all of those coalescing around Tom Bradley and his campaign for mayor.

Among them and particularly among the black and Jewish Angelenos who constituted his coalition's backbone, Tom Bradley's candidacy aroused the hope that these two historic outsiders could band together and at last become the city's insiders. Their time, they felt, had come.

For generations their credo in Los Angeles had been *macht nicht kein tummel*—"don't make noise"—and perhaps as a result the city's Jews had prospered. They had come after the Gold Rush. German Jews with pushcarts and names like Newmark and Hellman. By the 1890s they had become prosperous merchants, and when the city's new society gathered in 1888 to found the citadel of the Los Angeles establishment, the California Club, 12 of the 125 charter members were Jewish. But as they died off, no new ones were accepted. Nor were they welcomed at the Jonathan Club or the other hallowed halls of wealth, power, and influence or permitted to join the pinnacle of local society, the Los Angeles Country Club. The massive wave of Eastern European Jews immigrating into the United States during the 1890s had been the catalyst for the new exclusion, magnifying anti-Semitism in Los Angeles, as it had in the rest of the nation. Louis B. Mayer may have been the highest-paid man in America, but he like the other Jewish moguls—the Goldwyns and Warners—who built and controlled the film industry knew their place in Los Angeles. They were not men to rock the boat. And they would be right. America in the twenties and thirties, after all, maintained a full-fledged apartheid system in a quarter of its states, an unapologetic pattern of racial discrimination throughout much of the rest of them, and a pattern of anti-Semitism and quotas at its major universities, corporations, and law firms. Pogroms, the outer edge of racist thinking, were just a generation away for many Jews. And pogroms were possible anywhere. *Macht nicht kein tummel.*

The Reds, the socialists, the politically conscious Jewish proletariat, they could fight off the attacks of Red Hynes and James Davis, but they were of little consequence. Led by Rabbi Edgar Magnin, the builder of the mammoth, landmark Wilshire Boulevard Temple, most of the rest of L.A.'s tightly knit eighty thousand Jews, would live their lives in the manner of immigrants of the time, eager for acceptance and determined to prove themselves the most patriotic of Americans.

After the Second World War, hundreds of thousands of Jews poured into Southern California, first from the Midwest, then from the Bronxes and Brooklyns of the East Coast. By 1969 and Tom Bradley's run for mayor, over half a million of them were living in Los Angeles County. By then they had made their own power centers and affluent lives on L.A.'s Westside and were both hugely successful and extremely powerful within the entertainment, garment, savings and loan, and real estate industries.

But it wasn't until 1960 that L.A.'s older German Jews and the newer arrivals of Eastern European descent banded together into the Jewish Federation Council of Greater Los Angeles, giving the organized Jewish community a united, soon to be highly influential voice.

At about the same time, Paul Ziffren, Lew Wasserman, Howard Ahmanson, Mark Taper, and other prominent Los Angeles Jews were being wooed by Dorothy Chandler, wife of Norman and mother of Otis, the scion of the *Los Angeles Times*. She needed money to build the downtown Music Center and for other philanthropic endeavors. To get it, she was willing to merge her mainline, downtown-Pasadena–San Marino social order of conservative Protestant old money led by the *Times* with the new liberal Democratic Jewish money of West Los Angeles and Beverly Hills, Brentwood, Bel Air, and the Pacific Palisades. Dorothy Chandler got her Music Center in 1964, and with it the centerpiece Dorothy Chandler Pavilion, Ahmanson Theater, and Mark Taper Forum; and the wealthy Westside Jewish establishment gained the beginnings of the social acceptance that had previously eluded them.

But still, very few of them were being hired by the prestigious, power-brokering downtown law firms, corporations, banks, or insurance companies. And in spite of the fact that their L.A.—the cool, green hills and ocean-view homes of the West Side and movie industry—was increasingly *the* L.A., many Jews still wanted into Los Angeles' inner circle. Full participation in the eating clubs, old-line law firms, banks, and corporations of downtown Los Angeles, and equal footing with the old money of San Marino, meant more than jobs and wider social acceptance. Particularly for Jews like Maury Weiner, who would become Tom Bradley's campaign manager, and Ethel Narvid, who campaigned for Bradley and became one of his top aides. Weiner was nine when Hitler went into Poland, and nine when he'd overheard his uncle lamenting the fact that all their relatives there were already surely dead; and Narvid, overseas with her husband in the judge advocate's office after the war, had been one of the first American women to personally witness the horrors of the concentration camps. For Jews like them the elimination of discrimination meant the elimination of the assumptions that underlay anti-Semitism and that gave validity to the merest possibility of an American Holocaust ever taking place.

By the late 1960s, the great civil rights coalition of African and Jewish Americans had already started to crumble in places like New York City. But the wrenching power struggles that would destroy it—such as the ugly 1968 New York teachers' strike that pitted black activists against a largely Jewish teachers' union—had not yet taken place in Los Angeles. The city's Jews were still liberal, and much of the New Deal spirit of its older generation had fused with the New Frontier idealism and civil rights and antiwar passions of a younger one. In L.A. the ideals of the alliance still held. Of course there was friction in L.A. Jewish shopkeepers and landlords in Watts were vilified with the usual talk of how they were taking money out of South Central and giving nothing back. And there was fear among working-class and lower-middle-class Jews during and after the Watts insurrection, and racial tensions in the city's schools. But it was nothing compared to what was going on in places like the Bronx and Brooklyn, where countless Jewish neighborhoods were turning black, poor, and violent almost overnight. Vast geographic segregation and a less hard-edged nature of life still existed in Los Angeles then. And so did the coalition.

For all its members, Tom Bradley was the dream candidate. But this was particularly true of the city's white liberals. For them Tom Bradley was Sidney Poitier in *The Defiant Ones* and *Guess Who's Coming to Dinner* without the blazing eyes or irrepressible sexual tension. For them Bradley was the personification of every well-meaning, painfully hilarious, Stanley Kramer, do-good, feel-good movie ever made. For them he was perfect. Handsome, charming, and imposing, he was "dignified" in the way that white people like black professionals to be—a quality only highlighted by that winsome, ready smile so capable of putting you at ease. Cosmopolitan and well educated, he seemed as comfortable with them as he was with his fellow blacks, and he brought with him a political philosophy that soothed mainstream liberals. He shared their moral commitment to civil rights, had marched with the Urban League and the local branch of the NAACP, but his goals were always reasonable, and he was, in any case, a politician, not a civil rights leader. "It wasn't a politician's business to be a civil rights advocate or spokesperson," as he would later point out. There was nothing phony about that position, that *was* Tom Bradley. Yet it was also the perfect political position for a black man in a city where African-Americans constituted less than 17 percent of the population, and even less of the electorate. In fact, for a black man running for mayor of Los Angeles just four years after Watts, just four years after Bill Parker had warned of all those Negroes multiplying like cancer cells, well, it was the only position that held the possibility of citywide electoral success.

As Tom Bradley well knew. He'd won his council seat in 1963 from a constituency that was only about 30 percent black, and in which they comprised just 15 percent of the voters. That victory had been no accident. "One of the most satisfying experiences [to come out of] that campaign was a statement that was made on the day of the election," Bradley would later recount. "In the campaign headquarters there was a blind man who had been coming in on a regular basis, working on the campaign. He had heard radio broadcasts [about Bradley] and he called me over and said, 'You know, despite all of the time that I have worked on this campaign, today was the first day I knew you were black.' That said a great deal to me because it was the way in which we tried to run the campaign: not on the question of color, just on the basis of issues, of qualifications, and what I'd like to see done in the district." The lesson of a more innocent time—biracial cooperation—became the essence of his public character and political persona, an integral part of his campaign strategy, and the cornerstone of his political life. Never would he be a black-agenda man. There was, to cite the smallest of examples, the matter of parades. Once he was mayor, he became a prodigious marcher in every ethnic parade from those commemorating Mexican and Philippine independence through those such as the annual Nisei and Korean festivals. But the only parade he did not participate in for half a dozen years was the one held to revere Martin Luther King—the one that traversed the heart of South Central and down the boulevard that bore King's name. He had become engaged in a blood war with a political enemy who was the parade's organizer and decided as a result to boycott the King parade, correctly gauging that he could do so without political damage, so broad-based was his support.

And when the explosive, rubber-meets-the-road issue of crosstown busing hit Los Angeles in 1977, Tom Bradley—who in Los Angeles' weak mayoral system had no direct jurisdiction over the city's public schools in any case—refused to take a stand. And he'd been right. Nothing either the courts or liberal politicians did in the sixties and seventies to try to alleviate segregation did more to promote it than busing kids out of their neighborhoods in the name of racial integration. But it was also true that nothing would have been more counterproductive to Tom Bradley's political career.

Yes, he was perfect for L.A.'s liberals, and perfect for its Jews. His victory would be their victory. His victory would be a symbol of the outsider making it, and many of them, psychologically if not in fact, were still outsiders, too. In that sense Tom Bradley *was* a movement candidate.

*　　*　　*

In a four-man field, Tom Bradley did astoundingly well in the 1969 primary, garnering 42 percent of the vote to Sam Yorty's 26 percent. It was an eye-opening victory, achieved on a shoestring budget, and his supporters felt he could now really take off. Statewide, he was already becoming the darling of the political establishment. Both of California's U.S. senators—the liberal Democrat Alan Cranston and the conservative Republican George Murphy—had endorsed him, as had the powerful speaker of the California Assembly, Jesse "Big Daddy" Unruh. Nationally his supporters included former vice president Hubert Humphrey and Democratic senators Eugene McCarthy, George McGovern, Edmund Muskie, and Ted Kennedy, and the Republican senators Jacob Javits, Edward Brooke, and Charles Percy. Moreover, Adlai Stevenson, the grand old man of the Democratic Party and twice its candidate for president, had even done a radio commercial for him.

The list of stars and other entertainment heavyweights on the Hollywood Committee to Elect Tom Bradley was like an entertainment industry who's who: Samuel Goldwyn, Burt Lancaster, Jack Lemmon, Sidney Poitier, Carl Reiner, Debbie Reynolds, Gene Roddenberry, Barbra Streisand, Elizabeth Taylor, Frank Sinatra . . . it was endless. With that kind of support and the money now coming in, they couldn't lose.

Sam Yorty did not take this lying down. He had, after all, plans to go national. Why else was he having his staff regularly send out five thousand reprints of his speeches and interviews to newspapers and television stations all over America? Why else had he gone to the Middle East and met with Arab leaders? Why else had he taken a virtual nuke-them-if-you-must position on winning the Vietnam War? Why else had he been dubbed the only mayor in the country with a foreign policy? But his national and statewide plans were now in jeopardy. Not only had Tom Bradley humiliated him in the primary, the *Times,* the downtown law firms, and the city's more powerful bankers and CEO's were growing increasingly unhappy with Sam Yorty. They had never liked him to begin with, this little upstart from the San Fernando Valley, and along with most of the major media had opposed his campaign for mayor eight years earlier. That he had won was a sure sign that their grip on the city was starting to slip. His victory had been a triumph of the conservative home-owning suburban Valley over the centralized, monopolistic power of downtown. Once in office, he kept himself in power with a network of grassroots, volunteer, neighborhood organizations and as many as one hundred thousand voters to whom his office would mail cards, letters, and questionnaires. By 1965, he had moderated his populist stances and had become sufficiently pro-downtown-business growth so that the *Times* found it possible to endorse him for reelection.

But nevertheless, they could not bring themselves to *embrace* Sam Yorty. The sheen of polyester radiated off him. He was too gauche, too obviously ambitious: a yokel attracting exactly the wrong kind of attention to the embryonic, would-be capital of the Pacific Rim. There was, for example, the 1967 cover story on him in the *New York Times* Sunday magazine. The writer, Jack Langguth, did a serious profile to be read by serious people in the powerful New York–Washington–Harvard Yard East Coast axis of government, business, and academe. And his assessment of Yorty was there in every other line. Clearly he found Sam Yorty, the mayor of Los Angeles, hugely, inadvertently amusing. It was not the image of the new Los Angeles that the city's power brokers wanted projected to potential investors. Downtown Los Angeles was rapidly deteriorating, becoming an increasingly marginalized slum. The engagement of a mayor was important. And Sam Yorty had spent well over two of the first six and a half months of 1967—to take just one period of time—out of town. Over his years in office, in fact, he'd traveled to West Germany for a film festival; to Eilat, a sister city to Los Angeles in Israel; to Vietnam; and to Jordan, where he met "with Arab leaders on means of restoring peace with Israel." Yet he was oblivious to the details of running the city, to the ins and outs of legislation and its implementation. And that was not the kind of man the *Los Angeles Times* and others with vast downtown real estate holdings needed in their efforts to revitalize the area.

Nick Williams, the paper's editor, pointed out another Yorty liability in 1966. Yorty, he said, hadn't made any "wildly racial statements. . . . But he [had] presented the image of a man on the side of the white majority against the black minority." A city in racial turmoil was another image the new *Times* and the new L.A. did not want for the city. Not after Watts. They needed someone to bring back some of that good-government harmony to Los Angeles, someone who was not, as Tom Bradley later put it, "literally despised in Washington" by the very officials charged with dispensing federal grants and programs desperately needed by Los Angeles. It wasn't that Sam Yorty was exactly a loose cannon. He could be dealt with by the people who ran Los Angeles. But not with any comfort.

Nevertheless, Sam Yorty wasn't going anywhere. He was an old warhorse able to perfectly gauge the class resentment, racial antagonism, and free-floating anger in the political wind because he himself was part of the breeze. He'd spent his entire adult life running for office and was not about to let this fellow Tom Bradley end it all. Not without first applying the cardinal rule of campaigning for any candidate buried deep behind a front runner: go down and go dirty.

Tom Bradley, he knew, was vulnerable. Watts had taken place just four short years earlier. Sam Yorty had taken a hard stand against it, conceding no fault on the part of the white man or the LAPD, a righteous position only strengthened in the minds of many whites by the explosion in America's urban ghettos following the assassination of Martin Luther King in 1968. Now, a year later, there were all these raised black fists. All these people named Mohammad with Xs after their names. All those "black racists" as Sam Yorty never grew tired of saying. All these slogans and groups: Black Power. Black Pride. Black Panthers. They'd tried to take over Watts. Now they were trying to take over UCLA and other universities with their white radical friends. And, with Tom Bradley, they were trying to take control of Los Angeles itself.

The fact that Tom Bradley had nothing to do with any of this was of no matter. It was all to be his fault. If the chief of police, Tom Reddin, chose to resign from office to pursue a lucrative career as a local television commentator, Tom Bradley would be blamed. "I think the fact you could get an antipolice mayor [if Bradley won] weighed on his [Reddin's] mind and was part of his decision," said Sam Yorty of Tom Reddin's resignation, in spite of the fact that Reddin had publicly stated that his decision had "absolutely nothing to do with the current mayoral race."

If white cops on the street didn't like the idea of a liberal black mayor, then Sam Yorty would accuse him of being "the biggest enemy of the police department in city government today." And then follow up the accusation by challenging people to "ask any policeman." Go out, said Sam Yorty, and "stop one on the street . . . and ask him how they [feel] about Tom Bradley." Stop one on the street! It was brilliant. The department was still 5 percent black and over 90 percent white, and most white cops *were* contemptuous of Tom Bradley. So just stop one. He'll tell you.

That animosity toward Bradley extended so deep into the Organized Crime Intelligence Division, which normally provided security for political candidates, that Tom Reddin asked Jesse Brewer, a black lieutenant in charge of community relations, to head Bradley's security detail during the campaign.

Fair-skinned, soft-spoken and handsome, Brewer was a former student at the great Tuskegee, and as middle-class and respectable as a Mormon deacon. He was a charming man, "dignified," smart, and popular within the department, a man willing to keep his counsel and cool his role, to fit in, get by, keep his mouth shut, and not step on anybody's toes. Even more than Tom Bradley, he was a gradual-change Negro. He'd fought in Italy as an infantry captain during World War II and had served on the Chicago PD before becoming disgusted with its corruption. In 1952, twelve years after Tom Bradley had been initially disqualified from the LAPD because of a "heart murmur," Jesse Brewer had come to Los Angeles to take the test for the LAPD. Back in Chicago, he received two letters, a week apart. The first congratulated him on passing the LAPD exam. The second was a notice that he had been disqualified. His medical examination with a Dr. Vance had revealed inadequate muscular development and athlete's foot. Through his uncle, who was a member of Tom Bradley's church, Brewer got in touch with Tom Bradley, who said that the same thing had happened to him and to fly back out to L.A., appeal the decision, and get examined by another doctor. Brewer did so and was finally admitted to the force, where he was then voted president of his recruit class by his fellow cadets. But he was quietly, deeply enraged that a police department outside the Deep South was still pulling that kind of shit. By 1955, Brewer had become the LAPD's first not-passing-for-white motorcycle officer. In the years that followed, he kept pushing. Three times he tried to make lieutenant, and each time he was rejected. He'd done well on the written exam, but before the oral boards, he had felt either outright hostility or an attitude of "let's get rid of this guy; let's ask him a few questions and let him go." Finally he made it on his fourth attempt, in 1967. After Watts, after Bill Parker was gone. After the Civil Rights Acts of 1964 and 1965.

Tom Bradley welcomed both Brewer as chief of his security and the contingent of about twenty black officers who would back him up. One day during the campaign, Bradley was scheduled to make an appearance in the San Fernando Valley, and a security detail had been sent ahead to check the area out. The unit parked illegally to get their surveillance done quickly, and while they were looking the site over, several squad cars filled with white officers from the local division drove up and ordered them to get that car parked legally. Imagine. "Here we were," Jesse Brewer would later say with a joyless, indignant laugh, "police officers providing security to a mayoral candidate and they're saying that we can't park there!"

Over the following weeks, Sam Yorty's labeling of Tom Bradley as both "antipolice" and a closeted Black Panther began to pick up steam. That they were vile appeals to fear and to ignorance, hurt not at all. It wasn't beside the point, it was the point. They worked precisely because people—white people—wanted to believe them, wanted the excuse not to vote for Tom Bradley. Their city, as they saw it, was being destroyed by "those people." Tom Bradley's people.

Nevertheless, declared Sam Yorty, he was not "going to make racism an issue." Even if he felt compelled to "state as fact that Bradley ran a racist campaign among Negro voters and [that] it was effective." Even if he had to point out, as he had done on another occasion, how it was "this whole bunch—the SDS, the black militants, [who were] the gang behind Bradley."

In white areas of the San Fernando Valley, bumper stickers with a black fist proclaiming "Bradley Power" began mysteriously appearing on billboards, buildings, street signs, and cars driven by blacks cruising through white neighborhoods. Yorty campaign advertisements beneath a big picture of Tom Bradley asked: "Will you be safe with this man?" "Suspicious advertisements," as J. Gregory Payne and Scott C. Ratzan point out in their 1976 biography of Bradley, "unknown to the Bradley campaign, appeared in papers on the predominantly white West Side listing Black Muslims and some Black Panthers as key Bradley supporters." Meanwhile, stunning "make Los Angeles a black city" brochures—designed to look like Bradley campaign literature—were being left on the doorsteps of white homes in the San Fernando Valley.

But the best example of the type of campaign Sam Yorty waged was a picture taken the night of the primary, as Tom Bradley was delivering his victory speech. With "the cameras . . . flashing," as Stephen Reinhardt, a top Bradley campaign aide tells it, there inadvertently turned out to be "only blacks on the platform" with Bradley. The only exception was Reinhardt himself. The image was precisely counter to the rainbow coalition they were trying to project, and the next day when Reinhardt saw the picture in the papers, he winced and then forgot about it. "I thought," he would later say, "it was the last time I would see that picture. I was wrong. Miraculously, the picture appeared on a Yorty mailer the weekend before the general election—but there was one difference: my face was colored black, and the message underneath read, '*We* need a mayor for *our* city.' "

In South Central early that election morning, Ray Cunningham arrived at the Bradley campaign satellite headquarters she was running, only to be met by about twenty people waiting to get in. She was only ten or fifteen minutes late, but the people outside were angry nonetheless. They wanted in *now*, wanted to get down to work. Cunningham, who'd lived in South Central most of her life, had never seen anything like it. She'd worked in campaigns in both 1963 and 1967, and it had been like pulling teeth to get anybody to volunteer to do anything. Yet they were here today, worked up, and anxious to volunteer. It was like that all day. A black man running for mayor had won the primary. And they just knew he was now going to win the election for mayor.

That election eve, Jesse Brewer took personal charge of Tom Bradley's security. It was just a year since the assassinations of Bobby Kennedy and Martin Luther King. It was entirely reasonable that given Tom Bradley's fifteen-point lead in the polls and the bitter hatred roused by the campaign that some foul-tempered Bircher or secret cadre deep in the bowels of the government might now try to take out Tom Bradley as well. And if it was going to happen, thought Jesse Brewer, it would probably be on this day, before Bradley even took office. So Brewer beefed up the security around Bradley and clung to him like a Velcro rug, winding up that night at the Hollywood offices of a studio executive a few short blocks from where five thousand supporters were waiting. They were jubilant, brimming with that very special Dr. King, peace-and-love idealism of the time, which in little more than a decade would be held up to ridicule and scorn by Ronald Reagan's young trickle-downers and the black intelligentsia. But that was to come. Tonight, they could *feel* the victory.

Bradley's wife, Ethel, his mother, Crenner, and his two daughters were all over at the Palladium. There, they were waiting for his victory speech, which he'd already drafted. "The election," he had written, "was a victory—not of a man, but an attitude—proof that our democratic system is capable of peaceful change, a testimony that people should not live by fear but by hope, not by hate but by love.'' It was a speech that was all any black man could have done to reach out. There was nothing more those people in the Valley could have expected, no further he could have gone.

It was a beautiful evening, the culmination of the campaign, and of the civil rights movement in Los Angeles. Jesse Brewer sat there with Tom Bradley and a few others, feeling that moment, like the crowd at the Palladium. *Feeling it.*

First the absentee ballots came in. They weren't good, but then absentee ballots were never good for liberal black candidates trying to make fundamental change. *Their* voters didn't vote absentee; white, geriatric Republicans voted absentee. But by eleven that night the trend was holding. But it would change. It had to. They'd garnered an astounding 42 percent in the primary. They were fifteen points ahead in the polls. They'd spent more money this time, and their campaign had been better organized. They'd even received the *Times* endorsement. It would turn around. But it didn't. Tom Bradley, who hated confrontation, had believed that people wouldn't vote against him because of some black-power bullshit Yorty was trying to lay on him. People knew better than that. People were better than that. But for all of his comfort around white people, for all of his shrewd political instincts and cosmopolitan nature, he had failed to understand them as had Sam Yorty, one of their own.

Slowly the returns filtered in. Instead of Sam Yorty's vote diminishing as the pundits had predicted, it kept growing. And slowly, Bradley's people began feeling as if someone had stepped on their heads. Jesse Brewer looked at Bradley to gauge his reaction and could not believe what he was seeing. Tom Bradley had laid down on the sofa and within minutes was asleep. Asleep! As the returns continued in, they confirmed that Tom Bradley had not just lost, but had lost by an unambiguous six points in a remarkable turnout of registered voters that numbered over 75 percent. So they woke Tom Bradley. ''Tom,'' they told him, ''we have bad news. It's over. All over. You've lost.'' Tom Bradley sat up, and what he said, if anything, Jesse Brewer fails to recall. But what Brewer does remember, and vividly, is that not a flicker of emotion—not the pain of rejection, not a wince of disappointment or flash of rage—crossed the face of Tom Bradley as he received the news.

CHAPTER **2**

Crazy Ed

●●●●●●●●●●●●●●●●●●●●●●

In the waiting room of his sixth-floor office in the newly named Parker Center, Ed Davis kept an array of prominently displayed publications that included a pamphlet written by a conservative Glendale minister entitled, "The Attack on Your Local Police." This time Sam Yorty had chosen well.

Ed Davis, who'd been sworn in as chief in August of 1969, had the energy, had the edge, had the heart, for the fight then going on for the soul of America. Black Panthers and skinny kids with radical hair were on one side. Angry, middle-aged, white men with beer guts were on the other. Ed Davis stood with the beer guts. Years later he would hang on the wall of his outer office a quotation from Ezekiel that had been sent to him by a friend: "It is well and good to remember that the land is full of bloody crimes and the city is full of violence."

L.A. was his city, and it was being destroyed. That was the bottom line, and no matter the attempts to frame the issue in different terms, class, race and fear, formed the nucleus around which Ed Davis's public persona and public support centered. Like Sam Yorty, his implicit appeal was this: these people cannot be accommodated. The best we can do is contain them, keep the lid on, and marginalize their leadership. The cop's job is to do that. By its nature it's a dirty one. We expect your support, we're in this together.

Brash and mocking as he led the department in the tumultuous seventies, his hair now turned dramatically white, his ever-present pipe lending him even in uniform a somewhat professorial air, Ed Davis would build up a long list of enemies. There were the United States and California Supreme Courts, which had allowed "the North Hollywood area" to become a "cesspool of pornography, fruit bars, and bottomless bars." There were United States attorney general Edward Levi and U.S. senator Sam Ervin. Levi and Ervin had spoken of handgun control and were thus attempting to dilute the right of individual citizens to bear arms. "No thanks, King Edward; no, thank you, King Sam," Ed Davis told a National Rifle Association Convention to a thunderous standing ovation in 1975. There was Robert Strauss, the chairman of the national Democratic Party, who had decided to bypass Los Angeles as a Democratic Convention site, in part because he feared the LAPD's and Ed Davis's tendency toward "overreaction." Denouncing Strauss, Ed Davis promptly quit the Democratic Party. There was the *Los Angeles Times*. The "libertine" *Los Angeles Times,* his subscription to which he publicly and dramatically canceled, proclaiming that he was going "to pray for the *Los Angeles Times,*" and vowing that "if it ever again becomes a newspaper," to "immediately reinstate [his] subscription." There was "antipolice, antiestablishment, and anti-American" *Newsweek* magazine, which angered Ed Davis by doing a "hatchet job" on him. And there were the leaders of the African-American community. When they complained that far too many blacks were being killed by the LAPD, Ed Davis was ready with his answer. "More white people," he pointed out, had been "fatally shot by police officers last year than black people . . . so we don't discriminate." And there were the state prisons, with their "rapid release of felons in the minimum amount of time." "Bar [the] doors, buy a police dog, call us when we're available, and pray," warned Ed Davis.

At UCLA, there was another kind of warning during the climactic spring of 1970, the spring of Cambodia and Kent State and Jackson State. The LAPD would react with unforgettable violence to the antiwar demonstrators, and Ed Davis would dismiss criticism by calling the police response a "perfect operation," standing by that characterization even when a chancellor's investigative commission accused the department of "creating violence." He would also fight with the city attorney and with the governor of California. And they, not he, would back off.

He particularly despised rich and upper-middle-class liberals, "swimming-pool communists," as he called them. They were filled with excuses for criminals, bums, welfare mothers, and deviants. "Situational ethics," "doing your own thing," it was these kinds of things, said Ed Davis, that these people were pushing. Otis Chandler. He was the worst. This man who'd been handed the entire *Los Angeles Times* empire, this obscenely rich man—a kid really—had been given everything and knew nothing. He was the archetypical squishy liberal, "out of touch with mankind."

On occasion, Davis would even invoke the master's name. "Parker," he once said, had "found himself fighting off the evil forces from City Hall and the state capital and from various groups in the city, and I think it is absolutely vital that this department not be dominated by politicians."

The walls were being breached, and while Ed Davis was no less obsessive about it than Bill Parker, he was not nearly as frantic. He was too shrewd, too grounded in reality for that. He was a younger man than Bill Parker, younger by some fourteen years. At the time of the Watts insurrection and the years that followed, he was still robust, clear-minded, and able to absorb what was happening, unlike Parker, whose health was broken and for whom the tumult and riotous anarchy of the midsixties was incomprehensible.

The pithy quote, lively sound bite, and colorful phrase would become his trademark. Hijackers, he'd say, should be strung up and "hung at the airport." Homosexuals could not become LAPD officers because no one would be able to use the radio microphones in the patrol cars after they had. The quotes got Ed Davis some press and gave him a persona— "Crazy Ed"—that hurt him with no one who counted. But they had the ring of George Will talking about baseball, of George Will trying too hard to show that despite the bow ties and the constipation, he was really one of the boys. Davis himself called the image "country boy," and he would send back memos drafted by an aide with the notation, "I want more country boy in this." It all masked who Ed Davis really was: a deadly serious, supremely ambitious man.

He wanted to provide good police service. It was all in how you defined it. He wasn't just bombastic, he was smart, and he understood, twenty years before it would again become fashionable, the concept of community policing. He understood that impersonal, faceless police officers working different neighborhoods every shift, with no roots or ties to the community, was an ineffective method of policing that made the officer an alien among the people he was supposed to be serving. So he began what he called his Basic Car Plan, assigning officers to specific geographic locations and instructing them to meet with advisory committees made up of representatives of the neighborhood they were policing. They were to find out local concerns about crime and see if they could then address them. The concept was brilliant. And had its spirit been fully implemented, it might have led to an astounding turnabout in the LAPD. But Ed Davis would not take the crucial step of addressing the lethal problems between the LAPD and the black and Chicano communities. Of course those communities were not only concerned with crime, they were *obsessed* with crime, and any moves to fight it more effectively were welcome. But of equal if not greater obsession were police shootings, casual brutality, and continual harassment, all the issues that LAPD officers involved with the program wanted to avoid. The code of silence, the brotherhood in blue, discouraged that. As a result, the meetings were attended by those already friendly to the department, and those who weren't stayed home. "We told them what we wanted," says David Dotson, a former LAPD assistant chief, "rather than finding out what they wanted."

Ed Davis was not Bill Parker's clone. But he served the same masters. In every way that really mattered, he was more of the same. Throughout the seventies, he'd blast away at liberals, radicals, and critics and reinforce the department's tough proactive policing. His probing, formidable intellect and natural inclination to innovate made him aware of what needed to be done, but his conservative values and stubborn inability to accept a changing of the guard prevented him from actually doing it. When it came down to it, when it really came down to it, Ed Davis's heart always overruled his head.

CHAPTER 3

The Nigger Inspector
•••••••••••••••••••••••

Jim Fisk, 1939 graduate of UCLA, reflective elder of the Hollywood First Presbyterian Church, respected member of the Urban and Ministerial Relations Committees of Presbyterian, now twice passed over for chief of police and now post-Watts LAPD inspector in charge of coordination of community relations activities, had always been outside the parochial, reactionary mainstream of the LAPD. Perhaps that was why he was known as the "Nigger Inspector." Perhaps that was why he thought a sensitivity-training conference might work. He may have been unable to help Tom Bradley integrate a white neighborhood, but it said a great deal about Jim Fisk that he regarded that decision as cowardly and shameful, as an incident where he'd failed to show character.

Handsome in a Fred MacMurray, wavy-haired sort of way, the son of a circuit-riding Presbyterian preacher, he had that rare thing for a cop—a twinkle in his eyes. His manner was friendly, soft-spoken, folksy, not down-home folksy—but small-town, Midwest, plain-folks friendly. It was not an act. He believed in reconciliation and the reinforcement of people's self-esteem as basic to a Christian way of life. In later years, he'd deny being a liberal, as if he'd been accused of having some kind of contagious disease. But in the eyes of mainstream LAPD officers, who thought black

Supreme Court justice Thurgood Marshall an agent of the communist conspiracy, he *was* a liberal and therefore, beyond the pale. Honest, intelligent, personable—yes, that was Jim Fisk. But an officer, no. Never an officer. He was, after all, in charge of community relations. You might need a man like Fisk to take the heat off after Watts. But there were limits. Like the race-relations seminars for high-ranking LAPD officers that Jim Fisk had arranged at the USC Conference Center in the nearby mountain village of Idylwild in 1966. With the support of Tom Bradley and other council members, Fisk had applied for and received financing from the city council for the conferences. Then with the help of some professors from UCLA and Cal State, he'd put together a three-day seminar as part of his post-Watts community-relations program. The idea was for the officers to examine why they acted as they did, and in the process, to understand other people in the extraordinarily diverse city Los Angeles was becoming. But the department was not ready to interact with the downtrodden. Patrol had only been integrated for five or so years, and now, here comes Jim Fisk, working with these liberal professors at UCLA, wanting to put them through an honest interchange between white and black officers. They wanted men for whom personal reticence and the refusal to display emotions was a source of pride to open up! And to do so, a professor at one of the sessions—which had been deliberately designed to get people angry as a method of having them frankly express themselves—chose the issue of homosexuality. Homosexuality. It was enough to make the hairs on the back of your neck stand up. It was disgusting. What they did was disgusting. Negroes were one thing. There were, to be sure, officers who came to the conferences with racial attitudes they could not shake. Like the captain who approached Fisk, pointed at a black policeman, and asked, "Are *they* going to stay overnight [with us]?" But for the fast-track, high-ranking officers, it was clear, at least on a professional level, that they'd have to adapt to integration. That was one thing, but homosexuality was something even Jim Fisk felt was an abomination.

Ed Davis was sitting in the session where the whole issue of anger and homosexuality came out. Throughout most of his career, Ed Davis would be a notorious homophobe, even in a profession and an era when gays were routinely treated with disgust and ridicule. It was "one thing to be a leper," as he once said of gay prostitutes, "another thing to be spreading the disease." Following the session, recalls Jim Fisk, "Ed Davis just turned right around in his attitude . . . just became hostile to the whole [conference] procedure.'' Jim Fisk could actually feel the energy turning against him and the idea of community relations after that.

Which didn't mean he didn't have support. The *Sentinel* loved him, lauding his ''skill and sensitivity.'' The *Los Angeles Times* loved him, hailing his community-relations program for ''moving toward solution of a long-smoldering problem.'' Tom Reddin would call Jim Fisk a ''visionary,'' credit him for the momentary improved relations with the black community for which *he,* Reddin, had received credit, and show his faith in Fisk by expanding the staff of his program from 4 to 120 officers. Ed Davis himself would cite Jim Fisk as a major reason why Los Angeles did not explode with 150 other cities after the assassination of Dr. King in 1968. Jim Fisk had shown a willingness to listen to people, to go into Watts and South Central and as a deputy chief of police have eighteen-year-old black kids screaming in his face. It took a lot of strength.

And when two plainclothes officers shot and killed an innocent fifty-five-year-old film-studio carpenter they'd been following because he was ''driving [too] slowly'' and had failed ''to yield the right-of-way to three women in a crosswalk,'' Jim Fisk defended that killing. The man, who had no record, may have been confused and feared the plainclothes officers were attempting to rob him. But he had tried, the officers claimed, to run them down when they approached, so they fired their revolvers and shotgun five times, killing him. They couldn't shoot the tires because bullets might have ricocheted off the ''modern self-sealing tires.'' That was the story. ''A felony was not only committed in their presence, a felony was committed upon them,'' Jim Fisk said in their defense. No apology, no ''we'll look into this to see that such a tragic incident doesn't occur again.'' Jim Fisk *was* an LAPD officer.

CHAPTER 4

Fear and Loathing in South Central

••••••••••••••••••••••

Steve Fisk had never seen anything like it, had never even heard of anything like it. Not even as the son of a cop. Not even when he'd gone out with his father, Jim Fisk, after turning eighteen, and would view the corpses of people who'd been murdered or had been shot by cops. Not even when he'd ridden with the elite, head-busting troubleshooters of the Metro Squad and watched as they shaked and baked a neighborhood. Here I am, green as hell, Fisk would later say, and it's right after the [Watts] riots, which had just turned the whole city upside down. And I'm new on the job—working morning watch [the midnight shift] out in the Wilshire Division. It was all black down there, but Dad, who's no liberal, had always taught me not to be prejudiced, and I thought that once I was working, I was actually going to change society, change the way people view officers, the way they said we acted, because, you know, *I* wasn't prejudiced. But I start going into the homes of blacks all the time. And my insights start to change. I mean, I used to see them at Dorsey High all the time, our school was already about one-third black. And we got along, everything was fine. It was like, you know, the old saying "I have a lot of black friends." And I *did*. But school was one thing. You see them in their own environment, well, that's entirely different, it's a whole different lifestyle.

So anyway, we get this radio call, domestic dispute. Black guy comes home from work, his wife had prepared a special dinner. He says, "Fuck you, I'm going to bed. *You* eat it." He takes off his clothes, lays down naked on the bed, and goes to sleep. The wife gets pissed, heats this big pot of boiling water, and pours it all over him. Because he didn't like what was for dinner. It was unbelievable.

I'm on the job less than a year and all this stuff just keeps popping up. People getting shot and cut. I remember this one guy, he'd been cut from side to side. We get there and he's holding his intestines in his hands. . . . He's sitting on the curb, holding his intestines in his hands because he'd just been slit from side to side, and people are just sitting around talking to him about it. Nobody's too upset, and *he* doesn't seem to be upset either. It's just like, well, that's life in the neighborhood, you know? But I knew that wasn't life in *my* neighborhood. In my neighborhood people'd be scattered, screaming, going up the walls! Man, I'll tell you, I'd never seen anything like it.

And indeed, that level of violence was still all new then—or it was new to white people like Steve Fisk—when he started working patrol in the Wilshire Division in 1966.

The violence, the senseless violence over silly shit, that's what thousands—tens of thousands—of young cops like him were experiencing in the sixties and seventies as America's urban ghettos swelled; and the results of more than three hundred years of treating people like mules and came home to roost.

So Steve Fisk, son of a churchgoing graduate of UCLA, son of one of the fairer, more progressive ranking officers in the LAPD, found himself in a constant rage and started trying to square in his head what he was seeing with his eyes. And he came to this conclusion: "No way in hell am I like them. No way *these* people are the same as me." And from there, the next step was easy: "They are all like that." It was an attitude reinforced by the old vets, the Rudy Rednecks who made no bones about being prejudiced and didn't hesitate to put the peer pressure on and inculcate in the new green troops their views on the niggers and jungle bunnies. Less than a year went by before he began to think it wasn't worth trying to diminish the tension or to change their opinions that the people he was policing had of him and his fellow officers. There was no use. Besides, what they thought didn't really matter anyway. Because, as

Steve Fisk later told it, "we were right and they were wrong." After that he became convinced with a cynical, soul-diminishing clarity that "everything I'd always thought was true, wasn't." The Bible, which in his home had been The Book, became just a bunch of "malarkey" that no one could possibly believe in.

His metamorphosis was manifest first in his language, in the way he talked about people, in the way he joked about them, until "all of a sudden" they were no longer blacks, "they were niggers." And he became, as he himself later confessed, "your basic bigot." He was big and powerfully built and started to grow badge heavy—the cop term for being more than willing to demonstrate your authority, and for listening a little more closely to see if some asshole had that *tone* when he talked to you. It was a journey taken by thousands of other cops in scores of cities throughout America. Many, of course, were already predisposed to a racial prejudice that Black Panther leader H. Rap Brown had once correctly described as being as "American as apple pie." But to it, for many cops, was added a new element: loathing.

It was the angry, insistent, prophetic black writer James Baldwin who best spelled out the white cops' dilemma in *Nobody Knows My Name:* "He is facing, daily and nightly, people who would gladly see him dead, and he knows it. He moves . . . therefore, like an occupying soldier in a bitterly hostile country, which is precisely what, and where, he is." That was it. Exactly what Steve Fisk was experiencing, exactly how he felt.

Inevitably, he began to talk about it with his father. It wasn't long, however, before those conversations turned from discussion to argumentative anger—at least on the part of Steve Fisk. Finally they got to the point where he refused to share his experiences with his father. It was too frustrating. Here was Jim Fisk, so calm, so rational, so infuriatingly levelheaded: a man who's deep faith in Christ and the precepts of his religion compelled him to see the humanity of African-Americans, and here was Steve Fisk absolutely beside himself with rage at that kind of attitude. He'd shout: You're a cop, for Christ's sake! Don't you get it? Those people out there are trying to kill us! He and his partner had just been sniped at as they'd rolled onto a scene where some burglars were holed up in a building, and his partner had wound up shooting one while he'd had to jump out of the way to avoid getting run down by a truck the other guy was driving during his getaway. And here you are, *Dad,* talking about community relations. About how much the people out in South Central support us, while I'm rolling around in the dirt, getting my uniform torn, getting my nose punched, and all you see is the perspective of the top brass, all you do is meet with middle-class church groups, as if *they* were the community.

But there was more to it than that. There was the digging. The looking for that little weak spot, that vulnerability, that's so much a part of an exclusively male world, and then zeroing in and grinding away. With Steve Fisk, that spot was his father. "There were a lot of people [LAPD officers] who thought my father was a communist, a pinko," recalls Steve Fisk.

It was Steve Fisk's burden, as if defending his father from charges of ax-murder, to protest that Jim Fisk was not a liberal, just a guy doing his job. It wasn't like he'd exactly signed up for it. "Parker had told him," says Steve Fisk, " 'Hey, this is your assignment. Go to work.' So he did."

But for all that, Steve Fisk felt a need to put some distance between himself and the man whom he loved and admired, but who just wasn't quite one of the troops. To try to compensate, maybe overcompensate, for his father's involvement in community relations. To let it be known, as Steve Fisk himself put it, that "that's him over there, and I'm me over here. And we're two different people." That, in short, in the most crucial of ways, he wasn't Jim Fisk's boy.

After about a year on patrol, Steve Fisk took to stopping at various saloons with the troops, just drinking, having a good time. Then he took to staying and drinking for hours. Over time, he was drinking a fifth of Jim Beam a day. His mind was filled with one obsessive thought: get-me-the-fuck-out-of-here. It wasn't that he felt he had it so bad. Not relatively speaking. He was working the Wilshire Division, which was pretty mild stuff compared to working in South Central. Wilshire was a circus; South Central, a zoo.

But what ex-LAPD officer turned novelist Joseph Wambaugh called "the most dangerous job on earth emotionally" had gotten to Steve Fisk, as it had to so many police officers working in a profession with a 75 percent divorce rate, and one of the nation's highest rates of suicide. "The main killer of cops," as Wambaugh described it, was "premature cynicism—that producer of alcoholism and cop suicides and divorces and excessive force." It would be a long time before it let go of Steve Fisk.

CHAPTER 5

The Rise of the
People Shouters

• •

Over the years at the Academy the military tradition had deepened. The first day would start on the black line. You'd be brought up to the gymnasium at the Academy and made to stand at attention on this black line that ran through it. They'd start at one end and scream in the face of each cadet as they meandered down the line, just like John Wayne in *Sands of Iwo Jima.* If they didn't get the answer they wanted—and they rarely did—or didn't like your appearance, there'd be more yelling and push-ups to do. If they didn't like the look of you, they'd tell you to go home, change, and come back properly dressed. Oh, yes, they'd add, you have twenty minutes to do that. They'd tell you to do all kinds of impossible shit like that. People would literally break into tears. That was day one. From then on you'd be called names. Scum, worm, asshole, dirtbag. Whatever was the current tin-eared white-man, macho insult, that's what you'd be called.

On a doorframe in an office that housed the physical-training staff, they'd attached a big piece of plywood. Starting sometime in the 1960s, any recruit who wished to speak to someone in that room had to go up and pound on the knocking board three times and wait. The board had been mounted on the door after previous classes filled with pumped-up cadets had banged on the door so hard that it had literally fallen apart. The board, nailed to this very solid doorframe, had proven the answer. Now the cadets could hit that instead. After they'd pounded the knocking board the requisite three times, they'd then snap to, stand at rigid attention, and remain there until somebody felt like opening the door and talking to them. Sometimes that would take a very long time. There was no rational purpose for the knocking board. It was there for one reason: it had hard-man, urban-warrior appeal.

The heavy emphasis on military training had evolved in earnest in the early sixties, about the time of the 1962 raid and the shoot-outs with the Black Muslims at their South Central mosque when one police officer and six Muslims were shot, and had intensified after Watts. It was then that the military guys, the people shouters, the men who saw no difference between the airborne and cops were really let loose. It was bound to happen anyway. The LAPD never did anything halfway, and it was only appropriate that if they were going to have high-stress boot-camp military training, it would be the most stressful, the most bad-assed.

And, if, as a result of the mind-set it produced indiscriminate shootings, or people were shaken down on their way home from Burger King for no reason, it was the price you paid to keep control of the city. And if, God forbid, the guy you stopped said, "Hey, what the fuck you stopping me for?"—well, that might pose a danger. And if he's turning toward you, then you've got to whack him. If he's black, so much the better. Get rid of that fear of those wild, bred-for-strength Africans that most white boys have. Get it out in the open. Deal with it.

At the Academy, they, along with other Southern-California depart-ments, were using training films that were sending conflicting messages, making cadets paranoid, placing them in crazy-making situations. One that the department was using, had "re-created"—according to a Uni-versity of California study reported in the L.A. *Times*—was "an incident in which a liquor-store bandit killed a rookie officer. While the officer being trained could 'kill' the shotgun-toting bandit [in the film], to do so he must violate the department policy by firing his service revolver into a crowd, [thereby] risking the 'lives' of innocent bystanders."

By the early 1970s there was a real need for strategies to deal with dangerous situations. About 120 cops a year were being killed in the line of duty across the nation, and cops were shooting about 527 people to death every year in return. Police shootings—even "bad" or avoidable ones—were bound to occur. The task was to limit them. To provide the training to help officers avoid life-threatening situations, and to provide strong leadership from the top—an attitude that said that shooting someone when it can clearly be avoided will not be tolerated.

In Los Angeles that wasn't happening. As LAPD press spokesman Lt. Dan Cooke once put it, "We don't teach our officers when *not* to shoot, we mandate a set of circumstances when they *must* shoot."

During the 1970s, Dr. Martin Reiser, the first psychologist hired by the LAPD, concluded that if you want police officers who can go out and communicate, take charge of a situation, be confident, and have the public feel they can rely on them, then you had to train them that way. He tried to make the department hierarchy understand that if you wanted recruits to come out of the Academy radiating confidence, they couldn't be frightened all the time during their training. That they couldn't go through a program that was constantly overemphasizing the dangers of police work and not be overwhelmed by fear when they hit the street. That they couldn't be screamed at all the time, expected to do ridiculous shit, treated like idiots, and not go out on patrol and treat people the same way. The proof that Reiser and the other behavioral scientists were right was that when the cadets left the Academy, they did exactly that. And it became self-perpetuating. The rookie became the training officer and reinforced what the new probationary cadet coming out of the Academy had learned. You went along, joined the fraternity, and earned some respect or did what you had to in order to ignore it. No one dared turn in a partner, no one dared being labeled a sissy boy, snitch, and traitor. After a while, a saying developed with the troops: "If the trainer is 415"—415 being the LAPD code for fighting, choking people out, and kicking ass—"then his probationer is going to turn out 415, too."

CHAPTER 6

The Downtown Man

•••••••••••••••••••••••

It was no ordinary inaugural of an American mayor. For one, the former chief justice of the United States Supreme Court, Earl Warren, had agreed to swear him in. For another, Tom Bradley, the object of threats throughout his campaign, was wearing a bulletproof vest as he gave his inaugural address that July day in 1973. He wanted, he said, to "be the mayor of all of Los Angeles," of the San Fernando Valley, of San Pedro—of all those white, conservative areas that he would need if he was to govern effectively and be reelected. He also went out of his way to praise Chief of Police Ed Davis and to pledge that his administration would be dedicated to law and order. Tom Bradley had not lost once and then put it all together a second time to see it fall apart now that he was in office. And he *had* put it back together.

From his bedrock base of black ministers led by the Reverend H. H. Brookins—then perhaps the most influential person in South Central after Bradley himself—he had expanded outward. His vote among Jews had been phenomenal, perhaps 90 percent of the votes they'd cast. From wealthy, influential Westside Jewish liberals such as Stanley Sheinbaum, Harold Willens, Paul Ziffren, and Max Palevsky, he had obtained the serious money he needed for his campaign. It was to them, as much as to the downtown real estate interests and the South Central black ministers, that Tom Bradley would owe his allegiance. And it would be from that Jewish constituency of developers and businessmen that many of his most crucial appointments would come. With their support, and that of the blacks, liberals, environmentalists, and Asians, Tom Bradley had amassed 55 percent of the vote.

He'd done so by running a smart campaign. This time around he had not let Sam Yorty define him as this huge, dangerous black Goliath who was running against a little guy defending a white America under siege. Almost from the day of his 1969 defeat, Tom Bradley had worked eight to ten hours a day seven days a week to dispel that notion. Before his city council sessions, which began at ten A.M., he would make public appearances; then, after the council meetings, he'd make a couple more. Every chance he got he'd go out into the city, lunching in cafeterias where he could meet people and shake hands, going to dinners, going to festivals, taking the opportunity—not just on weekdays, but on Saturdays and Sundays and holidays as well—to portray himself as essentially what he was: safe, smart, cosmopolitan, and fundamentally conservative.

Then with his Westside money he hired the savvy, high-priced political media consultant David Garth, who produced highly effective television commercials for him.

Equally important, 1973 was not 1969. The memories of Watts, of the explosions of America's black ghettos in 1965, 1967, and 1968, and of the debacle of the '68 Democratic Convention in Chicago, were dimming. The Panthers were becoming marginalized. Sam Yorty's attempt to replay his racist campaign had little resonance. Bradley was appearing on television, showing himself to be this astounding combination of comforting black Buddha and intelligent Mr. Clean. Dignity. Tom Bradley had dignity and wonderful strength and integrity. You had to be a racist or a fool to be frightened by him. And a lot of people no longer *were*.

So Tom Bradley easily won election. Of all the victories of black mayors in the seventies and eighties, his would remain the most remarkable. Andrew Young and Maynard Jackson in Atlanta, Wilson Goode in Philadelphia, Harold Washington in Chicago, Coleman Young in Detroit, and David Dinkins in New York, all would be elected with huge black votes in cities with huge black populations. Only Tom Bradley's victory would come in a major American city with such a relatively small black population. He would be the first black mayor of one of America's ten largest cities, and he would be put into office not by blacks, but by whites.

Everywhere he went during that campaign and in the early days of his administration, they would play the song that he described as his favorite: "The Impossible Dream." But impossible dreams were not Tom Bradley's style. When he was a student at UCLA, Bradley's black fraternity used to argue about how much pressure they should exert in getting more blacks hired at the school's football games at the Coliseum. "Tom always supported as strongly as the most avid the need for all these kinds of things," Bill Elkins, a fraternity brother, would later say. "But he'd always be the kind of guy who would [also] say, 'Well, now, let's think it through and see if we can't conciliate and if we can't take half a loaf, or let's take three-quarters of a loaf and come back for the other piece later.' " That's what Tom Bradley was, a half-a-loaf man, not an impossible dreamer.

The half a loaf before him when he became mayor was gaining the support of the prodevelopment downtown business establishment, the people who could make or break any administration. Having the businessmen of the Jonathan Club whispering that this black man doesn't understand us and will not permit us to get things done could be devastating to his political career. So Tom Bradley turned his attention, his energy, and his resources to the development of downtown Los Angeles. Downtown, he said, belonged to all Angelenos. When he took office, there were only three buildings fifty stories or taller; only five, all told, above thirteen stories. Over the next two decades of his reign, that number would increase to almost fifty. Forging a powerful coalition of big business and big labor, Tom Bradley would preside over the greatest construction boom in the history of downtown Los Angeles. What could have turned into a great slum was turned instead into a vast sea of high-rise office buildings. Soulless, denuded, impersonal high rises to be sure, the same ones you could see in Atlanta, Denver, or Houston. But there they were. They may have constituted, as *Forbes* magazine described it, "an artificial heart" of Los Angeles. But they were there. Of course nobody *lived* downtown, except winos, crackheads, wacko artists, and Salvadoran domestics. But the high-rises were there. And Tom Bradley had done it. And the real players in Los Angeles, the Central City Association, the developers, the unions, the large law firms, Times Mirror and the other corporations, they loved him for it. And at the same time downtown was booming, so was the Westside of his Jewish supporters; and so was the San Pedro Harbor, which was undergoing a $500 million redevelopment that would greatly expand its facilities. Throughout much of L.A., real estate values were soaring and business was booming.

And in those downtown high-rises sat the corporate offices of many of the international conglomerates that were making it happen. The Pacific Rim was a brilliant concept, one that fit in perfectly with the image of Los Angeles as an ever-growing, ever-expanding economic behemoth. If Harrison Gray Otis and Harry Chandler had been alive, they would undoubtedly have been the staunchest supporters of the Pacific Rim concept. And presiding over it all—facilitating it all—was a black man raised in East and South Central L.A.

He'd been good for South Central, too, in those early years, getting as much state and federal money as possible: antipoverty funds, block grants, CETA money, those kinds of remedial maintenance funds. But as the economy of South Central began slowly to collapse as America moved from manufacturing to service-oriented jobs, Tom Bradley did not particularly concern himself with it. Nor did he act to alleviate the structural problems already existing in South Central. Development money was channeled downtown, and linkage of the entire city through taxes on the wealthier areas so that South Central could be redeveloped never took place. As federal and state money became tougher to get, South Central became more impoverished. Neither Tom Bradley nor the city council made much of an effort to see to it that South Central got its share of a rapidly disappearing pie. As Tom Bradley would be loved downtown, he would ever so slowly become despised in South Central. But it would take a very long time.

His style in those early years, his style throughout his life as a politician, would be to work behind the scenes, to avoid confrontation, and to avoid any battle he thought he could not win. "Sometimes black politicians have a tendency to scare [white people]," Joe Cerell, a veteran L.A. Democratic political consultant, once told the *Times*. "But Los Angeles can be the murder capital, the crime capital, the drug capital, and people don't think it's his fault, and I bless his [Bradley's] heart for being able to get away with it." "This is a strategy dating back to the beginning. His caution is almost legendary," David Garth would later say. "He plays it very, very, very, close to the vest. . . . I've never seen anyone like him in all my years in this business."

At the same time Bradley was being cautious and prudent, he could be seen everywhere. He went to weddings, he attended bar mitzvahs, he ate at pancake breakfasts, he cut ribbons at seemingly every opening, he went to festivals, banquets, anniversaries, and cocktail parties, rallies for Soviet Jews, protests against apartheid in South Africa. No event, it seemed, was too small for Tom Bradley to make an appearance. In 1989, the *Los Angeles Times* obtained Bradley's daily calendar for 1987, a nonelection year. It showed, the *Times* pointed out, that in that year he had "attended 512 such events—ten times the number of social appearances made that year by New York's Mayor Koch." In 1977 he would be reelected with almost 60 percent of the vote; in 1981 he'd win a third term with 64 percent.

PART 5

CIRCLING THE WAGONS

CHAPTER 1

The Master and the Novice

••••••••••••••••••••••

He was born into middle-class comfort in the summer of 1926, the second of three sons of Paul Gates, an Irish Catholic plumber from Ohio, and Arvilla Gates, a devout Mormon housewife. His older brother, Lowell, an epileptic, would die in a surfing mishap. His brother Steve, his junior by eleven years, would become an LAPD captain who would rise no higher after his romance with the owner of a San Fernando Valley whorehouse was revealed. Their childhood in blue-collar, small-town, suburban Glendale might have been commonplace had it not been for the intercession of two cataclysmic events that dominated their youth and formed the character of Daryl Gates: the Depression and Paul Gates's terrible, all-consuming drunkenness. Overnight, Daryl Gates's world was transformed from the golden-hued bliss of an untroubled four-year-old happily playing at home with his mother and brother, into the bleak turbulence of a poverty that would mark him as nothing else, other than his father's weakness, ever would.

With his father unable to find work, and without Daryl Gates really understanding why, one day in 1930 the family moved "... into a tired and ramshackle frame house that was quite small. There, in addition to losing the privacy of his own room, he found himself having to share the same bed with his brother.

With his father unemployed and so deep into the bottle he would disappear on drunken binges for days on end, it fell to Arvilla Gates to scrape out a meager living for her family. A practical, determined woman, she took a job as a nonunion pattern-cutter in a dress factory, worked nine or ten hours a day, and frequently returned home, Daryl Gates would later recall, with her "hands bleeding and her fingers gashed."

Although more neglectful than abusive toward his sons, Paul Gates's temper was such that it only required a few beatings for them to live in fear of its ever happening again. With alarming frequency, big men in uniform—Glendale cops and county marshals—would pound on the Gateses' front door, looking to haul Paul Gates away to jail on various charges having to do with his drinking, or to serve him with papers for indebtedness. "It was just devastating," Daryl Gates would later recount. ". . . Dad was still the authority figure in the family, and there he was, scurrying out the back door into the blackness of night, while these massive uniformed people were beating on the door, rushing in."

There were other wounds. The poor-boy lunches, which Daryl Gates, like Tom Bradley, was forced to eat—the mashed-potato sandwiches, the bean sandwiches, the nameless gooey, cheap, sweet paste spread on bread. Those sandwiches were symbols of the deep humiliation he felt at the squalid conditions to which he and his family had descended. And there were the times when his would be the only family on the block to receive a help-the-poor Christmas basket from his school, or when he stood in a breadline with his father as potatoes and heads of cabbage were chucked into the waiting gunnysack they held.

Later, Daryl Gates would make much of the scorn and contempt he held for the police when he was growing up, detailing in his biography the harassment that he, like so many other Southern California teenagers, suffered at their hands. And he would recall the horror he had felt as the cops knocked at his door and, with a macho pride, detail how at seventeen he had once punched a police officer who'd unjustly pushed his brother. But it was the police with whom he would later identify, and in a manner so thorough and complete that it blinded him to the feelings of others. It was the police, after all, who had what he wanted: the power to ensure that he would never be treated as his father had been. He would be nothing like his father. He would show no weakness, would understand no weakness, and admit no mistakes.

By the time he was a 165-pound high school fullback at Franklin High, Daryl Gates was, as he described himself, "brimming with competitiveness and ego." At seventeen he graduated from high school, joined the Navy, and spent most of his two years of service aboard ships in the Pacific before being discharged. Using the G.I. Bill, he enrolled in Pasadena City College in 1946 and met a "very attractive blonde" named Wanda Hawkins. They married within a year. By 1949, Gates had transferred to the University of Southern California and was preparing to enter his senior year. He had considered and dismissed careers in psychology and teaching and had just settled into the idea of going into law. But that summer his wife got pregnant. Broke, in debt, and tired of working part-time, he heard through a friend that the LAPD was hiring, and that the starting salary was $290 a month. That seemed an enormous amount of money to him at the time. It was also a way, he'd later say, to make some money and save up for law school. Never, ever, he would later recount, did he have it in his mind to stay on a police force and in the profession that would consume his life.

Daryl Gates was a shy, soft-spoken rookie barely on the street a year working traffic control, when, at age twenty-three, he was thrown face-to-face with Bill Parker.

It seemed inevitable. From the moment he'd applied to the department he'd been an "upstreamer," a climber, a man destined to go places. By his own account, he ranked ninth out of the five thousand applicants who took the LAPD test with him, and he continued to shine at the Los Angeles Police Academy, where he was his class's honor graduate. Everyone there had been impressed with him. "He was likable," says Tom Reddin, who was superintendent of training at the time, "he was physical, he was bright, he did everything well, and he was well regarded by his fellow officers. He had no negatives." In addition to Reddin, Daryl Gates had been noticed by Floyd Phillips, an influential physical-training sergeant at the Academy, and when he heard that Parker was looking for a full-time chauffeur/bodyguard, he recommended Gates. To his qualifications coming out of the Academy, Gates had one more that was essential.

Like Bill Parker, he was of no more than average height—five feet eleven inches, he would claim. (Although several high-ranking officers would maintain that it's only with the inch-and-a-half high-heeled ankle boots he habitually wears that he reached five-eleven.) In any case, it was an unspoken rule that none of Bill Parker's drivers/bodyguards could be taller than him; an accident of birth for which Daryl Gates was truly blessed. But as Gates himself would later tell it, it was a job in which he initially had little interest. And he said as much to Sergeant Phillips, declining his offer. He didn't want "to be somebody's toady, bowing and scraping along in the chief's ceremonial wake," an attitude that seemed, however, to disappear as soon as he took the job. After that, the course of Daryl Gates's career was set. Bill Parker took a look at him, noticed he was smart, noticed he looked just as he should, was taken with his aw-shucks charm, and suddenly he was driving Bill Parker's car and guarding Bill Parker's ass.

The department had a tradition of plucking bright young men out of the ranks and putting them in staff positions, where most would acquire captains, commanders, or deputy chiefs as mentors. But the break that Daryl Gates received was unquestionably the biggest and sweetest ever laid in the lap of a young LAPD officer: the chance to bond with and learn at the knee of the godfather of the modern LAPD. The assignment was, as Gates himself says, "an incredible, golden opportunity." Seated outside Parker's door or inside during important meetings, Gates saw who had clout, who had ability, and how to deal with the troops, the public, and the politicians.

Undoubtedly Daryl Gates also benefited far more from his relationship with Parker than Parker had from his with James Davis. Bill Parker trusted few people, least of all those in line to succeed him. And being driven around the vast expanse of Los Angeles in his official Buick Dynaflow by a young man who posed no threat, and who was the perfect symbol of what he wanted his officers to be, was an ideal opportunity for the aging Parker to grow expansive, share his thoughts, and discuss philosophy, law enforcement, current events, and even Gates's night-school studies at USC with his bright, awestruck young protégé. And Daryl Gates in return "just *adored* Bill Parker," says Ed Davis, becoming, as Gates himself later put it, "totally smitten." "Here I was, just a plain old police officer," Gates would reminisce on numerous occasions, "but he didn't close me off from anything. He'd discuss decisions as we'd drive, he'd philosophize a lot. . . ." "He didn't have any children, and I think he saw in me an opportunity to mold somebody. He knew I had tremendous respect for him and that I hung on every word." By the end of his fifteen-month stint with Parker, Daryl Gates had about him the knowing assurance and dismissive condescension of the true insider. "I could relate to various things that were happening in the department that other officers couldn't," he would later say. "They'd complain about personnel investigations, for example, but I could understand, clearly and perfectly, what Internal Affairs was all about, why we had strict personnel investigations. Why we disciplined and how. I understood the whole structure of the department . . . and the average officer just did not."

At just twenty-four, and at a time so early in his career that he was still very impressionable, Bill Parker also instilled in Daryl Gates—as he did in the entire department—a reverence for police authority that had about it the sanctimony of religion, reinforcing the rigidity that would define Gates and the LAPD for the next forty years.

And Bill Parker unquestionably liked Daryl Gates. "Now look at him," Bill Parker would sometimes urge his audience as he interrupted one of his countless speeches and pointed to Daryl Gates. "Stand up now," he'd say to Gates. "I want you to stand up!" And Daryl Gates would stand up. "This," Parker would say, "is a *policeman*. . . . Look at him!"

He was Parker's boy. And in the years that followed, Daryl Gates would find himself on the fast track, promoted through the ranks as quickly as civil service regulations permitted. When he went to take his oral exams before a board of high-ranking officers, why, they weren't blind, they knew he was Parker's boy, knew the chief thought him a star. And the orals, unlike the written part of the civil service exam, was subjective They accounted for 50 percent of a candidate's grade, were the place where being part of the club really mattered. It was naive to think that any oral board would fail to punch Daryl Gates's career ticket when Bill Parker had put him on the train.

Gates, moreover, had the kind of retentive mind that could absorb and hold the detailed information so prized by civil service test-makers—an ability that when combined with his ferocious determination and highly disciplined study habits enabled him to do extremely well on the written parts of the tests as well. And he had ample time to study. Bill Parker had three drivers, and Gates was primarily used as his day driver. When Bill Parker wasn't in his car, Daryl Gates's time was free. He had to be there, of course, outside the chief's office, but he could sit there and study. Which he did. In a little office that was set up right outside Parker's office. And when Bill Parker walked out, there would be Daryl Gates studying. Other people would go out to lunch, but not Daryl Gates. He would always stay in his little office, eating lunch at his desk, studying. Bill Parker admired that. But then Daryl Gates was an admirable young man. His demeanor was subdued, his manner calm, his image that of the straight-arrow family man whom you wished your eldest daughter had met before she'd gotten married. While on the job the words he uttered most frequently were "Yes, sir" and "No, sir." He was smart, insightful, and seemed to have instantly grasped the importance of saying and doing nothing remotely offensive that might have gotten back to Bill Parker.

Bill Parker was so notorious for his unapproachability that like airline pilots routinely asking about the weather, the men on Parker's staff, in an effort to catch him at just the right time, would routinely ask about his mood before taking up an issue with him. Gates's predecessor was great at letting you know if the time was right, recalls former deputy chief Harold Sullivan. And so was his successor. No, no, they would say, you don't want to go in there today. Not today. He's in a foul mood. "But Gates, Gates was noncommittal," says Sullivan. "You couldn't get anything out of him. He was self-centered."

He was also exceptionally vain about his appearance, a definite plus in a paramilitary police organization like the LAPD. He kept himself deeply suntanned and in superb physical condition and decades later would pride himself on the fact that he could still wear the same-size uniforms he wore when he joined the department.

Scoring first on every promotional exam he took up until the rank of chief, he made sergeant in six years, did some obligatory time in the field working juvenile and vice, and was right back in Bill Parker's office again. This time he was a lieutenant and Parker's adjutant, and in little more than nine years after joining the department. Shortly thereafter, Bill Parker made him his executive officer. For four years, he helped prepare Parker's speeches, advised him—to the extent that Bill Parker took anyone's advice—and was there at his side.

But in his years as Bill Parker's chauffeur and executive officer, Daryl Gates also saw Bill Parker at his worst: so drunk on bourbon that "his words slurred and stairs became a hazard." So drunk that "he would repeat the same thought over and over until he became a terrible bore."

So drunk that on some nights Parker "smelled embarrassing" to Daryl Gates "as he stumbled getting into the car and stumbled getting out," and as Gates had to help Parker in "negotiating a steep hill" that led to his house. Seeing Parker like that rekindled in Gates "bad long-ago" memories of his father. Bill Parker, Daryl Gates would ruefully recall, had become "a paternal image in more ways than I would have liked."

Four years after making lieutenant, Daryl Gates was promoted to captain, went out to a sleepy little division in Highland Park, and within six months was right back in Parker Center, heading Bill Parker's Intelligence Division, in charge of the division that was privy to many of the city's dirtiest little secrets. Bill Parker had chosen well.

Two years after making captain and as soon as he was eligible, Daryl Gates was promoted to inspector, the equivalent today of commander. It was 1965, the same year that a teeming section of South Central Los Angeles called Watts would sear itself into the national consciousness.

CHAPTER 2

The Protégé

••••••••••••••••••••••••

Shortly after Tom Bradley's mayoral victory, his new, ethnically diverse, mildly liberal police commissioners tried to find out if the department had any guidelines that distinguished intelligence-gathering on political activists from that on criminal activities. It was no easy task. Ed Davis and his staff didn't even want to reveal where the Public Disorder Intelligence Division's offices were located. That was the way it would go. If you were a commissioner, an outsider, a civilian, you had to work at knowing. They were masters of nondisclosure at the LAPD, revealing nothing in so skilled a manner you could never really call them on it. They'd always have fifty reasons why something couldn't be done, some of which—and this was their genius—seemed quite valid. Getting even a modicum of oversight of the department would prove no easy task for Tom Bradley.

Then there was the delicate issue of Bradley himself. Sam Yorty had already shown back in the '69 election how easy it was to play on white Los Angeles' fear of blacks and fear of crime—the two being indistinguishable in the eyes of many. It would not do, therefore, to tread too heavily on Ed Davis, a smart, conservative chief of police with political ambitions, lifetime tenure, a combative nature, a way with a colorful phrase, and the backing of an increasingly powerful and politicized Police Protective League. Not after Watts. Not with *that* wound still so fresh and vivid.

The commission could order a change in policy, but insuring the chief carried it out if he didn't want to required enormous tenacity and political will. And even if a chief and his command staff *were* willing to cooperate, meaningful change would come hard, thought Stephen Reinhardt, a lawyer who'd been one of Bradley's top campaign aides and was the president of Bradley's police commission. You can't change basic values and attitudes with specific orders.

As for the difficulty of penetrating the byzantine workings of the LAPD, well, Reinhardt (who later became a Carter-appointed federal judge) quickly realized, in the eyes of the department, that was the only way it could be. For them, it was intolerable that outsiders—the press, the city council, the mayor, even the police commission, would attempt to insert themselves in the running of *their* department. There was this monolithic resistance to and suspicion of the rest of the world—a wall the department was determined to keep unassailable.

Further, each LAPD generation, Reinhardt grew to understand, was training and promoting the next, and everybody was being ranked and promoted from the bottom. It was like this exclusive, inbred club, with so little cross-fertilization, and few new ideas. Every police department has a bunker mentality—it's the nature of the beast. But in the LAPD, after more than two decades of Bill Parker and Ed Davis fostering and building on that mentality, the attitude had deeply permeated the entire organization.

It was a pivotal time in the city's history, a time when the LAPD had become the most politically powerful institution in the government of Los Angeles. The department's power flowed not just from its autonomy, but from the expert manner in which Parker and Davis, who were exceedingly good politicians, had protected and expanded their turf. Parker had been the most powerful public official in L.A., and Ed Davis's close links to the city council made him at least as powerful a figure now as Tom Bradley. Tom Bradley may have appointed a mildly liberal police commission, but he didn't press Ed Davis. It was a fight he didn't need.

In January of 1978, it seemed Tom Bradley would finally have his opportunity to reform the LAPD. Davis, with nearly ten years in office and eager to make a run for governor of California, announced his retirement. Bradley would have a chance to select a new chief—one less bombastic, less contentious, less uncompromising, less tied to a vision of a police department at least a decade behind the city it was serving. It was a hope that proved illusory.

When Stephen Reinhardt and the rest of the commission saw their choices for the next chief of police, they realized that the selection process effectively precluded them from choosing anyone with fresh blood or new ideas.

One key problem was the longtime head of the Personnel Department—Muriel Morse—a strong-willed, powerfully entrenched political ally of Sam Yorty. An active, conservative Republican, her relationship with Yorty was close enough that he had at one time asked her to become one of his deputy mayors.

As the general manager of the Personnel Department, it was Morse who put together the generally conservative selection committee that insured that she got what she wanted. The highest civil service positions are not filled by applicants taking "objective" true-or-false tests but by written essays. Moreover, a large part of a candidate's final score is based on an entirely subjective oral exam, put together by a selection team generally in tune with the values and philosophy of the person who selected them. Usually that person gets the results he or she desires. That was the trick, and nobody understood it better than Muriel Morse, the veteran head of the department. Some maintained that Morse deliberately put off her retirement until she could participate in the selection of a new chief. In any case, it was to be her last major decision, for shortly thereafter she retired.

Twenty candidates were eventually permitted to take the written examination—six of them from outside the LAPD—but the three highest scorers were all departmental insiders: Daryl Gates at number one; the square-jawed, blow-dried, born-again deputy chief Robert Vernon, at number two; and the head of the department's planning and fiscal operations—Deputy Chief Charles D. Reese, in third place.

George Tielsch, the chief of police of the nearby beach town of Santa Monica, who'd written a book on how to take police examinations, had actually scored the highest. But Gates was awarded insider seniority points for his service in the LAPD, and additional points for being in the Navy, and moved to the top of the list. In the process—and due to another quirk in the civil service law favoring insiders—the next-highest-scoring LAPD candidates also moved up with him, and the outsider from Santa Monica was then excluded from further consideration.

"Had Davis retired a year or two later," Stephen Reinhardt later said, "there would have been people making and grading the tests more responsive to Bradley's philosophy and to our desire for an outsider. But that wasn't the way it was when we had to make the selection."

The commission asked each of the candidates to respond to a list of items they wanted the new chief to accomplish—relatively noncontroversial things like how to eliminate the high number of brass in the department's upper echelons, and how to get more officers on the street. Robert Vernon returned with a carefully prepared presentation, complete with detailed flip charts. Using a pointer, he went over each item. Daryl Gates responded with just two words: "Trust me." And in the end, it was he who was chosen, chosen with an enthusiasm as limited as had been the commission's alternatives. "Of the three names given to us, all had considerable negatives," says Reinhardt. "At least with Gates you knew what you were getting—a straight conservative. I didn't think Gates was the right person to lead the department into the future. He lacked both creativity and the desire to make the necessary changes. He was a police bureaucrat, someone who totally reflected the status quo, a Bill Parker product. But I felt he was clearly the best of the lot. In the end we simply had no other choice."

Sima Gates was feeling euphoric on that day in March of 1978 as her husband stood on the parade grounds of the Police Academy in Elysian Park and was sworn in as the forty-ninth chief of police of the city of Los Angeles. A former airline stewardess whom Gates had met on a flight, Sima was his second wife (his first marriage ended in divorce), and clearly this was among the crowning days of her life.

Sitting among the goodwill and festivities, Stephen Reinhardt, on the other hand, was feeling uncomfortable, and more than a bit hypocritical. It wasn't that he disliked Daryl Gates. In fact, he liked him personally, had found him quite reasonable to work with as a deputy chief, and was genuinely touched by Sima Gates's obvious joy. But he knew that this was not the man to bring about the change the department so desperately needed.

Sitting on the stage of the gymnasium during the ceremonies, Mariana

Pfaelzer (who also went on to become a federal judge), Gates's biggest advocate on the commission, turned to him and said, "Don't forget the commitments you made to us." Overhearing, Reinhardt tapped Jim Fisk (now retired and a Bradley-appointed police commissioner) on the elbow. "What commitments?" Reinhardt asked. Not long after, Gates said he'd do his "utmost to get along" with the commission, but that of course he was "going to take issue with them, and I've already told them that."

So Daryl Francis Gates, a man of quiet, boyish charm, narrow vision, enormous ego, and unlimited ambition was now the head of the Los Angeles Police Department. The chief for life, if he so desired. A man with the soul of a clerk had been raised to a height of unchecked power few in a democracy ever achieve. And in the years to follow it would be his policies—along with Ronald Reagan's war on the poor, the vagaries of the international economy, and the complexities of Tom Bradley's soul and political ambition—that would steer Los Angeles toward its cataclysmic destiny.

The disgrace of the Serpico scandals in the late sixties and early seventies had dimmed the prestige and tarnished the glitter of the New York Police Department. Daryl Gates would now head the most powerful, sacrosanct big-city police department in America. He had joined the department and risen through the ranks as the wealth of the city's real estate, entertainment, and defense industries were all coming together; at a time when the L.A. *Times,* the Chamber of Commerce, the Merchants and Manufactures Association, and a conservative WASP electorate were still one with its police department.

But just as cities like New York, Chicago, and Miami were undergoing wrenching, epoch-defining transformations in race, class, and culture, which brought with them an economic dislocation requiring whole new sets of answers, so, too, was Los Angeles. And if Daryl Gates was not the last to notice the change, he would certainly be among the last to understand it. As a result, he would almost immediately run into trouble.

CHAPTER 3

The Killing of Eulia Love

• •

What stood out even then, less than a year after Daryl Gates took office, was how ordinary the shooting seemed, how it was initially viewed by the press and public as perfectly normal—an acceptable, everyday, routine occurrence. How, for example, there was initially just the slightest mention of it in the media—a small, barely noticeable item on page 2 of the local news roundup in the L.A. *Times.*

But even more startling was the LAPD's behavior. How the officers involved made absolutely no effort to avoid the incident, but acted instead in the cool, almost casual manner of men performing a job of termite control. The whole episode, framed by Daryl Gates's response to it, would in fact speak more to the LAPD's long-unchallenged power in Los Angeles and the rage it was causing than to the life of a pitiful black woman named Eulia Mae Love whose fate would unlock a Pandora's box and make her the city's most unlikely cause célèbre.

A thirty-nine-year-old South Central housewife, Eulia Love had lost her husband, William Earl Love, to sickle-cell anemia in June 1978. Although he'd worked as a cook in big-time establishments such as the Brown Derby and the Beverly Hills Hotel, when Love died, he'd left his wife with no pension, three daughters, and a severe cash-flow problem.

The months that followed proved a daily struggle as Eulia Love tried supporting herself and her family on her late husband's $680 monthly social security benefits. The mortgage alone on her three-bedroom, yellow, stucco bungalow consumed $200 a month; food, at least another $200.

As Christmas approached and her bills mounted, Love's financial problems grew so severe she asked her eldest daughter, then seventeen, to find another place to live. By then, she owed $69 and was six months in arrears on her gas payments. A minimum of $22.09 would have to be paid on or about the first of the year, the Southern California Gas Company warned her, or they were going to turn off the gas. The gas Eulia Love used to cook her family's meals.

Although she'd applied to a state program designed precisely to help people like herself pay their utility bills, the application hadn't as yet been processed, and Love, consequently, hadn't received any money.

By the morning of January 3, 1979, when the meter man from the gas company came by either to collect some money or to shut her down, Eulia Love, not unlike many another impoverished recent widow with children to raise, had become a woman on the brink. Her house on Orchard Avenue, like so many in South Central, was on a quiet, palm-lined, neatly landscaped street of well-maintained homes with late-model cars parked in the driveways. And while unquestionably there was a lot of crime in her tough Athens Park neighborhood, Love's street was filled with L.A.'s striving black working and lower-middle class. Love, however, was no longer a part of that. She was barely hanging on.

So when John Ramirez, the meter man, laid out the pay-now-or-be-shut-down alternatives, Love told him that she'd already turned off the meter and, when he went to check it out, smashed him on the arm with a long-handled garden shovel. Without turning off the gas, Ramirez, who later described Love as "distraught" and "frothing at the mouth," quickly left, welts and abrasions on his arm, and a swelling beneath his elbow already starting to develop. Eulia Love then got her purse, walked about five blocks to the local Boy's Market, bought a money order for the exact minimum amount due on her gas bill—$22.09—and went home.

Ramirez, meanwhile, had reported the incident to his supervisor, Bill Jones, as well as to the LAPD. Around four P.M. Jones decided to go to Love's house himself and turn off the meter. But before going, he called

Southeast Division headquarters and asked for "officer assistance to ensure there would be no further violence."

Three gas company vehicles went to Eulia Love's and parked within two hundred feet of her house. There, according to Love's fifteen-year-old daughter, Sheila, her mother approached the truck in which Jones was sitting and tried to give him the money order. Jones and his driver responded by rolling up their windows, causing Love to became "irrational." Returning to her house, she emerged with an eleven-inch boning knife, stood on the sidewalk under the shade of two rubber trees, and began slashing away at them.

It was then that a black-and-white LAPD patrol car arrived. In it were Edward Hopson, a forty-three-year-old African-American with twelve years on the LAPD and several more on the Chicago police force, and Lloyd O'Callaghan, a beefy, five-foot-eleven-inch, four-year veteran of the department. Stepping out of their car, they immediately drew their guns and demanded Love drop the knife.

"She was there on the sidewalk," Jones later said, ". . . talking to them in a loud voice, and she sort of had the knife down . . . swinging it around, but not like she was cutting at anyone . . . more [like she was] gesturing as she was talking—back and forth with the knife."

Love's greeting to the cops was not cordial. She called them motherfuckers. She called them cocksuckers. She told them to kiss her ass.

Standing off to the side, Sheila and Love's youngest daughter, Tammy, twelve, watched as their mother turned and walked away from the officers, back again toward her home. Hopson and O'Callaghan followed, cornering her against the house. There, O'Callaghan swung his more-than-two-foot-long, fifteen-ounce baton and knocked the knife out of Love's hand.

Hopson, meanwhile, was off to Love's side, already locked into the department's recommended semicrouch shooting position: his arms outstretched, his .38—held in both hands—aimed directly at the distraught woman, who was standing no more than ten feet away. At this point Eulia Love made the biggest mistake of her life. She reached down and tried to pick up the knife.

According to the officers, Love was in the act of throwing it when, from less than a dozen feet, they opened up, firing off six rounds in less than four seconds, hitting Love eight times while she was turning and falling. Three of the shots punctured her right thigh, and one each entered her right foot, left thigh, left lower leg, and left upper arm. The eighth and fatal shot was "a penetrating wound of the chest." Later it was reported that a bullet had been flattened on the sidewalk after it had passed through Love's body—indicating she'd been shot at least once while on the ground.

Following the shooting, O'Callaghan and Hopson ejected their spent casings and reloaded their guns. Then, with Sheila and Tammy looking on, Hopson walked over to Eulia Love, put his foot on the neck of her still-struggling body, pushed down, and according to the girls, said, "Lay down, bitch." Then rolling her to the left, he handcuffed her.

Edward Hopson and Lloyd O'Callaghan had arrived at Eulia Love's house at four-eighteen in the afternoon. Two minutes and twenty-seven seconds later she was dead.

The best-case scenario for the killing of Eulia Love was that the officers were in fear for their lives and used poor tactics in not calling for some backup to help deal with the situation.

The worst was that this overwrought, overweight, five-foot-four-inch, 175-pound woman was scared, humiliated, and backed into a corner without a way out, and that Hopson and O'Callaghan had quickly grown impatient and annoyed at this screaming bitch busting their ass—challenging them both personally and professionally, threatening them, making their lives difficult.

It was, after all, neither the style nor the philosophy of the LAPD to give a person a little room, a chance to calm down. That, in fact, was exactly what the LAPD was not about. That kind of shit cut against the department's grain—against its training, its tactics, its soul. It was an approach suited for social workers, a style of policing for cops with leaders who wouldn't back the troops, who wouldn't defend them from the politicians and the liberals and the press when they did what had to be done to keep the lid on. It was, after all, their asses on the line, they themselves who had to ensure their safe return home to their families after every shift.

As LAPD spokesman Lt. Dan Cooke put it several years later when asked to account for a decrease in officer-involved shootings: "Maybe there has been less need to shoot, maybe the word has gotten out to the criminal element not to mess with us."

*   *   *

Throughout the 1970s it would be there, this clash of cultures in Los Angeles. The LAPD would continue to police L.A. as if the city consisted solely of the department itself, the straight-arrow, white, homeowning middle class, and the business community. And it would continue to defiantly ignore the desires of the people who were transforming Los Angeles into one of the most modern and cosmopolitan cities in the world.

Of course the remaining white community, increasingly peopled by a more sophisticated, less homogenized out-of-state immigrant, still didn't want to see three or four six-foot-five-inch black guys or tattoo-covered Cholos on *their* block. Of course they wanted them contained. But they wanted it done with some sense of proportion. Movies like *Death Wish* and *Dirty Harry,* and the fear and anger they represented, resonated in Los Angeles as well as in New York or Chicago. People were worried about crime, and L.A. crime rates *were* high. But crime was not yet daily staring the white middle class in the face as it would in the years to come and as it already was in a place like Manhattan. The underclass in L.A. was seen by white homeowners, business leaders, and corporate lawyers—the people who made the really important decisions in the city and county—only as they drove toward their freeway on-ramp. Los Angeles, after all, was a highly segregated city of vast distances separating the blessed from the despised. Tom Bradley's new, mildly progressive L.A. wanted protection, but without liberal guilt. The highly ambitious, independent people L.A. was attracting from New York, Boston, Chicago, and Europe were used to seeing cops—if they saw them at all—as part of the civic furniture, not the main actors in the life of a city. They didn't want to see blacks or whites shot in situations where the police seemed appallingly aggressive or dismissively careless, nor did they want to feel hassled at a rock concert or outside a club.

But the LAPD had had its way for so long that it refused to accommodate itself to L.A.'s changing face. In fact, the message in the street became even more emphatic: if you defy us, as the killing of Eulia Love demonstrates, we will not go out of our way to avoid killing you. And we will answer to no one.

David Klinger was not exactly from redneck country. In fact, Klinger, the son of a Jewish father and an Episcopalian mother, was from a family that had been active in the civil rights movement. When he graduated first

in his class at the Police Academy at the age of twenty-two, he specifically asked to be assigned to South Central, where he felt he could do the
most good. Four months later, he watched transfixed, as if he were an
actor in his own surreal dream, as a young black man reached into his
shoulder bag, pulled out a butcher knife, and like Anthony Perkins in
Psycho leaped on top of his partner, knocked him to the ground, and tried
to stab him in the neck. Running across the street, Klinger attempted to
pull the man off his partner's chest, but the guy was like a wild man and
flipped Klinger off instead. Simultaneously the butcher knife was pushing
down, inches from his fellow officer's throat. All Klinger could hear was
his partner shouting, "Shoot him, shoot him." Which David Klinger did.
From two feet away he aimed his service revolver, pulled the trigger, and
heard a muted pop as he shot the man in his left armpit. "Oh, shit," said
the man, and died right before Klinger's eyes. "I had always believed,"
he would later say, "that just about everybody could be controlled without using fatal force, but my idealism wasn't real. There are people out
there that are beyond the pale, beyond redemption."

David Klinger, like Steve Fisk, was an LAPD recruit at his best. Most
were from the city's outer limits or the lily-white suburbs, or from places
as far away as rural Iowa and Kansas, high school graduates lured to the
LAPD by its big salaries, plentiful benefits, and increasingly mythic reputation. For the most part they were better spoken and more formally
educated than their working-class counterparts back east. But deep down
they were the same: young white men with parts in their hair and mus-
taches, boys really, often with a spark of idealism, who nevertheless had
as little understanding of the people living in America's urban ghettos as
they might have had if they'd been sent to police the jungle tribes of
Borneo. Any empathy, idealism, or goodwill that existed was quickly
dispelled by the ugly daily occurrences of their working lives. It wasn't
surprising. A gut-level understanding of what was going on was easy to
acquire. One day on the street as a cop would do it. Understanding the
forces behind it—social, political, economic, even anthropological; being
able to truly see the world through other people's eyes—well, how much
can you expect from a twenty-two-year-old, working-class white kid with
a high school education? From someone preselected to fit a particular
profile, one that emphasized a strong sense of good and bad, us and them,
black and white. From someone who'd undergone a regimen and been
exposed to an ethos that would ensure that they saw no shades of gray.

What could you expect from kids, as Steve Fisk later put it, "who'd been given a gun and a badge and all the authority they needed . . . all the backup they needed to take somebody's life and ruin it, kill someone, destroy their family and their reputation. It was a very heady position for someone in his early twenties to be in."

How could they be expected to care about alien communities in which they had no stake, not even as local taxpayers? It was far easier to fall into telling cynical can-you-top-this war stories about the human garbage out on the street. Far easier to shrug your shoulders, as did Steve Fisk and David Klinger, and settle into the notion that no matter how hard you work it's not going to make a bit of difference—that people are still going to kill each other over whether the TV set should be tuned to channel five or channel seven. And as things progressed in the sixties and seventies, it grew hard to argue with them. An omnipresent fear of crime was permeating America's cities. The Age of the White Man, the conformity of the fifties, was dying. You could feel it. The social fabric of places like Los Angeles, New York, and Chicago was becoming a fragile thing that, in the decades to follow, would be stretched to the breaking point. The kinds of senseless, stomach-churning, violent crimes feared most— and committed most frequently by young blacks and Hispanics—were sharply rising, and rising each year over what seemed already intolerable levels. This hadn't always been the case. In the early sixties, crime rates were low, and prison cells in many parts of the country lay unoccupied. But by 1968, a Gallup Poll, for the first time in its thirty-three-year existence, found that the American people now regarded crime as the country's number one domestic problem. That same year the FBI reported that urban crime had risen 88 percent from the start of the decade through 1967. During the 1970s, in Los Angeles, the crime rate would increase by almost 70 percent.

Guns, thousands of guns, were flooding the streets of Los Angeles, filling police officers, like the residents of many of L.A.'s and America's impoverished urban neighborhoods, with a new and extraordinarily real fear. That fear, along with an LAPD training that focused inordinately on the dangers of police work, an attitude on the part of the LAPD hierarchy that refused to discourage indiscriminate shootings, and the alienation most cops were already feeling from the people they were both serving *and* repressing, would produce a potent combination and lethal results.

*　　*　　*

By themselves, the LAPD's numbers were not startling. The late sixties and seventies were characterized by high numbers of killings by police throughout big-city America. In 1970, for example, there were more than 350 killings by police in fifty cities. Taking 1975 as a base year, for instance, the LAPD shot and killed thirty people and wounded fifty-one. In comparison, the Chicago PD, in a city with a similar number of people, killed thirty-seven and wounded ninety-nine. So LAPD's shootings were not out of line.

No, it was rather the nature of so many LAPD shootings, and of the department's dismissive explanations after its investigations, that eventually provided the fuel for the firestorm of criticism in the months and years following the killing of Eulia Love. People were being shot or choked to death for wielding such items as a liquor decanter, wallets, sunglasses, gloves, a hairbrush, a silver bracelet, a typewriter, a belt, a key chain, even a bathrobe.

While working in a Sunset Boulevard high-rise, for example, a twenty-one-year-old maintenance man named Charles Chiarenza was shot and seriously wounded by one of several officers who had been pursuing an armed man into the building. Chiarenza had been repairing an electrical system on the building's roof. Passing through the door leading to the roof, the officer saw a glint from "a shiny object" and, firing once, hit Chiarenza, who had been holding two "shiny objects." One was a screwdriver, the other a chrome-plated flashlight.

There was the case of Martin (Meb) Brantly, a fifty-three-year-old mentally disturbed man who was holed up in his home, resisting efforts by police and psychiatric workers to take him to the mental ward of an L.A. hospital. Temporarily blinded by a chemical spray the police had used while attempting to subdue him, Brantly ran from his bathroom into the living room with a club in his hands. Bumping into the officer who had been chasing him, he dropped the club as both men fell to the ground. Then, without the club, Brantly stood up, whereupon the officer, who had remained on the ground in a crouched position, drew his gun, shouted, "Hold it," and according to witness and neighbor Herbey Hernandez, shot Brantly "right after he said [hold] it." Hernandez and his father would later say that Brantly had nothing in his hands when the officer fired, but an LAPD report would claim that Brantly was holding a type-writer over his head, ready to throw it, when the officer killed him.

And there was Alice English. During a 1983 drug raid on the house of a friend, as the *Herald Examiner* reported, English, twenty-eight, was standing naked in a shower stall.'' According to the police account, ''English was holding an object in both hands at chest height and lunged at the detective [who had entered the bathroom]. . . . [The] detective instinctively whirled to his left in a crouched position and fired one round from his service revolver at English, striking her in the left groin area.'' And killing her. In her hands was a dark rolled-up bathrobe. The district attorney, the police commission, and Chief Daryl Gates all found no violation of shooting policy in English's death.

In addition to objects held in hands, LAPD officers would use automobiles to justify shootings on at least seventeen occasions in the six-year period from 1980 to 1986, saying the cars had been used as deadly weapons against them.

There were other shootings—scores of them—involving unarmed people. There was the shooting of Kenneth Ramirez, nineteen, in October of 1980, at about one A.M. outside his parents' house. Ramirez had just arrived home from his job at Lockheed Aircraft where he worked the four P.M. to midnight shift. On the way he stopped for a short visit with his fiancée and three-month-old daughter.

Earlier that evening, two men in a car registered in the name of Ramirez's father had robbed a woman in Beverly Hills. Searching for the suspects, two LAPD officers drove up to the Ramirez house just as Kenneth Ramirez—who was unarmed and knew nothing of the robbery—was leaving his house and walking toward the parked automobile. Spotting the patrolmen pulling up, he turned and walked directly toward them. Then ''as the police car stopped, the passenger door immediately opened and [one of the police officers named] Rhinehard started out,'' according to a forty-page report by the Los Angeles district attorney's office. ''Ramirez had continued walking and was now abreast of the right front tire of the police car. Rhinehard withdrew his service revolver [and] within one second of Officer Rhinehard's exiting the police car, his gun fired once and Ramirez fell to the pavement.'' Although Ramirez was hit above the left eyebrow and killed instantly, Rhinehard refused to be interviewed by the district attorney's office, and no charges were filed. Those were some of the shootings.

Then there were all the guys dying from doing the chicken. That's what the cops out on the street called it, ''doing the chicken.'' Somebody gives a cop some lip or flips him the bird or takes a swing at him, and boom, the next thing he knows an officer's baton is around his neck and he's "doing the chicken," flopping around helplessly like a fool until he loses consciousness. It was an easy way to make anybody show a little respect, to cause a son of a bitch who didn't want to be cooperative to *be* cooperative. And afterward, there was always an excuse. He pushed me away, he flailed his arms. Almost any movement could be construed as offensive. And once you put that arm around him, and the guy started flopping around like a marionette, that further justified applying the pressure because the guy's damn sure resisting now. "I can remember," says former assistant chief David Dotson, "a jailer whacking a guy on the shins with his flashlight because he was walking up the wall with his feet. Well, the reason he was, was that they had him in a choke hold on his back and he was trying to get some air. I mean, what did they expect the guy to do?" Within the department, it was officially referred to as the "upper-body control hold," and unofficially as the choke hold. You placed a forearm or baton around a suspect's carotid artery and squeezed until the suspect stopped resisting or was rendered unconscious. It was a basic hold used unofficially by a lot of police departments in very violent situations when a guy *needed* to be controlled. But the LAPD was using it officially, routinely, and defiantly.

Over a seven-year period from '75 to '82 the LAPD would choke fifteen people to death. This, as opposed to only one choke-hold death each in New York, Chicago, San Francisco, and Dallas in the same period. There was Larry Morris, twenty-nine, who was choked to death in his apartment after exchanging taunts from his balcony with officers passing by. When the Police Commission criticized Morris's death, Daryl Gates let them know that Larry Morris was *supposed* to be doing the chicken. The officers who killed Morris, Gates wrote the Commission, "reacted aggressively to what they perceived to be a serious incident . . . it is this precious quality of service I feel we must do everything in our power to avoid losing. And there was Robert Ian Cameron, thirty-two, a passenger in a car stopped by LAPD officers, who then allegedly attacked them with a hairbrush and was also choked to death. And Hubert B. Avery, a black doctor who saw his son stopped by police officers and walked over to ask what the problem was. He was severely beaten with a nightstick and choked until he passed out. And Donald R. Wilson, a naked man who died when he was choked while handcuffed and manacled.

All of these incidents, as well as scores of others involving the killing of unarmed civilians by the LAPD (one in three civilians shot by the LAPD in the late seventies would prove to be unarmed), would have extenuating circumstances: PCP in the bloodstream; a struggle with police before a typewriter was raised to be thrown; a nervous officer in fear of his life. And the inquiries that followed would be characterized by a bending over backward to justify the officer's actions by a department investigating itself and operating under what seemed a set of unwritten but inviolable rules: (1) an officer involved in a shooting or choke-hold death is never wrong; (2) department policies and procedures are the best in the nation and therefore are in no need of change; (3) a story favorable to the officer will be released just hours after an investigation has begun and remain the department's official position no matter what evidence subsequently emerges.

In time the self-serving rationale the police department would issue after every controversial killing would engender a devastatingly accurate parody on the streets of South Central: "Subject reached into his waistband and pointed a black, shiny object at the officer, which subsequent investigation proved to be his finger."

CHAPTER 4

The Patsies

....

Sitting in his office, Jim Bellows, the newly hired editor of the *Los Angeles Herald Examiner,* spied the tiny paragraph of Eulia Love's killing in the local-news roundup of the *Times.*

As small as the item was, it nevertheless seemed to Bellows to be filled with passion and conflict: Eulia Love, a thirty-nine-year-old black mother of three, had been fatally shot eight times outside her home by two LAPD officers in a dispute over an unpaid gas bill.

Turning to one of his assistant editors, Frank Lalli, Bellows asked how such a killing could possibly have happened. "The image of this defenseless woman being shot multiple times just seemed all wrong," and it disturbed both of them, Lalli later said. There seemed, moreover, a pattern to too many of the LAPD shootings, and a pattern to the department's explanations. Something, thought Bellows and Lalli, had broken down.

But their interest in the story went beyond that. A year earlier—in January of '78—Bellows had been hired by the Hearst Corporation to try to turn around the *Herald,* which as L.A.'s second paper had been losing millions of dollars for well over a decade and was almost daily falling even further behind in circulation, advertising, and revenues.

The only way to compete with the *Times,* Bellows, the former editor of the *New York Herald Tribune,* believed, was to show L.A. as the city in flux that it was and hope people would turn to the *Herald* instead of the *Times*—which he regarded as a "mausoleum." "I told Bill Thomas [then the editor of the *Times*] that I was gonna try and get people upset," Bellows later said. "It's important for an underdog newspaper to do that. It forces the big dogs to get in the pond with you."

"Bellows knew the *Times* could kick our ass whenever they wanted to," recalls Joel Sappel, who was then reporting on the Love story and other police stories for the *Herald.* "There was just no way we could be the paper of record. But he also knew that we could beat them [the *Times*] on any one story." And Eulia Love and the whole issue of the LAPD's abuse of power was to be that story.

First, Bellows ran a twenty-two-paragraph story on page 3 of the *Herald.* Then, six days later, he ran another lengthy article, this time on page 1. A dozen days later, he followed up with an even longer front-page story. It had a picture of a youthful, attractive, smiling Eulia Love and the headline: "The $22.09 Gas Bill Tragedy."

The *Herald* had a large black readership, and the stories created an uproar in the city's African-American community, setting off a chain reaction of follow-up stories by the *Times* and the *Herald* on the LAPD shootings, choke-hold deaths, and spying. What everybody in L.A. with an ounce of street sense had known for years was finally being investigated and reported by the establishment press. Stories that in almost any other major American city would have been regarded as laudatory but unremarkable were soon to be hailed as watershed events.

For a quarter century, the LAPD had been largely unassailable in the local press. That was the atmosphere that existed in late 1976 when Wayne Satz, an investigative reporter for local television station KABC, wrote to Ed Davis and the police commission asking for detailed information about shootings involving its officers. He and his news director, Dennis Swanson, had been observing a pattern of unarmed civilians being shot and killed by the LAPD, followed only by a few terse lines in the city news service. That was it. No public discussion, no questions asked. He wanted to know, Satz wrote Davis, how many people they had shot in the past, what the circumstances were, how many of the suspects had been unarmed, and what the disposition of the cases had been.

They received no response. Nothing. Satz and Swanson were incredulous. "It was astonishing to us that we could make an inquiry and that it would simply be ignored," says Satz. "They didn't think they had any public accountability whatsoever. Their arrogance was incredible."

But Satz, an attorney turned reporter, and Swanson were from out of town and therefore had not understood the local ground rules: (1) The investigations of shootings by LAPD officers were solely the department's territory, as was any discipline to be meted out. (2) It was *they* who were the experts, not some asshole reporter or hotshot politician out there trying to make a reputation for himself.

They and KABC News responded with a critical report called "The Accountability of the LAPD" to be aired daily on or near the top of the six o'clock evening news. They interviewed witnesses to shootings whose versions or events often differed dramatically from the official LAPD version. They repeatedly asked why the LAPD alone was responsible for investigating the shootings and why other city agencies such as the district attorney, the coroner, the police commission, and the city council weren't more involved. Then the station's general manager started running editorials backing up the news division's efforts.

One day, in the most dramatic development of the coverage, an LAPD officer named John Mitchell, who worked out of South Central's Seventy-seventh division and had been watching Satz's futile attempt to get any information about the shootings, contacted the television station.

Mitchell volunteered to help, but refused to be publicly identified. So KABC aired a series of on-camera interviews with him disguised in a scuba diver's hood and a mask. Mitchell said that most of the officers he worked with were racist and, moreover, "extremely eager to be in a shooting."

Ed Davis was outraged. The ACLU, some ad hoc police abuse group run out of a South Central storefront, they were meaningless, but this was a sworn LAPD officer, a fifth columnist whispering institutional secrets and embarrassing the department. During one interview, the camera panned to the Masked Marvel's hands. So determined was Ed Davis to silence this affront to departmental publicity that he had the videotape of Mitchell's hands freeze-framed and then blown up and examined for any telltale marks or scars that might reveal his identity. Twice he then went on the LAPD's in-house, closed-circuit television system and denounced KABC and Satz by name, calling the reporter an enemy of law enforcement and making dubs of his statements to the troops available to other local stations. He hoped, said Davis, that the people of Los Angeles would watch Channel 2, not Satz's station, Channel 7. Luminous green bumper stickers announcing "Satz Sucks" began appearing on LAPD squad cars; calls came in telling him to back off if he wanted to stay alive; targets at the Academy firing range popped up with Satz's picture on them. Although the Masked Marvel broadcasts with Mitchell only lasted about a week, the police series itself ran five months and won a Peabody Award.

But the L.A. *Times* was the agenda-setting newspaper of record. And although it had already made its historic transformation from right-wing rag to one of the nation's best papers, hard-hitting investigative reporting—particularly of local institutions—was simply not its forte. As a major investor in the city's financial life and in the redevelopment of downtown L.A., it seemed disinclined to make waves. And like that of many big-city dailies at the time, the paper's local coverage was slim and inadequate, especially of the city's black and Hispanic communities.

On the few occasions when critical reporting of the department was done, as the *Times'* own media critic David Shaw later pointed out, the paper and its reporters were met with such a fierce counterattack that by the late seventies they'd simply backed off. Right after Eulia Love's shooting, in fact, a black *Times* journalist, Celeste Durant, wrote a story on Love's funeral and a demonstration against the police, and the paper decided not to run it. But the situation couldn't continue. Not if the *Los Angeles Times* wanted to maintain its newfound journalistic integrity. By the late sixties, the kind of submissive respect the media had given both the lords of foreign policy and the chiefs of law enforcement in Bill Parker and J. Edgar Hoover's post–World War II America had been shattered by both Vietnam and America's social revolution. Television news, moreover, was now bringing the breaking stories to the public, and daily newspapers like the *Times* were being forced to emphasize what television did not: investigation, analysis, and the placing of a story into a social and political context. Doing that meant understanding why so many people like Eulia Love were dying at the hands of the LAPD.

The *Herald*'s coverage of Eulia Love's killing would have the lasting effect that Wayne Satz and KABC had not. After her death, the LAPD would be critically covered by the *Times* on a day-to-day basis. Gradually, a detailed documentation of the department's successes, failures, follies, and excesses started accumulating. For the first time in decades, the local press would no longer be, in the words of Stephen Reinhardt, "a patsy for the police."

CHAPTER 5

Higbie

·····················

He wasn't bright, but Chuck Higbie damn sure knew how to follow orders. And he was dead loyal—which was what counted most to Daryl Gates. Once in a 1983 deposition, a civil rights attorney had asked him if he agreed with something Gates had said. "Well," replied Lt. Chuck Higbie, who was in his early fifties at the time, "he's the chief of police. Of course, I agree with anything the chief of police says." He seemed to regard his duty as head of the Officer Involved Shooting Team not as an investigator who gathered the facts and let the chips fall where they may, but as a protector of his officers and the department. And that was certainly appreciated. As an old friend of his once described it, Chuck Higbie was considered a kind of combination of St. Christopher and the Buddha by LAPD officers: "He is their guardian, so to speak," said defense attorney George Franscell. "He is loved, admired, and respected. The man is just recognized as Mr. Perfect." And celebrated among the troops, according to one LAPD officer, as "a major deity." And no wonder. By 1986 Chuck Higbie had headed his investigative unit for thirteen years. And in the seven-year period from 1980 through the end of 1986, not one LAPD officer would be charged for shooting someone in the line of duty. And prior to one indictment filed in 1979, the district attorney's office had not filed charges against any of his officers who'd been involved in a shooting for the previous eight years. Three hundred and seventy-two shootings by LAPD officers had occurred from 1980 to 1986, and many of those shot had been unarmed, but no officers had been indicted, and only one had been fired. In fact, when Chuck Higbie retired in 1987, he had investigated more than sixteen hundred use-of-force incidents involving LAPD officers, and only nine had resulted in criminal prosecutions. And three of those nine were indicted in just one case.

Not only was he loyal, but he was old-school dedicated, out on the street, clipboard in hand at every hour of the day or night, whenever an officer was involved in a shooting. He'd even left in the middle of his own daughter's wedding to investigate a shooting. Such dedication did not go unrewarded. In 1985, for example, Higbie, whose base pay as a lieutenant was then $53,000, made over $108,000 with overtime. His salary allowed him a Mercedes-Benz sedan and a comfortable suburban lifestyle in Orange County, away from the city in which he had so much power over people's lives. And he was also powerful within the department. A lowly lieutenant given his authority first by Ed Davis and then, and most especially, by Daryl Gates, Charles A. Higbie controlled not only the investigation of sixteen hundred cases from beginning through witness interviews to final report, but was also a key lecturer at the Police Academy, passing on his wisdom about what to do if one day an officer should become involved in a shooting or choke-out.

Having dropped out of Jordan High School in Long Beach after the tenth grade, he went into the Marine Corps at seventeen. When he was discharged in 1953 after serving in Korea, he had a high school equivalency diploma, a Purple Heart, and numerous other decorations. In 1957, Chuck Higbie joined the LAPD, keeping his fifties crew cut, big-man's fifties belly (he was six feet three inches and 240 pounds), and identity with the Corps well into the 1980s. Gates had first met him at the scene of a shoot-out during the 1960s. A suspect in a house had fired at the police and refused to surrender, and Higbie had volunteered to go into the tear-gas-filled house to get him. Daryl Gates was greatly impressed when he emerged with the wounded suspect. And although Higbie was already heading the Officer Involved Shooting Team when Gates became chief, it was under him that Chuck Higbie would become a departmental star.

*   *   *

It seemed a daily occurrence for David Dotson in the early 1980s. He could not pick up the *Times* or the *Herald* without seeing yet another embarrassing, page-one story about an LAPD shooting. A trim, cautious man from Iowa, Dotson had joined the LAPD three years after being discharged from the Air Force in the midfifties, and had steadily worked his way up to deputy and later assistant chief, one rank away from The Man himself, He was a strange guy for an LAPD cop. Easy-mannered and unassuming, he believed in management by consensus. A runaway who'd been on his own since the age of fourteen, he possessed only an associate's degree from the College of the Canyons, but nevertheless had a grasp of the historical and social forces shaping Los Angeles; that was a rare thing in the LAPD. He believed in following the book, the rules, and the chain of command, and although Chuck Higbie and his Officer In-volved Shooting Team had a good deal of independence, they were none-theless under his command in the Headquarters Bureau. And David Dotson was unhappy not only with the headlines, but with the investiga-tions Chuck Higbie was conducting.

Those investigations, he felt, were raising "really troubling questions," and the reports Higbie and his team were submitting were often "worth-less." That was a big problem, as Higbie's reports, according to one department expert, constituted "ninety-nine percent" of what the LAPD Board of Rights considered when reviewing the use of force by officers; and they were also highly influential as well in determining what action Gates, the police commission, and the district attorney took.

So one morning after yet another headline, Dotson picked up the phone and set up a meeting with Jim Hardin, the commander of robbery/homi-cide, and Chuck Higbie's immediate supervisor. "Look," he told Hardin when they met, "these investigations are terrible. I want you to tell Higbie to get with the goddamn program and start using the same inves-tigative techniques we use in our other investigations." It wasn't neces-sary for Dotson to add that he meant the same investigative techniques that were also used by police departments all over the country. Chuck Higbie, according to David Dotson, replied with clarity and unequivoca-tion: "Tell him," he said to Hardin, "that we don't have time for that shit, tell'm that it's crazy, tell'm I'm doing what Gates wants me to, and tell'm to mind his own fucking business." "And by God," says David Dotson, "after that I minded my own business." David Dotson had learned that Chuck Higbie, as he himself put it, was "a creation of the chief, answerable only to the chief.'' That Chuck Higbie ''was,'' in short, ''above the law.''

Unlike LAPD officers, most civil rights attorneys would roll their eyes skyward when Higbie was brought up. One characterized Higbie's investigations as ''shot through with poetic license.'' Another described Higbie's reports as ''setting the scene to explain what the civilian did to get himself shot.'' But in fairness to Chuck Higbie, shooting and excessive-force cases have always been difficult to investigate and discipline. Police work *is* repression, and physical intimidation and reasonable force are the ultimate guarantor of law and order. The line between doing your job and unnecessary brutality is often a fine one. As a result, officers are found guilty only in an extremely small percentage of excessive-force or shooting cases. That in itself sends a message: if you can fog up the facts, claim not to remember, say you didn't see what your partner did, or simply lie if there were no witnesses around, you can nudge a shooting or complaint over into the unsustained category.

''I've been there, I used excessive force on the street when I was a young cop,'' says Dave Dotson. ''So I *know* it happens. And subliminally the message is sent out about how to go about these things without having to pay the consequences.'' Once an officer *is* brought before a trial board, in L.A., as in many other cities, it's a board composed of other cops. And even if the evidence is overwhelmingly against the officer, there's always some excuse, some mitigation that the trial officers are open to seeing, because they, like David Dotson, have been there themselves and know how easy it is to lose it. So the discipline in excessive-force cases tends to be light, and the desire not to ruin an officer's career or send him to jail if it's a shooting case is very strong. Decisions are easier, situations more clear cut, when a cop shoots somebody off the job when he's drunk or does something that's really stupid or laughs at bureaucratic rules and knowingly breaks them. That's straight up and down, easy to define, and they frequently get nailed. The problem was both Chuck Higbie's investigations and the discipline that followed were going far beyond the normal loyalty that cops have for each other.

It had been set up that way even before Chuck Higbie. ''There was a period at the time when I entered the police department in the fifties until 1977,'' says former LAPD commander Jack White, ''when there was no shooting policy. And this was by design. It was felt that a shooting policy would further limit an officer's activities [as well as] subject the city to liability.'' Then, investigations and reports were confidential and not subject to discovery—that is, did not have to be given to a plaintiff's attorney if they decided to sue. The chief of police could read it, get a picture of what happened, and defend his officers. And the city attorney could use it to defend the city. But as the law evolved, the reports became discoverable and usable by the plaintiffs as well. Officers could be in serious trouble if the district attorney decided to indict, the city liable to heavy financial liability. The need to protect the officers and the city became compelling.

No one recognized that need more than Daryl Gates. His compassion was aroused by Eulia Love's killing, which he described as ''tragic.'' But despite the police commission's public condemnation of the shooting, Gates could not bring himself to do likewise. Instead he said that he didn't ''think there was one single good thing that came out of [the] Eulia Love [killing and investigation], not one single blessed good thing. The *Herald Examiner* finally found a story that was going for them . . . and just beat [it] to death.'' Yes, civil awards against his officers were rapidly growing, but there were reasons for that, too. As the city attorney had told him: ''in almost every case . . . 'there was either a sympathetic jury or there were witnesses who changed their views . . .' ''

In the wake of the public outcry over the shooting of Eulia Love, the district attorney, John Van de Kamp, finally found the need to do something. And in 1980 he commissioned a study funded by the Justice Department and conducted by the Washington D.C.–based Police Foundation. Its purpose was to evaluate the LAPD's and the DA's shooting investigations.

James Fyfe, a criminology professor and former NYPD lieutenant, was one of the investigators. ''What we found,'' says Fyfe, ''was that the primary purpose of the department's investigation was to protect itself from any liability or embarrassment. They would use irregular investigative procedures. When interviewing civilian witnesses, for example, they would immortalize their testimony on tape at the time of the initial interview. But civilians aren't professional witnesses. They're surprised by what's happened, often in a state of shock. So you can bet there'll be inconsistencies. But when the officers were interviewed, it was together, in a group session, with no tape. Questions were asked off the record—

and a version of events squared away. It gave them an opportunity to shoot holes in the civilians' stories and iron out inconsistencies in their own. *Later,* the cops would be taped, and their versions would all be the same. So their version was assumed to be the correct one. When I asked about this, the explanation that was given to me by Lieutenant Higbie for not immediately taping the cops was that police officers are very emotional and that they don't want to be embarrassed by breaking down and sobbing on tape.''

Fyfe's findings coincided precisely with the problems David Dotson had found in Higbie's investigations. Dotson, moreover, had been disturbed that civilian witnesses were not being interviewed by the Officer Involved Shooting Team, but instead by divisional detectives. The detectives had not heard the officers' statements and consequently did not know the right questions to ask to get at inconsistencies between the officers' and the civilians' versions of events.

Van de Kamp also established a special District Attorney's unit to investigate police shootings. Almost immediately its members began bitterly complaining about Higbie. He was, said the investigators, allowing civilian witnesses to slip out the back doors of police stations so they couldn't interview them and was failing to notify them beforehand of witnesses who spoke only Spanish and therefore needed an interpreter to be interviewed. He was ignoring the police-commission directive that the department deliver a preliminary report within a week of a shooting and was sometimes taking months before submitting a final report. In some cases, the DA's investigators were actually being denied close enough access to a shooting scene to get a good view of what had happened. ''I regretfully have come to the conclusion,'' Deputy DA Gilbert Garcetti, who headed the Special Investigations Division, told the *Times,* that ''he [Higbie] is playing games with us. He knows what kind of information we need. If he withholds information for hours, days or weeks he is impeding our investigation.'' ''He's just protective of the officers in every case,'' said Assistant DA Johnnie L. Cochran, Jr., then the number three man in the DA's office. ''I don't know of any case where they've come over and said, 'We've got a bad shooting here.' '' To which Chuck Higbie replied that he was tired of Garcetti and the DA's office ''whining and crying.'' ''I'm getting sick of it,'' he said. ''I do not welcome these people with open arms. Our dealings with them are purely professional. I don't serve tea or cookies at these unfortunate occurrences.''

Finally, in late 1983 (the year twenty-five unarmed civilians were shot by LAPD officers), the Los Angeles Police Commission issued another directive, this one requiring the LAPD to use "criminal investigative standards" in officer-involved shootings, and to, among other things, separate and tape-record officers when questioned.

But according to William D. Hall, who replaced Higbie as the head of the LAPD's Officer Involved Shooting Team, the directive wasn't followed. Instead, said Hall later in sworn testimony, the tape-recording of officers during initial questioning continued to be routinely ignored, despite the explicit orders to the contrary. The police commission policy, said Hall, "talks about tape-recording and interviewing the officers in a manner that's consistent with normal criminal investigations, [but] in reality that is not done." Instead, "verbal instructions" were given to the members of the Officer Involved Shooting Team that were "in opposition to what is in the Eulia Love report," which mandated the proper procedures. Officers were interviewed for up to ninety minutes, but were recorded only for fifteen-second monologues.

Following the uproar caused by the 1979 shooting of Eulia Love and the tightening of the department's shooting policy by the police commission, LAPD shootings dropped from sixty-one in 1979 to about forty-five in each of the subsequent two years. But after that, they rose to at least fifty a year. In 1983 there were sixty-six, and in 1985, sixty-eight. By 1986, a comparison of officers in the six largest American cities showed that members of the LAPD "killed or wounded the greatest number of civilians, adjusted to the size, of [any] police force. LAPD officers killed 3.0 persons per 1,000 sworn officers and wounded 8.1 persons per 1,000 sworn officers. In Detroit, with the second-highest violent- and property-crime arrest rate, the comparable numbers were 1.2 and 5.0 respectively."

The truth of an old saying in the department, "Don't worry, the pendulum will swing back, just wait them out," was once again proving true, as the public and the press became fixated on the Bloods and Crips, and LAPD shootings returned to page 3 of the *Time*'s Metro section. Oh, occasionally the subject would surface as it did in a special 1986 three-part report in the *Herald,* which was as good as anything ever written on the subject. But that was in a paper that was literally about to die and that few people were bothering to read.

Throughout the 1980s, Tom Bradley, the city council, and the police commission would either ignore the problem of excessive force and bad shootings or do the minimum required to curb them. But, it was really up to Daryl Gates. He could have said: I am by the book, gentlemen, and the reason I am by the book is because I don't want you to be hated in the community, I don't want people shot who shouldn't be, I don't want you to become professional liars, and I damn sure don't want to see you indicted. Instead, he used the opportunity to set the stage for things to come.

CHAPTER 6

The Macho Men

·······················

It was amazing how much Daryl Gates's modus operandi changed after he became chief of police. Bob Gaunt, an old assistant chief who'd worked with Gates when they were both up-and-comers, used to tell the most illustrative story about the Daryl Gates who'd so studiously climbed his way up the ranks. "What time is it?" he would ask Gates. And Daryl Gates would squint, look at his watch, pause for a moment, and then reply, "I'm not sure, Bob . . . what time do you have?"

During those years he'd been not just cautious but astute. At Jim Fisk's post-Watts community-relations seminars for the top brass at Lake Arrowhead, it was Daryl Gates who had proven the most instructive person to watch. Ed Davis would try to dominate every meeting. But Daryl Gates would quietly take it all in, carefully measuring everything that was being said and everybody who was saying it. Then when it became clear what the consensus was, he'd speak up, his comments always perfectly reflecting that consensus. The ability to say the right things without ever committing anything of his own had always been one of Daryl Gates's greatest talents as he rose to the top.

Which made his behavior when he finally became chief all the more inexplicable. At staff meetings and seminars he was now abrupt, unresponsive, aloof, his body language and attitude inattentive. He would push aside and simply not address some problems while using inappropriate forcefulness to deal with others, and, like Parker, he would lash out at any kind of criticism or threat to his position, whether perceived or real.

He was notoriously bad—perhaps as bad as Bill Parker in his final years—at accepting advice, criticism, or bad news from his deputy and assistant chiefs. He wasn't open, he didn't listen. Senior staff people would talk to him about internal problems, but problems would be left unresolved, decisions left unmade. "I don't believe," one of them would later say, "that he gave any credence, validity, or value to much of anything that anyone on the staff had to say."

According to David Dotson, Jim Jones, then Daryl Gates's chief of staff, once wondered aloud to Gates why he didn't simply get all his deputy and assistant chiefs together to hammer out solutions to nagging problems. Gates had let him know why: "Jim, you don't understand. I'm the chief. There's no way they can comprehend what the chief's responsibilities are, no way they can understand what it's like to be chief of police." The clear implication, at least as read by several assistant chiefs, was that they, his staff, had nothing to offer. It was a major miscalculation.

Like Bill Parker, Daryl Gates had little understanding of other points of view and none at all of the ways in which people of a different race, sex, or class perceived the world. Consequently, he was entirely missing the subtext of what was taking place in a city that was becoming increasingly, and extraordinarily, complex. He needed other voices. "Gates," a high-ranking officer told the *Times* in the early eighties, "is in over his head, that's the real problem. He hit his level of competence as an assistant chief and that's where he should have stayed. He doesn't have either the flexibility or the foresight to be chief of a department this large."

But Daryl Gates loved being chief of police, loved playing the role, loved the attention that came with the job. He was the protégé, Bill Parker's boy now heading the master's LAPD. He had risen under Parker and been director of operations, the second most powerful position in the department, for almost eight years under Ed Davis. And now he was chief. In Los Angeles the LAPD was omnipotent. Why shouldn't Daryl Gates believe he was omnipotent, too?

But one could never experience the essential Daryl Gates without understanding that he was a nice guy. That's the way he saw himself, and that's the way he wanted to be seen by the people whose opinion mattered most to him: his own troops. After the rocky start he'd gotten off to as chief—with all that carping from the Police Protective League and all those blind quotes in the L.A. *Times* about whether he could cut it or not—being a nice guy became, in fact, one of the cornerstones of his management style.

And as he grew into his job and took on the gravitas of a man nearing sixty, he seemed every day to more and more relish the role of paterfamilias within the LAPD family.

Some wondered if this wasn't just for expediency, since the backing of the troops was crucial for any chief of police. As one LAPD officer recalled, "It was very important that after those first years when he was constantly on the defense that the troops saw him fighting back, taking dominion, being the man, playing John Wayne. It was the part of the whole LAPD tradition and they needed that." Others felt it was something deeper.

"Gates," says Jesse Brewer, who became the department's first black assistant chief in the mid-eighties, "wanted so badly to be loved by the troops that everything he did was a defense of the department and the troops. 'They are attacking us unnecessarily, and we are the greatest police department in the world,' that was always his line. . . . He'd never just come out and say, 'Look, we just screwed up.' " "He wanted to be their father but a very benevolent father," says David Dotson, who, like Brewer, served directly under Gates as an assistant chief. "That's the way he approached the troops, ignoring the part of parenthood that requires sometimes that you take the kid by the scruff of the neck, take him out behind the woodshed, and tell him what it is you expect of him."

One thing was clear. The opinion of a narrow cadre of hard-nosed, old-line cops was inordinately important to Daryl Gates. They weren't just cops, but men of whom he seemed to be truly in awe: the guys who were at home on the street—the legendary characters who could spot a crook a mile away, feared nothing, and could take charge of any situation. He seemed to feel he needed their approval. But just as importantly, he liked those guys, he identified with them. And that fact was key in understanding his frequently bellicose public persona, his lenient attitude toward discipline in shooting and excessive-force cases, his disdain for affirmative action, and his intolerance of suggestions from outside the department. For the department's macho men—more than the city council, the businessmen, and the homeowner's associations—were his true constituency. The hard-driving troops in Metro, the men of SWAT, the guys in SIS, the old-time detectives, the dog men, OCID, PDID, the old vets constantly going around bitching about how it ain't like it used to be—all of them, all the special-unit boys, they were his real base, the people to whom he played. He needed them. They were the department's opinion-makers. Daryl Gates's reputation when he first became chief had been that of a "squint," of a Parker Center desk jockey who'd made his career busying himself studying for the next promotional exam. Like a young Army officer out of ROTC who's put in most of his time behind a desk and goes out at lunch and sees the airborne in training, sees the Green Berets with their Purple Hearts, Daryl Gates seemed awestruck. He had never put in serious years out in the street, in the field with the grunts and "gunslingers." He was not one of the legends, a John St. John or Thad Brown who'd seen, heard, and done it all, even though he had commanded Metro. But over the course of his almost thirty years on the force before he became chief, Daryl Gates, by his own count, had spent only six years in uniform, on the street. He had busted prostitutes and mah-jongg games and staked out public rest rooms frequented by homosexuals—an assignment, he later told the *Times*, that was "about as low as you can get." But the closest he'd come in those years to any real danger was when he'd been cut on the head by a hooker. He'd never been shot at or shot at anybody. It was the equivalent of a general never having been in combat. He'd never really walked the walk, so he definitely had to talk the talk.

For Steve Fisk, shootings were a part of the job. That's why he didn't have a problem with the killing of Eulia Love. Sure it could have been handled differently. But one thing that Steve Fisk, like most cops, hated was to second-guess another officer in a shooting situation. There were just too many variables, too many things moving too fast, too many split-second decisions to be made, too many times when something happens that you're not ready for. Steve Fisk tried to stay ready and was always amazed when he talked to other cops who hadn't already thought through what they were going to do *before* they got into a shooting situation.

That was his attitude even before he'd joined the Special Investigation Section, the secretive stakeout unit known as SIS. Even before that day in

1977 when he and eight other SIS officers were following around these four black kids in a car. Normally they didn't stake out and follow juveniles. It was taboo. It just wasn't done. If they thought some kids were about to commit a crime, they'd pick them up right there, nip it in the bud. SIS was too deadly a business to deal with kids. Its mission was to follow people around, sometimes for weeks. Violent people, rapists, armed robbers, burglars, suspects whom they knew were going to do it again, but didn't have the evidence to arrest or convict. So SIS tailed them and waited and watched as they did their crime (except, of course, for rape; they never let a rape go down). But an armed robbery, they'd let *that* happen, *then* go after the robbers as they left, and then take them out. Most big-city police departments didn't have full-time surveillance squads like SIS trailing habitual criminals, and most would never stand by and watch an armed robbery take place as SIS did. One out of three people gets hurt in armed robberies, according to the Justice Department, and 10 percent of all killings take place during armed robberies. But not the SIS. The job of the SIS was not to protect people being robbed, but to get the lice out of the street. Permanently. Within the department SIS was thought an elite unit doing elite work. But outside, among civil rights attorneys, they were considered an execution squad that had shot and killed twenty-three people between 1967 and 1990, and wounded at least twenty-three others. Many of those people had been gunned down in cold blood—deliberately, unnecessarily, they charged, in a kind of LAPD final solution. In 1988, in fact, the *Los Angeles Times* examined thirty-two shootings by the SIS and found that in twenty-eight of them the suspects had not fired at the officers; and that "SIS detectives over the years had shot thirteen unarmed people."

Steve Fisk had been on SIS for five years on that day in 1977 when he and the other SIS officers started following these black kids, waiting for exactly what went down: the four youths pulled into a gas station and two of them got out and robbed the station, while the cops stood by and watched. That's what they did: watch and wait. Wait outside a suspect's house in the morning and put him to bed at night. Wait until the crime they knew was coming finally went down. Then they'd take them *out.* From 1978 to 1987 the SWAT team shot fifteen people; SIS twenty-nine.

It wasn't exactly in the manual, but if you had a shooting or two in your jacket, you had a much better chance of getting into an elite unit such as Metro or SIS. Shootings were a badge of honor. Metro, in fact, had a tie tack made from the primer end of a shotgun shell. It was worn by those who had been in a shooting, worn as a badge of distinction. On their caps and T-shirts, many SIS members had a cloak-and-dagger emblem of a man dressed completely in black, wearing an oversize fedora, clutching a long knife, his cloak pulled up to cover his face in a secretive moment. That was SIS's mind-set when the two seventeen-year-old black youths emerged from inside the gas station, hopped into their car, and barreled out of their parking spot. "It's a good one! It's a good one!" Steve Fisk heard one of the detectives shout as a shot was fired from the car, and was answered by a shotgun blast from the detective.

The suspect's car took off down Western Avenue and finally screeched into a grocery store. Steve Fisk, who was following, screeched in behind him. As he did so, the kid in the car, the driver, bailed out and was wounded by another detective. He then headed directly toward Steve Fisk. There they were, Steve Fisk and this kid, maybe eight feet away from each other, holding guns, scared shitless. "Police officer, drop the gun! Police officer, drop the gun!" Fisk screamed. But the kid didn't drop it. His adrenaline was going, he was probably in shock, not even realizing that he's still holding the gun in his hands. So he just stared at Steve Fisk. And instead of just cutting the kid in half, like he was *supposed* to do, Steve Fisk jerked his gun up at the last moment and squeezed a blast over his head. Once the suspect heard the noise, he dropped the gun and that was the end of that.

Then he walked over and looked inside the car. Sprawled across a seat was thirteen-year-old Toni Hyams, her brains splattered everywhere, her brains just all over the car's interior. It was the most sickening thing Steve Fisk had ever seen. He didn't want to bad-mouth the judgment of the officer who'd shot her, but there was this young girl horribly dead, for, as far as he could see, no reason at all. She hadn't actually participated in the robbery, and whether she even knew what was going on or not has never been determined. "But, I mean," Steve Fisk would later say, "it just seemed like such a waste. A thirteen-year-old gal, bang, dead, just like that."

After the shoot-out, Steve Fisk couldn't come to grips with what had happened, not then. He wasn't drunk that day, he didn't drink on the job. But nevertheless he was still drinking hard off duty, his mind a constant bourbon haze. His confusion wasn't helped after his supervisor, who was angry, *very* angry, chewed his ass, or as Fisk himself later put it, in an oddly genteel choice of words, "chastised" him. "You had the opportunity to kill this kid and you didn't do it," his supervisor told him. "This kid's out there robbing places and you were the guy that could have ended this thing and he'd never do it again and he'd never hurt anybody again." That was his supervisor's mentality, that was the culture, as if they *were* executioners. And Steve Fisk couldn't argue with him. "I mean," as Steve Fisk would later allow, "the guy had a point. He had a point."

Steve Fisk had been drinking for a long time before that day that he'd fired in the air. Serious drinking. Drinking until he'd black out and wake up in his car someplace and not even remember where he'd been. But that had always been because he'd enjoyed it, enjoyed the drinking. Or so he says. But that night, after failing to kill the kid in the parking lot and seeing the brains of the thirteen-year-old girl in the front of the car, he started drinking to get away from the memory, to mellow out, to try to come to terms with all this killing he'd been involved in. The next day he called into work: "I'm not coming in today. I've got the flu." After that, things just got worse. For the next several days he stayed drunk. Once after a killing he had called his father, Jim. "Dad," he said then, near tears, "I murdered a man." This time Jim Fisk arranged for his son to go to see the department psychiatrist. Steve Fisk showed up drunk. But it didn't matter. The LAPD had nothing for officers going through that kind of stress at the time. They do now, but back then, they didn't know how to cope with a Steve Fisk.

He had to get away. In 1978 he was awarded a stress pension, and with his wife and family he moved to Idaho. Things didn't get any better, but his drinking got worse. He got divorced and then remarried. Then one day, driving in a pickup, Steve had a flash of insight. He was living where he wanted, had the woman he wanted, had all the material possessions he wanted, and he still wasn't happy. That's when he felt he had no choice. That's when he knew he had to go back to his childhood teachings, back to what he had learned about God and Jesus Christ. He hated to use the term, hated to use it because he knew the derisive snorts it evoked, but he was born-again. And after that, everything seemed to fall into place. In 1986 he returned to L.A. and the LAPD, becoming a highly successful homicide detective in Pacoima and Van Nuys.

For five years he had worked a secret unit that had no full-time equivalent in cities like New York, Chicago, or San Francisco. A unit that needed to be closely monitored and to have its officers regularly rotated. Neither of which had happened. And that was the very least. Whether a secret unit with SIS's kill rate should exist at all was another question entirely. (In 1988 when the *Los Angeles Times* asked the LAPD for details of the number of shootings and the officers involved, the department refused to give out the information on the grounds, according to the *Times,* that it would "violate laws guaranteeing the officers' privacy.")

But it had allowed Steve Fisk to live down his father's reputation as a liberal. Even if it had almost killed him.

CHAPTER 7

Stop the Band

•••••••••••••••••••••••

Soon after Daryl Gates was appointed chief in 1978, the voters of California passed a mundane-sounding ballot initiative limiting property taxes. Known as Proposition 13, it was a watershed event in California, the cataclysmic trigger for the great tax revolt that was about to sweep the nation, characterize the Ronald Reagan eighties, and decimate the social fabric of the once ''golden state.'' The mood of the country was shifting ever rightward. The revolt of the affluent, of the haves, had begun. In California, the ability of local government to raise property taxes—the heart of funding for local services such as police and fire protection and public school education—was now to be severely and permanently curbed throughout the state.

The bloom was off the California dream, and what had once been among the finest public service and social welfare systems in the country was about to shrivel up. Once the proud leader of the nation in funding for education, California would fall from second in state spending per student to forty-eighth.

It was in this atmosphere, and on the very day after the voters had passed Proposition 13, that the LAPD's top leadership met for their annual Staff Officers Retreat. The only subject that anybody wanted to talk about was how dramatically Proposition 13 was going to cut the tax base of the city and therefore the budget of the LAPD. The time was ripe and the staff retreat was the perfect opportunity to assess the cuts that the department would inevitably have to make. Suggestion after suggestion to scale back personnel, budgets, or matériel were made, but in the end, no plan to deal with the ramifications of Proposition 13 was adopted. Nothing. Even though *some* kind of a comprehensive plan was desperately needed.

In 1981, Keith Comrie, the city's chief administrative officer (CAO), came up with one: an exhaustive audit of the LAPD that suggested dozens of measures the department could take to slash its expenditures. Daryl Gates was infuriated. He hated Comrie, whom he regarded as Tom *Bradley's* CAO, "Bradley's hatchet man." A man who was now trying to eliminate the funds for his department. Was it any wonder that "communications ... between Parker Center and City Hall," as the *Times* pointed out shortly afterward, had "broken down almost entirely"? Was there any reason for Daryl Gates to walk "across the street [to the mayor's office and to the city council chambers unless] absolutely required"? "Why," as he rhetorically asked a *Times* reporter, "should I go?" He couldn't "get a damn thing through their sometimes very thick skulls ... and [he hadn't] heard a new idea from Bradley or the great Comrie since [he'd] been chief."

Some of the CAO's recommendations—and the cuts that were eventually made—*were* genuinely painful. This was true of the thirty full-time, uniformed officers who had been teaching law enforcement in predominately black schools, and of the seventeen lieutenants who had been working full-time in the community-relations programs Ed Davis had set up. But Tom Bradley, whom Daryl Gates regarded as a great antipolice liberal bent on emasculating the LAPD, had actually exempted the department from cuts until 1981, when he reduced its budget by just 3 percent, compared to 15 to 18 percent for other city agencies. According to the LAPD's own records, in fact, Bradley had been approving between 90 and 99 percent of the department's initial budget requests. Sam Yorty in his last five years in office, Sam Yorty, the "propolice" mayor with all that provocative law-and-order rhetoric, had granted between 84 and 94 percent of the department's requests.

But Daryl Gates was never a man confused by the facts, and what he saw was not an effort by City Hall to adjust now to a new fiscal era, but the stripping away of the department's independence and glory. The police band. They were even eliminating the funds for the police band! So with TV cameras rolling, Daryl Gates acted to dramatize his contempt. Calling the report "the worst I've ever seen, disastrous," Gates, without rancor and with a smile, took it, flung it to the ground, and stomped on it.

Despite intense lobbying, the city council finally told Daryl Gates that the mayor was right, cuts would have to be made. And they were. But once again nothing changed. "We didn't look at reorganization," David Dotson would later say, "we didn't look at reprioritization or . . . any . . . obvious solutions." In the years following Proposition 13 the department's sworn officers would decrease through attrition from 7,400 to about 6,700, with no fundamental change in the organization that Ed Davis had structured for 10,000 men during the heady days of free spending, a rubber-stamp city government, and a fat tax base. Far too many officers were still in special units, far too many in staff positions, and nine levels of bureaucracy still separated Gates from the street. And increasingly, there were too few officers on L.A.'s violent, gang-ridden streets.

By the mideighties, all of this had become impossible to ignore, and a complete reorganization was becoming critical. Key deputy- and assistant-chief positions were opening up as officers retired, but there was simply no money to fill them. The time when you could move a few people here, a few there, and let attrition do the rest was long since past. A major overhaul was imperative.

So a reorganization conference was arranged; for three extraordinarily full days and nights, Jesse Brewer, David Dotson, Deputy Chief William Rathburn, and other members of the department's senior staff worked on a reorganization plan. Putting aside their own fiefdoms and personal agendas, they were able to drastically reduce the department's bloated, high-salaried command staff and redesign it to reflect the city's new fiscal realities. They felt good when they finished. They'd come up with something that really worked. But Daryl Gates was not pleased. In fact, according to David Dotson, he told them that "they were crazy," that, as Jesse Brewer later put it, they were "a bunch of dummies" who didn't "know what the hell [they were] talking about." Didn't they understand what they were doing? he asked. Instituting those recommendations would be "deadly," would "cut out promotional opportunities" for younger officers. The structure of the department, he said, was going to stay the way it was. That was it. After that, it was as if the report and its recommendations had been written with invisible ink.

CHAPTER 8

Form the Wagons

The command staff restructuring might have been a flow-chart exercise to Dotson and Brewer and the rest of them, but for Daryl Gates the whole tradition of the LAPD was at stake. The idea that something extraordinary had been created and perfected and now had to be protected and insulated from change was, after all, the guiding principle out of which he operated. Like Bill Parker, he was the department and the department was him. Criticism of his person was criticism of his creature. Neither could be tolerated. And no mistakes would be acknowledged. The paranoia of Bill Parker and the line drawn in the sand by Ed Davis would be built upon by Daryl Gates. And as a result, as former LAPD deputy chief Lou Reiter would put it, there grew within the department "a siege mentality, form the wagons, if anyone talks out of shop about the LAPD, it's like they are a traitor, they are out to get us."

By the end of the 1980s it was impossible within the department to remember when this hadn't always been so. It was just about that time that George Felkenes, a professor of criminal justice at Claremont Graduate School, did a survey of more than fourteen hundred LAPD officers. He found a high degree of job satisfaction among most of the officers—including the women and minorities—whose pay and benefits were among the very best in the nation. But he also found that "once . . . in the department, they [the officers] are shaped and molded into what the department wants them to be . . . [and that] the subculture and peer pressure becomes very strong and breeds out any autonomy in an individual."

As every white cop knew, having blacks and women on any police department meant the possibility of a different consciousness and point of view, the possibility of a bleeding heart, the possibility of someone who could actually tell the difference between one black piece of shit and another, or who might not think it was funny when you humiliated some asshole. That was one reason why those who didn't quite fit in, who had the wrong background, who'd been rebellious, flirted with drugs, were rumored to be gay, or in fact were gay were weeded out beforehand. Those that did get in—and large numbers of blacks and women were getting in thanks to the courts—had to be held in check, had to be good white men, part of the club. And they would be made that way by their desire to be accepted, and by the internal and external need to prove themselves, to be part of the family, part of the police culture, one of the boys. It was a constant counterbalance to any real difference in perspective or willingness to speak out. The pull of the job is powerful indeed.

"Cops see themselves as having been given the very confusing and unpleasant task of being society's char cleaners . . . ," says former Minneapolis chief of police Tony Bouza. "They're asked to undertake a task that in large part is morally bankrupt. . . . So they lie . . . to you and to themselves, and stick together. They don't expect you to understand their plight or their dilemma . . . it's the code of silence, *omertà;* the closing of ranks, the keeping of organizational secrets."

But the world was filling up with assholes, with individuals who wanted to go their own way, and some were making their way to the LAPD.

Carl McGill was a good example. McGill, a thirty-one-year-old African-American, had moved to South Central from Connecticut with his family at fifteen. After joining the LAPD, he began working during his off-duty hours to try to stem the flow of gang warfare. He counseled the parents of preteens, gave antigang lectures to high school students, and joined the Black Chamber of Commerce. By June of 1988 he was gaining a national reputation for his antigang efforts in South Central, and ABC News, describing McGill as one of California's "leaders for the future," chose him as their Person of the Week. But ever since he'd entered the

Police Academy, says McGill, he'd had a reputation of "not walking like a duck." Once an instructor had observed him giving a soul shake to a black cop from the sheriff's department. "If I catch you doing that shit again," he was told by the instructor, "you'll be kicked out on your ass. You wanna do that, go out and sell bean pies."

It was the same with his antigang work. That independent shit. It affected people's mental attitude, gave them a false sense of themselves, eroded the department's cohesion, made them forget exactly who it was that was setting policy. Push came to shove, and Carl McGill was suspended and threatened with being fired for insubordination. "The department just doesn't like officers who do things on their own," the five-year LAPD veteran would later say. "They don't like officers who have their own ideas."

Sgt. Alex Gomez was another one. Assigned as a community-relations officer in the heavily Mexican-immigrant community of Boyle Heights, Gomez had gone beyond the traditional LAPD community functions of going out on the street glad-handing, speaking to kids about crosswalks, and eating rubber chicken at community-group luncheons. Instead he began holding fund-raisers to aid the neighborhood's many impoverished people. He worked with a rock station and with area businessmen to organize a concert starring Linda Rondstadt that raised over $100,000 for a local youth center. He worked locally with children who were terminally ill. But Gomez was involved in a fund-raiser that starred that mascara-wearing, painted-lipped former junkie Boy George, a choice about which people on Chief Daryl F. Gates's staff, among others, complained.

So in spite of the fact that Gomez had built and headed "one of the most prolific police fund-raising units in the country," as the *Los Angeles Times* put it, he was reassigned to patrol duties, and a new LAPD policy was promulgated. "Under the [new] rules," said the *Times*, "any officer who [now] wants to raise money—even by passing the hat for a crime victim—must seek permission from the brass downtown in Parker Center."

Diversity such as McGill's and Gomez's had to be kept in check if the department was to remain *Daryl Gates's* vision of the LAPD.

After becoming Fort Worth's police chief, Daryl Gates's former chief of staff Thomas Windham would point out how the system worked to fill the LAPD with little Daryl Gateses: "The people who get promoted [within the LAPD] don't have differing points of view. They've worked the right jobs, got to know the right people, and the department is very slow to change . . . and the rank structure, from top to bottom, thinks along the same lines, no matter what the issue might be. It made for situations where things had a tendency to become sacrosanct.'' Earlier, Sgt. Frank Grimes, a Protective League official, put it another way: ''No officer is going to advance . . . is going to make it through the orals [exam] unless he becomes a Gates clone.''

It wasn't, of course, that the thinking within the LAPD was monolithic, just what people were willing to say. Everything was centralized in Parker Center and ordered from the top down. There was no opportunity in the precincts to innovate and experiment—to adapt to local situations, as Alex Gomez found out. It was mandatory that you think like The Man. And it didn't hurt to look like him either. By 1980 blacks still only comprised about 6.5 percent of the force, Latinos under 11 percent, and women about 2.5 percent. That year, however, after a long, bitter court fight, the city and the LAPD entered into two consent decrees requiring the department to increase the number of females hired until they made up 20 percent of the department's officers, and the numbers of blacks and Hispanics to correspond to their percentage of the metropolitan Los Angeles workforce. So by the end of the decade the number of blacks and Latinos on the LAPD had doubled to 13.5 percent and 21.5 percent respectively, and increased fivefold for women to 12.5 percent. But 61 percent of the LAPD was still non-Hispanic white. So were 67 percent of its detectives and almost 80 percent of sergeants. But it was in the higher ranks where the discrepancies were far greater: 83 percent of lieutenants, 86 percent of captains, and 84 percent of commanders. One reason the higher ranks weren't better integrated, according to City Councilman Zev Yaroslavsky, was that ''Neither Gates nor his predecessors had ever dipped below number one on the [civil service] list, and if you have a guy with a 97 and a guy with a 96.8, he'll pick the 97, even though there may be a black, Hispanic, or woman within one-tenth or two-tenths of a point.'' So while blacks, Latinos, and women were being hired, they were getting promoted at a far slower rate than white males.

Nor were all those new hires forced upon the department being smiled upon as they positioned themselves for promotions. They weren't getting their fair share of positions in ''coveted'' units such as air support, SWAT, Metro, and Internal Affairs, or as adjutants to deputy chiefs and other high-ranking officers. Those assignments lay at the core of the promotional process, providing both the experience needed to do well on examinations and the opportunity to get known and meet mentors who'd serve as guides and put in a word for you with their fellow brass on oral boards. Working in the right place as an adjutant allowed an officer to meet the people at the top, see how they operated, and understand their concerns. "He sees them in staff meetings, reads their written communications—and that gives an officer a leg up," says Tom Windham. "The way promotions are made on the LAPD, you have these upper-level officers on interview boards, and most of the people who come before those boards are known. Their reputations and accomplishments follow." Daryl Gates couldn't stem the tide. Their day would come. But he could slow it down.

CHAPTER 9

Whispers in the Ear of the Chief

••••••••••••••••••••••

A new embarrassment. They were coming one after another. Eulia Love. Choke-outs. And now this, this spying thing. In April of 1975, Tom Bradley had held a press conference along with then chief of police Ed Davis to announce that the LAPD had destroyed 2 million dossiers on some fifty-five thousand individuals and organizations. Two thousand five hundred files would remain active, along with the LAPD's two intelligence divisions; the Organized Crime Intelligence Division (OCID) and the Public Disorder Intelligence Division (PDID). In 1975–76, they would still have almost 190 people working for them, and a total budget of close to $6 million, far more than either robbery-homicide, burglary–auto theft, or bunco-forgery had. Far more. But that was about as much as was known. Omerta was at work. "There is little we talk about as far as what PDID [the division charged with political surveillance] does or . . . how many men are assigned. . . . We don't talk about PDID at all," said Lt. Dan Cooke, the department spokesman at the time.

That was where it rested until 1978 when a group called the Coalition Against Police Abuse (CAPA) uncovered the names of some PDID members. They were surprised to learn that one of them had been their organization's secretary. CAPA went to the ACLU, and in 1981 the ACLU, CAPA, and one hundred individuals and twenty organizations filed lawsuits. They alleged that the LAPD had illegally spied on them, tapped their phones, and in at least one case, had had a PDID officer have a romantic affair with one of the plaintiffs. After hearing the evidence the court ordered the LAPD to release six thousand pages of intelligence documents. They showed Bill Parker's paranoia pushed over the top by the Panthers and the Social Worker's Party. The LAPD had been illegally spying on everybody: the National Organization for Women, Operation Breadbasket, the Beverly Hills Democratic Club; slightly liberal religious, civil rights, and environmental organizations. Over two hundred organizations and individuals in all. They had infiltrated private meetings attended by Mayor Tom Bradley, meetings of the city council and of the police commissioners. They had spied, according to former OCID detective Mike Rothmiller, on Democratic congressmen Edward Roybal and Mervyn Dymally, on L.A. city councilman Richard Alatorre, on State Senator Art Torres, on former governor Jerry Brown, and former Los Angeles district attorney and California attorney general John Van de Kamp. (The files on both Van de Kamp and Brown, said Rothmiller, were fishing expeditions to prove they were gay. In Brown's case "the files showed eavesdropping on his car phone conversations [and] intense surveillance [of his apartment].")

"I was chairman of the transition team that put together the report . . . for the dismantling of PDID . . . ," Jesse Brewer would later testify, "so I know that at the time there were files on elected officials because I observed some in my investigation. [They were] of elected officials who had run afoul of the law and who the department was aware of. . . . I think we are privy to a lot of information that is not necessarily positive about a lot of people, but I don't think that's in files."

Instead, both Ed Davis and Daryl Gates received secret briefings especially prepared for them. Whispers in their ear. "There was a weekly intelligence briefing that had been going on for years," says David Dotson. "The briefing would be all verbal. In the old days there would be reports. After PDID [the PDID scandal], everything was verbal, and if a captain had a couple of key words on a notepaper to jar his memory, that was destroyed. It never became a file. It never became discoverable. It never became damning in any way." But the information, or at least its threat, was there to be used. As Daryl Gates would later tell Ted Koppel on "Nightline," "If I really laid it on the line, and it may come down to exactly that, when I do, watch out."

CHAPTER 10

The Boxer

••••••••••••••••••••••

Daryl Gates reacted characteristically to the negative press coverage following the shooting, choke-hold, and spying controversies. Like a good lightweight boxer matched against a bigger man, he had a remarkable ability to go with the punch, to semi-admit to something, to appear, in fact, to actually *agree* with you as he meandered through his long, convoluted sentences. It was only toward the end, when you began to be taken with his reasonableness, that he would hit you with the rabbit punch. That was the genius of his style; that and his tenacity, his ability to make mistake after mistake, take punch and punch, and never be knocked out of the ring. Conceding nothing, he would turn around and blame his critics of the very problems for which they were attacking him.

He was, moreover, a perfect master of a certain kind of American idiom, a talk-radio brand of rancor-filled, chip-on-the-shoulder indignation. Early on, he had understood the free-floating anger and deep frustration that has increasingly characterized the public mood. Like Sam Yorty and Ed Davis, he understood The Fear. Instinctively, he seemed to know how to reach for that feeling. That feeling that had been out there ever since all those blacks, Mexicans, and Latinos from seemingly every isthmus and island in the Caribbean, started hitting America's big cities like a Florida hurricane. That feeling that had been manifest ever since the hippies, liberals, and faggots had taken over Hollywood, the courts, the universities, and the Democratic Party. He'd reach deep and pull out his ace in the hole, which was nothing less than the white man's fear of the insanity that he saw blossoming in the neighborhoods in which he once lived. Daryl Gates might sound mean-spirited, might act vengeful, yet because he was so well plugged into The Fear, he managed to come across to Richard Nixon's forgotten Americans as their defender, as one of them. As Rush Limbaugh later would, Daryl Gates understood that people like to identify a villain, focus aggression, and maintain hope by having someone with authority articulate what they're thinking. And America and Los Angeles were full of Daryl Gateses, full of people for whom it resonated when Daryl Gates spoke the truth: "I don't remember anybody ever telling us [his boyhood family] that just because we wanted a glass of milk for breakfast and didn't have it, we should steal milk from the neighbor's front porch. . . . Find a place in the desert . . . to send criminals. Give them a hoe, some seeds, and . . . put a mile of land mines all around a fence." At a press conference in England, he'd suggested that if President Jimmy Carter was finding it impossible to rescue the American hostages then held in Iran, then *he* could, simply by ordering in his LAPD SWAT team. To stop the export of cocaine from South and Central America, he suggested international sanctions. And if they didn't work, "a friendly invasion," adding, "I really don't give a damn if it's friendly or not." On the CBS television network in 1985, he would effusively praise Philadelphia mayor Wilson Goode for approving the police bombing of the headquarters of a black radical organization called MOVE, a bombing that was not only the first *aerial* bombing in history on mainland America, but that also resulted in the deaths of eleven people and the setting ablaze of blocks of housing. By his actions, Goode had become an "inspiration to the nation," Gates told a wide-eyed Leslie Stahl, and had "jumped on [his] heroes list." And "by golly," he added, "that's not a long list." Daryl Gates had simple answers. People liked that.

And if he sometimes sounded like Sinatra in Vegas at his Rat Pack petulant worst, people understood that, too. He was authorized to be petulant; his first four years in office, after all, had been "the most disappointing, frustrating period of [his] life,'' a time when he ''hadn't been able to do a damned thing except try to hold things together and avert real human tragedy . . . General Douglas MacArthur had just been trying to win his war, too, but they wouldn't let him either.''

Daryl Gates would say all these things and sound genuinely perplexed when criticized. After L.A. *Times* reporter Bella Stumbo had followed Gates around for a month in 1982 and then written a thirty-thousand-word profile that was devastating in its details, Gates simply took what for him was a pile of shit and turned it into gold. ''I think she [Stumbo] gave that impression [of] my being angry,'' said Daryl Gates. ''I am not an angry person. I am someone who, I believe, does what too few people do today—simply, I am willing to speak out on issues I think affect this police department. I feel good about the fact I can tell people what I think of them. And, as Bella will tell you, I never talk off the record or use that as a hiding place for my comments. Everything is on the record and I suppose that is why sometimes I find myself in difficult waters.'' He didn't seem to grasp the down side of playing Archie Bunker.

But Tom Reddin believed that it *all* trickled down: ''When Ed Davis fought with everybody, the man [the cop] on the street thought he could fight with anybody, too. And they would rather do that, listen to a policeman like that, than listen to a chief who is saying that we cannot and shouldn't engage in that type of behavior any longer because this is a different time in history. Cops like it when there's no gray area. If a guy gives you some trouble, whack him, and he's not going to give you any trouble anymore. He won't respect you, but he'll be afraid of you. Hand-to-hand combat is a lot simpler than having to deal with verbal judo. Law enforcement is about ninety percent gray area and about ten percent black and white, and the 10 percent black and white is at one end of the spectrum or the other and in the middle is the gray area. Well, the gray area is very difficult for the cop on the street. He would like it to be all black and white. If it's black and white, it's easy, much easier, to make a decision.''

Occasionally, Daryl Gates would miscalculate just how far he could go. His uttering of four words, ''blacks and normal people,'' during a 1982 interview with the *Los Angeles Times* would be such a case. It had started with the long-simmering controversy about the LAPD's use of the upper-body control holds, the chokes. The coroner at the time was attributing a lot of deaths to the use of the hold, and the negative press, now that the *Herald* and the *Times* were seriously covering the police department, was becoming intense. Choke-out deaths were all over the papers. In seven years fifteen choke-hold victims had died. So the LAPD did a study, and it showed that while the hold had been applied in approximately equal numbers to Hispanics, blacks, and whites, twelve blacks had died from them, two Hispanics, and just one white—numbers that were extremely disparate.

When David Dotson saw the statistics, it was clear to him that something was wrong, but he didn't know what. Why, if the choke hold was being applied in equal numbers, were there so many more blacks dying as a result? So he met with Daryl Gates, told him what they'd found, and suggested that they look at why so many blacks were dying from the holds.

It might have resulted from blacks resisting more when the hold was put on them, or blacks being more intoxicated or in poorer cardiovascular health. There were a number of possible explanations for the study's results, including cops applying the hold with more force on blacks.

But in his eagerness to defend his department rather than address the problem of unarmed citizens who had committed no capital crime dying at the hands of his police officers, Daryl Gates offered up the tentative results of the study to the *Los Angeles Times* during an interview. "We may be finding," said Daryl Gates by way of explaining the high percentage of black choke-hold deaths, "that in some blacks when [the choke hold] is applied, the veins or arteries do not open up as fast as they do in normal people."

"Normal people!" Nobody could believe it. "Normal people!" Where had this guy been for the past twenty-five years of the civil rights movement? Was it possible that the chief of police of a city that had been through Watts, that had a black mayor, black council members, and was vying with New York for the title of most cosmopolitan city in America could have been so . . . so . . . unaware? Was it really possible that he was actually insulting everybody's intelligence with this lame theory? That this was what he *really* meant to say? But there it was. In the days that followed, a tidal wave of criticism from the NAACP, from the ACLU, from the city council, and from the police commission would wash over Daryl Gates. Before it ended, David Cunningham, a black city councilman, was comparing Gates to white supremacist Lester Maddox and genetic determinist William Shockley. And Tom Bradley was uncharacteristically calling on the police commission to launch an unprecedented disciplinary investigation into the chief's "disparaging, intemperate, inappropriate, unfounded" remarks. The investigation, of course, went nowhere. And after a flurry of press coverage, the status quo returned.

CHAPTER 11

The Fear

....

It was silly. Dumb at worst, politically inastute and comically naive at best. There was Daryl Gates posing in a photo in the *Los Angeles Times* after announcing he was seriously considering running for mayor of Los Angeles. Facing the camera, Gates held up a large, dark T-shirt with the lettered slogan "Gates for Mayor 198-," the last numeral being deliberately left out. It was a big political mistake. But not untypical. For as Daryl Gates was uncanny in gauging the pulse of the public on gut issues, he otherwise had a way of expressing himself that was best summed up in a drawing by Conrad, the liberal L.A. *Times* editorial cartoonist. It showed Daryl Gates balancing on one foot as he attempted to place the other in his mouth. He knew his constituency. But that was all he knew. And as a result, his first years in office had often been public relations nightmares. Shortly after entering office, he had, as the L.A. *Times* put it, applied "the mañana stereotype" to his Latino officers—and before a Latino audience—by saying the reason they weren't promoted more rapidly within the LAPD was because they were lazy. Then in 1980 he'd incurred the wrath of women's groups by calling a local blond TV anchorwoman "an Aryan broad." After that, he'd enraged the black community with his "black and normal people" remark. Then he'd angered many Jews in 1982 when he'd allowed the release of a report that suggested that the Russians might be using the large number of Soviet Jews emigrating to Los Angeles as a way to infiltrate criminals, spies, and agent provocateurs into the city to disrupt the 1984 Olympics.

Several years later, seemingly still not having learned his lesson, he'd been publicly—humiliatingly—slapped down by the state's Republican hierarchy when he'd proclaimed that becoming California's next governor was his next goal. It was embarrassing. He seemed a lost political novice once he was out of his role as chief of police.

But in his sphere, he was really quite good. He knew how to hold on to what he had and to resist change and "interference" in the running of the department. And once it became clear to the city council, as well as to Gates himself, that he had as much chance of being elected mayor of L.A. as say Strom Thurmond would have had if he'd chosen to run for mayor of Detroit, his relationship with the city council improved significantly.

For Daryl Gates always knew how to take care of the city council. How to keep them satisfied: how to give what they asked for in terms of police services. How to keep them off his back and in his pocket.

There was, for example, Robert Farrell, the black city councilman from burglary-ridden South Central, who, according to former LAPD detective Zvonko G. Pavelic, had a patrol car pass by his house almost every day and night. And if his office called to complain, say about vandalism, a special patrol car would be sent out with officers particularly skilled in public relations and communications to make sure that Farrell or the constituent he was calling about got the best possible service.

Sooner or later city council members came around, either becoming ardent supporters of the department or learning at the very least to always support more cops on the street.

Zev Yaroslavsky was from L.A.'s largely white, largely Jewish fifth council district and had come to prominence in Los Angeles politics as the quintessential outsider. The only son of Ukrainian immigrants, Yaroslavsky was a brash, populist troublemaker who'd attended Fairfax High when it was 90 percent Jewish and one of the best public schools in the country, and then gone to UCLA. In 1972, at the age of twenty-one, Yaroslavsky, fifty pounds overweight, wearing polyester suits and Medusa hair, had been led away in handcuffs by the LAPD after protesting the treatment of Jews in the Soviet Union during a performance of Moscow's Osipov Balalaika Orchestra. That same year, he was fired from his

$150-a-week job as executive director of the Jewish Federation's Southern California Council on Soviet Jewry. A federation official later told the L.A. *Times,* "He was fat, unkempt . . . a radical. He was persona non grata around here." But just three years later, after walking almost every block in the fifth council district passing out plastic bottle caps with his name on them, he scored a monumental upset, defeating both Bradley aide Fran Savitch and ex-councilwoman Rosalind Wyman.

Then, in the early eighties, Yaroslavsky, one of the those on whom the LAPD had kept a dossier, led the fight against the department over the issues of police spying and choke holds. Putting himself on the line, Yaroslavsky directly challenged the LAPD, something no other local politician, including Tom Bradley, had been willing to do at the time.

But by the mideighties, and the rise of the Bloods and the Crips, Yaroslavsky's concerns had changed. With one eye on his constituents' fear of crime and the other on the mayor's office, Yaroslavsky began playing "Can you top this?" with Bradley and other city council members, voting for increased funds for manpower and technology for the department and saying little publicly about ever-accelerating LAPD brutality. His Jewish constituency's demand for law and order and his political viability had become far more important than a no-win issue like police reform.

Meanwhile, the city's black and Latino leaders in areas like South Central and Pico-Union were also demanding that something be done about street crime and gang violence. Richard Alatorre was the chair of the city council's Public Safety Committee, which oversaw the LAPD at the time. A Mexican American who'd started out as a liberal, his district was 70 percent Latino and many of the young men in it were being rousted or beaten by the LAPD, yet he had become even more uncritical of the department than Yaroslavsky. His constituents, he said, "all wanted more police, and more people sent to jail. And they will almost tolerate anything [to see that achieved]."

Charles Stewart, the press secretary to black state senator Diane Watson of South Central and himself an African-American, best summed up the attitude of L.A.'s black and Latino politicians on the issue as the decade neared its close: "As long as you have this sort of fear, then the perception of law-abiding minorities is going to be that the police are not as bad as the gangs. When you have a state of war, civil rights are suspended for the duration of the combat."

CHAPTER 12

The Weepers

· ·

It was an outrage. One so unprecedented and intolerable that the entire physical-training staff of the Los Angeles Police Academy felt that they had no choice but to act collectively and demand that something be done. Things were bad enough already having the courts and the liberals pushing these women and so-called minorities into the Academy, and mandating that all these females and underqualified blacks and Hispanics be admitted. In all, 25 percent of each cadet class now had to be composed of women and minorities to reach the court's quotas. The blacks and Hispanics—the men that is—you simply dealt with, even if you knew they wouldn't be there without special treatment. What else could you do?

But the women, the women were a different story entirely. No upper-body strength. No balls. Pun intended. In general, they were weepers, weepers who were quitting or getting pushed out of the Academy at a rate of close to 70 percent just two years after this consent decree had gone into effect. What did they expect when they started sending all the females up to the Academy in those kinds of numbers? The men, for God's sake, were being thrown out at a rate somewhere between 37 and 38 percent.

Then, they'd hired this new psychologist, Dr. Martin Reiser, who'd started telling David Dotson things like, ''We're not training combat units to take machine guns in a war situation." And then in comes Dotson, along with a black deputy chief, Bernard Parks, and they want to build on that kind of attitude, and to use it as a way of changing the Academy's training. And they weren't just talking about nipping and tucking around the edges. They wanted to transform the whole training program at the Academy, the entire philosophical approach. They wanted a cadet's time in the Academy to be "a developmental experience," one where he or she would receive information and learn how to practically apply it. They wanted to measure how well each cadet was doing in each area, then "address" those areas where he or she was falling short. To develop each cadet in all aspects of training up to his or her absolute potential. "We should be enhancing those attributes," Dotson was saying, "not continuing to try and stifle them. We should be encouraging them to integrate their skills into the police work that they were going to be doing." The most successful cops out on the street, according to Dotson, were precisely those who could use their life experiences and knew what the fuck was going on at a visceral level.

Dotson and Relser wanted, in other words, to change the Academy training from a military model to "one that stimulated independent thought and action, and to get them away from rote classroom lectures." Why not? After all, the training staff at the Academy had only been turning out the best damn police officers in the world for the past thirty years. And Gates was going along with it. This was, after all, science talking, and the LAPD that Bill Parker and his disciples had built had always respected science.

The objects that David Dotson focused on as a symbol of everything that was wrong with the Academy's training were the knocking boards on the doors of the trainers. Bang! Bang! Bang! the cadets would knock like some kind of brainless automatons.

So Dotson told the training staff that he wanted the knocking boards down. When he returned two weeks later, they were still up. "I thought I told you that I wanted those knocking boards down," Dotson said. And the instructors replied, "Well, yeah, but if you take the knocking boards down, you'll have to keep repairing the doors." It was unbelievable. They were going to make him spell it out! "Look," said Dotson, "I want the practice of people being forced to act like an idiot to stop; I want them to be able to get the attention of someone in that room in a much more civilized way, and I want them to be accorded some kind of respect as human beings.''

Eventually, the knocking boards did come down. But it took literally months even to start to get some of the changes he wanted made.

The instructors did not take this shit lightly. Twice, *twice,* the entire eleven-man, one-woman physical-training staff of the Los Angeles Police Department met with Daryl Gates to protest the changes, threatening to resign en masse if they weren't rescinded. That was how strongly they felt. Not that they were exactly experts. They'd gotten their jobs either because they'd impressed an instructor with their physical prowess for something like setting a record in sit-ups, or because they fit the department's image or had caught someone's eye out in the field or were born-again protégés of born-again assistant chief Bob Vernon, which by Dotson's calculation was about half the training staff. The selection wasn't driven by education and background. Certainly none of them was exactly a trained kinesiologist. Bob Smitson was in charge of physical training. He was a great, huge hulk of a man, a weight lifter, one of the first SWAT guys, and among the most macho men on the force. If you were his peer, Bob Smitson was a nice guy. But his idea of training recruits was to keep them so goddamned scared that if you cleared your throat, they'd jump three feet and hover there, like a helicopter, while they looked around to see what was going on. These were old-school people, on the training staff; people who cared about standards, standards that were now being compromised. That was why they'd demanded the meeting with Daryl Gates. And when they met, Gates listened to their complaints but held fast. "It was," says Dotson, "one of the rare occasions that he called me as the manager of a particular area and actually asked, 'Look, what's going on here?' " And when Dotson told him Daryl Gates replied that he was absolutely right, the instructors' resignations were accepted, and they were transferred out.

But later, after David Dotson himself was transferred, the knocking boards went back up, and things settled back down to normal at the Academy. What had caused Daryl Gates to return to the military model of training remained a mystery to Dotson. But he had his suspicions. "In his gut," says David Dotson, "Daryl Gates knew that a cop ought to be six feet tall, one hundred eighty-five pounds, male, and that it would help if he was blond and blue-eyed. In his gut, that's what a cop was."

James Edgar Davis, 1938. The man and his image: right-handed, left-handed pistol champion of the United States. (Hearst Collection, USC Library)

James Edgar Davis (center) and family, setting the example according to the *Los Angeles Examiner,* "to other families on 'how to protect your home.'" (Hearst Collection, USC Library)

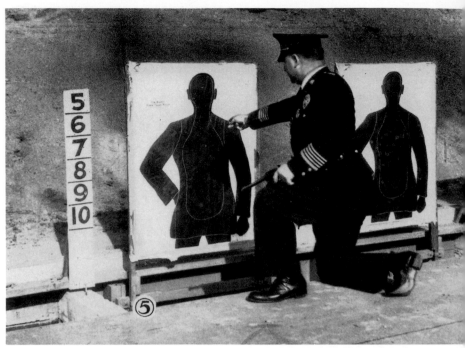

James Davis in 1936 at the pistol range after squeezing off a few. (Hearst Collection, USC Library)

James Davis shoveling "bundles of salacious literature" into a police incinerator in 1935. (Hearst Collection, USC Library)

Down in Mexico: Mayor Frank Shaw (second from left) with James Davis (center), in Mexico City in 1938. (Hearst Collection, USC Library)

Clifford Clifton examines Harry Raymond's bombed-out car in 1938. (Hearst Collection, USC Library)

Earle Kynette reads the United States Constitution after refusing to testify before the Los Angeles Grand Jury in 1938. (Hearst Collection, USC Library)

James Davis passing a courthouse crowd on his way to the trial of Earle Kynette in 1938. The judge called his testimony "a debris of words." (Hearst Collection, USC Library)

Jesse Brewer, the LAPD's first not-passing-for-white black motorcycle officer. (Jesse Brewer)

Rumbling by. The LAPD motorcycle squad in 1941. (Hearst Collection, USC Library)

The raw-boned rookie from the South Dakota badlands: Bill Parker in 1927. (*Herald Examiner* Collection/Los Angeles Public Library)

Bill Parker as chief of police in 1951. *"Il capo di tutti capi."* (*Herald Examiner* Collection/Los Angeles Public Library)

"We are sitting on a powder keg." Bill Parker displaying a Molotov cocktail before the City Council following the 1965 Watts insurrection. *Herald Examiner* Collection/Los Angeles Public Library)

Bill Parker in October 1965. The stress of Watts, and of his heart condition, showed on his face. (*Herald Examiner* Collection/Los Angeles Public Library)

Comedian Ed Wynn with the sign that said it all in 1950. (Hearst Collection, USC Library)

Captain Bill Parker (left) and his future P.R. specialist, Sgt. Stanley Sheldon, in 1941. (Stanley Sheldon)

The old western myth meets the new: Gene Autry and his horse, Champion, with two LAPD officers before a Los Angeles Police Show at the Shrine Auditorium in 1954. (Hearst Collection, USC Library)

Worshipping the god of technology: one fixed-wing, seventy-five officer Air Support Division. (Hearst Collection, USC Library)

"You are trying to pin this [uprising] on the police. [And] I'll go to the grave thinking this was your intention." Bill Parker arguing with Councilman Tom Bradley at a hearing after Watts. (*Herald Examiner* Collection/Los Angeles Public Library)

"Crazy Ed" Davis wearing an eye patch given to him by his press relations staff as "an act of love" after an eye injury in 1973. (*Herald Examiner* Collection/Los Angeles Public Library)

The American Nazi Party welcomes Tom Bradley to his inauguration as L.A.'s first black mayor in 1973. (*Herald Examiner* Collection/Los Angeles Public Library)

Tom Bradley being sworn in as mayor in 1973 by former Chief Justice Earl Warren, as Bradley's wife, Ethel, looks on. (*Herald Examiner* Collection/Los Angeles Public Library)

The more things change, the more they remain the same. Daryl Gates's wife, Sima, checks out his badge at his 1978 swearing-in ceremony as chief of police. (*Herald Examiner* Collection/Los Angeles Public Library)

"The Nigger Inspector" on the Police Commission in 1979. "The central issue here," said Jim Fisk, "is that Eulia Love could be and should be alive today." (*Herald Examiner* Collection/Los Angeles Public Library)

Using a bomb to kill a bug: Daryl Gates with the battering ram in 1985. (*Herald Examiner* Collection/Los Angeles Public Library)

The beginning of the end: Tom Bradley after winning the Democratic nomination for governor of California in 1982. (*Herald Examiner* Collection/ Los Angeles Public Library)

Mayor Tom Bradley with his longtime colleague, ally, and friend, Jesse Brewer. (Jesse Brewer)

The future commander-in-chief pays a visit to the assistant chiefs (from left): David Dotson, Robert Vernon, presidential candidate George Bush, and Jesse Brewer. (David D. Dotson)

Korea Town, 1989: the dream candidate of L.A.'s disintegrating rainbow coalition. (*Herald Examiner* Collection/Los Angeles Public Library)

Tarnished star—Tom Bradley in 1989 just before addressing the City Council about allegations of ethical misconduct. (*Herald Examiner* Collection/Los Angeles Public Library)

Warren Christopher hands the chief of police a copy of his commission's report. "There was nothing in there that was new or startling to us," said Daryl Gates shortly afterward. (Ted Soqui)

Rodney Glen King. As the city burned, they dragged him out to help douse the fires. ''Can't we all get along?'' (Ted Soqui)

Los Angeles, May 1992. (Ted Soqui)

Coin Laundry

FUCK THA POIICE

CHAPTER 13

Riding Shotgun

•••••••••••••••••••••

The first time Daryl Gates used the armored personnel carrier with the fourteen-foot protrusion known as the battering ram was in 1985. It was his prelude to the drug war that was now really heating up in earnest, and he used the occasion to christen his new weapon just a few blocks from the suspected rock house whose wall was about to be knocked down. With the press in attendance, he hopped aboard, and riding shotgun, watched as the vehicle smashed a huge, gaping hole in the house. Who knew that a simple media event staged to garner a little publicity in the department's war on drugs would turn into another public relations disaster? Who knew that when they busted down the wall all they'd find was two women transfixed with fear and a few kids eating ice cream? Who knew there'd be no stash, no pounds of cocaine, and just one-tenth of one gram? Nobody. He had dropped a bomb on a bug and emerged with nothing.

The intelligence he'd received from the narcotics officers had been terrible. They hadn't done their follow-up. Hadn't verified their information. They let him drive up there and bust a hole in the wall while saucy-eyed kids sat there holding plates of chocolate swirl in their laps. As a result, Daryl Gates and the LAPD looked like fools. And who was he angry with when it was over? Himself for his overkill? The narcotics guys whose intelligence was so bad that they allowed him to go into something like that? No, he was angry at the *media* for reporting it. Nobody in the department, according to David Dotson, was ever disciplined or even chewed out for their terrible police work.

PART 6

THE BLOODS AND THE CRIPS

CHAPTER 1

Where Do These Animals Come From?

•••••••••••••••••••••••••

It was they, the Bloods and the Crips, who owned the eighties in L.A., not the LAPD. It was the time of the economic collapse of South Central. A time of the massive loss of jobs in the steel, auto, and rubber industries to the sweatshops of Mexico and East Asia. A time obsessed with mendacity. In the name of making war on welfare queens, L.A.'s own Ronald Reagan was cutting back federal jobs, grants, programs, and social services, as he paid his debt to the already obscenely rich men who had created him by making them richer. In the governor's mansion in Sacramento, George Deukmejian, a mediocrity out of Long Beach as conservative as Reagan, was doing the same. At the same time, a conservative majority was being elected to the Los Angeles County Board of Supervisors—the body responsible for providing health and social-welfare programs to the entire county, including the city of Los Angeles. Within the city, Tom Bradley, whose fiscal hands were tied by federal, state, county, and Proposition 13 cutbacks, seemed far more intent on rebuilding downtown L.A., catering to corporate C.E.O.'s, and running for governor than in helping prop up South Central. It was a stunning convergence of events, a series of judo chops that knocked South Central to the ground and left it for dead. When that happened, what remained of the area's black middle and professional classes moved out, thereby exacerbating an already untenable situation.

To all this was added rock cocaine. South Central's collapse had converged with the federal government's turning up the law enforcement heat in south Florida, thereby shifting the principal port of entry for cocaine from there to Mexico, and then into Southern California. At the same time the transformation of cocaine—an expensive drug in its powdered form—into a cheap, hard, smokable "rock" that was readily affordable on the streets was hitting the area.

Left behind in hypersegregated, increasingly worsening conditions was the black underclass. They were joined by hundreds of thousands of Salvadorans fleeing civil war and American-trained death squads and settling into the city's Pico-Union district, and equally large numbers of newly arrived impoverished Mexicans, who were settling everywhere—including South Central. From its charred shell rose the fellas, the boys, the Niggas With Attitude straight out of Compton, the Bloods and the Crips. And the fate of South Central was sealed.

It was a quiet evening in February of 1985, and Jay-Rock and Coco were spending it as they had many others, idly cruising around in Coco's fading blue-and-white Dodge Dart. As they passed L&E liquor, they spotted Erica Johnson, arms wrapped around a bag of groceries, emerging from the store. Instantly, Jay-Rock spun their car around, tooled into the parking lot, and offered her a ride.

Erica was well acquainted with the young men, having once even introduced Jay-Rock to her sister. And although the seventeen-year-old had good reason to fear them, she seemed, that night, happy to accept their offer of a ride home.

All three were from the vast, nameless, working-class black area of West Los Angeles that sprawls from the Salvadoran and Korean neighborhoods east of Crenshaw Boulevard to within blocks of Venice beach.

They'd grown up just a fifteen-minute or twenty-minute drive from Beverly Hills, the trendy shops frequented by the weekend punks on Melrose Avenue, and the scores of movie theaters that dot the UCLA-campus town of Westwood. The palm-lined streets, modest, well-maintained homes, and small, neat apartment buildings all disguised the area's high level of crime and violence. Only the gang graffiti on the signs, stores, and apartment buildings gave, to an outsider, a hint of the darker side of the neighborhood that had been spilling over from South Central for the past decade.

In their late teens, the two young, streetwise black men were both semiliterate high school dropouts from broken homes who'd already acquired multiple-arrest records. Glenn "Coco" Martell, tall and light-skinned, and Jederick "Jay-Rock" Bond, his coal black partner, had been fast friends since their early years at John Burroughs Junior High School, where they'd hooked up with about a dozen other brothers and formed the Mansfield Hustlers in order to make a little change dealing weed and rock. But belonging to a minor organization was no way for Coco and Jay-Rock to carve a niche in a world of "chump change" jobs at McDonald's and 45 percent unemployment rates. They had ambitions.

What they sought was membership in the Playboys, one of the baddest of the Crip gangs that, along with the rival Bloods, were blanketing South Central and their area of West Los Angeles. Crip gangs, or "sets," like the Playboys and the School Yards, and Blood gangs like the Swans and the Roy Campanella Boys, had been increasing in those sections of the city ever since the midseventies.

Prior to that, when gangs were mentioned in Los Angeles, people thought of the zoot-suited, low-riding Cholos of the city's Chicano East Side. There, gang affiliations were traditional and ran deep—often going back four or five generations. Over the years in neighborhoods like Maravilla, the *vatos locos* would hang out drinking their T-bird, and rum, popping their reds, and painting their gang signs: Lopez Maravilla, Lota Maravilla, Arroyo Maravilla. They talked about who had *palabra*—the balls to keep his word at any cost—and who didn't; who was in jail and who was dead; and laugh about the suffering they'd inflicted like dead-eyed cops over beers.

There had been black gangs in L.A. in the thirties, midfifties, and midsixties, but they'd never become neighborhood institutions as they had with the Cholos. And by the mid-1980s, the majority of L.A. County's fifty thousand gang members were still Latino, but black gang members, numbering about fifteen thousand, were becoming the majority within the city. And in both teeming South Central and in adjacent parts of West Los Angeles where Jay-Rock and Coco made their home, a new breed of violent gangsters was emerging.

Among the most notorious of the gangs was the Playboy Gangster Crips. "Man, cuz," Jay-Rock used to tell Coco, "Playboys got a sign, that big black sweatshirt with a pretty white bunny.'' That sign, Jay-Rock would say, really made him "trip." And, as Erica was to discover, he would do anything to earn the right to wear it.

After reaching the corner of Erica's house, Jay-Rock waited in the car while Erica stood and talked with Coco. Several minutes later, Jay-Rock got out, too, and walked up to them, and faced Erica. Though she was normally feisty and adventurous, the dark, pretty girl had grown uncharacteristically somber over the past several months. But tonight, staring down at Jay-Rock, she seemed like her old self.

That is, until he asked about Kevin Goff. "What's up with the homeboy?''

Goff, known as No-Brain, was an older, influential leader of the Playboys whom both Coco and Jay-Rock idolized. Erica was due to testify against him the following Monday. As he put the question to her again, Jay-Rock, not really waiting for an answer, raised a .38 to Erica's head. When she grabbed it, he very deliberately told her to let go. As she did, he shot her four times in the face. One slug went through the right side of her nose, another through her left front hairline. But any of the shots— according to the autopsy—would have killed her.

Erica was already dancing at the house of a friend when the Playgirls decided to crash the party. That was how it all began. At first they left her alone, but after a while, about seven of them surrounded Erica and, as always, began calling her a Scrap and a School Yard, just as they had ever since that day in junior high when Erica had boldly strolled in wearing a sweatshirt with the name DION on it. Dion was a Scrap—the derisive name given by the Playboys to their archrival Crip gang, the School Yards. But Erica wasn't and never had been. She'd worn that sweatshirt really only because she liked Dion. But for the Playboys and Playgirls she would forever remain a despised Scrap. It was bullshit, a sweatshirt, but Erica was living in a world with its own weird logic. At a South Central high school a seventeen-year-old girl new to the school unknowingly wore blue Puma sneakers—the color of the Crips—into a Blood-controlled area and was killed at lunchtime. A black woman in her twenties, unrelated to any gang, had her car break down in an unfamiliar neighborhood. When she got out to try to fix it, she was shot to death because of the red bandanna she wore, red being the color of the Bloods. It was all part of the gang style. Their clothing and colors told what gangs they were from. Their pants sagged off their bodies—they called it the sag look. Then there were their sneakers. Crips wore a suede Puma with a blue stripe on each side and blue shoestrings. The Puma company also had them for Bloods: black with a red stripe and red shoestrings. Later both groups would change to Adidas. Sometimes they wore an earring and had a blue or red rag hanging out of their pockets or wrapped around their heads in "do-rag" fashion. Most gangs used hand signs and signals to further identify themselves. To delineate their territory they scrolled their graffiti, both as a warning and a statement of possession.

But Erica was no impoverished street kid. Her mother, who looked like the actress-model Shari Belafonte, sold clothes in the junior miss department of Bullock's Westwood, a block from UCLA; her dark, soft-spoken father managed a neighborhood Sav-On. But she was tough when she had to be, and although not in a gang herself, she dated gangsters.

Now, trying to have a good time, she was again being challenged by some of the same girls who'd been hassling her ever since junior high. She had committed the cardinal sin in the eyes of many Playgirls: she had "crossed lines" by dating boys from both gangs.

Taking the lead taunting Erica that night at the party was No-Brain's girlfriend, Sonja Key. At sixteen, Sonja was already one of the toughest Playgirls. She had tattooed No-Brain's real name, Kevin, on her back, and on her wrist was a tattoo of her own street name, Puppet. She, in particular, seemed to hate Erica, for Erica, she said, was "from School Yard and had turned an enemy."

After repeatedly ignoring Sonja's invitation to "step outside," Erica—who "never would," according to her sister, "put up with their mess"—left the house to accept Sonja's challenge. Immediately, she was jumped by Sonja and another girl and surrounded by Playgirls. Before the fight was broken up, Sonja had pulled a knife and slashed Erica in the ribs.

At her mother's insistence, Erica reported the assault to the LAPD. Sonja, already on parole, was sent to California Youth Authority camp in Ventura, where she served two and a half years.

Five weeks before Erica was killed, Sonja, in one of her letters to No-Brain, wrote: "Baby, I feel real bad because the homies be kicking it with them Scraps," and "about Erica, I don't know why they be kicking it with her." Three weeks later, No-Brain placed a .22 automatic to Erica Johnson's face and threatened to kill her for what she'd done to Sonja. "I could kill you anytime, bitch," he said, "whether I'm in jail or out of jail."

* * *

On a wall in a room of the narcotics section of the LAPD's Hollywood Division was a cutout gang photo. It showed the oversize head of a detective attached to a lean, brown, remarkably muscular body covered with tattoos. The body was of No-Brain.

At twenty-eight, No-Brain should have been too old for gangs, but he liked being perhaps the most influential leader of the Playboy Gangster Crips.

With his wire-rimmed glasses, No-Brain didn't look particularly menacing, despite his muscular build and tattoos. But looks were deceiving. He'd been arrested at least three times for murder but had done time only once for manslaughter. Witnesses had memory lapses. Street-smart and extremely bright, his reading material included the philosophy of Mao Tse-tung. In the sixties he might have been a Black Panther. But these were the eighties. He was a Crip.

Although everybody in the Playboys looked up to No-Brain, nobody seemed to lionize him more than Jay-Rock and Coco. "[Most] niggers, cuz," Jay-Rock used to tell Coco, "ain't do or die." When Coco would offer that perhaps Scoobie or Insane-D were, Jay-Rock would shake his head. "The only one I know is do or die," he would say, "is No-Brain." Coco could only agree.

Several days after No-Brain had threatened Erica, officers from the LAPD's West Bureau Community Resources Against Street Hoodlums (CRASH) heard about it and went to Erica's house and asked if she'd press charges. For the second time Erica was willing to break the street code of silence and testify against a gang member. Perhaps she was tired of the threatening phone calls that had been plaguing her for months. She *was* scared—uncharacteristically breaking out in tears of exasperation when her mother insisted she go to school. "It got to the point," says Dorothy Johnson, "that Erica would refuse to leave the house. She'd just hang around the steps [outside the Johnsons' apartment] and refuse to go beyond them."

A couple of weeks after his threat, No-Brain was arrested for intimidating a witness and assault with a deadly weapon. Bail was set at $50,000. He remained in jail, where he made calls to his fellow Playboys. Several were to Coco.

The morning after Erica was killed, No-Brain made another, this one to Gina Brown, a Playgirl who knew and hated Erica and had herself threatened her. "Poor, poor Loopie," said No-Brain to Gina. "We'll never see her again." Erica was dead, and so was the DA's case against him.

Two days after the murder of Erica Johnson, there was a picnic in a vest-pocket park in the heart of the tight, isolated little neighborhood surrounded by freeways that comprises the turf of the Playboy Gangster Crips. Anthony "T-Bone" Williams, an "OG," or original gangster, was returning from "camp"—that is, state Youth Authority prison—and about fifty of the Playboys and Playgirls were throwing him a welcome-home party.

Among those attending was T-Bone's cousin, Gina Brown, twenty-one. Gina was not only a rare female gang member but, like T-Bone, an original gangster as well.

Throughout the afternoon the death of Erica Johnson, Gina would later recall, was "the talk of the whole park." Although "not," she pointedly adds, "in the manner of which they cared."

Gina was standing by a barbecue pit with several other people when Jay-Rock came over and started, she says, speaking "in my mouth." It was strange, his being there. In addition to being a former Hustler, Jay-Rock was perhaps the only School Yard ever to become a Playboy. Such lines are usually never crossed, and Jay-Rock was aware of it.

One of four children by the same mother but different fathers, Jay-Rock "wasn't nothin" in junior high, according to those who knew him then. But after the Mansfield Hustler, he got some backing. And that "really pumped up Jay-Rock's head." He began to emulate the far more self-assured, sophisticated Coco, who by nineteen had been arrested thirteen times and had fathered, he thought, three children.

"Guys like Jay-Rock and Coco," LAPD gang detective Kevin Rogers would observe, "don't work and never will. They're basically losers in society with no niche other than gangs to fit into. They join gangs for power and recognition, jack up people for entertainment, and have no fear of going to jail. Because in jail they do just what they would on the street—hang out with their friends, kick back, jive, and tell stories about how they stole an apple from some punk's [prison] chow tray or knocked him down and made him grovel. It makes them feel they have some power."

For Jay-Rock on the afternoon of the picnic, that sense of power must have combined with the giddiness one feels on fulfilling a dream. There he was talking to Gina at a Playboy party and having Coco as his "ace boon-coon main nigger.'' He didn't want to blow any of that, and so he tried hard, that day, to fit in, to make a good impression. And Gina, an OG, was one of the Playgirls he wanted most to impress. No-Brain had told him that Gina was "do or die." So why not? There was a party going down and a buzz in the air. Why not tell her? So Jay-Rock told Gina about the killing—all about the killing. And how he and Coco had picked up Erica at the L&E, about getting out of the car, about asking if she was going to testify against No-Brain, about the chips and soda she was carrying, about how she grabbed for the gun, and about shooting Erica Johnson four times in the head.

Three days later, officers from CRASH picked up Gina for questioning. They knew she'd threatened Erica herself and been present when No-Brain had done the same with his .22. They came down hard on Gina, threatening to send her to Sybil Brand—L.A. County's tough, over-crowded women's prison. That and the fact that it was a girl who'd been gunned down, and just days before, seemed to overwhelm Gina. She broke down and told them—on videotape and in front of a judge—everything, and in detail, of what Jay-Rock had said at the picnic. Only in her later testimony, when asked why she had been willing to "put it on" Jay-Rock, did Gina explain why: "That nigger used to be a Scrap. As far as I'm concerned, once a Scrap, always a Scrap."

On March 7, two days after Gina's videotaped testimony and seven days after the murder, LAPD detectives William Cox and Michael Mitchell arrested Coco and Jay-Rock. But they weren't talking, and Gina's testimony wasn't enough to hold them. They would have to let them go. Before they did, however, Mitchell, a thirty-one-year-old, nine-year veteran of the force, had an idea: he'd leave them sitting in a police car and tape them surreptitiously.

Mitchell took the unmarked CRASH police car to the scientific investigation unit and had it wired, then left Coco and Jay-Rock handcuffed in the car with the tape running, while he and Cox went up to the DA's office to present what they knew would be insufficient evidence.

During the next hour, Coco and Jay-Rock talked about everything from prison food and cops to women and welfare checks. Coco told Jay-Rock how the deputies at the county jail had almost mistakenly put him in the Blood tank instead of the Crip tank, a practice that's forbidden and would almost certainly have gotten him killed or seriously injured. And Jay-Rock told Coco how he thought they should let their hair grow out and braid it up even though it would take a "long-ass time for it to grow." Coco told him, "Yeah, [and] we got a long-ass time for it to grow, too." And they talked, of course, about the Playboys and how as Coco put it, "Crippin' ain't easy." And just as Mitchell had hoped, they also quite naturally talked extensively about their case.

Near the end of the tape, after much jive about who could better satisfy a woman, they went into a little cheerleading rap:

Jay Rock: "What's happenin'? The PBGs." (Playboy Gangster Crips)
Coco: "Fuck SYC." (School Yard Crips)
Jay Rock: "Playboy, Playboy."
Coco: "Playboy, Playboy."

Then, after a little more of this talk, Coco suddenly said to Jay-Rock, "Hey, cuz, I talk too much, cuz, like I think T-Bone and Gina told. [But] I didn't tell T-Bone nothing, cuz. The niggers I told, cuz, they didn't say nothing, cuz. That's why I'm tripping, Jay-Rock."

And with that, Jay-Rock looked at Coco, opened his mouth, and helped seal their doom: "Cuz, *I* told Gina, cuz."

In itself Jay-Rock's taped admission wasn't enough to convict him and Coco, but at the trial it proved to be the prosecutor's most damning piece of evidence. Back in March of 1985, however, it still wasn't quite enough for the DA to file charges. But what Jay-Rock hadn't given the police, Coco would.

Coco had run into a homegirl named Demenia Duvall and had talked with her about the night Erica was killed. They had a lot to talk about. Right before they'd picked up Erica, Coco and Jay-Rock had also given Demenia a ride and during it had flashed the .38.

As he spoke about that night and about Erica, Coco started to laugh. Then, he yelled, "Playboy," shrugged, and said, "The next thing I know, she was dead." He laughed again, then added, "Yeah, I killed the bitch." The police found out about Demenia's conversation with Coco, and her meeting with the boys the night of the murder. Under pressure, she agreed to give the detectives a statement. The DA now had a motive, had placed the suspects in the vicinity of the crime, and had each of them separately admitting to the killing. That, other evidence, and some additional corroborating statements finally gave the DA enough evidence to file charges.

On September 16, 1986, Coco and Jay-Rock were found guilty of murder in the first degree and shipped to the California State Prison at Chino to do twenty-five years to life.

The day of the sentencing, they sat in the courtroom laughing. Or rather, Coco was laughing. He'd been laughing ever since they were arrested, and he was laughing even as his life was ending. "Where," someone said, walking out the courtroom after the sentencing, "do these animals come from?"

By the end of the eighties, the sheer mindlessness of it all had become numbing. "Gang-related" killings in Los Angeles County had risen to 570, 303 of which were in the city. The media loved the story. It was "Hard Copy"–sexy. It was Rambo-Uzi-violent, it was good-guy, bad-guy uncomplicated. Cops jacking up punks and breaking down doors was great television.

Estimates of the number of gang members would rise almost exponentially as both law enforcement, always hungry for more money, and the media pursued their agendas. First it was ten thousand. Then fifty thousand. Then seventy thousand. Then as many as a hundred thousand. No care was taken to differentiate between an awestruck wanna-be and a genuine stone killer, or to thoughtfully analyze just what the fuck was going on. Instead, as a justification for cracking down *hard*, law enforcement in L.A. portrayed the gangs as a new, more ruthless breed of Mafia, not what they were, which was teenagers and young men who were hapless, stupid, violent, and high. They were branching down and into the Southwest, up deep into the Pacific Northwest. They were making millions selling crack, as *Newsweek* magazine breathlessly told it in a March 1988 cover story entitled "The Drug Gangs: Waging War in American Cities."

But the reality was far different. The violence, the sociopathic sickness, and the dealing were there, as they were in impoverished black ghettos throughout America. But the rest was hype, at least according to research and studies done by UCLA, USC, and the LAPD. "Despite the Los Angeles high-profile gang culture," wrote UCLA sociology professor Jack Katz in 1989, "criminal homicide has for years been close to the rate in New York City, which has not been publicized as having youth gangs since the seventies." USC examined the arrests of over 700 suspects for cocaine sales in gang-plagued neighborhoods in the mid-'80s and found that 75 percent of those arrested had no gang affiliation. In the LAPD study, the department selected a block and then a violent gang associated with it called the Rolling 60s. And what they found was that the teenagers and young men on that block and in the neighborhood surrounding it associated with one another, but that there was no formal structure, no real leadership, other than some of the older OGs, who had some influence on the neighborhood kids. But not because of any organizational structure but because the teenagers saw them as romantic figures. Within the gang, there were two or three cells of associates who *were* engaged in criminal activities, but not as members of the Rolling 60s. The car thefts and robberies they did, they did as people who knew each other and could depend on one another, not as gang members. Many of the killings were gang related, of course, but few of them were sitting around drawing organizational flow charts or masterminding plots to take over Seattle. In fact, according to Katz's research with street level police officials and social scientists, "well under five percent [of gang members] engaged in serious criminal violence."

Whether or not there were actually seven hundred gangs in L.A. County, and approximately thirty thousand principally black Bloods and Crips in the city, those that did belong to gangs and were criminally active would generate enough fear, violence, and media coverage so that by the late eighties, they would supersede the LAPD, the Beach Boys, and Beverly Hills and become the new symbols of L.A. This, even though the Reagan and Bush administrations' war on drugs was having its effect in places like South Central, whose young men were increasingly going on to prison instead of a job.

Many of them had been arrested for the murders, rapes, robberies, and assaults that were terrorizing urban America. But it was small-time drug crimes, combined with a lack of good jobs and training, and a war on drugs that emphasized incarceration over treatment, that was increasingly responsible for California's and the nation's huge numbers of prisoners. In 1988, for the first time, more adults in California were arrested for felony drug crimes than felony property crimes like burglary, auto theft, and forgery. By the end of the Reagan-Bush era, the United States would have higher percentages of its population in prisons than any other industrial nation in the world, except for the then Soviet Union and South Africa. From 1980 to 1990, the prison populations in eighteen states, the District of Columbia, and the federal penal system would more than double; while in such diverse states as California, Alaska, New Hampshire, and New Jersey, it would triple. California's increase alone accounted for 19 percent of the nation's growth. In 1980, almost 8 percent of the nation's prisoners were in California. By 1988 that figure had risen to more than 13 percent, and California would officially shift the purpose of imprisonment from rehabilitation to punishment. By 1990, the prison population of California, which had been twenty-five thousand in 1980, had risen to almost ninety thousand. In Los Angeles, 25 percent of all inmates in the L.A. County Jail were there for possession or sale of drugs.

Meanwhile, the California Department of Corrections was releasing an unprecedented number of paroled convicts—mainly small-time drug dealers and users—back into Los Angeles. By the end of the eighties the figure would reach almost 14,500 annually, more than twice that of 1984. And as he or she walked out the prison gates, each was being given $200 to start a new life. Sixty percent of those very same prisoners would return to jail within two years for parole violations—mostly for drug-related crimes or testing dirty. Sixty percent. Major crimes in Los Angeles were going up at the time at a rate of over 8 percent a year, and all these uneducated, unskilled people were being released back into places like South Central—back into a cold job market, and now with criminal records—and were being told to change deeply embedded habits, habits like crack addiction, the use of violence to solve problems, hustling to get by, and contempt for straight work, all of which had just been reinforced in prison. And they were going back into areas like South Central that were economic disaster zones, without treatment to keep them away from the terrible plague of crack, without professional guidance or a place to get unstuck and make a transition into a semblance of normal life. It was they who would perpetuate themselves and who would be looked up to for being ex-cons by the young brothers fueling the ranks of the Bloods and Crips. But they were black and Mexican, they were wild, and they were killing each other. It didn't matter. Not until Karen Toshima.

One minute she was young, vivacious, and full of life at just twenty-two. The next she was dead.

Karen Toshima had been innocently strolling through Westwood Village in late January of 1988 when she got caught in the cross fire between two warring black gangs and was shot dead in the head. It should have been no big deal. Toshima was just one of ninety-six homicide victims to die at the hands of alleged gang members in the city of Los Angeles in the first five months of 1988. Nevertheless, Karen Toshima's death would prove different from the other ninety-five. Hers would count. Hers had taken place in Westwood, a former sleepy college village abutting UCLA that had grown into a maze of cinemas, restaurants, shops, and high-rise office towers. The area was just a ten-minute ride from Brentwood, Holmby Hills, Beverly Hills, and Ron and Nancy Reagan's retirement home in Bel Air, and an even shorter distance from the million-dollar Wilshire Boulevard condos known as the Gold Coast. Throughout the seventies and early eighties it had been a weekend haunt of the sons and daughters of the affluent, a place to see a movie, have dinner, and mingle with the passing parade. That Karen Toshima could be killed in such an area was shocking. If Westwood wasn't safe, what was next? Rodeo Drive? As the L.A. *Times* would later write in a follow-up story about her killing, Karen Toshima "came to represent 'every woman,' and her death made all of Los Angeles feel more vulnerable." More precisely, Karen Toshima, although an Asian American, would come to represent every *white* woman—"white" in the same sense that Bill Cosby and Eddie Murphy counted as white to Sal's bigoted son in *Do the Right Thing*. And when her head was splattered in Westwood, it spurred Tom Bradley and the city council into action.

Not only was the largely white middle class being threatened, so was business. A killing like hers could scare people away permanently. Why take in a movie or eat out or go shopping if there's a chance—no matter how slim—of winding up like Karen Toshima? Why go to Westwood when you could find some place safer? Westwood's businessmen and merchants were in an understandable uproar. In response, the LAPD quickly tripled its patrols in the area and thirty officers were assigned to work on Toshima's murder. Meanwhile, the city council and the L.A. County Board of Supervisors simultaneously voted $6 million in emergency funds to pay for expanded special patrols. Less than two weeks later the financially strapped city council also approved the hiring of one hundred and fifty additional police officers and within months voted to add five hundred more.

The crisis born out of South Central's economic disintegration had finally come home to roost for white L.A. People were convinced that the Crips and the Bloods were now swirling out of control, and all of a sudden any heat or any will to truly reform the police department after the shooting, spying, and choke-hold controversies dissipated. The political trigger had been pulled for the LAPD to do what it had to to get the job done. Contain the animals was the message. Karen Toshima was dead and it could have been me.

Shortly thereafter, Daryl Gates would respond, and in the only way he knew. And with almost everybody's blessing.

With the drumbeat for him to do something pounding like an ache in Daryl Gates's ear, he answered the killing of Karen Toshima with Operation Hammer, a massive series of indiscriminate "gang sweeps" in which at least twenty-five thousand mostly young black men were arrested. (Some put the number, when combined with the arrests of the sheriff department's operations at the same time, as high as fifty thousand.) The LAPD had used sweeps before: during the great Red Scare of the First World War, in the thirties with James Davis's raids on the city's skid-row unemployed, and in the hype sweeps of the twenties and sixties when heroin was big and the department would round up every junkie in town.

But the Hammer, the Hammer was a whole different order of magnitude. And posting those stats required huge numbers of busts for the pettiest of crimes: failure to carry proper identification, loitering, spitting on the sidewalk.

The "tag teams" were a beautiful example. You assigned a bunch of motorcycle cops to a CRASH (Community Resources Against Street Hoodlums) detail, that is, the gang police, and watched them go to work. They knew the vehicle code backward and forward, every clause in the section. *Every* clause. They knew that a car had to be parked eighteen inches from the curb, and if it was twenty-two, it was a ticket. If the windshield wipers didn't work, it was a ticket. If there were no floor mats, it was a ticket. They knew everything and could get anybody. *Then*, the guy gets his car impounded because it's unsafe. He can't pay the car out, can't afford it, so he can't drive and go around town and do a drive-by. Sure you pissed off a lot of people, and sure most of them weren't involved in killings or serious violence, but it was a way, the LAPD way, of getting at the problem.

Afterward, many of those hauled in were released when the DA determined there wasn't sufficient cause to charge them. How many is hard to say. In 1988 the L.A. *Times* reported that in one sweep the DA filed just 103 cases out of over 1,400 arrests.

The sweeps weren't only useless as a long-term solution but were also mindless in their execution, according to several officers.

Other than the admonishment to, as one LAPD spokesman put it before a sweep, "pick 'em up for anything and everything," nobody clearly informed the officers involved exactly what to do. A sweep would be announced, they'd arrive at work, go to roll call, and be told to do something about the gangs. But they never really knew what that "something" was. So they'd drive around, and if they saw some brothers hanging around on a corner, they'd shake them down, see if they could ID them as gang members, run a check on them for outstanding warrants (and in L.A. an overdue parking or jaywalking ticket is an outstanding warrant), and generally, as David Dotson later put it, "mess around with them." Each cop made up his or her own criteria for what constituted a gangster. With no clear guidelines they generally went out and harassed and arrested people who looked as if they *might* be gangsters. And the department tallied up lots of numbers, lots of people were talked to, lots of people were arrested, and a few were actually charged. But what was left in its wake was not a bunch of kids saying let me out of gangs, not a bunch of kids with a new respect for the law, but a lot of young men with even deeper negative feelings about the LAPD.

Daryl Gates had three very different assistant chiefs: David Dotson, Jesse Brewer, and Bob Vernon. The tall, starched, blow-dried, born-again Vernon was the director of the Office of Operations; he oversaw all of the LAPD's patrols, recruitment, promotions, and most of its detectives. In short, just about all the officers who came in contact with the public— nearly 85 percent of the department's sworn personnel. He was, in effect, first among equals among the three assistant chiefs, powerfully positioned within the department. Known as the Reverend Bob, Vernon also stayed busy, as Brewer and Dotson tell it, facilitating promotions and desirable assignments for people who met his particular Christian criteria, and who had made the pilgrimage out to the San Fernando Valley to hear him preach in the Grace Community Church. The God Squad, they were called. But Vernon emphatically denied all charges of favoritism. By the mideighties, as some say his born-again protégés were spreading throughout the department, Bob Vernon was recording a series of audiotapes entitled *The True Masculine Role*. "I am convinced," he said on one, that "because God has said that women's role is to be submissive, that what they really want [is] for you to be the decision-maker. . . . Wives ought to be subject to their husbands in everything. That includes physical relationships.'' On another he discussed disciplining children: ''I've spanked boys as old as sixteen or seventeen. . . . I hit them with a boat oar. . . . I tell them, if you use drugs, I'm going to spank you with a boat oar. But I don't do that with girls once they start puberty.''

Bob Vernon and his born-again fraternity within the LAPD were making people nervous. And not just his fellow assistant chiefs, Brewer and Dotson, who both thought that what Vernon was doing was wrong, but were, in any case, locked in a power struggle with him, jockeying for position, always hoping one day to be chief if and when Gates ever left.

Vernon's tapes and his God Squad were also one of the few issues during the late eighties that would lift the city council out of its somnolence concerning the LAPD's brutality. Bob Vernon might have been fine for the people of Dallas, but he was three or four decades too late for Los Angeles. It was the worst time for a proselytizing, antifeminist, pro-corporal-punishment, fundamentalist Christian to be near the pinnacle of the LAPD hierarchy and a contender to be the next chief of police. Council members, particularly Zev Yaroslavsky, were watching him. He wasn't going any higher, but he was already right below Gates.

In many ways Brewer and Dotson felt that Bob Vernon was part of the LAPD's problem. At meetings, after Vernon had finished speaking, he would pick up a folder he'd brought and, and like a busy schoolteacher marking tests at a faculty meeting, begin doing paperwork, ignoring Brewer and Dotson's concerns about the tinderbox that South Central was becoming. Which really pissed them off because it was Vernon's people that they—and particularly Brewer—were complaining about. But Vernon seemed as disinterested as Gates, who never thought it necessary to give Vernon a verbal punch in the arm by saying, ''Hey, Bob, come on, pay attention, these things fall under your purview.'' That he failed to do so was no small matter. For what Brewer and Dotson were telling them went to the very heart of the rage at the LAPD in South Central, a rage that was incrementally reaching a Watts-like boiling point.

Their complaints were the same as those leveled at the department by Deputy Chief Lou Reiter following police shootings and choke-outs of the late seventies and early eighties. In a 1981 retirement speech Reiter had accused the officers in South Central of acting like a ''hard-charging street army'' and treating ''everyone who is black as a bad guy.'' In the five or six years since, blatantly outrageous shootings had decreased, and the use of the choke hold had been all but outlawed. But the Bloods and the Crips had risen, and sweeps, harassment, humiliation, intimidation, dog teams, and beatings had replaced deadly force. But the attitude was the same. A fact immediately noticed by Jesse Brewer when he took over as commander of Bureau South in 1986. "I was appalled by how awful the department was treating people," he later said. "There seemed to be a feeling [among the officers] that you could walk into a situation, say, 'Hey, I'm the man; get the hell out of my way'—and that was the way to do police work."

Brewer and Dotson were also concerned about Daryl Gates's John Wayne rhetoric. In Gates's 1986 videotaped end-of-year address to the troops, which was played at roll calls throughout the department, he had compared the LAPD to the United States Marine Corps and identified the city's gang members—the fringe hangers-on and wanna-bes as well as the hard core—as the enemy. "It's like having the Marine Corps invade an area that is still having little pockets of resistance; we can't have it . . . we've got to wipe them out," he said. Got to be aggressive.

Aggressive. He would repeat the world proudly, almost daily it seemed, as if a mantra. And when relaxed, even expound upon it. Like the time he was sitting in a Parker Center conference room with a reporter and brought up a movie he'd just seen, the Eddie Murphy, Nick Nolte film *48 Hours.* It was, said Gates, "kind of interesting, because they were following the shift of some gang drug sellers [from Los Angeles] into other communities . . . Seattle was one. . . . And a drug dealer was talking about why he'd gone there . . . because he wanted to get a better price [for his drugs.] *And* because," Daryl Gates continued, leaning forward now, "the police there weren't as *aggressive* as the LAPD. And they said, 'Well what do you mean by *aggressive?*' And he replied . . . '[Here] the police see me, and we wave and they wave back. . . . In L.A., if they saw you on the street . . . you'd be stopped immediately and examined from the standpoint of what you were doing.' And that is . . . the difference between the LAPD and some other departments. And we are forever moving in on those areas and those people we think are dealing drugs." If there was a problem with that, Daryl Gates didn't see it.

But black men do not like taking orders from white men with attitudes putting them through deeply humiliating procedures because they *might* be dealing drugs, or for any other petty-ass reason. The consequence, as

David Dotson would later put it, was that "the guy [who's been stopped by the police] knows, 'You don't have anything on me, you don't have any reason to stop me' . . . and that [got] us, time after time, into these conflict situations that end[ed] up frequently with uses of force, frequently with manufacturing or at least puffing of the probable cause. . . . We reward[ed] our people . . . for what we call hard-nosed, proactive police work. We expect[ed our officers] to go out and aggressively identify people and investigate them, and that put these police officers in the middle between what we evaluate them on and what they [were] able to do legally." It was nothing new. It just intensified when the sweeps came down. Generations of African-Americans, of high school and college students, teenagers, professionals, working men as well as crackheads, thieves, and gangsters—all had matter-of-fact stories that by their very mundaneness were more telling than any horrific story of brutality.

There was Derrick Mims, who worked his way through USC, became an aide to legendary black congressman Augustus Hawkins, and was then an administrator at UCLA. When he was fifteen, his uncle T.C. sat him, his brother, and his cousins down and told them what to expect when stopped by the LAPD: "They'll pull you over, lay you down, kick you, step on your fingers, stomp on your neck, and make you feel like a chump—just to let you know they have control." About a year later, exactly that happened to Mims's brother and cousins as they were on their way to get something to eat at McDonald's. The word was out, the drill well-known. You had to shuck, shuffle and jive, to make sure when stopped that you didn't give them any reason to kick your ass or use their gun. You had to clasp your hands—fingers intertwined in the approved manner—behind your neck. And if you were smart, you minimized your chances of being stopped by never riding in a car with three or more black friends. But often no precautions sufficed. As longtime South Central resident Rodney Williams, a twenty-seven-year-old college student and teacher's aide at a local high school, described it to the *Times:* "When you see their [officers'] heads swivel as you drive by, it's not even worth driving further. Just pull over and wait for the routine. They'll say, 'Stick your right hand out the window, now your left. Open the door with your left hand. Keep your hands out and exit with your hands out, sir.' If you get out facing them, they'll say, 'Do not face me! Turn around!' Then they tell you to interlock your hands behind your head, back up three steps, and get down on your knees. Then they put you into the ground.

"I know [the routine] better than the Lord's Prayer, man. Just about every black man does."

Those were the central lessons of growing up with the LAPD in South Central. Lessons for which Daryl Gates made no apologies. "If you look like a gang member and [are] just cruising around . . . you're liable to get stopped, and I think with good reason," he would later say. "Everybody thinks that there's some special reason that they're going to be stopped . . . that the police have some ability, an innate ability, to separate the good people from the bad people before they'd made an inquiry. And there isn't any way to do that. . . . All people . . . in certain circumstances are stopped because of the circumstances and not what they look like." Although it was clear that being black and in a car with other black males was the "circumstance," Gates failed to make clear how his officers— barring someone's driving down the street with a blue or red flag wrapped around his head or flashing gang signs—could determine who "looked" like a gang member while sitting in a car. Or who was "just cruising around." But, nevertheless, there was a certain logic to the LAPD's tactics. If you saw a carload of blacks, they might very well be gang bangers. And if they were gang bangers, well, then those people needed to be talked to. Needed to be dragged out of their car, put up against a wall, and talked to. They might be on their way to a shooting. Wasn't that what aggressive policing was all about?

Officer safety. That was another thing. One of the reasons for tactics like the prone-out. As Capt. James Tatreau, who was a ranking officer in the Southeast Division, put it, "It's police work, pure and simple. When you're on patrol in a place where you have a lot of crime, you have to watch out for yourself and your partners. Our lives are on the line every time we stop someone. And we're not going to tell our people to ease up so that some idiot can have a fairer fight and maybe go for our guns or pull out one of their own."

And of course it was frightening. But despite soaring images of Uzi shoot-outs and cops being mowed down fighting gangs in the great drug war, police work, in some ways, was becoming *safer,* not more danger-ous. FBI statistics on the nation's five largest cities (New York, Los Angeles, Chicago, Houston, and Philadelphia) showed that the number of officers killed in the line of duty had *declined* by almost 40 percent during the 1980s. In 1990, sixty-five officers were killed nationwide, the lowest number since 1968, and about half the peak rate of one hundred and twenty officers slain during the early seventies. "Based on exposure to potential hazard (as measured by violent felony arrests), American police on average are 300 percent less likely to be killed feloniously in the line of duty today than they were in the mid-1970s," wrote William A. Geller, the associate director of the Police Executive Research Forum at the end of the 1980s. "And, by the same measure, they are 150 percent less likely to be assaulted (with or without injury) by assailants armed with deadly weapons." From 1984 through 1988 an average of two officers a year were killed in the line of duty in all of Los Angeles *County,* which included the LAPD, the 11,800 officers of the L.A. County Sheriff's Department, and the police forces of scores of cities within the county. In comparison 108 civilians were killed by the LAPD alone in those years. The fact of the matter is, as Prof. James Alan Fox of the National Crime Analysis Project at Northeastern University in Boston told the *New York Times,* the danger to police officers is less than at any time in recent years. "For your average cop," said Professor Fox, "it's *not* a jungle out there." All of which did not mean that cops didn't have to be cautious. They would have had to be insane not to be. But there had to be limits. "It's been a long-standing concern of mine that officer safety has been a sacred cow in the LAPD," says William Rathburn, a former LAPD deputy chief who left the department and became chief in Dallas. "Anything, or almost anything, done in the name of officer safety is okay. That's the perception. And it's *not* okay, you know. You can't prone everybody out just because there's an officer-safety consideration. You can't make everybody kneel down."

Often with the backing of David Dotson, Jesse Brewer would try to tactfully hammer home the problems that rolling over people like the Israeli airborne was causing, and to do so without directly confronting Daryl Gates. Jesse Brewer, after all, was a system man, a man who'd spent his entire adult life in uniform. You could spend days talking to LAPD officers and never hear a harsh word about Jesse Brewer. Except, of course, from the most malcontent of the officers. From those few men and women who were revolted by what they saw their fellow officers doing and knew that Jesse Brewer, with his sensibility and innate decency, was revolted, too. He knew. So where, they asked, was his commitment to the principles of professionalism and his oath of office? Where was his loyalty to his fellow African-Americans? Where was the character it took to speak out against racism and bias within the LAPD? Where, in short, were his balls? But those were questions only Young Turks or failed idealists would ask. They didn't understand that confrontation wasn't in Jesse Brewer's nature, wasn't how he'd survived, wasn't how he'd become the highest-ranking African-American in the history of the LAPD. Or, equally as important, that confrontation wasn't always how you played high-stakes political poker, particularly in an organization as intensely political and inherently hierarchical as was the LAPD.

Take the simple fact of Jesse Brewer's popularity. There wasn't anyone, including the carping Young Turks, who didn't like him. And Daryl Gates was no exception. But did they or anybody else believe that Gates had elevated Jesse Brewer to assistant chief just because Brewer was well qualified and Gates liked him? No. Daryl Gates might have worn his chief's stars like an imperial crown, but his power rested not only in the city charter but in the fact that within his sphere he was a savvy politician. He'd shown that by cementing his power with the old-line troops within the department, by catering to key city council members, by marginalizing the mayor when it came to police affairs, and by finessing the police commission and returning it to its traditional rubber-stamp status. And while he wasn't about to modify his proactive policing philosophy to mollify the leaders of South Central, he, or at least the department, *did* have a constituency there: the black middle and working class, the entire lawful black and Latino population, in fact, who were literally terrified by the accelerating street violence that had permeated the area for decades. And in spite of the fact that their sons, brothers, husbands, uncles, and cousins were constantly being hounded, *that* constituency—the voters of South Central—were proving the department's most faithful allies whenever a proposition appeared on the ballot to raise money to build more police stations, to upgrade the department's communication system, to buy more police cars. Thanks to Proposition 13, however, it now took a two-thirds vote to raise the property tax to pay for those things. And it had been South Central, and *not* Daryl Gates's white, law-and-order constituency in the San Fernando Valley, that had consistently voted for them. So it was a shrewd political move to appoint Jesse Brewer an assistant chief and then give him nominal command of South Bureau. Brewer was *very* popular with the black leadership of South Central. Moreover, the appointment was in a sense a political and administrative "twofer"—

both a bone to South Central as well as a necessary nod to the intense pressure facing Gates over the issue of affirmative action. It would have been stupid really to have denied him the job.

Undoubtedly, Jesse Brewer understood all this. He had had to work twice as hard, be three times as smart, and four times as astute as Daryl Gates just to have gotten where he was. And where he was, as Jesse Brewer could justifiably point out to his critics, was just a short step away from *really* being able to change the LAPD. For if and when Daryl Gates ever left, Jesse Brewer had the inside shot at being the next chief—the first black chief in the city's history.

Gates, after all, had been making noises about leaving for years. During the selection process for chief in 1978, he told the police commission that if appointed he intended to serve no longer "than three or four years." Then in 1984, during the planning for the Los Angeles summer Olympics, he talked about leaving after the successful completion of the games, and again in 1987 he'd mentioned resigning following Pope John Paul II's visit to the city. He kept threatening to run for mayor or governor, kept talking about receiving an appointment from the Republican administration in Washington. And Jesse Brewer, with his long friendship with Tom Bradley, with the high regard in which he was held in the department, in the police commission, and in the city council, would be at the top of the short list if Gates left. But Bob Vernon, Bill Rathburn, David Dotson, and half a dozen high-ranking officers within the department also wanted Gates's job. For Jesse Brewer to publicly challenge and embarrass Daryl Gates on the fundamental question of policing philosophy would in all probability take him out of the running. In the closed world of the LAPD he'd be regarded as a bad soldier, as a man—a black man like Tom Bradley—who'd betrayed a trust, broken the code, sucked up to the liberals.

And while some in the political establishment might hail him for speaking out, among others he'd be damaged goods, a lightning rod whose appointment as chief would cause dissension and turbulence within the department at a time when worry about the Bloods and Crips and the downward spiral of the city was spreading like cancer.

It was the same for Dotson. He and Brewer were *management,* ambitious bureaucrats, not heroes. They'd been part and parcel of what had been going on in the LAPD for over thirty years. Part of whatever it was that had to be covered up and spliced over.

And Daryl Gates held an additional trump card. Jesse Brewer and David Dotson served at his pleasure. Their civil service position was *deputy* chief, one very big rank below their current prestigious, inner-circle, next-in-line-for-the-throne positions of assistant chief. Gates could bump both of them back a grade if either publicly defied him. That meant a loss of options as well as a lot of pension money when they retired. If Gates chose to demote David Dotson one rank to deputy chief, as was his right, Dotson would lose at least $1,300 a month in retirement pay. An amount that would increase annually with the cost-of-living adjustments to which retired LAPD officers were entitled. Brewer, with his forty years of service, would have lost even more. If you cared about that, you'd better keep your mouth shut.

Besides, what good would it do them to go public? The story would just play itself out after three or four days on the pages of the Metro section of the *Times,* while Gates made some of his patented scornful or condescending remarks.

So Jesse Brewer tried to tactfully address what he and David Dotson considered the "appalling" way the troops of the LAPD, Gates's troops, were dealing with the public. "We did not just go in there and say, 'Goddamn it, we've got to do something to change this,' " says David Dotson. "We tried instead to point out the problems, but in a way that didn't make it appear as if we were fighting with Bob Vernon."

It wasn't only South Central that was the problem, Brewer told Gates. And it wasn't just racism that was causing the problem—the attitude was citywide. Pico-Union, teeming with tens of thousands of Salvadoran refugees and impoverished immigrants, was a white-hot cauldron of hatred and resentment of the LAPD, just inches away from boiling over. Moreover, Brewer's *white* friends were complaining to him about the arrogant, high-handed way LAPD officers were acting, about their cavalier rudeness, about the feeling they radiated that they "didn't have to show any courtesy at all to the public."

Nor was it only Brewer and Dotson telling Gates these things. Other officers—black and white—were bringing up the same concerns at the general staff meetings. And Gates was hearing it for himself when he went into the black community with Brewer. Hearing it at community forums in the Crenshaw Plaza shopping center at the foot of the upper-middle class African-American enclave of Baldwin Hills. Hearing it from the leaders of the most mainstream of the city's black organizations: from

Joe Duff, the president of the local chapter of the NAACP, from John Mack, the president of the Los Angeles branch of the Urban League, and from Mark Ridley-Thomas of the Southern Christian Leadership Conference. People were outraged and in an incendiary mood as a result of having their sons, brothers, husbands, and fathers constantly proned-out, beaten up, and talked down to.

In response, Gates would get up and try to explain this away. Sometimes, he managed to do so with great effect, the halting, adjective-starved, tongue-twisting syntax that marked his usual public utterances giving way—as they sometimes did when he spoke about things of which he cared, to a presentation that, if not bordering on eloquence—was solid and impassioned. That was the case when he once spoke before the organization known as 100 Black Men, a group of doctors, lawyers, educators, administrators, elected officials, and other black professionals. They, too, were highly critical of the LAPD, and Daryl Gates had sat there and listened, then stood up, defended the department, explained some of his actions, and at the end of his speech received a standing ovation. But nothing changed. "It was like Gates had built this wall," says David Dotson, "and cut himself off from any real communication . . . like he was hearing our words but not understanding the meaning."

It was all there for anyone to see even without Brewer and Dotson speaking out, there in the excessive-force civil suits against the department. In 1989 the city paid $6 million in excessive force settlements, in 1990, $11.1 million, and in 1991 over $14,500,000. To Daryl Gates it seemed not to matter. It was all bullshit. City attorneys, he said in 1986, had explained to him that the reason there were so many awards against his officers was because "in almost every case . . . there was either a sympathetic jury or there were witnesses who changed their views or a whole variety of reasons." Or as he later told *Playboy* magazine as he summarized some case reports he was holding in his hands: "This is what we settled in 1990 . . . a shooting case, a shooting case, pursuit, traffic, pursuit, traffic, pursuit, traffic—an awful lot of them are traffic accidents. We bump into somebody and they file a traffic complaint." That was it. It was bumps, it was sympathetic juries. It was bullshit. And he did not want to hear it. In June of 1991 there was a staff officers retreat where the question of civil suits and the large amounts being awarded in settlements was discussed at length. A panel of judges were invited to the retreat, and

"Gates kept steering the discussion to these goddamn juries," said David Dotson, "these crazy goddamn juries. And we finally got on the subject of dogs." Over the past three years LAPD dogs had bit nine hundred people. Philadelphia, with twice as many dogs as L.A., had had just twenty bites. The reason for the large number of bites, according to a dog handler who had been at a Parker Center staff meeting, was that the bites were the dogs' reward. And that if a dog wasn't allowed to bite someone once in a while, he'd lose interest in the search. (Later Daryl Gates would publicly defend the dogs, calling them "the sweetest, gentlest things you'll ever find," who "only bite if attacked.") Anyway, as David Dotson would recall it, this judge, Judge Arabian, said to Gates, 'Look, you've got to make a decision about whether it's in your best interest to deploy dogs. Juries can't make it for you. I can't make it for you. You have to make it.' But Gates didn't do anything. He could not recognize that we had some power over the way we did things. He ended up believing he was a victim, and the police department was a victim."

In March of 1992, the city's chief legislative analyst issued a report on lawsuits filed against the LAPD for the four-year period from 1986 to 1990. It focused on one hundred and three cases, excluding traffic accidents, that cost the city over $15,000 each: shootings, excessive use of force, attacks by police dogs, and civil rights violations. According to the report, only thirty-six of those were even investigated by LAPD's Internal Affairs. And of the officers involved in the cases that were investigated, twenty-four received no penalty whatsoever, seventeen temporary suspensions, and four received admonishments or official reprimands. Only two were removed from the force.

Three-quarters of the settlements or judgments of over $100,000 were not even investigated by Bill Parker's tough, much vaunted Internal Affairs Division. And of those that were investigated, close to 75 percent resulted in no suspensions, with the longest suspension for any of the cases being just *one day*. "Obviously," as Councilman Zev Yaroslavsky put it, "there's a problem with the message being sent through the disciplinary system. And when people shoot people and make them quadriplegics or kill them, and they get *no* investigation at all . . . and a guy gets a thirty-three-day suspension for being caught reading a magazine while on duty . . . there seems to be a greater importance placed on disciplining people who engage in bureaucratic infractions than excessive use of force." It was nothing new. "Years ago, when I was a young lieutenant,'' former deputy chief William Rathburn would later say, ''I remember an officer that worked for me who tried to shoot somebody when he shouldn't have, and the department's reaction was: 'Well, that's not too big a deal.' And another officer was involved in a traffic accident . . . and he didn't even hurt anybody, it was just a traffic accident, but a preventable traffic accident . . . and we said, 'That *is* a big deal.' We wanted to suspend the officer in the traffic accident, but we didn't want to do anything about the shooting. There was something *real* inconsistent and *real* wrong with that.''

The *Los Angeles Daily News* would also later examine the LAPD discipline practices during the mid and late eighties and come to the very same conclusions. Based on LAPD Board of Rights and other police documents, the *News* detailed what happened to thirty-five officers who, from 1985 to 1991, were ruled by Gates to have shot people unnecessarily or in avoidable situations. Of the thirty-five, only two were fired. (The same two as in the legislative analyst's report.) The vast majority, twenty-three, received either ''verbal admonishments'' or suspensions of less than twenty-two days. Moreover, according to the *News*, ''no consistent pattern of punishment was found with regard to the severity of the violation, injury or death. . . . For instance, one officer was suspended five days for fatally shooting an unarmed motorist, while in a separate case an officer was suspended ten days when his gun accidentally fired while he was trying to shoot a dog.''

In another case, a Board of Rights panel suspended rather than fired an officer who'd shot an unarmed man in the back who was in the act of surrendering because, said the panel, the officer had previously been cited for bravery. This despite the fact that the cop, nicknamed Hernando the Commando, had been involved in at least nine other shootings.

The *News* then followed up the investigation with another, this one looking at the department's procedures for investigating and punishing officers who used unnecessary or excessive force from 1983 through mid-1988. Based on Internal Affairs documents, it showed that ''the LAPD, which investigates its own officers . . . concluded that of the 254 officers [who had] three or more complaints'' against them, only ''1.6 percent should be fired and 11 percent should be suspended,'' and that ''more than 50 percent of those suspensions were for five or fewer days.'' And that ''the LAPD's investigations of its own officers very seldom conclude that any officer did anything wrong.''

The *Los Angeles Daily News* would also report, and in stunning detail, on ten excessive-force cases they reviewed involving twenty-one police officers. They found that while juries or the city attorney had awarded the victims in the cases $752,000 after they'd sued the city, all of the officers involved had nevertheless been cleared by LAPD investigators. In one incident the city attorney settled a suit out of court for over $177,000 because he felt if it went to trial a jury would award the victim much more because he'd been blinded in one eye. Perhaps the city hadn't a leg to stand on. The LAPD division commander, after all, had said that his men had acted intolerably, had acted like a "lynch mob." Yet the department's investigation found they hadn't done anything wrong. In none of the ten cases was the victim convicted of a crime. Their injuries, in addition to the blinded eye, included "a fractured skull, a seriously damaged pancreas . . . cuts, bruises, abrasions and a loss of hearing in one ear."

"This is dynamite," thought Jesse Brewer as he read through the report. Pure dynamite. And as such, he didn't want to send it over to Bob Vernon cold. Some groundwork would have to be laid. He'd have to go and see Vernon in person. So he called and made an appointment.

As head of two of the four vast LAPD bureaus into which the department divided Los Angeles, Brewer was ostensibly an integral link in the disciplinary process for cops accused of serious offenses—that is, in those cases that could result in punishment ranging from a twenty-one-day suspension up to an officer's firing. Over time, reading the disciplinary reports sent to him by the division captains in South Central, Brewer began to detect a disturbing pattern: their disciplinary recommendations, especially those for knocking heads, were light, way light. And were light in spite of the fact that Brewer had put out the word upon assuming command that those types of violations were not going to be tolerated. So when an excessive-force report came into his office coupled with a captain's slap-on-the-wrist punishment recommendation, Brewer would overrule it and recommend a harsher punishment. Then he'd send it on to Daryl Gates for final disposition. And in every case—*every* case, according to Brewer—Gates had gone along with the captain's light recommendations.

Once Jesse Brewer noticed the pattern, he had his adjutant conduct a study—the result of which was the dynamite now lying on his desk. It showed that in every one of the cases where Brewer had submitted a higher penalty and Gates had gone along with the lighter one advocated by a captain, the officer was in trouble again within a year for an identical violation. There it was. Proof that the spirit of the department's written use-of-force policy—and in many cases the policy itself—was being subverted by Daryl Gates and his use of the bureaucratic equivalent of a wink and a nod. He was giving the green light to a lot of cops to do whatever they wanted; he was failing to set limits as to how far they could go in using force. The Internal Affairs Division, which had the expertise and brought most of the misconduct cases, only investigated the most major of the police-abuse cases, and not a great many of those. That was a message right there. The vast bulk of the rest were left to field supervisors who at the very least had working relationships and often friendships with the cops they investigated. It was Chuck Higbie and the shooting investigations all over again.

And the implications were just as enormous. If this was happening with Jesse Brewer and his men in Southwest Division, what was going on in the black and brown ghettos in Pico-Union, out in the Valley, over in Pacific? What else was being neglected? What else wasn't being controlled? Moreover, how could all this be happening when police psychologists all over the country were constantly repeating what was clearly self-evident: that police will behave properly only when management and supervisors put out the word that violations of policy and the law simply will not be tolerated?

When Jesse Brewer saw Bob Vernon, he knew by Vernon's reaction that he'd been right: the report *was* hot. So hot, as Jesse Brewer tells it, that Vernon told him he didn't want to send it through to Gates without laying the groundwork. Everybody knew, he said, how much the chief hated to be criticized about his disciplinary decisions. "Let me talk to Gates about it first, feel him out," said Vernon. And that was the last Jesse Brewer heard of the report from either Bob Vernon or Daryl Gates. And Jesse Brewer never pushed it. The time wasn't right. But the copy he'd given to Bob Vernon wasn't the only one he had.

The LAPD's troubles in South Central and Pico-Union went far beyond just lax discipline. Beyond even the incendiary, wrongheaded messages Daryl Gates was sending. The department's philosophy of policing was not only inappropriate and untenable, it was at the very heart of so much that was wrong. Proactive policing had become not only a philosophy, but a reward mechanism, a promotional system. The guy who had made the most arrests, busted the most assholes, was being the most aggressive, was the guy who made detective, was named a training officer, got promoted. You had to produce arrests, a lot of arrests, to be considered a hard-charger. To be labeled a good street cop, to be known as a "gunfighter." Conversely, the information that civil service promotional boards were receiving regarding patterns of excessive force was extremely limited and often glossed over in their evaluation reports.

Moreover, the fruits of years of experience—the true coin of the realm in policing—was tucked away in special units, not out on the street where the need for them was overwhelming. By the late 1980s, almost 40 percent of the department's field officers and 36 percent of its sergeants had four years or less on the job. The general consensus was that it took between six and ten years for a cop to become really good. To have your game plan in your head so you knew what you were going to do in the vast majority of situations. Guys with three years didn't know anything. And they were making *them* field training officers. A cadet comes out of the Academy with his books down pat but no street experience, looks around for some guidance, and what does he get? A training officer almost as green as he is. And when a sampling was taken of those training officers, what did they find? That almost half of them were already badge heavy and had had "disciplinary problems." It was all inevitable. The blind leading the blind.

Rarely did anybody want to remain in the field, work nights and weekends, bust his or her ass, and then turn around and *not* be regarded as the cream of the crop because they had stayed. After all, if you were any good, then what the fuck were you still doing working patrol? No, you made your arrests, made your rep, and got into a special unit. The arrests, that was the ticket out and into Daryl Gates's beloved specialized units, the units that were bleeding the institutional heart out of patrol. The LAPD, particularly on the street, had become a department filled, as Joseph Wambaugh put it, with "superaggressive twenty-two-year-olds, full of testosterone, full of energy, absolutely immortal, and unable to admit fear, unable to verbalize fear, even to themselves." Instead of a seasoned cop stopping a guy and shrugging it off when he's called a motherfucker, what was happening were countless challenges to some kid's manhood, to some young female officer's ability to appear tough and be counted as one of the boys, which then led to fights, beatings, arrests, and simmering hatred.

Proactive policing had been Bill Parker's dream. And like Parker, Gates totally lacked the soul needed to imagine what it would feel like if the situation had been reversed. If black cops from South Central and Latinos from Pico-Union got up each morning, drove thirty or forty miles to Canyon Country or Simi Valley and in the normal course of policing rousted and beat up and jailed their young—and sometimes not so young men—on petty pretenses. What it would feel like to have a black chief of police and a black district attorney proclaim that the way to deal with the problems in South Central and Pico-Union was to "write off" thousands of young men, as L.A. County DA Ira Reiner had said should be done on more than one occasion.

Meanwhile, Daryl Gates and the district attorney, the noble-headed, earnest-voiced Ira Reiner, were trying to outcoon each other, as Huey Long used to say about Louisiana politicians upping the ante defending segregation, by vying for the title of LA's toughest cop.

Like Zev Yaroslavsky, Reiner had started his career as a liberal and as city attorney had been critical of the department, but now that he was DA, he'd come around. He had plans to run for attorney general of California. To stamp out gangs, he announced, his office would stop plea bargaining with them. "The objective," as Reiner explained it, was "to use each occasion that a gang member was arrested for a crime, no matter how minor, as a means to remove him from the streets for as long as possible." (Six months in jail, for example, for drinking in the park.) Since more than seventy thousand young men in the county had been identified as gang members, the result could be exactly what Reiner felt was needed: thousands of young black and brown men "written off." Written off! They were too far gone to save. So write them off. Cut your losses. Daryl Gates could make his "black and normal people" remark in 1981 and create an uproar. And now just five or six years later, here was this Jewish American DA, who presumably should have known something about people being written off, telling black and Latino mothers, sisters, fathers, and uncles their kids had to be "written off." And nothing was said. It was a measure of just how far rightward the insanity of the Bloods and Crips and the media hype that accompanied it had moved the political spectrum in Los Angeles in so short a time.

Gates and Reiner's tough statements were now exactly what many of their white constituents wanted to hear. As one of the city's top Democratic consultants put it when asked why the Westside's powerful white liberals weren't pressuring Gates, Reiner, and the city council to get a grip and stop playing political football with a serious, complex problem: "Those people have no interest in what takes place east of La Brea. Let the blacks and Hispanics burn each other down!"

At the same time, Daryl Gates had been transformed into the New Nixon. He was the same old Gates but the times had changed. If he was willing to appear with you in your district, it made *you* look good. After all, he looked good in his uniform or his Johnny Carson pastel sport coats. He was tough, honest, independent, and out there fighting crime. He enjoyed a public reputation as a serious, able administrator. And he appeared sincere, with a certain up-front, soft-spoken charm about him that he usually dropped only when castigating criminals and fool politicians. He offered simple solutions to complex social and criminal issues, promised a return to the safe good old days if only the politicians would stop handcuffing the police and free them up to do their job. And there was always the fear of Gates's intelligence dossiers, or what had been whispered in his ear. Of Daryl Gates being moved, as he once threatened, to "clear out his [intelligence] files."

Neighborhood Watch. That was another thing. After the rebellion and riot in Watts, Ed Davis had set up the program, in which neighborhood groups regularly met with sworn LAPD officers and talked about neighborhood crime prevention. In concept, it seemed solid, progressive community policing. But it had become politicized, and some of the officers involved were going around slamming Bradley every chance they got. No member of the city council ever wanted uniformed cops or the chief of police going around his or her district saying that he or she was soft on crime. As Zev Yaroslavsky once put it, "I think a lot of people are afraid to be critical of the police department. They don't want to get into arguments with their local police chief. . . . It can do a lot of damage to a person's reputation if the chief of police says you're antipolice or you are aiding and abetting criminals or that you're really proterrorist. You can deny it all you want, but unless you're willing to accept that criticism, and most people aren't willing, you don't get into an argument with the police department. And most people take the path of least resistance in life." Like the council. Like the police commissioners.

So as federal juries were awarding the LAPD's brutality and shooting victims tens of millions of dollars in settlement awards, the response of the city council would be not to ask why the department was so violent, but to authorize $900,000 for a special police litigation unit to better defend the city and police department from lawsuits. "It's cost-effective, plain and simple," Councilwoman Joy Picus would say.

CHAPTER 2

Not White Enough

•••••••••••••••••••••••

Tom Bradley's 1986 campaign song was the theme from *Rocky,* that ultimate Hollywood schlock emblem of triumph over adversity. It should have been "The Impossible Dream" again, this time without the poignancy. His era had passed. Only he didn't know it. After thirteen years as mayor he was still doing good work, still engaged. Just a year earlier, he'd helped save thousands of unskilled jobs at the Central City Produce Mart and in 1984 had presided over the hugely successful Los Angeles Olympics, following it up with a fourth-term victory as mayor of Los Angeles with close to 70 percent of the vote.

But now as he was running hard for governor, the dynamic was all wrong. Liberalism was spent. Reagan was near his peak, the country full of his disciples anxious to lead the country back to 1928.

Nineteen eighty-two had been his real shot for governor. He'd lost that race by an infuriatingly thin margin, less than 1 percent of the vote. And he'd lost it to George Deukmejian, an anemic Republican hack with so little charisma it was often difficult to know if he was dead or alive. That had to have hurt. But most infuriating was the role South Central had played in that loss. There was Tom Bradley, running to become the nation's first black governor since Reconstruction, running to become the governor of the most populous state in the nation, running in an election so close that it would be decided by a margin of less than 1 percent, and South Central, and black areas like South Central, and like Oakland, had simply not voted in significant enough numbers to put him over the top. It was part of Tom Bradley's special bind, part of having to be whiter than white without becoming Sammy Davis, Jr. In the mayoral elections of 1969 and 1973, Tom Bradley had been regarded as an almost Christ-like savior by L.A.'s blacks. But by '82, reality was setting in. Bradley was still thought of as a good role model for their kids—someone who could greet the crown prince of Japan or the British royal family and make them, and all Americans, feel good about themselves. And all you had to do was walk into City Hall to see the racial progress that had been made; you'd see it in the vastly increased number of blacks, browns, and females working there, see it in the way he'd opened up so much of city government for them.

Yet, after eight years of Tom Bradley's leadership, little had changed in the lives of most of South Central's residents. The LAPD was just as brutal, disrespectful, and unaccountable as it had ever been. Crime was getting worse every year, jobs harder to find, the schools more of a joke. They had watched, worked, and applauded as Tom Bradley had put his show together, and now they still weren't part of the act.

Bradley's representatives, even Bradley himself, had been available to the people of South Central, had met with them and listened to their problems. But there was little Tom Bradley could, or in the case of the LAPD, would do.

The issues in Tom Bradley's second run for governor were all about class and race presented as law and order: gun control, the death penalty, and whether or not Tom Bradley supported liberal California Supreme Court justice Rose Elizabeth Bird for reconfirmation. And the LAPD was already working hard pinning the scarlet letter of antipolice on Tom Bradley's black breast. The Police Protective League endorsed George Deukmejian, as it had done in 1982. Daryl Gates, maintaining the fiction that because of his position he was apolitical and officially neutral, had written a letter to Deukmejian (which somehow became public) pointing out: ''My admiration for you and for the job you are doing as Governor of California is the highest. . . . I could go on, and on, and on in praising you and your dignified, stable, aggressive, common sense leadership''; a letter that Gates had written after he'd publicly called Bradley a ''lousy mayor." Ed Davis also had something to say about Tom Bradley's candidacy: "There is no doubt that Tom Bradley set himself up as the enemy and the critic of the police department. For thirteen long years . . . as the leader of a police department, Tom Bradley has been an unmitigated disaster." OCID, meanwhile, was leaking negative stories about Bradley to the press. If they were after him for the mild reforms he'd tried, how much could he do about the LAPD in South Central and maintain his statewide political viability?

As for doing something about South Central, there were just too many people, too much need. Out of South Central's 630,000 residents, about 230,000—over one in three—were living at or below the poverty line. Thirty-seven percent of all the city's poor people lived right there. Those people never *did* understand what the city could do, and what it couldn't. The social services in Los Angeles, all the social services, were controlled by the county, state, or federal governments. The schools were run by an independently elected school board over which the mayor had no control. Police, fire, the airport, the harbor, street maintenance, yes, the city ran those, but through commissions appointed for five years, and through entrenched, often independent civil service boards, or civil servants like Daryl Gates. You want your trees trimmed? That was something City Hall could help you with; they could send someone out to do that, but not much else in the way of services. Or at least that would later be the position of Tom Bradley's loyalists.

As for building up the infrastructure of South Central, the whole idea of Tom Bradley somehow bucking the massive economic restructuring taking place all over the country, all over the *world,* the idea of him halting the inexorable pull of manufacturing jobs out of areas like South Central into Mexico or some dime-an-hour Asian city was simply naive. He was a mayor, not the president. Community activists and liberals liked to talk about "alternative models" of development for downtown and South Central, of a "working-class enclave of light, nonpolluting industry and sturdy and attractive low-income housing, one interlaced with a strong infrastructure of schools, health establishments, and social-service and community organizations." But really, where was that successfully being done on a large scale in an impoverished area anywhere in the country? Where did they expect him to get the money? Jobs were leaving America. Proposition 13 in 1978 and then Ronald Reagan's 1980 election had underscored the fact that white people didn't want their money spent redeveloping black slums. Walter Mondale's humiliating defeat in the 1984 presidential race had emphasized that Americans didn't want to pay any more taxes. The mass influx of poor Latinos into L.A. only exacerbated poverty in the city. There were precious few funds to do anything in South Central.

As for the private sector, whom are you going to get to invest in an area like South Central? Who was investing in the south Bronx? On the south side of Chicago? People with money wanted to invest on the Westside, in Orange County, or in downtown L.A., wanted to make downtown the high-rise corporate headquarters of the Pacific Rim. Who wanted to buck a trend and build a factory in South Central when factories there were closing up, and those still operating were cementing up their windows to keep the dope fiends out at night? It was all Tom Bradley had been able to do to get a Broadway and May Company to remain in the area to anchor a new shopping mall.

Still, Tom Bradley could have used more of his political capital, some of that enormous popularity he'd accrued by the late seventies, to assist South Central. Could have expended some of the enormous energy, political savvy, and persuasive powers he'd used to obtain billions of dollars in mass transit funds from the Reagan administration, on South Central. And he had not.

Nineteen eighty-two had been Tom Bradley's year to win California's state house and he'd just missed. In 1986, he never really had a chance. No matter how hard he tried, he'd just never been able get away from race. By 1985, even as he was garnering almost 70 percent of the vote for mayor, it was already tearing at his political coalition. Like Jews across America, like *white* people across America, the Jews of Los Angeles were turning rightward. Burgeoning crime, deteriorating schools, crosstown busing, were their concerns. Most of the prominent leaders of the anti-busing movement in the San Fernando Valley were Jewish, and a housewife named Bobbi Fiedler had even ridden the issue into a congressional seat.

It was then that Louis Farrakhan, the dynamic disciple of the Honorable Elijah Muhammad, the charismatic leader of the Nation of Islam, came to Los Angeles. He had, as usual, been spouting his obscenely comic racial and religious theology about how the human race had originally been black before a mad, big-headed scientist had created a bleached-out white race of devils; and about how Judaism "was a gutter religion."

So L.A.'s Jewish leadership turned to Tom Bradley, turned to their Sidney Poitier, and demanded—*demanded*—that he denounce Louis Farrakhan before Farrakhan had even spoken. Bradley refused. It was a mistake. When the time came, and he really needed them, the powerful organized Jewish community of Los Angeles would no longer be there for him.

But he'd never really had a chance in '86. Just two years earlier, Ronald Reagan had demolished Walter Mondale, an old-style Democrat very much like Bradley. By 1986, the bloom was off Tom Bradley, and his coalition was a creature of the past. On the west side of Los Angeles, the liberal, Jewish eleventh district, previously a staunch Tom Bradley stronghold, went to George Deukmejian. In 1982 close to 60 percent of the black voters had turned out for the governor's race. In 1986 that number dropped to 40 percent.

Tom Bradley had always had his integrity. But by the late eighties, that, too, was being dragged through the mud, as Bradley found himself in a series of stupid, venal, and highly embarrassing situations. Individually, each could be explained away. Together, they were devastating: A telephone call from Bradley to the city treasurer suggesting that he deposit $2 million in city funds in a bank that had paid Bradley $18,000 the previous year to serve as an adviser. Allegations of conflict of interest and insider trading with the likes of Michael Milken, from whom Bradley had bought junk bonds. A failure to disclose more than $200,000 in investments in public filings and reports of his financial holdings, for which he had to pay a $20,000 penalty. The conviction of Juanita St. John, a Bradley friend and business associate, on charges of tax evasion and embezzlement after she'd been awarded a plum city contract. Allegations that Bishop H. H. Brookins, a longtime political mentor and key South Central supporter of Bradley's, used $336,000 in city controlled antipoverty funds to renovate a building he owned in secret. Fund-raising by Bradley's staff and commissioners from special interests that often did frequent business with the city; intervention by his staff with city agencies on behalf of a businessman who'd donated large sums of money to Bradley's reelection campaign. Allegation after allegation. Tom Bradley was convicted of nothing. Yet the allegations were so numerous and so sordid that they would not, could not, go away. Tom Bradley had gone from high patron saint in Martin Luther King's dream of integration to ambitious politician, to finally, what seemed, as he neared twenty years in office, to a bored, quietly disgruntled power broker. All of the snide whispers from the closet racists in the LAPD, from the chiefs like Ed Davis and Daryl Gates who could not control him, had now, in the eyes of many, been given validity. It didn't happen all at once. The allegations played themselves out over several years. But the harm was cumulative, and by the end of the decade Tom Bradley seemed weary, disengaged, his star tarnished, his light dimmed, unprepared for what was slowly building.

CHAPTER 3

The Raid on Dalton Avenue

••••••••••••••••••••••

It began on an August evening in 1988 with the whirl of a circling helicopter and the beam of its spotlight shining directly into the South Central living room of a heavyset black woman named Rhonda Moore. Startled, Moore, twenty-four, peered outside and saw an LAPD patrol car pull up and an officer jump out with his gun drawn. "Uh-oh," she thought, "they after someone." Then at about eight-thirty the streetlights went dark.

Meanwhile, Johnnie Mae Carter, who lived two doors down from Moore in a similar tiny duplex, was settling in to watch "Jake and the Fatman." The show was just getting interesting when Carter and her granddaughter, Amber Green, fifteen, heard some noise. As they turned, their door burst open and five or six LAPD officers, guns in hand, rushed in.

"Get up," one of them commanded. Dazed, Carter and Green were quickly handcuffed and ordered onto the floor. Carter, sixty, overweight and recovering from an appendectomy, followed the officers' instructions exactly. Their voices had *that tone.*

The streetlights going out had signaled the start of an LAPD raid on four apartments in two small buildings on a well-maintained block on

Dalton Avenue, not far from the Coliseum where the 1984 summer Olympics had been held. As neighbors watched in awe, nearly eighty officers carrying guns, sledgehammers, and crowbars stormed the apartments looking for drugs. Rushing through Rhonda Moore's door, police began kicking her, while a visiting friend named Tommy was knocked to the floor, handcuffed, and then thrown like a cord of wood through the open door and onto Moore's brown, parched front lawn.

Carter and her granddaughter, meanwhile, were led outside and ordered to sit on the stoop. Their lawn, like Moore's, was already overflowing with residents of the raided apartments and with passersby randomly netted by the police. Most had been handcuffed and were now lying facedown where they'd been thrown. One was Carter's son Raymond, twenty-one, who'd been dragged from his car with his four- and five-year-old nephews as they returned home with pizza for the family. Crying, the boys ran to their grandmother, who could do nothing but tell them to hush.

Among those manacled on Rhonda Moore's lawn was her upstairs neighbor Gloria Flowers, who'd been grabbed naked from her bathtub by onrushing police while her young children watched. Clothed now, she was lying not far from Carl DeLoach, a passerby whom Moore and her sister particularly noted because the police had "kicked his mouth so much that there was just blood all around him."

For the first half hour, Carter was conscious of what was taking place. Then, hearing the shattering of her second-floor rear windows as her possessions were thrown through them, she went blank. Over the course of the next several hours, Johnnie Mae Carter, Rhonda Moore, Gloria Flowers, and the others watched while their homes were systematically destroyed.

Nobody was killed or seriously injured. But there was nonetheless something chilling, something out of proportion, something not quite comprehensible about the methodical damage caused by more than eighty officers as they searched through four apartments looking for drugs on what turned out to be a bullshit tip.

All the toilets, for example, were broken to pieces and torn from the floor, leaving water running everywhere. The plaster walls were smashed in with sledgehammers, and so, too, were bedroom and living room sets, televisions, VCRs, and typewriters. Couches and chairs were cut and slashed with knives, jars of baby food and bottles of wine were emptied onto clothes and bedding, dishes and glasses were shattered, light fixtures were destroyed or torn out, phone wires were cut, and frozen food and furniture were sent crashing through windows. Finally, before leaving, the officers spray-painted—gang style—some graffiti on a large board down the street. "LAPD Rules" and "Rolling 30's Die" were among the slogans written.

Then thirty-three people were brought to the Southwest Division police station and six were booked on various misdemeanor charges. While there, according to eyewitness Hildebrandt Flowers, brother of Gloria Flowers, whose home was destroyed, they were forced to whistle the tune from the old Andy Griffith television show, and to run a gauntlet of police officers who allegedly struck them with fists and steel flashlights.

Later, Moore, Carter, Flowers, and the others learned that their apartments had been targeted for the raid after a series of gang-related shootings in the neighborhood. But no gang members lived in the four apartments, and eventually only one person—from outside the neighborhood—was ever successfully prosecuted. Moreover, only a small amount of cocaine and marijuana and no weapons were found in the apartments. "They told me later," says Johnnie Mac Carter, "that they was looking for drugs. And I remember very clearly saying back to them that the only ones acting like they was on drugs that night was you."

Daryl Gates sought nobility in his officers' actions. Although he transferred and reduced the pay of the captain who had ordered the raid (and who had absented himself while it was taking place), Daryl Gates pointedly praised him as "a very, very fine captain" who had a bright future with the department. And while the chief ordered either days off without pay or independent hearings likely to result in minor discipline for thirty-seven other officers involved, he seemed more preoccupied with defending them and the department's image than in acknowledging the horrors they had wrought and the troubling questions their actions raised. At a press conference held almost a year after the raid to announce his disciplinary actions, Gates allowed that "clearly the situation got out of control." But he added, "The officers were trying very hard to do the right thing—to solve the narcotics trafficking problem. Unfortunately, while doing the right thing, they were doing it the wrong way."

"While I vigorously defend my officers, I also vigorously and tenaciously defend the very strict discipline that we have in this system."

But the discipline seemed later to be more in the chief's rhetoric than in actuality. To be sure, two officers were forced to resign, but when Officer Carl A. Sims, Jr., was unanimously found by a departmental tribunal to have submitted a false affidavit (on which the search warrant for the raid was based), he was given just two days off without pay.

The district attorney's office, long criticized by local civil-rights advocates for its reluctance to prosecute all but a few of the high number of police-abuse complaints it received, also responded minimally. While alleging that the police captain who ordered the raid, Thomas Elfmont, had told his officers at a roll call that they had ''carte blanche'' with ''bureau backing'' to ''level'' and ''make uninhabitable'' the Dalton Avenue apartments, the charges the DA decided to file against Elfmont and three other officers were misdemeanors, not the far more serious felonies they could have been charged with. Moreover, the misdemeanor charges were for vandalism, conspiracy, and delaying or obstructing the investigation of the case.

Even with the minimal charges, the three indicted LAPD officers were acquitted, one in a long line of high-profile cases the DA's office under Ira Reiner had been losing. But a secret, internal LAPD report showed that there had been a serious managerial breakdown from the very beginning of the department's war on gangs in early 1986, and that Dalton Avenue was only one example.

The report, written by Assistant Chief Robert Vernon, and dated April 1989, called the Dalton Avenue raid ''a poorly planned and executed field operation [that] involved many simultaneous failures. Among those factors were an improperly focused and supervised aggressive attitude of police officers, supervisors, and managers . . . directed toward being 'at war with' gang members. . . . [A] disregard for the chain of command . . . [and] a lack of overall supervision of the [task force] and search warrant operations.''

According to an internal LAPD memo, in fact, just days before the Dalton Avenue raid, the captain in charge of the operation—which was aimed at a street gang but had been misdirected—told his officers at roll call that ''it would not be a loss to the community'' if they shot a gang member, and that ''management would not view it negatively.''

Four apartments on a quiet South Central street had been targeted for a drug raid. The warrant obtained was based on deliberately fraudulent information and issued by a woman notorious for being a ''sweetheart judge.'' The damage was so extensive that the city later paid the residents over $3 million in an out-of-court settlement. And Daryl Gates's response had been to bend over backward to defend his officers. Meanwhile, the president of the police commission would say in a deposition that he was aware in only a general way of the raid. And no one from the mayor's office or city council publicly complained or made a critical statement.

That same year, Daryl Gates held an impromptu press conference outside a federal courtroom. A jury had just awarded more than $90,000 to a family named Larez as a result of their being rousted, punched, kicked, and thrown to the ground by LAPD CRASH officers in an early-morning raid on the Larezes' home in a search for a gun allegedly used in a murder. Among other things, Jessie Larez, fifty-five, had had his nose broken during the search. At the press conference, Gates said that Larez was ''probably lucky that's all he had broken. How much is a broken nose worth? Given the circumstances in this case . . . I don't think it's worth anything.'' After the chief's remarks, the jury was so outraged they awarded the Larezes an additional $170,000 and ordered Gates to pay it out of his personal funds. Subsequently the award was overturned by a judge on appeal.

CHAPTER 4

The Grand Old Man

•••••••••••••••••••••••

Eulia Love, "normal people," battering rams, spying, the Hammer, Dalton Avenue, over $11 million in 1990 in judgments against his men—none of it seemed to matter. Nobody was calling him on it. In fact, it was just the opposite. As Daryl Gates sat in a conference room in Parker Center looking back at the 1980s, he was a man at the top of his game. After thirteen years in office he'd quieted his critics and was actually cashing in on his reputation as a loose cannon and taking on the sheen of irascible Grand Old Man.

In September of 1990, he testified before the Senate Judiciary Committee in Washington, D.C., and had made headlines not just locally but throughout the country. "Casual drug users," he said, "ought to be taken out and shot." They were "treasonous." They were "aiding and abetting the enemy."

Daryl Gates's own son, Lowell Scott Gates, was a serious, perhaps lifelong drug addict who had gone to jail for a year in 1985 for breaking into a pharmacy and stealing drugs. "Clearly my son is an addict," Gates would later say. "If anything, he's a prime example of a young person who has everything in this world. God was so good to that kid you couldn't believe it. He's not a kid anymore, he's thirty-five, [but] he had everything you'd want—good looks, tremendous physique, smart, tremendous personality—everything you would think would be a road to success." Gates would momentarily pause and shake his head as he said this, seemingly unable to grasp, despite his forty years in the business of human behavior, what drove his son or the fact that he might have an interior life or self-image vastly different from what his father saw. It was "the Pied Pipers down the road—the casual drug users—who told him it was okay [to use drugs]," Gates would say. And his father wasn't smart enough to do anything about it. Gates wasn't talking about killing his own son when he was talking about shooting casual drug users, because his son was a *hard-core* addict, living under "a terrible, terrible compulsion."

But the national publicity from the remark helped get him a $300,000 book contract for an autobiography. President George Bush had just singled him out for special praise on a recent trip to Los Angeles. He had kept Bill Parker's LAPD largely intact and maintained its forty-year tradition of honesty. And in spite of the carping of the ACLU types, the department had received a 74 percent approval rating in a 1988 *Los Angeles Times* poll.

But his problems were waiting, just waiting, to bubble to the surface. Another, more recent *Times* poll showed that more than one-third of the blacks in Los Angeles and Orange counties said that "they or a family member had been intimidated or harassed by law-enforcement officers." Over the past thirty years, moreover, violent crime in L.A. had grown at more than twice the national average. According to figures compiled by the Police Foundation, during 1986 Los Angeles had the highest number of reported violent crimes per 100,000 (9.2 compared with 5.2 in New York, the second highest), and the highest number of property crimes. In 1989 alone, major crimes in the city had risen over 8 percent. And although the increase in 1990 had been only 1 percent over that, murders were still up by more than 11 percent and robberies by more than 16. (In 1989 both murders and robberies had risen by about 18 percent.)

The LAPD may have been far more "aggressive" than the NYPD, but the gangs, drugs, shootings, and violence were there in about the same or in higher numbers as other big cities. And Daryl Gates had utterly failed to understand the root causes of crime or to present any real long-term solutions to them. As Tony Bouza, the liberal former chief of police of Minneapolis, would put it, "He thinks Willie Horton's a monster that needs to be destroyed, and so do I. But I'm also interested in the forces that shaped him. Minneapolis is safer than New York because it has the lowest [big-city high school] dropout rate in the country; *Roe vs. Wade* has been the biggest deterrent to crime because poor teenagers are producing fewer children who become criminals—you've got to see these indirect connections.''

But Daryl Gates and the system he'd inherited and perpetuated chose neither to see nor to make those connections. And as a result it was failing. But few people in Los Angeles and almost no one in local government had the courage to say so. The LAPD had produced some good men like Jesse Brewer and some thoughtful ones like David Dotson, but no outspoken fresh and independent thinkers such as the NYPD had done with James Fyfe, Tony Bouza, or Joseph McNamara.

Instead, the LAPD had brought to the forefront Daryl Gates, who, with the exception of his antidrug DARE program in the public schools, hadn't had a new idea in years.

The 1980s in Los Angeles had begun with Eulia Love. They ended with a federal grand jury awarding $540,000 to former major-league baseball player Joe Morgan after he had been mistaken for a drug courier, thrown to the floor, handcuffed and publicly humiliated. With Jamaal Wilkes, the former basketball star for UCLA and the Los Angeles Lakers being pulled over in a white neighborhood because his license was ''about to expire'' and handcuffed while his name was run through a computer. And with LAPD officers firing eighteen shots and killing a seventeen-year-old unarmed boy who they believed had a gun hidden under a sweatshirt wrapped around his hands. Eighteen shots. In between Eulia Love and that shooting, nothing had really changed.

The police commission, which was supposed to oversee the department and set broad policy, had reverted back from its mild activism in the early eighties to its traditional post-Parker function as a rubber-stamp. During the late seventies and early eighties, when Stephen Reinhardt and Jim Fisk were leading the commission, it had at least occasionally asserted itself—making or expediting changes in shooting policy and the department's spying and intelligence gathering. But after them, the commission's new members were all but comatose. As was the city council as far as Daryl Gates was concerned.

Tom Bradley, too, had refused to provide any real counterweight to

Gates and the department's excesses. Through seventeen years in office and two runs for the governorship, Bradley had sought to avoid a confrontation with the LAPD's tenured, conservative, outspoken chiefs of police. When Daryl Gates was new and weak in the late seventies and early eighties and Tom Bradley was one of the most powerful mayors in the city's history, he could have seriously tried to transform the department. But he'd chosen not to. The cost would have been too great.

"The problem [with the LAPD has been] a problem of leadership," Zev Yaroslavsky would later say. "Leadership at the top. It wasn't just Daryl Gates, particularly, although he was part of the leadership. It was the mayor, the police commission, and the city council. That's where the tone had been set for as long as I'd been here. There'd been absolutely no interest in investigating police-abuse cases until they became public embarrassments to the political leadership."

There was no one in Los Angeles to combine wisdom with courage and do something. They just let it drift. From 1986 through 1990, Daryl Gates had received "outstanding ratings" from the police commission, the mayor, and the city council, all of whom had input and signed off on Gates's ratings and evaluations—which Gates himself would write.

Tom Bradley too had no place to go. Nothing to do now but to reclaim his place in history and perhaps shape his political epitaph, which was soon to be written. He was a two-time loser for the governorship, beset now by allegations of financial improprieties, and past seventy. It was not only understandable but entirely proper that he now regain a modicum of his righteous indignation. He and Gates hated each other, had not spoken in almost a year. So in November of 1990, after Gates had made his "shoot casual drug users" remark, Tom Bradley's office finally announced that "the mayor want[ed] an active, progressive police commission." It was none too soon. The police commission's reaction to Gates's "shoot casual drug users" statement had been to brush it aside "as simply a graphic figure of speech," and to rise in celebratory applause on the occasion of Daryl Gates's forty-one years of service on the LAPD. In late 1990, two of those commissioners resigned. One of them was Stephen Yslas, who, when he had headed the commission's use-of-force panel told a reporter that while he looked at the department's use of force, his real area of concern was insuring the promotion of Hispanics within the department. The other who resigned was the commission's president, Robert Talcott, who before resigning said in a sworn deposition that he had only a "general idea" of what had happened at the Dalton Avenue raid that cost the city $3.5 million in damages, and that he was unfamiliar with the investigation. Bradley replaced them with two strong political allies. The first was Dan Garcia, who once headed the powerful City Planning Commission and had been a longtime backer and big-time fund-raiser for Bradley. A Mexican American who'd made it on his own, Garcia, like Tom Bradley, had become an establishment insider and wheeler-dealer. He was shrewd and alive, too tough to be bulldozed by Gates and too smart to be charmed.

Bradley's second appointment to the commission was, given what had gone before, almost daring: thirty-nine-year-old Melanie Lomax, a fiery, African-American civil-rights attorney with a finely tuned race and class consciousness. In selecting her, Bradley not only chose an activist but the first civil-rights lawyer ever appointed to the commission.

Lomax was not shy in expressing her views. Shortly after taking office she promised that the department was going to be made more accountable, pointedly criticized Gates, and laid down the gauntlet, saying, among other things, "You can never have anyone who makes policy make public statements and not have that person have an effect on eight thousand four hundred officers with revolvers on their hips," and, "The legal mandate of the police commission is to be independent and review and evaluate police functions in this city. . . . and, someone said they needed a pistol over there; with me, they're getting a shotgun." When now federal judge Stephen Reinhardt, the former president of the police commission that had selected Gates as chief, was told by a reporter of Lomax's remarks in late 1990, he said that he wished her well. But, he added, if "he was a betting man, he'd bet on Daryl." "The only way any meaningful change would take place in the LAPD," Reinhardt insisted, was "if the city reformed its charter to allow the mayor to select his own chief of police." An event he thought highly unlikely. Not unless some major event happened. "Not unless," said Stephen Reinhardt," there were to be some kind of very serious scandal within the LAPD." The speed with which that was about to occur would be dazzling to behold.

PART 7

CAN'T WE ALL GET ALONG?

••••••••••••••••••••••••

CHAPTER 1

The Aberration

••••••••••••••••••••••

The evening began in a manner so quintessentially male and American that it's hard to imagine a young man alive over the last fifty years who hadn't experienced almost a carbon copy. William Rehnquist perhaps. But surely not many more.

Sometime between five and six P.M. on Saturday, March 2, 1991, Rodney Glen King, a twenty-five-year-old high school dropout just out of prison, hopped into his white, economy-size Hyundai and headed for the family home of Bryant Allen, a long-haired, still-boyish-looking friend of his whom everybody called Pooh. After picking Allen up, the two drove over to Freddie G.'s, that is, to Freddie Helms's house, got him, and before going to a local park, stopped at a liquor store.

The three black men, in their early to mid twenties, were hanging-out buddies—Rodney King and Pooh since they were teenagers—and on this quiet evening in suburban Altadena, about ten miles northeast of downtown L.A., that was exactly what they planned to do: hang out, get high, talk about girls and each other, laugh and goof, mellow out, and maybe later, go out and look for the heart of the night.

So at the liquor store they each purchased the preferred drink among many of the penny-wise young brothers in Southern California, a forty-ounce bottle of Olde English 800 malt liquor. Eight Balls, as they were called, gave you a bang for your buck.

For the next several hours, the three men sat in the park, slowly downing their Olde English. At about ten, they drove to Pooh's mother's house, where they watched a little basketball on television. Then they went back to the Hyundai, turned on the radio, and sat there singing and laughing, feeling nice, feeling comfortable after finding a little release. Then, all of a sudden, Rodney King put the car into drive and took off. Pooh wasn't sure where King was going, but he figured it was out to cruise some girls, probably over at Hansen Dam, a local park and recreation area where, if they wanted, they might be able to score some reefer from the dealers that infested the place. Pooh was feeling good, feeling *right*, but not drunk, and Rodney King, at least to Pooh, seemed to be in exactly that same place.

When they hit the 210—the Foothill Freeway—Pooh and Rodney King were singing and rapping, while Freddie G. was sleeping in the back. It was past midnight, late for that part of Los Angeles, even for a Saturday night, and Rodney King was hauling ass, changing lanes, lost in the music, lost in the moment. His timing couldn't have been worse. Zooming past vehicle after vehicle, he streaked by a California Highway Patrol car, which immediately switched on its flashing red lights, activated its siren, and sped off after him.

In their report, the highway patrol officers, a married couple named Melanie and Timothy Singer, would give Rodney King's speed as 110 to 115 mph, although people familiar with Hyundais, including company officials, thought that King's vehicle would have had to have been shot out of a cannon to go any higher than 100.

When Pooh noticed the flashing red lights behind them, he got that sinking feeling and told King he'd better pull over and stop. But pulling over was the last thing Rodney King wanted to do. He was out on parole after a year in jail for second-degree robbery, a stupid crime of opportunity that had landed him in the state prison at Susanville among Bloods, Crips, and Cholo gangsters with tattooed tears on their cheeks and dramatic crucifixes over what seemed like every square inch of their bodies. Rodney King might have been big, semiliterate, and black, but he was no Blood or Crip, no bad-ass from the 'hood, getting off with being with his boys and enhancing his reputation by doing time. Singing on the corner, hanging out in the park, was his style, Baby Huey his image on the street. He had grown up, after all, in Pasadena and its middle-class suburb, Altadena, not the searing streets of South Central. He had hated prison and didn't want to go back to Susanville. He was fucked up and irresponsible—he'd fathered two children out of wedlock by two different women and was now married to a third, and he'd done that stupid robbery—but bad, no, Rodney King was not *bad*. That was the thing that later, by necessity, would be obfuscated by some and totally missed by others whose lives had always been so constricted, and whose spirits were so existentially dead, that they had no idea of the difference between the two.

Although reared in relatively tranquil Altadena, Rodney King's life had hardly been bucolic. He'd grown up one of five children of a construction worker and maintenance man named Ronald King and his wife, Odessa. Their existence was an exhausting struggle, the family's life one of impoverishment and despair. After a deep descent into alcoholism, Ronald King died at forty-two, and Odessa withdrew almost entirely from the temporal world, living the narrowed life of a deeply devout Jehovah's Witness. The children grew up in the kind of poverty, as Rodney King's aunt related to *Vanity Fair,* "where they didn't have no food, and [the] kids were walking around with T-shirts for diapers." As they matured, their lives, according to the aunt, all seemed to take wrong turns: one sister taking up and moving in with a man who regularly beat her; another who disappeared without a trace; a younger brother involved in a fight with a policeman and sent to jail for over a year.

John Muir High School was Rodney King's first turning point. With the exception of frequent lateness, he was never in trouble, but he had serious reading problems. So one year they didn't promote him, and he was placed in the retard special education class. Six months before his scheduled graduation, he dropped out of school. After that, his life seemed preordained. He worked sporadically, fathered the two children by two different girlfriends, and married a third, Crystal Waters, who herself had two young sons. Always, it seemed, he was broke. Then came the event that proved to be the second defining moment in Rodney King's life: the robbery.

One day in 1989 Rodney King walked into the 99 Market in nearby Monterey Park, bought a piece of bubble gum, and reached under his jacket and came out with a two-foot-long tire iron. Looking at the store's

Korean owner, Tae Suck Baik, he said four words: "Open the cash register." Which Tae Suck Baik did. But the cash in the register was one thing—Baik was willing to give up the cash—but not the checks that were also there. And when Rodney King dumbly reached for them—what after all, was he going to do with *checks?*—Tae Suck Baik freaked out. Using a three-foot-long metal rod he began smacking Rodney King. Instead of hitting Baik back with the tire iron, Rodney King dropped it and tried to run away. Enraged now, Baik ran around the counter after King, raining a second barrage of blows on him. At which point Rodney King picked up a small bread rack, swung it once and hit Baik, and ran out of the store with about $200. Baik followed and, as Rodney King drove away in his white Hyundai, jotted down his license number. Later Baik would tell the *Los Angeles Times* that he did not believe that King had the heart to hurt him. "He just wanted the money," said Baik. "I held him . . . I hit him first. If I didn't hit him, he wouldn't have hit me." It was armed robbery, Baby Huey style.

He was sentenced to two years in Susanville, and as a first offender, thinking it might do some good, he wrote a letter to his judge: "I have all good time work time. . . . I have a good job and I have two fine kid who wish me home. Have so much at stake to lose if I don't get that chance. My job and family awaits me. So please reconsider your judgement, your honor. The sky my witness and God knows." The judge was not touched and Rodney served about a year before being released on parole. He'd played on the baseball team in high school, and when he got out of prison, he landed a job that was perfect for him as a laborer at Dodger Stadium, where he proceeded to rack up an exemplary record.

But now, with the CHP car bearing down on him, it looked as if he was once again going to be caught short, once again going to be locked up. There was an Olde English in the car, he'd been drinking, and he was speeding. Probably, he thought, all violations of his parole, cumulative tickets to ride back to Susanville. (And in fact, five hours later, his blood-alcohol level would be just under the recently lowered legal minimum, but almost surely high enough, if it had been taken earlier, for Rodney King to have been found legally drunk.) And there was something else. Rodney King—not unreasonably for a black man in Southern California in 1991—was physically frightened. As he himself later told it: "When police pull you over, man . . . your heart start jumping a little bit, you know, boom, boom, [and you] hope they don't beat [you] with anything. That thought always go through your mind.'' So Rodney King panicked when he saw those red lights flashing and heard that siren wailing, and he slowed down, but did not stop. Instead, he drove at a reduced speed for what seemed like a long five minutes to Pooh, who was still trying to tell him, goddamn it, to pull over. ''I was scared,'' Pooh would later say, wondering, ''why doesn't he pull over?'' But Rodney King, recalls Pooh, wasn't responding, in fact, ''wasn't saying nothing, just driving.''

And just when Pooh thought that King *was* going to stop as they approached an off-ramp, he drove down it instead and, at its end, according to the CHP, barreled through a stop sign at 50 mph.

Realizing that they were now entering LAPD jurisdiction, the CHP car had meanwhile radioed the department's local command, the sprawling, sixty-square-mile Foothill Division, and with that, an LAPD squad car occupied by Laurence Powell and Timothy Wind joined the pursuit. Simultaneously, a Los Angeles Unified School District Police car also entered the chase.

With Freddie G. still asleep in the backseat and Pooh pleading with him to pull over, Rodney King decided to take off westbound. According to Pooh, King obeyed all the traffic lights and stop signs once they were on the surface streets. According to the CHP, however, he was driving at upward of 80 mph and ran at least one red light. At one point in the chase, according to Melanie Singer, she and her husband actually pulled their patrol car abreast of King's and told him to ''pull over to the right'' and that he ''wouldn't get hurt.'' But Rodney King ignored them. Through a darkened neighborhood, he led the cops in a circle, at a speed of about 55 mph in a 40-mph zone, stopping for at least one red light, according to a police transmission, but ''failing to yield'' to them and surrender. Pooh could see the police lights steadily flashing behind them, and now he was starting to hear what sounded like a lot of police cars. But Rodney King wasn't reacting. He seemed, thought Pooh, to be out of it, as if he were ''in a trance.''

Finally they came to yet another red light in an integrated, middle-class area of the San Fernando Valley known as Lake View Terrace. On one side of the road was Rodney King's probable destination, Hansen Dam Recreation Area; on the other, a long series of two-story apartments known as the Mountain-Back Apartments. There Rodney King waited until the light turned green, slowly drove through the intersection, and finally pulled over and stopped. An LAPD unit at the scene then radioed ''Code 6'': the chase was over; and then, about one minute later, a Code 4, indicating that no further assistance was needed and that all other units should return to routine patrol.

Immediately the Hyundai was surrounded by squad cars. Using the loudspeaker, Melanie Singer's CHP partner and husband, Timothy, ordered Rodney King, Pooh, and Freddie G.—who was still sleeping—out of the car. Driver, Singer's voice echoed through the night: put your hands up toward the windshield. . . . Using your left hand, open the car door from the outside. . . . Put your other hand outside the car door. . . . Now step out. As Rodney King attempted to do so, however, his seat belt yanked him back in. That, sensed Pooh, who was very nervous, was ''getting [the police] nervous, too.'' King then unlocked the belt ''real fast,'' causing Pooh to feel even more nervous. Black men know cops don't like any sudden movements during routine traffic stops, and this situation was certainly more than routine. Pooh feared he might get shot at any moment. Immediately, Rodney King was ordered to lie down flat, in the approved, arms-stretched-out prone position. Pooh and Freddie G., meanwhile, were stepping out on the opposite side of the car, next to the park. Like Rodney King, they, too, were ordered to prone-out, but unlike King, they were immediately handcuffed when they did so.

The scene outside the Hyundai as the three men stepped out of the car was astounding: a circus in which the cops were the spectators and Rodney King the center-ring attraction. At least ten officers, according to one eyewitness, had their guns trained on King. Circling above, its rotors reverberating that ungodly, predatory noise, its floodlights glaring down— giving an eerie, ghostlike pall to the tableau—was an LAPD helicopter. But what really gave the scene its circuslike atmosphere were the police themselves. Twenty-seven of them, including twenty-three LAPD officers, who had raced to the scene of Rodney King's arrest. At least twelve of those officers had arrived *after* the broadcast of the Code 4 announcing that no further assistance was needed, and that the units should return to normal patrol. And ''five of [those] officers,'' as an investigative commission would later point out, ''were at Foothill Station doing paperwork at the end of their shift when they heard the pursuit broadcast over the radio. The five took two separate cars, joined the pursuit, and continued to its termination after the Code 4 [broadcast]. One of those officers [later] told district attorney investigators that he proceeded to the scene after the Code 4 'to see what was happening.' '' It would be their milling about, their socializing, their laughing, their posturing, and their taking in everything that was about to unfold as if it were some kind of a performance, something that happened every day, that would give the event an almost surreal feeling. Not that the arrival of so many of them should have been totally unexpected. Young cops, particularly in a relatively quiet division like Foothill, live for the chase. In the minds of many of them, the chase is what they do. As Tom Reddin would later put it: ''Everybody wants to get there for that action.'' But behind the thrills and the obvious desire to assist a fellow officer, there were definite problems with police officers of whatever number responding to a chase. A cop's adrenaline is flowing and tempers are flaring. Someone's running, after all, someone who's potentially endangering the lives of both the officers and innocent bystanders. And someone, therefore, has to pay. Bill Parker had recognized that tendency for retribution, according to Tom Reddin, and had responded by instituting a policy mandating that in a pursuit situation a sergeant would have to answer the call and be there at the chase's termination. The sergeant who responded on this night was Stacey Koon.

As the ranking officer at the scene, Stacey Koon waved Melanie Singer off when she approached Rodney King to place him in the ''felony kneeling'' position, telling her, said Singer, to stay back, and ''that they [the LAPD] would handle it.'' What happened next depends on whom you believe.

According to Stacey Koon and Officer Laurence Powell, Rodney King did not follow directions, first getting out of and then reentering the car (the unbuckled-seat-belt episode), and then, when he did get out, refusing to lie on the ground as ordered. Instead, they said, he got down on all fours and slapped the ground. Moreover, according to Koon, Rodney King looked ''very muscular,'' ''very buffed-out,'' and as a result he suspected that King ''was probably an ex-con'' who had spent a lot of time working out in jail. He ''felt threatened,'' said Koon, a fifteen-year veteran of the force. He thought Rodney King to be ''disoriented and unbalanced'' and—using the perennial favorite excuse among cops since the brief popularity of PCP or angel dust in the late seventies and early eighties—that King was dusted out on the drug. Rodney King looked glassy-eyed and spaced-out, and with his size and with the dust, who knew, Koon later said, if the guy might at any moment turn into the Hulk.

Yet whether Stacey Koon did, in fact, feel threatened seems highly problematic. He himself would later say that he "felt enough confidence in his officers to take care of the situation." And Stacey Koon was hardly a man to blink when confronting a single suspect with twenty-six other armed officers—many with drawn guns—on the scene to back him up.

A well-built, balding man of forty with a tendency to tilt his head and thrust his prominent jaw outward in the manner of a Prussian general in an American World War II propaganda movie, Stacey Koon would be the only one who would emerge from his and his fellow officers' subsequent ordeal iron-willed and uncontrite, admitting no wrong and apologizing for nothing—the G. Gordon Liddy of the whole sorry Rodney King affair. A veteran of South Central's notoriously tough Seventy-seventh Street Division who had transferred only within the past year to the relatively tranquil San Fernando Valley, Stacey Koon was the kind of cop that the LAPD had been encouraging for decades. One who placed a premium on macho posturing and displays of physical prowess, who sought to become a legend among his fellow officers and then to feed off that legend and become it.

Once, so Stacey Koon's legend goes, while working the Seventy-seventh Street Division, he did what for most people and most cops—white or black—would have been unimaginable. A hooker, according to the L.A. *Times,* a black transvestite hooker whose mouth was covered with prominent sores, suddenly collapsed of a heart attack in the station house, and Stacey Koon got down and gave him mouth-to-mouth resuscitation. The man, who had AIDS, died despite Koon's CPR attempts, but Christ, who else in his normal mind would do a thing like that?

Then there was the time, as Stacey Koon would tell it, when he was investigating a serious traffic accident. At the scene was a man, a Latino, who was acting insane, acting PCP-crazed, jumping around, getting in the officers' faces, screaming at them, interfering as they tried to help an accident victim. Stacey Koon stunned the guy—that is, shot him with fifty thousand volts from a dart propelled from a Taser electric stun gun—and when the man pulled the dart out and made his way toward him, Stacey Koon dealt with him. He later wrote: "My boot came from the area of lower California and connected with the suspect's scrotum about Lower

Missouri. My boot stopped about Ohio, but the suspect's testicles continued into upper Maine. The suspect was literally lifted off the ground. The suspect tried to speak, but it appeared he had something in his throat—probably his balls.'' Later, the incident, which was videotaped by a film crew, would be used as a training tool at the Police Academy, "used," according to LAPD spokesman Comdr. Rick Dinse, "in training how to deal with a PCP suspect, and [in] the proper use of force."

Then there was the shoot-out with a man who'd been drinking in his house and came out holding an AK-47 assault rifle and pointing it at a fellow officer of Koon's. When the man went into a crouch, Koon shot the man four times, possibly saving the life of his fellow officer. Later he was commended by the police commission for his tactics and common-sense coolness during the incident; and by his fellow officers, who joked to him that the man would surely survive because blacks were "too dumb to go into shock." But Stacey Koon was no LAPD clone. On at least two occasions he had pissed off officers he worked with, for, in their estimation, too vigorously pursuing complaints of brutality lodged against fellow officers. But he himself had been suspended for five days in 1986 for kicking a robbery suspect after a chase, then failing to report that fact. The suspect's charge, like most, went unsustained, but Koon was suspended anyway for failing to *report* it.

Above all, Stacey Koon loved the street as if he were a rookie. He'd been on the job for fifteen years, but still he wasn't angling for one of the straight-days, weekends-off special assignments that most veterans crave. No, he loved the street. "That was where," he would later say, "you do real police work" . . . where you didn't "have to deal with the bureaucracy" . . . where you could "make quality arrests" . . . be an "aggressive police officer" . . . the place where you could, in fact, "make fabulous arrests." You had to be an "idiot," Stacey Koon would later point out, if you wanted to be promoted and you stayed on the street as long as he had. But the street was his "whole thing," his "calling in life." And despite two master's degrees, one from Cal State, Los Angeles, in criminal justice and another in public administration from USC, the street was where he would stay. He was a street cop, a "shit magnet," as they said in the department, and that was what he wanted to remain.

But like so many white LAPD officers—like so many cops throughout big-city America—those streets were also the last place Stacey Koon wanted to live. He was the son of an electrician and an office clerk and had primarily grown up in the same general area of Los Angeles as Daryl Gates, the then largely white, working and lower-middle-class areas of Lynwood and Glendale, and had graduated with honors from Glendale High. After serving in the Air Force, he'd joined the department in 1976. Then, with his wife, Mary, a registered nurse whom he'd married in 1971, he moved forty miles north of Los Angeles into the hilly, former-ranch country of the Santa Clarita Valley. There they would raise five children and he would hear himself described by Father Robert Rankin—the parish priest at Koon's local Roman Catholic church, Our Lady of Perpetual Help—as ''the ideal Catholic family man.''

There is no telling what traveling from the quiet suburban bliss of the Santa Clarita Valley into the violent, sometimes crazed world of South Central had done to Stacey Koon's psyche over all those years. But he would see the events about to unfold in a very different light from Rodney King, or for that matter, much of the rest of the world. Or at least that would be his position.

The fear, although hard to swallow given the overwhelming force the LAPD had on the scene and the ten guns trained on Rodney King and his passengers, might initially have been responsible for what followed. Who knew, after all, what Rodney King and the others might be packing, or why he'd taken so long to pull over? And, surely, too, was the fact that the rabbit had run. You engage in a high-speed chase, you're gonna get whacked. As an LAPD dispatcher put it after it all went down and an ambulance was being requested: ''They should know better than [to] run. They are going to pay a price when they do that.'' Guys like Rodney King, after all, needed a whack, needed someone to knock some sense into him. If you let them run, what have you got? What kind of respect? To run is an affront to a cop's dignity, to the whole system. And surely no major police department in the country felt that more keenly than did the LAPD.

Retribution, street justice, ''givin' them one,'' as the old Irish cops used to say, ''to remember you by,'' was always a strong possibility. But it was probably more what Rodney King did as Melanie Singer approached him with her gun drawn that set up the horror of what transpired. Melanie Singer, her partner-husband, Timothy Singer, and Stacey Koon all distinctly remember it. As Rodney King came out of the car, he was ''moving his feet and shaking his hips, like in a dance,'' said Timothy Singer. He seemed "almost happy and jovial," remembered Melanie Singer. "He was smiling . . . [and] dancing around, almost like a pitter-patter." It was strange. Then, after getting down on all fours as she'd ordered him, Rodney King began to "parade around, almost like he was a dog." What Stacey Koon saw, however, was a lot more than just a prance or dance. As he would later describe it, Rodney King "grabbed his butt with both hands and began to shake and gyrate his fanny in a sexually suggestive fashion. [And] as King sexually gyrated, a mix of fear and offense overcame Melanie [Singer]." The fear, thought Stacey Koon, "was of a Mandingo sexual encounter." There it was. Rodney King had touched the Travis Bickle, had touched the *Taxi Driver*, dwelling deep in the libido of every straight, white, Catholic male who'd ever been exposed to the church's powerful Madonna-whore teachings. His dance called up that strange, potent mixture of rage, revulsion, incredulousness, and envy that demands the annihilation of every black pimp and white girl's black boyfriend on the planet. And Stacey Koon had put it all right out there. A Mandingo sexual encounter. A Mandingo, a black slave, a big black buck, was terrorizing this poor white female officer. It wasn't enough that he had dared defy them, turning a Saturday-night cruise into a high-speed chase. It wasn't enough that he was laughing and pointing at the whirling LAPD helicopter, and diddy-bobbin' around like this was all some kind of goddammed joke. No, he was also challenging every white man there by shaking his ass, Mandingo-style, at Melanie Singer, treating them all like they were some kind of fucking fools. It was all too much. Clearly, "a group beat," as Stacey Koon later called the arrest of Rodney King, was in order.

As King lay on the ground, surrounded by police, Officer Laurence Powell, a twenty-eight-year-old, weak-jawed, puffy-faced, three-year veteran of the LAPD, bent and grasped Rodney King's wrists to handcuff him.

Like Koon, Powell had previously had brutality charges lodged against him. In 1986, while police searched for a man who'd been seen with a gun, Powell, still in the police reserve, had grabbed a temporarily handcuffed black suspect by the throat and forced him back against a police car, injuring the man's back. Then, in 1989, a factory worker named Salvador Castaneda claimed that Powell had broken his arm with his police baton, striking him at least four times while he stood still, unarmed and unresisting. Of course, Castaneda had been drunkenly chasing a drinking partner down the street with a machete when Powell arrived on the scene—which in the eyes of a lot of people totally mitigated Powell's actions, even if Castaneda *had* dropped the machete when he saw the cops. Nevertheless, by both department policy and state law cops are not out there to punish people like avenging angels, and the city finally settled Castaneda's brutality suit for $70,000.

But Laurence Powell—the son of a lieutenant for the L.A. County Marshal's office; the son of a man and woman who provided foster care to children, some of whom were black, Latino, abused and drug addicted; Laurence Powell, who had grown up in middle-class comfort in suburban Los Angeles and been an honor student in high school—seemed to have a great deal of the avenging angel in him.

And in late 1990, he was once again accused of excessive force, this time for hitting an already handcuffed suspect six to ten times in the legs with his heavy metal flashlight, which, after his encounter with Rodney King, would lead to a severe reprimand from the department for "serious misconduct." Laurence Powell was, as a former supervisor would put it, "trying to prove he was tough." Janine Bouey, an African-American officer and occasional partner of Powell's, put it another way: "He treated everybody like crap. He always had his hand on his gun. . . . If things didn't happen during the course of a normal tour, he would be out looking for problems. . . . He was always bragging about altercations he was in and how he kicked butt."

Now, Laurence Powell did indeed seem ready to kick some butt. Face-down on the pavement, Rodney King felt Laurence Powell reach down, grasp his wrists, twist them up, and "apply pressure," as Rodney King later described it, like "he was trying to snap my wrist in half." As he did so, Rodney King screamed in pain and "flinched." Then someone yelled, "Back!" and Powell and the other officers all jumped back away from him. It was at that point that Stacey Koon, off to the side, stunned Rodney King, shooting two darts attached by wires to his Taser gun, each sending fifty thousand volts of electrical shock through King's body. Watching as the darts hit, CHP officer Timothy Singer noted what was happening to King's face, noted that it was "vibrating," that it was "convulsing." Rodney King felt as if his "blood was boiling inside" him. Then, according to King, the officers around him started a steady singsong taunt: "What's up, killer? How you feelin', killer? What's up, nigger? How you feelin'? How you feelin'?'' They asked him this as he coughed and made noises that sounded like laughs but were really efforts to try to get the blood out of his mouth. Rodney King wasn't sure of the word following ''how you feelin'.'' Whether they were saying ''How you feelin' *killer?*'' or ''How you feelin' *nigger?*'' But he did know he was feeling this enormous pain. And that he was scared shitless. ''I was just trying to stay alive, trying to stay alive, and they never gave me a chance to stay still. I never had a chance to stay still,'' he'd later say. It was then, according to Melanie Singer, that Laurence Powell, like a baseball player at the plate swinging a bat, and with what's known in law enforcement as ''a power swing,'' struck Rodney King once across his face, once across his knuckles, and then four more times in rapid succession on the right side of his head with his heavy metal baton. Rodney King was now on his knees. ''I saw the blood come out of the right side of his cheek,'' Melanie Singer would later testify, and ''I heard the driver scream. The driver then clasps both hands into his face as Officer Powell delivers another power swing.'' ''There is no doubt in my mind that he [Laurence Powell] hit Mr. King repeatedly in the face,'' Melanie Singer would later recall in sworn testimony, her voice cracking. It was something, she said, ''I will never forget . . . until the day I die.'' The hitting of Rodney King in the face, a violation of LAPD policy, was intentional, said Singer later, there was no question in her mind. Nor in Rodney King's. ''They shocked me . . . ,'' he would later testify, then ''they paused for a moment and then they struck me across the face real hard with the billy club.''

Timothy Singer remembers it slightly differently, saying that King had not fallen down after the second shot from the stun gun but was staggering around and that was when Laurence Powell struck the first blow. Laurence Powell, too, would dispute this, saying he did not hit King until he'd risen from the ground and was charging at him in a threatening fashion. But Rodney King would have an answer for that. ''No, no, no,'' he would say, ''I wouldn't strike back. I don't think no one would strike back against four or five guns aimed at him.''

Then, says Rodney King, they told him to run. Dazed, literally stunned, probably still a little drunk, Taser darts and wires still attached to his body, Rodney King got up and did try to run, stumbling in the direction of Laurence Powell.

* * *

On the balcony of the Mountain-Back Apartments, meanwhile, Josie Morales had been awakened by the sound of the LAPD helicopter's blades slicing through the air and the sirens of the pursuing police cars. She saw about ten officers in a loose circle surrounding Rodney King, and Rodney King flat on his face. Then she saw Stacey Koon fire the stun gun and some officers begin to club him. "He didn't touch anybody," said Morales. "He got up and ran blindly but not running at anyone, just trying to get away. We thought maybe they stopped him for guns or drugs or even murder. . . . There was nothing that the guy did that could warrant that kind of a beating."

The two-foot-long, solid-aluminum Monadnock PR-24 baton that Laurence Powell was swinging like an ax-wielding lumberjack was a terrible weapon. As Steve Fisk would later say about the Rodney King beating, "they were kicking, and kicking's not fair, but I'd rather be kicked than hit with that PR-24 because it breaks bones." Rodney King had a way of describing what it felt like to be hit by one, to be hit by a solid-metal bar twenty-four inches long that weighs two pounds. It was like, he would say, when "you would get up in the middle of the night and jam your toe on a piece of metal. That's what it felt like every time I got hit." Once Rodney King got to his feet and ran toward Laurence Powell, it was all over for him. Ten quick smacks brought him quickly to his knees. Rolando Solano, one of the 23 LAPD officers at the scene, stared "shocked at the . . . chops which hit King's face" and was "surprised King could be hit so hard and still be standing." Laurence Powell was now joined by another officer, Timothy Wind. Responding to orders from Stacey Koon, they unmercifully smashed Rodney King with bursts of "power strokes." But Rodney King was, as Stacey Koon later said it, like "a Bobo doll." "Ever hit one?" he would ask a reporter. "Comes back and forth, back and forth. That's exactly what he's [King's] doing."

Of course, Rodney King *was* popping up and down like a Bobo doll. What could Koon or anyone else expect? People are tied down when they're whipped. That's the way the human body reacts when it's hit. Nevertheless, it would become Stacey Koon's position that Rodney King was a threat and had to be beaten down. "Prone is safe," he would later say. "Up is not. That is what we're trying to do, to keep him on the ground, because if he gets up, it's going to be a deadly force situation." "My intent was to cripple Rodney King. That is a better option than having to use deadly force, having to choke or having to shoot Rodney King.''

So Stacey Koon then ordered Laurence Powell and Timothy Wind to *get down* on Rodney King. ''Hit his joints, hit his wrists, hit his elbows, hit his knees, hit his ankles,'' Stacey Koon screamed. In eighty-one seconds Rodney King was pounded with fifty-six blows, all but one of which was from the batons of Laurence Powell and Timothy Wind. One blow every 1.5 seconds. The other blow was from a third officer, Theodore Briseno, who tried to intervene and stop Powell and Wind from hitting Rodney King and, all of a sudden, appeared frustrated and stomped down hard on King's neck. Like Koon and Powell, Briseno, too, had his problems with civilian complaints. Known within the department for his hot temper, Briseno was suspended in 1987 by the LAPD for sixty-six days without pay for kicking a handcuffed prisoner and using his baton to strike him.

As the beating continued, not one of the mass of officers at the scene (with the possible exception of Theodore Briseno) lifted a finger to stop the beating. Nor was there any effort to conceal it. It was as if they knew that they had carte blanche, nothing to fear and no price to pay. Cars passed, witnesses were visible both on the balconies of the nearby apartment complex and standing outside it. But not one law enforcement official at the scene seemed to think that made any difference.

By the end of the eighty-two seconds, Rodney King had suffered a broken cheekbone, permanent cracks to the bones that hold his right eye in its socket, eleven fractured bones at the base of his skull, a serious concussion, facial-nerve damage, a broken ankle, and the loss of several of the fillings from his teeth. But for Stacey Koon it was just another night's work. ''We take Rodney King into custody,'' he would later say. ''He doesn't get seriously injured. We don't get injured. He goes to jail. That's the way the system's supposed to work.''

If getting up and running was what did Rodney King in, it was the Mountain-Back Apartments that would seal the fate of the four LAPD officers involved in his beating. More than twenty residents of that apartment building had, like Josie Morales, been awakened by the clamorous events outside. They were ordinary people, plain citizens, and they were horrified by what they saw. Elois Camp, a sixty-five-year-old retired teacher, said King was lying ''in a fetal position trying to avoid the blows

... [and] we were yelling, 'No, don't kill him!' [but] they paid us no attention.'' Said Dorothy Gibson, a registered nurse, ''He was just dodging blows. He was on the ground. It sounded like I heard him scream out, 'Please stop.' ... I saw them kick the man ... any way they could get a lick in, they were kicking him.'' After Rodney King was totally subdued, she recalled of the officers, ''they were talking and they were laughing.'' Javier Martinez, a bus driver at the scene, later told a law enforcement official that ''he considered getting out of the bus to help King, [but] decided against doing that for fear of also being hit himself.'' Dawn Davis, twenty-six, said she saw King on the ground ''facedown and he wasn't fighting or anything, and ... they were still hitting on him ... Every time he'd move, they'd hit him again. I was crying. I was praying for the guy ...'' The sounds of the batons on Rodney King's flesh and bones, thought Ned Camp as he heard the officers ''grunt'' as they swung their nightsticks, was like the sound of someone ''hitting a tree.'' But the observations of all of these witnesses, even collectively, mattered little. Over the years, on numerous occasions, groups of civilians had witnessed what they considered atrociously brutal behavior and little had been done and nothing had changed. On a second-floor balcony that night, however, was a man who would have more to offer to the LAPD, the district attorney, the press, and the world than just his word. On a balcony that night shooting away with his new Sony Handycam was a thirty-one-year-old manager of a North Hollywood plumbing company named George Holliday.

In the days before the Rodney King beating, George Holliday had been like a kid with a new toy; ''trigger-happy,'' he called his infatuation with his new camera. Ever since he'd gotten his Handycam, he'd felt almost compelled to point and shoot at anything that moved. He'd taped his neighborhood bar, where a portion of the film *Terminator II* had been shot. He'd taped a cat licking its paw. And when he awoke that early Sunday morning in March of 1992, he taped the beating of Rodney King, catching it from the time King rose from the ground, whirled, and found his face meeting the slashing solid metal of Laurence Powell's baton, to its exhaustive end. Like the other residents of the Mountain-Back he'd been awakened by the sirens, noise, and light outside, and as he sleepily aimed his camera from his second-floor patio, he was only dimly aware of just exactly what he was shooting. Without the bright glare from the streetlights, from the squad-car headlights, and most especially from the helicopter spotlights, the tape would have been worthless. With their illumination it was grainy but clear—the video equivalent of a just-dropped atomic bomb. But that night George Holliday had little conception of this. He planned on getting up early the next morning to view the L.A. marathon and wanted to get back to sleep. All George Holliday knew for sure when he went back to bed was that there'd been an arrest and that a man had been spread-eagled, surrounded by police. It wasn't until the next day, when he shoved the tape into his VCR, sat down, and stared transfixed, that he saw, in graphic detail, the pictures that would outrage the world.

Pooh had been exposed to "whuppings" when he was a child, had grown used to them, and knew their sound. But as he lay handcuffed and facedown on the ground with Freddie G., he knew what he was hearing was something different, something on a whole other level. Freddie G. (who later died in an unrelated automobile accident) knew, too, that something dreadful was happening, that they were beating Rodney King and "doing him real bad." It wasn't only the intensity of Rodney King's screams, but the sound of the metal batons on King's flesh and bones. It sounded to Pooh "like bones being cracked, like being beat, [like] loud thumps, [like] gushy sounds." He was frightened, "definitely frightened." A School District Police officer had his gun drawn on them, and Pooh had already been kicked twice, before being ordered to crawl, flat down in a kind of scooting movement over to "somewhere real dark" (the park), where, feared Pooh, they might beat or shoot him. Like Pooh, Freddie G. had been kicked and hit in the head with a baton, he'd later claim, after he'd raised his face in an effort to get it out of the dirt. The blow drew blood, which then ran down his neck into his shirt collar.

As the whacks to Rodney King's body echoed in the night, one of the officers turned to Freddie G. and asked, "Do you want to be like your homeboy?" Meanwhile Pooh, who'd been "slapped twice against the car"; was asked, like Freddie G., if he, too, would like a beating; and was ordered not to look in King's direction. But that was unnecessary. Pooh already had his eyes closed. "Whatever was happening to [Rodney King]," Pooh would later say, "I didn't want to see it."

Meanwhile, as the beating concluded, Melanie Singer briefly considered giving Rodney King first aid. Clearly King needed it. But she didn't want to face the jeers and heckling that she was sure would come from the arresting cops, didn't want to place herself that far outside the fraternity. So she left Rodney King lying there, facedown—hog-tied by his hands and feet like a dazed, wounded animal—in the street.

Just seconds after Laurence Powell had stopped beating Rodney King, he grabbed his squad-car radio and requested an ambulance: "We need an RA [a rescue ambulance] at Foothill and Osborne [for a] victim of ah . . . ah . . ." And he paused, as if groping for a word. As he did so, the word he wanted floated from the background and into the microphone. "Beating," someone, probably Timothy Wind, called out. This was followed by a laugh, a kind of chuckle or giggle, as Laurence Powell, picking up on it, added, "Yeah . . . numerous head wounds."

Then, just two minutes later, shortly before one A.M. on Sunday morning—right after Rodney King had been swarmed over by the LAPD and hog-tied—Stacey Koon sent a computer message over the department's Mobile Digital Terminal (MDT) system, which was hooked up by small computers placed inside LAPD squad cars to the station house, informing the watch commander's office about what had happened. "U[unit] just had a big-time use of force," he reported. "Tased and beat the suspect of CHP pursuit, Big Time." One minute later, the reply came back: "Oh, well . . . I'm sure the lizard didn't deserve it . . . Ha, Ha, I'll let them know, O.K."

Responding to Laurence Powell's call for a rescue ambulance, meanwhile, an LAPD dispatcher was contacting the L.A. County Fire Department. The exchange, like others that night, was filled with gallows humor—which later offended a lot of people who could *feel* those baton blows hitting Rodney King and thought that the laughing merely underscored the callousness of the brutality. But cynical, unfeeling humor is a cop characteristic, a defense mechanism used by those who deal with death and squalor. More interesting was the fact that, like the beating itself, the conversations over the radio and the computer system were startlingly casual and matter-of-fact, as if it happened every day, and as if they could say anything they wanted with an absolute disregard for any possible retribution:

LAPD dispatcher: "Foothill and Osborne. In the valley, dude . . ."
Fire department: (laughs)
LAPD: ". . . and like he got beat up."

FD: (laughs) "Wait." (laughs)

LAPD: "We are on the scene."

FD: "Hold, hold on, give me the address again."

LAPD: "Foothill and Osborne. He pissed us off, so I guess he needs an ambulance now."

FD: "Oh, Osborne. Little attitude adjustment?"

LAPD: "Yeah, we had to chase him . . . that kind of irritated us a little."

FD: "Why would you want to do that for?"

LAPD: (laughter) "Should know better than [to] run. They are going to pay a price when they do that."

Shortly before the Rodney King chase, Powell and Wind had swapped messages with a female officer on foot patrol over the MDT computer system telling her how they'd broken up a domestic quarrel involving African-Americans:

Powell and Wind: "Sounds almost [as] exciting as our last call. . . . It was right out of *Gorillas in the Mist.*"

Foot-patrol officer: "Ha, ha, ha, ha . . . let me guess who be the parties."

Then, fifteen minutes after the King beating, Laurence Powell and Timothy Wind had another conversation, this one also over the MDT computer system, again with the officer on foot patrol. "Oops," they typed. "Oops, what?" came the reply. "I haven't beaten anyone this bad in a long time." "Oh, not again . . . ," wrote the foot-patrol officer. "Why for you do that? . . . I thought you agreed to chill out for a while." So, it had all happened before. One of the officers, probably Powell, had a reputation for this sort of thing. He wasn't alone. Foothill Division, as David Dotson would later somewhat delicately put it, was known for its "lack of sensitivity" when dealing with brutal cops. There was, for example, the officer who had been involved in the debacle of the Thirty-ninth and Dalton raid who had been transferred out to Foothill. Almost immediately he challenged someone to a fight on the street, head-butted him, and broke his lip. Then he was permitted to work as a detective, where he made an unlawful arrest. After that, Dotson told the Foothill commander, " 'My God, don't you guys understand? He can't be out there. He can't be trusted.' . . . So, a couple of weeks later, I discovered where . . . they put [him]. In [the] Foothill jail. Now there is not a place that I know of where, if you have a tendency toward abusing people, you can do it more easily than in jail. The management out there didn't understand those kinds of sensitivities."

Later, after Daryl Gates referred to Rodney King's beating as an "aberration," Ed Davis, now a state senator and a death-bed convert to officer accountability, would have an answer for Gates: "I don't think that [when you have] all those communications between radio cars [they] are a one-night aberration."

Hog-tied and lying facedown in the back of the ambulance just as he had been on the street, Rodney King was transported to Pacifica Hospital for emergency treatment. With the exception of CHP officer Melanie Singer, nobody had seemed much concerned with his condition prior to his arrival. Certainly not paramedic Kathleen Bosak, who, along with her partner, had found King lying on the side of the road. To her, Rodney King, as she later said in careful police–fire-fighter–paramedic jargon, simply "looked like he had been in some kind of ground confrontation." On the way to the hospital Rodney King seemed to her at times to be "combative and uncooperative," but then he was hog-tied and facedown in a vulnerable, painfully uncomfortable position, as Bosak could see, had a body aching from a beating, and was only acting "uncooperative" when he was lying in that uncomfortable position.

Riding with them was Timothy Wind and another LAPD officer, Susan Clemmer. She never saw Rodney King acting "combative" but he did spit "blood on [her] legs and shoes" and started to laugh when she told him to stop. Then, as he was being taken into the hospital emergency room, he even smiled at the young, white female officer and said something to her that she couldn't hear. So she asked him to repeat it. Rodney King looked at Stacey Koon, smiled and said "I love you." Then he started laughing.

Inside the Pacifica Hospital emergency room where Rodney King had his broken cheekbone and right ankle treated and had his body and face sewn with twenty stitches—five on the inside of his mouth—Laurence Powell still hadn't had enough of him. Still hadn't rubbed Rodney King's nose deep enough in the shit to suit him. So when King indicated that he worked at Dodger Stadium, Laurence Powell had a question: "Did you see the game we played tonight?" When Rodney King looked at him quizzically, he went further: "Don't you remember the hardball game?

We hit quite a few home runs." Then, when Rodney King allowed that now he understood what he meant, Laurence Powell closed in with what he must have thought was a killer line: "Yeah, and you lost the ball game, didn't you?"

That same Sunday morning at about four A.M., Pooh awakened Rodney King's brother Paul and told him what had happened. The next morning Paul King went to the Foothill station to register a complaint. Nobody wanted to hear it. After about an hour he left, knowing, as he later said, that he "hadn't made a complaint." The officer at the front desk had essentially just ignored him, while a sergeant who finally brought him into a detective's interview room left him sitting there for thirty minutes. Before doing so, however, the sergeant had asked Paul King if *he'd* ever been in trouble. Later, he also informed Paul King that his brother Rodney was in "big trouble," and if Paul was able to obtain a video of the incident (Pooh had told Paul King that he thought a video might have been made) that he should then go ahead and bring it in. But Paul King had been right. No complaint form had been made or filed by the sergeant. Instead, he noted in his daily log that nothing further needed to be done unless additional evidence was presented or there was a problem with the officer's use-of-force report.

So brazen was Laurence Powell's arrest report, and so bold-faced were the lies in Stacey Koon's daily sergeant's log, that in a curious way they substantiated Koon's later contention that he and his men had done nothing out of the ordinary and were simply doing what they'd been taught, and what was expected of them. Rodney King's ankle was broken and so was his cheek and eleven bones at the base of his skull. His face was puffed out like a watermelon. Dozens of cops had witnessed what had happened, as had perhaps that many civilians. Cars passed by and slowed down to get a look; a *bus* actually did the same. Yet, so secure were Laurence Powell and Stacey Koon in their invulnerability to complaint or retribution that they made no effort to cover up. Clearly there was, in their minds, no need to cover up. As the Singers' supervisor, California Highway Patrol Lieutenant John M. Kielbasi told CHP investigators from Sacramento after the King beating: "If there was not a video on it, you wouldn't be down here. That's the only difference between what goes on down here in Los Angeles—I would say half a dozen times a week, any given week—the fact that it hasn't been recorded. And these things do go on.''

So Laurence Powell was remarkably straightforward when he described King's alleged resistance and subsequent beating: King had ''recovered almost immediately [from the Taser shots] and resumed his hostile charge in our direction. [Ofcr.] Wind and I drew out batons to defend against deft's [defendant's] attack and struck him several times in the arm and leg areas to incapacitate him. Deft continued resisting, kicking and swinging his arms at us. We finally kicked deft down and he was subdued by several officers using the swarm technique.'' The almost sixty blows had become ''several.'' Out-of-policy hits to the face and head had never happened. Rodney King's failure to comply immediately with every instruction like a highly trained show dog, Rodney King's baying at the moon, Rodney King's insolent, ass-shaking dance, Rodney King's probably involuntary physical reaction to being stun-gunned, to having his wrists twisted and then being beaten, had become a simple, clear-cut case of ''resistance.''

And King's numerous injuries, according to Stacey Koon, no more than your five-year-old might sustain if she fell off her tricycle. King had suffered, wrote Koon, ''several facial cuts due to contact with asphalt. Of a minor nature. A split inner lip.'' About the only concession made to the possibility of the incident's being questioned, to his assumption of absolute invulnerability, was Koon's notation that the ''suspect [was] oblivious to pain''—a setup for the PCP excuse. But perhaps there was another reason for the notation. One beyond Koon's covering his ass or the possibility that King *was* dusted (he wasn't). Stacey Koon, in the tradition of white men down through the ages, may really have believed that Rodney King was so big, so black, so animallike, such a buck, that he *didn't* really feel pain.

There were also, of course, the reports that didn't come in from the two dozen or so officers at the scene who were witnessing a brutal out-of-policy beating. A beating, after all, not of a child-molesting ax-murderer caught in the act, but of a motorist who cruised too long and played the fool at the wrong time.

Only in the movies, of course, would someone have stepped up and actually stopped the beating. To inject yourself into a violent situation like that requires not only an extraordinary act of physical will, but a willingness to take on the people you work with and the ethos of an entire institution. Even reporting it would have required a willingness to be ostracized from your fellow cops and branded a traitor and a snitch. The code required you turn away and ignore it, and if necessary to protect a fellow officer, to lie. As LAPD officer Scott Kennedy put it on another occasion when his partner was charged with using excessive force: "It's basically an unwritten rule; you don't roll over, [you don't] tell on a partner." Rodney King put it another way: "They are all a family, a big family. They're one family, and we're another family."

When he woke up on Monday morning, an enormous question was weighing on George Holliday's mind: just what could that man on the ground have done to deserve such a vicious pounding. George Holliday was no political activist. He was a person whom news director Warren Cereghino of local TV station KTLA would later perfectly describe as "low-key, noncomplex . . . a person without a lot of guile."

But nonetheless, George Holliday was disturbed enough that he decided to call the LAPD's Foothill Division. He told the desk officer that he'd witnessed a beating of a man by LAPD officers, then inquired about his condition. It was a frustrating conversation. The desk officer didn't want to know him or to hear anything he had to say. He didn't offer to take an incident report of personal complaint, asked Holliday no questions, and responded to his inquiry regarding King with a curt, "We [the LAPD] do not release information like that." Then, says George Holliday, he "pretty much hung up."

After talking it over with his wife, George Holliday decided to call CNN's L.A. bureau and give them the tape. But the phone kept ringing and no one answered. So he contacted KTLA, Channel 5. They told him, sure, they'd be interested in taking a look at the tape and to bring it down. He had a busy day planned, so he dropped it off at the station and left. Then an assignment manager and two veteran local reporters—Warren Wilson and Stan Chambers—viewed it. Instantly they recognized the video for what it was: a *very* serious piece of tape. Their assessment went beyond the fact that this was a *story*, and certainly beyond ideology. Wilson and Chambers were solid, durable reporters, but hardly crusading investigative journalists. They'd been in L.A. for years, did their jobs, knew the score, and rarely questioned it. But clearly this video was *television*, amazing, sit-up-in-your chair, holy-shit television. It was a bridge collapsing as an earthquake hit. It was a young Marine with a

Zippo lighter torching a Vietnamese village while an old peasant woman wails and pleads with him to stop. It was the essence of TV: an entire story in pictures. Immediately they brought it to Warren Cereghino, the news director. He too was "blown away" by what he saw.

They called the LAPD's Press Relations section and told them what they had. The attitude there wasn't much different from the desk sergeant's at Foothill. They were not about to come down to KTLA. If the station wanted someone from the LAPD to view it, well, they'd have to bring it to Parker Center. In most cities a news department would have felt that by offering a police department a viewing of the tape, they had gone the extra mile, completed their obligation to get the other side of the story, and then told them that if that was their attitude, fine, just be sure to watch the news tonight. But this was Los Angeles, and KTLA was one of the most conservative of the local stations. So they made a full copy of the tape and sent a reporter and crew down to LAPD headquarters. There, they showed it to Lt. Fred Nixon, a gruff, impatient, middle-aged African-American who could barely conceal his contempt and hostility toward reporters not following the LAPD's line. But after Nixon viewed the tape, what could he say? David Gergen himself couldn't have put a good spin on *that* tape. He murmured some inanities, but the tape was far beyond both his bureaucratic station and capacity for damage control. Clearly, it would have to be handled by someone much higher up in the command structure. It wasn't just dynamite for television viewing, it was clearly dynamite for the LAPD as well.

After agreeing to pay George Holliday $500 for the tape, KTLA played the video that Monday night as its lead story in the second section of its ten-o'clock news. The reaction was instantaneous, and the phones at the station blew off the hook. One of the calls was from CNN. They had a reciprocal agreement with KTLA, and they wanted the tape. When KTLA provided it, the beating of Rodney King ran all night long on CNN. In the days that followed, it would literally be beamed around the world almost every five minutes, becoming in the weeks to follow among the most famous news videos in broadcast history.

CHAPTER 2

The Reaction
······················

Standing in a hallway deep within the downtown headquarters of the Los Angeles Police Department, the young reporter from the L.A. *Times* presses Daryl Gates for an answer as CNN is busy beaming George Holliday's video around the world at the top of the hour. Thus far, over a thousand outraged calls have come into City Hall—some from as far away as New Hampshire.

"I want to go back to the time frame of the investigation," says the reporter, one of at least a dozen the *Times* will assign to work this, what is fast becoming the biggest story to hit Los Angeles since Bobby Kennedy's assassination. "You said you were expediting the investigation. Just what exactly does that mean, 'expediting'? A week, two weeks, a month?"

It's perhaps the fifth time the reporter has put the same question to Gates, a fact that causes a cameraman from one of the most sycophantic of L.A.'s local television stations to stage-whisper, "He's already answered that." But Daryl Gates shakes off his protector, spreads his arms slowly—palms up, as if imploring God for patience—and turns to the reporter. "I already *told* you we're expediting the investigation, why do you persist in this?" he says, allowing a note of sarcasm to creep into his voice. "It's dictionary-clear what *expedited* means. Look it up. We intend to conduct our investigation as quickly as possible. Period." But if Daryl Gates thought that would be enough, and that it would all blow over, he was wrong. Within two weeks, nearly nine in ten Americans would say that they had seen, heard, or read about the beating of Rodney King.

About a dozen days after the beating of Rodney King, Daryl Gates again walks into Parker Center. In a hallway, he's greeted by over one hundred applauding detectives and clerical workers, some wearing yellow ribbons. The show of support had been orchestrated by a local PR firm, but the warmth of his reception seems nonetheless entirely genuine. "What about resigning, Chief? Are you going to resign?" asks a reporter from a local radio station. "How," replies Gates in a low and plaintive voice, indicating his supporters, "could I resign after this?" Then, as if to show that the city still belonged to him and that nothing was really going to change, he said of Rodney King, "We regret what took place. I hope he gets his life straightened out. Perhaps this will be the vehicle to move him down the road to a good life instead of the life he's been involved in for such a long time." There it was. The beating had been good for the rabbit.

But the list of those calling on him to resign was growing daily. Something deep in Tom Bradley's soul that had almost been lost seemed to have been awakened by Rodney King's beating, and within days he had called for Gates's resignation. Then George Will, Gates's favorite columnist, ran a piece dripping with contempt, echoing Bradley. Jesse Jackson flew to L.A. to support their demand. Willie Brown, the African-American speaker of the California State Assembly, also called on Gates to leave, and so, too, did U.S. Senate Judiciary Committee chairman Joseph R. Biden, Jr. Biden, who'd lavished praise on Gates at a hearing the previous September (when Gates had made his "shoot casual drug users" remark before Biden's committee), made his resignation call on "Meet the Press." Seated next to him was Attorney General Dick Thornburgh, who, while not echoing Biden, did not exactly leap out of his chair in Gates's defense. His silence was, in fact, deafening. Only weeks before, Thornburgh's boss, Pres. George Bush, had singled out Gates as one of his "all-American heroes" in front of an audience to which he was proposing a new crime bill. Now, the FBI was investigating the LAPD, and at the urging of the congressional Black Caucus, George Bush's

Justice Department was announcing a review of all complaints of police brutality to the federal government over the past six years—about fifteen thousand cases in all.

The L.A. *Times, La Opinión,* the *Daily News,* the *LA Weekly,* local television station KCBS, the ACLU, the area's three most powerful congressmen, Henry Waxman, Howard Berman, and Tony Beilenson—all of them were also telling Daryl Gates to get out of town. And, to cap it all off, the *Los Angeles Times* had just run a front-page poll in the wake of the airing of the King video showing that two-thirds of the respondents believed that police brutality was common in Los Angeles. It was an astounding statistic, even given the King tape's saturation broadcasting.

Overnight, it seemed, Los Angeles was being branded the Selma, Alabama, of the 1990s. And while nobody was going around polling the heads of the city's banks, corporations, and old-line law firms (at least publicly), it was clear that Selma was hardly the image of Los Angeles they wanted. When police dogs, water cannons, and clubbings on the Edmund Pettus Bridge in the days of the civil rights movement began to negatively define a South looking for a new place in an expanding national and world economy, it became clear cops like Bull Connor had to go. Daryl Gates, too, was now bad for business. He had kept the city's business titans reasonably satisfied, but he was a functionary, and his leaving would be no loss. Who needed people referring to their city as sports columnist Mike Lupica had in *Esquire* magazine when he wrote that "National Football League Commissioner Paul Tagliabue took the 1993 Super Bowl away from Phoenix because Arizona voters would not approve an official state holiday for Martin Luther King. It looked like a tough stance, but it wasn't. Tagliabue . . . then sent the '93 Super Bowl to Southern California, that cradle of civil liberties, a great place for a big football game, but an awful place to get pulled over by the cops." Who needed that?

Under pressure Daryl Gates would be left with little alternative but to recommend that felony charges be filed against the four officers involved in the beating, insist that under no circumstances would he resign, and declare at every opportunity that the incident was an aberration. Meanwhile, other reactions were being played out.

Halfway through the speech that opens the meeting and sets its tone, Carl McGill starts to fidget with his Malcolm X watch. The speaker,

Marguerite Justice, the self-described "first black woman in the world appointed to a police commission," has been talking now for about ten minutes in the broadest of platitudes, saying nothing McGill wants to hear.

Elderly, pale-skinned, and precisely turned out, Justice speaks of small triumphs while serving on the Los Angeles Police Commission in the early seventies: of obtaining promotion manuals for black cops, of the removal of "clichés from the files of black officers."

McGill—the five-year African-American LAPD veteran who is still on suspension for insubordination growing out of his off-duty antigang work—Justice, and about twenty black police officers are gathered in a South Central LAPD substation for a meeting of the Oscar Joel Bryant (OJB) Foundation. The gathering of the association of African-American police officers from the LAPD and other local departments is hardly the well-attended, highly charged event one might have expected. This, after all, is their first general meeting since Rodney King's beating weeks ago. Instead, on this March night in 1991, the organization's board of twelve outnumbers the eight general members present. And given the outrage and unity in the black community over King's flogging, Justice seems a strange choice as sole guest speaker. She speaks of her affection for Daryl Gates, and of how she has always supported him and always will, and of how grateful she is that Gates had often brought his wife when he came to OJB meetings. There's good and bad in the department just as there is in the rest of the community, she says, adding, "I still believe we have the greatest police department in the world, and that the training you men receive is the best in the world. . . . Remember, your commissioners are the head of the police department. Your commissioners carry a badge of five stars. . . . The chief of police has only four stars. Your commissioners are appointed by your mayor, who is a black man, confirmed by your city council, where you have strong representation. . . ." Finishing, she receives a warm round of applause. McGill does not join in.

Then James Craig, the Foundation's president, reads a statement strongly denouncing King's beating but supporting "Chief Gates," who "over the past thirteen years has provided strong leadership to the finest police agency in the nation."

With the exception of McGill, the statement seems favorably received. Are there any questions? Craig then asks. "Was there a vote among the members [approving the statement] or did just the board of directors vote?'' inquires McGill. Immediately the tension level in the room shoots up. There was, it turns out, no general membership vote.

Thanks to the consent decree of 1980 there were now more than 1,100 black cops on the LAPD. But they and the OJB Foundation remained divorced from any real power within the department, in spite of the fact that first Jesse Brewer, and now Deputy Chief Bernard Parks, were highly placed.

What follows as the meeting continues only makes that case. As McGill sits stoically by, a kind of melding of Robert Townsend's *Hollywood Shuffle* and Adolph Caesar's agony in *A Solder's Story* unfolds. It's painful to watch. Five or six officers step to the podium, denounce the beating, deny that anything like that ever took place on *their* watch, and then, sometimes emotionally, sometimes personally, testify to their unswerving support of Daryl Gates. The talk is all of due process for the officers involved in King's beating; of not seeing white, black, or green but only blue; of how only Daryl Gates can turn things around; and of how people are using the beating to get at the chief. There is no dissension.

By late April, something had snapped. About 150 African-American officers joined Carl McGill and packed the next OJB meeting, demanding in a near-unanimous vote that the association's board retract their statement of praise and support for Daryl Gates. ''It was really something to see,'' Officer Ed Williams, a ten-year veteran of the force, would later say. ''Before I'd felt like the Lone Ranger, but the King beating really'd laid the grounds for people to come out.''

At one point, OJB's entire board, with the exception of LAPD officer and Inglewood city councilman Garland Hardeman, threatened to walk out of the meeting. Never before in the history of the Oscar Joel Bryant Foundation had such a thing occurred. The inherent contradiction of black cops who'd come of age in a post-civil-rights atmosphere joining a police department hated by a vast number of the African-Americans it was policing, and then being expected to be good soldiers—to be good *boys*— had finally surfaced. The only surprise at the revolt now unfolding—at the rank and file raucously shouting down the leadership of what amounted to a company union—was that it had taken so long. And that, *that* was testimony to the extraordinary cohesion demanded in the ranks of the LAPD. It was easy enough to blame it all on Daryl Gates. But John

Mitchell, the LAPD officer known as the Masked Marvel, the officer who had agreed to appear on television and criticize the department's shootings only if scuba-diving gear was placed over his head, had happened on *Ed Davis's* watch. Not Daryl Gates's. It was the institution, not only the man.

In any case, the board *would* have walked out had not Hardeman, its only subversive member, told them to go ahead and he would reconvene the meeting alone if they left. That statement, that statement praising Daryl Gates after all that had gone down, could not be allowed to stand. "It simply did not," Officer Garland Hardeman would later say, "represent the general membership's views." For the first time an organized break from the LAPD hierarchy by a significant number of its black officers had occurred. And Rodney King had been the catalyst.

Meanwhile, the April issue of the Police Protective League's *The Thin Blue Line,* representing the thinking of not some fringe radicals over at the OJB Foundation but of your basic, hard-core LAPD troops, was being sent out to the membership. If ever anyone doubted the great divide separating that rank and file of the LAPD from the editorial page of the *Los Angeles Times;* from the L.A. of balding Hollywood screenwriters from the Bronx tooling down Sunset in their mauve Mercedes convertibles, ponytails flapping in the breeze; from the L.A. of hip-hop brothers and West Hollywood drag queens; well, here it was, prima facie evidence bursting out of the pages of the latest issue of the *Blue Line.* The issue, given over almost entirely to letters to the editor, was marked by the same blazing outrage and high indignation that had characterized the black protesters who had been disrupting the police commission's weekly meetings ever since the beating of Rodney King.

The attacks on the department were, wrote Det. William Lacey, "making him angry and sick to his stomach" and were "just another of a long list of injustices to affront the men and women of the Los Angeles Police Department." The King beating was described by various officers as "the King encounter," "the Foothill incident," "the pursuit termination." LAPD sergeant Don Schwartzer wrote that "the media has printed and spoken Rodney King's name so much. . . . I demand to know why names like Danny Pratt, Duane Johnson, Paul Verna, Tom Williams, Oscar Bryant, Tina Kerbrat, and James Pagliotti are virtually unknown to the public. . . . Those officers are heroes and no one remembers them. They all took bullets and died violent deaths . . . but after the last shovelful of dirt went into their graves, you folks forgot the names of those heroes who died for you. How cold can you get?'' ''The accused officers shall be punished to a vastly greater extent than their culpability in any alleged crimes,'' Det. Chad Wetzel pointed out. ''Their rights have already been sacrificed through political and media hyperbole.''

As for the beating itself, Foothill Division Sergeant Jay Fry, and eighteen-year LAPD veteran and League official, summed that up to a reporter: ''If the individual had done what he was told to do, it wouldn't have happened. He keeps trying to get up. He has a long criminal history. . . . Their [the officers'] adrenaline is going—the person goes down. It happens in families all the time. Your kid is beating on his brother so you swat him on the head. Just because he stops doesn't mean you don't pop him in the head.''

Out in the Valley, in the Foothill Division where the Rodney King beating occurred, LAPD captain Tim McBride works the crowd at the Moose Lodge. Located in Sylmar, an old, low-slung desert town, the Lodge is only about a ten-minute drive from the LAPD's fifties, box-shaped station house. In spite of his best efforts, McBride's enthusiasm on this night hardly seems reciprocated. Not that the sixty or so casually dressed people present—an assortment of truly ancient Anglos breathing hard through their mouths, and younger Latinos with their kids—are hostile. They just seem weary and indifferent.

McBride is a powerfully built man in his early fifties dressed in torso-tailored blues, oversize LAPD badge, and various ribbons and pins: one from the pope, a Medal of Valor for a shoot-out, another for his work during the Olympics. As he talks into a portable microphone about the LAPD and the division he commands, people get up and quietly meander to the bar for a Friday-night drink, or to the Dutch door of the kitchen, where they receive a hot-dog dinner from a gray-haired woman with an I've-seen-it-all demeanor.

Along with five of his officers, McBride has come to the Moose Lodge to engage in what the LAPD is now calling ''public awareness'' seminars or ''community-based policing.'' One cop, a canine man who's brought his German shepherd along, talks about sniffing out suspects, struggling as he does so in that stiff, unnatural way of speakers who'd rather be elsewhere. A second tells about a graffiti-removal program called Operation Sparkle; a third about what to do if you think your child might be inclined to join a gang.

Their appearance at the Lodge is part of a new series of forums the LAPD has been holding throughout the Foothill Division ever since Rodney King's pounding. But the forums have the whiff of damage control about them, as if someone from on high had grabbed Daryl Gates and the department's ranking officers collectively by the scruff of the neck and said, "Look, this beating has exploded on television screens throughout the *world*. Get your image together." Listening to McBride, a twenty-six-year veteran of the force, adds to the feeling. It's not that he displays any of the righteous indignation of the officers whose letters flooded the April issue of the *Thin Blue Line*. (He's in no position to be publicly outraged in any case. They were *his* men, after all, who were on the video wailing away on King.) There is none of that from McBride. Nor is there any of the attitude that L.A. district attorney Ira Reiner described as "of great concern to professional law enforcement": the fact that "to this very day, some of the officers present [at the King beating] do not acknowledge that the incident should have been handled any differently than it was."

Instead, McBride says all the right things. He's "ashamed" of the beating; it's "very difficult to explain the last few seconds of that tape." Then he shifts gears: "I want to talk a little bit about the use of force and arrests. The first thing is, if stopped by a police car, keep your hands where the officer can see them. . . . Don't make any quick moves, particularly if you're in a van or a vehicle with blackened windows. Move slowly, take your time, and just talk normally when the officer talks to you." There it was. Tim McBride was laying out the LAPD's conception of community policing under Daryl Gates for the ordinary citizens of sleepy Sylmar. He was giving them a lesson on how to be arrested without getting shot.

In the days that followed, City Councilwoman Joan Milke Flores, a strong Gates supporter, would lob Daryl Gates that same softball during a council hearing, as if she herself had been sitting there at the Moose Lodge. Did he see a need, she asked, for a program to make the public aware of "how to be arrested"? "No question," replied the chief.

CHAPTER 3

The Suspension

Over the weeks following King's beating, the pressure on Tom Bradley to do something other than impotently implore Daryl Gates to resign intensified. Ever since Bill Parker had demonstrated the ease in which the police commission could be rendered cravenly malleable rubber stamps, its members had, at best, done little more than just nibble at the edges of the department's omnipotence. Now for the first time in a decade a police commission was in place that gave some indication, even before the beating of Rodney King, that they took their job of overseeing the department seriously. And for the first time in forty years there was a mayor not only willing, but almost seized by a compulsion, to do something about a department and a situation that was making everybody involved look ridiculous. Gates had to go. That much was clear. If he stayed, nothing would change. Asking him to fundamentally reform the LAPD would be akin to asking him to perform his own castration. No, Daryl Gates remaining in power was out of the question. The ante had to be raised, the stress, the urgency, intensified until he was eliminated. It was the only way. Otherwise, Daryl Gates could, and would, drag this thing out for years and wait, as he and others had done so many other times in the department's history, for all this shit to die down and go away.

They couldn't fire Daryl Gates, not with his civil service protection and all those years of excellent and outstanding ratings written by no less an authority on his performance than Daryl Gates himself. But they could suspend him, say for sixty days. Out of sight, out of mind. The suspension was no great answer, but at least they'd be doing something. So they summoned Daryl Gates to an extraordinary hour-long, closed-door meeting with the commission, on April 4, and told him that in the "best interests of the police department" they were temporarily suspending him. It would be for sixty days, they said, until the commission had completed a wide-ranging investigation. David Dotson would be acting chief. "I feel that I have been disgraced and defamed," said Daryl Gates as he left the police commission chambers. "I have done nothing wrong. What they have done is improper and we're going to prove that."

The next day, Daryl Gates, dapper in a blue suit and matching tie, and looking as tanned and rested as if he'd just come off a two-week idyll in the Caribbean, strides into the ballroom of the Sportsmen's Lodge in suburban Studio City and smiles broadly. Passing a table laden with petitions, bumper stickers, blue-ribbon lapel pins, and $8 white T-shirts emblazoned with LAPD badges and his name, Daryl Gates hits the main ballroom and moves past the hordes of TV cameras and photographers who've been awaiting his arrival.

First the rear, then the center tables, spot him, and the entire place breaks into a ten-minute standing ovation. Women with that special glow they reserve for dream lovers rush up to kiss and hug him, men to shake his hand as a bouquet of red roses is placed in his arms. Arriving at a table near the front of the stage, Gates turns, faces the crowd, and takes their continued applause. Then he applauds back.

You had to hand it to Daryl Gates. He was a player. Just twenty-four hours earlier, "disgraced and defamed," unable "to remember [a time] when [he'd] felt worse," Daryl Gates had been placed on a sixty-day suspension by the police commission. And now here he was basking in applause.

The $25-a-plate luncheon, sponsored by Citizens in Support of the Chief of Police (CISCOP), was for his adulation, and for the denigration of Tom Bradley and Councilman Mike Woo, who had only recently stood up to Gates in a face-to-face confrontation on the city council floor, after Gates, in open session, had threatened to withhold police services from those council members who didn't support his struggle to survive. And in perhaps the tensest moment anyone could remember in the council chambers since Tom Bradley had challenged Bill Parker's post-Watts testimony, Woo called Gates on it. Woo had been the only one on the fifteen-member city council to have done so. And these people hated him for it, as they hated Bradley for demanding Gates's resignation.

The tables are filled with blue-haired matrons from Hancock Park; cops, white and black, in and out of uniform; Republican women from Encino; Chatsworth real estate salesmen; and Van Nuys businesspeople and housewives. Each time a black baritone belts out the line "I'm proud to be an American where at least I know I'm free" from a then-popular patriotic country song, the room bursts into applause. In the back of the room, two Mexican-American coeds sparkle as they gaze at Daryl Gates. They'd dug deep into their pockets, along with about a thousand others, and come up with the $25 to eat and show solidarity with their "great, I mean magnificent, police chief." Criminology majors at Cal State, L.A., they were sweet and earnest, awed by Gates as chief and father protector, motivated by the idealism of youth and not that home brew of patriotism, resentment, insularity, and fear that gave Daryl Gates meaning for most of the rest of the people present.

The rest of the afternoon was a triumph of image over substance. Orchestrating the day was a local Republican political consultant who undoubtedly had a hand in crafting Daryl Gates's generally good-natured speech, one that was uncharacteristically lacking in recrimination or self-pity. ("If it wasn't for the helicopter, the lighting would have been horrible," said Gates about George Holliday's video of King's beating.) And it is the consultant, a young man named Eric Rose, who pulls off the master PR coup of the whole sorry Rodney King affair. With TV cameras rolling and flashbulbs popping, he has Daryl Gates present an award to George Holliday. An award to George Holliday! Think of it. The liberal media and the black politicians were all saying Daryl Gates was at fault for the trashing of Rodney King, as if he himself had been there. Now he was giving an award to the man who took the video of the beating. It was brilliant.

And the next day, sure enough, the color photo—in deep reds, whites, and blues—of George Holliday clutching his award alongside Daryl Gates—makes page one, front and center, above the fold, of the *Los Angeles Times*. The coverage in the *Daily News* was almost as good.

Under the headline "Jovial Chief Jokes With Supporters" was a color picture of Daryl Gates sucking his thumb and holding a "100 percent true-blue" teddy bear that had been given to him by an admirer. (By contrast, that Sunday, a black-and-white photo of Jessie Jackson leading five thousand demonstrators in a Gates-must-go protest march to Parker Center appeared on page 32 of the *Times,* even though Jackson had flown into L.A. for the march. Even though he called for a boycott of the 1993 Super Bowl, which was coming to L.A., and called for Gates's removal while thousands cheered, page 32 was all he could get.)

As Holliday made his way to the stage, which was festooned with a banner saying "Stay," to receive his award, the applause was less than thunderous, but that was understandable. And inconsequential. For that evening it would be apparent what *was* important, and why Gates had been so cool all afternoon. That evening the rest of the city would find out what Daryl Gates already knew, and what had caused him to "return to Parker Center feeling like General MacArthur." Daryl Gates knew that *he,* not Tom Bradley, had the votes. That in a closed, four-hour session, the city council would choose by the embarrassing margin of ten to three to invalidate the Bradley police commission's temporary removal of Gates from office. Daryl Gates's camp had pulled off the week's PR coup while he and his lawyers had totally outflanked the police commission and the mayor's office. Bradley had been under intense pressure to do something about Gates. And he did. But the evening, like the afternoon, belonged to Daryl Gates. The commission and the mayor's office had gambled big and lost big, had chosen a hazardous way to go and misjudged every step. The three council members who voted to uphold the suspension were Robert Farrell, who represented South Central and who was retiring in any case and had nothing to lose; Ruth Galanter, a white, former sixties radical whose district also included parts of South Central and who, locked in a tight election campaign, needed every black vote she could get; and third, liberal Michael Woo, who was genuinely appalled by both the King beating and Daryl Gates's threat to withhold services, and who was also positioning himself as the candidate of brown, black, and Asian L.A. when Tom Bradley left office.

But the lopsided vote in favor of reinstating Gates was causing a lot of people to ask just what power Gates had over the council. One answer came after his "shoot casual drug users" remark. The *Los Angeles Times* asked a number of council members about what they thought of Gates's comment. Gloria Molina, a populist who as a representative of the city's teeming Hispanic underclass should have been no friend of Gates's, said that he "had been very responsive whenever I've had problems with officers in my area." She then offered no complaint about his remark. Black, South Central councilman Robert Farrell responded that he was "shocked [but that Gates] is a very good administrator . . . he's responsive to me." The city's most sought-after service was police protection, and Gates had been answering council members' specific concerns. They could only deliver police service to the extent that the chief of police cooperated—that is, used his discretionary power to deploy his police when and where a council member asked. Gates had always been good at that. "He's demonstrated his ability to deliver," said one council aide, "so why should they support a vacancy in the post when they don't know what they'll get instead?"

Rumors were also rampant about what Gates might have on various members of the council. Zev Yaroslavsky, on whom the PDID had kept a file, voted to reinstate Gates. He maintained that the reinstatement was more a reaction to Bradley's tactics than anything else. "If the commission's intent was to remove Gates, and to make a change of leadership, they should have laid the groundwork pursuant to the civil service laws for his removal," said Yaroslavsky in the weeks after the council vote. "They should have started citing him for his deficiencies. . . . That would have made sense. Suspending Gates without a hearing was absolutely foolish. . . . Now you have a situation where Gates is ahead of the game. And it makes it that much more difficult to make the reforms the department is crying out for. . . . Gates should retire," Yaroslavsky concluded, "but I'm not calling for his resignation. That would just make it less likely that he would go of his own volition."

But the problem was more than just tactics. It was a question of an institution so powerful that a major local political player like Yaroslavsky felt so constrained he would still not call for the resignation of the civil servant who headed it.

The official reason for reinstating Gates, however, was given by council president John Ferraro, who said it would cost the city several hundred thousand dollars if Gates had sued and won. No mention was made by Ferraro of the $11 million the city had paid in police-abuse cases the previous year.

By the following Monday, when a Superior Court judge officially reinstated Gates, Tom Bradley's police commission had been totally emasculated and undermined. Both it, and Tom Bradley, looked dead as the battle for the soul of a city played itself out. For seventeen years Los Angeles had tried to have it both ways—a liberal black mayor and an ironfisted throwback to another era as chief of police. Now it was being forced to choose.

Following the reinstatement, it became clear that only a smoking gun was going to get the political and economic establishment of Los Angeles to move against Daryl Gates and start serious police reform. They were all waiting for *the* definitive judgment on the LAPD and indicating who could give it to them: Warren Christopher and the commission that he would head, a commission that Tom Bradley had impaneled on April 1 to launch a sweeping investigation of the LAPD.

The ten-member commission was the bluest of blue-ribbon panels, starting with Christopher himself, who would go on to become Bill Clinton's secretary of state. The world was full of high-priced lawyers, but there were few Warren Christophers, few power-brokering attorneys with real behind-the-scenes weight and power. He'd been a deputy United States attorney general, a deputy secretary of state under Jimmy Carter, and was currently serving as chairman of Los Angeles' prestige-laden, old-line downtown law firm O'Melveny & Myers. At sixty-five, he was stiff, button-down, careful, precise, made few mistakes, and rarely permitted a public smile to light his hound-dog face. If respectability was what you wanted, you could do no better than Warren Christopher. It was the same with the rest of the commission. The vice chair, John A. Arguelles, was a conservative Republican who'd retired from the California Supreme Court and was with the law firm of Gibson, Dunn & Crutcher, a downtown powerhouse the equal of O'Melveny & Myers. Among the commission's other members were Roy Anderson, chairman emeritus of the Lockheed Corporation, and Mickey Kantor, a partner in yet another highly influential local law firm, Mannatt, Phelps and Phillips, and soon to play a major role in Bill Clinton's campaign before being named his U.S. Trade Representative. The entire panel was like that. So heavy-duty respectable that from the moment of its inception, there were fears that it would produce a whitewash. The commission's mandate was strong and sweeping, covering every base, including the proper roles of the police commission and the chief of police; departmental discipline, supervision, and training; the investigation of citizen complaints and how they'd been responded to; and the city-charter provisions governing the hiring, disciplining, and firing of the chief.

But Warren Christopher had also been the vice chairman of the Mc-Cone Commission, a body that had deliberately missed its opportunity to dig at the real meaning of Watts, squandering a once-in-a-generation opportunity at the altar of Establishment Brotherhood. And there was also the time frame the commission had been given: three months. "Mr. Christopher and Judge Arguelles have indicated that we want to finish our work in ninety days—by the end of June," the commission's general counsel, John Spiegel, announced. "They feel the city needs to hear from us in a short period of time." Three months. Long enough to look serious and to provide damage control, but not enough time to do a probing investigation and to arrive at any meaningful conclusions. It looked like 1965 all over again, as the comfortable smells of the status quo mingled with the stench of the whitewash.

Neither David Dotson nor Jesse Brewer was comfortable about testifying before the Christopher Commission. They knew what it would entail. About two days before appearing, David Dotson sat down in an easy chair and jotted down some key words on index cards. As he fingered these cards at the hearing, all the years of pent-up frustration and quiet, understated rage came pouring out. Provocative policing, the ethos of the macho man, disengaged management, lax, uneven discipline, discipline by imperial fiat, retrenchment, retreat. All of it came out. "In a lot of cases . . . an officer will appeal to the chief, and the chief will [lessen] whatever the decision may have been—whether it be discipline, administrative transfer, an appointment or an upgrade, or whatever. And he frequently does that without informing the chain of command," said Dotson. Gates, by his statements, was causing rank-and-file officers to "believe that there are different classes of people that can be treated in different ways." David Dotson had a lot of things like that to say during his hour-long testimony. As he left, he thanked the panel. "This was a rare opportunity for me," he said, "and I let it all hang out, whether I should have or not."

Jesse Brewer, too, let it all hang out. He was retired now, after almost thirty-nine years, and when Tom Bradley had called and asked him to be a member of the Christopher Commission, he'd turned him down. He knew the commission's report would be controversial and he didn't want to be part of it. He wanted to stay retired. But Bradley had urged him to at least meet with Warren Christopher, who said, "We'd love to have you, and call me Chris." Brewer was more than impressed and shortly afterward agreed to work with the commission as a consultant, providing advice and information. Once signed on, Jesse Brewer went home, rifled through his files, and came up with information that he thought "would give people a picture of what was going on [in the LAPD]." Among those pieces of information was "the dynamite" study he had commissioned while commanding South Bureau, the report showing how he had over-ridden the consistently lenient disciplinary recommendations of his captains, and how Daryl Gates, in turn, had overridden *him*. The time for that report, which Jesse Brewer had carefully filed away, had now come. All his life he'd eaten it. In Dallas, growing up, he'd watched a friend almost beaten to death by the Dallas police because he got on a bus in front of some white people and refused to leave when the bus driver ordered him off. He'd been called a nigger and told to get his black ass back on the curb by a Dallas cop after *he'd* called *them* following an auto accident. He'd seen his cousin, who was married to a beautiful fair-skinned woman, get into a fight with some white guys over her and wind up dead. Then he'd watched impotently as afterward the police did nothing. He'd sat in a foxhole in the mountains of Italy with German artillery raining down on him, thinking that he must be a damn fool to be fighting for a country that despised him. And finally as a mature man he'd watched as his people, the LAPD, treated his people, the citizens of South Central, as if they were coons in Dallas in the thirties. *Now,* finally, his time had come.

And like David Dotson he was not shy when he testified before the commission. "We knew who the bad guys are. . . . We know the [officers] who are getting into trouble more than anyone else. But I don't see anyone bringing these people up [for discipline]. . . . I don't see that occurring," said Jesse Brewer.

One of the bright young commanders Daryl Gates had surrounded himself with, Michael Bostic, buttressed Dotson's and Brewer's accounts. Testifying about a survey he'd done on the LAPD's use of force that had been requested by Daryl Gates after Rodney King's beating, Bostic said, "I've interviewed several hundred people in the organization—from lieutenants and captains and all of the commanders and deputy chiefs—and the kind of reoccurring theme that I've heard that's really bothered me . . . they say that the organization is light on excessive force. Light in punishment. . . . They said if you lie, cheat, and steal, we'll fire you; if you use drugs, we'll fire you. But if you use excessive force, we won't.''

Warren Christopher allowed a slight, enigmatic smile to play across his face as he handed Daryl Gates a copy of his commission's final report on July 9, 1991. No stiletto had ever been more subtly placed. If, as one commissioner later said, ''Christopher was really trying to atone for what went wrong in 1965,'' and that ''he [had] vowed [to the commission members] that this would not be another McCone Commission,'' his atonement was complete, his word golden. There had been no whitewash. Virtually every page of the 228-page report, in fact, was an extraordinary, unanimous indictment of the LAPD and Daryl Gates's leadership. Over the course of one hundred days, the commission and its staff of over fifty volunteer attorneys and accountants had interviewed almost eight hundred people, taken testimony from over two hundred, and reviewed more than 1 million documents. Then they wrote their report and left no room for ambiguity.

It was time, said the report, for new leadership in the LAPD. Daryl Gates, along with the police commission, should retire. Then in a long, detailed critique of the department it said among other things, that ''the LAPD has an organizational culture . . . that isolates the police from the communities and the people they serve'' . . . ''that witnesses testify to unnecessarily aggressive confrontations between LAPD officers and citizens, particularly members of minorities'' . . . ''that LAPD officers are encouraged to command and confront, not to communicate'' . . . that ''the LAPD rewards officers for a hard-nosed, aggressive style of policing, especially in dealing with minority communities; [and that] it is apparent that too many LAPD officers view citizens with resentment and hostility; too many treat the public with rudeness and disrespect.'' That there were at least several hundred [officers] who ''repeatedly misused force,'' and that ''the department not only failed to deal with [this] problem group of officers but it often rewarded them with positive evaluations and promotions.''

''The failure to control these officers is a management issue that is at the heart of the problem,'' the report continued. ''The LAPD's failure to analyze and act upon these revealing data evidences a significant breakdown in the management and leadership of the department.''

Then it continued, ''The Commission's review of MDT [Mobile Digital Terminal] transmissions revealed an appreciable number of disturbing and recurring racial remarks. Some of the remarks . . . ('sounds like monkey slapping time') . . . ('I would love to drive down Slauson with a flamethrower . . . we would have a barbecue') . . . ('I almost got me a Mexican last night but he dropped the damn gun too quick, lots of wit'). The officers typing the MDT messages, said the commission, "apparently had little concern that they would be disciplined for making such remarks."

And it was those remarks that would turn the tide for the members of the panel according to commission member Leo Estrada. "Even the commissioners who had expressed the least concern about the police really shifted that day," said Estrada. It was "a crystallizing moment," confirmed another commission member, Mickey Kantor.

Among a number of profound reforms, the Christopher Commission recommended "the most fundamental change of values within the LAPD" and the implementation of community policing, a model of which "treats service to the public and prevention of crime as the primary function of police in society. Instead of viewing 'the community as enemy,' community policing will emphasize patrol officers interacting positively with the public."

Almost every line in the report was an implicit and frequently overt criticism of the protégé turned Grand Old Man's leadership. Daryl Gates may have had his allies on the city council, but Tom Bradley had found the man willing to search for and discover the smoking gun in the person of Warren Christopher. But Bradley himself would not go unscathed. First his ambition and then his inertia had set him apart from his younger, better self. "His unwillingness over the years to exert more leadership using the inherent powers of his office has contributed to the police commission's ineffectiveness," the report would point out. In his testimony before the commission, Bradley, not usually given to making excuses, told them that there had been "no way to rein him [Gates] in." To which the commission report replied that the problem had been partly his. Like his police commission and the city council, which had all given Gates those outstanding ratings, Tom Bradley had failed to use a major oversight tool he had, Gates's job evaluations, "to evaluate the chief critically," said the commission. It was not good news for Tom Bradley, but it was a couple of sentences buried deep within the report's pages. Daryl Gates's usually unnamed presence *permeated* the critical document, although as usual Daryl Gates failed to admit it. "There was nothing in there that was new or startling to us," he told local radio talk-show host Michael Jackson shortly after its release. Nevertheless, Daryl Gates had no more cover. He was going. The only question was when.

Like his father almost sixty years earlier, Daryl Gates had no idea that after the binge, there'd be someone knocking on the door, demanding payment for his sins. He could not accept it, even after his allies on the city council, with the solicitude of loving sons trying to ease their geriatric father out of the daily running of the family business, told him it was no use going on. The Christopher Commission report had been too specific, too well crafted. The evidence was undeniable; his chief accusers had not been Ramona Ripston of the ACLU or those NAACP types, but two of his top three assistants, two men with more than seventy-five years between them as cops. His judge and jury had not been his critics at the L.A. *Times,* but the cream of the city's establishment. He had become a permanent lightning rod. There was nothing left. You could almost smell his reluctance, that's how strong it was. But finally he announced his retirement date: April 1992. Then he changed it. It would now be June. *Then* Daryl Gates started saying that he could legally remain substantially beyond that by spreading out his unused vacation time. June, however, seemed the real goal. It was a pivotal month for him. The Christopher Commission reforms would be placed on the ballot then. Together, those reforms represented a dramatic transformation of the department. They would institute far greater oversight of the department by the police commission and give the commission the right, with the approval of the city council, to fire the chief, while putting a limit on his tenure to two five-year terms. Gates had sworn to campaign against them. And June was also the month his autobiography was to be published. The link between the book and Gates's revised retirement plans wasn't to be underestimated. Interest and sales in such books are almost always much higher for a sitting officeholder than for one who's retired. By June, Gates would also have stayed long enough to claim that his retirement was unforced, just as James Edgar Davis had done in 1938.

The public, the good, decent law-abiding public, had never been his problem. Their rejection of the Christopher Commission's reforms would be his true vindication—an affirmation by them of his position that, yes, there were problems, but they were aberrations that he had already taken care of before he left.

CHAPTER 4

The Trial

`•••••••••••••••••••••••`

They were so guilty on the face of it, all the proof needed so obviously there, cut and dried, on George Holliday's video, that little attention was paid to the stunning break that was given to Stacey Koon, Laurence Powell, Timothy Wind, and Theodore Briseno even before their trial began. The press duly noted it, of course. But the news was largely overshadowed by the continuing headlines generated by the Christopher Commission's searing report, and by the embarrassing spectacle of an impotent city desperately pleading with its chief of police to *please* resign his office. They were the powerful, drama-laden stories. Not this other, this change-of-venue business, which seemed a mere legal technicality.

In the turbulence of the weeks following the beating, the four LAPD officers had been indicted for assault with a deadly weapon and unnecessarily beating a suspect under color of authority. Additionally, Stacey Koon and Laurence Powell had been charged with filing a false police report. They were now facing the horrific possibility of seven years and eight months in state prison, while Timothy Wind was looking at seven years, and Theodore Briseno—for his one boot stomp on Rodney King's neck and all its potential to have crippled King—four years. Nor was that all. The full force of the entire system was now bearing down on the unquestioning men who were its enforcers. Soon after their indictments, Daryl Gates had fired Timothy Wind—who, with less than one year on the force, was still on probation and thus *could* be fired—and suspended the other three officers without pay pending a Board of Rights hearing. (Daryl Gates had recommended only the indictments of the three officers who had actually done the beating, and not Stacey Koon, who'd been directing it.) Afterward, following the DA's advice, the grand jury had decided not to indict the other twenty-three officers on the scene. Stacey Koon and his men would stand alone and scorned, publicly defended initially only by their attorneys and the right-wing commentator Pat Buchanan, provided for only by the deep pockets of the Police Protective League.

For decades the Ed Davises and Daryl Gateses, the district attorneys, the members of the city council, Sam Yorty, and even Tom Bradley had either condoned and winked or chosen to ignore exactly what had happened to Rodney King, and worse. Rodney King, at least, was alive. The same could not be said for scores of unarmed people shot and killed by the LAPD when Chuck Higbie was conducting his darkly comic investigations of officer-involved shootings in the 1970s and 1980s. Now George Holliday's video had brought the winking to a halt. To defend it was to turn the whole notion of right and wrong, of good and bad, of blind, fair, impartial justice right on its head. *That* video would have embarrassed Bull Connor. Of course, the officers were entitled to a fair trial, but its result was a foregone conclusion. There was nothing to be done by Daryl Gates and by the city's establishment really but to leave them, as John Ehrlichman had said of John Dean during Watergate, to twist slowly in the wind. Or at least that was the way it appeared until the defense's motion for a change of venue was granted. After that, all bets were off.

The events leading to the trial's move out of Los Angeles County unfolded in a tortuously convoluted sequence of events. Originally, the Superior Court judge assigned to the case had denied the defense attorneys' requests that the trial be held in another location. "The tape is what makes this case unique," declared the judge, Bernard Kamins, in May, and "it doesn't matter where you play [it] . . . the proof will be the same, the uniqueness [of the tape] will be the same." To bolster his contention, Kamins had held up a recent front-page *New York Times* story about the beating and asked the essential question: "Where else are you going to take the case where jurors haven't heard about it?"

By June, however, Kamins, a forty-eight-year-old former public defender, was having second thoughts. So in a startling breach of judicial etiquette, he wrote a letter to the appellate court then considering the police officers' appeal of his decision and told them that he'd changed his mind and was now willing to move the trial. He was still "100 percent" certain that an unbiased jury could be found in L.A. Los Angeles County had a potential jury pool of nearly 4 million people, he pointed out. But still, if moving the trial was what was required to get it started, then he was willing to go along. When the appellate court dismissed his offer, Kamins publicly dismissed them. "All I can say," he declared, "is to heck with the letter [he'd sent] . . . the case will stay here."

At about the same time, Kamins took another injudicious step, sending a message to the DA's prosecutors. They, of course, had been opposing any move out of Los Angeles. The county, after all, was rich with potential black and Latino jurors all too familiar with the LAPD's brutality. "Don't panic," he told them. "You can trust me." Well, you didn't have to be Miss Manners to know that a message like that went beyond just the *appearance* of impropriety. "Trust me"! What in the hell did he mean "trust me"?

As a consequence of both *that* message and his public letter to the appellate court, he was removed from the case, and a new judge, Stanley Weisberg—an appointee of the conservative, law-and-order Republican governor George Deukmejian, and a prosecutor for eighteen years—was named.

The importance of that change in judges quickly became apparent when the Second Court of Appeals then overturned Kamins's decision and ordered the trial moved out of Los Angeles. "So extensive and pervasive has been the [media] coverage, and so intense has become the political fallout . . . ," wrote the appeals court, "[that] there is a reasonable likelihood that a fair and impartial trial cannot be had in Los Angeles County."

It was an extraordinary decision. Only two other changes of venue—both in relatively obscure cases—had ever been granted in modern Los Angeles' history. Charles Manson, the Night Stalker, the Hillside Strangler, and the defendants in the McMartin Preschool child-molestation debacle had all been tried in Los Angeles with jurors presumably oblivious to the publicity and above the fray. But that was not the only problem with the decision. Its real flaw lay in the fact that this was a highly charged political case *throughout* the United States. Daryl Gates and Tom Bradley were merely players in the drama—symbols of two different ways of viewing crime in America, its causes, and how to deal with it. Ronald Reagan's extraordinary popularity and the triumph of conservatism during the eighties had rendered much of the debate on crime moot. Education, early-childhood intervention, job training, and drug-treatment programs had become anathema, nothing more than thoroughly discredited liberal cant. Wars on drugs and crime were the way to go. And in war you supported your troops, even if they sometimes crossed that line and breached the rules of engagement. The only question was how far. That was the only issue still outstanding in American law enforcement as the 1990s began. That was to be the bottom-line question at the trial. Not local politics or how potential jurors felt about Daryl Gates or Tom Bradley. And that debate was taking place everywhere in America since CNN had run George Holliday's tape. As Tom Bradley put it after the change-of-venue decision was announced: "Is it necessary to move that trial just because people have seen that video? Everybody has seen that video."

If the appeals court ruling had indeed contained a certain logic, Stanley Weisberg, the thin, balding, scholarly looking judge who would now preside over the case, failed utterly to recognize it. In fact, it was as if he had not even read the very reasons the appeals court cited for moving the trial out of Los Angeles. Left to pick a new site for the trial from the state jurisdictions both able to accommodate a trial-of-the-century proceeding and willing to suffer the accompanying media circus, Stanley Weisberg had few choices. There was, however, Alameda County, which, if one wanted to shield the trial from L.A.'s political currents, seemed perfect. It was located 350 miles north of Los Angeles, far enough so that the political futures of Tom Bradley and Daryl Gates—other than as symbols—were of small import to the people there. And within Alameda were Oakland and Berkeley, both of which had large black populations. And when added to the rest of the county, the racial composition more than approximated that of Los Angeles. But Weisberg rejected it. Instead, he chose his only other real option: the nearly lily-white, distant bedroom suburb of Los Angeles known as Simi Valley, which was in southern

Ventura County—just north of L.A. ''The focus of the Court of Appeals was on the political atmosphere that had been generated by the media coverage and the unique events that were occurring . . . the political careers that were at stake,'' declared Weisberg as he announced his ruling. ''[Ventura County] has its own politics, its own political officials, and its own police department. My view is that the proper venue for the trial of this case . . . is the County of Ventura.'' It was an insane argument, one so ill-informed that it showed, at the very least, that Stanley Weisberg was not nearly as scholarly as he looked. Had he been, he would have discovered what enterprising reporters did within days of his announcement: that Simi Valley was as emotionally invested in the upcoming trial as any area of Los Angeles other than South Central. And a big reason why was precisely its proximity to Los Angeles. It was ''impossible,'' as the appeals court had written, to ''pick up a copy of the *Los Angeles Times*'' or to listen to the radio or to watch TV without hearing about the Rodney King beating. Yet the people of Simi Valley read many of the same newspapers, viewed many of the same television stations, and heard many of the same radio talk shows as did the people of Los Angeles. The media saturation of the case was nearly as pervasive there as in L.A. One would have been hard put, in fact, to find a *more* passionately partisan area for the trial than Simi Valley.

Nestled in the hills and mountains about an hour's drive north of downtown L.A. and just twenty-five miles from the scene of Rodney King's beating, Simi Valley and its sister municipality, Thousand Oaks, might more accurately have been named Cop Haven. About four thousand active law enforcement officers lived in the two areas, among them more members of the LAPD than in almost any city in *Los Angeles* County. They dwelled there in semirural comfort among dwindling citrus orchards and strawberry fields in a county that was still almost 70 percent white and only 2 percent black, with most of the rest of the population Asian or Latino.) Their neighbors were much like themselves, people who had made their choices about crime, race, and the quality of life and saw no gradation between a Rodney King and the cold-blooded drive-by gang killers of South Central Los Angeles. They not only revered Bill Parker's thin blue line, they—or their cousins, uncles, brothers, sons, and friends— *were* the thin blue line. A line that stretched tightly around their communities. In 1992, as the King beating trial ran its course, Thousand Oaks and Simi Valley would rank number one and two on the FBI's list of

America's safest cities. (Lying just northeast, Santa Clarita ranked fourth safest in the nation.) "Thousand Oaks and Simi Valley," as the senior FBI agent in Ventura County pointed out, were "usually the two lowest [ranking cities in crime totals] in the country, and have been for a couple of years." And the people who lived there, even more than most, were determined to keep it that way. At least according to John R. Hatcher III, the president of the Ventura County chapter of the NAACP who described Ventura as "the home breeding ground for the David Dukes, Tom Metzgers, and skinheads of America." Hatcher, who had "We is Apes" spray-painted on his garage in two-foot-high letters in 1990, seemed to have a better insight than Judge Stanley Weisberg into the potential ramifications of moving the trial to Simi Valley. "They would be better off going to Mississippi," said Hatcher before the newly moved court proceedings had begun. "Rodney King is on trial, not those officers. King will lose and the officers will win."

With the change of venue, Stanley Weisberg had dealt the prosecution some bad cards. And as was the fashion of the Los Angeles County district attorney's office under the perennially inept eight-year tenure of DA Ira Reiner, the prosecution then proceeded to play the worst possible game it could. Reiner, a white-haired, noble-headed, resonant-voiced man in his midfifties, looked just as he should. But by the early nineties, his record in the high-profile, career-making cases that ambitious DAs live for had turned into an embarrassing litany of defeats.

First, he had inherited the McMartin Preschool child-molestation case from his even more publicity-obsessed predecessor, Robert Philibosian. Philibosian, a Republican who'd been appointed to fill a Democratic vacancy, had been running hard for election in his own right when he charged seven employees—six of them women—with child molestation. Their indictments were based on patently absurd accusations involving satanic rites and animal sacrifice. Eventually Reiner dismissed the indictments against five of the defendants, but let the cases against the other two play out for years, never obtaining convictions in what turned out to be one of the most bizarre, long-running, headline-generating cases in California history.

Then in 1986, Reiner, a Democrat, also brought charges of political bribery against Republican congresswoman Bobbi Fiedler, who was running for her party's nomination for the United States Senate. Before a trial could even take place, Reiner dropped the charges, but by then Fiedler's career was ruined.

Next came the thumping defeat his office suffered at the trial of *Animal House* and *The Blues Brothers* director John Landis and four associates, who'd been indicted on involuntary manslaughter charges. The indictments followed the decapitation of two children in a helicopter accident on the set of *Twilight Zone: The Movie*. Given that two children, aged six and seven, were working illegally at two in the morning with a helicopter hovering just twenty-four feet above their heads, many in Hollywood felt it was an open-and-shut case. But all five defendants were found not guilty on all five counts.

Then after a rare indictment of four LAPD officers for their thuggish behavior during the raid on Dalton Avenue, Reiner's office lost that case as well.

Defeat in any one of the trials might have been understandable. But together they constituted a record of incompetence that would eventually cost Ira Reiner. In 1990, during the Democratic primary for attorney general of California, the obscure DA of San Francisco, Arlo Smith, defeated Reiner, the far better known, presumptive favorite.

Reiner's reputation was certainly not enhanced by the way he went about preparing for what was certain to be the most closely watched, politically explosive trial in Los Angeles since that of the McNamara brothers eighty years earlier. Instead of studiously, carefully, judiciously selecting a star litigator familiar with police cases to lead his prosecution team, Reiner's office chose a thirty-five-year-old African-American deputy D.A. named Terry White. Like Stanley Weisberg's selection of Simi Valley, Reiner's choice of the balding, bespectacled White seemed to defy logic. It wasn't that White lacked prosecutorial experience; he'd worked for the Los Angeles district attorney's office for his entire eight-year legal career. But he'd never before prosecuted a police officer and had only just joined the DA's Special Investigations Unit—under whose jurisdiction the misconduct of police and other public officials fell—weeks earlier. Incredibly, a spokeswoman for Reiner would actually cite White's recent transfer to the unit as a reason for his being assigned to the case. "His [White's] schedule was not full, as the other lawyers' were," she explained to the *New York Times*. His schedule wasn't full! What could *that* mean? Did Reiner want to win or what? Of course experienced lawyers such as White's cocounsel, Alan S. Yochelson, would be assisting him, but the case was *Terry White's*. He wasn't just a front-man mouthpiece for the others. Reiner's mammoth office, which employed over eight hundred deputy DAs, was not known to operate that way. Generally once an attorney was assigned a case it was his or hers. And Terry White, with absolutely no experience in the extremely complex, extraordinarily difficult task of gaining convictions against police officers acting in the line of duty, would have to carry the ball. And to do so in Simi Valley, a jurisdiction where his black face was certain to be no assistance. It was inconceivable that Reiner and his office weren't proceeding in good faith. But after deciding that the chances of winning an appeal of the change of venue were "low," and that they didn't want to see the trial delayed any further, they had failed to appeal a decision that they knew could have deadly possibilities for their case. And then they had chosen Terry White. It made one wonder whether they were simply in over their heads or really didn't want to win very badly.

It was the ones and twos, the alarmingly small number of ones and twos, that was driving Terry White crazy. Out of a jury pool that had been narrowed down to just 264 potential candidates, White and his fellow prosecutors had been able to come up with only twenty-seven people who rated the top scores of a one or a two in the system they'd devised to rate possible jurors. In their accounting, they gave a grade of one—their highest score—to a juror who they believed had the greatest potential to decide in their favor, and a five to those they thought would be most sympathetic to the indicted officers. After examining the questionnaires returned by the prospective jurors, that was the best they could come up with: twenty-seven jurors who might be good for them. Those rated as a five—that is, the worst prospects from the prosecution's point of view— were, on the other hand, so numerous that Terry White began desperately reevaluating them, separating the absolutely disastrous, as he later told the *Los Angeles Times,* from those he felt had only the potential for disaster.

Moreover, out of the 264 potential jurors, there were only about half a dozen African-Americans, and most of them were buried so far down on the list that White knew they'd never be called. And when a juror to White's liking did get as far as to be questioned by Judge Weisberg and the attorneys, he or she was invariably eliminated. They simply could not contain their emotions. This was the case when a black woman had watched the police officers in court "as they talked with their attorneys and smiled from time to time [and] thought: 'I wonder if having your jaw broken two or three times stops you from smiling a full smile.' I'm sure Rodney King didn't smile after his dog beating.''

But for the most part, that kind of outrage was rare, and the jury selection would end with Terry White feeling it was hopeless to try to get an impartial jury. End with him failing to even use all of his preemptory challenges. End with him failing, for the first time in his career, to get even *one* juror he wanted. Instead, the jury would consist of "jurors [who]," as White later described them, "were very pro-law-enforcement . . . [of] people who believe there is this 'thin blue line' . . . [of] people who put police officers on a pedestal . . . [of people who] have had very positive experiences with police officers even when they get a traffic ticket.''

The jury was everything that Terry White feared and more. On it sat ten whites, one Hispanic woman, one Filipino woman, and no blacks. Zero. Zero in a case that, above all, was about the police and their relationship to and treatment of African-Americans. It was the worst possible jury the prosecution could have hoped for, and its awfulness went beyond just its racial composition. The jurors were almost exclusively lower-middle class, the very people who most loathed predatory hordes out there just waiting to bring them down to their level. They were separated from those people by geography and values. Differentiated from them by their just-making-it jobs. And above all protected from them only by the police. There was a cable splicer for Southern California Edison; a service technician for Pacific Bell; a park ranger; a printer; a nurse; a computer programmer; a retired teacher; a housekeeper; a retired mental-health worker; a program manager for a company that provided video training manuals for the Navy; a retired real estate broker; and a garbageman. At an average age of fifty, they were precisely the people least capable and least inclined to distinguish between Rodney King and the violent criminal underclass they so feared. Precisely the people least likely to identify with Rodney King's pain, and most likely to be sympathetic to Stacey Koon and his men. Barry Goldwater and then Ronald Reagan had instinctively understood their fears and their outrage at America's moral decline. Like John Wayne, Goldwater and Reagan had ridden in from the same physical and psychic West in which the jury members dwelt and had promised to make it all right again. But still it continued. And their disenchantment seemed magnified precisely because they lived in a safe, white shelter from the storm. Precisely because it was a rest area and a staging site for the war being waged in the third world that was Los Angeles. Simi Valley was Cop City, that was the truth of it. And for better or worse, the Simi Valley jury reflected that reality. One of the jurors had a brother who was a retired LAPD sergeant. Another had worked as a security guard. A fifth had been a U.S. Navy shore-patrol officer. A sixth had been a military-police officer in the Air Force. A seventh was a park ranger. Three—the fifty-year-old park ranger, the sixty-five-year-old jury forewoman, and the forty-nine-year-old cable splicer—were members of the National Rifle Association. Eight had either been in the military or had a spouse who was. It was, in short, a prosecutor's jury, a prosecutor's dream, a jury that Terry White would normally have killed for. But this was that rarest of prosecutions— especially in Southern California—the prosecution of police officers for their actions in the line of duty. That fact alone made this jury not Terry White's dream, but his worst nightmare.

The genius of their defense would be in its bold-faced, unabashed shamelessness; in its willingness to use every stereotype and to play on every cliché they could. It seemed a desperate, even reckless strategy. But it was really their only option. The tape showed what the tape showed (or at least it seemed so at the time). And with it as a key piece of evidence, a plea bargain without jail time was out of the question. So what did they have to lose by going to trial?

As Laurence Powell's attorney, Michael Stone, an ex-police sergeant who'd also worked as the general counsel for the L.A. Police Protective League, put it on the trial's eve, "In talking to a number of people about this case, there's very few of them who acknowledge there's any defense at all. And these are people who are open-minded and propolice. They're asking me, 'Gee, what are you going to do? How are you ever going to overcome the prejudice of the tape?' "

Well, there were ways.

First, and above all, they would blame Rodney King for his own beating. If he hadn't been speeding, if he hadn't fled, if he hadn't charged Laurence Powell, if he'd just stayed down, none of this would have happened. As Stacey Koon's attorney, Darryl Mounger, would sum it up, "Stacey Koon was not in charge of this incident. The only one person who was in charge of this incident was Rodney Glen King.'' It was a hard sell, this aspect of the defense. It meant, in effect, convincing a jury that if a person doesn't immediately, completely, and absolutely comply with a police officer's instructions with robotic precision, then he deserves to be beaten half to death. To make it work, the defense would have to blur the distinction between resistance and noncompliance so that it became nonexistent. The defense's bottom-line rationale for this would be laid out by LAPD sergeant Charles Duke, their use-of-force expert. When asked if he'd equate overcoming resistance with beating someone into submission, Duke replied, ''If that's what it takes. If it takes one blow . . . or if it takes eight thousand blows to overcome resistance, then that's what it takes.'' You can beat them, in other words, until they're as still as a corpse. Doubtless, such a concept existed in no police manual in the United States. But defense attorneys and prosecutors can find expert witnesses to testify to anything. And with the careers and lives of fellow officers at stake, such experts were not hard for the defense to find.

Next, the beating would be portrayed as ''a controlled application of force.'' Far from being an object lesson for the local brothers, it would be transformed instead into ''a classic example of proper form and proper control of batons.'' The officers had been dealing, after all, ''with an assaultive person,'' one ''who was engaging,'' as Timothy Wind's lawyer, Paul DePasquale, pointed out, ''in assaultive behavior . . . that was intended to aid his escape.'' Rodney King was the wild man. They were not the mad dogs, *he* was. He kept trying to get up, would not lie still. Each time he was whacked he moved, which in and of itself was reason to hit him again. What they had done, as Stacey Koon described it, was nothing more than ''control an aggressive, combative suspect.'' After all, as Koon pointed out with undeniable truth, ''police work is [sometimes] brutal, [and] that was just a fact of life.''

Third, they would demonize Rodney King. They would show him to be the monster that was turning America's streets into war zones that could not be walked at night. They would cast him as the marauder who had made America's parks and public schools unfit for decent kids. He was a drunk, a felon, and a convicted armed robber (the latter a fact that Judge Weisberg would rule the jurors could not be told but which the defense would manage to sneak in anyway).

Conversely, the officers would be portrayed as vital links in Bill Parker's thin blue line, as all that stood between *them*—the jury—and anarchy. This was the essential fourth element of the defense on which all others rested, and Powell's lawyer, Michael Stone, had it down. "When you make a decision on whether these officers are guilty or not guilty, you're not going to be able to look through the eye of the camera. You're going to have to stand in their shoes," Stone would tell the jury. The job of police officers was not to be risking their lives "rolling around in the dirt with the likes of Rodney King." They were not "robocops, they hurt, and . . . they bleed and they die, just like everybody else."

And lastly, the lawyers would seek to convince the jury members that they, in fact, could not really believe their eyes. That what they were seeing on the tape wasn't what they *thought* they were seeing, but an "optical illusion." "The tape," as Michael Stone would put it, was "almost an illusion. It's a one-dimensional thing . . . filmed under the worst possible conditions. There are things you can't see on the tape that we know are happening."

So there in court Stacey Koon would stand, wooden pointer in hand, in front of a huge television set. At its bottom would run a time code as George Holliday's videotape of Rodney King's beating was continuously flashed across the screen. Frame by frame, second by second, Koon— dressed in a dark suit and red-striped tie, head characteristically cocked back, mouth slightly twisted— would point to a series of frames shown either in slow motion or in isolated freeze-frame, cutting off all that proceeded or followed it. There, he would say, indicating Rodney King's ankle as King writhed in pain. See that, he moved his ankle, he was trying to get up. Look, he would note, he's "rigid and tense when handcuffed," a clear sign "he was trying to resist us." It was a brilliant tactic. Simultaneously, it neutralized the relentless nature of the beating, eliminated the sounds of the action, and made the entire incident look softer, almost dreamlike. The raw disturbance, the visceral fear and empathy that radiated in the pit of your stomach as you watched the batons doing their work in real time disappeared as you watched in slow motion without sound. (The sound is lost in slow motion.) And, yes, Rodney King *had* moved his ankle, and there he was rolling over. So maybe he *was* trying to get up and fight back, or to reach into his "waistband" for a weapon. It wasn't much, but it was a defense. Something for the jury to hang on to, if, that is, they wanted to *believe.*

* * *

In spite of their misgivings about the jury, the prosecution's strategy was to err on the side of caution by making no major mistakes and relying heavily on George Holliday's video. That tape, after all, was really all that they needed. Or at least that was the general consensus as the trial began. As criminal-defense attorney Charles English told the *New York Times* in a reflection of the prosecution's tactics: "You could damn near put somebody on the stand, point out the people on the videotape, and rest your case. As a general rule, the stronger your case is, the closer to the vest to play it." It was good, sound, coolly calculated insider reasoning. But it was also the approach of the wise guy, of someone who knew more than he should—a decision straight from the head, not the gut. And as such it was terrible. With the jury they'd drawn they'd need *all* their guns firing full blast. But as they had no faith in their gut instincts, they had no faith in their two biggest guns other than the video itself: the horrified civilian witnesses to the beating, and Rodney King himself. Of the thirty civilians who watched the incident, only George Holliday was called. Yet it was precisely the testimony of those people, those average, normal, over-whelmingly *white* people, people like those sitting on the jury, that was so compelling. Almost to a person, they had condemned the officers' actions and were shocked, horrified, and outraged by what they had seen. The testimony of several dozen ordinary people grimly recounting their re-vulsion at what they'd witnessed—coupled with their firsthand accounts of how it was the *officers,* not Rodney King, who had been the real out-of-control threats—might well have softened up some of the jurors. Might well have convinced them that what they were seeing on the tape *was* in fact what happened, and not an "optical illusion." But then there were always problems in preparing such witnesses. Inevitably they wound up giving conflicting versions of events, or blurting out something that the defense might use against you. So the civilian eyewitnesses were never called. Instead, the prosecution chose to rely far too strongly on the testimony of CHP officer Melanie Singer. Unfortunately, her version of events in court, while vivid, telling, and helpful to the prosecution, dif-fered in some key points from what she'd written in her initial incident report, creating credibility problems for both her and the prosecution.

But nothing reflected the caution of the DA's office more than its decision not to call Rodney King to testify. There were reasons for the decision and they were all good. Rodney King's behavior since the beat-ing had become highly erratic. He was spending long hours alone watching television or sitting and staring off into space. He was on antidepressant medication. He was moody. He had headaches, he was worried about the damage done to his face and teeth, of which he had always been inordinately vain, and wondered if they could be repaired so he could look good again. His lips were numb with that just-got-a-shot-of-novocaine-at-the-dentist feeling, and he couldn't purse them well enough to speak properly. Often when he spoke, his manner was brusque. He felt, according to his now ex-wife, deeply humiliated by his beating, robbed, in her words, of "his manhood." Rarely did he venture out, and when he did, he was always getting involved in something, always there was some bullshit that seemed to come up. In mid-May of '91, just about ten weeks after the beating, he'd taken a drive and was stopped by sheriff's deputies in Santa Fe Springs and given a warning for driving with tinted windows, an expired registration, and no driver's license. He was also told at the time there was a $1,000 traffic warrant out on him in Orange County. Two weeks later, he'd driven around to Hollywood, picked up a transvestite hooker, parked his car, and while he was being served, was being watched by the two LAPD undercover officers on a stakeout. When they approached the car, King, who said he feared he was getting rolled, gunned the car and peeled off. Several blocks later, he flagged down an LAPD patrol car and told them that somebody had tried to rob him. The undercover officers claimed King had tried to run them over, and he was arrested for assault on a police officer with a deadly weapon, but no charges were filed.

King and his attorneys had also filed an $83 million lawsuit against the City of Los Angeles, but that suit was far from being settled, and he was caught in the middle of a byzantine dispute between his lawyer and his family over exactly who was going to profit from the expected bonanza as a result of his notoriety.

Rodney King, as a result of all this, was now a deeply angry man. After CHP officers Melanie and Tim Singer had testified that they never hit him, for example, Terry White received a call from King's lawyer, who then put King on the phone. Then with "profanity," according to White, "spewing out," Rodney King told him that "Melanie Singer kicked me. Tim Singer kicked me, and they're lying!" "It was 'Fuck this,' and 'Motherfucker that,' " White recounted to *Vanity Fair* magazine, and "right then I knew we had made the right decision."

Buttressing White's decision and his anxiety about him as a witness was King's street-easy propensity to lie to avoid trouble, just as he had run to avoid it on the night of his beating. Rodney King was not some rebellious left-wing lawyer who instantly grasped the meaning of Bob Dylan's line that You got to be an honest man to live outside the law. He was a street guy caught short. So he had initially lied. Lied badly and reflexively. Lied about not having been drinking that night. Lied about not running away from the CHP. Lied about not immediately complying with the officers' instructions. Lied that he was certain the officers called him a nigger as they beat him.

The defense, as it later freely admitted, and as White well knew, could barely wait to zero in on those inconsistencies. Or on Rodney King's criminal record, which if the prosecution called him as witness, the defense was free to delve into. And what would White be able to answer? "Well, ladies and gentlemen of the jury, you know he *dropped* the tire iron during the robbery. He's not really violent." Or could he say, "Yes, I know he has a record, but so does one in three black men his age in California. It doesn't really mean that much, it happens all the time, he's not a white boy, you know." Forget that. The defense attorneys would love it, love making King, and not the four LAPD officers, the focus of the trial. It all made perfect sense.

Except that this was a case that cried out for a flesh-and-blood victim, a human being whom the jury could see was real—like the cops they were being asked to send to jail—and not just a grainy abstraction. It was critical, in fact, for them to see him, to see that Rodney King was not a demon, was not the lurking savage they so feared, but a shy, stuttering, mixed-up, and oddly likable man. But nevertheless, there were few lawyers who responded affirmatively when asked by reporters if *they* would have called King. One was the tough, brilliant strategist Howard Weitzman, who had successfully defended automaker John DeLorean on drug-dealing charges. Weitzman said that he might have called King to "provide some insight as to why he moved around while they beat him." That was the mundane rationale. The better explanation was given by defense lawyer Johnnie L. Cochran, Jr., a well-known Los Angeles specialist in police-abuse cases. "When you have a case like this," said Cochran, "the jurors would expect and would want to hear from the victim." And indeed that was the case. "Had King been able to talk to us, the video might have been looked at differently," said one juror after the trial. An alternate juror, Lindy Miller, was more emphatic: "My mouth just dropped open [when he wasn't called]. It was like, where's Rodney? My feeling was that the defense didn't need to come on at all [and present its case], it had reasonable doubt all over it. Surely, we thought, he *had* to come and tell his version." But of course, he didn't.

The tension in the city those last days of the trial of Stacey Koon and his men was palpable. You could taste it, feel it. The local talk shows were consumed with it. People were talking about nothing else.

When the jury came in with its verdict on April 29, 1992, after deliberating for seven days, Laurence Powell's heart was pounding with anticipation. It was three-fifteen in the afternoon. Fifteen minutes later, as the verdicts were being read, he could barely contain his joy. Not guilty. Ten times the court clerk said it. Not guilty. Not guilty on all counts except one against Laurence Powell, on which the jury was hung, and on which Judge Stanley Weisberg promptly declared a mistrial. The verdicts had never been in question. The jury had actually decided on the acquittals during the first day of deliberations; the other six days had been spent debating that lone assault count against Powell. There were sobs of relief from the defendants' families. There were hugs, handshakes, smiles, and backslaps among the four officers and their attorneys. Outside the courthouse, Laurence Powell's twenty-two-year-old sister, Leanne, told reporters, "It hurts to see what they have done to my brother, to hear people telling lies about him. He did nothing wrong. And today I saw his first real smile since March third, 1991."

At Parker Center, meanwhile, detectives watching the verdicts being read were equally ecstatic. "Yes!" they shouted. "Go get 'em"; while near the scene of the beating, at the LAPD's Foothill Station, a young female officer, Corina Smith, almost bubbled over. "I'm elated, absolutely elated," she told the *Times* as she raised her fist in the air. "It's like this sick feeling is finally going to go away." "I feel the truth came out and that the verdicts are a reflection of the truth," said another Foothill officer. That was the message as she saw it. The message millions of black Americans received was different. Eat it, man, that was the message *they* got. Among many of them their reply would be just as unequivocal: Fuck it. Fuck it all.

CHAPTER 5

The Insurrection

······················

Throughout Los Angeles, throughout America, people kept changing channels to see what was going on, but always they kept going back to that one horrific image now seared into America's collective consciousness: thirty-six-year-old, blond-haired Reginald Denny lying on his knees and elbows outside his eighteen-wheel, big-rig truck after being pulled out of its cab for having the misfortune to be a white man in South Central just after the Simi Valley acquittals were announced. With helicopters hovering like vultures and broadcasting it all live and in living color, his ass is literally being kicked by two or three rioting brothers, who then turn to his head. One after another, they approach him like he's a vicious, rabid pit bull who's been weakened, and whose life they are now determined to stamp out. But to party as they do so. And it was a party. Up ran one man, his arms raised above his head, who, after taking careful aim, hurls a fire extinguisher he grabbed from the truck directly on Reginald Denny's head. Then up steps another, who, as Denny rises slightly, casually kicks him in the back before proceeding to repeatedly beat his cranium in with a metal hammer. He's replaced by a third, a local young man named Damian Williams, who will render the coup de grâce: walking up to Denny's right, and standing not more than a foot away, he fires a brick into Denny's temple before raising his leg in a triumphant little jig. Then he spits on Denny, points disdainfully at him, and dances away. The message is clear: if you're white, you're dead.

Click. Over to channel nine, to seven, to eleven, to see what else is happening as the city breaks out in rioting and looting, but always, always, it is back to Reginald Denny to see if it's possible that the poor guy is *still* lying there. Back and forth. It couldn't be live, could it? He was there a half hour ago. He must have been picked up. Then you'd turn and, with the rest of the nation, ask the question that would be asked for the next thirty-six hours as massive sections of Los Angeles are burning to the ground. The question you'd ask as cars driven by whites, Asians, and Latinos are being pelted with rocks, bricks, and chunks of concrete and their occupants are being pulled out by about two hundred people dressed in shorts and T-shirts, milling about sipping Buds and sodas, shaking their fists and beating people right next to Denny. The question you ask as "the rocks . . . slam into car after car," as L.A. *Times* reporter Shawn Hubler wrote, and "you . . . hear the shouts [of] 'Yeah, motherfucker, oh, yeah!' " The question you ask as the police who had been there retreat back to a staging area at a bus depot and the lieutenant in charge refuses to deploy them without orders that are not forthcoming. As South Central and Pico-Union are being looted, and while the rage and mayhem are spilling over into Hollywood, into West L.A., into Culver City, into mid-Wilshire, into Beverly Hills, into Compton, Carson, and San Pedro, Pacioma, Pomona, El Monte, and into Long Beach. The question you asked as the sons of South Central hopped on city buses, pulled off the terrorized passengers, and beat them senseless and robbed them. The question you asked when once again you turned back and Reginald Denny still lay sprawled on the asphalt on the corner of Florence and Normandie for what seemed like an eternity: Where the *fuck* are the cops?

The next morning, day two of the insurrection and riot, is a sunny Thursday. At eight o'clock local radio station KNX is blaring: "The Anaheim Police Department said that about five last night their 911 number was jammed with people calling after seeing the violence in Los Angeles saying, 'Do something—send police into Los Angeles and help them out . . . !' " Heading south on Normandie into the heart of South Central, smoke frames the background of the steeple of the Abundant Life Christian Church on Jefferson and Normandie, not far from the campus of

USC. It turns out to be coming from Frankie and Anne's Beauty Salon on Thirty-ninth Street—just a few blocks down from the LAPD's mammoth raid on the two apartment houses on Thirty-ninth and Dalton. The four other small stores next to Frankie and Anne's have already burned to the ground. Straight down Normandie, in fact, as far as the eye can see, stores are ablaze.

On the street corners mostly black men—a few Latinos—restlessly mill about, many with forty-ounces of Olde English or bottles of Bud in their hands. At Fifty-first Street four teenagers in identical black pants and T-shirts shout menacingly at a lone white motorist, "Hey, yo, what's up? What's up, fuck-head?" On *every* corner is another store, mainly liquor stores and mom-and-pop groceries, that is burning or is already a smoldering, looted hulk.

At Fifty-fourth Street four LAPD motorcycle cops stand on the corner drinking coffee and bullshitting after having set a green Dumpster across Normandie to block traffic. The few drivers out this early simply cut down a side street. At Fifty-fifth and Normandie two Latinos and an elderly Korean woman with garden hoses are busy watering down the embers of the blackened skeleton of what the night before had been a grocery store.

The woman keeps hosing down the embers as she repeats over and over, "Three times fire department come. I don't know what happen. . . . I lose everything." Her son joins her. "All they [the fire department] could do," he says, "is let the roof [come] down and let it burn, they had to go to other places. . . . I don't think we'll rebuild, under the insurance policy we can't rebuild another store."

Just then a black woman with braided hair walks across the street, comes up, stops, and says, "My store, my store, what have they done to my store? . . . I shopped here every day. These people were *wonderful*. Now there's no place to shop. I mean I need *milk*." She gestures down Normandie. "This store is gone, that store's burned down, that store is looted. *All* the stores in this area are gone. It's like they've shut down the neighborhood. I have two grandchildren to look after. Where am I gonna shop? The Valley?"

Down another side street are the neat bungalows and craftsmen cottages with their well-landscaped front yards that are the wonder of visitors from New York or Chicago who are used to seeing Harlem or the Southside. *This* is South Central? You mean this is really South Central? they would say. Everything is remarkably still and calm, seemingly as far from the madness of Normandie as a street in Beverly Hills. Of course it's only eight-twenty in the morning, and people are just getting up and about, standing outside their houses, quietly talking.

Two black women, Lisa, who's heavyset and wears a T-shirt with an old lady sitting in a rocking chair that says, "I've still got it but nobody wants to have it," and Brenda, thirty-four, thin and wearing burgundy sweats, stroll by. "It's not only gang members doing the fires and looting," says Lisa. "Yesterday evening we seen for *ourselves*. The Crips and the Bloods tied their rags together and said they wuz united. That it was now a black thing. The Crips drove up in cars. And the Bloods, you know, thought they wuz fixin' to bust them, and the Crips said no, and they just started huggin' each other sayin' they wanted to unite, that it was [now] a black thing."

"That's right," says Brenda, "they said it was all over for gang-banging. . . . But it wasn't only Bloods and Crips out there [burning and looting]. It's *everybody*. You can't just put it on those gang-bangers."

"This *was* a Blood neighborhood," says Lisa.

"That's right, it *was*," echoes Brenda. "Now we united. When we took that walk down there by Sixtieth and over by Florence, we united. See, the news didn't get that. They don't want to get nothin' like that because they want to keep it goin'."

"The media," says Lisa, "they don't know what's going on. They [the people doing the rioting] wanted to get these Korean stores out of the neighborhoods."

On Normandie and Sixtieth Place three black men in their thirties and a fourth, who's in his late teens wearing Raiders gear, stand with a beautiful young African-American woman holding an infant in her arms. Cecil, tall and light skinned, about thirty-five, confirms the gang story: "They tied their rags together."

"The red and the blue," says Kenny, a balding man of thirty-seven, nodding his head. "And they held up the power sign."

"Now they all be wearing black rags."

"We was real happy," says Eric, the teenager. "We were sad it had to come like this, but now we won't have to worry about gettin' shot."

"That's right," says Kenny, picking it up. "We were observers last night, and we actually had no fear of the gunfire because they were shooting up in the air, they weren't shooting *at* each other."

"And I'll tell you," says Cecil, "it was *organizzzed!* They had generals . . ." Everybody starts laughing knowingly. Cecil smiles back at them. "You know what I'm talkin' about. There was generals and soldiers and it was just like an ant colony, and when they started burning down that liquor store, they sent some of them out to the street to direct traffic, and some others, they had brought tools."

"Uh-huh," says Kenny, "they all for one purpose. And the Koreans, well, you know they gonna pay. That's why they hit all them swap meets." And indeed, they did pay. The Korean who wouldn't look you in the eye, who wouldn't touch your hand when he gave you change, the Korean who followed you around his store as if you were some kind of klepto, and jacked up the prices as if you were some kind of fool; the Korean who only hired his own, like the kids comin' up in the neighborhood didn't even *exist,* did pay. From South Central all the way up to Koreatown—you could trace it in a line—they paid. From Florence and Normandie to Sixth and Western, they paid as hundreds of their stores and businesses were looted and went up in flames.

Around the corner, Nathaniel, fifty-five, and William, seventy-four, are already into their forty-ounces of Olde English and a bag of reefer. "That verdict, that little girl getting killed, that a *wrong* verdict," Nathaniel says of Korean shopkeeper, Soon Ja Du, who had shot a black, fifteen-year-old girl named Latasha Harlins in her grocery store and had recently gotten off with just probation. "That Korean woman, she didn't get as much as they charge a man for drunk driving," he adds of the sentence, which was regarded as an outrage in the local black community second only to the King beating. "And the King stuff, man, that's been goin' on *forever* in this city."

"I'm not part of all this [the rioting]," says William, "but the bullshit that's going on—well, you got to be black to understand that. You know, I came up in the South, but the youngsters, they ain't gonna put up with the shit I used to."

By early morning J.J. Newberry's department store is already a gutted, charred shell. The store's located in a shopping center on Venice and Western on the far northern fringes of South Central, and the looting is well under way as two long hook-and-ladder fire engines guarded by four police cars, each packed with five cops in riot gear, pull out of the parking lot.

Watching as people walk out of a Sav-on, a black man of about thirty says, "They *have* to loot, they showin' it on the news, they see it, and most of them don't have anything." People stream through the store's broken front door. Many are Latino, perhaps 70 percent, reflecting the population of this neighborhood bordering the main riot area. The rest are black. One guy, looking like John Belushi at his most bloated, walks out with fingers entwined around four gallons of burgundy, the pockets of his red nylon shorts bulging with pints of whiskey. Following him is his look-alike with two twelve-packs of Miller.

Meanwhile, a Greek chorus of eight black men in their fifties and sixties, sounding much like Sweet Dick Willie and the corner men in *Do the Right Thing,* stand about twenty feet from the doorway. "Help yourself, help yourself," they shout as a big-bellied Latino wearing a FUCK YOU T-shirt wheels out a shopping cart filled to the brim with double-A batteries and Ramses condoms.

The first flash of anger comes from a balding black man about forty in a gray ski jacket and glasses. Earlier, four teenagers looking like starters for UCLA's freshman basketball team had ran into the store, each carrying empty suitcases. Now they were coming out, suitcases bulging. "I got a calculator, home," says one. "I got some ice cream," says another. The man in the ski jacket walks up to the tallest of the kids: "Man, all the shit that you take, it's gonna come back to you. It's real stupid shit you're doin'. Leave it and *respect* yourself."

For a moment the young brother looks uncertain, until his friend in a Miami Heat cap looks at him: "Man, if you feel like you need this, then *take* it."

"Take it?" says the man. "And give up your respect?"

"Fuck respect," replies Miami Heat, "they don't give *us* no respect."

As they stroll away, two black women call out, "No shame, no shame."

Meanwhile, the chorus gives its views. "All the people of color that was injured," says one man, "they took 'm over to Daniel Freeman. . . . But that white fireman that got shot, they took over to Cedars-Sinai. You see what I'm saying?"

"And Westwood, Westwood," says another, "man, they were down there en *masse.* Stuff was happening since three o'clock down in South Central and they did not go down there—*not once.*"

"That's right," says a third, "let them niggers destroy their *own* neighborhood."

As they talk, a dark, angry-looking man of about thirty drives up in a beat-up white Mazda, scowls, and starts yelling, "Fuck'm, take everything; fuck'm, take everything." Then a wiry-looking black kid, maybe nineteen, starts doing the Ali shuffle around a lone white reporter chanting, "You in the wrong neighborhood, man, you in the wrong neighborhood." The guy in the Mazda walks over and says two words, "Get going," as the reporter moves quickly to his car.

Daryl Gates's explanation for the thirty-six-hour debacle in which there was no coherent police response while Los Angeles was burned, trashed, and looted on national TV was a rambling mix of contradictions, factual distortions, and denial.

On Sunday, May 3, on "Meet the Press," he said that one of the reasons the department had been so unprepared was that "no one knew when the verdict was going to come out." No one, that is, except every person in the L.A. basin with a radio or TV turned on—the court having announced at ten in the morning that verdicts on all the counts save one would be read at three o'clock that afternoon.

Then, at a press conference the day after the rioting started, he attributed the department's failure to rescue people such as Reginald Denny, who'd been pulled from their vehicles at the now infamous corner of Florence and Normandie, then thrown gape-mouthed and terrorized into a wave of crashing fists and bricks, to the fact that his troops had been too busy protecting firefighters. But when a reporter pointed out that the assaults had taken place *before* the fires had been set, Gates backtracked, saying instead that he didn't want his troops to appear too aggressive or provocative, the subtext being that he'd been handcuffed by his critics. There was something to that, except that he himself had done the handcuffing. His relationship with the black community was now so abysmal, and the department so hated, that Daryl Gates had been precluded from using the massive display of force that might have immediately snuffed out the riot before it really got started. In fact, he had been warned the day before the verdicts were handed down *not* to do that. Speaking for a coalition of South Central ministers, business leaders, and civil rights organizations, the area's fiery new councilman, Mark Ridley-Thomas, said at a news conference that "we should not repeat the errors of the past. A massive show of force would be a mistake. These are very tough times." Daryl Gates by his total disdain for the black community in the past had placed himself in the position where a preventive show of force would now have been considered a gross provocation, and he chose not to do it.

Commander Ron Banks, the officer in charge of the riot area at the time the motorists were being pulled out of their cars, offered a different explanation. "Our units that responded initially were assaulted," Banks told the L.A. *Times.* "Windows were broken out of their police cars. Several received minor injuries . . . we were not going to go back and be taken hostage or incur more injuries until we had sufficient personnel." That outraged former San Jose Chief of Police Joseph McNamara, who was monitoring the riots: "I can understand firefighters not wanting to go into an area where people are shooting at them. But the police? That's their job, that's what they're getting paid for. It's unthinkable for them to say they didn't want to risk their lives to save others."

The LAPD leadership in South Central, like Daryl Gates downtown, seemed paralyzed as well as unprepared. "If they had been even minimally ready," LAPD detective Zvonko G. Pavelic would later reflect, "they'd at least have sent their undercover men to assess the situation— see if there are any snipers, how large the crowd was, that sort of thing, and then stopped and rerouted traffic so innocent people weren't driving into harm's way."

There were also no groups of police stationed on reserve, out of sight so that their presence wouldn't provoke tensions, but who could move quickly to protect people, make arrests, and quickly take the ringleaders out of circulation—a now-standard policy in riot control. People thought that Daryl Gates was spitting at them. They could not conceive the truth of the matter: that it was an extraordinary, ill-prepared, undirected fuckup.

First, Daryl Gates appeared genuinely surprised by the not-guilty verdicts, even though it didn't take a cultural anthropologist to know that given the ultraconservative nature of Simi Valley, and the makeup of the jury, not-guilty verdicts were a distinct possibility. "I don't think he understood the ramifications of acquittals," said police-commission president Stanley Sheinbaum, "because he was so sympathetic to acquittals." So, despite the escalating violence and arson, Gates left his post at the most crucial hours in the city's history—and in a highly charged political atmosphere where other high-ranking LAPD officials were not about to go out on a limb and make a decision—and went off to a Brentwood political fund-raiser to defeat Proposition F, the Christopher Commission reforms coming up on the June ballot. Second, there was the matter of a contingency plan. If it existed, nobody saw it. "To my knowledge there never was a contingency plan," Stanley Sheinbaum would later say. "The commission was never able to get Gates to tell them what it was. It was nonexistent."

Earlier, Daryl Gates had taken several divisions, including South Central's Seventh-seventh, and placed them under his personal command. He was going to show the department and the city his version of community policing. But things were left hazy. And at staff meetings the deputy chief nominally in charge of the divisions, Matthew Hunt, according to David Dotson, kept pressing Gates for a clear line of command, for the definitive word on who exactly was in charge, so that plans could be made and Hunt would know who had the authority to call officers in if they were needed, and to deploy them. As a result, when the mayhem broke out at Florence and Normandie, Gates was busy with his fund-raising in Brentwood, Matthew Hunt was with Tom Bradley and much of the city's black leadership at the First AME Church, and *nobody* was in charge. Consequently, the majority of the department's one thousand detectives—who work between six A.M. and two in the afternoon and live outside the city—were permitted to go home as usual. And when the rioting started, the tough, elite Metro Squad, the Narcotics and CRASH gang units, and the hundreds of officers who work at Parker Center were not deployed, and hundreds of officers and hundreds of desperately needed vehicles and radios remained in safe, relatively tranquil areas of the Valley. At the same time, LAPD officers in South Central, once they *were* dispatched, were riding around packed five to a car. Meanwhile, forty miles northwest of L.A., most of the department's critically important field captains were sitting together attending a seminar in Oxnard.

The failure to swiftly deploy the National Guard and other police agencies was also a monumental breakdown, one both the offices of Mayor Bradley and California governor Pete Wilson were blaming on the LAPD. Gates should have asked for assistance sooner, everyone was saying. But the very word *assistance* was insulting. "This department has never reached out to others like the sheriff's department, the Santa Monica PD, or the Highway Patrol—the attitude has always been, 'We are the LAPD, the best, why should we?' " said a police commissioner later. "So the sheriff was offering assistance for twelve hours and there was no response to it." The calling up of the National Guard, that, too, was asking for assistance, as was the specter of federal troops on the streets of L.A. It would be a blot on the city's reputation, and Daryl Gates didn't want to be taking orders from a general, he told local KNBC reporter Linda Douglas.

In June of 1992, a nine-page internal LAPD report criticizing the department's performance during the riot surfaced. A large number of officers, said the report, were untrained and unfamiliar with the Field Command Post (FCP) operations used during emergencies, causing "substantial delays in the deployment of officers." Some officers didn't even know where to report for emergency duty and went to their regular roll call instead. Once there, they had to learn what to do as they went along. Adding to the disarray, according to the report, was a serious shortage of equipment such as police cars, computers, radios, and maps. But perhaps the biggest reason for the department's disastrous response was that Daryl Gates himself, the king of modern, high-tech policing, the father of SWAT, had to direct the LAPD during the riot. Gates hadn't run that department in an operational sense for many years. That was Bob Vernon's job. And Vernon had retired from the department just a week earlier. Daryl Gates, moreover, hadn't spoken to David Dotson since Dotson had been critical of him in his testimony before the Christopher Commission, just as he hadn't spoken to Tom Bradley or Jesse Brewer (who was now retired and the vice president of the police commission) in a year. And the people who knew "which side their bread was buttered on," says Dotson, weren't talking to Dotson either. As the riot spread, Dotson went to the command post to direct the refueling of the department's vehicles, a job that fell under his purview and that he'd been doing. But he was told by a junior officer, commander Frank Persol, "to get the hell out of the command post and quit bothering him." There were no repercussions. The LAPD command structure was in a shambles. Gates had isolated and surrounded himself with a few young commanders, and when the riot was dumped into his lap, he couldn't handle it. All of which was later underscored by the official conclusions of an independent investigative commission headed by former FBI Director William H. Webster. Three days after it began, it was over. More than twenty thousand police and soldiers had been used to quell the insurrection. There were large demonstrations in Harlem, stones and bottles hurled through store windows and whites assaulted by bands of young blacks in Atlanta. In San Francisco, demonstrators shut down the San Francisco–

Oakland Bay bridge, as downtown crowds rioted and the city was placed under a state of emergency. In Madison, Wisconsin, the windshields of police cars were smashed in, and in Las Vegas the National Guard had to be activated. In Los Angeles fifty-eight people had been killed, 2,383 injured, and the damage to property totaled almost $800 million.

The point in time when people say I won't take this anymore, I will fight back, I will seek retribution, had been reached. It was a feeling so widespread in South Central and Pico-Union that what was really amazing was not what broke out during those days, but that so many white people were totally blind to what had led up to it. The tragedy was that L.A.'s black mayor, once a symbol of transformation, had been blinded, too. By the time he opened his eyes, it was too late.

What Daryl Gates had shown by his performance after the beating of Rodney King was that he had learned nothing from the killing of Eulia Love. What he had now shown with his actions after the King verdict was that he had learned nothing from Watts. Nothing at all. The beating had tarnished Daryl Gates's reputation; now—as 81 percent of those polled told the *Los Angeles Times* that they disapproved of the job he was doing—it had been destroyed. And with it, Bill Parker's protégé, his keeper of the flame, took all that was left of the LAPD's mystique, and of the legend of the Golden Boys.

PART 8

EPILOGUE

Epilogue

●

He left the LAPD in June. But he was still The Chief. That's how all those computer salesmen from Canyon Country, all those housewives from Orange County, all those Rush Limbaugh–loving ditto-heads, still addressed Daryl Gates on his local talk radio show, as The Chief. They were his bedrock listeners, but occasionally some irate brother from South Central would call in, and he and Gates would go at it. It was good for ratings. But for the most part the boxer had transformed himself into the most genial of talk-show hosts. He was "pleasant," he was "charming" to local ACLU head Ramona Ripston. He was almost "too nice" to city councilman Zev Yaroslavsky. It was just as he'd always maintained. Daryl Gates *was* a nice guy. Rambling, inarticulate, George Bush on Valium, but nice. After a time, however, his ratings weren't all that KFI-AM had hoped for, and they went to promos like the one featuring The Chief and the former Black Panther and perennial police-abuse activist Michael Zinzan:

Gates: "You're a loudmouth, Michael . . . a jerk."

Zinzan: "There you go name-calling. . . . I haven't called *you* a scummy, low-life pig."

But they hadn't really worked, and as 1994 dawned, Daryl Gates was off the airwaves. He had, nevertheless, managed to hold center stage in Los Angeles for a *long* time. And in his wake he'd left his monument. In the midsixties, Watts had been only one of literally hundreds of insurrections and riots that had broken out in America's black ghettos. But the rebellion of 1992 had belonged to Los Angeles. And to Daryl Gates. It was his insurrection, his riot, as the LAPD had been his department.

In September of 1992, Tom Bradley held a press conference to announce that he would not run for a sixth consecutive term as mayor. The collective sigh of relief that whooshed out of the city's liberal establishment could be heard all the way to Fresno. In the astoundingly tense days leading up to the second trial of Stacey Koon and his men on federal civil-rights charges, Bradley had outraged them and the entire city by going off on a promotional junket to Asia. Why not? It was over. Barely 38 percent of the people approved of the job he was doing, and it had been like that for a year. Daryl Gates had gone beyond his capabilities; Tom Bradley, as he knew better than anyone else, had never been permitted to reach his. He'd let others dream about what might have been and view him as an American tragedy. Now was his time to go to work as a senior counselor for the downtown law firm of Brobeck, Phleger & Harrison. Now was his time to play in the big-money league.

David Dotson took the examination to succeed Daryl Gates, but was not selected. Afterward, he retired before Gates, at whose pleasure he served as assistant chief, could demote him back to deputy chief and cost him $1,300 a month in pension benefits tied to the cost of living. Earlier, he'd provided Gates with the justification by becoming romantically involved with a female officer under his command. She was married. He was married. He was twenty-eight years her senior. That, and an allegation that Dotson hadn't fully investigated some charges against a deputy chief, were all Gates needed. Dotson then applied for jobs at other police agencies in southern California, but was not hired. He was persona non grata, a man not to be trusted. He had opened his mouth and spoken the truth. It wasn't done. He was out of the club. Daryl Gates had said it all: "In my opinion, Brewer and Dotson sold us out."

Jesse Brewer was named to the police commission by Tom Bradley in July of 1991, later becoming both its vice president and president and significantly influencing the choice of a new police chief. When Richard Riordan, downtown multimillionaire, behind-the-scenes puller of strings, and the Valley's new white hope in City Hall was elected mayor in 1993,

Brewer was asked to step aside with the rest of Bradley's liberal appointees.

Jim Fisk and his son Steve have reconciled. The elder Fisk is retired and lives in the Hollywood Hills. Steve Fisk is the head of detectives at the LAPD's Van Nuys station.

Sam Yorty, too, is long retired and lives in a house, formerly owned by Mickey Rooney, on a hill in the San Fernando Valley. There, every chance he gets, he sits and rails at L.A.'s "black racists."

Ed Davis ran unsuccessfully for the Republican nomination for governor and then became a state senator from the Valley. In the months following the beating of Rodney King, he called on Daryl Gates to resign ("I think the fat lady has sung. Everybody has to know he has a boss") and sponsored legislation making it a felony for a police officer to witness a fellow officer using unnecessary force and not taking steps to stop him or to later report the incident. The legislation went nowhere. Nor did three similar bills vetoed by the lawman's friend in Sacramento, California's Republican governor Pete Wilson. The state's almost ninety-thousand-member law-enforcement unions—representing California's police officers and prison guards—had hated those bills. They were a threat to them, a threat to the order of things. And it was the police unions—an integral part of California's burgeoning law-enforcement industry—acting together as a block to form one of the most formidable lobbying groups in the state, that saw to it that those bills were killed. It wasn't hard. Just one of the unions—the state's prison guards—had, after all, contributed more than $760,000 to support Pete Wilson's run for governor in 1990, a contribution second in generosity only to that of the national Republican Party. Then, with the obliviousness to appearance of the truly powerful, the union's lobbyists turned around and began pushing a bill that would permit police officers to refuse to cooperate with internal-affairs investigators from their own departments. The legislation, a representative of the guards' union told the *Los Angeles Times*, would protect officers from "overzealous" supervisors. As for Ed Davis, whose heart had failed to bleed for all those victims of police abuse when he was chief, well, he had done his part and shown as well an eye for history.

In June of 1992, following the insurrection and riot, Charter Amendment F, the Christopher Commission reforms designed to serve as the basis for rebuilding and reforming the LAPD, passed by an overwhelming margin of two to one. Prior to the vote, a full-page ad appeared in the *Los*

Angeles Times urging the amendment's passage. It was signed by, among others, the chairmen and CEOs of TransAmerica, First Interstate, Arco, GTE, UNOCAL, Disney, Lockheed, Times Mirror, Northrop, and Bank of America, and by senior partners in L.A.'s most powerful law firms. Their sense of justice had been aroused. Reform would have to proceed.

And for a huge, rusted hulk that takes forever to turn around, for the big ship that is the LAPD, the reforms *were* incontestably revolutionary. No longer would the chief be chief for life. Exempted from civil-service protection, with tenure limited to two five-year terms, he or she could now be fired. Training and discipline were to be placed under far greater civilian control and accountability. A system for tracking problem officers and a police-commission watchdog unit to oversee the disciplinary process would be established. Community-based policing—working *with* the public instead of riding herd over it—was to become the new operating philosophy of the department.

But two years after the vote, many of the commission's key proposals had not been implemented. The city was broke. And although the new mayor, Richard Riordan, had signed that full-page ad and claimed to support the reforms, money could somehow not be found to implement the new system for tracking officers with a history of civilian complaints. It would, after all, cost $39,000. Thirty-nine thousand dollars out of a city budget of $4.6 billion, of which the LAPD's share was $500 million. And it could not be found.

The new mayor had campaigned and won with the strong and vocal support of the Police Protective League, and many officers didn't like the tracking system, or another of the proposals, which mandated that a civilian sit on the LAPD's disciplinary boards. As of April of 1994, that reform, too, was languishing.

Prone-outs continued, despite a promise by the department over a year earlier that they would be discontinued.

The LAPD's definition of, as well as its plan for, community policing remained "vague," according to police-commission staff members.

The controversial head of the officer-involved-shooting team, William Hall, was still in place, and the LAPD was refusing to hand over documents to the district attorney pertaining to the death of a black woman who was shot ten times by LAPD officers—seven times in the back—and killed.

The man responsible for bringing the fervent hopes of L.A.'s blacks and liberals to fruition was Willie Williams, who entered office the same month that Charter Amendment F passed. Williams, the moonfaced, easy-mannered head of the Philadelphia PD, replaced Daryl Gates and became the first black chief in the city's history. In Philadelphia, Williams liked community policing and liked affirmative action. What he didn't like was Rodney King's beating. After he'd seen it, he ordered the videotape played at training classes for veterans and recruits and was quick to denounce the officers' actions. About three weeks after the incident he told the *Philadelphia Inquirer* that he was "embarrassed as a police officer . . . I was shocked. I had not seen pictures of Vietnam or Korea where I saw one human being try to kill another human being the same way some of those officers tried to do to that man." After he arrived in L.A., Willie Williams said that he wanted to "serve a new customer base" of multiracial city dwellers; that he wanted to double the number of Internal Affairs investigators; and that he wanted to get more officers out on patrol. The city's black and liberal leadership was, well, ecstatic with his choice. And everybody was happy with the way he trained and prepared the department for possible riots after the federal trial of Stacey Koon and his men.

But as 1994 dawned, Willie Williams was in a bind, caught between the expectations of the city's liberals and the realities of L.A. Not only was the city broke, but the rank and file were demoralized and petulant, and literally under fire, with at least seven officers wounded in 1993. The Protective League, without a contract for years, launched a stay-out-of town-it's-too-dangerous campaign, complete with billboards of Angelenos getting mugged, in an effort to extract money from the city. Meanwhile, people began to wonder if Willie Williams was in over his head.

Then there was the mayor, Richard Riordan, who was elected in June of 1993. A rich, high-profile businessman, Riordan poured hundreds of thousands of his own dollars into his campaign and easily defeated the hapless efforts of his chief rival, the liberal city councilman Michael Woo, who, in the tense days after King's beating, had been the only member of the city council to strongly oppose Daryl Gates. Woo ran in support of the Christopher Commission reforms; Riordan ran to expand the LAPD to ten thousand officers. The outcome was never in doubt. Richard Riordan received the overwhelming support of white Angelenos—particularly in the Valley—who still made up two-thirds of the electorate.

In two of his first acts in office, Riordan appointed Bill Violante, the Police Protective League president, as a deputy mayor and his liaison to the police department. It was as if Bill Clinton had appointed Pat Robertson to shepherd his gays-in-the-military proposal through Congress. The heart of the Charter Amendment F reforms had been about officer and departmental accountability, and Violante, as head of the Protective League, had been among its fiercest opponents.

Then Riordan went to an LAPD roll call at the department's Van Nuys station. There, to the cheers of the officers, he said, "I know that when you're put in situations where you have to be tough and make tough arrests, you are subject to criticism. I think we have to step back and give some latitude, to know that you've got to be tough, and when you're tough, things don't always come out the way everybody wants them to." Daryl Gates would have taken heart.

In April of 1993, Stacey Koon and Laurence Powell were convicted by a federal jury for violating Rodney King's civil rights. The other two officers, Timothy Wind and Theodore Briseno, were exonerated. The streets were saturated with thousands of LAPD officers and sheriffs on patrol when the verdicts were announced, but there were no incidents. Koon and Powell were sentenced to eighteen months in federal prison, the bare minimum they could have gotten. The jury had not bought the defense's argument, but the judge had. Rodney King, he said, as he announced Koon's and Powell's sentences, had indeed been responsible for his own beating.

For three years Rodney King sat at home dreaming of his forthcoming multimillion-dollar settlement from the city of Los Angeles, which in 1992 paid out almost $20 million to its citizens in atonement for the sins of its police officers. The city offered him $800,000. Rodney King said no. He wanted $15 million. In April of 1994, a federal jury awarded him $3.8 million. Several weeks later, Judge John G. Davies, the same Judge Davies who had declared Rodney King responsible for his own beating, dismissed King's suit against Daryl Gates for punitive damages. Daryl Gates would not have to reach into his deep pockets and personally pay retribution to Rodney King. "Bad management is not enough, allowing racism is not enough, poor supervision is not enough" to make Daryl Gates pay, said Judge Davies. It had not been shown that he was *directly* responsible for Rodney King's beating.

Meanwhile, the ship, the big ship, is moving. But with an angry Police Protective League, a mayor calling for more—if not better—cops, and mandatory minimums, three strikes you're out, regional prisons, and everybody scared shitless of thirteen-year-olds with semiautomatics, who knows which way it will turn?

The thoughts and quoted dialogue come from a variety of sources, including the recollections of persons who participated in the conversations or who observed them or took notes, from public documents, published sources, and other written accounts. Some of the background in the sections dealing with Tom Bradley and some of Bradley's quoted remarks come from interviews with him which were conducted under the auspices of the oral-history program of U.C.L.A.

Source Notes

∙∙∙∙∙∙∙∙∙∙∙∙∙∙∙∙∙∙∙∙∙∙∙

ABBREVIATIONS

LADN	Los Angeles *Daily News*
LAHE	Los Angeles *Herald Examiner*
LAR	*Los Angeles Record*
LAT	*Los Angeles Times* (note that when the *Times* is cited in the text, *LAT* is implied)
NYT	*New York Times*

AUTHOR'S NOTE: The following are a list of abbreviations of the major sources used in TO PROTECT AND TO SERVE. These sources will be referred to by their abbreviations throughout the source notes.

Borough	Reuben W. Borough, "Reuben W. Borough and California Reform Movements," Oral History Program, University of California, Los Angeles, 1968.
Caplan	Gerald Saul Caplan, "The CIVIC Committee in the Recall of Mayor Frank Shaw" (master's thesis, University of California, Los Angeles, 1947).
Domanick 1	Joe Domanick, "Why Glenn Martell and Jederick Bond Killed Erica Johnson. No Good Reason," *California Magazine,* July 1987, 71ff.
Domanick 2	———, "Stop the Presses," *L.A. Weekly,* November 3–9, 1989, cover story.
Domanick 3	———, "The Black Cop Speaks Out and Others Don't, *L.A. Weekly,* March 29–April 4, 1991.
Domanick 4	———, "The First Jewish Mayor of L.A.?" *Jewish Journal of Greater Los Angeles,* August 8–14, 1986, cover story.
Domanick 5	———, "What's with Zev?" *L.A. Weekly,* June 7–13, 1991, 12.
Domanick 6	———, "Police Power: Why No One Can Control the LAPD," *L.A. Weekly,* February 16–22, 1990, cover story.

Source Notes

Domanick 7 ———, "Trouble at the D.A.," *Los Angeles,* April 1988.

Domanick 8. ———, "Gates's People," *L.A. Weekly,* April 12–18, 1991, 13.

Donner Frank Donner, *Protectors of Privilege: Red Squads and Police Repression in Urban America* (Berkeley: University of California Press, 1980).

Eulia Love Report L.A. Board of Police Commissioners, *The Report of the Board of Police Commissioners Concerning the Shooting of Eulia Love and the Use of Deadly Force* (Los Angeles, October 1979), 1–56.

Galm Bernard Galm, "The Impossible Dream: Thomas Bradley," Oral History Program, University of California, Los Angeles, 1984.

Gates Daryl Gates, *Chief: My Life in the LAPD* (New York: Bantam Books, 1992).

Gottlieb and Wolt Robert Gottlieb and Irene Wolt, *Thinking Big: The Story of the Los Angeles Times, Its Publishers and Their Influence on Southern California* (New York: G. P. Putnam's Sons, 1977).

Henstell Bruce Henstell, *Sunshine and Wealth: Los Angeles in the Twenties and Thirties* (San Francisco: Chronicle Books, 1984).

LAPD Comm Los Angeles Police Revolver and Athletic Club, *LAPD Commemorative Book, 1869–1984* (Los Angeles: Los Angeles Police Revolver and Athletic Club, n.d.).

Leader Leonard Leader, *Los Angeles and the Great Depression* (New York: Garland Publishing, 1991).

McWilliams Carey McWilliams, *Southern California Country: An Island on the Land* (New York: Duell, Sloan & Pearce, 1946).

Owens and Browning Tom Owens and Rod Browning, *Lying Eyes: The Truth Behind the Corruption and Brutality of the LAPD and the Beating of Rodney King* (New York: Thunder's Mouth Press, 1991).

Payne and Ratzan J. Gregory Payne and Scott C. Ratzan, *Tom Bradley: The Impossible Dream* (Santa Monica, Calif.: Roundtable Publishing, 1986).

RIC Independent Commission on the Los Angeles Police Department, *Report of the Independent Commission on the Los Angeles Police Department* (Los Angeles, 1991).

Rothmiller and Goldman Mike Rothmiller and Ivan G. Goldman, *L.A.'s Secret Police: Inside the LAPD Spy Network* (New York: Pocket Books, 1992).

Schiesl Martin J. Schiesl, "Behind the Badge: The Police and Social Discontent in Los Angeles Since 1950," in Norman M. Klein and Martin J. Schiesl, eds., *20th Century Los Angeles: Power, Promotion, and Social Conflict* (Claremont, Calif.: Regina Books, 1990).

Sjoquist Arthur W. Sjoquist, "From Posses to Professionals: A History of the Los Angeles Police Department" (master's thesis, California State University, Los Angeles, 1972).

Starr Kevin Starr, *Inventing the Dream: California through the Progressive Era* (New York: Oxford University Press, 1985).

Source Notes

Turner   William W. Turner, *The Police Establishment* (New York: G. P. Putnam's Sons, 1968).

Understand-   Los Angeles Times, *Understanding the Riots: Los Angeles before and after the Rod-*
ing the   *ney King Case* (Los Angeles: Los Angeles Times, 1992).
Riots

Webb   Jack Webb, *The Badge* (Englewood Cliffs, N.J.: Prentice-Hall, 1958).

Woods   Joseph Gerald Woods, "The Progressives and the Police: Urban Reform and the Professionalization of the Los Angeles Police" (Ph.D. diss., University of California, Los Angeles, 1973).

INTERVIEWS: In researching this book, the author interviewed the following persons; dates of the interviews are specified. The interviews are abbreviated in the notes as follows:

Aliano   George Aliano, former president, Police Protective League, May 20, 1991.

Bellows   Jim Bellows, editor, L.A. *Herald Examiner,* 1989.

Bouza   Tony Bouza, former Minneapolis chief of police, April 1991.

Brewer   Jesse Brewer, former LAPD assistant chief and former L.A. Police Commission president, October 9, 1991.

Burnham   David Burnham, author and journalist, April 19, 1991.

Caldwell   Bernard Caldwell, former LAPD deputy chief, July 11, 1991.

Cortez   Leo Cortez, Community Youth Gang Services (social service agency), April 1987.

Cunningham   Raye Cunningham, former campaign worker and aide to Mayor Tom Bradley, October 2, 1991.

Davis,   Charles Davis, son of former L.A. chief of police James Davis, May 11, 1992.
Charles

Davis, Ed   Ed Davis, former L.A. chief of police and California state senator, December 18, 1991.

Dederick   Jack Dederick, former LAPD sergeant, October 29–30, 1991.

Dircks   Joe Dircks, former LAPD lieutenant, November 26, 1991.

Dotson   David Dotson, former LAPD assistant chief, July 1992–May 1993.

Driscoll   Jack Driscoll, L.A. city Personnel Department, March 16, 1991.

Duvin   Mike Duvin, L.A. County Probation Department, April 1987.

Fabiani   Mark Fabiani, former aide to Mayor Tom Bradley, April 18, 1991.

Felkenes   George Felkenes, professor of criminal justice, Claremont Graduate School, Claremont, California, May 1, 1991.

Source Notes

Fisk, Jim   Jim Fisk, former LAPD deputy chief and former L.A. Police Commission president, April 25–26 and December 10, 1991.

Fisk, Steve   Steve Fisk, LAPD officer and former member of Special Investigation Section (SIS), October 30 and November 12, 1991.

Fry   Jay Fry, LAPD sergeant, May 22, 1991.

Fyfe   James Fyfe, former New York Police Department lieutenant and professor at American University, Washington, D.C., winter 1989 and spring 1991.

Garcia   Dan Garcia, L.A. police commissioner, April 29, 1991.

Gates interview   Daryl Gates, former L.A. chief of police, winter 1990–91.

Hardeman   Garland Hardeman, LAPD officer, spring 1991.

Harrison   Paul Harrison, former LAPD deputy chief, March 21, 1992.

Henning   Phil Henning, L.A. city Personnel Department, May 16, 1991, and June 8, 1992.

Holsted   Jack Holsted, former LAPD officer, October 2 and 28, 1991.

Jackson   Don Jackson, former Hawthorne, California, police officer, now police-abuse activist, March 13, 1991.

Johnson   Dorothy Johnson, mother of Erica Johnson, and family members, spring 1987.

Kinsling   John Kinsling, former LAPD officer and aide to LAPD chief William Parker, December 12, 1991.

Klinger   David Klinger, former LAPD officer, winter 1989–spring 1990.

Lacky   Ray Lacky, LAPD detective, May 24, 1991.

Lalli   Frank Lalli, former assistant editor, L.A. *Herald Examiner,* 1989.

Leader   Leonard Leader, instructor of journalism, University of Southern California, October 10, 1991.

Lester   Irvis Lester, former LAPD deputy chief, March 18–19, 1992.

Lomax   Melanie Lomax, L.A. police commissioner, May 3, 1991.

Manes   Hugh Manes, civil rights attorney, winter 1989.

McBride   Tim McBride, LAPD captain, spring 1991.

McGill   Carl McGill, LAPD officer, April 1991.

McNamara   Joseph McNamara, former chief of police, San Jose, California, May 1, 1992.

Mims   Derrick Mims, former aide to Congressman Augustus Hawkins, April 12, 1991.

Murdock   Roger Murdock, former LAPD deputy chief, November 4, 1991.

Narvid   Ethel Narvid, former campaign aide and assistant to Mayor Tom Bradley, April 26 and November 11, 1991.

Niles   Larry Niles, L.A. city Personnel Department, May 8, 1991.

Patterson   Pat Patterson, L.A. city Personnel Department, June 11, 1992.

Source Notes

Pavelic	Zvonko G. "Bill" Pavelic, former LAPD detective, November 5, 1991, and April 1, 1992.
Paz	R. Samuel Paz, civil rights attorney, April 1991.
Rathburn	William Rathburn, as LAPD deputy chief in winter 1989, and as Dallas chief of police, May 21, 1991.
Reddin	Tom Reddin, former Los Angeles chief of police, July 15, 1992.
Reinhardt	Stephen Reinhardt, former president, L.A. Police Commission (now a federal judge), winter 1990.
Rogers	Kevin Rogers, LAPD detective, spring 1987.
Rothmiller	Mike Rothmiller, former detective, LAPD Organized Crime Intelligence Division, April 11, 1994.
Sappel	Joel Sappel, reporter for *L.A. Times*, 1989.
Satz	Wayne Satz, reporter for television station KABC, winter 1990.
Sheinbaum	Stanley Sheinbaum, then president, L.A. Police Commission, September 23, 1991.
Sheldon	Stanley Sheldon, former LAPD captain, November 6, 1991.
Stewart	Charles Stewart, press secretary for state senator Diane Watson, April 1991.
Storm	Daisy Storm, former LAPD officer, November 6, 1991.
Sullivan	Harold Sullivan, former LAPD deputy chief, November 1, 1991.
Swanson	Dennis Swanson, former news director for television station KABC, March 1994.
Valdivia	Steve Valdivia, Community Youth Gang Services (social service agency), April 1987.
Wambaugh	Joseph Wambaugh, former LADP officer and novelist, December 30, 1991.
Washington	Rocky Washington, former LAPD lieutenant, October 12 and December 11, 1991.
Weiner	Maury Weiner, former campaign aide and assistant to Mayor Tom Bradley, October 14, 1991
Weiss	Clifford Weiss, member of L.A. Police Commission staff, March 11, 1994.
White	Jack White, former LAPD commander and chief investigator for the L.A. District Attorney's Office, winter 1989.
Wilkinson	Frank Wilkinson, political activist, November 26 and December 3, 1991.
Williams	Ed Williams, LAPD officer, May 1991.
Windham	Thomas Windham, former LAPD officer and Fort Worth chief of police, May 13, 1991.
Yagman	Stephen Yagman, civil rights attorney, winter 1989.
Yaroslavsky	Zev Yaroslavsky, Los Angeles city councilman, 1986; May 22, 1991; and 1992.
Yorty	Sam Yorty, former Los Angeles mayor, April 26, 1991.

PART 1—PROLOGUE: SILENCE OF THE LAMBS

CHAPTER 1: The Black Prince

The author attended the community meeting at the First AME Church in Los Angeles on the evening of April 29, 1992.

Rocks fly: *Understanding the Riots,* 49; *U.S. News and World Report,* May 11, 1992; *NYT,* December 9, 1993.

Eulia Love: *LAHE,* January 23, 1979.

Black population below 18 percent: *LAT,* April 8, 1989.

Hooked up with ... then-liberal: Weiner; *LAT,* April 8, 1989.

LAPD "exported": confirmed with police departments in Ft. Worth, Dallas, Beverly Hills.

Summed up the stance: Harold Meyerson, *L.A. Weekly,* March 29–April 4, 1991; *LAT,* May 26, 1991.

Spied on the state attorney general: Rothmiller, *L.A.'s Secret Police,* 171–80.

Check rearview mirrors: police commissioner (not for attribution), 1989.

King's kidneys ... Monadnock: *Village Voice,* April 16, 1991.

Bradley almost first black governor: *LAT,* August 15, 1992; February 24, 1994.

CHAPTER 2: The Keepers of the Flame

Gates speech: The author attended the graduation exercises on November 2, 1990.

Watts insurrection: *Author's note:* Throughout the text when I refer to the violence in Watts in 1965 and in South Central and many other areas of Los Angeles in 1965, I use the terms *insurrection, riot,* and sometimes *rebellion.* In their initial stages, both episodes were expressions of rage that disintegrated into mindless rioting and looting.

Consent decree: *LAT,* October 22, 1982, December 19, 1990, February 2, 1994.

Latinos 40 percent/blacks declined to about 14 percent: *1990 U.S. Census of Population and Housing Summary,* cited in *RIC.*

11 percent ... voted: *LAT,* September 25 and November 30, 1992.

3.5 million people: *RIC,* 2.

641,000 kids, 70 percent of parents: *NYT,* November 29, 1992.

"Who would want to work with one?": *LAT,* August 15 and 16, 1992.

Rookie ... chauffeur: Gates, *Chief,* 25.

Parker basis for Spock: *Philadelphia Inquirer,* July 19, 1992.

"I run the police"/didn't want to be mayor: *LAT,* December 18, 1977.

"Casual drug users ought to be ... shot": Gates, *Chief,* 286; *LAT,* March 17, 1991.

Reporters had examples: *LAT,* March 17, 1991.

8,400 officers, eighteen geographic divisions: *RIC,* 22.

2.5 officers per 1,000 residents: *LAT,* December 17, 1990.

Source Notes

Top-heavy in special units: Willie Williams cited in *LAT,* April 8, 1993, Dotson.

If you beat the shit: *LAT,* April 4, 1991; *LADN,* July 10, 1991.

Head of CIA: Gates interview.

Whites ... 65 percent of registered voters: *LAT,* September 25, 1992.

Condo in San Clemente: Dotson.

Milken paroled: Gates interview; *LAT,* December 14, 1990.

Unemployment ... 45 percent: estimate of South Central Organizing Committee in 1988, quoted by Mike Davis, *City of Quartz* (New York: Verso, 1990), 321; *Village Voice,* April 16, 1991.

Gang killings topped three hundred a year: *LAT,* January 12, 1990; *NYT,* December 9, 1991.

Bell Jet Rangers: *LAT,* April 3, 1988; *LADN,* October 31, 1991.

IN JAIL, IN PRISON, ON PROBATION: Susan Fry and Vincent Schiraldi, "Young African-American Men and the Criminal Justice System in California." Formerly *The National Center on Institutions and Alternatives,* now *The Center on Juvenile and Criminal Justice, October 1990, Page 2.*

$300,000 book advance: *LAT,* December 28, 1990.

"Hunter": author's observations; *NYT,* March 26, 1991.

Nancy ... cokeheads: *LAT,* April 7, 1989.

74 percent ... approved: Bill Boyarsky, "Governing," *LAT,* December 1988.

PART 2—PEORIA WITH PALMS

CHAPTER 1: The Past Meets the Future

1937 shooting exhibition/shooting demos since 1929: Kinsling; Dircks, *LAT,* September 30, 1931. Much of the material in this chapter regarding Davis, marksmanship, and the Academy derives from the interviews with Kinsling and Dircks. Additional sources follow:

DAR meetings: Borough, 8.

Five feet seven inches: Lester.

"Fighting Bob" Shuler: Henstell, 50.

"Distinguished expert": LAPD Historical Society.

Depression vagrants: Charles Davis.

Two-by-twelve-inch board: Ed Davis.

Academy via Chavez Ravine: Sheldon.

Red Squad "lawless and brutal": ACLU *Open Forum,* July 7, 1934; Woods, 244.

Harold Story: Gottlieb and Wolt, 199.

"Citizens of economic value": *LAR,* November 16, 1929, September 21, 1938. *Author's note:*

Without the *L.A. Record,* the only populist newspaper at the time in Los Angeles, it would have been virtually impossible to decipher a meaningful account of political events.

Blue-gray eyes, bull neck: Lester; *LAR,* November 29, 1929.

"Even if he hadn't": *LAR,* November 29, 1929.

"Throw up his hands": ACLU *Open Forum,* July 7, 1934.

Elysian Park: *LAT,* June 29, 1949; *LAPD Comm;* Sheldon.

Five feet ten inches: Lester.

"Put himself through law school": *LAPD Comm;* Sheldon.

CHAPTER 2: Fighting Bob's People

1923 protest by Shuler and Briegleb: *LAR,* June 12, 1923.

Born in a log cabin: Henstell, 50; Woods, 141; McWilliams, 343; *LAT,* September 12, 1965.

Shuler's magazine: Henstall, 50.

St. Paul's Church: *LAT,* August 24, 1937, May 22, 1943.

Regulate public dancing: Woods, 140–41.

Duncan barred: *LAR,* November 21, 1922.

Lysistrata: LADN, January 26, 1922.

Purity squad: Henstell, 49.

Tenderloin: Interview with William Mason, Curator of History, Los Angeles County Museum of Natural History, Summer 1992.

Arriving in earnest in 1883: McWilliams, pp. 150–164; Mike Davis, *City of Quartz* (New York: Verso, 1990), 111.

Ticket prices one dollar: McWilliams, 88.

1887, one hundred thousand tourists: Davis, op. cit., 111.

"Least heroic migration": McWilliams, 150.

"White spot": McWilliams, 293.

Volstead Act: Woods, 69n.

"Tracking down candy machines": Woods, 90.

William Huntington Wright: McWilliams, 158.

Fatty Arbuckle: *LAT,* August 31, 1992; Carl Sifakis, *Encyclopedia of American Crime* (New York: Facts on File, n.d.), 29.

Pueblo with population of about fifteen hundred: Zena Pearlstone, *Ethnic L.A.* (Beverly Hills, Calif.: Hillcrest Press, 1990), 98.

Chinatown Massacre: Caroline Gabard, "The Development of Law Enforcement in Early Southern California" (master's thesis, University of Southern California, 1960), 150–51; *LAT,* May 24, 1992; Robert Eshman, "The 'Macher' Who Tamed L.A.," *Los Angeles,* November 1991, 76–88.

Full-fledged in 1877: Eshman, op. cit.

Widespread corruption scandals: Sifakis, op. cit., 24.

Taking of payoffs ... inevitable: Woods, 24; *LAR,* March 16 and August 6, 1920.

Source Notes

The department's dual allegiance: This analysis, like much of the department's early history, is based on Joseph Gerald Woods's extraordinarily insightful 1973 doctoral dissertation.

CHAPTER 3: San Francisco Blues

First in vigilante excess/highly unionized: McWilliams, 275–76; Mike Davis, *City of Quartz* (New York: Verso, 1990), 25.

Marietta, Ohio: David Halberstam, *The Powers That Be* (New York: Alfred A. Knopf, 1979), 147; author interview by telephone with Tim Knight, archivist for the *Los Angeles Times,* February 1994.

Harry Chandler: Gottlieb and Wolt, pp. 121–26, Halberstam, op. cit., 152.

Had city charter changed: McWilliams, 13.

"Connected to vast trade": Mike Davis, op. cit., 113.

1890, 20 percent wage cut: Halberstam, op. cit., 155–56.

Merchants and Manufacturers (M&M)/law curtailing: McWilliams, 281.

Red Flag Law: McWilliams, 287.

Twenty *Times* employees: *A Chronological History of the Los Angeles Times,* issued by Los Angeles Times History Center. Gottlieb and Wolt, 85.

McNamara brothers: Geoffrey Cowan, "The Trials of Clarence Darrow," *Los Angeles Times Magazine,* May 16, 1993, 26ff.

"Last citadel": McWilliams, 293.

Haymarket Square, 1886: Donner, 364.

Doubled to five hundred: Woods, 41; *LAPD Comm.*

Files on three hundred thousand people: LAPD, *Annual Report of the LAPD, 1913. Author's note:* According to the report, over 290,000 records of criminals are contained in the Bertillon cards.

"Strong-arm Squad": Woods, 73.

CHAPTER 4: The Company Man

James Davis arrived 1911: *LAR,* December 2 and 3, 1929.

Davis birth and childhood: *LAR,* November 29 and 30, 1929.

"One small sin": Charles Davis, May 1, 1992.

Within month: *LAR,* December 3, 1929.

No written exam: Dircks.

Two months after arrival/early employment with LAPD: *LAR,* December 3, 1929.

Returned to Los Angeles, 1912: Woods, 211.

"I determined at that time": *LAR,* December 3, 1929.

Chicken-fried steak: Dircks: Charles Davis.

Vice squad: *LAR,* December 4, 5, 7, and 9, 1929.

Edna Kline: *LAR,* December 4, 1929.

Salary never exceeded $100: *LAR,* December 12, 1929; Sjoquist.

$600 lot in Silverlake: *LAR,* December 4, 1929; Charles Davis.

Lived there rest of their lives: Dircks; Charles Davis.

By the end of 1914: *LAR,* December 5, 7, and 9, 1929.

Earle Kynette: Harrison; Gottlieb and Wolt, 223; Donner, 62.

Would be chosen: Harrison, Washington.

Armory on Jefferson Boulevard: *LAPD Comm.*

Albert Marco: Woods, 261; *LAPD Comm.*

Nine hundred new men: *LAR,* December 17, 1929; Woods, 202.

Reaching about 1.5 million: Population was 1,238,048, according to U.S. Bureau of the Census, *Fifteen Census,* 1930.

Picking up the payments: Harrison; Washington.

One fifteen-month period: Woods, 149. *Author's note:* In 1931, the *L.A. Record,* ran a series of articles on LAPD officers being fired for brutality and rehired, and on ''cossackism'' throughout the 1920s. See in particular July 28 and July 30, August 8 and August 15, 1931.

Milton B. ''Farmer'' Page . . . Jack Dragna: *LAR,* August 4, 5, and 21, 1926; Charles Rappleye and Ed Becker, *All-American Mafioso* (New York: Doubleday, 1991), 47; Woods, 233.

''Swaggering, more or less insolent'': Gottlieb and Wolt, 198.

''The place to get action'': Woods, 233.

''His man Cryer in office'': *LAR,* November 15, 1929.

Charlie Crawford, a local saloon owner: Rappleye and Becker, op. cit., 46.

Ganz, McAfee, ''Listen to the Mockingbird'': Henstell, 47; Rappleye and Becker, op. cit., 47.

Marco who ran . . . prostitution: Woods, 110.

Began to challenge: LAPD, *Gangland Killings, Los Angeles Area, 1900–1951* (Los Angeles: LAPD, 1951), 2–5; Rappleye and Becker, op. cit., 46–49.

Central City Jail: Sjoquist, p. 244; Starr, p. 170; *LAR,* March 24, 1929; December 13, 1929; Woods, p. 230.

Tony Cornero paid out $100,000: Woods, 237; *LAR,* August 7, 1925.

Added eight hundred: *LAPD Comm;* Lester; Starr, 172.

CHAPTER 5: The Survivor

Banquet: *LAR,* March 19, 1926.

Four hundred thousand new people: Starr, 135.

Preeminent member . . . land baron: Gottlieb and Wolt, 151, 396–97; Joan Didion, ''Letter from Los Angeles,'' *New Yorker,* February 26, 1990, 87–88.

Board of directors: Gottlieb and Wolt, pp. 396–97; Mike Davis, *City of Quartz* (New York: Verso, 1990), 114; Leader, 31.

Guy Barham . . . Rufus B. von Kliensmid: *LAR,* March 19, 1926; Woods, 242.

''Gun Squad'': *LAPD Comm.*

''Refusal of brother officers'': *LAR,* December 23, 1929.

Mexican *federales:* Charles Davis.

"Davis quite honestly": *LAR*, May 11, 1929.

Fingerprinting: Lester; Woods, 246.

"Suspicious characters"/Glendale and Beverly: *LAR*, December 14, 1929.

"Today the public": *LAR*, December 5, 1929.

Carl Jacobson: *LAR*, August 6, 1927; Woods, 252.

Callie Grimes, Frank Cox: Woods, 253

The man he finally chose: Harrison; Woods, 261; Donner, 62.

Marco indicted and convicted: *LAPD Comm;* Woods, 264.

Walter Collins: *LAR*, September 17, 19, 21, and 22, 1928; November 16, 1929; August 5, 1931; Henstell, 51; Woods, 249.

"Bathhouse" McDonald: *LAR*, October 2, 1929; November 16, 19, and 20, 1929; *LAPD Comm;* Woods, 109, 265.

"Incompetent and unqualified": *LAR*, December 14 and 26, 1929.

McDonald himself named: *LAPD Comm; LAR*, November 18, 1929; Woods, 265.

Demotion to deputy chief: *LAR*, December 30 and 31, 1929; Woods, 268; Sjoquist, 231.

Roy "Strongman Dick" Steckel: *LADN*, January 1, 1930; *LAR*, January 1, 1930.

Venice Beach shooting: *LAR*, January 1, 1930; Harrison.

John Porter ... to victory: *LAPD Comm;* Woods, 264; Leader, 24.

Refused to toast: Lester.

Stop all traffic: Woods, 298.

Frank Shaw: Harrison; Woods, 315; Gates, *Chief,* 28.

"Good care of his friends": interview with Frank Shaw, cited in Caplan, 9.

Investigating the food service: interview with John Anson Ford, cited in "Report on Food Service at the General Hospital," November 10, 1934, cited in Caplan, 3; Gottlieb and Wolt, 222.

"Local political figures": *LADN*, August 5 and 9, 1933; December 12, 1933.

"That jobs paid for": *LAT*, June 1, 1933.

Times would keep: Gottlieb and Wolt, 194, 220-22.

CHAPTER 6: Bum Blockades

Jobless rate of 25 percent: *LAPD Comm.*

Seven hundred thousand ... off trains: William Manchester, *The Glory and the Dream* (Boston: Little, Brown & Co., 1973), 21.

Thirty-nine states ... residency requirements: Lester Chandler, *America's Greatest Depression, 1929–1941* (New York: n.p., 1970), 47, cited in Leader, 196.

"Invading hordes": *LAT*, February 8, 1936.

"This transient thing": cited in Leader, 195.

"All-Year Club"/"sleep under a blanket": Norman M. Klein and Martin J. Schiesl, eds., *20th Century Los Angeles* (Claremont, Calif.: Regina Books, 1990), 7.

One hundred thousand destitute, seventy thousand to Los Angeles: Chandler, op. cit., 47.

"As illegal as hell": Caldwell.

"The refuse of other states": Woods, 342.

The bum blockade: *LADN*, February 4, 7, and 8, 1936: *LAT*, February 4, 7, and 8, 1936; Leader, 204, 206, 212.

"Tangled other-world"/"flying squadron": *LADN*, February 7 and 8, 1936; *LAT*, February 7 and 8, 1936.

"Let's have more outrages": Woods, 343.

"A report on the effects": Caldwell.

Fourteenth Amendment: *LADN*, February 7, 1936.

25 percent drop in purse snatchings: *LAT*, February 13, 1936.

"Launched the first war on bums": Leader, 207.

William H. "Red" Hynes: Hannah Bloom, "The Passing of 'Red' Hynes," *The Nation*, August 2, 1952, 91–92; *LAT*, May 18, 1952.

IWW: *LAT*, May 18, 1952.

Hynes . . . provided the key testimony: *LAT*, December 2, 1943; Bloom, op. cit.; Borough, 221–22.

"Of sedition and treasonable activities"/House Special Committee: Donner, 59–60.

Sold embarrassing information: Dircks.

"Primitive or even savage": *LADN*, February 19, 1934.

Wirin . . . sued officials: *LADN*, January 26, 1934.

"The 'mysterious' documents"/other efforts against labor: *LAR*, August 7, 1929; ACLU *Open Forum*, October 2 and November 7, 1931, January 30, March 19 and 26, April 16, and December 10, 1932, January 31, 1933, July 7, 1934; Woods, 293.

"Shove Days": McWilliams, 291.

"Side by side": Jerome Hopkins, "Our Lawless Police," ACLU *Open Forum*, November 24, 1931.

Pasadena to break up meetings: Woods, 296; ACLU *Open Forum*, January 30, 1932.

Refuse to allow the Reds: ACLU *Open Forum*, December 10, 1932.

"The damnable vilification": *LAR*, October 30, 1931.

"You'll learn pretty soon"/Gallagher/Communists on the floor: Bloom, op. cit.

Quarter of America's workforce: *LAPD Comm.*

"Bunch of bums": Woods, 294.

Three hundred thousand unemployed . . . 1933: Gottlieb and Wolt, 205.

Wagner Act: Woods, 166; Gottlieb and Wolt, 204; Bloom, op. cit., 91; Dircks.

Harry Bridges: *LADN*, July 18, 1934.

Thirty-seven thousand longshoremen: *LADN*, May 10, 1934.

Union membership sixty-five thousand: Leader, 169.

Upton Sinclair: *LADN*, February 2 and November 7, 1934.

"Revolution": *LADN*, February 2 and November 7, 1934.

CHAPTER 7: Clark Kent

1938 International Pistol Matches: Lester; Dircks.

January 14, 1938; Woods, 358; Lester; Caplan, 59.

Harry Raymond ... Mary Pickford ... Carl Jacobson: Marvin Wolf and Katherine Mader, *Fallen Angels* (New York: Ballantine Books, 1986), 151–52; Borough, 224; Gottlieb and Wolt, 55–56; Woods, 357; Caplan, 58.

CIVIC: Woods, 252, 261, 357, 365; *LAPD Comm;* Wolf and Mader, op. cit., 151; Webb, 247; *LAR,* January 28, 1920.

Campaign aide ... into crisis: Caplan, 6–8, 14; radio broadcast by CIVIC Committee, February 28, 1938, cited in Caplan, 83–84.

Federation/Clinton: Caplan, 2–4, 7, 19–20, 23, 83; Wolf and Mader, op. cit., 150, 173; Gottlieb and Wolt, 222; Caplan, 19–20; Woods, 350.

"Shaw spoils system": *LADN,* February 9, 1934; Borough, 200; *LAPD Comm.*

Joe Shaw ... John Rosselli: Henstell, 54; Harrison; Wolf and Mader, op. cit., 150; *LAPD Comm;* Lester.

Old guys ... Crawford: LAPD *Gangland Killings, Los Angeles Area, 1900 1951* (Los Angeles: LAPD, 1951), 19; Charles Rappleye and Ed Becker, *All-American Mafioso* (New York: Doubleday, 1991), 86–87.

Pete Del Gado: Dircks; Caldwell; Dederick; Woods, 382; Wolf and Mader, op. cit., 153.

"Sunny Jim" Bolger: Caplan, 14 (see also part 3, chapter 1)

Exams ... for $500: Gates, *Chief,* 28.

Motorcycle meant $25/other corruption: Lester; Sheldon; Kinsling; Sullivan; Sjoquist, 234;Woods, 383.

"Organized racketeering": *LADN,* February 21, 1936; *LAPD Comm.*

The old syndicate guys: *Gangland Killings,* op. cit., 19–20, 26; Rappleye and Becker, op. cit., 81 88.

"Floppers": Woods, 355; Borough, 214.

$10,000 in improvements: Gottlieb and Wolt, 222; Clifford Clinton, cited in Caplan, 22.

"Forthright action": Borough, 209; Woods, 380

As they made their raid: Caplan, intro. and 43; *LAPD Comm;* Woods, 352.

Issued subpoenas: Rappleye and Becker, op. cit., 86; *Hollywood Citizen News,* October 14, 1937.

Les Bruneman: *Gangland Killings,* op. cit., 20; Rappleye and Becker, op. cit., 84–86; Woods, 352, 356.

Vital positions: *Los Angeles Grand Jury Minority Report,* cited in Caplan, 46–47.

Lukewarm support: *LAT,* September 16, 1938; Gottlieb and Wolt, 109, 224–25.

Petitions ... circulated: Borough, 239; radio broadcast, February 28, 1938, cited in Caplan, 83–84.

"Keep your mouth shut": *LADN,* April 23 and 27, 1938; L.A. *Examiner,* May 18, 1938; L.A. *Examiner,* May 6, 1938, cited in Caplan, 31; Gottlieb and Wolt, 223; Borough, 224.

"To check on the activities of": L.A. *Examiner,* May 18, 1938.

"Buron Fitts": Caplan, 68.

"A debris of words": Woods, 361; Caplan, 70.

"Not sufficiently clear": *LADN,* April 27, 1938.

Guilty verdict ... returned to duty: *LAT,* June 28, 1938.

Or abolish the Red Squad: Harlan Palmer, cited in Caplan, 110.

Forced into retirement: Lester.

Twenty-three high-ranking: *LAT,* May 24, 1992; *LAPD Comm;* Sjoquist, 236; Harrison; Dircks.

Married well: Dircks; Woods, 382.

Abolished 1938: *LAT,* December 2, 1943; Hannah Bloom, "The Passing of 'Red' Hynes," *The Nation,* August 2, 1952, 91–92.

Douglas Aircraft ... Biltmore: Dircks: *LAT,* June 21, 1949.

"Dominated by women": Charles Davis.

PART 3–THE GODFATHER AND THE SUBVERSIVE

CHAPTER 1: The Godfather and the Subversive

Seventy-eight: *LAT,* September 3 and November 29, 1940.

Copyrighted badges: *LADN,* September 8, 1990.

Five thousand applicants: Reddin.

Protective League activist: Sullivan; O. W. Wilson, ed., *Parker on Police* (Springfield, Ill.: Charles C. Thomas Publisher, 1957), xi.

"You don't hit him in here": Washington.

"The most lawless nation on earth": *L.A. Daily Journal,* November 2, 1950.

"Man the most predatory": *LAT,* July 17, 1966.

"The nigger inspector": so-called by the LAPD officers because his rank was inspector and he worked primarily in the black community.

Tom Reddin: Jim Fisk.

UCLA quarter miler: *LAT,* October 1, 1991.

"Statuesque": Ed Davis; Sullivan; Reddin; Payne and Ratzan, 51; Narvid.

Four children ... weight of the cotton sack: Galm, 5; Payne and Ratzan, 4.

No diners would serve them: Payne and Ratzan, 6.

Crenner Hawkins/Bradley's upbringing: Galm, 15–17, 47, 50.

"In my neighborhood": *LAT,* January 26, 1986.

Polytechnic High: Galm, 25.

440 dash, All City Tackle: Galm, 23.

"Like a pink poodle": Marshall Frady, "The Children of Malcolm," *New Yorker,* October 12, 1992, 64–81.

Boys League/"cleanliness": Galm, 27.

"You could know": Narvid; Cunningham.

"Even in high school": *LAT*, October 21, 1982.

"Realistic about being a nigger": Frady, op. cit.

"Just break your heart"/scholarship/patrolman's exam: Galm, 12, 24, 39.

Dr. Vance: Brewer; Dederick.

"We can't take you": Galm, 43; Payne and Ratzan, 34.

Parker ... Lead ... Deadwood: Webb, 245; *L.A. Police Beat,* September 1966.

"Was buried in same cemetery": *L.A. Daily Journal,* December 29, 1952; April 24, 1959.

"One of the great frontier"/altar boy: Webb, 245–46.

"Display lingerie": *L.A. Police Beat,* September 1966.

"Less excuse": Wesley Marx, "Parker: The Cop as Crusader," *Los Angeles Magazine,* August 1962, 19–20, 47–48.

Moved ... 1923: *L.A. Daily Journal,* December 29, 1952; *LAT,* July 17, 1966; *The Eight Ball* (publication of the Los Angeles Press Club), March 1966.

Los Angeles College of Law: *L.A. Police Beat,* September 1966; LAPD biographical profile on Parker (LAPD Library); *L.A. Daily Journal,* December 29, 1957.

$225 a month: *L.A. Daily Journal,* December 29, 1957.

Obstinate: Kinsling: Jim Fisk; Ed Davis; Dircks.

Miss about fifteen/shared suite with "Sunny Jim": Lester.

Fishing trips: Ed Davis.

First teethed on political: Woods, 280–81, 421; Sheldon.

Section 202 ... trial board: City Charter amendment, 1925.

1931 ... "right": City Charter amendment, 1931.

1934, 1937, Earle Cooke ... rewrote: City Charter amendment to section 202, 12a, 1934; Wilson, op. cit.; *LAPD Comm; Police Commission Report 200;* Sheldon; Woods, 283.

Names from box ... free from chief's discipline: City Charter amendment, section 202, part 6.

"Substantial property right": City Charter amendment; *Police Commission Report 200.*

Chief would be entitled: *RIC,* 187.

If a chief were fired: City Charter amendment, section 202.

Captain in Europe: *L.A. Police Beat,* September 1966.

Purple Heart: According to Ed Davis, Parker suffered a shrapnel wound in the buttocks.

Brenda Allen: Sjoquist, 241.

Became lovers: Sheldon; Woods, 406.

Horall ... not sophisticated: *LAPD Comm;* Schiesl, 154; Woods, 385, 408; Dederick; Sullivan.

Elizabeth Short: Marvin J. Wolf and Katherine Mader, *Fallen Angels* (New York: Ballantine Books, 1986), 203–04; Sjoquist, 256–58.

IATSE: Denise Hartsough, "Crime Pays: The Studios' Labor Deals in the 1930s," 49–63, and Larry Ceplair, "A Communist Labor Organizer in Hollywood: Jeff Kibre Challenges the IATSE, 1937–1939," 64–74, both in *The Velvet Light Trap* (Austin: University of Texas Press, 1989).

Closed them down in 1939: *LAT,* November 17, 1991.

Source Notes

Head and neck splattered: LAPD, *Gangland Killings, Los Angeles Area, 1900–1951* (Los Angeles: LAPD, 1951), 26; Dennis Eisenberg, Uri Dah, and Eli Landau, *Meyer Lansky: Mogul of the Mob* (New York: Paddington Press, 1979), 239.

Ties to sheriff's department: Nick Tosches, *Dino* (New York: Dell Publishing, 1992), 270.

Protected gambling ring/betting markers: Jim Fisk; Woods, 398.

160 agents ... $7 million annually: *LADN,* June 15, 1949; L.A. *Evening Herald & Express,* December 8, 1949; Woods, 401–03.

Bowron had been mayor: Leader; Schiesl, 154.

Forced the resignation: Schiesl, 155.

Personal stamp: Sheldon; Reddin; Woods, 409.

Intelligence squad: Jim Fisk; Webb, 249.

How strongly the chief wanted to pursue: *LAT,* December 18, 1977.

Any complaint of misconduct: Woods, 411; LAPD Public Affairs, March 10, 1994.

Three top-scoring/"A piss-poor one": Lester.

Thad Brown: *LAPD Comm;* Reddin; Sullivan; Dederick; Dircks; Lester.

Stable of informants: Reddin.

Commission was divided: Woods, 418; *LAT,* August 3, 1950.

"With his knife out": Sullivan; Webb, 250–51.

Refused ... integration: Brewer.

1949 ... Rocky Washington: Washington.

"All the fiber": *LAT,* August 3 and 9, 1950; July 17, 1966.

Dinner and drinks: Sullivan.

CHAPTER 2: The Grip

He would take it: Ed Davis.

"Daily Training Bulletin": Ed Davis; Sheldon; Sullivan; Jim Fisk; Dederick; Woods, 426–27.

Table ... USC: *LAT,* August 16, 1967; Ed Davis.

Dyer ... "average man": *LAT,* December 18, 1977; Ed Davis.

Reduced people reporting from fourteen to eight: Woods, 425; *LAPD Comm.*

Plotted the sick days: Ed Davis.

Streamlining booking: Woods, 427–28; Gates, *Chief,* 270–71.

1953 ... deaths dropped: LAPD, *LAPD Annual Report, 1953* (Los Angeles: LAPD, 1953).

Fifteen thousand jaywalking tickets: Sullivan.

"Or they don't ride bikes": *LAPD Comm.*

Dart throwers arrested: *LAT,* March 21, 1991.

Professionals: Schiesl, 155.

1956 ... best-paid: Domanick 6.

Ten-point bonus: Pavelic.

Height requirement: Murdock.

Frank Walton ... Merrill Duncan ... Pappy Boyington: Sullivan.

"Permissive": Reddin.

Addressed by your title: Dotson.

Five thousand men ... 450 square miles: *LAT,* October 14, 1986.

"Proactive policing": Schiesl, 155.

"Someone looked out of place": Gates, *Chief,* 34.

Arrest 220,000/twice the number: radio broadcast by Bill Parker, KFI, June 2, 1957.

Couple of drunks: Dotson.

Seventeen-helicopter ... Air Support Division: *LAT,* March 7, 1988; *LADN,* May 16, 1987, April 3, 1988, October 31, 1991.

"Who aren't joggers": *LAT,* April 3, 1988.

No longer would it be legal: Dotson.

Charles Cahan: L.A. *Herald-Express,* March 7, 1961; *L.A. Daily Journal,* November 7, 1955; Webb, 260–61.

Exclusionary rule: Woods, 453; Gates, *Chief,* 258–59.

"A death warrant": Woods, 454.

"Could not believe": White.

"Find the best way": Dotson.

"National conspiracy": Schiesl, 159.

"Entire essence": White.

"If you'd gone": Fyfe.

"West Point": Woods, 429.

CHAPTER 3: The Mythmakers

Much of the information in this chapter derives from the author's interviews with Stanley Sheldon. Other sources for particular passages are cited below.

Nancy Davis: Stephanie Salata, public affairs officer, Ronald Reagan Library, Simi Valley, California.

MGM publicity people: *San Diego Tribune,* June 28, 1985; *LADN,* July 20, 1953, cited in Woods, 604.

"They haven't been out there": *San Diego Tribune,* June 28, 1985.

Star-studded stage shows: program of the Eighteenth Annual Los Angeles Police Show, May 1–14, 1952.

"Stirring patriotic prologues"/song lyrics: police-show program, op. cit.

Its own movies: L.A. *Evening Herald & Express,* March 5, 1942.

Reshape the ... image: Dederick.

Insurance industry: Jim Fisk.

Motors on Parade: William Stull, "Police Make Films to Teach Traffic Safety," *American Cinematographer,* July 1942, 316, 326.

Second only to agriculture: McWilliams, 339.

Twenty-five national radio shows: McWilliams, 340–41.

Distorted the record: David Halberstam, *The Powers That Be* (New York: Alfred A. Knopf, 1979), 117.

Erroll Flynn/Howard Hughes/Busby Berkeley: Dederick.

Stopped a prominent person: Rothmiller interview.

All criticism of the FBI: Curt Gentry, *J. Edgar Hoover, the Man* (New York: W. W. Norton & Company, 1991).

"Correct standards": Charles Aaronson, ed., *International Motion Picture Almanac 1960* (New York: Quigley Publishing, 1960), 712.

$125 a week: Sheldon.

"He duplicated": *San Diego Tribune*, June 28, 1985; *LAT*, December 18, 1977.

Broderick Crawford: Author interview with John Schultheiss, professor, Department of Radio, Television, and Film, California State University, Northridge, March 20, 1994.

NYPD: Mark Crispin Miller, "Boxed In: The Culture of TV," *NYT*, March 26, 1991.

"You get this through your head": *LAPD Comm.*

By 1953–54 season: Alex McNeil, *Total Television* (New York: Penguin Books, 1991).

"Detrimental": letter from Jack Webb to Chief William Parker, August 4, 1953.

"Except for some deviations": *LAT*, December 18, 1977.

Letter of complaint: letter from Geoffrey M. Shurlock, vice president and director of production code, to Capt. Stanley Sheldon, June 20, 1956.

Felt-lined box: Dederick; Murdock.

The New Centurions/**it weighed:** *LAT*, May 25, 1992.

"Long-bladed knife": Karl Detzer, "Why Hoodlums Hate Bill Parker," *Reader's Digest*, March 1960, 239–45.

Twenty employees: Dederick.

"The Thin Blue Line": *LAT*, December 18, 1977.

An actual set: *LAT*, December 18, 1977.

Wanted Persons . . . Missing Juveniles: Sheldon; McNeil, op. cit.

Real muckraking: Gottlieb and Wolt, 223.

Impossible to have written thesis: Woods, 516.

His job was to manage the news: *LAPD Comm.*

More than twenty-five LAPD police shows: *LAT*, December 18, 1977; *NYT*, March 26, 1991; *Spy*, May 1991.

Local press people: *Los Angeles Enterprise*, June 26, 1970.

CHAPTER 4: Whiter Than White

Fan-tan: Connie G. Bunch, "A Past Not Necessarily Prologue," in Norman M. Klein and Martin J. Schiesl, eds., *20th Century Los Angeles* (Claremont, Calif.: Regina Books, 1990), 113.

Not permitted to teach: *Understanding the Riots.*

In their neighborhood: Galm, 7.

Humanity: Jim Fisk.

Worst of his entire LAPD career: Galm, 40.

Five or six years/"wherever my natural work": Galm, 54, 58.

Zoot Suit: Galm, 86.

Electric red cars: Galm, 88

1920 ... fifteen thousand: Payne and Ratzan, 7.

Two hundred thousand African-Americans: Bunch, op. cit., 115, 117.

1950, more than 170,000: Bunch, op. cit., 119.

Sleepy Lagoon, 110,000 Japanese-Americans: Gottlieb and Wolt, 299.

Turn of the century: Washington.

Forbidden to work together ... motorcycles or accident: Brewer.

"A whole new standard": Galm; Bradley confirmed by fax, March 1994.

"The white law!": Brewer.

"You could send Negro officers": Woods, 46.

2 to 4 percent: *Time*, July 1968; Woods, 459; Galm, 42, 64.

Oscar DePriest: Brewer.

"Blacks couldn't work": Sheldon.

Become ... supporters: Galm, 60

Sentinel, Sun: Sheldon.

First black motorcycle officer: Brewer.

Community organizations: Bradley confirmed by fax, March 1994.

Roddenberry had rented: Sheldon.

CHAPTER 5: The Seven Dwarfs

1957, radio station KMPC: L.A. *Herald-Express*, August 7, 1957; *L.A. Daily Journal*, August 9 and 30, 1957.

Chester Gould: *LAT*, August 8, 1957.

Already started to rival: *LAT*, December 1, 1959; Reddin; Sullivan.

"Crime Center": *LAT*, September 2, 1958.

"Compiler of statistics": *LAT*, December 1, 1959.

"Security reasons": *LAT*, July 18, 1966; *LAPD Comm.*

Thirteen cosponsors: L.A. *Herald-Express*, August 7, 1957; *L.A. Daily Journal*, August 9, 1957.

George Murphy: *L.A. Daily Journal*, August 9, 1957.

"A model for police": *L.A. Daily Journal*, July 30, 1957.

"One of the top"/ninety seconds: *L.A. Daily Journal*, August 9, 1957.

Sun Valley: Sullivan; Murdock.

Parker specials: Kinsling.

"Zoo": Murdock.

Literally carried home: Dotson.

His life was the LAPD: Kinsling; Sheldon.

CHAPTER 6: The Victorian

"To believe that society": *LAT,* May 13, 1962; *L.A. Daily Journal,* July 18, 1961.

"The crime-increase rate": radio broadcast by Chief of Police William Parker, KFI, June 2, 1957.

"Feeding upon": *L.A. Daily Journal,* September 12, 1956.

"The major responsibility": *LADN,* January 21, 1954.

"Crime for a known prostitute"/"policeless state": Woods, 442, 454.

"Most lawless nation"/compiled dossiers: Police Division Municipal Reference Library, Los Angeles.

"Been well noted in the Kremlin": Woods, 455.

"Impotent rubber stamp": Woods, 466.

Five businessmen or lawyers: Woods, 488; Reinhardt.

Granting or rescinding/limo to lunch: Jim Fisk.

"Relied on Parker": *LAT,* July 10, 1991.

"Really didn't have anything": White.

Herbert Greenwood: *LAT,* June 19, 1959.

"We know all about that": L.A. *Herald-Express,* June 19, 1959.

"Rule the force": Woods, 466.

"We don't tell him": *LAT,* June 19, 1959.

CHAPTER 7: The Property of the Chief

"Seen as a gathering": Dederick.

"Soviet-style": Dotson.

"Somebody went to a meeting": Woods, 420, 491.

Small unit: Reddin.

Eighty-four by 1969: *LAT,* December 28, 1975.

Drooling to make: Woods, 446.

Airport Squad: Rothmiller and Goldman, 143–44.

Ethel Narvid: L.A. City Council Index.

Asked . . . to become his deputy: City of Los Angeles, *Administration Code,* vols. 1–2. A council member's deputy must be approved by a vote by the entire city council, or by a special council.

Stanley Mosk: Charles Rappleye and David Robb, "The Judge, the Photos, and the Senate Race," *L.A. Weekly,* March 4–10, 1994, 17–28.

Massive file on Pat Brown: independent interviews with two former Organized Crime Intelligence Division officers, March 22 and 25, 1994 (not for attribution). The officers corroborated one another.

Frank Wilkinson/background: Wilkinson interview.

1951, social activist/ten thousand units of public housing: Frank Wilkinson, "How Integrated Housing in Los Angeles Was Destroyed," *Heritage* newsletter, spring 1991, 5–6. *LAT*, October 18, 1987.

"Creeping socialism": Wilkinson interview, *LAT*, October 18, 1987.

"Adjacent areas": Wilkinson, op. cit., 6.

"Subversive associations"/1953 mayoral campaign: Wilkinson, op. cit., 6.

2 million dossiers: *LAT*, December 28, 1975.

Undercover agents: *LAT*, December 28, 1975; *Municipal Guardian*, September 30, 1962; Jim Fisk.

Secret caches: Rothmiller and Goldman, 11, 106–07, 156; Gates, *Chief*, 72; Dotson; Dircks.

CHAPTER 8: The Betrayer

1959, *Los Angeles Sentinel*: Dederick; Reddin; Kinsling.

"Contacts": *Municipal Guardian*, September 30, 1962.

1.5 million citations: *LAT*, January 8, 1960.

"Hardly a day": *L.A. Sentinel*, August 17, 1961.

"By his public": *L.A. Sentinel*, July 13, 1961.

"Research a complaint": Sheldon.

"Instead of talking": Gates, *Chief*, 66.

"Freedom Award": Woods, 472.

"Some of these people": *LAT*, January 29, 1959.

Christmas Eve of 1951: *LAT*, March 27 and 28, 1952.

Official reprimands: *LAT*, April 23, 1959.

"Vicious physical assaults": *Municipal Guardian*, September 30, 1962.

"Certain racial groups": Webb, 157–58.

"Get rid of Bradley": Kinsling; Gates, *Chief*, 66.

"We oughta"/that man: Reddin.

Remained in Wilshire: *LADN*, September 8, 1990; Payne and Ratzan, 58.

About to finish: Payne and Ratzan, 46.

Lieutenant in 1960: Sheldon; Payne and Ratzan, 55; Galm, 67.

"Very sick": Galm, 68.

Relegated to South Central: Brewer.

Four times/"Lieutenant, have you made captain?": Washington.

"Quietly he sent out the word": Jim Fisk; Woods, 466; Sheldon; Galm, 68.

Family/fraternity: Jim Fisk.

Bradley's reputation: Galm, 68.

"Viewed as": Gates, *Chief*, 66.

Publicly supporting: Galm, 72.

No motel would take him in/other discrimination/running record: *LAT*, October 21, 1982.

"I didn't have the guts": Jim Fisk.

Letters to Gillette: *LADN,* September 8, 1990.

"Like Daddy": *LAT,* October 21, 1982.

CHAPTER 9: Integrating the Garbage

Yorty's background: Jack Langguth, "Yorty's Eye Is on the Big Apple," *New York Times Magazine,* September 17, 1967.

Squeaked into office: Galm, 123.

To the housewives: Galm, 123; Langguth, op. cit., 128.

Promised to integrate: Galm, 123.

Rubber stamp: Schiesl, 157; Woods, 468.

"I wouldn't have faith": L.A. *Herald-Express,* May 24, 1961.

"Perfectly obvious": L.A. *Herald-Express,* June 9, 1961.

"I've survived": *LAT,* June 6, 1961.

"Clarified": *LAT,* June 13, 1961.

Case bulging: Woods, 467; Reddin.

Lover of . . . Dorothy Healy: Woods, 359.

"Not take Kennedy": Payne and Ratzan, 93; Langguth, op. cit., 122.

"Red-baiter": Borough.

"Mayor going to work"/"get something on Otis": Reddin.

CHAPTER 10: The Black Nirvana

"Growing hostility": Galm, 127.

Speedy Curtis: Galm, 99–100; *LAHE,* May 5, 1965. After Bradley had made various charges against the LAPD as a councilman, a "stinging" seven-page public reply to Bradley's charges was issued by police-commission president Dr. Francisco Bravo, who "suggested," according to the *Herald Examiner,* that Bradley mind his own business.

Comprised one-third/15 percent voters: Galm, 80.

Billy Mills, Gilbert Lindsay/voting as block: Cunningham.

Less than twenty-five years: *Understanding the Riots,* 11.

Gangs . . . low-income housing . . . high school dropout rates: Wanda Coleman, "Voices from the Curfew Zone," *L.A. Weekly,* December 30, 1988–January 5, 1989.

60 percent . . . welfare: *Los Angeles,* September 1965; Schiesl, 163.

Sixty . . . twenty-seven: Gottlieb and Wolt, 376.

Specifically criticized: Woods, 476.

Seventy-five LAPD officers/Muslim temple: Schiesl, 161; *LAT,* August 5, 1962.

"Manufactured incidents": *LAT,* August 11, 1962.

Negro Urban League: Reddin; Gates, *Chief,* 94; Woods, 488.

"No realization": Ed Davis.

CHAPTER 11: Caught Flat-footed

"See that man"/Marquette Frye incident: *LAT*, August 19, 1990.

"Idle hands": *Los Angeles*, September 1965.

Four hundred: Schiesl, 164.

Smashed his baton: *LAT*, August 19, 1990; Woods, 483–84.

Heart aneurysm: *LAHE*, October 7, 1965.

Violent protests: *LAT*, May 11, 1992.

Riot control back then: Reddin.

Seventy-five thousand: Robert Fogelson, *The Los Angeles Riots*, cited in John Gregory Dunne, "Law and Disorder in L.A.: Part Two," *New York Review of Books*, October 24, 1991, 62.

"Like monkeys": Dunne, op. cit., 62; Gottlieb and Wolt, 378; *LAT*, May 25, 1992.

"Fight the riot"/"call me every"/"make up your mind": Reddin.

150 sheriff's: Reddin; *LADN*, May 16, 1992.

"Handcuffed some people": *LADN*, May 10, 1992.

"To pull back": Reddin, *LAPD Comm.*

"Not equipped": Gates, *Chief*, 91.

"Lack of sufficient": *LADN*, May 11, 1992.

Fourteen thousand National Guardsmen: *Time*, July 19, 1968; *LAPD Comm.*

"Burn, baby, burn!": Wanda Coleman, "Voices from the Curfew Zone," *L.A. Weekly*, December 30, 1988–January 5, 1989, 53.

Thirty-four died: *LAT*, May 11, 1992; Woods, 483–84; Schiesl, 164.

Four thousand arrested: Gottlieb and Wolt, 379.

103 LAPD patrol cars: Reddin.

Two weeks afterward: Transcript of "Meet the Press," August 29, 1965; Dunne, op. cit., 63.

45 percent: *LAT*, May 25, 1992; Dunne, op. cit., 62.

CHAPTER 12: Insulting Reactions

"Not yet been established"/"recent public"/"deeply resent"/key recommendation/Billy Mills: *LAT*, February 22, 1966; Galm, 129.

"Legal evidence"/Bradley-Parker confrontation: *LAT*, September 15, 1965.

"Two or three votes": Galm, 129.

"For his conduct": *LAT*, March 29, 1966.

"Seeds of disaster": Galm, 145.

"Irritates me": Ed. Donald Freed et al., *The Glass House Tapes* (New York: Avon, 1976), 418.

John A. McCone/limousine: *LAT*, May 11, 1992.

"Existing breach": *LAT*, May 11, 1992; Schiesl, 165.

"Economic conditions": *LAT*, May 25, 1992.

150 American cities: *LAT*, May 11, 1992.

Kerner Commission/"two societies": *NYT*, May 8, 1992.

"Walk out of a party"/seventy-five thousand wrote: Jack Langguth, "Yorty's Eye Is on the Big Apple," *New York Times Magazine*, September 17, 1967.

"Urban guerrilla warfare"/"flyspeck"/"highly inflammatory": *LAT*, June 26, 1966.

"Recuperating": *LAT*, July 17, 1966.

Antiriot Act: *LAT*, June 26, 1966.

Protest a speech: Turner, 103.

"Smeared themselves": Langguth, op. cit., 123.

CHAPTER 13: The Legacy

More than one thousand: *LAT*, July 17, 1966.

Replete with glowing: *LAHE*, March 3, 1966; *LAT*, March 3, 1966.

"Holy impatience"/"loss in the sense": *LAT*, December 3, 1965.

"Devoted his life": *LAT*, July 21, 1966.

$13,500 in personal property: *LAT*, July 18, 1966.

"We're on the top": Woods, 494.

"The L.A. cops": *Village Voice*, April 16, 1991.

PART 4–UNDER SIEGE

CHAPTER 1: False Breezes

"Attended college sporadically": "A Very Uncoplike Cop," *Time*, July 19, 1968, 17–19; Reddin.

"Bookish man/a PR man": Yorty.

Attending virtually: "A Very Uncoplike Cop," op, cit., 17.

UCLA called Kosher Canyon: "The Superchief," *West* magazine, *LAT*, June 9, 1968, 11–18.

Becomes a 100 percent: Reddin.

From about 4 to 120: *LAT*, August 17, 1970: Schiesl, 167.

Goddamn headlights: Reddin; Woods, 503.

"Roust anything strange": Gates, *Chief,* 112–14; "The Heir to Red Hynes' Red Squad" in Donald Freed, ed., *The Glass House Tapes* (New York: Avon 1976), 207.

$500,000 for three years/"broaden the base"/SWAT: Reddin.

Gates would claim credit/trained deep in the Valley: Gates, *Chief,* 114–15. *Guns and Ammo*, July, 1975, p. 65.

Detroit and Chicago: Todd Gitlin, *The Sixties: Years of Hope, Days of Rage* (New York: Bantam Books, 1987), 393; John Hersey, *The Algiers Motel Incident* (New York: Bantam Books, 1968).

Symbionese Liberation Army: Gitlin, op. cit., 422; *LAT*, Editorial Library, *Facts on File*, 420; *LAPD Comm*, 130.

Source Notes

"The memory of the fire devouring"/"They were intrepid": Gates, *Chief*, 138–39.

Five thousand volunteers: Galm, 150.

1890s . . . 12 of the 125 Jewish: Robert Scheer, "Line Drawn between Two Worlds," *LAT*, January 30, 1978.

Rabbi Edgar Magnin . . . eighty thousand Jews: Scheer, op. cit., January 29, 1978.

Wooed by Dorothy Chandler: Robert Scheer, op. cit.; Gottlieb and Wolt, 309–17; David Halberstam, *The Powers That Be* (New York: Alfred A. Knopf, 1979), 385–87; Joan Didion, "Letter from Los Angeles," *New Yorker*, April 24, 1989.

"It wasn't a politician's business": *LAT Magazine*, January 19, 1992.

"One of the most satisfying": Galm, 81.

1967 cover story: Jack Langguth, "Yorty Has His Eye on the Big Apple," *New York Times Magazine*, September 17, 1967.

Spent well over two/"Arab leaders"/"wildly racial statements": Langguth, op. cit.

Literally despised": Galm, 121.

"Black racists": *LADN*, May 28, 1991.

"The biggest enemy": "Ask any policeman," editorial, *LAT*, April 11, 1969.

5 percent black: *Time*, July 19, 1968.

"Antipolice": *LAT*, April 10, 1969; editorial, *LAT*, April 11, 1969; Payne and Ratzan, 96.

"Going to make racism"/"state as fact": Payne and Ratzan, 95.

"Bradley Power": Galm, 163; Payne and Ratzan, 102.

"Will you be safe with this man?": Payne and Ratzan, 95.

"The cameras . . . flashing": Payne and Ratzan, 91.

"The election was a victory": Payne and Ratzan, 106.

"We have bad news": Brewer; Galm, 159.

CHAPTER 2: Crazy Ed

"It is well and good": Author's observations, Ed Davis's office, December 18, 1991.

"North Hollywood area": *West* magazine, *LAT*, August 15, 1971, 7.

Edward Levi, Sam Ervin/"no thanks": *LAT*, April 24, 1975.

"Overreaction": *LAT*, September 5, 1975.

"Libertine *Los Angeles Times*": Gottlieb and Wolt, 536.

"To pray for"/"becomes a newspaper": *LAPD Comm*, 135.

"More white people": *LAPD Comm*, 135.

"Perfect operation"/"swimming-pool communists": *West* magazine, *LAT*, August 15, 1971, 7.

"Out of touch": Gottlieb and Wolt, 535.

"Hung at the airport": *LAPD Comm*, 135.

Not able to use radio microphones: Reinhardt.

"More country boy": *LAT*, December 18, 1977.

CHAPTER 3: The Nigger Inspector

"Nigger inspector": Jim Fisk.

Applied for and received financing: Jim Fisk; Reddin; Dotson.

"One thing to be a leper": *LAT,* January 24, 1972.

"Skill and sensitivity": *Los Angeles Sentinel,* August 7, 1969.

"Moving toward solution": *LAT,* January 20, 1966.

From 4 to 120 officers: Jim Fisk.

Did not explode: Ed Davis.

Driving slowly/not only committed: *LAT,* February 26, 1965.

CHAPTER 4: Fear and Loathing in South Central

Here I am, green as hell: Steve Fisk.

"He is facing, daily and nightly": James Baldwin, *Nobody Knows My Name* (New York: Dell Publishing, 1961), 62.

"Most dangerous job on earth/premature cynicism": Wambaugh, cited in John Gregory Dunne, "Law and Disorder in L.A.: Part Two," *New York Review of Books,* October 24, 1991, 62–70.

CHAPTER 5: The Rise of the People Shouters

One police officer and six Muslims shot: Schiesl, 161; Dotson.

"Re-created ... an incident": *LAT,* February 25, 1982.

120 cops killed a year: *NYT,* April 25, 1991.

527 people ... in return: April 25, 1991.

Martin Reiser: Dotson.

"If the trainer is 415": Pavelic.

CHAPTER 6: The Downtown Man

"Be the mayor of all": Payne and Ratzan, 135.

90 percent of the Jewish vote: Weiner; Narvid.

Sheinbaum, Willens, Ziffren, Palevsky: Glam, 170.

Only three buildings fifty stories: *LAT,* September 25, 1992.

"Tendency to scare"/"bless his heart"/"very close to the vest"/ 512 events: *LAT,* April 8, 1989.

Source Notes

PART 5—CIRCLING THE WAGONS

CHAPTER 1: The Master and the Novice

"Tired and ramshackle"/"hands bleeding": Gates, *Chief,* 50.

"It was just devastating": Gates, *Chief,* 80.

"Brimming with competitiveness": Gates, *Chief,* 11.

"Very attractive blonde": Gates, *Chief,* 14.

"Upstreamer"/"likable": Reddin.

None could be taller: Dotson; confirmed by two other LAPD officers (not for attribution).

"Somebody's toady"/"You're on the transfer": Gates, *Chief,* 25–26.

"Golden opportunity": *LAT,* August 16, 1982.

"Totally smitten": Gates, *Chief,* 32.

"Didn't close me off": *LAT,* August 16, 1982.

"Mold somebody": Gates interview.

"Now look at him": Reddin.

"Gates ... noncommittal": Sullivan.

"Stairs became a hazard/Parker's drunkenness": Gates, *Chief,* 32.

CHAPTER 2: The Protégé

Information in this chapter derives substantially from the author's interviews with Stephen Reinhardt and Jim Fisk.

Put off retirement: Reinhardt.

Position of twenty candidates for chief: Reinhardt; Fisk; Niles; Driscoll, Henning; Patterson.

Eliminate ... bruoe . "trust me"; Jim Fisk.

"Don't forget the commitments": Jim Fisk.

"Utmost to get along": *RIC,* 202.

CHAPTER 3: The Killing of Eulia Love

The information and quoted material in this chapter are based upon L.A. Board of Police Commissioners, *The Report of the Board of Police Commissioners Concerning the Shooting of Eulia Love and the Use of Deadly Force* (herein called *Eulia Love Report*), (Los Angeles, October 1979), 1–56; Steven Comus's comprehensive January 23, 1979, lead story in the L.A. *Herald Examiner;* an interview with Jack White; and John Gregory Dunne, "Law and Disorder in L.A.: Part Two," *New York Review of Books,* October 24, 1991.

$69 in arrears: district attorney report, Special Investigation Section Division, case No. 100-2070, April 16, 1979, as cited in Dunne.

Applied to state programs: Cunningham.

Welts and abrasions. district attorney's report as cited by Dunne. The *Eulia Love Report* has "contusion."

Lt. Dan Cooke, "Maybe less need to shoot": *LAT,* 1987.

David Klinger shooting incident: Klinger.

"Who'd been given a gun": Steve Fisk.

Crime rates low in early sixties . . . risen 88 percent: *Time,* July 19, 1968.

Almost 70 percent: Domanick 2.

LAPD in 1975/killed thirty, wounded fifty-one: Domanick 2.

Such items as a liquor decanter: *LAT,* December 16, 1981; March 13, 1987; *LAHE,* April 26, 1982, October 22 and 23, 1986; "The Dead," L.A. *Reader,* August 11, 1980; *New West,* September 26, 1977.

"Shiny object": *LAT,* July 17, 1981.

Martin "Meb" Brantly: *LAT,* November 14, 15, and 27, 1980.

"English was holding": *LAHE,* October 22, 1986; Dotson.

Kenneth Ramirez: *LAT,* October 16, 1980; April 8 and May 2, 1981.

"Doing the chicken": Dotson.

1975 to 1982 LAPD choked fifteen: *LAHE,* April 20 and 26, 1982.

Larry Morris: *LAHE,* April 26, 1982; October 23, 1986.

"Precious quality": letter from Daryl Gates to police commissioners, cited in *LAHE,* October 23, 1986.

Robert Ian Cameron: *LAHE,* April 26, 1982.

CHAPTER 4: The Patsies

"Image of this defenseless": Lalli; Domanick 2.

"I was gonna try": Bellows.

"Could kick our ass": Sappel.

"Gas Bill Tragedy": *LAHE,* January 23, 1979.

1976, Wayne Satz: letter from Wayne Satz, October 1, 1990; Satz.

"The Accountability of the LAPD": Satz; Swanson; Howard Rosenberg, "LAPD Sins Are Old Hat to KABC," *LAT,* August 5, 1991.

"Extremely eager": Rothmiller and Goldman, 85.

Targets with Satz's picture: Satz; Rosenberg, op. cit.

"Patsy for the police": *LAT,* May 24, 1992.

CHAPTER 5: Higbie

The information in this chapter on Chuck Higbie is based on interviews with David Dotson, James Fyfe, civil rights attorneys Stephen Yagman and Hugh Manes, and most especially on Lennie LaGuire and Mark S. Warnick's L.A. *Herald Examiner* profile on October 24, 1986.

Source Notes

"The chief of police says"/"Guardian, so to speak"/"major deity": *LAHE*, October 24, 1986.

Statistics on police shootings: *LAHE*, October 22 and 27, 1986; *LAT*, March 30, 1993.

99 percent of what the LAPD considered: *LAHE*, October 22 and 24, 1986.

"Poetic license"/"civilian did to ... get himself shot": *LAHE*, October 24, 1986.

"In the fifties until 1977": White.

Gates calls Love's death/"tragic" ... sympathetic jury: *LAHE*, October 22, 1986.

James Fyfe: Fyfe.

Van de Kamp ... tea or cookies: *LAT*, October 12, 1980.

William Hall/"in reality that is not done": Paz; *LAT*, May 1, 1991; *LAHE*, May 1 and 12, 1991.

Sixty-three shootings in 1979 ... LAPD killed or wounded: *LAHE*, October 22, 1986; LAPD Public Affairs Office.

"3.0 persons per 1,000"/other statistics: *RIC*, 23–24.

CHAPTER 6: The Macho Men

The sections of this chapter dealing with SIS are based on my interviews with Steve Fisk, David Dotson, and Zvonko G. "Bill" Pavelic, and on David Freed's remarkable investigative piece for the *LAT*, "Citizens Terrorized as Police Look On," September 25, 1988. See also *LAT*, August 16, 1991, March 31, 1992, January 10, 1991, and especially "Police Surveillance Unit Kills Three Robbery Suspects," March 19, 1990.

"What time is it?": Dotson.

"Anything that anyone ... had to say": Dotson.

"In over his head": *LAT*, August 16, 1982.

"Fighting back, taking dominion": Author interview with LAPD officer (not for attribution), December 1989.

"Wanted so badly": Brewer.

"About as low": *LAT*, August 16, 1992.

Never been shot at: *LAT*, August 16, 1992.

One out of three hurt in armed robberies: 1987 U.S. Justice Department survey, cited in *LAT*, September 25, 1988.

SIS killed 23/other shooting statistics: *LAT*, September 25, 1988.

Toni Hyams: *LAT*, September 25, 1988.

"Violate laws guaranteeing": *LAT*, September 25, 1988.

CHAPTER 7: Stop the Band

"Bradley's hatchet man"/"broken down"/"absolutely required"/"Why ... should I go?": *LAT*, August 16, 1982.

"Sometimes very thick skulls"/exempted ... from cuts until 1981: *LAT*, August 16, 1982.

Reduced ... by just 3 percent ... compared to: *LAT*, October 22, 1982.

Source Notes

Approving between 90 percent and 99 percent/Yorty . . . granted: *LAT,* October 22, 1982.

"The worst I've ever seen, disastrous": *LAT,* August 16, 1982.

"We didn't look at reorganization"/"deadly": Dotson; Brewer; transcript of Dotson's testimony before the independent commission (supp. to *RIC*), 8–10; transcript of Brewer's testimony (supp. to *RIC*), n.p.

CHAPTER 8: Form the Wagons

"A siege mentality": *LADN,* April 29, 1991.

Job satisfaction/"breeds out any autonomy": *LAT,* September 20, 1990; Felkenes.

"Cops see themselves": author interview by telephone, April 1991.

Carl McGill . . . "have their own ideas": McGill; *LAT,* September 20, 1990; December 20, 1990; *L.A. Weekly,* March 29–April 14, 1991.

Gomez . . . raised $100,000/"must seek permission": *LAT,* December 31, 1990.

"Differing points of view": Windham.

"Going to advance/Gates clone": *LAT,* August 16, 1982.

Increase the number of females hired/statistics on minorities in LAPD: LAPD, "Sworn Personnel by Rank, Sex, and Ethnicity," March 24, 1991.

"Neither Gates . . . ever dipped": Yaroslavsky, *LAT,* May 8, 1991.

Weren't getting . . . positions in "coveted" units: Hardeman; *LAT,* December 19, 1990, January 24 and November 5, 1991.

CHAPTER 9: Whispers in the Ear of the Chief

April 1975, 2 million dossiers . . . We don't talk about PDID": *LAT,* December 28, 1975.

Coalition Against Police Abuse incident . . . over two hundred in all: Schiesl, 182; *LAT,* December 17, 1984, January 11, 1985; *Philadelphia Inquirer,* June 3, 1993.

They had spied (Roybal, Dymally, Alatorre, Torres, Brown, Van De Kamp): Rothmiller interview; Rothmiller and Goldman, 22–23, 146–48, 156, 171–95.

"I was chairman"/"privy to . . . information": transcript of Brewer's testimony before the independent commission (supp. to *RIC*), 37–38; *LAT,* July 21, 1991.

Weekly intelligence briefing/everything verbal: Dotson, Rothmiller.

"If I really laid it on the line": *LAT,* May 23, 1991; author's observation.

CHAPTER 10: The Boxer

"I don't remember": *LAT,* July 15, 1992.

"Mile of land mines": From the documentary *Police Chiefs,* "POV Series," PDR Productions, New York.

By ordering in SWAT team: *LAT,* September 8, 1990, March 17, 1991.

Source Notes

"A friendly invasion": Bill Boyarsky, "Daryl F. Gates: A Cowboy Cop with a Thoughtful Side Confronts the L.A. of the Eighties," *Governing,* December 1988, 43–47.

1985 Philadelphia bombing of radical organization: "Face the Nation," May 19, 1985.

"Inspiration to the nation": *LAT,* May 23, 1985.

Frustrating first four years/Bella Stumbo: *LAT,* August 15, 1982.

"Not an angry person": as quoted by Lewis S. Snow, consultant to *LAPD Comm.*

When Ed Davis fought: Ed Davis.

Twelve blacks died: *Newsweek,* May 24, 1982.

Dotson saw statistics: Dotson.

"We may be finding ... normal people"/disparaging: *LAT,* May 11 and August 15, 1982; *Newsweek,* May 24, 1982.

CHAPTER 11: The Fear

"Gates for Mayor 198–": *LAT,* August 16, 1982.

Latinos lazy: *LAT,* July 15, 1982, March 17, 1991.

"An Aryan broad": *LAT,* July 24, 1991.

Soviet Jews ... infiltrate: *LAT,* March 17, 1991.

Robert Farrell: Pavelic.

Yaroslavsky/LAPD dossier: *LAT,* April 9, 1981, August 18, 1985; Domanick 4.

Richard Alatorre, Public Safety Committee: Alatorre.

Charles Stewart: Stewart.

CHAPTER 12: The Weepers

Women pushed out ... 70 percent, men thirty-eight percent: *LAT,* November 6, 1982. The dropout rate was among the highest in the country, *LAT,* November 6, 1982.

Dr. Martin Reiser/"not training combat": *NYT,* July 14, 1991; *LAT,* November 6, 1982.

Dotson's philosophy of training: Dotson; *LAT,* March 25, 1992.

Size of physical training staff: *LAT,* November 6, 1982, March 25, 1992; Dotson.

Bob Smitson: Dotson.

CHAPTER 13: Riding Shotgun

Fourteen-foot battering ram/two women ... kids eating ice cream: *LAT,* February 8, 1985.

One-tenth gram cocaine: *Understanding the Riots,* 29, has "only one-tenth of a gram of cocaine"; *LAT,* February 8, 1985, has "only a small amount of marijuana."

PART 6–THE BLOODS AND THE CRIPS

CHAPTER 1: Where Do These Animals Come From?

The story of Jay-Rock and Coco's killing of Erica Johnson is from the author's July 1987 article in *California Magazine* (Domanick 1) and is based on DA transcripts and on interviews with the victim's parents and sister; with friends and associates of the victim and the perpetrators; with LAPD detective Kevin Rogers and members of the LAPD's West Bureau Community Resources Against Street Hoodlums (CRASH) unit; and with Steve Valdivia and Leo Cortez, Community Youth Gang Services members.

The following stories corroborate much of the culture and history of the gangs that appeared in the *California Magazine* piece: *LAT,* November 6, 1987, June 26, 1988, May 13, 1992; *L.A. Weekly,* November 3, 1980, April 22, 1988.

Massive loss of jobs: *L.A. Weekly,* December 30, 1988–January 5, 1989, May 19–25, 1989; Richard J. Riordan, "Rescue Plan for a City at Risk," *LAT,* July 28, 1991; *U.S. News and World Report,* May 11, 1992.

Maravilla . . . batos locos/palabra: Valdivia; Cortez; Duvin; author's observations.

"Gang-related killings" 570, 303 in city: *LAT,* January 12, 1990.

March 1988 cover story: *Newsweek,* March 28, 1988.

"Despite the Los Angeles high-profile gang culture"/under 5 percent of gang members: Jack Katz, "If Police Call It Gang Crime, That Doesn't Make It True," *LAT,* September 28, 1989.

Seven hundred suspects, 75 percent no gang affiliation: *LAT,* October 8, 1988.

1988 . . . more adults in California: "Crime and Delinquency in California," cited in *LAT,* August 9, 1989.

Higher percentages in prison: *LAT,* January 5, 1991.

Prison population statistics: Bureau of Justice Statistics, U.S. Department of Justice, "Prisoners in 1988," *LAT,* February 20, 1990.

Karen Toshima's murder: *LAT,* September 11, 1989.

150 additional, within months 500 more: *LAT,* September 11, 1989; for cost of sweeps, see "Guns, No Butter," *L.A. Weekly,* December 30, 1988.

Huge number of arrests during sweeps: *LAT,* April 12 and 15, 1988, August 20, 21, and October 2, 1989.

"Tag Teams": Steve Fisk; Dotson.

Filed just 103 . . . out of 1,400: *LAT,* April 15, 1988.

"Pick 'em up for anything": *LAT,* April 3, 1988.

Everybody's blessing: *LAT,* April 13, 1988.

Reverend Bob: Dotson; Brewer; Yaroslavsky; *LAT,* June 11 and 15, 1991; transcript of Brewer's testimony before the independent commission (supp. to *RIC*), June 19, 1991, 12; Gates's wife, Sima, regularly attended Grace Community Church, where Vernon preached, *LAT,* June 15, 1991.

"I've spanked boys"/"women's role": *LAT,* May 23, 1991; *Spy,* August 1991, cited in John Gregory Dunne, "Law and Disorder in L.A.: Part Two," *New York Review of Books,* October 24, 1991, 62–70.

Source Notes

"Hard-charging": *LAT,* June 29, 1981.

"I was appalled": Brewer.

1986 end-of-year address/"like having the Marine Corps": *LAT,* December 25, 1986.

"Kind of interesting"/"the guy knows": Gates interview.

Derrick Mims, Augustus Hawkins/"They'll pull you over": Mims.

Rodney Williams: *LAT,* December 16, 1991.

"If you look like a gang member": *LAT,* December 17, 1991.

"Pure and simple": *LAT,* December 12, 1991.

"Declined by almost 40 percent . . . half the peak rate: *NYT,* April 25,1991.

"Based on exposure"/150 percent less likely: William A. Geller, "Don't Multiply the Mixed Messages," *LAT,* July 11, 1991.

Peace officers killed in line of duty: *California Bureau of Criminal Statistics and Special Services,* September 1989.

108 civilians: Los Angeles Police Department statistics, on file in public-affairs office at Parker Center.

"For your average cop": *NYT,* April 25, 1991.

"A long-standing concern": Rathburn.

Bump them back a grade/lose $1,300 per month: Dotson.

"Didn't . . . show courtesy"/Joe Duff, John Mack, Mark Ridley-Thomas: Brewer.

"Gates had built this wall": Dotson.

"Gates kept steering": Dotson.

Dogs bit nine hundred people: *LADN,* May 18, 1991; *LAT,* December 12, 1991.

Philadelphia 20 bites: *LAT,* December 12, 1991; CBS evening news, December 10, 1991.

"The sweetest, gentlest things": *Los Angeles Times Magazine,* February 9, 1992, 23.

"Only bite if attacked": Dotson.

103 cases cost the city over $15,000/"obviously there's a problem": *LADN,* March 25, 1991; the article was based primarily on the "Report of the Chief Legislative Analyst" (City of Los Angeles), March 25, 1991; see also *RIC,* 35–36.

"Years ago when I was": Rathburn.

Twenty-three received "verbal admonishments": *LADN,* March 25, 1991.

Suspended for five days . . . accidentally fired: *LADN,* May 12, 1991.

"The LAPD, which investigates": *LADN,* May 12, 1991.

Ten excessive force cases: *LADN,* May 12, 1991.

$752,000 after they'd sued . . . a fractured skull: *LADN,* September 6, 1991; the article was primarily based on the "Report of the Chief Legislative Analyst," March 25, 1991.

"This is dynamite"/"way light": Brewer.

"Let me talk to Gates": Brewer.

40 percent field department, 36 percent sergeants: *Time,* April 1, 1991.

"Disciplinary problems": *RIC,* 127; *LAT,* September 17, 1991.

"Superaggressive": *LAT,* August 14, 1991, cited in Dunne, op. cit.

Over 80 percent lived outside: *LAT,* March 24, 1994.

"The objective": *LAT,* October 20, 1989.

"Written off": *L.A. Weekly,* March 21–27, 1990.

"Those people have no interest": author interview (not for attribution), winter 1989.

CHAPTER 2: Not White Enough

"My admiration for you" ... **"set himself up":** *LAT,* October 14, 1986, December 14, 1991.

Poverty statistics in South Central/"working-class enclave of light": *L.A. Weekly,* December 30, 1988–January 5, 1989.

Anchor a shopping mall: *LAT,* November 25, 1991.

1985, 70 percent vote for mayor: *LAT,* September 25, 1992.

Highly embarrassing situations: *Los Angeles Times Magazine,* January 19, 1992, October 13, 1991, September 25, 1992.

CHAPTER 3: The Raid on Dalton Avenue

The information in this chapter is based on Joe Domanick, "Police Power: Why No One Can Control the LAPD," *L.A. Weekly,* February 16–22, 1990 (herein Domanick 6); *LAT,* August 5, 1988, January 6, June 23, July 26, August 26, October 2, 1989, December 6, 1990, May 12, 1991; L. A. *Sentinel,* August 11, 1988; *L.A. Weekly,* December 30, 1988–January 1, 1989; author interviews with victims Johnnie Mae Carter, Rhonda Moore, and Tammy Moore; *Onie Palmer, Rhonda Jean Moore et al. v City of Los Angeles et al.,* U.S. District Court, Central District of California, case no. CV 88-06376 RMT (JRX).

"Very, very fine captain": Domanick 6.

Thomas Elfmont/"carte blanche": Domanick 6.

"Sweetheart judge": Dotson.

Larez family incident: Domanick 6; *LADN,* April 2, September 28, 1991; *LAT,* November 30, December 2 and 24, 1988; April 2, 1991.

CHAPTER 4: The Grand Old Man

"Over $11 million in 1990": *LAT,* March 29, 1991.

Gates on casual drug users: *LAT,* September 6, 7, and 8, 1990.

$300,000 book contract: *LAT,* December 28, 1990.

74 percent approval: Bill Boyarsky, "Daryl F. Gates: A Cowboy Cop with a Thoughtful Side Confronts the L.A. of the Eighties," *Governing,* December 1988, 43–47.

Twice the national average/highest number per 100,000/9.2 compared to 5.2: *RIC,* 23.

Major crimes 8 percent: *LAT,* January 10, 1990.

Percent increase in major crimes in 1990/murders up 11 percent robberies up 16 percent: *LAT,* January 8, 1991.

Both risen by 19 percent: *LAT*, January 10, 1990.

"Willie Horton's a monster": Bouza.

Joe Morgan settlement: *Vanity Fair*, August 1991, 168.

Jamaal Wilkes: *LAT*, February 28, 1991.

Eighteen shots killing seventeen-year-old: *LAT*, November 2, 1990.

"Problem of leadership": Yaroslavsky.

"Superior ratings": *RIC*, 203.

"The mayor wanted": *LAT*, October 11, 1990.

Stephen Yslas: *LAT*, November 7, 1990.

Robert Talcott: *LAT*, October 11, 1990.

Melanie Lomax: Lomax.

Stephen "Reinhardt/"bet on Daryl": Reinhardt.

PART 7—CAN'T WE ALL GET ALONG?

CHAPTER 1: The Aberration

Between five and six/liquor store/since they were teenagers: *LADN*, March 6, 1992.

Allen called "Pooh": Owens and Browning, 47. Owens, a former LAPD officer, was the investigator for Rodney King and his attorneys.

Forty-ounce bottle Olde English: LAPD Internal Affairs report, cited by *LAT*, March 21, 1991; *NYT*, March 21, 1991.

Watched basketball: *LAT*, March 10, 1993.

Cruise some girls: *LADN*, March 6, 1992.

Hansen Dam: *LAT*, March 7, 1991.

Speed from 110–15: *LAT*, March 7, 1991.

On parole: *NYT*, March 20, 1991.

Middle-class-suburb Altadena: *LAT*, March 17, 1991.

Two children out of wedlock: Peter J. Boyer, "The Selling of Rodney King," *Vanity Fair*, July 1992, 81.

Maintenance man Ronald King: "didn't have no food": *LAT*, March 17, 1991; Boyer, op. cit., 82.

Serious reading problems: *LAT*, March 17, 1991; King had trouble reading during trial (*NYT*, March 11, 1993).

Crystal Waters had two sons: *LAT*, March 17, 1991.

99 Market, Tae Suck Baik, "open the cash register": *LAT*, March 17, 1991; *NYT*, March 20, 1991. This account closely follows that of the *NYT* and particularly that of the *LAT*, whose reporters Ashley Dunn and Andrea Ford interviewed the grocer for a story that appeared on March 17, 1991. Tom Owens, a former LAPD officer and the private investigator hired by Rodney King and his attorneys, in his book *Lying Eyes* (coauthored with Browning, see abbreviations list at beginning of notes), however, gives a somewhat different account on page 74: "In this complaint to the police, the Korean store-owner alleged King assaulted him when he refused to allow King to pay for cigarettes and soda with food stamps. He told the police King got angry, threw the food stamps down on the counter, opened the cash register, and removed the money. While King was attempting to flee, the store-owner tried to stop him by grabbing a tire iron from under the counter."

"I hit him first": *LAT,* March 17, 1991.

"I have all good time work time": *LAT,* March 17, 1991; *NYT,* March 20, 1991.

Laborer at Dodger Stadium: *LAT,* April 19, 1993.

Locked up: *NYT,* March 10, 1993.

Five hours later, King's blood alcohol under minimum: *NYT,* March 21, 1991.

Legally drunk: *LAT,* March 22, 1991, *RIC,* 8; *LAT,* April 24, 1991.

"When police pull you over, man": Boyer, op. cit., 82.

"I was scared"/"wasn't saying nothing, just driving": *NYT,* March 21, 1991; *LADN,* March 6, 1992; Owens and Browning, 47.

Stop sign at 50 mph: *RIC,* 4.

Ran at least one red: *RIC,* 4.

"Pull over to the right"/"wouldn't get hurt": *LAT,* March 7, 1992.

"Failing to yield": *RIC,* 4.

"In a trance": *LADN,* March 6, 1992.

Code 6/Code 4: *RIC,* 4–5.

Freddie G. still sleeping: *LAT,* March 20, 1991; Owens and Browning, 46.

Seat belt yanked him back in: *RIC,* 6; *NYT,* March 21, 1991.

"Real fast": *LADN,* March 6, 1992.

At least ten officers: *RIC,* 11.

Twenty-seven of them; twenty-three LAPD: *RIC,* 11.

"Five of those officers": *RIC,* 5; *LADN,* July 10, 1991.

"Everybody wants to get there": Reddin.

Parker policy that sergeant had to be there in pursuit situation: Reddin; Owens and Browning, 49.

"Felony kneeling" position: *RIC,* 6.

"they would handle it": *RIC,* 6; *LAT,* March 7, 1992.

"Very muscular"/"very buffed-out"/ "probably an ex-con": *LAT,* March 20, 1992.

Koon fifteen-year veteran: *NYT,* March 19, 1991.

"Disoriented and unbalanced": *RIC,* 6.

"dusted out on the drug"/could turn into the "Hulk": LAPD Internal Affairs report, excerpted in *LAT,* March 21, 1991.

"Glassy-eyed": *LAT,* March 21, 1992.

"Felt enough confidence": *RIC,* 6.

Transvestite: *LAT,* February 3, 1992.

Source Notes

Fifty thousand volts: *LAT*, March 7, 1992.

"Lower California": *LAT*, May 16, 1992.

"How to deal with a PCP suspect": *LAT*, May 16, 1991.

Holding an AK-47, four times, commended by Commission: *LAT*, February 3, 1992; *NYT*, March 19, 1991.

Suspended for five days: *LADN*, February 2, 1992.

"Where you do real police work" ... "shit magnet": *LADN*, February 2, 1992.

"Ideal Catholic family man": *NYT*, March 19, 1991.

"They should know better than to run": *RIC*, 15.

"Moving his feet ... like a pitter-patter": *LAT*, March 7, 1992.

"Parade around": *LAT*, March 10, 1992.

"Grabbed his butt ... sexual encounter": *LAT*, May 16, 1992; *NYT*, May 17, 1992.

"A group beat": *LAT*, May 16, 1992.

Forced him against police car: *LADN*, June 3, 1991.

1989, Castaneda claimed that Powell: *LAT*, July 24, 1991, February 3 and April 20, 1992.

"Serious misconduct": *NYT*, August 16, 1993.

"Prove he was tough": *LAT*, February 3, 1992.

"Treated everybody like crap": *LAT*, February 3, 1992.

"Apply pressure": *LAT*, March 10, 1993.

"Flinched": *NYT*, March 10, 1991.

Fifty thousand volts: *LAT*, March 7, 1991.

Two darts: *RIC*, 6.

"Vibrating" ... "convulsing": *LAT*, March 10, 1992.

"Blood was boiling": *LAT*, March 10, 1993.

"What's up, killer" ... "trying to stay alive": *LAT*, March 10, 1993; *NYT*, March 10, 1993.

"Power swing": *NYT*, March 7 and 10, 1991.

"Rapid succession": LAPD Internal Affairs report, excerpted in *LAT*, March 21, 1991; *LAT*, March 27, 1993; *NYT*, March 10, 1991.

"I saw the blood" ... "I heard the driver": *NYT*, March 27, 1993; *LAT*, March 7, 1992.

"No doubt in my mind": *LAT*, March 30, 1993.

"Struck me": *LAT*, March 7, 1991; *NYT*, March 18, 1991.

Timothy Singer remembered/four or five guns: *LAT*, March 10, 1992.

Taser darts: *NYT*, March 18, 1991.

Did try to run: *NYT*, March 11, 1993.

Josie Morales/"didn't touch": *LAT*, March 7, 1991; *LADN*, July 10, 1991.

"Kicking's not fair": Steve Fisk.

Twenty-four inches long: *NYT*, March 21, 1991.

"Jam your toe": *LAT*, March 10, 1993; *NYT*, March 10, 1993.

"Shocked at the ... chops": LAPD Internal Affairs report, excerpted in *LAT*, March 27, 1993.

Source Notes

"Power strokes": *LAT*, March 7, 1992.

"Comes back and forth": *NYT*, February 2, 1993.

"Prone is safe": *LAT*, February 27, 1993.

"Intent to cripple": *LAT*, March 25, 1993.

"Hit his joints, hit his wrists": *RIC*, 7.

Eighty-one seconds ... fifty-six blows: *LAT*, April 1, 1992; *LADN*, January 26, 1992. Various accounts of the length of the beating have been given, ranging from eighty-one to ninety seconds, depending on the point at which the action on Holliday's tape becomes discernible.

Briseno was suspended: *LAT*, April 20 and 24, 1991; *LADN*, June 3, 1991.

Permanent cracks: *LAT*, March 17, 1991; *NYT*, March 20, 1991.

"Supposed to work": *NYT*, February 2, 1993.

Twenty residents awakened: *NYT*, March 18, 1991.

"Fetal position": *LAT*, April 17, 1991.

"Don't kill him": *NYT*, March 18, 1991.

Dodging blows/"Please stop"/talking and laughing: *LAT*, February 27, 1993.

For fear of being hit: *LAT*, March 21, 1991.

"Facedown": *LAT*, March 7, 1991.

"Grunt": *LAT*, April 17, 1991.

Manager ... Holliday: *NYT*, March 18, 1991; *LAT*, March 7, 1991; *LADN*, March 7, 1991.

"Trigger happy": *LADN*, March 17, 1991.

"Whuppings": *NYT*, March 21, 1991.

"Doing him real bad": *LAT*, April 9, 1991.

"Like bones being cracked": LAPD Internal Affairs report, excerpted in *LAT*, March 21, 1993.

"Somewhere real dark"/Freddie G. kicked: *NYT*, March 21, 1991; Owens and Browning, 46.

"Like your homeboy?"/"whatever was happening": *LAT*, March 20, 1991; *NYT*, March 21, 1991.

Considered first aid: *LAT*, March 30, 1993.

"Need RA at Foothill": *LAT*, March 19, 1991; March 12, 1992; *LADN*, March 12, 1992.

"Big-time use of force": *LAT*, March 20, 1991.

LAPD dispatcher ... FD: *RIC*, 14–15.

Gorillas in the Mist: *RIC*, 14; *LAT*, March 20, 1991.

"Oops": *RIC*, 14; *Time*, April 1, 1991.

"Lack of sensitivity"/broke lip/"don't you guys understand?": transcript of Independent Commission on the Los Angeles Police Department executive session, 21.

"Aberration": *LADN*, March 30, 1991; *NYT*, May 21, 1992.

"All those communications": Ed Davis.

Hog-tied, handcuffed ... "I love you": *LAT*, March 19, 1992; *NYT*, March 18, 1991.

Broken cheekbone: *NYT*, March 20, 1991.

Twenty stitches: *RIC*, 8.

"Game we played": *LADN*, March 14, 1992; *LAT*, March 23, 1991.

Paul King's attempt to register complaint: *RIC*, 9–10.

Eleven skull bones broken: *RIC*, 8; *LAT*, April 24, 1991.

"If there was not a video": *LADN*, May 2, 1991.

"Recovered ... immediately": *RIC*, 9.

"Facial cuts" ... "oblivious to pain": *LAT*, March 20, 1991; LAPD Internal Affairs report excerpted in *LAT*, May 21, 1991; *RIC*, 9.

"Don't roll over": *LAT*, May 31, 1991.

Man on the ground have done: *NYT*, March 7, 1991.

"Low-key, noncomplex"/Cereghino "blown away" by tape: transcript of symposium held at California State University, Northridge, April 29, 1991.

"Pretty much hung up": *LADN*, March 7, 1991.

CHAPTER 2: The Reaction

"Back to the time frame": author's observations, March 5, 1991.

Thousand calls: *LAT*, March 15, 1991.

In a hallway/"What about resigning, Chief?" ... "We regret what took place": *LAT*, March 20, 1991; author's observation of television news broadcast, March 20, 1991.

Ran a piece dripping with contempt: George Will, "Daryl Gates Is the Cop's Own Worst Enemy," *LAT*, March 13, 1991.

Jesse Jackson: *LAT*, March 17, 1991.

Brown ... called on Gates to leave: *LAT*, April 5, 1991.

Urging of ... Black Caucus: *LAT*, March 13, 1991.

L.A. *Times*, *La Opinión*: *LAT*, March 23 and April 5, 1991.

First black woman/"clichés from the files": Domanick 3.

1,100 on the LAPD/150 joined Carl McGill: *LAT*, April 30, 1991.

"I'd felt like the Lone Ranger": Williams.

Hardeman threatened to walk: *LAT*, April 30, 1991.

Did not ... represent/"making him angry"/"I demand to know"/"sacrificed through ... hyperbole"/"if the individual had done": *The Thin Blue Line* (LAPD Protective League), April 1991.

McBride works the crowd at seminar: author's observations, May 24, 1991; McBride.

CHAPTER 3: The Suspension

"Disgraced and defamed": *LAT*, April 5, 1991.

"Great, I mean magnificent": Domanick 8.

"Wasn't for the helicopter"/"Jovial Chief Jokes": *LADN*, April 6, 1991.

Eric Rose: Domanick 8.

Gates-must-go protest: *LAT*, April 7, 1991.

Woo versus Gates: *LADN*, March 28, 1991; *LAT*, March 21, 1991.

Source Notes

"Return to Parker Center": *LAT*, April 4 and 5, 1991; *LADN*, April 5 and 6, 1991, editorial, April 9, 1991; Santa Monica *Evening Outlook*, April 6, 1991.

"Very responsive"/"shocked": *LAT*, September 8, 1990.

"Ability to deliver": Bill Boyarsky, "Why the L.A. City Council Backs Gates," *LAT*, May 22, 1991; author interview (not for attribution).

"Laid the groundwork": Yaroslavsky; Domanick 5.

"Finish our work in ninety days": *RIC; LADN*, July 10, 1991.

Different classes/"let it all hang out": *LAT*, July 12, 1991.

Bostic buttressed Dotson and Brewer/"reoccurring theme"/"light on excessive force": *LAT*, July 10, 1991.

"Really trying to atone": *L.A. Weekly*, July 19–25, 1991.

Interviewed almost eight hundred: *RIC*, appendix 2, 1; *LADN*, July 10, 1991.

"The commissioners . . . shifted that day": *L.A. Weekly*, July 19–25, 1991.

CHAPTER 4: The Trial

Four officers indicted: *LAT*, April 24, 1991; April 30, 1992; *NYT*, April 30, 1992.

Gates had recommended: *LAT*, March 15, 1991.

Grand jury decided: *LAT*, May 11, 1991, *NYT*, May 11, 1991.

Judge denied request to move trial: *LAT*, June 24, 1991.

"Tape . . . makes this case": *NYT*, May 16, 1991.

Letter to appellate court/"100 percent" certain/"Don't panic": *LAT*, June 21 and August 22, 1991.

As a consequence of: *LAT*, February 4, 1992.

Weisberg replaced Kamins: *LAT*, November 23, 1991.

"So extensive and pervasive": *LADN*, July 24, 1991.

Two other changes of venue/"is it necessary to move": *LAT*, July 25, 1991.

"The focus of the court": *LADN*, November 27, 1991.

Four thousand law enforcement officers: *LAT*, February 4, 1992; *U.S. News and World Report*, May 11, 1992.

More members of the LAPD: Sally Ogle Davis, "The Last Angry Woman," *Los Angeles*, July 1992, 68ff.

Three hundred LAPD in Simi Valley: *LAT*, March 29, 1994.

Almost 70 percent white in Ventura County: U.S. Bureau of the Census, 1990 (Washington: GPO); *LADN*, November 27, 1991; *LAT*, February 4, 1992; *U.S. News and World Report*, May 11, 1992. *Author's note: LAT*, May 4, 1992, lists ethnic breakdown of Los Angeles County, quoting the 1990 census, as 66 percent white, 26 percent Latino, 5 percent Asian, and 2 percent Afro-American.

Thousand Oaks, Simi Valley, Santa Clarita safe: *LADN*, April 30, 1992.

"Breeding ground for Dukes, Metzgers": *LAT*, December 5, 1992.

"Offices will win": *LAT*, December 5, 1991.

No convictions in McMartin trial: Domanick 7, 138.

Source Notes

Twilight Zone: May 17, 1992; Domanick 7, 133.

Raid on Dalton Avenue: *LAT,* November 26, 1990.

Arlo Smith: Laureen Lazarovici, "Men with Convictions," *L.A. Weekly,* March 21, 1990.

White inexperienced: *NYT,* March 25, 1992; *LAT,* April 30, 1993.

No experience in gaining convictions: *LADN,* May 8, 1992.

264 potential jurors: *NYT,* May 9, 1992; *LAT,* May 8, 1992.

"I wonder if . . . jaw broken": *LAT,* February 22 and 25, 1992.

"Very pro-law": May 8, 1992.

Jury makeup: *NYT,* May 5, 1992; *LAT,* March 3, 1992; *LADN,* March 3, 1992.

"Prejudice of the tape": *LADN,* January 26, 1992.

"Only one person in charge": *LAT,* March 6, 1992; *NYT,* April 10, 1993.

"If that's what it takes": *LAT,* March 23, 1993; *LADN,* March 25, 1992.

"Controlled application": *NYT,* April 10, 1993.

"Classic example": *LAT,* March 6, 1992.

"Assaultive person": *LADN,* March 5, 1992.

Would not lie still: *LADN,* March 25 and 30, 1992.

"Control an aggressive": *LAT,* March 20, 1992.

"Make a decision"/Stone's words to jury: *LAT,* April 22, 1992; *NYT,* April 10, 1993.

"Optical illusion": *LADN,* January 26, 1992; *NYT,* February 3, 1992.

"Rigid . . . when handcuffed": *LAT,* March 31, 1992.

Relentless nature of beating: Patricia Greenfield, professor of psychology at UCLA, and Paul Kibbey, second-degree black belt in aikido, "Picture Imperfect," *NYT,* April 1, 1993.

"Waistband": *LAT,* March 20, 1992.

"You could damn near put": *NYT,* March 25, 1992.

Only George Holliday: *NYT,* March 6, 1993; *LADN,* March 18, 1992. Although Bryant "Pooh" Allen was called by the prosecution and had heard Rodney King's screams, he was handcuffed on the other side of the car and saw little of the beating.

Robbed of "his manhood": *LAT,* April 4, 1991.

Being watched by LAPD *LADN,* May 30, 1991; Peter J. Boyer, "The Selling of Rodney King," *Vanity Fair,* July 1992, 159.

Assault on officer: *LADN,* May 30, 1991.

$83-million lawsuit: Boyer, op. cit., 159.

Who would profit/Melanie Singer kicked: Boyer, op. cit., 160.

Buttressing White's decision: *LAT,* May 8, 1992.

Howard Weitzman: *LAT,* April 30, 1993.

Johnnie Cochran, Jr.: *LAT,* March 19, 1992.

"Had King been able": *U.S. News and World Report,* May 11, 1992, 24.

"Mouth just dropped": Sally Ogle Davis, op. cit., 64.

April 29, 1992/reaction to acquittals: *LAT,* April 30, 1993.

CHAPTER 5: The Insurrection

Reginald Denny beating: *U.S. News and World Report,* May 11, 1992, 25; *Understanding the Riots,* 49; *NYT,* December 9, 1993; author's observations.

"You could hear the shouts"/other riot details: *Understanding the Riots,* 49–52.

"The Anaheim police": heard by author, April 30, 1992.

"What's up fuck-head?"/Burned-out grocery: author's observations and interviews, Thursday morning and afternoon, April 30, 1992.

Brenda and Lisa/Bloods and Crips: author's observations and interviews, April 30, 1992.

Nathaniel and William/Latasha Harlin's killing: author's observations and interviews, April 30, 1992; *L.A. Weekly,* January 3 and 9, 1992; *Understanding the Riots,* 38, 68, 71, 77.

J. J. Newberry's: author's observations and interviews, April 30, 1992.

"No one knew when the verdict": Gates interviewed on "Meet the Press," May 3, 1992.

Busy protecting firefighters: *LADN,* May 1, 1992.

M. Ridley-Thomas: *LAT,* April 29, 1992.

"Our units that responded": Lt. Michael Moulin, when initially responding to the disturbance at Florence and Normandie with twenty-five officers, ordered them out of the area—"immediately." See *Understanding the Riots,* 50, 52.

McNamara/"I can understand firefighters": McNamara.

Zvonko/"at least have sent their undercover": Pavelic.

"I don't think he understood": Sheinbaum.

Went to Brentwood: *NYT,* May 1, 1992; *LADN,* May 1, 1992.

"To my knowledge": Sheinbaum.

Placed them under his command: Dotson; Pravelic.

Matthew Hunt: *NYT,* May 1, 1991.

Detectives went home: *Understanding the Riots,* 74; Pavelic.

Metro Squad not deployed: Pavelic.

Seminar in Oxnard: Rothmiller and Goldman, 4.

Packed five to a car: Observations of author, April 30, 1992; Pavelic.

Late deployment of National Guard: *LADN,* May 1, 1992; *NYT,* May 1, 1992.

"This department has never reached out": author interview with police commissioner (not for attribution), May 2, 1992.

Blot on city's reputation: Gates interview by KNBC reporter, April 1, 1992.

Nine-page internal report: *Philadelphia Inquirer,* July 23, 1992.

Gates hadn't run department/"get the hell out": author interview with police commissioner (not for attribution), May 2, 1992.

Gates hadn't spoken to Dotson: Dotson; William H. Webster and Hubert Williams, *The City in Crisis: A Report by the Special Advisor to the Board of Police Commissioners on the Civil Disorder in Los Angeles, October 21, 1992* (Los Angeles: n.p., 1992), 15.

"Couldn't handle it": All of the problems with Gates's and the LAPD's response to the insurrection are abundantly documented in Webster and Williams, op. cit.

Source Notes

Largest insurrection: *Understanding the Riots,* 49.

Demonstrations in New York: *NYT,* July 21, 1993.

Fifty-eight killed, almost $800 million: *LAT,* May 11, 1992.

81 percent disapproved: *LAT,* May 15, 1992.

PART 8—EPILOGUE

"Pleasant," "charming": Claudia Puig, "From Tough Cop to Talk Jock," *LAT,* November 1, 1992; "Ex-Chief Displays a New Calmness," *NYT,* August 7, 1992.

"Too nice": *LAT,* November 1, 1992.

"Gates-Zinzan dialogue: author's notes on KFI promotional broadcast, 1993.

Junket to Asia: *LAT,* March 28, 1993.

38 percent job approval: *LAT,* June 27, 1993.

Brobeck, Phleger & Harrison: *LAT,* October 22, 1993.

Pension benefits/romantically involved: Dotson; *LAT,* March 4 and 25, 1992; *LADN,* November 23, 1991.

"Sold us out": Gates, *Chief,* 346.

"The fat lady has sung": *LADN,* July 11, 1991.

Making it a felony: *LAT,* May 16, 1991.

Bills vetoed by Wilson: *LAT,* February 15, 1992. After a three-strikes law sailed through the state legislature and was signed by Wilson in March 1994, Wilson—whose poll numbers were still staggeringly low and who was up for reelection in November—immediately turned around, upped the ante, and proposed one-strike legislation for rape and child molestation.

Ninety-thousand-member . . . $760,000/second in generosity/"overzealous": *LAT,* February 15, 1992.

Full-page ad: *LAT,* May 28, 1992.

System for tracking: *LAT,* July 11, 1993.

Key proposals/"vague": *LAT,* July 11, 1993; April 5, 1994; Weiss.

Refusing to hand over: *LAT,* February 4, 1994.

Played at training classes/"embarrassed": *Philadelphia Inquirer,* March 24, 1994.

"New customer base": *L.A. Weekly,* April 30–May 6, 1993.

Double Internal Affairs investigators: *LAT,* June 3, 1993.

City broke: *LAT,* March 31, 1993.

"When you're put in situations": *LAT,* July 16, 1993.

"Bad management Is not enough": *LAT,* May 10, 1994.

Index

Index

Index

Davis, Edna Kline, 43, 79
Davis, Edward M., 6, 12, 13, 17, 18, 85–86,
   90, 96, 106, 115, 136, 155, 203, 204, 207,
   271, 278, 287, 289, 296, 298, 341, 390
   on Bradley, 345, 348
   chief of police, 235, 250–52
   on Gates, 246
   homophobia, 226–27
   and intelligence files, 294, 295
   and police brutality, 380
   and police shootings, 267–69
   production of new police manual, 104–05
   as state senator, 435
Davis, James Edgar, 17, 18, 84, 95, 110, 111,
   119, 156, 157, 197, 210, 324
   background, 40–41
   bum blockade, 60–63
   chief of police, 21–28, 50–54, 55–58,
      221–24
   and communist threat, 67
   exposé of LAPD run by, 74–75
   forced into retirement, 78–79, 83, 403
   LAPD career, 41–44, 45, 46, 47
   on Parker, 147, 246
   Parker assistant to, 85, 92–93, 118, 246
   power of, 27–28
   and professionalization, 48–49
   and Raymond bombing, 69, 70–71, 75–78
   and Red Squad, 63–65
   and vice squad, 29, 30, 73
Dawson, William L., 140
Deadwyler, Leonard, 194
Del Gado, Peter, 72, 78
Democratic National Convention (1968), 207,
   236
Denny, Reginald, 4, 420–21, 426
DePasquale, Paul, 414
Depression, 59–60, 71, 83, 89, 91, 107, 122
DePriest, Oscar, 140
Desmond, William, 122
Detroit, 67, 199, 207
Deukmejian, George, 311, 343, 344, 347, 406
Dinkins, David, 236
Dinse, Rick, 369
Dircks, Joe, 21–23, 24–25, 26, 42, 64, 65, 73,
   79, 84
District attorney(s), 46, 352
   and police shootings, 272, 275
Dotson, David, 155, 224, 264, 288, 295, 308,
   325, 330, 332, 356, 428
   acting chief, 394
   assistant chief, 325–28, 333
   on choke-hold deaths, 299
   on Gates, 279, 280, 334, 335
   on police brutality, 379–80
   and police shootings, 272–73, 275
   retired, 434

testimony, Christopher Commission, 399,
   400, 429
   and training, 304–06
Downtown Business Association, 119
Downtown Business Men's Association, 103,
   144
Dragna, Jack, 46, 47, 72, 73, 75, 97–98, 197
Dragnet, 27, 53–54, 60–61, 110
"Dragnet" (radio show), 6, 123–29, 131, 132,
   133, 151, 197
   technical authenticity, 124
Drug trade, 35, 313, 321–22
Duff, Joe, 334
Duke, Charles, 414
Duncan, Isadora, 31
Duncan, Merrill, 109
Dymally, Mervyn, 295

East L.A., 10, 15, 111, 136, 163
Educational films, 120–21
End Poverty In California, 68
Elfmont, Thomas, 352
English, Charles, 416
Estrada, Leo, 402
Eubank, Harvie, 183–84
Excessive force, 276, 339, 401
Excessive-force suits, 334–37, 342, 353, 372

Farmer, James, 177
Farrakhan, Louis, 346–47
Farrell, Robert, 302, 396, 397
FBI, 107, 120, 122, 123, 154, 155, 160, 329
   investigation of LAPD, 386
Fear
   of crime, 250, 261, 303
   of moral decline, 412–13
Fear, The
   Gates's understanding of, 296–97, 301–03
Federation for Civic Betterment, 71
Felkenes, George, 289–90
Ferguson, Helen (Mrs. Callie Grimes), 54–55
Ferraro, John, 152, 397
Fiedler, Bobbi, 346, 409–10
Film industry, 121–22, 209, 210
   production code, 122
Fire and Police Protective League, 93–95, 196
Fisk, Jim, 90, 96, 98, 136, 167, 203, 254, 356
   and Bradley, 141, 169
   called "nigger inspector," 86, 204, 225–27
   director, community relations, 182, 205, 278
   and son, 228, 230–31, 284, 435
Fisk, Steve, 228–31, 260, 261, 281–85, 374, 435
   drinking problem, 283–85
Fitts, Byron, 76, 77
Flint, Frank, 52
Flores, Joan Milke, 392
Fox, James Alan, 330

• 488 •

Index

Index

Index

Index

Index

Index

Index

paramilitary, 49
pattern of, 47
social-work, 164
in South Central, 228–31
Policing philosophy, 12, 33, 198, 258, 331, 332, 338–40, 436
of Parker, 110–13
Political power
Parker and, 93–95
Political surveillance, 156–58
Politics (L.A.), 5, 33, 35, 39
blacks in, 140, 175
Porter, John, 32, 56–57
Poulson, Norris, 147, 159
Powell, Adam Clayton, 5
Powell, Laurence, 365, 367, 371–73, 374, 375, 376, 378, 379, 380–81
arrest report, 381–82
convicted, sentenced, 438
trial, 404, 413, 415, 419
Press, 76, 78
black, 161–62
and LAPD, 161, 267–69
LAPD public relations and, 103, 131
and social decline, 150
Press corps, 133–34
Prison population, 321–22
Proactive policing, 44, 110–13, 198, 331
blacks and, 161, 162
problems with, 339–40
Professionalization, 48–49, 101, 107, 108, 198–99
Progressive Labor Party, 192
Prohibition, 33, 46, 47, 158
Prone-outs, 329, 436
Proposition 13, 286–87, 288, 311, 331, 345
Prostitution, 31, 35, 42, 45, 75, 76, 150
laws prohibiting, 32
legalized, 98
organized, 46, 47, 55, 58
Public housing, 159–60
Public relations, 117–34, 143, 197
Pursuit situation(s), 367, 370

Race, 135, 137
Race-relations seminars, 226–27
Racial confrontation(s), 178, 181
Racism, 135–36, 210, 230
as issue in mayoral race, 218–19
in LAPD, 161, 331, 333
Radio industry, 119, 122
Rathburn, William, 288, 330, 332, 336
Ratzan, Scott C., 218
Raymond, Harry, 69–71, 75–78, 84
Reagan, Nancy, 15, 16–17, 117–18
Reagan, Ronald, 11, 15, 84, 145, 172, 199,

219, 254, 286, 311, 321, 323, 343, 345, 347, 407, 412
Real estate, 51, 159–60, 238
Red Flag Law, 38
Reddin, Tom, 86, 105, 124, 136, 165, 227, 298
chief of police, 172–73, 203–07, 217
on Gates, 245
intelligence file, 155–56
on King arrest, 367
on Parker, 147, 178
resignation, 206–07, 216
and training, 109, 110
and Watts insurrection, 182–83
on Yorty, 172
Reed, Joe, 96
Reese, Charles D., 252
Reform, reformers, 35, 54, 74–75, 78
see also Police reform
Reiner, Ira, 340–41, 352, 392, 409–11
Reinhardt, Stephen, 218–19, 251, 252, 253, 254, 269, 356, 358
Reiser, Martin, 234, 304–05
Reiter, Lou, 289, 326
Report writing, 114–15
Richardson, F. W., 74
Ridley-Thomas, Mark, 334, 426
Riordan, Richard, 434–35, 436, 437–38
Riot control, 181, 182, 427
Riots, 191
see also Watts insurrection
Robinson, Edward G., 122
Roddenberry, Gene, 12, 131, 141–42, 149, 214
Rogers, Kevin, 317
Rolling 60s (gang), 320–21
Roosevelt, Franklin D., 67, 84, 158
Rosselli, John, 47, 72, 73, 75, 97–98, 197
Rothmiller, Mike, 295
Roybal, Edward, 295

Sakalis, George, 76, 77
Salvadorans, 209, 312, 333
San Fernando Valley, 9, 10, 37–38, 166, 207, 214, 331, 346
and Bradley candidacy, 217–18
San Francisco, 34, 36, 264, 429–30
San Pedro, 37, 63, 65, 238
Sarnoff, David, 128
Satz, Wayne, 267–69
Scandals, 48, 70, 96, 254
movie industry, 121–22
Scientific management, 105–06, 197–98
Sebastian, Charles, 42
Segregation, 135, 178
LAPD, 138, 140, 142, 161, 167
Los Angeles, 212, 213

Index

Index